ENGLISH PROSE

H. CRAIK

VOL. II

FROM THE SIXTEENTH CENTURY TO THE RESTORATION

ENGLISH PROSE

SELECTIONS

WITH CRITICAL INTRODUCTIONS
BY VARIOUS WRITERS
AND GENERAL INTRODUCTIONS TO EACH PERIOD

EDITED BY
HENRY CRAIK

VOL. II

SIXTEENTH CENTURY TO THE RESTORATION

New York
MACMILLAN AND CO.
AND LONDON
1894

700

CONTENTS

INTRODUCTION

THE authors represented in this volume begin with men whose
life belonged in part to the reign of Elizabeth ; they end with
those who had reached manhood before the close of the Commonwealth. The period was a critical one for English prose. The
glory and the daring, the marvellous creative power of the
Elizabethan age—these were gone, and our literature was about
to pass through a severe ordeal. The rich harvest which the
Elizabethans had gathered was drawn from two sources. Something had been inherited from the native stock, which could trace
its origin back to ages long before that of Chaucer. There had
been no slight intermixture therein of the formal and unnatural—
of the pedagogic, and even of the pedantic. But it had its
excellences as well. It saved itself by its simplicity and directness ; by its marvellous power of using for literary purposes the
language of everyday life ; above all, by its faculty of assimilating
the romantic spirit, which set it free from the artificialities of the
homily, and gave to it the quickening force of artistic effort. The
native stock, then, was barren neither in promise nor in performance when there came to it the breath of a new life, partly
stimulating, partly controlling, from the Classical and Romance
literatures. It was the glory of the Elizabethans to absorb these
without losing what was best and most characteristic in the native
stock. It was through this added wealth that they achieved
their greatness. But their achievements did not belong, in any
large part, to the domain of prose. What they did in that domain
was, at the best, to show what were the possibilities of English
prose. We have books, indeed, both before the age of Elizabeth,

and others produced in that age, which show a charm of diction that later ages may strive in vain to reproduce. But such books belong to no school ; they conform to no set mode ; they haunt us with a reminiscence of the poetical romance, and contain no germ that can develop into a full tree, much less spread into a forest. It would be possible to speculate how the defects might have been supplied, how the secret might have been solved, and a standard for prose fixed as securely as for poetry. All that was hardest of attainment it would seem that the Elizabethans had attained. What they wanted we might judge was but a trick of art. But whether they cared not for the achievement, or the achievement was impossible, they reached to no such perfection, and left no such memory of their sway, in prose as in poetry. The Elizabethan prose did, indeed, in some high examples, show that it had not forgotten the simplicity, the directness, the wealth of romance, and that it was ready also to claim its inheritance in a larger language, enriched by the classics ; but for the most part these two streams run apart and do not mingle, and even in such a detail as the choice of words, the Elizabethans often indicate their debt to each rather by a copious variation of their vocabulary, by a deliberate repetition of the same word in its native and in its classical dress, than by any power of moulding a new and richer language, and a more lissome style, out of the double storehouses at their disposal. The poets and the dramatists of the age of Elizabeth completed their work quickly, and attained, by leaps and bounds, to the consummate perfection of their diction. But prose style grows more slowly ; and its growth is hindered rather than quickened by the very variety of its subject. Poetry is more apt to reflect the forms of monarchy ; it has its set usages, its prescribed modes, its court terms ; and even he who can do but little towards extending its sway, generally recognises and obeys its current fashions. But prose, on the other hand, governs only as a republic. Each individual writer would fain interpret its dictates after his own fashion. According to what he has to say, according to the story he has to tell, the argument he has to support, the theory he has to develop, his prose style must vary. More than half of those who write scarcely think of the form in which they cast their story or their thoughts. It is only when they have passed their apprenticeship in the art that they become conscious of the rules, and recognise with submission how few those are, and how consummate should be their endowments, who dare attempt to deviate from these rules, and impose upon the republic a style of their own.

It is quite possible to conceive that a new and stronger effort of the glory and the rapture of the Elizabethans might have done much to enrich us with a prose style as consummate and as commanding as that of their poetry. Whether it could have endured is another matter. Prose has to serve purposes so various, and often so vile, that it is hard to conceive it possible for it to abide by any type of perfect and unadulterated form. However that might have been, no such conquest was achieved by the age of Elizabeth. Its glories faded, its rapture grew cold, its creative power waned, before it accomplished for prose what it did for poetry ; and it was left for future generations slowly to travel, step by step, to a prose style ; first, to become artificial and involved ; then, by means of individual whims and caprices, to learn variety ; thereafter to conform to rule, and to acquire stateliness and formality ; then to dwindle off, in the decrepitude of age, to modishness, tawdriness, slipshod familiarity, or, worse than all, the narrow groove of technicality—leaving it to the unaided power of each writer to rescue himself from the prevailing vice of the style of his day. To understand how different is our debt to the Elizabethans in poetry and in prose, let us remember how close is the bond that binds Tennyson to Spenser, and how hopeless it would be for any one to repeat the style of Bacon without suggesting the impression of a masquerade.

But if the age of Elizabeth did not leave to us in prose, as in poetry, the rich inheritance of its imperial sway, it yet gave us an indication of what it might have achieved in prose. This volume opens with Bacon ; and in scarcely any author can we trace such possibilities of style as in his pages. It is true that much of Bacon's work loses its place as the highest literature by reason of its technicality. We have to study his style at its best, not in his most recondite, but in his most popular books. Setting aside that one amongst the Elizabethans who brooks no comparison, either in his own or any age, there is none in whom the rich endowment of his generation centres more notably than in Bacon. More than any one he showed in perfection that union of literature with practical wisdom which we can trace in so many from the days of Sir Thomas More to his own. None showed such variety of expression, and none with more consummate skill could bend to his purpose the resources of his own tongue blended with the added stores of classicism. He could bring to his prose just the right tincture of classical dignity, without losing that pungency of savour which came from the tradition of direct and familiar speech which was of native growth. Never losing its characteristic individuality, he can yet vary his style with his theme ; and the expression fits his thought with such perfection that (as is remarked in the introduction to the extracts which follow) it seems as if his aphorisms, and the thoughts that flower about them, often grew out of the aptness of a phrase that has suggested itself to his fancy.

But the promise of Bacon did not endure. The conditions of the time were adverse, even had the genius of the Elizabethans not waned, after the efforts they had made and the achievements they had won. To an age of creation there succeeded one of analysis. One of the first to point out the decadence in prose which followed the age of Elizabeth was Dean Swift ; and this decadence he finds to consist chiefly in the loss of simplicity— " the best and truest ornament of most things in human life." It is to that loss of simplicity that Swift traces back even the vices of English prose in his own day, which he would fain correct by the dictates of an Academy—a device least of all suited for a style so defiant of all rule and fashion as that of Swift himself.

Swift's proposal was due to his conviction that the loss of simplicity was owing to the absence of any controlling force, and such a force, it is conceivable, might have come through the instinctive obedience which is paid to genius. The genius of the Elizabethans did not exact that obedience in prose as it did in poetry. And the altered conditions soon made it impossible. New inquiries aroused curiosity, new interests claimed attention, new controversies occupied the field ; it soon became impossible that prose style should conform to one simple fashion, or mould itself after one type, however perfect. Before English prose came to acquire regularity, and established for itself some sort of standard, more than three generations—each of them eventful, stirring, and contentious—were to pass ; the old simplicity and directness, the old echo of a homely colloquialism, were almost overwhelmed beneath an unavoidable artificiality ; and the new style was evolved out of a century of struggle and disorder.

One conspicuous fashion in the prose of the Elizabethans

transmitted itself to the Jacobean age—that of Euphuism. We may easily exaggerate the evils of the fashion, and caricature its absurdities. But it was not the product solely of affectation. It was its misfortune rather than its fault that it never commanded the allegiance of any consummate artist, who might have used what was good in it, and discarded what was bad. In the instinct that prose style must, in order to attain literary perfection, set before itself a certain standard of grace, and not be too timid of formality, Euphuism was right; and we are the richer for the efforts of the Euphuists. The fashion lingered on to the next generation; but it lingered with more depth and earnestness of feeling. Take, for instance, the Euphuism, if we may so call it, of Donne. His quaintnesses and oddities are not due to extravagance, but rather to the very earnestness which seeks to enforce itself by strained expressions. It is to this quality that we owe what the seventeenth century called wit. Its object was not to excite laughter, but to compel attention, and stimulate curiosity, by a subtle intricacy which aroused and startled the reader, and which reveals the writer's inmost personality. To a later age it may seem quaint and curious, even affected; but to understand it so in a seventeenth-century writer is to misread the literature of the day.

But side by side with this many influences were at work. As the century advanced men took sides in the pitched battles of religion and politics; and the literary instinct was often overpowered by the controversial. The works of the time inevitably fell into groups according to their adherence to one side or the other, and each of these groups had its own fashions and modes. Men wrote too hotly and too eagerly to study style. We must add to this, that even on the literary side they were torn in different directions. There was an antagonism in their minds between the reverence for authority, the imitation of classical works, and the stubbornness of independence. The antagonism is often seen working in the same men —conspicuously in the case of such a man as Ben Jonson. The very multiplicity of their subjects bewilders them, and gives them something of fantastic variety by their discursiveness, as in the case of Burton. The force and directness of the drama had given place to minute analysis of character, as in Overbury, Earle, and Samuel Butler. Sometimes the classicism overpowers originality, as in the slavish copying of classical models by Hayward and

May.   Sometimes style seems to be everything, and a writer
never loses sight of the formal dignity of address befitting his calling, as in Sir Thomas Browne or Sir Kenelm Digby, or Drummond.   Sometimes, again, style seems to be altogether neglected,
and the writer is absorbed only in his subject, as with Selden,
Lord Herbert of Cherbury, and Ussher.   Sometimes the most
fantastic, either in style or subject, seems to be the only object of
pursuit—as with the extravagances of Urquhart, the odd eccen-
tricities of Fuller, or the whimsical theories of Harrington.   No
literature ever passed through the throes of a severer struggle ;
none was ever more near to losing all balance in the wilderness
of variety, the only saving quality of which was its thorough
earnestness.

But with all this, there was a steady development.   English
prose had perhaps lost its best chance of rising to the highest
level when the Elizabethan age passed without leaving a standard
warranted by its authority.   The floods of controversy, of mis-
directed effort, of exaggerated individualism, passed over it.
But in time it attained to a more serene atmosphere.   In Jeremy
Taylor, and we might add, in a lesser degree, in Leighton, we
see the evolution of order from disorder.   Taylor inherited something from the Euphuists : he caught his note of earnestness from
such a man as Donne ; but in his prose we have a sense of greater
security and restfulness than in any that had gone before.   The
fretfulness of controversy, the restlessness of individualism, the
perpetual pursuit of intricacy, and the ceaseless desire to startle
the reader, all the seare calming down.   The note of his books is
earnestness ; but it is earnestness which flows calmly.   Contrast
his prose with that of Milton, powerful as that is with the very
heat of the fight, and sounding as it were with the echo of the
war-trumpet.   We cannot deny its power, we cannot resist its
excitement.   But yet we are compelled to hear in it rather the
echoes of what had gone before than to recognise it as the har-
binger of a new and more self-contained prose.   To Milton prose
was an unnatural medium, which he never subdued to his purposes.
As a prose writer he commands admiration only where he enlists
sympathy.   He used the weapon provided for him by his age
with consummate power : but it was a weapon which he seized
as he found it, which owed its force to the arm that wielded it,
and which he left with no sharpness added to its temper, no
new polish to its surface, no new facility in its contrivance.

On the whole the elements of greatest hopefulness for English prose—its earnestness, its dignity, its conscious grace—were perhaps best summed up, in that age, in Jeremy Taylor : and to him more than to any other may be ascribed the handing on of the torch from the preceding to the next generation, and the preserving of its flame clear and undimmed amidst the heated struggles and cloudy controversies of the time. But others played no small part in the development of English prose. The glory of Taylor is shared by Clarendon, whose work, with all the occasional involution and irregularity of his style, stands unrivalled for its vivid picture of the Epic struggle in which he had played so conspicuous a part : for its careful adjustment of the parts, and above all for the surpassing skill of its character drawing. The chief impression of his prose is its studied restraint, and the instinct which makes him feel the exact point at which description should cease, and which compels his readers to accept each sentence, not as a mere literary ornament, but as contributing something essential to the description in hand. A history written under such conditions as that of Clarendon can never, in the nature of things, become a type which any successors could follow ; but none the less, in spite of all its irregularities, his prose has left as distinct an impression on our literature as his personal action has upon our constitution.

Another strain of English prose has to be taken into account in estimating the inheritance which this age bequeathed. From Hales and Chillingworth to Cudworth and Henry More there is a distinct genealogical connexion. Prose style was in no wise the aim, nor did it engage much of the attention of the English Rationalists or Platonists. But undoubtedly their work, in its care, its balanced thought, its elaborate arrangement of argument, above all in its air of philosophic calmness, did impart something of its character to later English prose. Doubtless the range of such writings must be small, and their influence cannot tell powerfully on the form of a general literary movement. Fancy, imagination, humour—these stand outside their sphere, and yet by these literary form must be largely shaped. But the language of the schools must still play its part ; and it was something that alongside of the strained but powerful phrases of a philosopher like Hobbes, and the amorphous diction of such a writer on religion as Lord Herbert of Cherbury, there should be carried on the sane, albeit somewhat tame, moderation of the school of Hales and Chillingworth, of Henry More and Cudworth.

Before the period closes we have a foretaste in L'Estrange of the literary craftsman of another age and type. His task came perilously near to hackwork, but he discharged it with something of the rollicking boldness, if with all the slipshod carelessness, of a generation to which, although older in years, he essentially belongs.

H. CRAIK.

FRANCIS BACON

[Francis Bacon, son of Queen Elizabeth's Lord Keeper, Sir Nicholas Bacon, and nephew of her Treasurer, Lord Burghley, was born on the 22d January 1561. In his twelfth year he was sent to Cambridge, in his sixteenth he was admitted to Gray's Inn, and went to complete his education by a three years' residence with Sir Amyas Paulet, the English Ambassador in France. He naturally looked to public life, having been saluted in his boyhood by the Queen as "her young Lord Keeper"; but his advancement, in spite of urgent solicitation on his part, was slow, probably owing to the jealousy or the distrust of his powerful relatives. His first employment of State was as Queen's Counsel in the trial of Essex in 1601, his conduct in which has been much discussed. It was an embarrassing position for him in consequence of his previous relations with that nobleman. Under James, at first, there was little improvement in his fortunes, but he became Solicitor-General in 1607, and his foot once on the ladder, he kept it there till he reached the top, being charged with the Great Seal in 1617. He was dismissed from this high office in 1621, upon impeachments which have since been the subject of prolonged and keen controversy, and spent the rest of his life in retirement. His literary and philosophic works were the occupation of his leisure, voluntary and enforced. The first edition of his *Essays*, numbering ten only, appeared in 1597; these were enlarged, and the number increased in successive editions (1612, 1625) to fifty-eight. The *Advancement of Learning* was issued in 1605; the *Novum Organum* in 1620. The *History of Henry VII.* was his first work after his fall; the *New Atlantis* was written about the same time; the *Sylva Sylvarum* was his last occupation. He died on the 9th April 1626.]

ANY attempt at analysing Bacon's style convinces us of the futility of trying to separate matter and manner, if by matter we understand more than the mere subject of discourse. The charm of Bacon's writings lies in his "wit," in the broad old sense of the word, in which it means intellect as well as expression. The sagacity of the underlying thought on which we rest when we apprehend the meaning of his words is as potent an element in our impression of delight as the aptness of the phrase and the ingenuity of the allusion. It is the style, as including both matter

and manner, that is the man.   To read him, is to put ourselves in
invigorating contact with an intellect of the utmost keenness and
force, steadily centred but wide in its scope and alive at every
point with a buoyant and intense vitality.

Taking style in the narrower sense of "expression," but still
as including both diction and method, we find that Bacon had
more than one style.   Essentially a man of calculation and contrivance, he adapted his style to his purposes.   His Essays have
always been, as he himself says they were in his own time, the
"most current" of his works.   In substance the very quintessence
of the worldly wisdom of his age, they have been most influential
in the history of English prose.   They have fixed the form of one
of our chief kinds of prose writing—the essay.   The Essays are sometimes spoken of as if they were models of good prose for all
purposes ; but this, as Bacon himself would have been the first to
discern, is an indiscriminate praise that is virtually a detraction,
inasmuch as it obscures the adaptation of the expression to the
design.   We miss in them the luminous sequence that we find in
his exposition of more definite themes, the close coherence that
made Ben Jonson say of his speeches that "his hearers could not
cough or look aside without loss."   The Essays are, as he said
himself, "dispersed meditations," detached thoughts on such topics
as Studies, Friendship, Ambition, Cunning, Praise, written down
as they occurred, without any other connection than their general
relevance to the topic.   In the original edition of ten, this was
indicated by prefixing to each separate "meditation" the now
obsolete mark ¶.   Mr. Arber's careful "Harmony" of the various
editions printed in parallel columns shows how he added to these
reflections and illustrated them here and there by happy anecdotes
and quotations at each revision.   It was a natural incident of
this "dispersed" way of writing that the expression of each
thought should have a felicity of its own, independent of its
relation to the others ; and the author did not mar this by trying
to force them into a sequence such as they might have had if one
had risen out of another in a continuous stretch of thought.   If
we forget this, we are apt to do another injustice to Bacon, and
to suspect him of a wilful and artful contravention of one of his
own precepts.   In a passage which we quote from the *Advancement of Learning*, he deprecates "hunting more after words than
matter," and after "the choiceness of the phrase" and "the
illustration of the work with tropes and figures," rather than

"weight of matter, width of subject, and depth of judgment." The words and the matter are certainly well matched in Bacon's Essays, but, as we can well suppose that it was the casual occurrence of a happy phrase or an apposite figure that moved him to take out his tablets and set his thoughts down, so it is really the choiceness of phrase and figure that has kept his wisdom from perishing. In weight of matter, and depth of judgment, Burghley's "Precepts to his Son" are at least equal to Bacon's "Counsels, Civil and Moral"; without the saving grace of wit in expression, Bacon's wisdom might have sunk like his kinsman's. And yet he could easily have defended himself from a charge of not "recking his own rede" against "hunting more after words than matter." These Essays are really not so much set compositions as collections of thoughts that have happily shaped themselves in epigrammatic and ornate phrase, that have flowered, as it were, spontaneously. Their diction has much in common with Lyly's Euphuism, which was the literary fashion of his youth, only there is more body in Bacon's epigrams, and his similitudes, while often equally far-fetched, are not so unscrupulously fantastic and flimsy. Bacon is distinguished on the one hand from Lyly by his incomparably greater weight of matter and depth of judgment, just as he is distinguished on the other from Burghley by his being an artist in choiceness of phrase. How dearly Bacon loved a brilliant phrase or an ingenious conceit, in spite of his protest against hunting after words, is seen by the care with which he gathered and stored in his Essays any flower of speech that incidentally came to him. In reading his State papers and private letters we often encounter felicities which have been thus carefully garnered.

But it would be a mistake to suppose that the style of the Essays is Bacon's only style. For the reasons we have indicated, this is much more thickly ornamented, much more alive with epigram and ingenious fancy, and much more inconsecutive than when he wrote with a definite end in view. In his *Advancement of Learning*, where he maps out and describes the provinces of knowledge, in his State papers, where he has a policy to recommend, and in his pleadings, where he has a complicated case to present for judgment, what principally strikes us is the compact grouping of details and the luminous order of the whole. It is when we read these works of his that we understand the full force of Ben Jonson's famous eulogium. "He was full of gravity in his speaking. His language, when he could spare or pass by a jest, was nobly censorious. No man ever spoke more neatly, more prestly, more weightily, or suffered less emptiness, less idleness in what he uttered. No member of his speech but consisted of his own graces. His hearers could not cough or look aside from him without loss. He commanded when he spoke, and had his judges angry and pleased at his devotion. No man had their affections more in his power. The fear of every man that heard him was lest he should make an end." A good way of appreciating the different " styles " that this wonderful wit had at command for different purposes is to compare his essay, " Of the True Greatness of Kingdoms and Estates," with the paper, " Of the True Greatness of the Kingdom of Britain," which he presented to King James at his accession.

" If his wit be not apt to distinguish or find differences," Bacon says in the essay " Of Studies," " let him study the Schoolmen." In his own set expositions he defines, divides, and subdivides with all the formal precision of a Schoolman, but his strong, ever-present sense of the necessity of keeping to a point saves him from becoming tedious. Thus his influence on expository prose told in the direction of what Jonson calls neatness and " prestness," and against superfluous finicking and irrelevant disquisition. And always anxious as he was to drive a clear impression home, his prose is much less involved in structure than that of many of his contemporaries. He does not, like Hooker, pile clause on clause ; he shows a much sounder judgment of what a reader can take in without confusion. He does not seem to have had Hooker's ear for the music of long periods, which often betrayed the great churchman into intricacy of syntax. Thus, on the whole, Bacon's prose helped the tendency to avoid cumbrous and involved structure, the tendency that was finally confirmed by Dryden.

WILLIAM MINTO.

LETTER TO LORD BURGHLEY IN 1591

My Lord—With as much confidence as mine own honest and faithful devotion unto your service and your honourable correspondence unto me and my poor estate can breed in a man, do I commend myself unto your lordship. I wax now somewhat ancient; one-and-thirty is a great deal of sand in the hour-glass. My health, I thank God, I find confirmed; and I do not fear that action shall impair it, because I account my ordinary course of study and meditation to be more painful than most parts of action are. I ever bare a mind (in some middle place that I could discharge) to serve her majesty; not as a man born under Sol, that loveth honour; nor under Jupiter, that loveth business (for the contemplative planet carrieth me away wholly); but as a man born under an excellent sovereign, that deserveth the dedication of all men's abilities. Besides, I do not find in myself so much self-love, but that the greater parts of my thoughts are to deserve well (if I were able) of my friends, and namely of your lordship; who being the Atlas of this commonwealth, the honour of my house, and the second founder of my poor estate, I am tied by all duties, both of a good patriot and of an unworthy kinsman, and of an obliged servant, to employ whatsoever I am to do your service. Again, the meanness of my estate doth somewhat move me; for though I cannot accuse myself that I am either prodigal or slothful, yet my health is not to spend, nor my course to get. Lastly, I confess that I have as vast contemplative ends, as I have moderate civil ends: for I have taken all knowledge to be my province; and if I could purge it of two sorts of rovers, whereof the one with frivilous disputations, confutations, and verbosities, the other with blind experiments and auricular traditions and impostures, hath committed so many spoils, I hope I should bring in industrious observations, grounded conclusions, and profitable inventions and discoveries; the best state of that province. This, whether it be

curiosity, or vain glory, or nature, or (if one take it favourably)
philanthropia, is so fixed in my mind as it cannot be removed.
And I do easily see, that place of any reasonable countenance doth
bring commandment of more wits than of a man's own ; which is
the thing I greatly affect. And for your lordship, perhaps you
shall not find more strength and less encounter in any other. And
if your lordship shall find now, or at any time, that I do seek or
affect any place whereunto any that is nearer unto your lordship
shall be concurrent, say then that I am a most dishonest man.
And if your lordship will not carry me on, I will not do as Anaxa-
goras did, who reduced himself with contemplation unto voluntary
poverty : but this I will do ; I will sell the inheritance that I have,
and purchase some lease of quick revenue, or some office of gain
that shall be executed by deputy, and so give over all care of
service, and become some sorry book-maker, or a true pioneer in that
mine of truth, which (he said) lay so deep. This which I have writ
unto your lordship is rather thoughts than words, being set down
without all art, disguising, or reservation. Wherein I have done
honour both to your lordship's wisdom, in judging that that will
be best believed of your lordship which is truest, and to your
lordship's good nature, in retaining nothing from you. And even
so I wish your lordship all happiness, and to myself means and
occasion to be added to my faithful desire to do you service.
From my lodging at Gray's Inn.

OF STUDIES

STUDIES serve for delight, for ornament, and for ability. Their
chief use for delight is in privateness and retiring ; for ornament,
is in discourse ; and for ability, is in the judgment and disposition
of business. For expert men can execute, and perhaps judge of
particulars, one by one ; but the general counsels, and the plots
and marshalling of affairs come best from those that are learned.
To spend too much time in studies is sloth ; to use them too much
for ornament is affectation ; to make judgment wholly by their
rules is the humour of a scholar. They perfect nature, and are
perfected by experience : for natural abilities are like natural plants
that need *proyning* by study ; and studies themselves do give forth
directions too much at large, except they be bounded in by experi-

ence. Crafty men contemn studies, simple men admire them, and wise men use them ; for they teach not their own use ; but that is a wisdom without them, and above them, won by observation. Read not to contradict and confute ; nor to believe and take for granted ; nor to find talk and discourse ; but to weigh and consider. Some books are to be tasted, others to be swallowed, and some few to be chewed and digested ; that is, some books are to be read only in parts ; others to be read, but not curiously ; and some few to be read wholly, and with diligence and attention. Some books also may be read by deputy, and extracts made of them by others ; but that would be only in the less important arguments, and the meaner sort of books ; else distilled books are like common distilled waters, flashy things. Reading maketh a full man ; conference a ready man ; and writing an exact man. And therefore, if a man write little, he had need have a great memory ; if he confer little, he had need have a present wit ; and if he read little, he had need have much cunning, to seem to know that he doth not. Histories make men wise ; poets, witty ; the mathematics, subtile ; natural philosophy, deep; moral, grave; logic and rhetoric, able to contend. *Abeunt studia in mores.* [The studies pass into the manners.] Nay there is no *stond* or impediment in the wit, but may be wrought out by fit studies : like as diseases of the body may have appropriate exercises. Bowling is good for the stone and reins ; shooting for the lungs and breast ; gentle walking for the stomach ; riding for the head ; and the like. So if a man's wit be wandering, let him study the mathematics ; for in demonstrations, if his wit be called away never so little, he must begin again. If his wit be not apt to distinguish or find differences, let him study the school-men ; for they are *cyminisectores* [splitters of hairs]. If he be not apt to beat over matters, and to call up one thing to prove and illustrate another, let him study the lawyer's cases. So every defect of the mind may have a special receipt.

(From the *Essays.*)

OF MARRIAGE AND SINGLE LIFE

HE that hath wife and children hath given hostages to fortune ; for they are impediments to great enterprises, either of virtue or mischief. Certainly the best works, and of greatest merit for the public, have proceeded from the unmarried or childless men ;

which both in affection and means have married and endowed the public. Yet it were great reason that those that have children should have greatest care of future times ; unto which they know they must transmit their dearest pledges. Some there are, who though they lead a single life, yet their thoughts do end with themselves, and account future times impertinences. Nay, there are some other that account wife and children but as bills of charges. Nay more, there are some foolish rich covetous men that take a pride in having no children, because they may be thought so much the richer. For perhaps they have heard some talk, *such an one is a great rich man*, and another except to it, *yea, but he hath a great charge of children;* as if it were an abatement to his riches. But the most ordinary cause of a single life is liberty, especially in certain self-pleasing and humorous minds, which are so sensible of every restraint, as they will go near to think their girdles and garters to be bonds and shackles. Unmarried men are best friends, best masters, best servants ; but not always best subjects ; for they are light to run away ; and almost all fugitives are of that condition. A single life doth well with churchmen ; for charity will hardly water the ground where it must first fill a pool. It is indifferent for judges and magistrates ; for if they be facile and corrupt, you shall have a servant five times worse than a wife. For soldiers, I find the generals commonly in their hortatives put men in mind of their wives and children ; and I think the despising of marriage amongst the Turks maketh the vulgar soldier more base. Certainly wife and children are a kind of discipline of humanity ; and single men, though they may be many times more charitable, because their means are less exhaust, yet, on the other side, they are more cruel and hard-hearted (good to make severe inquisitors), because their tenderness is not so oft called upon. Grave natures, led by custom, and therefore constant, are commonly loving husbands ; as was said of Ulysses, *vetulam suam prætulit immortalitati* [he preferred his old wife to immortality]. Chaste women are often proud and froward, as presuming upon the merit of their chastity. It is one of the best bonds both of chastity and obedience in the wife, if she think her husband wise ; which she will never do if she find him jealous. Wives are young men's mistresses ; companions for middle age ; and old men's nurses. So as a man may have a quarrel to marry when he will. But yet he was reputed one of the wise men that made answer to the question, when a man should marry ? *A young man not yet, an elder man not at all.* It is often seen that bad husbands have very good wives ; whether it be that it raiseth the price of their husband's kindness when it comes ; or that the wives take a pride in their patience. But this never fails, if the bad husbands were of their own choosing against their friends' consent ; for then they will be sure to make good their own folly.

(From the Same.)

OF VAINGLORY

IT was prettily devised of Æsop ; *the fly sat upon the axle-tree of the chariot wheel, and said, What a dust do I raise!* So are there some vain persons, that whatsoever goeth alone or moveth upon greater means, if they have never so little hand in it, they think it is they that carry it. They that are glorious must needs be factious ; for all bravery stands upon comparisons. They must needs be violent, to make good their own vaunts. Neither can they be secret, and therefore not effectual ; but according to the French proverb, *Beaucoup de bruit, peu de fruit; much bruit, little fruit.* Yet certainly there is use of this quality in civil affairs. Where there is an opinion and fame to be created either of virtue or greatness, these men are good trumpeters. Again, as Titus Livius noteth in the case of Antiochus and the Ætolians, *There are sometimes great effects of cross lies;* as if a man that negociates between two princes, to draw them to join in a war against the third, doth extol the forces of either of them above measure, the one to the other : and sometimes he that deals between man and man, raiseth his own credit with both, by pretending greater interest than he hath in either. And in these and the like kinds, it often falls out that somewhat is produced of nothing ; for lies are sufficient to breed opinion, and opinion brings on substance. In militar commanders and soldiers, vainglory is an essential point ; for as iron sharpens iron, so by glory one courage sharpeneth another. In cases of great enterprise upon charge and adventure, a composition of glorious natures doth put life into business ; and those that are of solid and sober natures have more of the ballast than of the sail. In fame of learning, the flight will be slow without some feathers of ostentation. *Qui de contemnendâ gloriâ libros scribunt, nomen suum inscribunt.* [They that write books on the worthlessness of glory, take care to put their names on the title page.] Socrates, Aristotle, Galen, were men full of ostentation. Certainly vain-glory helpeth to perpetuate a man's memory; and virtue was never so beholding to human nature, as it received his due at the second hand. Neither had the fame of Cicero, Seneca, Plinius Secundus, borne her age so well, if it had not been joined with some vanity in themselves; like unto varnish, that makes ceilings not only shine but last. But all this while, when I speak of vain-glory, I mean not of that property that Tacitus doth attribute to Mucianus; *Omnium, quæ dixerat feceratque, arte quâdem ostentator* [a man that had a kind of art of setting forth to advantage all that he had said or done]: for that proceeds not of vanity, but of natural magnanimity and discretion; and in some persons is not only comely, but gracious. For excusations, cessions, modesty itself well governed, are but arts of ostentation. And amongst those arts there is none better than that which Plinius Secundus speaketh of, which is to be liberal of praise and commendation to others, in that wherein a man's self hath any perfection. For saith Pliny very wittily, *In commending another you do yourself right; for he that you commend is either superior to you in that you commend, or inferior. If he be inferior, if he be to be commended, you much more; if he be superior, if he be not to be commended, you much less.* Glorious men are the scorn of wise men, the admiration of fools, the idols of parasites, and the slaves of their own vaunts. (From the Same.)

OF BUILDING

HOUSES are built to live in, and not to look on; therefore let use be preferred before uniformity, except where both may be had. Leave the goodly fabrics of houses, for beauty only, to the enchanted palaces of the poets; who build them with small cost. He that builds a fair house upon an ill seat, committeth himself to prison. Neither do I reckon it an ill seat only where the air is unwholesome; but likewise where the air is unequal; as you shall see many fine seats set upon a knap of ground, environed with higher hills round about it; whereby the heat of the sun is pent in, and the wind gathereth as in troughs; so as you shall have, and that suddenly, as great diversity of heat and cold as if you dwelt in several places. Neither is it ill air only that maketh an ill seat, but ill ways, ill markets ; and, if you will consult with Momus, ill neighbours. I speak not of many more ; want of water ; want of wood, shade, and shelter ; want of fruitfulness, and mixture of grounds of several natures : want of prospect ; want of level grounds ; want of places at some near distance for sports of hunting, hawking, and races ; too near the sea, too remote ; having the commodity of navigable rivers, or the discommodity of their overflowing : too far off from great cities, which may hinder business, or too near them, which lurcheth all provisions, and maketh everything dear ; where a man hath a great living laid together, and where he is scanted : all which, as it is impossible perhaps to find together, so it is good to know them, and think of them, that a man may take as many as he can ; and if he have several dwellings, that he sort them so, that what he wanteth in the one he may find in the other. Lucullus answered Pompey well ; who, when he saw his stately galleries, and rooms so large and lightsome, in one of his houses, said, *Surely an excellent place for summer, but how do you do in winter ?* Lucullus answered, *Why, do you not think me as wise as some fowl are, that ever change their abode towards the winter ?*

To pass from the seat to the house itself ; we will do as Cicero doth in the orator's art : who writes books *De Oratore,* and a book he entitles *Orator ;* whereof the former delivers the precepts of the art, and the latter the perfection. We will therefore describe a princely palace, making a brief model thereof. For it is strange to see, now in Europe, such huge buildings as the Vatican and Escurial and some others be, and yet scarce a very fair room in them.

First therefore, I say you cannot have a perfect palace, except you have two several sides ; a side for the banquet, as is spoken of in the book of Hester, and a side for the household ; the one for feasts and triumphs, and the other for dwelling. I understand both these sides to be not only returns, but parts of the front ; and to be uniform without, though severally partitioned within ; and to be on both sides of a great and stately tower in the midst of the front, that as it were, joineth them together on either hand. I would have on the side of the banquet, in front, one only goodly room above stairs, of some forty foot high ; and under it a room for a dressing or preparing place at times of triumphs. On the other side, which is the household side, I wish it divided at the first into a hall and a chapel (with a partition between), both of

good state and bigness ; and those not to go all the length, but
to have at the further end a winter and a summer parlour, both
fair.   And under these rooms, a fair and large cellar sunk under
ground : and likewise some privy kitchens, with butteries and
pantries, and the like.   As for the tower, I would have it two
stories, of eighteen foot high a piece, above the two wings ; and
a goodly leads upon the top, railed with statua's interposed ; and
the same tower to be divided into rooms, as shall be thought fit.
The stairs likewise to the upper rooms, let them be upon a fair
open newel, and finely railed in with images of wood, cast into a
brass colour ; and a very fair landing-place at the top.   But this
to be, if you do not point any of the lower rooms for a dining
place of servants.   For otherwise you shall have the servants'
dinner after your own : for the steam of it will come up as in a
tunnel.   And so much for the front.   Only I understand the
height of the first stairs to be sixteen foot : which is the height of
the lower room.

Beyond this front is there to be a fair court, but three sides of
it of a far lower building than the front.   And in all the four
corners of that court fair stair-cases, cast into turrets, on the
outside, and not within the row of buildings themselves.   But
those towers are not to be of the height of the front, but rather
proportionable to the lower building.   Let the court not be paved,
for that striketh up a great heat in summer, and much cold in
winter.   But only some side alleys, with a cross, and the quarters
to graze, being kept shorn, but not too near shorn.   The row of
return on the banquet side, let it be all stately galleries : in which
galleries let there be three, or five, fine cupolas in the length of
it, placed at equal distance ; and fine coloured windows of several
works.   On the household side, chambers of presence and ordinary
entertainments, with some bed-chambers ; and let all three sides
be a double house, without thorough lights on the sides, that you
may have rooms from the sun, both for forenoon and afternoon.
Cast it also, that you may have rooms both for summer and
winter : shady for summer, and warm for winter.   You shall have
sometimes fair houses so full of glass that one cannot tell where
to be come to be out of the sun or cold.   For inbowed windows,
I hold them of good use (in cities, indeed, upright do better, in
respect of the uniformity towards the street) ; for they be pretty
retiring places for conference ; and besides, they keep both the
wind and sun off ; for that which would strike almost through the

room doth scarce pass the window. But let them be but few, four in the court, on the sides only.

Beyond this court, let there be an inward court, of the same square and height; which is to be environed with the garden on all sides; and in the inside, cloistered on all sides, upon decent and beautiful arches, as high as the first story. On the under story, towards the garden, let it be turned to a grotta, or place of shade, or estivation. And only have opening and windows towards the garden; and be level upon the floor, no whit sunken under ground, to avoid all dampishness. And let there be a fountain or some fair work of statua's in the midst of this court; and to be paved as the other court was. These buildings to be for privy lodgings on both sides, and the end for privy galleries. Whereof you must foresee that one of them be for an infirmary, if the prince or any special person should be sick, with chambers, bedchamber, antecamera, and recamera, joining to it. This upon the second story. Upon the ground story, a fair gallery, open, upon pillars; and upon the third story likewise, an open gallery, upon pillars, to take the prospect and freshness of the garden. At both corners of the further side, by way of return, let there be two delicate or rich cabinets, daintily paved, richly hanged, glazed with crystalline glass, and a rich cupola in the midst; and all other elegancy that may be thought upon. In the upper gallery too, I wish that there may be, if the place will yield it, some fountains running in divers places from the wall, with some fine avoidances. And thus much for the model of the palace; save that you must have, before you come to the front, three courts. A green court plain, with a wall about it; a second court of the same, but more garnished, with little turrets, or rather embellishments, upon the wall; and a third court, to make a square with the front, but not to be built, nor yet enclosed with a naked wall, but enclosed with tarrasses, leaded aloft, and fairly garnished, on the three sides; and cloistered on the inside, with pillars, and not with arches below. As for offices, let them stand at distance, with some low galleries, to pass from them to the palace itself.

(From the Same.)

ON THE VANITY OF WORDS WITHOUT MATTER

THERE be therefore chiefly three vanities in studies, whereby learning hath been most traduced. For those things we do esteem vain, which are either false or frivolous, those which either have no truth or no use : and those persons we esteem vain, which are either credulous or curious ; and curiosity is either in matter or words : so that in reason as well as in experience, there fall out to be these three distempers (as I may term them) of learning ; the first, fantastical learning ; the second, contentious learning ; and the last, delicate learning ; vain imaginations, vain altercations, and vain affectations ; and with the last I will begin. Martin Luther, conducted (no doubt) by an higher Providence, but in discourse of reason, finding what a province he had undertaken against the Bishop of Rome and the degenerate traditions of the church, and finding his own solitude, being no ways aided by the opinions of his own time, was enforced to awake all antiquity, and to call former times to his succours to make a party against the present time ; so that the ancient authors, both in divinity and in humanity, which had long slept in libraries, began generally to be read and revolved. This by consequence did draw on a necessity of a more exquisite travail in the languages original wherein those authors did write, for the better understanding of those authors and the better advantage of pressing and applying their words. And thereof grew again a delight in their manner of style and phrase, and an admiration of that kind of writing ; which was much furthered and precipitated by the enmity and opposition that the propounders of those (primitive but seeming new) opinions had against the schoolmen ; who were generally of the contrary part, and whose writings were altogether in a differing style and form ; taking liberty to coin and frame new terms of art to express their own sense and to avoid circuit of speech, without regard to the pureness, pleasantness, and (as I may call it) lawfulness of the phrase or word. And again, because the great labour then was with the people (of whom the Pharisees were wont to say, *Execrabilis ista turba, quæ non novit legem*) [the wretched crowd that has not known the law], for the winning and persuading of them, there grew of necessity in chief price and request eloquence and variety of discourse, as the fittest and forciblest access into the capacity of the vulgar sort. So that these four causes concurring, the admiration of ancient authors, the hate of the school-men, the exact study of languages, and the efficacy of preaching, did bring in an affectionate study of eloquence and *copie* of speech, which then began to flourish. This grew speedily to an excess; for men began to hunt more after words than matter; and more after the choiceness of the phrase, and the round and clean com-position of the sentence, and the sweet falling of the clauses, and the varying and illustration of their works with tropes and figures, than after the weight of matter, worth of subject, soundness of argument, life of invention, or depth of judgment. Then grew the flowing and watery vein of Osorius, the Portugal bishop, to be in price. Then did Sturmius spend such infinite and curious pains upon Cicero the orator and Hermogenes the rhetorician, besides his own books of periods and imitation and the like. Then did Car of Cambridge, and Ascham, with their lectures and writings, almost deify Cicero and Demosthenes, and allure all young men that were studious unto that delicate and polished kind of learn-ing. Then did Erasmus take occasion to make the scoffing echo; *Decem annos consumpsi in legendo Cicerone* [I have spent ten years in reading Cicero]: and the echo answered in Greek, *one*, *Asine*. Then grew the learning of the schoolmen to be utterly despised as barbarous. In sum, the whole inclination and bent of those times was rather towards *copie* than weight.

Here therefore is the first distemper of learning, when men study words and not matter: whereof though I have represented an example of late times, yet it hath been and will be *secundum majus et minus* in all time. And how is it possible but this should have an operation to discredit learning, even with vulgar capacities, when they see learned men's works like the first letter of a patent or limned book; which though it hath large flourishes, yet it is but a letter? It seems to me that Pygmalion's frenzy is a good emblem or portraiture of this vanity: for words are but the images of matter; and except they have life of reason and invention, to fall in love with them is all one as to fall in love with a picture.

But yet, notwithstanding, it is a thing not hastily to be con-demned, to clothe and adorn the obscurity even of philosophy itself with sensible and plausible elocution. For hereof we have great examples in Xenophon, Cicero, Seneca, Plutarch, and of Plato also in some degree; and hereof likewise there is great use; for surely to the severe inquisition of truth, and the deep progress into philosophy, it is some hindrance; because it is too early satisfactory to the mind of man, and quencheth the desire of further search, before we come to a just period ; but then if a man be to have any use of such knowledge in civil occasions, of conference, counsel, persuasion, discourse, or the like ; then shall he find it prepared to his hands in those authors which write in that manner. But the excess of this is so justly contemptible, that as Hercules, when he saw the image of Adonis, Venus's minion, in a temple, said in disdain, *Nil sacri es* [you are no divinity] ; so there is none of Hercules's followers in learning, that is, the more severe and laborious sort of inquirers into truth, but will despise those delicacies and affectations, as indeed capable of no divineness. And thus much of the first disease or distemper of learning.   (From *The Advancement of Learning.*)

OF THE TRUE GREATNESS OF A STATE

AND therefore we may conclude, that as largeness of territory, severed from military virtue, is but a burden ; so, that treasures and riches severed from the same is but a prey. It resteth therefore to make a reduction of this error also unto a truth by distinction and limitation, which will be in this manner :

Treasure and moneys do then add true greatness and strength to a state, when they are accompanied with these three conditions :

First, the same condition which hath been annexed to largeness of territory, that is, that they be joined with martial prowess and valour.

Secondly, That treasure doth then advance greatness, when it is rather in mediocrity than in great abundance. And again better, when some part of the state is poor, than when all parts of it are rich.

And lastly, That treasure in a state is more or less serviceable, as the hands are in which the wealth chiefly resteth.

For the first of these, it is a thing that cannot be denied, that in equality of valour the better purse is an advantage. For like as in wrestling between man and man, if there be a great overmatch in strength, it is to little purpose though one have the better breath ; but, if the strength be near equal, then he that is short-winded will, if the wager consist of many falls, in the end have the worst ; so it is in the wars, if it be a match between a valiant people and a cowardly, the advantage of treasure will not serve ; but if they be near in valour, then the better moneyed state will be the better able to continue the war, and so in the end to prevail. But if any man think that money can make those provisions at the first encounters, that no difference of valour can countervail, let him look back but into those examples which have been brought, and he must confess that all those furnitures whatsoever are but shows and mummeries, and cannot shroud fear against resolution. For there shall he find companies armed with armour of proof taken out of the stately armouries of kings who spared no cost, overthrown by men armed by private bargain and chance as they could get it : there shall he find armies appointed with horses bred of purpose, and in choice races, chariots of war, elephants, and the like terrors, mastered by armies meanly appointed. So of towns strongly fortified, basely yielded, and the like ; all being but sheep in a lion's skin, where valour faileth.

For the second point, that competency of treasure is better than surfeit, is a matter of common place or ordinary discourse ; in regard that excess of riches, neither in public nor private, ever hath any good effects, but maketh men either slothful and effeminate, and so no enterprisers ; or insolent and arrogant, and so over-great embracers ; but most generally cowardly and fearful to lose, according to the adage, " *Timidus Plutus* "; so as this needeth no farther speech. But a part of that assertion requireth a more deep consideration, being a matter not so familiar, but yet most assuredly true. For it is necessary in a state that shall grow and enlarge, that there be that composition which the poet speaks of, " *Multis utile bellum* " : an ill condition of a state, no question, if it be meant of a civil war, as it was spoken ; but a condition proper to a state that shall increase, if it be taken of a foreign war. For except there be a spur in the state, that shall excite and prick them on to wars, they will but keep their own, and seek no farther. And in all experience and stories you shall find but three things that prepare and dispose an estate to war : the ambition of governors, a state of soldiers professed, and the hard means to live of many subjects. Whereof the last is the most forcible and the most constant. And this is the true reason of that event which we observed and rehearsed before, that most of the great kingdoms of the world have sprung out of hardness and scarceness of means, as the strongest herbs out of the barrenest soils.

For the third point, concerning the placing and distributing of treasure in a state, the position is simple ; that then treasure is greatest strength to a state, when it is so disposed, as it is readiest and easiest to come by for public service and use : which one position doth infer three conclusions.

First, That there be quantity sufficient of treasure as well in the treasury of the crown or state, as in the purse of the private subject.

Secondly, That the wealth of the subject be rather in many hands than in few.

And thirdly, That it be in those hands, where there is likest to be the greatest sparing, and increase, and not in those hands, wherein there useth to be greatest expense and consumption.

For it is not the abundance of treasure in the subjects' hands that can make sudden supply of the want of a state ; because reason tells us, and experience both, that private persons have least will to contribute when they have most cause ; for when there is noise or expectation of wars, then is always the deadest time for moneys, in regard every man restraineth and holdeth fast his means for his own comfort and succour, according as Solomon saith, " The riches of a man are as a stronghold in his own imagination " : and therefore we see by infinite examples, and none more memorable than that of Constantinus the last Emperor of the Greeks, and the citizens of Constantinople, that subjects do often choose rather to be frugal dispensers for their enemies, than liberal lenders to their prince. Again, wheresoever the wealth of the subject is engrossed into few hands, it is not possible it should be so respondent and yielding to payments and contributions for the public, both because the true estimation or assessment of great wealth is more obscure and uncertain ; and because the burden seemeth lighter when the charge lieth upon many hands ; and farther, because the same greatness of wealth is for the most part not collected and obtained without sucking it from many, according to the received similitude of the spleen, which never swelleth but when the rest of the body pineth and abateth. And lastly, it cannot be that any wealth should leave a second overplus for the public that doth not first leave an overplus to the private stock of him that gathers it ; and therefore nothing is more certain than that those states are least able to aid and defray great charge for wars, or other public disbursements, whose wealth resteth chiefly in the hands of the nobility and gentlemen. For what by reason of their magnificence and waste in expense, and what by reason of their desire to advance and make great their own families, and again upon the coincidence of the former reason, because they are always the fewest ; small is the help, as to payments or charge, that can be levied or expected from them towards the occasions of a state. Contrary it is of such states whose wealth resteth in the hands of merchants, burghers, tradesmen, freeholders, farmers in the country, and the like, whereof we have a most evident and present example before our eyes, in our neighbours of the Low Countries, who could never have endured and continued so inestimable and insupportable charge, either by their natural frugality or by their mechanical industry, were it not also that there was a concurrence in them of this last reason, which is, that their wealth was dispersed in many hands, and not engrossed into few ; and those hands were not much of the nobility, but most and generally of inferior conditions.

(From *Of the True Greatness of Britain.*)

THE CHARACTER OF HENRY VII

HE was of an high mind, and loved his own will and his own way ; as one that revered himself and would reign indeed. Had he been a private man he would have been termed proud : but in a wise Prince, it was but keeping of distance ; which indeed he did towards all ; not admitting any near or full approach either to his power or to his secrets. For he was governed by none. His Queen (notwithstanding she had presented him with divers children ; and with a crown also, though he would not acknowledge it) could do nothing with him. His mother he reverenced much, heard little. For any person agreeable to him for society (such as was Hastings to King Edward the fourth, or Charles Brandon after to King Henry the Eighth) he had none ; except we should account for such persons Foxe and Bray and Empson, because they were so much with him. But it was but as the instrument is much with the workman. He had nothing in him of vain-glory, but yet kept state and majesty to the height ; being sensible that majesty maketh the people bow, but vain-glory boweth to them.

To his confederates abroad he was constant and just ; but not open. But rather such was his inquiry and such his closeness, as they stood in the light towards him, and he stood in the dark to them ; yet without strangeness, but with a semblance of mutual communication of affairs. As for little envies or emulations upon foreign princes (which are frequent with many kings,) he had never any ; but went substantially to his own business. Certain it is, that though his reputation was great at home, yet it was greater abroad. For foreigners that could not see the passage of affairs, but made their judgments upon the issues of them, noted that he was ever in strife and ever aloft. It grew also from the airs which the princes and states abroad received from their ambassadors and agents here ; which were attending the court in great number ; whom he did not only content with courtesy, reward, and privateness ; but (upon such conferences as passed with them) put them in admiration to find his universal insight into the affairs of the world ; which though he did suck chiefly from themselves, yet that which he had gathered from them all seemed admirable to every one. So that they did write ever to their superiors in high terms concerning his wisdom and art of rule. Nay, when they were returned, they did commonly maintain intelligence with him ; such a dexterity he had to impropriate to himself all foreign instruments.

He was careful and liberal to obtain good intelligence from all parts abroad ; wherein he did not only use his interest in the liegers here, and his pensioners which he had both in the court of Rome and other the courts of Christendom, but the industry and vigilancy of his own ambassadors in foreign parts. For which purpose his instructions were ever extreme curious and articulate ; and in them more articles touching inquisition than touching negotiation : requiring likewise from his ambassadors an answer, in particular distinct articles, respectively to his questions.

As for his secret spials which he did employ both at home and abroad, by them to discover what practices and conspiracies were against him ; surely his case required it ; he had such moles perpetually working and casting to undermine him. Neither can it be reprehended ; for if spials be lawful against lawful enemies, much more against conspirators and traitors. But indeed to give them credence by oaths or curses, that cannot be well maintained ; for those are too holy vestments for a disguise. Yet surely there was this further good in his employing of these flies and familiars : that as the use of them was cause that many conspiracies were revealed, so the fame and suspicion of them kept (no doubt) many conspiracies from being attempted.

Towards his Queen he was nothing uxorious ; nor scarce indulgent ; but companiable and respective, and without jealousy.

Towards his children he was full of paternal affection, careful of their education, aspiring to their high advancement, regular to see that they should not want of any due honour and respect; but not greatly willing to cast any popular lustre upon them.

To his counsel he did refer much, and sat oft in person; knowing it to be the way to assist his power and inform his judgment; in which respect also he was fairly patient of liberty both of advice and of vote, till himself were declared.

He kept a strait hand on his nobility, and chose rather to advance clergymen and lawyers, which were more obsequious to him, but had less interest in the people; which made for his absoluteness, but not for his safety. Insomuch as I am persuaded it was one of the causes of his troublesome reign. For that his nobles, though they were loyal and obedient, yet did not co-operate with him, but let every man go his own way. He was not afraid of an able man as Lewis the Eleventh was. But contrariwise he was served by the ablest men that then were to be found; without which his affairs could not have prospered as they did. For war, Bedford, Oxford, Surrey, Dawbeny, Brooke, Poynings. For other affairs, Morton, Foxe, Bray, the Prior of Lanthony, Warham, Urswick, Hussey, Frowick, and others. Neither did he care how cunning they were that he did employ: for he thought himself to have the master-reach. And as he chose well, so he held them up well. For it is a strange thing, that though he were a dark prince, and infinitely suspicious, and his times full of secret conspiracies and troubles; yet in twenty-four years reign he never put down or discomposed counsellor or near servant, save only Stanley the Lord Chamberlain. As for the disposition of his subjects in general towards him, it stood thus with him: that of the three affections which naturally tie the hearts of the subjects to their sovereign,—love, fear and reverence,—he had the last in height; the second in good measure; and so little of the first, as he was beholding to the other two.

He was a prince, sad, serious, and full of thoughts and secret observations; and full of notes and memorials of his own hand, especially touching persons; as whom to employ, whom to reward, whom to inquire of, whom to beware of, what were the dependencies, what were the factions, and the like; keeping (as it were) a journal of his thoughts. There is to this day a merry tale: that his monkey (set on as it was thought by one of his chamber) tore his principal note-book all to pieces, when by chance it lay forth;

whereat the court, which liked not those pensive accounts was almost tickled with sport.

(From the *History of Henry VII.*)

THE DUTIES OF JUDGES OF ASSIZE

THE SPEECH WHICH WAS USED BY THE LORD KEEPER OF THE GREAT SEAL IN THE STAR CHAMBER, BEFORE THE SUMMER CIRCUITS, THE KING BEING THEN IN SCOTLAND, 1617.

THE King by his perfect declaration published in this place concerning judges and justices, hath made the speech of his Chancellor, accustomed before the Circuits, rather of ceremony than of use. For, as in his book to his son he hath set forth a true character and platform of a king, so in this his speech he hath done the like of a judge and justice ; which showeth that as his majesty is excellently able to govern in chief, so he is likewise well seen and skilful in the inferior offices and stages of justice and government ; which is a thing very rare in kings.

Yet nevertheless somewhat must be said, to fulfil an old observance ; but yet upon the king's grounds, and very briefly : for as Solomon saith in another case, *In these things who is he that can come after the king?*

First, you that are the Judges of Circuits are as it were the planets of the kingdom (I do you no dishonour in giving you that name), and no doubt you have a great stroke in the frame of this government, as the other have in the great frame of the world. Do therefore as they do ; move always and be carried with the motion of your first mover, which is your sovereign. A popular judge is a deformed thing ; and *plaudites* are fitter for players than for magistrates. Do good to the people, love them and give them justice. But let it be, as the Psalm saith, *nihil inde expectantes* ; looking for nothing, neither praise nor profit.

Yet my meaning is not, when I wish you to take heed of popularity, that you should be imperious and strange to the gentlemen of the country. You are above them in power, but your rank is not much unequal ; and learn this, that power is ever of greatest strength when it is civilly carried.

Secondly, You must remember, that besides your ordinary administration of justice, you do carry the two glasses or mirrors of the state ; for it is your duty in these your visitations to represent to the people the graces and care of the king ; and again, upon your return, to present to the king the distastes and griefs of the people.

Mark what the king says in his book : *Procure reverence to the king and the law; inform my people truly of me* (which we know is hard to do according to the excellency of his merit, but yet endeavour it), *how zealous I am for religion; how I desire law may be maintained and flourish ; that every court should have his jurisdiction; that every subject should submit himself to the law.* And of this you have had of late no small occasion of notice and remembrance, by the great and strait charge that the king hath given me, as keeper of his seal, for the governing of the Chancery without tumour or excess.

Again, *e re nata*, you at this present ought to make the people know and consider the king's blessed care and providence in governing this realm in his absence ; so that sitting at the helm of another kingdom, not without great affairs and business, yet he governs all things here by his letters and directions, as punctually and perfectly as if he were present.

I assure you, my Lords of the Council and I do much admire the extension and latitude of his care in all things.

In the High Commission he did conceive a sinew of government was a little shrunk ; he recommended the care of it.

He hath called for the accounts of the last circuit from the judges to be transmitted unto him in Scotland.

Touching the infestation of pirates, he hath been careful, and is, and hath put things in way.

All things that concern the reformation or the plantation of Ireland, he hath given in them punctual and resolute directions. All this in absence.

I give but a few instances of a public nature ; the secrets of counsel I may not enter into ; though his dispatches into France, Spain, and the Low Countries, now in his absence, are also notorious as to the outward sending. So that I must conclude that his majesty wants but more kingdoms, for I see he could suffice to all.

As for the other glass I told you of, of representing to the king the griefs of his people, without doubt it is properly your part ; for the king ought to be informed of anything amiss in the state of his countries from the observations and relations of the judges (that indeed know the pulse of the country) rather than from discourse. But for this glass (thanks be to God), I do hear from you all that there never was greater peace, obedience, and contentment in the country ; though the best governments be always like the fairest crystals, wherein every little icicle or grain is seen, which in a fouler stone is never perceived.

Now to some particulars, and not many. Of all other things I must begin as the king begins ; that is, with the cause of religion ; and especially the hollow church-papist. St. Augustin hath a good comparison of such men, affirming that they are like the roots of nettles, which themselves sting not, but yet they bear all the stinging leaves. Let me know of such roots, and I will root them out of the country.

Next, for the matter of religion. In the principal place, I recommend both to you and to the justices the countenancing of godly and zealous preachers. I mean, not sectaries or novellists, but those which are sound and conform ; but yet pious and reverend. For there will be a perpetual defection, except you keep men in by preaching, as well as law doth by punishing ; and commonly spiritual diseases are not cured but by spiritual remedies.

Next, let me commend unto you the repressing (as much as may be) of faction in the countries, of which ensue infinite inconveniences, and perturbations of all good order, and crossing of all good service in court or country, or wheresoever. Cicero, when he was consul, had devised a fine remedy (a mild one, but an effectual and apt one), for he saith, *Eos qui otium perturbant, reddam otiosos. Those that trouble others' quiet, I will give them quiet :* they shall have nothing to do, nor no authority shall be put into their hands. If I may know from you of any who are in the country that are heads or hands of faction, or men of turbulent spirits, I shall give them Cicero's reward, as much as in me is.

To conclude, study the king's book, and study yourselves how you profit by it, and all shall be well. And you the Justices of Peace in particular, let me say this to you. Never King of this realm did so much honour as the king hath done you in his speech, by being your immediate director and by sorting you and your service with the service of ambassadors, and of his nearest attendants. Nay more, it seems his majesty is willing to do the state of Justice of Peace honour actively also ; by bringing in, with time, the like form of commission into the government of

Scotland, as that glorious king, Edward the third, did plant this commission here in this kingdom. And therefore you are not fit to be copies, except you be fair written, without blots or blurs, or anything unworthy your authority. And so I will trouble you no longer for this time.

THE POISONING OF SIR THOMAS OVERBURY

FIRST, therefore, for the simple narrative of the fact. Sir Thomas Overbury for a time was known to have had great interest and great friendship with my Lord of Somerset, both in his meaner fortunes and after ; insomuch as he was a kind of oracle of direction unto him ; and if you will believe his own vaunts (being of an insolent Thrasonical disposition), he took upon him, that the fortune, reputation, and understanding of this gentleman (who is well known to have had a better teacher) proceeded from his company and counsel.

And this friendship rested not only in conversation and business of court, but likewise in communication of secrets of estate. For my Lord of Somerset, at that time exercising (by his majesty's special favour and trust) the office of the Secretary provisionally, did not forbear to acquaint Overbury with the king's packets of dispatches from all parts, Spain, France, the Low Countries, etc. And this not by glimpses, or now and then rounding in the ear for a favour, but in a settled manner ; packets were sent, sometimes opened by my lord, sometimes unbroken unto Overbury, who perused them, copied, registered them, made tables of them as he thought good ; so that I will undertake the time was when Overbury knew more of the secrets of state than the Council-table did. Nay, they were grown to such an inwardness, as they made a play of all the world besides themselves ; so as they had ciphers and jargons for the king, the Queen, and all the great men ; things seldom used, but either by princes and their ambassadors and ministers, or by such as work and practice against, or at least upon princes.

But understand me (my lord) I shall not charge you this day with any disloyalty ; only I lay this for a foundation, that there was a great communication of secrets between you and Overbury, and that it had relation to matters of estate, and the greatest causes of this kingdom.

But (my lords) as it is a principle in nature, that the best things are in their corruption the worst, and the sweetest wine makes the sharpest vinegar ; so it fell out with them, that this excess (as I may term it) of friendship ended in mortal hatred on my Lord of Somerset's part.

For it fell out, some twelve months before Overbury's imprisonment in the Tower, that my Lord of Somerset was entered into an unlawful love towards his unfortunate Lady, then Countess of Essex : which went so far, as it was then secretly projected (chiefly between my Lord Privy Seal and my Lord of Somerset) to effect a nullity in the marriage with my Lord of Essex, and so to proceed to a marriage with Somerset.

This marriage and purpose did Overbury mainly oppugn, under pretence to do the true part of a friend (for that he counted her an unworthy woman) ; but the truth was that Overbury, who (to speak plainly) had little that was solid for religion or moral virtue, but was a man possessed with ambition and vain-glory, was loth to have any partners in the favour of my Lord of Somerset, and especially not the house of the Howards, against whom he had always professed hatred and opposition. So all was but miserable bargains of ambition.

And (my lords) that this is no sinister construction, will well appear unto you, when you shall hear that Overbury makes his brags to my Lord of Somerset, that he had won him the love of the lady by his letters and industry ; so far was he from cases of conscience in this matter. And certainly (my lords) howsoever the tragical misery of that poor gentleman Overbury ought somewhat to obliterate his faults ; yet because we are not now upon point of civility, but to discover the face of truth to the face of justice ; and that it is material to the true understanding of the state of this cause ; Overbury was naught and corrupt, the ballads must be amended for that point.

But to proceed ; when Overbury saw that he was like to be dispossessed of my lord here, whom he had possessed so long, and by whose greatness he had promised himself to do wonders ; and being a man of an unbounded and impetuous spirit, he began not only to dissuade, but to deter him from that love and marriage ; and finding him fixed, thought to try stronger remedies, supposing that he had my lord's head under his girdle, in respect of communication of secrets of estate (or, as he calls them himself in his letters, secrets of all natures) ; and therefore dealt violently with him to make him desist, with menaces of discovery of secrets, and the like.

Hereupon grew two streams of hatred upon Overbury ; the one from the lady, in respect that he crossed her love and abused her name, which are furies to women ; the other of a deeper and more mineral nature, from my Lord of Somerset himself; who was afraid of Overbury's nature, and that if he did break from him and fly out, he would mine into him and trouble his whole fortunes.

I might add a third stream from the Earl of Northampton's ambition, who desires to be first in favour with my Lord of Somerset ; and knowing Overbury's malice to himself and his house, thought that man must be removed and cut off. So it was amongst them resolved and decreed that Overbury must die.

Hereupon they had variety of devices. To send him beyond sea, upon occasion of employment, that was too weak ; and they were so far from giving way to it, as they crossed it. There rested but two ways, quarrel or assault, and poison. For that of assault, after some proposition and attempt, they passed from it ; it was a thing too open and subject to more variety of chances. That of poison likewise was a hazardous thing, and subject to many preventions and cautions, especially to such a jealous and working brain as Overbury had, except he were first fast in their hand.

Therefore the way was first to get him into a trap, and lay him up, and then they could not miss the mark. Therefore in execution of this plot it was devised, that Overbury should be designed to some honourable employment in foreign parts, and should underhand by the Lord of Somerset be incouraged to refuse it ; and so upon that contempt he should be laid prisoner in the Tower, and then they would look he should be close enough, and death should be his bail. Yet were they not at their end. For they considered that if there was not a fit lieutenant of the Tower for their purpose, and likewise a fit under-keeper of Overbury : first, they should meet with many impediments in the giving and exhibiting the poison : secondly they should be exposed to note and observation, that might discover them ; and thirdly, Overbury in the meantime might write clamorous and furious letters to other his friends, and so all might be disappointed. And therefore the next link of the chain was to displace the then lieutenant Waade, and to place Helwisse, a principal abettor in the imprisonment : again, to displace Cary, that was the under-keeper in Waade's time, and to place Weston, who was the principal actor in the imprisonment :

and this was done in such a while, that it may appear to be done as it were with one breath ; as there were but fifteen days between the commitment of Overbury, the displacing of Waade, the placing of Helwisse, the displacing of Cary the under-keeper, the placing of Weston, and the first poison given two days after.

Then when they had this poor gentleman in the Tower close prisoner, where he could not escape nor stir, where he could not feed but by their hands, where he could not speak nor write but through their trunks ; then was the time to execute the last act of this tragedy.

Then must Franklin be purveyor of the poisons, and procure five, six, seven several potions, to be sure to hit his complexion. Then must Mris Turner be the say-mistress of the poisons to try upon poor beasts what's present, and what works at distance of time. Then must Weston be the tormentor, and chase him with poison after poison ; poison in salts, poison in meats, poison in sweetmeats, poison in medicines and vomits, until at last his body was almost come, by use of poisons, to the state that Mithridates' body was by the use of treacle and preservatives, that the force of the poisons was blunted upon him ; Weston confessing, when he was chid for not dispatching him, that he had given him enough to poison twenty men. Lastly, because all this asked time, courses were taken by Somerset both to divert all means of Overbury's delivery, and to entertain Overbury by continual letters, partly of hopes and projects for his delivery, and partly of other fables and negotiations ; somewhat like some kind of persons (which I will not name) which keep men in talk of fortune-telling, when they have a felonious meaning.

And this is the true narrative of this act of impoisonment, which I have summarily recited.

(From the *Charge against the Earl of Somerset.*)

A HAVEN AFTER STORM

WE sailed from Peru (where we had continued by the space of one whole year), for China and Japan, by the South Sea ; taking with us victuals for twelve months ; and had good winds from the east, though soft and weak, for five months' space and more. But then the wind came about, and settled in the west for many days, so as we could make little or no way, and were sometimes in purpose to turn back. But then again there arose strong and great winds from the south with a point east ; which carried us up (for all that we could do) towards the north ; by which time our victuals failed us, though we had made good spare of them. So that finding ourselves in the midst of the greatest wilderness of waters in the world, without victual, we gave ourselves for lost men, and prepared for death. Yet we did lift up our hearts and voices to God above, who *showeth His wonders in the deep;* beseeching him of His mercy, that as in the beginning He discovered the face of the deep, and brought forth dry land, so He would now discover land to us, that we might not perish. And it came to pass that the next day about evening, we saw within a kenning before us, towards the north, as it were thick clouds, which did put us in some hope of land ; knowing how that part of the South Sea was utterly unknown ; and might have islands or continents, that hitherto were not come to light. Wherefore we bent our course thither, where we saw the appearance of land, all that night ; and in the dawning of the next day, we might plainly discern that it was a land ; flat to our sight, and full of boscage ; which made it shew the more dark. And after an hour and a half's sailing, we entered into a good haven, being the port of a fair city ; not great indeed, but well built, and that gave a pleasant view from the sea ; and we, thinking every minute long till we were on land, came close to the shore, and offered to land. But straightways we saw divers of the people, with bastons in their hands, as it were forbidding us to land ; yet without any cries or fierceness, but only as warning us off by signs that they made. Whereupon, being not a little discomforted, we were advising with ourselves what we should do. During which time there made forth to us a small boat, with about eight persons in it ; whereof one of them had in his hand a tipstaff of a yellow cane, tipped at both ends with blue, who came aboard our ship, without any show of distrust at all. And when he saw one of our number present himself somewhat afore the rest, he drew forth a little scroll of parchment (somewhat yellower than our parchment, and shining like the leaves of writing tables, but otherwise soft and flexible) and delivered it to our foremost man. In which scroll were written in ancient Hebrew, and in ancient Greek, and in good Latin of the school, and in Spanish, these words ; " Land ye not none of you ; and provide to be gone from this coast within sixteen days, except you have further time given you.   Meanwhile, if you want fresh water, or victual, or help for your sick, or that your ship needeth repair, write down your wants, and you shall have that which belongeth to mercy." This scroll was signed with a stamp of cherubins' wings, not spread, but hanging downwards, and by them a cross. This being delivered, the officer returned, and left only a servant with us to receive our answer. Consulting hereupon amongst ourselves, we were much perplexed. The denial of landing and hasty warning us away, troubled us much ; on the other side, to find that the people had languages and were so full of humanity, did comfort us not a little. And above all, the sign of the cross to that instrument was to us a great rejoicing, and as it were a certain presage of good. Our answer was in the Spanish tongue ; "That for our ship, it was well ; for we had rather met with calms and contrary winds than any tempests. For our sick, they were many, and in very ill case ; so that if they were not permitted to land, they ran danger of their lives." Our other wants we set down in particular ; adding, "that we had some little store of merchandise, which, if it pleased them to deal for, it might supply our wants without being chargeable unto them." We offered some reward in pistolets unto the servant, and a piece of crimson velvet to be presented to the officer ; but the servant took them not, nor would scarce look upon them ; and so left us, and went back in another little boat which was sent for him.

About three hours after we had dispatched our answer, there came towards us a person (as it seemed) of place. He had on him a gown with wide sleeves, of a kind of water chamolet, of an excellent azure colour, far more glossy than ours ; his under apparel was green ; and so was his hat, being in the form of a turban, daintily made, and not so huge as the Turkish turbans ; and the locks of his hair came down below the brims of it. A reverend man was he to behold. He came in a boat gilt in some part of it, with four persons more only in that boat ; and was followed by another boat, wherein were some twenty. When he was come within a flight-shot of our ship, signs were made to us that we should send forth some to meet him upon the water ; which we presently did in our ship-boat, sending the principal man amongst us save one, and four of our number with him. When we were come within six yards of their boat, they called to us to stay, and not to approach farther ; which we did. And thereupon the man whom I before described stood up, and with a loud voice in Spanish, asked, " Are ye Christians ?" We answered, " We were "; fearing the less, because of the cross we had seen in the superscription. At which answer the said person lifted up his right hand towards heaven, and drew it softly to his mouth (which is the gesture they use when they thank God), and then said : " If ye will swear (all of you) by the merits of the Saviour that ye are no pirates, nor have shed blood lawfully nor unlawfully within forty days past, you may have licence to come on land." We said, " We were all ready to take that oath." Whereupon one of those that were with him, being (as it seemed) a notary, made an entry of this act. Which done, another of the attendants of the great person, which was with him in the same boat, after his lord had spoken a little to him, said aloud ; " My lord would have you know, that it is not of pride or greatness that he cometh not aboard your ship ; but for that in your answer you declare that you have many sick amongst you, he was warned by the Conservator of Health of the city that he should keep a distance." We bowed ourselves towards him, and answered, " We were his humble servants ; and accounted for great honour and singular humanity towards us that which was already done ; but hoped well that the nature of the sickness of our men was not infectious." So he returned ; and a while after came the notary to us aboard our ship ; holding in his hand a fruit of that country, like an orange, but of colour between orange-tawney and scarlet, which cast a most excellent odour. He used it (as it seemeth) for a preservative against infection. He gave us our oath ; " By the name of Jesus and his merits ;" and after told us that the next day by six of the clock in the morning we should be sent to, and brought to the Strangers' House (so he called it), where we should be accommodated of things both for our whole and for our sick. So he left us ; and when we offered him some pistolets, he smiling said, " He must not be twice paid for one labour ;" meaning (as I take it) that he had salary sufficient of the state for his service. For (as I after learned) they call an officer that taketh rewards, *twice paid.*

(From the *New Atlantis.*).

ON THE TRANSMISSION OF IMMATERIATE
VIRTUES

IT is mentioned in some stories that where children have been exposed, or taken away young from their parents, and that afterwards they have approached to their parents' presence, the parents (although they have not known them) have had a secret joy or other alteration thereupon.

There was an Egyptian soothsayer, that made Antonius believe that his genius (which otherwise was brave and confident) was, in the presence of Octavianus Cæsar, poor and cowardly : and therefore he advised him to absent himself as much as he could, and remove far from him. This soothsayer was thought to be suborned by Cleopatra to make him live in Egypt, and other remote places from Rome. Howsoever the conceit of a predominant or mastering spirit of one man over another is ancient, and received still, even in vulgar opinion.

There are conceits that some men, that are of an ill and melancholy nature, do incline the company into which they come to be sad and ill-disposed ; and contrariwise, that others, that are of a jovial nature, do dispose the company to be merry and cheerful. And again, that some men are lucky to be kept company with and employed ; and others unlucky. Certainly it is agreeable to reason, that there are at the least some light effluxions from spirit to spirit, when men are in presence one with another, as well as from body to body.

It hath been observed that old men who have loved young company and been conversant continually with them, have been of long life ; their spirits (as it seemeth) being recreated by such company. Such were the ancient sophists and rhetoricians ; which ever had young auditors and disciples ; as Gorgias, Protagoras, Isocrates, etc., who lived till they were an hundred years old. And so likewise did many of the grammarians and schoolmasters ; such as was Orbilius, etc.

Audacity and confidence doth, in civil business, so great effects, as a man may reasonably doubt that, besides the very daring and earnestness and persisting and importunity, there should be some secret binding and stooping of other men's spirits to such persons.

The affections (no doubt) do make the spirits more powerful and active ; and especially those affections which draw the spirits into the eyes : which are two : love, and envy, which is called *oculus malus.* As for love, the Platonists (some of them) go so far as to hold that the spirit of the lover doth pass into the spirits of the person loved ; which causeth the desire of return into the body whence it was emitted : whereupon followeth that appetite of contact and conjunction which is in lovers. And this is observed likewise, that the aspects that procure love, are not gazings, but sudden glances and dartings of the eye. As for envy, that emitteth some malign and poisonous spirit, which taketh hold of the spirit of another ; and is likewise of greatest force when the cast of the eye is oblique. It hath been noted also that it is most dangerous when an envious eye is cast upon persons in glory and triumph and joy : the reason whereof is, for that at such times the spirits come forth most into the outward parts, and so meet the percussion of the envious eye more at hand ; and therefore it hath been noted, that after great triumphs, men have been ill-disposed for some days following. We see the opinion of fascination is ancient, for both effects : of procuring love, and sickness caused by envy : and fascination is ever by the eye. But yet if there be any such infection from spirit to spirit, there is no doubt but that it worketh by presence, and not by the eye alone ; yet most forcibly by the eye.

Fear and shame are likewise infective ; for we see that the starting of one will make another ready to start : and when one man is out of countenance in a company, others do likewise blush in his behalf.

Now we will speak of the force of imagination upon other bodies, and of the means to exalt and strengthen it. Imagination in this place I understand to be the representation of an individual thought. Imagination is of three kinds : the first joined with belief of that which is to come : the second joined with memory of that which is past : and the third is of things present, or as if they were present : for I comprehend in this, imaginations feigned and at pleasure ; as if one should imagine such a man to be in the vestments of a pope, or to have wings. I single out, for this time, that which is with faith or belief of that which is to come. The inquisition of this subject in our way (which is by induction) is wonderful hard : for the things that are reported are full of fables ; and new experiments can hardly be made but with extreme caution, for the reason which we will hereafter declare.

The power of imagination is in three kinds : the first upon the body of the imaginant, including likewise the child in the mother's womb ; the second is, the power of it upon dead bodies, as plants, wood, stone, metal, etc. ; the third is, the power of it upon the spirits of men and living creatures : and with this last we will only meddle.

The problem therefore is, whether a man constantly and strongly believing that such a thing shall be (as that such an one will love him, or that such an one will grant him his request, or that such an one shall recover a sickness, or the like), it doth help any thing to the effecting of the thing itself. And here again we must warily distinguish ; for it is not meant (as hath been partly said before) that it should help by making a man more stout, or more industrious (in which kind constant belief doth much) ; but merely by a secret operation, or binding, or changing the spirit of another : and in this it is hard (as we began to say) to make any new experiment ; for I cannot command myself to believe what I will, and so no trial can be made. Nay, it is worse ; for whatsoever a man imagineth doubtingly, or with fear, must needs do hurt, if imagination have any power at all ; for a man representeth that oftener that he feareth, than the contrary.

The help therefore is, for a man to work by another in whom he may create belief, and not by himself until himself have found by experience, that imagination doth prevail ; for then experience worketh in himself belief ; if the belief that such a thing shall be, be joined with a belief that his imagination may procure it.

(From the *Sylva Sylvarum.*)

HAYWARD

[John Hayward (1564-1627) was born at Felixstowe and educated at Pembroke College, Cambridge. In 1599 he wrote a *History of the First Year of Henry IV.*, and, through the fulsome flattery which he addressed to Essex in the dedication, he brought himself, as it would appear, unintentionally, under the displeasure of Queen Elizabeth, and was imprisoned on suspicion of sympathy with the designs of Essex. After the accession of James I. he was patronised by the court, practised with profit as a lawyer, and was knighted in 1619. He wrote on the *Succession to the Crown*, as a defender of divine right, and was involved in a controversy thereon with Parsons the Jesuit, who wrote under the name of R. Dolman. Encouraged by Prince Henry he wrote lives of William I., William II., and Henry I.; and his works comprise a *History of the Reign of Edward VI.*, and one of the beginning of the reign of Elizabeth, which was not printed till 1840. He also wrote many forgotten works on religious topics.]

ALTHOUGH Hayward holds no high place even amongst the historians of his own age, there is much that is characteristic about him, and he marks a distinct phase of literary style. Anthony Wood thought his historical work good, but too "dramatic"—that is to say, in modern language, too much coloured for the sake of effect, and written with too little regard to strict historical accuracy. A certain interest attaches to him as the colleague of Camden in Chelsea College, founded by James I.; but there is no such permanent value in his work as there is in that of his colleague. Hayward makes much show of learning. He adduces proofs and illustrations from a very wide range of subjects, but he has no idea whatever of historical proportion; he drags in his authorities with no thought of their appositeness, and he has no conception whatever of criticism. But in spite of this his history marks a distinct step forward in the historical style. He sets before himself clearly the aim of rising out of the track of the older annalists, and of giving some literary finish to history. He has recounted a conversation between himself and Prince

Henry, in which his patron urges him to undertake what he himself admits to be a want in the English language, a style of historical narrative which shall more nearly approach the classical models, and shall be more worthy of the part which England played in history. With this end in view Hayward has drawn abundantly upon the Latin historians—upon Livy, to a large extent, but still more markedly upon Tacitus. Nothing could illustrate Hayward's position better than the discussion between Queen Elizabeth and Bacon, of which Bacon himself has left the record. Elizabeth complained to Bacon of Hayward's unlucky first attempt, and asked if Bacon " could not find places that might be drawn within the case of treason." " For treason surely," answered Bacon, " I find none, but for felony very many." " And when Her Majesty asked me hastily, ' Wherein ? ' I told her the author had committed very apparent theft ; for he had taken most of the sentences of Cornelius Tacitus and translated them into English, and put them into his text. And another time when the Queen would not be persuaded that it was his writing whose name was to it, but that it had some more mischievous author, and said, with great indignation, that she would have him racked to produce his author, I replied, ' Nay, Madam, he is a doctor ; never rack his person, but rack his style, and let him have pen, ink, and paper, and help of books, and be enjoined to continue the story where it breaketh off, and I will undertake by collating the style to judge whether he were the author or no.' " Hayward's style could indeed be " racked " without any undue cruelty. There is very little art in his imitation of his models, and he has scarcely mastered the manner so far as to give much attention either to the selection or critical examination of the matter. But it is something that he pursued, according to his lights, a distinct literary style in history, and thereby produced a noticeable effect on his successors. He is frequently dramatic in the better sense, and not only in the worse sense condemned by Wood. His diction is formal, and though sometimes forcible, often involved and confused. One of the most artificial features in his writing is the frequent introduction of imaginary speeches on the classical model : and the historical value of such speeches may well be tried by the following fantastic passage, which Hayward puts into the mouth of Edward VI. as expressing the boy's regret for his part in the death of his uncle, the Protector Somerset. " And where then," said he, " was the good nature of a nephew ? Where was the clemency of a prince ? Ah, how unfortunate I have been to those of my blood! My mother I slew at my very birth, and since have made away two of her brothers, and haply to make a way for the purposes of others against myself. Was it ever known before that a king's uncle, a lord protector, one whose fortunes had much advanced the honour of the realm, did lose his head for a felony, a felony neither clear in law, and in fact weakly proved! Alas, how falsely I have been abused! How weakly carried! How little was I master over my own judgment, that both his death and the envy thereof must be charged upon me!"

The history was certainly not very critical that could tolerate rhodomontade such as this; and such "dramatic" qualities as it has are drawn from the very worst stage models of Hayward's own days. But it would be unjust to measure his style by such an example. It was an honest though mistaken result of his study of his models : and that study led to much that was good, along with a considerable mixture of what was absurd.

H. CRAIK.

DIFFICULTIES IN REIGN OF EDWARD VI.

ON the other side King Edward added to his glory, courtesy, and liberality, showing himself most gracious in countenance to all, and giving rewards suitable to every man's performance or place. The lord protector he rewarded with lands of the yearly value of £500; and certain it is that these first fortunes raised unto him a great respect both in other countries and among his own people, and the rather because he was discerned to be much searching both into the counsels and after the events of all his affairs, and likewise into the condition and state both of his own strength and of the countries near unto him.

But these prosperous proceedings were not only hindered, in their fairest course, but altogether stayed, and in some measure turned back, by reason of the unadvised forwardness of divers chief counsellors, in making both sudden and unseasonable alterations in matters of state, whose greedy desires of having their wills in all they liked bred both trouble to the realm and to themselves danger. For great and sudden changes are never without danger, unless the prince be both well settled in government and able to bear out his actions by power; but while King Edward was both unripe in years and new in government, to attempt a change both sudden and great could not but be accompanied with many mischiefs. The great matters wherein alteration was wrought were especially two, religion, and enclosures.

Now for that religion is of so high and noble a nature, of so absolute necessity in a commonwealth, that it is esteemed the foundation of laws, and the common band of human society, no sudden alteration can almost be made therein, but many will be induced thereby to attempt some alteration in rule, whence (saith Dio) conspiracies and seditions are often occasioned. For religion being seated in the high throne of conscience, is a most powerful ruler of the soul, and far preferred before estimation of life, or any other worldly respect; for this advanceth man to the highest happiness, it leadeth him to his last end; all other things are but instruments, this is the hand; all other things are but accessories, this is the principal. And therefore as all men are naturally moved by religion, so when they are violently thrust forward by those who (as Livy speaketh) make it their purpose to possess souls by superstition, then do they break all bands of reason and of rule, no persuasion of the one, no command of the other can then restrain them. *Multitudo ubi religione capta est, melius vatibus quam ducibus suis paret* (Curt. lib. iv.)

I will not deny but that some change in religion is often expedient and sometimes necessary; because, more in that than in any other thing, it is hard to contain men from running into one of these extremes, either of vain superstition, or of careless contempt. But this must be done with a soft and tender hand, and as Cicero speaketh, *Ut quam minimo sonitu orbis in republica convertatur.* Some respect should also have been given to those green times, to the monstrous multitude muffled with two great plagues and corruptions of judgment, custom, and ignorance, whereto may be added grief at their own wants and envy at the prosperity of others, especially for that many bold spirits were busied, not only to incense, but to lead them into much variety of mischief. And if it be said that King Henry the Eighth had quietly passed the like change before; I answer, the example was not then to be followed, the kings were not equal either in spirit or in power. Even as it is in the fable, that albeit an eagle did bear away a lamb in her talons with full flight, yet a raven endeavouring to do the like was held entangled and fettered in the fleece.

Touching enclosures, I am not ignorant what a profitable purchase is made thereby, not only to particular persons, but generally to the whole commonwealth, in case it be without depopulation, because a company of lands enclosed are thereby improved in worth two or three parts at the least; hereby two great commodities ensue, riches and multitude of people, because the more riches are raised out of lands, the more people are thereby maintained. This doth plainly appear by two shires, almost equal, both in greatness and in goodness of soil: Northampton much champaign and Somerset altogether enclosed. For if estimation be made by musters, and by subsidies, tenths, and fifteenths, enclosure hath made the one county more than double to exceed the other, both in people and in wealth.

Notwithstanding the Lord Protector gaping after the fruitless breath of the multitude, and more desirous to please the most than the best, caused a proclamation to be set forth against enclosures, commanding that they who had enclosed any lands accustomed to lie open should, upon a certain pain, before a day assigned lay them open again. This proclamation, whilst few were forward to obey, gave occasion to the mutinous multitude, instable in judgment, and tempestuous when they are stirred, all carried with a headlong rashness, and one following another, as wiser than himself, immoderately both in desire and hope to be easily drawn by others who had deeper reaches than themselves, to matters which at the first they had the least intended.

(From *History of Edward VI.*)

THE PROTECTOR SOMERSET AND HIS BROTHER

WHILST these two brothers held in amity, they were like two arms, the one defending the other, and both of them the king. But many things did move together to dissolve their love, and bring them to ruin : first, their contrary disposition, the one being tractable and mild, the other stiff, and impatient of a superior, whereby they lived but in cunning concord, as brothers glued together, but not united in grain : then much secret envy was born against them, for that their new lustre did dim the light of men honoured with ancient nobility. Lastly, they were openly minded, as hasty and soon moved, so uncircumspect and easy to be blinded. By these the knot, not only of love but of nature, between them was dissolved ; so much the more pity, for that the first cause proceeded from the pride, the haughty hate, the unquiet vanity, of a mannish, or rather of a devilish woman.

For the Lord Sudley had taken to wife Katharine Parr, Queen-Dowager, last wife to King Henry the Eighth : a woman beautified with many excellent virtues, especially with humility, the beauty of all other virtues. The Duke had taken to wife Anne Stanhope, a woman for many imperfections intolerable, but for pride monstrous : she was exceeding both subtle and violent in accomplishing her ends, for which she spurned over all respects both of conscience and of shame. This woman did bear such invincible hate, first against the queen-dowager, for light causes and womens' quarrels, especially for that she had precedency of place before her, being wife to the greatest peer in the land ; then to the Lord Sudley for her sake, that, albeit the queen-dowager died by childbirth, yet would not her malice either die or decrease, but continually she rubbed into the duke's dull capacity, that the Lord Sudley, dissenting from him in opinion of religion, sought nothing more than to take away his life, as well in regard of the common cause of religion, as thereby happily to regain his place. Many other things, she boldly feigned, being assured of easy belief in her heedless hearer, always fearful and suspicious (as of feeble spirit), but then more than ever by reason of some late opposition against him. Her persuasions she cunningly intermixed with tears, affirming, that she would depart from him, as willing rather to hear both of his disgraces and dangers, than either to see the one or participate of the other.

The duke embracing this woman's counsel (a woman's counsel indeed, and nothing the better), yielded himself both to advise and devise for destruction of his brother. The Earl of Warwick had his finger in the business, and drew others also to give either furtherance or way to her violent desires ; being well content she should have her mind, so as the duke might thereby incur infamy and hate. Hereupon the Lord Sudley was arrested, and sent to the Tower ; and in very short time after, condemned by Act of Parliament. And within few days after his condemnation, a warrant was sent under the hand of his brother the duke, whereby his head was delivered to the axe. His own fierce courage hastened his death, because equally balanced between doubt and disdain, he was desirous rather to die at once, than to linger long upon courtesy and in fear.

The accusations against him contained much frivolous matter, or call it pitiful, if you please. The Act of Parliament expresses these causes of his attainder. For attempting to get into his custody the person of the king and government of the realm ; for making much provision of money and of victuals; for endeavouring to marry the Lady Elizabeth, the king's sister ; for persuading the king in his tender age to take upon him the rule and order of himself. The proofs might easily be made, because he was never called to his answer. But as well the protestations at the point of his death as the open course and carriage of his life, cleared him in opinion of many. So doubtful are all weighty matters, whilst some take all they hear for certain, others making question of any truths, posterity enlarging both. Dr. Latimer pretending all the gravity and sincerity of a professed divine, yet content to be serviceable to great men's ends, declared in a sermon before the king that whilst the Lord Sudley was a prisoner in the Tower he wrote to the Lady Mary and the Lady Elizabeth, the king's sisters, that they should revenge his death ; which indeed the Lady Mary afterwards more truly did, by executing the Earl of Warwick, than either she was, or at that time could in particular be required. Many other imputations he cast forth besides, most doubted, many known to be untrue. And so, whereas Papinian, a civil lawyer but a heathen, chose rather to die than to defend the murder which the Emperor Caracalla had done upon his brother Geta, some theologians have been employed to defile places erected only for religion and truth by defending oppressions and factions, staining their professions and the good arts which they had learned, by publishing odious untruths upon report and credit of others.

O wives ! the most sweet poison, the most desired evil in the world ! Certainly as it is true, as Syracides saith, that there is no malice like the malice of a woman, so no mischief wanteth where a malicious woman beareth sway. A woman was first given to man for a comforter, but not for a counsellor, much less a controller and director ; and therefore in the first sentence against man this cause is expressed, Because thou obeyedst the voice of thy wife. And doubtless the Protector by being thus ruled to the death of his brother, seemed with his left hand to have cut off his right ; for hereupon many of the nobility cried out upon him, that he was a blood-sucker, a parricide, a villain, and that it was not fit the king should be under the protection of such a ravenous wolf. Soon after it was given forth, and believed by many, that the king was dead ; whereupon he passed in great state through the city of London, to manifest that he was both alive and in good health. Whether this speech were spread either by adventure or by art, it is uncertain ; certain it is, it did something shake the strength of the king's affection towards the Protector.

(From the Same.)

PUBLIC FEARS

THE last sickness of Queen Mary was both exceeding sharp and of long continuance, her body being wearied, and almost wasted, with the violence of her disease; her mind anguished with thoughts, no less strange for variety, than strong for the great importance they drew, whereof some (doubtless) were secret and singular. And whilst she lay thus languishing under the heavy hand of death, many false rumours were spread abroad that she was dead : whereupon a notable example might have been seen how in a royal state the surety of the common people depends much upon the life and safety of their prince. For every man's mind was then travailed with a strange confusion of conceits, all things being immoderately either dreaded or desired. Every report was greedily both inquired and received, all truths suspected, divers tales believed, many improbable conjectures hatched and nourished. Invasion of strangers, civil dissension, the doubtful disposition of the succeeding prince, were cast in every man's conceit as present perils ; but no man did busy his wits in contriving remedies. They who held themselves in danger, seemed to desire nothing but safety ; they who apprehended any opinion of safety, did rise into unreasonable desire of liberty ; wherein they were as various as in anything beside, as well for the particulars, as for the limits of that which they desired. In this medley of thoughts, some thought to save themselves by adherents, some by adjoining to those who had more to lose than themselves ; some stood upon their proper strength, either for their own preservation, or for abating of such as they esteemed too great. Generally, the rich were fearful, the wise careful, the honestly-disposed doubtful, the discontented and the desperate, and all such whose desires were both immoderate and evil, joyful, as wishing trouble, the gate of spoil.

(From *Annals of Elizabeth.*)

QUEEN ELIZABETH

AND for that the presence of the prince is of greatest moment to establish affairs, the queen, the next day after her title was proclaimed, removed from Hatfield, in Hertfordshire, where she then lay, towards London ; and was upon the way encountered and entertained in all places with such a concourse of people, with so lively representations of love, joy, and hope, that it far exceeded her expectation. The people of all sorts (even such whose fortunes were unlike either to be amended or impaired by change) went many miles out the city to see her, some upon particular affection to her person, some upon opinion of good to the State, some upon an ordinary levity and delight in change, and not a few because they would do as others did ; all with like fervency contending who should most nearly approach unto her, who should most cheerfully bestow upon her all honourable titles and happy wishes.

Now, if ever any person had either the gift or the style to win the hearts of people, it was this queen ; and if ever she did express the same, it was at that present, in coupling mildness with majesty as she did, and in stately stooping to the meanest sort. All her faculties were in motion, and every motion seemed a well guided action ; her eye was set upon one, her ear listened to another, her judgment ran upon a third, to a fourth she addressed her speech ; her spirit seemed to be everywhere, and yet so entire in herself, as it seemed to be nowhere else. Some she pitied, some she commended, some she thanked, at others she pleasantly and wittily jested, contemning no person, neglecting no office ; and distributing her smiles, looks, and graces, so artificially, that thereupon the people again redoubled the testimonies of their joys ; and afterwards, raising everything to the highest strain, filled the ears of all men with immoderate extolling their prince.

She was a lady, upon whom nature had bestowed, and well placed, many of her fairest favours ; of stature mean, slender, straight, and amiably composed ; of such state in her carriage as every motion of her seemed to bear majesty : her hair was inclined to pale yellow, her forehead large and fair, a seeming seat for princely grace ; her eyes lively and sweet, but short-sighted ; her nose somewhat rising in the midst ; the whole compass of her countenance somewhat long, but yet of admirable beauty, not so much in that which is termed the flower of youth, as in a most delightful composition of majesty and modesty in equal mixture. But without good qualities of mind the gifts of nature are like painted flowers, without either virtue or sap ; yea, sometimes they grow horrid and loathsome. Now her virtues were such as might suffice to make an Ethiopian beautiful, which, the more a man knows and understands, the more he shall admire and love. In life, she was most innocent ; in desires, moderate ; in purpose, just ; in spirit, above credit and almost capacity of her sex ; of divine wit, as well for depth of judgment, as for quick conceit and speedy expedition ; of eloquence, as sweet in the utterance, so ready and easy to come to the utterance ; of wonderful knowledge both in learning and affairs ; skilful not only in the Latin and Greek, but also in divers other foreign languages : none knew better the hardest art of all others, that is, of commanding men, nor could more use themselves to those cares without which the royal dignity could not be supported. She was religious, magnanimous, merciful, and just ; respective of the honour of others, and exceeding tender in the touch of her own. She was lovely and loving, the two principal bands of duty and obedience. She was very ripe and measured in counsel and experience, as well not to let go occasions, as not to take them when they were green. She maintained justice at home, and arms abroad, with great wisdom and authority in either place. Her majesty seemed to all to shine through courtesy : but as she was not easy to receive any to especial grace, so was she most constant to those whom she received ; and of great judgment to know to what point of greatness men were fit to be advanced. She was rather liberal than magnificent, making good choice of the receivers ; and by this cause was thought weak by some against the desire of money. But it is certain that beside the want of treasure which she found, her continual affairs in Scotland, France, the Low Countries, and in Ireland, did occasion great provision of money, which could not be better supplied than by cutting off either excessive or unnecessary expense at home. Excellent queen ! what do my words but wrong thy worth ? what do I but gild gold ? what but show the sun with a candle, in attempting to praise thee, whose honour doth fly over the whole world upon the two wings of magnanimity and justice, whose perfection shall much dim the lustre of all other that shall be of thy sex ? I will no longer stay upon general descriptions, but proceed to such particular acts as shall justify much more than I have said.

When she came to London, she was lodged the first night in the Charter-house, where many great persons, either for birth, or worthiness (or place in the state) resorted unto her ; and now rising from dejected fears to ambitious hopes, contended who should catch the first hold of her favour. The Queen did bear herself moderately and respectively to all, desiring them, if they would not be deceived in her, that they would not be the first to deceive themselves : that they would not prejudice her in their opinions, as not by uncourteous suspicions and doubts, so not by immoderate expectations and hopes, promising unto themselves out of a sudden liking more than is fit, or peradventure possible, to be performed : the failure whereof would either change or abate their loves : that they would lay aside all fore-taken conceits, which, like painted glass, doth colour all things which are seen through it.   Lastly, that they would not too rashly judge of her actions, as being privy neither to the occasions of them, nor to their ends.

So, after she had passed the offices of court done to her by the nobility and others, the day following, in the afternoon, she rode from thence to the Tower.   At the Charter-house gate the mayor of the city met her, and the recorder with a short speech saluted her in the name of the whole city.   She rode in great state through Barbican, the mayor riding with Garter King-at-Arms, and carrying a sceptre before her ; she entered at Cripplegate, and so passed by the wall to Bishopsgate.   This gate was richly hanged, and thereupon the waits of the city sounded loud music.   At the head of the street a scholar of Paul's School made to her a short speech in Latin verses ; next unto him stood the Company of Mercers within their rails, and after them all the other companies, extending to the farthest end of Mark Lane.   When she entered Mark Lane a peal of ordnance began at the Tower, which continued half an hour or thereabouts.   The presence of the queen gave perfection and life to all these solemnities.   She answered such speeches as were made to her ; she graced every person either of dignity or employment ; she so cheerfully both observed and accepted everything, that in the judgment of all men, all these honours were esteemed too mean for her worth.   When she was entered into the Tower, she thus spoke to those about her ; " Some have fallen from being princes of this land, to be prisoners in this place ; I am raised from being prisoner in this place, to be prince of this land.   That dejection was a work of God's justice ; this advancement is a work of His mercy ; as they were to yield patience for the one, so I must bear myself towards God thankful, and to men merciful and beneficial for the other."

(From the Same.)

THE JESUITS

IT is a rule in nature that one contrary is manifested by the other. Let us compare then your boisterous doctrine with that of the apostles and ancient fathers of the Church, and we shall find that one is like the rough spirit which hurled the herd of swine headlong into the sea ; the other like the still and soft spirit which talked with Elias.

Neither was the devil ever able, until in late declining times, to possess the hearts of Christians with these cursed opinions, which do evermore beget a world of murders, rapes, ruins, and desolations. For tell me, what if the prince, whom you persuade the people they have power to depose, be able to make and maintain his party, as King John and King Henry the Third did against their barons ! What if other princes, whom it doth concern, as well in honour, to see the law of nations observed, as also in policy, to break those proceedings which may form precedents against themselves, do adjoin to the side ! What if whilst the prince and the people are (as was the frog and the mouse) in the heat of their encounter, some other potentate play the kite with them both, as the Turk did with the Hungarians ? Is it not then a fine piece of policy which you do plot ? or is it not a gross error to raise those dangers, and to leave the defence to possibilities doubtful ?

Go to, sirs, go to, there is no Christian country which hath not by your devices been wrapped in wars. You have set the empire on float with blood ; your fires in France are not yet extinguished ; in Polonia and all those large countries, extending from the north to the east, you have caused of late more battles to be fought, than had been in five hundred years before. Your practices have heretofore prevailed against us : of late years you have busied yourselves in no one thing more, than how to set other Christian Princes on our necks ; stirring up such a store of enemies against us, as, like the grasshoppers of Egypt, might fill our houses, and cover our whole land, and make more doubt of room than of resistance. Our own people also you have provoked to unnatural attempts : you have exposed our country as a prey to them that will either invade or betray it ; supposing belike that you play Christ's part well when you may say as

Christ did :—Think not that I came to send peace : I came not to send peace, but a sword.   But when, by the power and providence of God, all these attempts have rather shown what good hearts you bear towards us, than done us any great harm ; when in all these practices you have missed the mark, now you do take another aim : now having no hope by extremity of arms, you endeavour to execute your malice, by giving dangerous advice ; now you go about to entangle us with titles, which is the greatest misery that can fall upon a State.

You pretend fair shows of liberty and of power, *Sed timeo Danaos et dona ferentes :* we cannot but suspect the courtesies of our enemies : the power which you gave us will pull us down ; the liberty whereof you speak will fetter us in bondage.   When Themistocles came to the Persian court, Artabanus, captain of the guard, knowing that he would use no ceremony to their king, kept him out of presence, and said unto him :—You Grecians esteem us barbarous for honouring our kings, but we Persians esteem it the greatest honour to us that can be.   The like answer will we frame unto you :—You Jesuits account it a bondage to be obedient unto kings, but we Christians account it the greatest means for our continuance both free and safe.

(From *The Right of Succession Asserted.*)

JAMES VI.

[James VI. of Scotland and I. of England was born in 1566, and died in
1625. From his fourth till at least his twelfth year James was educated at
Stirling Castle with several youths of noble family, under the care of George
Buchanan and Peter Young. He was naturally clever, and made rapid progress in his studies, which included Latin, Greek, French, history, logic, and
rhetoric. We are told by Killigrew that at the age of ten he "translated a
chapter of the Bible from Latin into French, and from French into English,
extempore"; and James Melville, speaking of a visit he paid the King, says,
that "it was the sweetest sight in Europe that day for strange and extraordinary gifts of ingine, judgment, memory, and language." At twelve years
of age he had nominally to take the government into his own hands. His
tender age was, as his tutor laments, "engrossed by the attentions of
flatterers," and distracted by the "fechting and flyting" of those whom
Melville terms "bot factious, fasschious, ambitious, greedy, vengeable, warldly,
wretchit creatours." James's juvenile production, *Essays of a Prentice in the
Divine Art of Poetry* (1584), was probably written as themes for his tutors.
Two *Meditations on the Revelations* (1588-89) are indicative of his theological
bent. *Demonology* (1597), *Basilikon Doron* (1599), and *A Counterblast to
Tobacco* (1604), are his best known essays. The remainder, and much the
larger portion, of his writings deals with political and theological questions,
which have for their centre his cherished tenet of the "divine right of
kings." The most important of these are *The True Law of Free Monarchy*
(1603), *An Apology for the Oath of Allegiance* (1607), and *A Defence of the
Right of Kings* (1615). The Bishop of Winton published in 1616 an
edition of his prose works, which included his speeches and some occasional
tracts.]

IT is usual to introduce James I. among the writers of his reign
with an apology; and it is commonly, and perhaps justly, held
that his works would long ago have been forgotten, had they not
been written by a monarch. Yet there is another side to this;
for it is none the less true that his name as an author has suffered
from his notoriety as a king. In spite of the somewhat more
favourable estimate of later historians, such as Gardiner and
Ranke, James I. retains an unenviable reputation. His position,

moreover, has given an undue prominence to certain weaknesses characteristic of his time. The belief in witchcraft which he shows in his *Demonology*, and the pedantry of his disquisitions against Bellarmine and Vorstius, in which, according to his first editor, "his Majesty fought with beasts at Ephesus, and stopped the roaring of the Bull," were an inheritance shared by most of his contemporaries. To charge him with these faults is merely to say that he was not greater than his age. Yet, though James was a scholar and writer of at least more than average talent and attainments, it has to be admitted that under no circumstances could he have taken high rank in literature. His prosaic and pragmatical nature was too rocky a soil for even Buchanan to cultivate to any purpose. Without genuine spontaneity of emotion, originality of thought, or expanse of outlook, his mind, as has been said, "was essentially of that type which knowledge neither broadens nor enriches." The charge of pedantry is in this sense valid against all his writings. But from its more aggressive form of ostentation of learning and irrelevant quotation they are moderately free. The margin of *Basilikon Doron* teems with references to Plato, Aristotle, Isocrates, Cicero, and the Bible ; but they do not, as a rule, burden the text. And in such treatises as *A Defence of the Right of Kings* an exhibition of learning was unavoidable ; for he was attacking the parade of learning by his opponents. If tediously scholastic, their scholarship is thorough, and their logic so far sound. His errors, like those of his age, lay latent in his premises.

The *Basilikon Doron* is James's most readable production ; containing some good sense, shrewd advice, and worldly wisdom. But unfortunately the reader cannot avoid estimating these in the light of James's after conduct. He is reminded of Polonius. When the writer of *Demonology* warns his son against the evils of superstition, or the patron of Carr and Villiers denounces "that filthy vice of flattery, the pest of all princes," and urges upon his son the choice of his counsellors from the wisest among the "bornmen of each country, if God provide you with more countries than this," the reader is almost justified in taking in his own way the King's assurance to his Parliament of 1609: "In faith, you never had a more painful King."

James's compositions have none of the subtler qualities of literary excellence. The construction of his sentences is usually correct and careful, his expressions and metaphors are often pointed and forcible, but he rarely attempts any flight of rhetoric ; and when he does, he is rarely successful. The only subject on which he approaches to dignity of style is that in which alone he seems to have had an absolutely sincere conviction—the divinity of kingship. " It becometh a King," he was in the habit of reminding his Commons, "to use no other eloquence than plainness and sincerity." He held, "that which we call wit consists much in quickness and tricks, and is so full of lightness that it seldom goes with judgment and solidity." It was to the latter qualities that James laid claim in his works. Though he seems in conversation to have been addicted to punning, in his *Basilikon Doron* he but once falls into the fashionable word-play of his age, when he reminds his son that he is "born to *onus*, rather than *honos*." There is almost no trace of the far-fetched conceits and antitheses of his contemporaries ; for these his mind was probably too heavy, his nature too phlegmatic. He jokes after a lumbering fashion—' with difficulty.' His cast of thought is seen in the artificial division under heads, with which he opens and arranges every essay : a habit so ingrained, that in his speech after the Gunpowder Plot, he has under his first head a subdivision to consider "the three ways how mankind may come to death " : "The first, by other men and reasonable creatures, which is least cruel ; " "the second way more cruel than that, by animal and unreasoning creatures ; " "the third, which is most cruel and unmerciful of all, the destruction by insensible and inanimate things ; and amongst them all, the most cruel are the two elements of water and fire ; and of those two the fire most raging and merciless." Yet amid the diffuse formalism of his scholastic and theological argumentation, there is frequently a pithy saying or apt allusion, which recalls the best of Overbury's *Crumbs fallen from King James's Table*. If these are authentic notes, it is unfortunate that, in his case as in that of many others, he did not write as he spoke.

Pedant as he was, James refused to follow the practice of writing in Latin, which was kept up among scholars of even later times. This is the one point in which he wisely departed from the example of his master. With the exception of his youthful essay on poetry in the Scots dialect, James wrote in English ; but he continued, consciously or not, to make frequent use of Scots words. These are especially noticeable in his works before he became king of England : in his later writings they are more occasional. Had James succeeded in originating a movement whereby the English vocabulary could have been enriched by Scots words, he would have done English literature a permanent service. But, though he was not great enough to take any new departure, it must not be forgotten that he was the most learned of our monarchs.

W. S. M'CORMICK.

ON THE EDUCATION OF A PRINCE

THE next thing that ye have to take heed to, is your speaking and language; whereunto I join your gesture, since action is one of the chiefest qualities that is required in an orator: for as the tongue speaketh to the ears, so doth the gesture speak to the eyes of the auditor. In both your speaking and your gesture, use a natural and plain form, not *fairded* with artifice; for (as the Frenchmen say) *Rien contrefait fin:* but eschew all affectate forms in both.

In your language be plain, honest, natural, comely, clean, short, and sententious, eschewing both the extremities, as well in not using any rustical corrupt *leide*, as book-language and pen and ink-horn terms, and least of all, *mignard* and effeminate terms. But let the greatest part of your eloquence consist in a natural, clear and sensible form of the delivery of your mind, builded ever upon certain and good grounds; tempering it with gravity, quickness or merriness, according to the subject and occasion of the time; not taunting in theology, nor alleging and profaning the Scripture in drinking purposes, as over many do.

Use also the like form in your gesture; neither looking sillily, like a stupid pedant, nor unsettledly with an uncouth *morgue* like a new-come-over cavalier: but let your behaviour be natural, grave, and according to the fashion of the country. Be not over-sparing in your courtesies, for that will be imputed to incivility and arrogancy; nor yet over prodigal in *jowking* or nodding at every step, for that form of being popular becometh better aspiring Absaloms than lawful kings: framing ever your gesture according to your present actions: looking gravely and with a majesty when ye sit in judgment or give audience to ambassadors; homely, when ye are in private with your own servants; merrily, when ye are at any pastime or merry discourse; and let your countenance smell of courage and magnanimity when ye are at the wars. And remember (I say over again) to be plain and sensible in your language : for besides that it is the tongue's office to be the messenger of the mind, it may be thought a point of imbecility of spirit in a King, to speak obscurely, much more untruly ; as if he stood in awe of any in uttering his thoughts.

Remember also to put a difference betwixt your form of language in reasoning, and your pronouncing of sentences, or declarator of your will in judgment, or any other ways in the points of your office. For in the former case, ye must reason pleasantly and patiently, not like a king, but like a private man and a scholar ; otherwise, your impatience of contradiction will be interpreted to be for lack of reason on your part. Where in the points of your office, ye should ripely advise indeed, before ye give forth your sentence ; but fra it be given forth, the suffering of any contradiction diminisheth the majesty of your authority, and maketh the processes endless. The like form would also be observed by all your inferior judges and magistrates.

Now as to your writing, which is nothing else but a form of en-registrate speech ; use a plain, short, but stately style, both in your proclamations and missives, especially to foreign princes. And if your engine spur you to write any works, either in verse or in prose, I cannot but allow you to practise it : but take no long-some works in hand, for distracting you from your calling.

Flatter not yourself in your labours, but before they be set forth, let them first be privily censured by some of the best skilled men in that craft that in these works ye meddle with. And because your writes will remain as true pictures of your mind to all posterities, let them be free of all uncomeliness and unhonesty ; and according to Horace his counsel, *Nonumque premantur in annum.* I mean both your verse and your prose ; letting first that fury and heat, wherewith they were written, cool at leisure ; and then as an uncouth judge and censor, revising them over again before they be published, *quia nescit vox missa reverti.*

If ye would write worthily, choose subjects worthy of you, that be not full of vanity, but of virtue ; eschewing obscurity, and delighting ever to be plain and sensible. And if ye write in verse, remember that it is not the principal part of a poem to rhyme right, and flow well with many pretty words : but the chief commendation of a poem is, that when the verse shall be shaken sundry in prose, it shall be found so rich in quick inventions, and poetic flowers, and in fair and pertinent comparisons, as it shall retain the lustre of a poem, although in prose. And I would also advise you to write in your own language; for there is nothing left to be said in Greek or Latin already, and ynew of poor scholars would match you in these languages; and besides that, it best becometh a King to purify and make famous his own tongue, wherein he may go before all his subjects, as it setteth him well to do in all honest and lawful things.

And amongst all unnecessary things that are lawful and expedient, I think exercises of the body most commendable to be used by a young Prince, in such honest games or pastimes as may further ability and maintain health. For albeit I grant it to be most requisite for a King to exercise his engine, which surely with idleness will rust and become blunt; yet certainly bodily exercises and games are very commendable, as well for banishing of idleness (the mother of all vice) as for making his body able and durable for travel, which is very necessary for a King. But from this count I debar all rough and violent exercises, as the foot-ball; meeter for laming than making able the users thereof: as likewise such tumbling tricks as only serve for comedians and balladines, to win their bread with. But the exercises that I would have you to use (although but moderately, not making a craft of them) are running, leaping, wrestling, fencing, dancing, and playing at the catch or tennis, archery, palle maillé, and such like other fair and pleasant field-games. And the honourablest and most commendable games that ye can use, are on horseback: for it becometh a Prince best of any man, to be a fair and good horseman. Use therefore to ride and *danton* great and courageous horses; that I may say of you as Philip said of great Alexander his son, Μακεδονία οὔ σε χωρεῖ. And specially use such games on horseback, as may teach you to handle your arms thereon; such as the tilt, the ring, and low riding for handling of your sword.

I cannot omit here the hunting, namely with running hounds, which is the most honourable and noblest sort thereof; for it is a thievish form of hunting to shoot with guns and bows; and grey-hound hunting is not so martial a game. But because I would not be thought a partial praiser of this sport, I remit you to Xenophon, an old and famous writer, who had no mind of flattering you or me in this purpose, and who also setteth down a fair pattern for the education of a young king, under the supposed name of Cyrus.

As for hawking I condemn it not, but I must praise it more sparingly, because it neither resembleth the wars so near as hunting doth, in making a man hardy, and skilfully ridden in all grounds, and is more uncertain and subject to mischances ; and (which is worst of all) is therethrough an extreme stirrer up of passions. But in using either of these games, observe that moderation, that ye slip not therewith the hours appointed for your affairs, which ye ought ever precisely to keep ; remembering that these games are but ordained for you, in enabling you for the office, for the which ye are ordained.

(From *Basilikon Doron.*)

TOBACCO AND GOOD MANNERS

AND for the vanities committed by this filthy custom, is it not both great vanity and uncleanness, that at the table, a place of respect, of cleanliness, of modesty, men should not be ashamed, to sit tossing of tobacco pipes and puffing of the smoke of tobacco one to another, making the filthy smoke and stink thereof, to exhale athwart the dishes, and infect the air, when very often men that abhor it are at their repast ? Surely smoke becomes a kitchen far better than a dining chamber, and yet it makes a kitchen also oftentimes in the inward parts of men, soiling and infecting them with an unctuous and oily kind of soot, as hath been found in some great tobacco takers, that after their death were opened. And not only meal time, but no other time nor action is exempted from the public use of this uncivil trick : so as if the wives of Dieppe list to contest with this nation for good manners, their worst manners would in all reason be found at least not so dishonest (as ours are) in this point. The public use whereof, at all times, and in all places, hath now so far prevailed, as divers men very sound both in judgment and complexion hath been at last forced to take it also without desire, partly because they were ashamed to seem singular (like the two philosophers that were forced to duck themselves in that rain water and so become fools as well as the rest of the people), and partly to be as one that was content to eat garlic (which he did not love) that he might not be troubled with the smell of it in the breath of his fellows. And is it not a great vanity, that a man cannot heartily welcome his friend now, but straight they must be in hand with tobacco? No, it is become in place of a cure, a point of good fellowship, and he that will refuse to take a pipe of tobacco among his fellows (though by his own election he would rather feel the savour of a sink) is accounted peevish and no good company, even as they do with tippling in the cold eastern countries. Yea the mistress cannot in a more mannerly kind entertain her servant, than by giving him out of her fair hand a pipe of tobacco. But herein is not only a great vanity, but a great contempt of God's good gifts, that the sweetness of man's breath, being a good gift of God, should be wilfully corrupted by this stinking smoke, wherein I must confess, it hath too strong a virtue; and so that which is an ornament of nature, and can neither by any artifice be at the first acquired, nor once lost be recovered again, shall be filthily corrupted with an incurable stink, which vile quality is as directly contrary to that wrong opinion which is holden of the wholesomeness thereof, as the venom of putrefaction is contrary to the virtue preservative.

Moreover, which is a great iniquity, and against all humanity, the husband shall not be ashamed to reduce thereby his delicate, wholesome, and clean complexioned wife to that extremity, that either she must also corrupt her sweet breath therewith, or else resolve to live in a perpetual stinking torment.

Have you not reason then to be ashamed, and to forbear this filthy novelty, so basely grounded, so foolishly received, and so grossly mistaken in the right use thereof? In your abuse thereof sinning against God, harming yourselves both in person and goods, and raking also thereby the marks and notes of vanity upon you; by the custom thereof making yourselves to be wondered at by all foreign civil nations, and by all strangers that come upon you to be scorned and contemned : a custom loathsome to the eye, hateful to the nose, harmful to the brain, dangerous to the lungs, and in the black stinking fume thereof, nearest resembling the horrible Stygian smoke of the pit that is bottomless.

(From *A Counterblast to Tobacco.*)

JOHN SPOTTISWOODE

[Spottiswoode was born of a good Scottish stock in 1565, seven years before Knox's death. He was educated at Glasgow University, and succeeded his father as minister of Calder in West Lothian. In 1601-2, as chaplain to the Duke of Lennox, he visited the French and English Courts. On the accession of James VI. to the throne of England he accompanied the king to his new capital, and was sent back to Scotland as Archbishop of Glasgow. He became Archbishop of St. Andrews in 1615, and Lord High Chancellor of Scotland in 1635. He was a favourite with both James VI. and Charles I., and wrote his *History of the Church of Scotland* (first published in 1665) at the instigation of the former monarch. He died in 1639, and is buried in Westminster Abbey.]

" In Scotland," says Lord Clarendon, speaking of the time of James VI. and I., " though there were bishops in name, the whole jurisdiction and they themselves were subject to an Assembly which was purely presbyterian : no form of religion in practice, no liturgy, nor the least appearance of any beauty of holiness." Spottiswoode was one of the prelates who found themselves in this unfortunate position, against which his life and his works were one constant protest. He seems to have been rather a counter than a player in the game between priest and presbyter which in Scotland preluded the Great Rebellion, and it was his fate, like Clarendon's, to record the contest from the standpoint of the losing side. But his *History of the Church of Scotland* is all the more valuable on that account. A successful party never wants defenders, and posterity is too ready to condemn a failure. Spottiswoode's *History* enables us to appreciate the royal policy as it presented itself to a man, not indeed of high genius, but gifted with sufficient insight to make his record both interesting and instructive.

Spottiswoode was bred in the atmosphere of authority. A sentence from his will sums up the tenor of his writings :—
" Touching the government of the Church, I am verily per-

suaded that the government Episcopal is the only right and apostolic form. Parity among ministers is the breeder of confusion, as experience might have taught us ; and for these ruling elders, as they are a mere human device, so will they prove, if they find way, the ruin both of Church and State." " No bishop, no king," was for him the final expression of the truth upon questions of government ; and it is evident that the state of mind which, accepting the axiom, could carry it without flinching to one of its logical conclusions, a Republic, was to him quite incomprehensible. " James Melville," he says, " lost the king's favour *and so* made himself unprofitable to the Church." That subjects may lawfully rise and take the sword out of the king's hand is " a most execrable doctrine." King James was " the Solomon of this age." Among his ancestors " during 1400 years " on the Scottish throne—" If a careless or dissolute king (*which in so long a succession of princes is not to be wondered*) happened to reign, the same was abundantly repaired by one or other of the kings that followed."

Enough has been said to illustrate the temper in which Spottiswoode wrote. But if he was a courtier, he had all the graces, and far more than the virtues, of the Court. It is natural to compare his work with that of Knox. Readers will declare for or against the sentiments of either according to their prepossessions. In energy, in narrative power, and in the general impression of genius produced, the earlier writer must be pronounced by far the superior. Spottiswoode's merits are of a different order. His style is smooth, but seldom strikes any high note. There is no display of enthusiasm ; the reader is rarely warmed into strong approval or censure ; the tone is that of gentlemanly compromise or bland remonstrance. The really notable point about the book is the breadth of its charity. In this Christian virtue it must be acknowledged that the earlier Scottish Reformers were sadly deficient. Knox was most intolerant of opposition. Spottiswoode, in the whole of his *History*, has not a bitter word for foe or friend, unless it be one about Andrew Melville, who had indeed been a sore thorn in His Grace's flesh.

JAMES MILLER DODDS.

THE EXECUTION OF QUEEN MARY

AFTER this, she [Queen Mary] was brought to the hall, in the midst whereof, over against the chimney (where was a great fire), a scaffold was erected of two feet high and twelve feet broad, having two steps to ascend : the scaffold was railed about almost a yard high, and all covered with black cloth, as were the chair, stools, and block, and cushions to kneel upon. Before she went up, turning to the earls, she requested that her servants might stand by at her death. They answered, that their passionate weeping would disquiet her, and do no good else. "Nay," said she, "I will promise for them, they shall not do so : it is but a small favour, and such as Queen Elizabeth would not deny me, to have my maids present." She named Melvill her steward, Burgoin her physician, her apothecary and chirugeon, with two maids.

Being on the scaffold and silence made, the clerk of the council did read the commission, which she listened to as it had been some other matter. That ended, the dean of Peterborough began to remember her of her present condition, and to comfort her in the best sort he could. She, interrupting his speech, willed him to hold his peace, for that she would not hear him. And when, excusing himself that what he did was by command of her majesty's council, he began again to speak,—"Peace, Mr Dean," said she ; "I have nothing to do with you, nor you with me." The noblemen desiring him not to trouble her further, she said, "That is best, for I am settled in the ancient Catholic religion wherein I was born and bred, and now will die in the same." The earl of Kent saying, that as yet they would not cease to pray unto God for her, that He would vouchsafe to open her eyes, and enlighten her mind with the knowledge of His truth, that she might die therein, she answered, "That you may do at your pleasure, but I will pray by myself." So the dean conceiving a prayer, and all the company following him, she likewise prayed aloud in the Latin tongue : and when the dean had finished, she, in the English language, commended unto God the estate of His afflicted Church : prayed for her son, that he might prosper and live happily, and for Queen Elizabeth, that she might live long and govern her subjects peaceably ; adding, that she hoped only to be saved by the blood of Christ, at the feet of Whose picture presented on the crucifix she would willingly shed her blood. Then, lifting up the crucifix and kissing it, she said, "As Thy arms, O Christ, were spread abroad on the cross ; so with the outstretched arms of Thy mercy receive me, and forgive me my sins."

This said she rose up, and was by two of her women disrobed of her upper garments. The executioners offering their help, and putting to their hands, she put them back, saying, "She was not accustomed to be served with such grooms, nor dressed before such a multitude." Her upper robe taken off, she did quickly loose her doublet, which was laced on the back, and putting on her arms a pair of silken sleeves, her body covered with a smock only, she kissed her maids again, and bade them farewell. They bursting forth in tears, she said, "I promised for you that you should be quiet ; get you hence, and remember me." After which, kneeling down most resolutely, and with the least token of fear that might be, having her eyes covered with a handkerchief, she repeated the Psalm, *In te, Domine, confido ; ne confundar in æternum.* Then stretching forth her body with great quietness, and laying her neck over the block, she cried aloud, *In manus tuas, Domine, commendo spiritum meum.* One of the executioners holding down her hands, the other at two blows cut off her head, which falling out of her attire seemed to be somewhat gray. All things about her were taken from the executioners, and they not suffered to carry their aprons, or anything else with them that her blood had touched ; the clothes and block were also burned, her body embalmed, and in solemn manner buried in the cathedral church at Peterborough ; and after many years taken up by the king her son, and interred at Westminster amongst the rest of the kings.

This was the end of Queen Mary's life ; a princess of many rare virtues, but crossed with all the crosses of fortune, which never any did bear with greater courage and magnanimity to the last. Upon her return from France, for the first two or three years, she carried herself most worthily; but then giving ear to some wicked persons, and transported with the passion of revenge for the indignity done unto her in the murder of David Rizzio, her secretary, she fell into a labyrinth of troubles, which forced her to flee into England, where, after nineteen years' captivity, she was put to death in the manner you have heard.

(From the *History of the Church of Scotland.*)

THE ADVENTURES OF MR. JOHN CRAIG

IN the end of the year (1600) Mr. John Craig, that had been minister to the king, but through age was compelled to quit the charge, departed this life. This man whilst he lived was held in good esteem, a great divine and excellent preacher, of a grave behaviour, sincere, inclining to no faction, and, which increased his reputation, living honestly, without ostentation or desire of outward glory. Many tossings and troubles he endured in his time; for being left young and his father killed at Flodden, after he had got an entrance in letters and passed his course in philosophy in St. Andrews, he went to England, and waited as pedagogue on the Lord Dacres his children, the space of two years. Wars then arising betwixt the two realms, he returned home, and became one of the Dominican order; but had not lived long among them when, upon suspicion of heresy, he was put in prison. Being cleared of that imputation, he went back again into England, and thinking by the Lord Dacres' means to have got a place in Cambridge, because that failed, he went to France, and from thence to Rome. There he found such favour with Cardinal Pole, as by his recommendation he was received among the Dominicans of Bononia, and by them first appointed to instruct the novices of the cloister: afterwards, when they perceived his diligence and dexterity in businesses, he was employed in all their affairs throughout Italy, and sent in commission to Chios, an isle situated in the Ionic sea, to redress things that were amiss amongst those of their order.

Therein he discharged himself so well, that at his return he was made rector of the school, and thereby had access to the libraries, especially to that of the Inquisition; where falling on the Institutions of John Calvin, he was taken with a great liking thereof, and one day conferring with a reverend old man of the monastery, was by him confirmed in the opinion he had taken, but withal warned in any case not to utter himself, or make his mind known, because the times were perilous. Yet he, neglecting the counsel of the aged man, and venting his opinions too freely, was delated of heresy, and being sent to Rome, after examination imprisoned. Nine months he lay there in great misery ; at the end whereof, being brought before the judge of the Inquisition, and giving a clear confession of his faith, he was condemned to be burnt the next day, which was the nineteenth of August.

It happened the same night Pope Paul the Fourth to depart this life ; upon the noise of whose death the people came in a tumult to the place where his statue in marble had been erected and pulling it down, did for the space of three days drag the same through the streets, and in the end threw it in the river of Tiber. During the tumult all the prisons were broken open, the prisoners set free, and among those Mr. Craig had his liberty. As he sought to escape (for he held it not safe to stay in the city), two things happened unto him not unworthy of relation. First, in the suburbs, as he was passing, he did meet a sort of loose men, whom they called banditti ; one of the company, taking him aside, demanded if he had been at any time in Bononia. He answered that he had been some time there. Do you not then remember, said he, that walking on a time in the fields with some young noblemen, there came unto you a poor maimed soldier, entreating some relief ? Mr. Craig replying that he did not well remember. But I do, said he, and I am the man to whom you showed kindness at that time : be not afraid of us, ye shall incur no danger. And so conveying him through the suburbs, and showing what was his safest course, he gave him so much money as might make his charge to Bononia, for he intended to go thither, trusting to find some kindness with those of his acquaintance ; yet at his coming he found them look strange, and fearing to be of new trapped, he slipped away secretly, taking his course to Milan.

By the way another accident befell him, which I should scarce relate, so incredible it seemeth, if to many of good place he himself had not often repeated it as a singular testimony of God's care of him, and this it was. When he had travelled some days, declining the highways out of fear, he came into a forest, a wild and desert place, and being sore wearied lay down among some bushes on the side of a little brook to refresh himself. Lying there pensive and full of thoughts (for neither knew he in what part he was, nor had he any means to bear him out the way), a dog cometh fawning with a purse in his teeth, and lays it down before him. He stricken with a fear riseth up, and looking about if any were coming that way, when he saw none, taketh it up, and construing the same to proceed from God's favourable providence towards him, followed his way till he came to a little village, where he met with some that were travelling to Vienna in Austria, and changing his intended course went in their company thither.

Being there, and professing himself one of the Dominican order, he was brought to preach before Maximilian the Second, who, liking the man and his manner of teaching, would have retained him, if by letters from Pope Pius the Third he had not been required to send him back to Rome, as one that was condemned for heresy. The emperor not liking to deliver him, and on the other part not willing to fall out with the Pope, did quietly dimit him with letters of safe conduct. So travelling through Germany he came to England, and being there informed of the Reformation begun at home, he returned into Scotland, and made offer of his service to the Church. But his long desuetude of the country language (which was not to be marvelled, considering that he had lived abroad the space of twenty-four years,) made him unuseful at first; now and then to the learneder sort he preached in Latin in the Magdalen's Chapel at Edinburgh, and in the year 1561, after he had recovered the language, was appointed minister at Halyrudhouse. The next year he was taken to Edinburgh, and served as colleague with Mr. Knox the space of nine years. Then by the ordinance of the Assembly he was translated to Montrose, where he continued two years, and upon the death of Adam Heriot was removed to Aberdeen, having the inspection of the Churches of Mar and Buchan committed to his care. In the year 1579 he was called to be the King's minister, and served in that charge till, borne down with the weight of years, he was forced to retire himself. After which time, forbearing all public exercises, he lived private at home, comforting himself with the remembrance of the mercies of God that he had tasted in his life past; and this year, on the twelfth of December, without all pain died peaceably at Edinburgh in the eighty-eighth year of his age.

(From the Same.)

SIR HENRY WOTTON

[Born 9th April 1568, at Boughton Hall, in the Parish of Boughton, Malherbe, Kent ; educated at Winchester, and New and Queen's Colleges, Oxford ; travelled on the Continent from about 1590 to 1599, spending five of these years in Italy ; on his return attached himself to the Earl of Essex, whom he accompanied on two sea-voyages and on his Irish expedition ; on the discovery of Essex's plot secretly quitted the country for Italy ; about 1602 was, under the assumed name Octavio Baldi, admitted to an audience by James VI. at Stirling.   After the accession of James I. he was three times sent ambassador to Venice, besides being charged with several diplomatic missions in Germany, including an embassy to the Emperor Ferdinand II., in the affairs of the dethroned Queen of Bohemia and her family.   On his retirement in 1623 he was promised the reversion of the Mastership of the Rolls, but obtained the Provostship of Eton College.   In 1627 he took deacon's orders.   He died at Eton in December 1639.]

THE roll of our notable prose writers, like that of our poets of genius, would be incomplete without the name of Sir Henry Wotton, which is illuminated by something beyond the afterglow of the great age to which, both by his nurture and by his sympathies, he belonged. For he represents more distinctly perhaps than any other of his contemporaries the militant Protestantism which counted for so much in the whole life of their age. Like Bacon, he formed part of the younger generation which passed from the service of the great Queen into that of her successor. Had it been morally possible for James I. to allow their counsels to determine permanently the balance of his judgment, European history might have taken a different course. But this by the way. What concerns us is the type which in Wotton is so cherished by Englishmen. Advanced Protestants in their religious views (for to call them Puritans would be a misnomer), these heroes of an unheroic age were, it must be confessed, unhampered by too nice a scrupulosity in their methods of political conduct, and well fitted to co-operate with the statesmen who enjoyed the confidence of Henry IV., or contributed despatches to the Chancery of militant Calvinism in the Empire. Wotton, before he became a diplomatist himself and wrote despatches which lie outside our present range, and of which, for the rest, but few seem to have been preserved, took occasion to put forth a manifesto of his opinions which is certainly not lacking in plainness. In his later days he advised a young aspirant in his profession always to tell the truth, more especially since nobody would ever believe it to be such. But the spirit of *The State of Christendom*, written shortly before the death of Queen Elizabeth, and the largest and most important of Wotton's extant prose writings, is that of a self-confident aggressiveness without *arrière-pensées*. It opens with a plain statement that in the weary days of the author's foreign exile there had occurred to him, among other possible ways of bringing about his return, the notion of "murdering some notable traitor to his prince and country"; but that on second thoughts he had not carried out the scheme, as likely to entail upon him both danger and disquietude. In the body of the essay he argues very audaciously, and at the same time very subtly, in defence of such disputable acts as the execution of Mary Queen of Scots and the murder of the Duke of Guise, but he is not less prepared to show cause why King Philip of Spain should be lawfully excommunicated and deposed, and dealt with accordingly. An argument conducted in this practical fashion may serve to show that revolutions, such as were attempted in the state of Western Christendom alike by the Calvinist propaganda and by the Catholic reaction, are not made with rose-water; but no refinements of style could render it pleasant reading, and to these indeed it makes no pretence. With this treatise should be compared Wotton's youthful letters to Lord Ford from Germany, which breathe the same defiant spirit. I have extracted from *The State of Christendom* part of an interesting passage on the relations between the King of Spain and "the Turk" of the period, in order to show the forcible directness of which Wotton was capable when he allowed his English Prose to remain unadorned by the quaint conceits and Italian phrases which abound in his "familiar" letters. His chief attempt in the field of natural science, for which he always retained a keen interest, was in Latin, and the work of his Oxford days; but his treatise on *The Elements of Architecture* is in the vernacular, and to the full as readable as any modern pamphlet on house-decoration. More ambitious in design, but, like nine-tenths of his writings, only fragmentary in execution, is the *Survey of Education; or, Moral Architecture*, which consists of aphorisms and a preface, the latter interesting as seeking to place education on its true, *i.e.* psychological, basis. The historical pieces are similarly unfinished, unless we should except the not very profound quasi-Plutarchian parallel between Essex and Buckingham, and the servile panegyric "to" Charles I. This king loved epigrams, and Wotton the making of them—witness his famous definition of an ambassador, as sent to 'lie abroad,' on behalf of his country—a witticism, wickedly published by Scioppius several years after date. The panegyric contains a more academic saying of which its author wished mention to be made in his epitaph, thus "Englished" by Izaak Walton:

> "Here lies the first author of this sentence:
> 'The itch of disputation will prove the scab of Churches.'
> Inquire his name elsewhere."

We might well wish that he had, among his many designs, carried out that of a Life of Luther, with a history of the German Reformation; for nobody better knew how to correlate a great man and his times, and he had in him both enthusiasm and humour enough to understand the genius of the great Reformer. Wotton's own religious meditations have nothing specially characteristic in them, but they breathe the fervent piety which lends their deepest charm to his later letters, and which reveals itself even in the chance expressions of so personal a "report" as that which I have extracted from his letters to Sir Edmund Bacon,—to my mind next to the *Poems* the pleasantest part of the *Reliquiæ Wottonianæ*. It is necessary to turn to this varied collection from Izaak Walton's delightful but imperfectly balanced *Life*, which presents to us the Provost of Eton in his cloistered retirement—a solitude of study and prayer—rather than the enthusiastic "servant" of Elizabeth of Bohemia, the eager friend of Father Paul, the courtier, the politician, and the wit. And to those who are not content with a mere glance at Wotton's prose, fragmentary as it is, most passages of his *Remains* will I think suggest a combination of characteristics rare in the style even of a highly cultivated writer, unless he is at the same time a man of convictions rooted in principle and matured by experience.

A. W. WARD.

HOW TO MEET THE TURK

THE Turk he (the Spanish king) knoweth to be a Prince greatly to be feared of all Christians, as well in regard of his great power, as in respect of his subtile policy. His power is terrible, because he armeth speedily, and that in such multitudes, as both the number and the expedition terrifieth all Christendom. For when he armeth, he most commonly bruiteth it abroad, that he meaneth to carry his Forces to one place, when indeed, he conveyeth them to another; yea, and sometimes he sendeth Ambassadors to will them to be assured and out of all doubt, that he will not in any wise molest or trouble them, whom his full intent, purpose, and resolution is to invade upon a sudden. Considering therefore his strength, his religion, his natural hatred against Christians, together with the continual emulation, quarrels, and contentions that are betwixt Christian princes, he holdeth it most convenient and necessary to have always a vigilant eye over such an adversary. For of Christian princes, he considereth who they be whom he most envieth, whose states he most longeth for, after whose dominions he most thirsteth, and unto which he hath best access, and easiest possibility to attain them. The House of Austria are his nearest kinsmen, and on one side, the next adjoining neighbours unto the Turkish territories. With them for kindred's sake he entertaineth perpetual amity, and is loth to offer them any occasion of discontentment because he knoweth that of late years they have not only possessed the Empire, but also been greatly favoured in Germany, with whose invincible power and puissance, they are both able and ready, when occasion shall be offered, to offend and defend the Turk. For it is their dominion unto which the Turk hath an especial eye, and an unsatiable desire, and by them and their means, Christian princes most annoy him; because by the country of Hungary the way lieth open unto these regions, which he lately subdued; and a

Christian prince leading an army through the country against the Turk, may undoubtedly have good success against his forces, if he shall observe these conditions following :—

First.   If in conducting his army he shall avoid and decline the wide plains, and come not near unto the river Danubius ; of the commodity whereof, the Turk by reason of his great courage, standeth always in need.

Secondly.   If he shall not come nigh unto such places where the Turk may have convenient use of his horsemen and innumerable footmen ; with the excessive multitudes of which, he will easily oppress and suppress a Christian army, if they should chance to encounter in those plains.

Thirdly.   If the Christian prince shall arm this year, and proceeding slowly on his journey not meet with the Turk, but fortify and strengthen such places as he shall get and conquer ; and the next year, when, as the Turk neither is wont, nor can arm with the like number and quantity, proceed manfully ; for the Prince in thus doing, shall compel him to stand continually upon his guard, and always to entertain great and gross armies, which he should not be able to endure long ; or else enforce him to use such forces as might be more easily conquered, and so consequently drive him to change the accustomed course and custom of his wars, which would be as much as half a victory gotten against him.

Fourthly.   If the Christians shall endeavour to draw him into some strait, and there with some warlike stratagem enforce him to a battle, and with a troop of well-ordered footmen, encounter his Janizaries, which he usually reserveth for some extremity, and some unknown and unusual exploit, drive them to the worst, or put them out of their array and order ; there is no doubt but with the strangeness thereof he might obtain a notable victory against him ; whose horsemen are most easily overthrown, because they are for the most part unarmed.

Fifthly.   If he shall mark and observe when there is a mutiny, sedition, or secret dissension, disturbance, or discontentment betwixt the Turk and his subjects, and by all cunning and policy entertain the same, maintain the procurers and heads thereof, and in the very heat of their tumult be ready to invade them. For indeed, the especial means to weaken the Turk, is to assault him when he is otherwise busied in wars with the Sophi, or with any other enemies, or when his successors are at contention for the crown, or his people divided amongst themselves, or he did lately receive some notable overthrow; for he, tyrannising his subjects in such manner as he doth, the least overthrow that can be, must needs endanger his State greatly, because he feareth that his own people will be ready to give entertainment, aid, and succour unto any, by whom they may have certain hope to wind their necks out of the yoke of that intolerable servitude which they now suffer.

This is so true, that it is credibly affirmed by the best warriors of our age : that if the Christians had proceeded with their invincible navy, when Don John de Austria gave the Turk the famous overthrow (for which all Christendom greatly rejoiced) they might haply have gotten Constantinople, and have recovered most part of the Turkish dominion.

(From *The State of Christendom.*)

TO SIR EDMUND BACON

O (MY most dear nephew, for so I still glory to call you, while Heaven possesseth her who bound us in that relation) how have I of late after many vexations of a fastidious infirmity, been at once rent in pieces by hearing that you were at London : what ? said I, and must it be at a time when I cannot fly thither to have my wonted part of that conversation ; wherein all that know him enjoy such infinite contentment ? Thus much did suddenly break loose from the heart that doth truly honour you. And now (Sir) let me tell you both how it hath gone with me, and how I stand at the present. There is a triple health. Health of body, of mind, and of fortune ; you shall have a short account of all three.

For the first : it is now almost an whole cycle of the sun, since after certain fits of a quotidian fever, I was assailed by that splenetic passion, which a country good fellow that had been a piece of a grammarian meant, when he said he was sick of the *flatus*, and the other hard word, for *hypocondriacus* stuck in his teeth ; it is the very Proteus of all maladies ; shifting into sundry shapes, almost every night a new, and yet still the same ; neither can I hope that it will end in a solar period ; being such a saturnine humour ; but though the core and root of it be remaining, yet the symptoms (I thank my God) are well allayed, and in general I have found it of more contumacy than malignity ; only since the late cold weather, there is complicated with it a more asthmatical straightness of respiration than heretofore ; yet those about me say I bear it well, as perchance custom hath taught me, being now familiarised and domesticated evils, in the tragedian's expression : *Jam mansueta mala.* And thus much of the habit of my body. On the other side : my mind is in a right philosophical state of health ; that is, at an equal distance both from desire and hope ; and ambitious of nothing, but of doing nothing and of being nothing ; yet I have some employment of my thoughts to keep them from mouldering, as you shall know before I close this letter. But first, touching the third kind of health. My condition or fortune was never better, than in this good Lord Treasurer's time ; the very reverse of his proud predecessor, that made a scorn of my poverty, and a sport of my modesty ; leaving me in a bad case ; and the world, so as though we now know by what arts he lived, yet are we ignorant to this hour by what religion he died, save only that it could not be good, which was not worthy the professing. This free passage let me commit to your noble breast, remembering that in confidence of the receiver, I have transgressed a late counsel of mine own which I gave to a young friend, who asking me casually of what he should make him a suit, as he was passing this way towards London ; I told him that in my opinion, he could not buy a cheaper nor a more lasting stuff there than silence. For I loved him well, and was afraid of a little freedom that I spied in him. And now, Sir, I must needs conclude (or I shall burst) with letting you know, that I have divers things in wild sheets that think and struggle to get out of several kinds, some long promised, and some of a newer conception ; but a poor exercise of my pen (wherewith I shall only honour myself by the dedication thereof unto your own person) is that which shall lead the way by mine and your good leave, intending (if God yield me his favour) to print it before it be long in Oxford, and to send you thence, or bring you a copy to our Redgrave. What the subject is you must not know beforehand, for I fear it will want all other grace, if it lose virginity. And so the Lord of all abundant joy keep you long, *con quella buona Ciera*, which this my servant did relate unto me,

Who live, at all your commands,

HENRY WOTTON.

From your College,
this Ashwednesday, 1637.   (From *Reliquiæ Wottonianæ.*)

JOHN DONNE

[John Donne was born in London in 1573, his father being a tradesman or merchant of means, his mother a daughter of Heywood the epigrammatist, and a relation of Sir Thomas More. He was brought up in a Roman Catholic circle, if not actually as a Roman Catholic; but was admitted at Hart Hall, Oxford. Perhaps (for Walton could hardly be wrong here, though later biographers doubt) he was also entered at Cambridge. He travelled, and became a member of Lincoln's Inn in 1592, now definitely casting in his lot with the English Church; but it was long before he took orders. He went the Cadiz voyage in 1596, and on his return became a member of the household of Lord Keeper Egerton. Here he fell in love with and clandestinely married Anne More or Moore, a connexion of the Lord Keeper's wife. Her father, Sir George, was very angry, and procured Donne's dismissal and imprisonment; but this difficulty blew over. Donne would apparently have chosen lay preferment, but, though he was a favourite with James the First, none came, and at length, in 1615, he took orders. The king made him his chaplain, and he received several livings and the readership of Lincoln's Inn. His wife, whom he idolised, died in 1617, and his heart seems to have been broken : his appointment to the Deanery of St. Paul's in 1621 making no change in the ascetic and mystical tincture which his life and thought had taken. He held his post ten years, and died on the 31st March 1631. Of his various poems nothing need be said here, and, indeed, few of them were published during his life. His first published work was prose — a treatise entitled *Pseudo Martyr*—written at the king's desire to reconcile Roman Catholics to the oath of allegiance (1610). He also wrote essays, "devotions," and miscellaneous tractates, of which the chief, not published till after his death, was a paradox on suicide, entitled *Biathanatos*. But his principal work in prose is composed of sermons which fall but little short of the second hundred in number. It is unlucky that the only full edition of his works, that of Alford in 1839, is not complete, and is very badly done.]

THE characteristics of Donne's voluminous and now little read prose are not on the whole very different from those of his strange and frequently exquisite but far less voluminous and better known verse. The differences, indeed, are little more than might be expected to be caused by the variation of subject and the advance of years. If he seldom, in prose, reaches the highest efforts of his unique imagination in verse, the removal of the restraints of verse frees his prose for the most part from the extreme obscurity and the labyrinthine conceit of his poetry. The latter traits appear chiefly in his Letters. These are sometimes charming, and they often display the wit with which Coleridge (in the modern sense rather than that in which the word was used of Donne by his own contemporaries) credits him. But elsewhere they are far from clear, and the forlorn condition, dateless and of uncertain address, in which we sometimes have them, aggravates their difficulty. The chief fault of the Sermons is again different. There are magnificent passages in them, but these passages are too often brief, and hardly separable from the context. They sometimes contain the germ of much more elaborate things written subsequently; for instance, one of Jeremy Taylor's most celebrated pieces—that on the fragility of human life and health —is little more than an amplification of Donne. But something of the same want of perfect command of his wide learning, his profound thought, his soaring imagination, which mars the Poems, appears likewise in the Sermons. It is sometimes rather hard for the modern reader to discern what Donne, in modern phrase, is "driving at"; and the same reader is apt to be teased and annoyed by the perpetual running accompaniment of Protestant and Papist controversy, natural and indeed inevitable in the time and circumstances, but too omnipresent, and yet not sufficiently raised to the great scale. The learning also, like the imagination, may seem not sufficiently under control.

But the saving grace of Donne, in prose as in poetry, is the strength and savour of his *quality*, in the strict sense of the word. In this quality he has no rival in English; no rival, I think, anywhere except in the author of the *Confessions*. Donne, indeed, and St. Augustine stand almost alone in the temper of thought and sentiment which a youth of passion followed by a middle age of devotion has impressed upon them, and which utters itself perpetually in their style. Even the translators of the *Confessions* have not been able entirely to obliterate the tone of mingled asceticism and regret for things quite other than ascetic which echoes from page after page of the original; and this same tone is found in Donne, heightened and deepened during his later days to an almost unearthly pitch by the death of his wife and the bodily feebleness which seems to have come on him. Many who know little else about him know the strange fancy which caused him to have his portrait painted coffined and shrouded, as well as Walton's description of the famous last sermon, from which an extract is given below. But this same sentiment or mixture of sentiments pervades his work as an undertone even where it does not come to the surface. It is a tone which, in a younger man, or less constantly maintained in less voluminous work by a man of equal experience of life, might arouse a strong suspicion of insincerity. But such a suspicion would be utterly out of place in the case of Donne.

In the minor particular of quaintness he is more on a par with others of his time ; but here also he excels them. Even the most careless reader must note in him expressions of a racy oddity not surpassed by Fuller or Burton, by Glanville or Browne. " False and *fashional* Christians " ; " ragefully " ; " Who would be loth to sink by being over freighted with God, or loth to overset by having so much of that wind the breath of the Spirit of God." These are but specimens of the things that meet the mere turner-over of the Sermons *passim* and without the trouble of minute attention. A little, but a very little, more may be required to do justice to the extraordinary profundity of Donne's thought, and the accuracy of his observations of human nature, such as that given in our last extract, which might be taken as a motto describing the sin or mental disease which in the Middle Ages men called " accidia." " In a dark sadness indifferent things seem abominable or necessary, being neither ; as trees and sheep to melancholy night-walkers have unproper shapes." But the most careful reading will be the best repaid by discoveries of this sort. And before long the reader will perceive, everywhere rising from the page, and expressed in it with a power extremely rare in prose, and not very common even in poetry, that mood which has been already referred to :—a mood in which the memory of bygone earthly delights blends inextricably with the present fervour of devotion, and which to a fancy resembling his own might suggest a temple of Aphrodite or Dionysus turned into a Christian church, and served by the same priest as of old, with complete loyalty to his new faith, but with undying consciousness of the past.

GEORGE SAINTSBURY.

OCCASIONAL MERCIES

IF I should declare what God hath done (done occasionally,) for my soul, where He instructed me for fear of falling, where He raised me when I was fallen, perchance you would rather fix your thoughts upon my illness, and wonder at that, than at God's goodness, and glorify Him in that ; rather wonder at my sins than at His mercies, rather consider how ill a man I was, than how good a God He is. If I should enquire upon what occasion God elected me, and writ my name in the book of life, I should sooner be afraid that it were not so, than find a reason why it should be so. God made sun and moon to distinguish seasons, and day and night, and we cannot have the fruits of the earth but in their seasons ; but God hath made no decree to distinguish the seasons of His mercies ; in Paradise, the fruits were ripe the first minute, and in Heaven it is always autumn, His mercies are ever in their maturity. We ask our daily bread, and God never says you should have come yesterday. He never says you must again to-morrow, but *to-day if ye will hear His voice*, to-day He will hear you. If some king of the earth have so large an extent of dominion in north and south, as that he hath winter and summer together in his dominions, so large an extent east and west as that he hath day and night together in his dominions, much more hath God mercy and judgment together ; He brought light out of darkness, not out of a lesser light ; He can bring thy summer out of winter, though thou have no spring ; though in the ways of fortune, or understanding, or conscience, thou have been benighted till now, wintred and frozen, clouded and eclipsed, damped and benumbed, smothered and stupified till now, now God comes to thee, not as in the dawning of the day, not as in the bud of the spring, but as the sun at noon, to illustrate all shadows, as the sheaves in harvest, to fill all penuries, all occasions invite His mercies, and all times are His seasons.

(From *Sermons preached on Christmas Day.*)

SALVATION

HERE then salvation is eternal salvation; not the outward seals of the church upon the person, not visible sacraments, nor the outward seal of the person to the church, visible works, nor the inward seal of the Spirit, assurance here, but fruition, possession of glory, in the kingdom of heaven; where we shall be infinitely rich, and that without labour in getting, or care in keeping, or fear in losing; and fully wise, and that without ignorance of necessary, or study of unnecessary knowledge, where we shall not measure our portion by acres, for all heaven shall be all ours; nor our term by years, for it is life and everlasting life; nor our assurance by precedent, for we shall be safer than the angels themselves were in the creation; where our exaltation shall be to have a crown of righteousness, and our possession of that crown shall be, even the throwing it down at the feet of the Lamb; where we shall leave off all those petitions of *Adveniat regnum*, Thy kingdom come, for it shall be come in abundant power; and the *Da nobis hodie*, Give us this day our daily bread, for we shall have all that which we can desire now, and shall have a power to desire more, and then have that desire so enlarged, satisfied; and the *Libera nos*, we shall not pray to be delivered from evil, for no evil, *culpæ* or *pænæ*, either of sin to deserve punishment, or of punishment for our former sins, shall offer at us: where we shall see God face to face, for we shall have such notions and apprehensions as shall enable us to see him, and he shall afford such an imparting, such a manifestation of himself, as he shall be seen by us; and where we shall be as inseparably united to our Saviour, as His humanity and divinity are united together; this unspeakable, this unimaginable happiness is this salvation, and therefore let us be glad when this is brought near us.

And this is brought nearer and nearer unto us, as we come nearer and nearer to our end. As he that travels weary, and late towards a great city, is glad when he comes to a place of execution, because he knows that is near the town: so when thou comest to the gate of death, glad of that, for it is but one step from that to thy Jerusalem. Christ hath brought us in some nearness to salvation, as he is *vere Salvator mundi*, in that we *know, that this is indeed the Christ, the Saviour of the world*: and He hath brought it nearer than that, as he is *Salvator corporis sui*, in that we know *that Christ is the head of the church, and the Saviour of that body* : and nearer than that, as he is *Salvator tuus Sanctus*, in that we know, *he is the Lord our God, the Holy One of Israel, our Saviour :* but nearest of all, in the *Ecce Salvator tuus venit*, Behold thy salvation cometh. It is not only promised in the prophets, nor only writ in the Gospel, nor only sealed in the sacraments, nor only prepared in the visitations of the Holy Ghost, but, *ecce*, behold it, now, when thou canst behold nothing else : the sun is setting to thee, and that for ever ; thy houses and furniture, thy gardens and orchards, thy titles and offices, thy wife and children are departing from thee, and that for ever ; a cloud of faintness is come over thine eyes, and a cloud of sorrow over all theirs ; when his hand that loves thee best hangs tremblingly over thee to close thine eyes *ecce Salvator tuus venit*, behold then a new light, thy Saviour's hand shall open thine eyes, and in His light thou shalt see light ; and thus shalt see, that though in the eyes of men thou lie upon that bed, as a statue on a tomb, yet in the eyes of God, thou standest as a colossus, one foot in one, another in another land ; one foot in the grave, but the other in heaven ; one hand in the womb of the earth, and the other in Abraham's bosom ; and then *vere prope*, salvation is truly near thee, and nearer than when thou believedst, which is our last word.

(From *Sermon to the Prince and Princess Palatine.*)

THE ARITHMETIC OF SIN

THE pureness and cleanness of heart which we must love, was evidently represented in the old law, and in the practice of the Jews, who took knowledge of so many uncleannesses ; they reckon almost fifty sorts of uncleannesses, to which there belonged particular expiations ; of which, some were hardly to be avoided in ordinary conversation : as to enter into the courts of justice ; for the Jews that led Christ into the common hall, would not enter, lest they should be defiled. Yea, some things defiled them, which it had been unnatural to have left undone ; as for the son to assist at his father's funeral ; and yet even these required an expiation ; for these, though they had not the nature of sin, but might be expiated (without any inward sorrow or repentance) by outward ablutions, by ceremonial washings, within a certain time prescribed by the law, yet if that time were negligently and inconsiderately overslipped, then they became sins, and then they could not be expiated, but by a more solemn, and a more costly way, by sacrifice. And even before they came to that, whilst they were but uncleannesses and not sins, yet even then they made them incapable of eating the Paschal Lamb. So careful was God in the law, and the Jews in their practice (for these outward things) to preserve this pureness, this cleanness, even in things which were not fully sins. So also must he that affects this pureness of heart, and studies the preserving of it, sweep down every cobweb that hangs about it. Scurrile and obscene language : yea, misinterpretable words, such as may bear an ill sense ; pleasureable conversation and all such little entanglings, which though he think too weak to hold him, yet they foul him. And let him that is subject to these smaller sins, remember, that as a spider builds always where he knows there is most access and haunt of flies, so the devil that hath cast these light cobwebs into thy heart, knows that that heart is made of vanities and levities ; and he that gathers into his treasure whatsoever thou wastest out of thine, how negligent soever thou be, he keeps thy reckoning exactly, and will produce against thee at last as many lascivious glances as shall make up an adultery, as many covetous wishes as shall make up a robbery, as many angry words as shall make up a murder ; and thou shalt have dropped and crumbled away thy soul, with as much irrecoverableness, as if thou hadst poured it out all at once ; and thy merry sins, thy laughing sins, shall grow to be crying sins, even in the ears of God ; and though thou drown thy soul here, drop after drop, it shall not burn spark after spark, but have all the fire, and all at once, and all eternally, in one entire and intense torment. For, as God, for our capacity, is content to be described as one of us, and to take our passions upon Him, and be called angry, and sorry, and the like ; so is He in this also like us, that He takes it worse to be slighted, to be neglected, to be left out, than to be actually injured. Our inconsideration, our not thinking of God in our actions, offends him more than our sins. We know, that in nature, and in art, the strongest bodies are compact of the least particles, because they shut best, and lie closest together ; so be the strongest habits of sin compact of sins which in themselves are least ; because they are least perceived, they grow upon us insensibly, and they cleave unto us inseparably. And I should make no doubt of recovering him sooner that had sinned long against his conscience, though in a great sin, than him that had sinned less sins, without any sense or conscience of those sins ; for I should sooner bring the other to a detestation of his sin, than bring this man to a knowledge, that that that he did was sin. But if thou couldst consider that every sin is a crucifying of Christ, and every sin is a precipitation of thyself from a pinnacle : were it a convenient phrase to say, in every little sin, that thou wouldst crucify Christ a little, or break thy neck a little.

(From *Sermon to the Lords of the Council.*)

DEATH

NOW this which is so singularly peculiar to him, that His flesh should not see corruption, at His second coming, His coming to judgment, shall be extended to all that are then alive, their flesh shall not see corruption ; because (as the apostle says, and says as a secret, as a mystery, *Behold I show you a mystery ; we shall not all sleep*) that is, not continue in the state of the dead, in the grave ; *but we shall all be changed.* In an instant we shall have a dissolution, and in the same instant a redintegration, a recom- pacting of body and soul ; and that shall be truly a death, and truly a resurrection, but no sleeping, no corruption. But for us, who die now, and sleep in the state of the dead, we must all pass this posthume death, this death after death, nay this death after burial, this dissolution after dissolution, this death of corruption and putrefaction, of vermiculation and incineration, of dissolution and dispersion, in, and from the grave. When those bodies which have been the children of royal parents, and the parents of royal children, must say with Job, *To corruption, Thou art my father, and to the worm, Thou art my mother and my sister.* Miserable riddle, when the same worm must be my mother, and my sister, and myself. Miserable incest, when I must be married to mine own mother and sister, and be both father and mother, to mine own mother and sister, beget and bear that worm, which is all that miserable penury, when my mouth shall be filled with dust, and the worm shall feed, and feed sweetly upon me. When the ambitious man shall have no satisfaction if the poorest alive read upon him, nor the poorest receive any contentment, in being made equal to princes, for they shall be equal but in dust. One dieth at his full strength, being wholly at ease, and in quiet, and another dies in the bitterness of his soul, and never eats with pleasure ; but they lie down alike in the dust, and the worm covers them. The worm covers them in Job, and in Esay, it covers them, and is spread under them, (the worm is spread under thee, and the worm covers thee). There is the mats and the carpet that lie under ; and there is the state and the canopy that hangs over the greatest sons of men. Even those bodies that were the temples of the Holy Ghost, come to this dilapidation, to ruin, to rubbish, to dust : even the Israel of the Lord, and Jacob himself had no other specification, no other denomination but that, *Vermis Jacob*, Thou worm Jacob. Truly, the considera- tion of this posthume death, this death after burial, that after God, with whom are the issues of death, hath delivered me from the death of the womb, by bringing me into the world, and from the manifold deaths of the world, by laying me in the grave, I must die again, in an incineration of this flesh, and in a dispersion of that dust ; that all that monarch that spread over many nations alive, must in his dust lie in a corner of that sheet of lead, and there but so long as the lead will last : and that private and retired man, that thought himself his own for ever, and never came forth, must in his dust of the grave be published, and (such are the revolutions of graves) be mingled in his dust, with the dust of every highway, and of every dunghill, and swallowed in every puddle and pond ; this is the most inglorious and con- temptible vilification, the most deadly and peremptory nullification of man, that we can consider. God seems to have carried the declaration of His power to a great height, when He sets the prophet Ezekiel in the valley of dry bones, and says, *Son of man, can these bones live* ? as though it had been impossible ; and yet they did ; the Lord laid sinews upon them, and flesh, and breathed into them, and they did live. But in that case there were bones to be seen : something visible, of which it might be said, Can this, this live ? but in this death of incineration and dispersion of dust, we see nothing that we can call that man's. If we say, Can this dust live ? perchance it cannot. It may be the mere dust of the earth which never did live, nor shall ; it may be the dust of that man's worms which did live, but shall no more ; it may be the dust of another man that concerns not him of whom it is asked. This death of incineration and dispersion is to

natural reason the most irrevocable death of all; and yet *Domini
Domini sunt exitus mortis, Unto God the Lord belong the issues of
death*, and by recompacting this dust into the same body, and re-
animating the same body with the same soul, He shall in a blessed
and glorious resurrection give me such an issue from this death,
as shall never pass into any other death, but establish me in a
life, that shall last as long as the Lord of life himself.

(From *Donne's Last Sermon*.)

TO MY VERY TRUE AND VERY GOOD FRIEND,
SIR HENRY GOODYERE

SIR—At some later reading, I was more affected with that part
of your letter, which is of the book, and the nameless letters, than
at first.   I am not sorry, for that affection were for a jealousy or
suspicion of a flexibility in you.   But I am angry, that any should
think you had in your religion peccant humours, defective, or
abundant, or that such a book (if I mistake it not) should be able
to work upon you ; my comfort is, that their judgment is too
weak to endanger you, since by this it confesses, that it mistakes
you in thinking you irresolved or various ; yet let me be bold to
fear that that sound true opinion, that in all Christian professions
there is way to salvation (which I think you think) may have
been so incommodiously or intempestively sometimes uttered by
you ; or else your having friends equally near you of all the
impressions of religion, may have testified such an indifference,
as hath occasioned some to further such inclinations, as they have
mistaken to be in you.   This I have feared, because heretofore
the inobedient puritans, and now the over-obedient papists,
attempt you.   It hath hurt very many, not in their conscience,
nor ends, but in their reputation, and ways, that others have
thought them fit to be wrought upon.   As some bodies are as
wholesomely nourished as ours, with acorns, and endure nakedness, both which would be dangerous to us, if we for them should
leave our former habits, though theirs were the primitive diet and
custom ; so are many souls well fed with such forms, and dress-
ings of religion, as would distemper and misbecome us, and
make us corrupt towards God, if any human circumstance moved
it and in the opinion of men, though none.   You shall seldom

see a coin, upon which the stamp were removed, though to imprint it better, but it looks awry and squint. And so, for the most part, do minds which have received divers impressions. I will not, nor need to you, compare the religions. The channels of God's mercies run through both fields ; and they are sister teats of His graces, yet both diseased and infected, but not both alike. And I think, that as *Copernicism* in the mathematics hath carried earth farther up, from the stupid centre ; and yet not honoured it, nor advantaged it, because for the necessity of appearances, it hath carried heaven so much higher from it : so the Roman profession seems to exhale, and refine our wills from earthly drugs, and lees, more than the reformed, and so seems to bring us nearer heaven ; but then that carries heaven farther from us, by making us pass so many courts, and offices of saints in this life, in all our petitions, and lying in a painful prison in the next, during the pleasure, not of Him to whom we go, and who must be our Judge, but of them from whom we come, who know not our case.

Sir, as I said last time, labour to keep your alacrity and dignity in an even temper ; for in a dark sadness, indifferent things seem abominable, or necessary, being neither ; as trees, and sheep, to melancholy night-walkers, have unproper shapes. And when you descend to satisfy all men in your own religion, or to excuse others to all : you prostitute yourself and your under-standing, though not a prey, yet a mark, and a hope, and a subject, for every sophister in religion to work on. For the other part of your letter, spent in the praise of the countess, I am always very apt to believe it of her, and can never believe it so well, and so reasonably, as now, when it is averred by you ; but for the expressing it to her, in that sort as you seem to counsel, I have these two reasons to decline it. That that knowledge which she hath of me, was in the beginning of a graver course, than of a poet, into which (that I may also keep my dignity) I would not seem to relapse. The Spanish proverb informs me that he is a fool which cannot make one sonnet, and he is mad which makes two. The other stronger reason is my integrity to the other countess, of whose worthiness, though I swallowed your opinion at first upon your words, yet I have had since an explicit faith, and now a knowledge : and for her delight (since she descends to them) I had reserved not only all the verses, which I should make, but all the thoughts of women's worthiness. But because

I hope she will not disdain, that I should write well of her picture, I have obeyed you thus far, as to write : but entreat you by your friendship that by this occasion of versifying, I be not traduced, nor esteemed light in that tribe, and that house where I have lived. If those reasons which moved you to bid me write be not constant in you still, or if you meant not that I should write verses : or if these verses be too bad, or too good, over or under her understanding, and not fit ; I pray receive them, as a companion and supplement of this letter to you ; and as such a token as I use to send, which use, because I wish rather they should serve (except you wish otherwise) I send no other : but after I have told you, that here at a christening at Peckham, you are remembered by divers of ours, and I commanded to tell you so, I kiss your hands, and so seal to you my pure love, which I would not refuse to do by any labour or danger.—Your very true friend and servant,

J. DONNE.

BEN JONSON

[Born at Westminster in 1573 ; known as a playwright in or before 1597 ; finished his first extant play in the following year ; died 6th August 1637.]

APART from his dramatic prose, which, as he would readily have asseverated, "none but himself" could have produced, Ben is entitled to some sort of niche of his own among our prose writers. It may be going rather far to say, like his most recent biographer Dr. Herford, that "no other contemporary prose equals the *Discoveries* in ripe wisdom or sinewy vigour"; for, whatever opinion may be held concerning the claims of aphoristic composition, Ben Jonson's only extant prose work (with all respect to the *English Grammar*) can hardly be said to belong to any other species. If it, more or less remotely, "approaches the type of the Baconian Essay," it savours far more noticeably of the qualities pervading the *collectanea* of Jonson's friend and master Camden, the scholar extolled by him for his skill and faith

"in things ;
[His] sight in searching the most antique springs."

Yet it would be a short-sighted exclusiveness which should altogether shut the doors of the temple of classic prose to the literature of annotations, albeit the contributions of so many dunces have swelled its total bulk. At all events we have no other prose (outside his plays and their paraphernalia) remaining from Ben Jonson's prolific pen. His *English Grammar*, patriotically designed

"To teach some that their nurses could not do,
The purity of Language,"—

was consumed, together with much else which posterity has more largely lamented, by the fatal conflagration commemorated in his genial *Execration upon Vulcan ;* and only its dry bones or materials, including, however, an instructive series of quotations, have come down to us. His unpublished translation of Barclay's *Argenis*—that typical scholar's delight, the last book of which the hand of Leibniz turned the pages—has likewise passed out of reach.

But the *Discoveries*, which "contain matter" like everything from their author's pen, will serve. They very evidently belong to his declining years, when, though his creative powers were on the wane, his critical faculty, in which he had stood supreme among his fellows, was stronger and more conscious of its strength than ever. With a great reverence for authority, such as that of the ancients in literary matters, he combined a perfectly fearless independence of thought and judgment ; and while as full of reading as he was of experience of life, he digested whatever he read, and was no mere walking mirror of Fleet Street. Thus, although the *Discoveries* contain little or nothing that is original in the sense of being absolutely new, they fully justify their claim to have " flowed out of his daily readings, *or had their reflux to his peculiar notion of the times.*" It is the prerogative of a mind so powerful, so well equipped and so well balanced as his, to be able to form and express all its judgments in its own character, and thus to stamp each of its criticisms with that other kind of originality which renders them invariably interesting.

The complement of Ben Jonson's *Discoveries* is his so-called *Conversations with William Drummond of Hawthornden*, as reported by his host unextenuatingly, but presumably with a touch here and there heightened, and a qualification here and there left out. In these discourses, or heads of discourse, there are passages which once more irresistibly remind us of Jonson's great later namesake, or rather (since it would be an error to regard these *Conversations* as more than the merest rough notes of Ben's actual talk) which suggest that the same versatility, the same precision, and the same force marked much of the spoken as well as of the written criticism of both. Neither in the Devil Tavern nor in the Mitre was the law laid down with a waste of words or with a side-appeal to the audience ; and it is this freedom of spirit, born of self-knowledge and of good faith, to which both the one and the other of these great critics owed their " dictatorships." Beyond a doubt, there are other passages in the *Conversations*, as condensed by Drummond, perhaps after suffering from his part of *auditor tantum*, which are mainly attributable to bile, and resemble some of the incidental utterances of Carlyle,—

of Annandale stock like Ben. Such are the pronouncements : " That Sharpham, Day, Dekker, were all rogues, and that Minsheu was one." "That Abraham Fraunce, in his English Hexameters, was a fool."

But of this there is nothing in the *Discoveries*, which are marked by genuine sobriety of spirit as well as by a dignity of tone which is not least noticeable in so personal a passage as the fine reference to the poet's own career cited below. At the same time the general style of these aphorisms, or notes for essays never intended to be written, is quite unforced ; and we may perhaps have reason to be glad that they were not over-elaborated for publication.

A. W. WARD.

DE MALIGNITATE STUDENTIUM

THERE be some men are born only to suck out the poison of
books : *Habent venenum pro victu ; imo, pro deliciis.* And such
are they that only relish the obscene and foul things in poets ;
which makes the profession taxed. But by whom ? Men that
watch for it ; and (had they not had this hint) are so unjust
valuers of letters, as they think no learning good but what brings
in gain. It shows they themselves would never have been of the
professions they are, but for the profits and fees. But if another
learning, well used, can instruct to good life, inform manners, no
less persuade and lead men, than they threaten and compel, and
have no reward : is it therefore the worse study ? I could never
think the study of wisdom confined only to the philosopher ; or of
piety to the divine ; or of state to the politic : but that he which
can feign a commonwealth (which is the poet) can govern it with
counsels, strengthen it with laws, correct it with judgments, inform it with religion and morals is all these. We do not require in him mere elocution, or an excellent faculty in verse, but
the exact knowledge of all virtues, and their contraries, with
ability to render the one loved, the other hated, by his proper
embattling them. The philosophers did insolently, to challenge
only to themselves that which the greatest generals and gravest
counsellors never durst. For such had rather do, than promise
the best things.

> (From *Timber : or, Discoveries made upon Men and
> Matter.*)

DE BONIS ET MALIS.—DE INNOCENTIA

A GOOD man will avoid the spot of any sin. The very aspersion
is grievous ; which makes him choose his way in his life, as he

would in his journey. The ill man rides through all confidently; he is coated and booted for it. The oftener he offends, the more openly; and the fouler, the fitter in fashion. His modesty, like a riding coat, the more it is worn, is the less cared for. It is good enough for the dirt still, and the ways he travels in. An innocent man needs no eloquence; his innocence is instead of it; else I had never come off so many times from these precipices, whither men's malice hath pursued me. It is true, I have been accused to the lords, to the king, and by great ones: but it happened my accusers had not thought of the accusation with themselves; and so were driven, for want of crimes, to use invention, which was found slander: or too late (being entered so far) to seek starting holes for their rashness, which were not given them. And then they may think what accusation that was like to prove, when they that were the engineers feared to be the authors. Nor were they content to feign things against me, but to urge things feigned by the ignorant against my profession; which though, from their hired and mercenary impudence, I might have passed by, as granted to a nation of barkers, that let out their tongues to lick others' sores; yet I durst not leave myself undefended, having a pair of ears unskilful to hear lies, or have those things said of me, which I could truly prove of them. They objected making of verses to me, when I could object to most of them, their not being able to read them, but as worthy of scorn. Nay, they would offer to urge mine own writings against me, but by pieces (which was an excellent way of malice): as if any man's context might not seem dangerous and offensive, if that which was knit to what went before were defrauded of his beginning; or that things by themselves uttered might not seem subject to calumny, which read entire, would appear most free. At last they upbraided my poverty: I confess she is my domestic; sober of diet, simple of habit, frugal, painful, a good counsellor to me, that keeps me from cruelty, pride, or other more delicate impertinences, which are the nurse-children of riches. But let them look over all the great and monstrous wickednesses, they shall never find those in poor families. They are the issue of the wealthy giants, and the mighty hunters: whereas no great work, or worthy of praise or memory, but came out of poor cradles. It was the ancient poverty that founded commonweals, built cities, invented arts, made wholesome laws, armed men against vices, rewarded them with their own virtues, and preserved the honour and state of nations, till they betrayed themselves to riches. (From the Same.)

NOTÆ DOMINI S. ALBANI DE DOCTRINÆ INTEMPERANTIA

It was well noted by the late lord St. Alban, that the study of words is the first distemper of learning ; vain matter the second ; and a third distemper is deceit, or the likeness of truth ; imposture held up by credulity. All these are the cobwebs of learning, and to let them grow in us is either sluttish, or foolish. Nothing is more ridiculous than to make an author a dictator, as the schools have done Aristotle. The damage is infinite knowledge receives by it ; for to many things a man should owe but a temporary belief, and suspension of his own judgment, not an absolute resignation of himself, or a perpetual captivity. Let Aristotle and others have their dues ; but if we can make farther discoveries of truth and fitness than they, why are we envied ? Let us beware, while we strive to add, we do not diminish, or deface ; we may improve, but not augment. By discrediting falsehood, truth grows in request. We must not go about, like men anguished and perplexed, for vicious affectation of praise ; but calmly study the separation of opinions, find the errors have intervened, awake antiquity, call former times into question ; but make no parties with the present, nor follow any fierce undertakers, mingle no matter of doubtful credit with the simplicity of truth, but gently stir the mould about the root of the question, and avoid all *digladiations*, facility of credit, or superstitious simplicity, seek the consonancy and concatenation of truth ; stoop only to point of necessity, and what leads to convenience. Then make exact animadversion where style hath degenerated, where flourished and thrived in choiceness of phrase, round and clean composition of sentence, sweet falling of the clause, varying an illustration by tropes and figures, weight of matter, worth of subject, soundness of argument, life of invention, and depth of judgment. This is *monte potiri*, to get the hill ; for no perfect discovery can be made upon a flat or a level.

(From the Same.)

SAMUEL PURCHAS

[Samuel Purchas (1577-1626) of St. John's College, Cambridge, some time "minister at Estwood in Essex," afterwards "parson of St. Martins, near Ludgate," wrote (1) *Purchas, his Pilgrimage, or Relations of the World and the Religions observed in all Ages* (1613), a careful abstract of histories of travel; (2) *Purchas, his Pilgrim: Microcosmus, or the Historie of Man, relating the Wonders of his Generation, Vanities in his Degeneration, Necessity of His Regeneration* (1619), a treatise the scope of which is sufficiently indicated by its title; (3) *Purchas his Pilgrims* (1625), a collection of voyages, including those left unprinted by Hakluyt.]

THE most important original work of Purchas is his *Pilgrimage*. In the *Pilgrims*, as in Hakluyt's voyages, the editor is editor and not author. *Microcosmus* is a discourse on the infirmities of the human estate, written with some liveliness, yet hardly escaping from the commonplaces of the subject. *Purchas his Pilgrimage* is a digest of all the accessible information about the inhabitants of different countries and their religions, a successful attempt to bring together and arrange in one large volume the most important observations of voyagers. As an original author, Purchas is more copious than Hakluyt; his style has little of Hakluyt's eloquence, but it is generally adequate to the matter. His industry was well bestowed in his *History of Religions*, and his desultory learning is not unworthy of the approval given by Selden in his preliminary Greek and Latin verses. Four lines of the book stand out from the rest :—

"In Xaindu did Cublai Can build a stately pallace, encompassing sixteen miles of plaine ground with a wall, wherein are fertile meddowes, pleasant springs, delightful streams, and all sorts of beasts of chase and game, and in the middest thereof a sumptuous house of pleasure."

The description of the Mount Amara of the "Abassin Kings" has also an accidental value, from the honour rendered to that mountain by the poets.

W. P. KER.

OF THE HILL AMARA AND THE RARITIES
THEREIN

THE hill Amara hath already been often mentioned, and nothing indeed in all Ethiopia more deserveth mention, whether we respect the natural site, or the employment thereof. Somewhat is written thereof by geographers, and historians, especially by Aluarez, whom we have chiefly followed in the former relations of this country, as an eye-witness of the most things reported ; but neither they, nor he, have anything but by relation, seeing that he passed two days' journey along by the said hill, and that also had almost cost him his life. But John de Baltasar (saith our Friar) lived in the same a long time, and therein served Alexander which was afterwards emperor, and was often by commandment of the same man, when he was emperor, sent thither : out of his relations, Friar a Luys saith he hath borrowed that which here we offer you. And here we offer you no small favour to conduct you into, and about this place, where none may come but an Ethiopian, and that by express licence, under pain of leaving his hands, feet, and eyes behind, in price for his curiosity, and not much less is the danger of such as offer to escape from thence : Aluarez himself being an eye-witness of some such cruel executions inflicted for that offence. This hill is situate as the navel of that Ethiopian body, and centre of their empire, under the equinoctial line, where the sun may take his best view thereof, as not encountring in all his long journey with the like theatre, wherein the graces and muses are actors, no place more graced with nature's store, or furnished with such a storehouse of books, the sun himself so in love with the sight, that the first and last thing he vieweth in all those parts is this hill ; and where antiquitie consecrated unto him a stately temple : the gods (if ye believe Homer, that they feasted in Ethiopia) could not there, nor in the world find a fitter place for entertainment, all of them contributing their best store (if I may so speak) to the banquet, Bacchus, Juno, Venus, Pomona, Ceres, and the rest, with store of fruits, wholesome air, pleasant aspect and prospect ; secured by Mars, lest any sinister accident should interrupt their delights ; if his garrisons of soldiers were needful where nature had so strongly fortified before ; only Neptune with his ruder sea-deities and Pluto with his black-guard of barking Cerberus, and the rest of that dreadful train (whose unwelcome presence would trouble all that are present) are all, save Charon, who attends on every feast, yea now hath ferried away those supposed deities with himself, perpetually exiled from this place. Once, heaven and earth, nature and industry, have all been corrivals to it, all presenting their best presents, to make it of this so lovely presence, some taking this for the place of our forefathers' paradise. And yet though thus admired of others, as a paradise, it is made a prison to some, on whom nature had bestowed the greatest freedom, if their freedom had not been eclipsed with greatness, and though goodly stars, yet by the sun's brightness are forced to hide their light, when gross and earthly bodies are seen, their nobleness making them prisoners, that one sun only may shine in that Ethiopian throne.

It is situate in a great plain largely extending itself every way without other hill in the same for the space of thirty leagues, the form thereof round and circular, the height such, that it is a day's work to ascend from the foot to the top ; round about, the rock is cut so smooth and even, without any unequal swellings, that it seemeth to him that stands beneath, like a high wall, whereon the heaven is as it were propped ; and at the top it is over-hanged with rocks, jutting forth of the sides the space of a mile, bearing out like mushrooms, so that it is impossible to ascend it, or by ramming with earth, battering with cannon, scaling or otherwise to win it. It is above twenty leagues in circuit, compassed with a wall on the top, well wrought, that neither man nor beast in chase may fall down. The top is a plain field, only towards the south is a rising hill, beautifying this plain, as it were with a watch-tower, not serving alone to the eye, but yielding also a pleasant spring which passeth through all that plain, paying his tributes to every garden that will exact it, and making a lake, whence issueth a river, which having from these tops espied Nilus, never leaves seeking to find him, whom he cannot leave both to seek and find, that by his direction and conveyance he may together with him present himself before the father and great king of waters, the sea. The way up to it is cut out within the rock, not with stairs, but ascending by little and little that one may ride up with ease ; it hath also holes cut to let in light and at the foot of this ascending place, a fair gate, with a *Corpus du Guarde*. Half way up is a fair and spacious hall cut out of the same rock, with three windows very large upwards : the ascent is about the length of a lance and a half : and at the top is a gate with another guard. The air above is wholesome and delectable ; and they live there very long, and without sickness. There are no cities on the top, but palaces, standing by themselves, in number four and thirty, spacious, sumptuous, and beautiful, where the princes of the royal blood have their abode with their families. The soldiers that guard the place dwell in tents.

There are two temples, built before the reign of the Queen of Saba, one in honour of the sun, the other of the moon, the most magnificent in all Ethiopia, which by Candace, when she was converted to the Christian faith, were consecrated in the name of the Holy Ghost, and of the Crosse. At that time (they tell) Candace ascending with the eunuch (whose proper name was Indica) to baptize all of the royal blood, which were there kept, Zacharie the eldest of them, was in his baptism named Philip, in remembrance of Philip's converting the eunuch, which caused all the emperors to be called by that name, till John the Saint, who would be called John, because he was crowned on St. John's day : and while they were busy in that holy work of baptising the princes, a dove in fiery form came flying with beams of light, and lighted on the highest temple dedicated to the sun, whereupon it was afterwards consecrated to the Holy Ghost by St. Matthew the Apostle, when he preached in Ethiopia. These two temples were after that given to the monastical knights of the military order of Saint Anthony, by Philip the seventh, with two great and spacious convents built for them. I should lose both you and my self, if I should lead you into their sweet, flourishing, and fruitful gardens, whereof there are store in this plain, curiously made, and plentifully furnished with fruits both of Europe plants there, as pears, pippins, and such like ; and of their own, as oranges, citrons, lemons, and the rest ; cedars, palm-trees, with other trees, and variety of herbs and flowers, to satisfy the sight, taste, and scent. But I would entertain you, only with rarities, nowhere else to be found ; and such is the cubayo tree, pleasant beyond all comparison in taste, and whereunto for the virtue is imputed the health, and long life of the inhabitants ; and the balm-tree, whereof there is great store here : and hence it is thought the Queen of Saba carried and gave to Solomon, who planted them in Judæa, from whence they were transplanted at Cairo long after. The plenty of grains and corn there growing, the charms of birds alluring the ear with their warbling notes, and fixing the eyes on their colours, jointly agreeing in beauty, by their disagreeing variety, and other creatures that adorn this paradise, might make me glut you •(as sweet meats usually do) with too much store. Let us therefore take view of some other things worthy our admiration in this admired hill, taking the Friar for our guide, whose credit I leave to your censure.

(From *Purchas, His Pilgrimage.*)

SIR THOMAS OVERBURY

[Sir Thomas Overbury (1581-1613) was the son of Nicholas Overbury, a squire in Gloucestershire. After three years at Queen's College, Oxford, where he took the degree of B.A., he travelled for some time on the Continent. His introduction to the Court was doubtless due to Carr, who was, till close upon Overbury's death, his most intimate and constant companion. In 1608 Overbury was knighted ; in the following year he visited France and the Low Countries, and wrote his *Observations Upon the State of the Seventeen Provinces*. On his return he was regarded as the most accomplished of James's courtiers, and the wits and poets vied with each other in soliciting his patronage. Ben Jonson, with whom he quarrelled afterwards, ascribes in some complimentary verses the saving of wit and manners at Court to Overbury's presence. In 1613, as "oracle of direction" to Carr, now Lord Rochester, Overbury strongly opposed his friend's marriage with the Countess of Essex, who had obtained a divorce with this purpose. The countess in revenge secured his imprisonment in the Tower, where, after five months of lingering suffering, he died of poison at the age of thirty-eight. In 1616 Rochester (then Somerset) and his wife were found guilty of the murder. Some contemporary records suggest that James I. was implicated. It is possible that the pride and insolence of bearing with which one contemporary, Weldon, charges Overbury, may have made him enemies at Court. But even this writer admits him to have been "a man of excellent parts." Overbury's works, published after his death, gained an immense popularity. His poem of *The Wife*, written, according to Overbury's father, "to induce Viscount Rochester to make a better choice than of the divorced Countess," appeared in 1614. To the second edition in the same year were "added many witty Characters and conceited News, written by himself and other learned gentlemen his friends." There are only twenty-one characters in this issue. By the ninth impression in 1616 the number had swelled to eighty. An excellent comparison of Theophrastus and his English followers— Hall, Overbury, and Earle—is to be found in Mr. Jebb's introduction to his edition of *Theophrastus* (Macm. 1870).]

SHORT sketches of character and manners form a feature of our seventeenth-century literature. Over two hundred "characters," or books of characters, are said to have been published between the years 1605 and 1700. Casaubon had published in 1592 a Latin translation of Theophrastus. But though the Greek author is taken as a model in some of these works, the main causes of their prevalence are to be sought in the age itself. "There was," says Mr. Jebb, "in one particular, a rough analogy between the literature of that century in England and the Greek literature of the age of Theophrastus ; both were marked by the reaction from creating to analysing, and in both ethical analysis was a favourite subject." Church and stage alike fostered a taste for these character sketches. Of these the earliest of any importance— Hall's *Characterisms of Virtues and Vices* (1608), which have an avowedly didactic purpose—shows the tendency to ethical intro- spection which Puritanism brought with it. Overbury's *Characters*, which followed Hall's, take their cue rather from the comedy of the time ; they are framed pretty much after the model of the descriptions of contemporary manners, that are occasionally to be found in such plays as *Cynthia's Revels.* Hall's *Characters* are illustrations for sermons ; Overbury's, for the most part, echo the wit and gossip of court and tavern. Further, euphuism was a dialect specially adapted to personal criticism of this kind. But while it lent itself to this taste, it at the same time led off the writer from simple description into elaborate comment. Hall, though following in the main the manner of Theophrastus in giving characteristic anecdotes, is affected to some extent by the prevalent taste for conceit and antithesis. In Overbury it reaches its height. As a rule, illustrations are sacri- ficed to make room for epithets ; and even when he does illustrate traits by examples, they are given neither simply nor concretely enough to be effective. A comparison of one of Theophrastus' characters—say, *The Shameless Man*—with *An Affectate Traveller*, one of the best of Overbury's, will show how Overbury's wit is apt to spoil his humour. The following is an average specimen of his style, "*A Dissembler* is an essence needing a double definition, for he is not that he appears. Unto the eye he is pleasing, unto the ear not harsh, but unto the understanding intricate, and full of windings ; he is the *prima materia*, and his intents give him form ; he dyeth his means and his meaning into two colours ; he baits craft with humility, and his countenance is the picture of the present disposition. He wins not by battery, but undermining, and his rack is smoothing. He allures, is not allured by his affections, for they are the brokers of his observa- tion. He knows passion only by sufferance, and resisteth by obeying. He makes his time an accountant to his memory, and of the humours of men weaves a net for occasion : the inquisitor must look through his judgment, for to the eye only he is visible." Overbury is constantly on the track of the ingenious. He places subtlety of words before subtlety of invention and characterisation; the originality of the idea rarely justifies the novelty of its expression. Many of the sketches, as *A Sailor*, *A Tailor*, and others, are little more than a succession of puns. Yet most are to some extent redeemed by a sentence or two. "*A Flatterer* is the shadow of a fool." Of an *Ignorant Glory-hunter :* "He confesseth vices he is guiltless of, if they be in fashion." Of a *Timist :* "He never praiseth any but before themselves or friends ; and mislikes no great man's actions during his life." Of a *Good Woman :* "Dishonesty never comes nearer than her ears, and then wonder stops it out, and saves virtue the labour. . . . She hath a content of her own, and so seeks not a husband, but finds him." This last portrait, which comes first in the collection, shows, like *A Franklin* and *A Fair and Happy Milkmaid*, a sincere appreciation of virtue ; but, as a rule, Overbury's style is more serviceable in satire.

Only a small proportion of Overbury's sketches are "characters" in the Theophrastian sense. Seven-eighths of them are descriptive of callings or professions rather than of moral qualities ; and the majority of these, again, seem portraits rather of individuals than of types. The character given to an *Old Man*, or a *Country Gentleman*, is evidently coloured by personal animus. The writer, or writers, of *An Apparitor*, *A Creditor*, *A Sergeant*, and *A Jailor* had probably suffered at their hands. There can be little doubt that *A Tailor* was drawn by a customer who could not pay his bill. Overbury is at his best in the portraiture of manners. He has not his successor Earle's sympathetic insight, nor does he attempt in his characters, as Earle does, a sober estimate of both sides. This can be seen by comparing Earle's with Overbury's *Flatterer*, and Earle's *Downright Scholar* with Overbury's *Mere Scholar*. But Overbury has a quicker eye for small vagaries of behaviour, and for superficial oddities of character ; and he has a wider and more intimate experience to draw from. His *Characters* are valuable as a reflection of the times. The courtier "in Paul's, with a pick-tooth in his hat, a capecloak and a long stocking" ; the button-maker of Amsterdam whose "zeal consists much in hanging his Bible in a Dutch button" ; the sailor whose "language is a new confusion, and all his thoughts new nations" ;

the braggadocio Welshman who "prefers Owen Glendower
before any of the nine worthies :" these and others serve to
bring the age before the modern reader, and at times throw an
interesting light upon the Elizabethan drama.

It is convenient to speak of the *Characters* as Overbury's, but
it must not be forgotten that he is mentioned on the title-page of
every edition merely as joint-author. The method of their publication justifies the inference that Overbury wrote only a few of
them. It is impossible, however, to say which are his, and which
belong to the " other learned gentlemen, his friends." The dialect
and accent are much the same in all, though more pronounced in
some. Some doublets occur, which seem as if they were rival
exercises on the same theme. There are two portraits of *A
Mere Fellow of an House* ; and it is hard to distinguish between
A Wise Man and *A Noble Spirit*. Some of the sketches have
so little unity of purpose that they might be taken as the result
of a game in which each of a company of wits had taken his turn.
It may be fairly said of most of them that they served to their
writers as butts for " taffeta phrases, silken terms precise."

W. S. M'CORMICK.

AN AFFECTATE TRAVELLER

Is a speaking fashion; he hath taken pains to be ridiculous, and hath seen more than he hath perceived. His attire speaks *French* or *Italian*, and his gait cries, *Behold me.* He censures all things by countenances, and shrugs, and speaks his own language with shame and lisping: he will choke, rather than confess beer good drink; and his pick-tooth is a main part of his behaviour. He chooseth rather to be counted a spy, than not a politician; and maintains his reputation by naming great men familiarly. He chooseth rather to tell lies, than not wonders, and talks with men singly: his discourse sounds big, but means nothing; and his boy is bound to admire him howsoever. He comes still from great personages, but goes with mean. He takes occasion to show jewels given him in regard of his virtue, that were bought at S. Martin's; and not long after having with a mountebank's method pronounced them worth thousands, impawneth them for a few shillings. Upon festival days he goes to court, and salutes without resaluting: at night in an ordinary he canvasseth the business in hand, and seems as conversant with all intents and plots as if he begot them. His extraordinary account of men is, first to tell them the ends of all matters of consequence, and then to borrow money of them; he offereth courtesies, to show them, rather than himself, humble. He disdains all things above his reach, and preferreth all countries before his own. He imputeth his want and poverty to the ignorance of the time, not his own unworthiness; and concludes his discourse with half a period, or a word, and leaves the rest to imagination. In a word, his religion is fashion, and both body and soul are governed by fame; he loves most voices above truth.

(From *The Characters*.)

A MERE FELLOW OF AN HOUSE

HE is one whose hopes commonly exceed his fortunes, and whose mind soars above his purse. If he hath read Tacitus, Guicciardini, or Gallo-Belgicus, he contemns the late Lord Treasurer, for all the state-policy he had ; and laughs to think what a fool he could make of Solomon, if he were now alive. He never wears new clothes, but against a commencement or a good time, and is commonly a degree behind the fashion. He hath sworn to see London once a year, though all his business be to see a play, walk a turn in *Paul's,* and observe the fashion. He thinks it a discredit to be out of debt, which he never likely clears, without resignation money. He will not leave his part he hath in the privilege over young gentlemen, in going bare to him, for the empire of Germany : he prays as heartily for a sealing as a cormorant doth for a dear year ; yet commonly he spends that revenue before he receives it.

At meals, he sits in as great state over his penny commons, as ever Vitellius did at his greatest banquet : and takes great delight in comparing his fare to my Lord Mayor's. If he be a leader of a faction, he thinks himself greater than ever Cæsar was, or the Turk at this day is. And he had rather lose an inheritance than an office, when he stands for it. If he be to travel, he is longer furnishing himself for a five miles' journey, than a ship is rigging for a seven years' voyage. He is never more troubled, than when he is to maintain talk with a gentlewoman : wherein he commits more absurdities, than a clown in eating of an egg. He thinks himself as fine when he is in a clean band and a new pair of shoes, as any courtier doth, when he is first in a new-fashion. Lastly, he is one that respects no man in the University, and is respected by no man out of it.

(From the Same.)

A ROARING BOY

HIS life is a mere counterfeit patent : which nevertheless makes many a country justice tremble. Don Quixote's watermills are still Scotch bagpipes to him. He sends challenges by word of mouth : for he protests (as he is a gentleman and a brother of the sword) he can neither write nor read. He hath run through divers parcels of land, and great houses, beside both the counters. If any private quarrel happen among our great courtiers, he proclaims the *business*, that's the word, the *business;* as if the united forces of the Romish Catholics were making up for Germany. He cheats young gulls that are newly come to town ; and when the keeper of the ordinary blames him for it, he answers him in his own profession, that a *woodcock* must be pluckt ere he be drest. He is a supervisor to brothels, and in them is a more unlawful reformer of vice, than prentices on Shrove-Tuesday. He loves his friend, as a councillor-at-law loves the velvet breeches he was first made barrister in ; he'll be sure to wear him thread-bare ere he forsake him. He sleeps with a tobacco-pipe in's mouth ; and his first prayer i' th' morning is, he may remember whom he fell out with overnight. Soldier he is none, for he cannot distinguish between onion-seed and gunpowder : if he have worn it in his hollow tooth for the toothache, and so come to the knowledge of it, that's all. The tenure by which he holds his means, is an estate at will ; and that's borrowing. Land-lords have but four quarter-days ; but he three hundred and odd. He keeps very good company ; yet is a man of no reckoning : and when he goes not drunk to bed, he is very sick next morning. He commonly dies like Anacreon, with a grape in's throat ; or Hercules, with fire in's marrow. And I have heard of some (that have scap't hanging) begged for anatomies ; only to deter man from taking tobacco.

(From the Same.)

A FRANKLIN

HIS outside is an ancient yeoman of England, though his inside may give arms (with the best gentlemen) and ne'er see the herald. There is no truer servant in the house than himself. Though he be master, he says not to his servants, Go to field, but, Let us go ; and with his own eye, doth both fatten his flock, and set forward all manner of husbandry. He is taught by nature to be contented with a little ; his own fold yields him both food and raiment ; he is pleas'd with any nourishment God sends, whilst curious gluttony ransacks, as it were, Noah's Ark for food; only to feed the riot of one meal. He is ne'er known to go to law ; understanding, to be law-bound among men, is like to be hide-bound among his beasts ; they thrive not under it : and that such men sleep as unquietly, as if their pillows were stuft with lawyer's pen-knives. When he builds, no poor tenant's cottage hinders his prospect : they are indeed his alms-houses, though there be painted on them no such superscription : he never sits up late, but when he hunts the badger, the vow'd foe of the lambs : nor uses he any cruelty, but when he hunts the hare ; nor subtlety, but when he setteth snares for the snite, or pit-falls for the black-bird ; nor oppression, but when in the month of July, he goes to the next river, and shears his sheep. He allows of honest pastime, and thinks not the bones of the dead any thing bruised, or the worse for it, though the country lasses dance in the church-yard after evensong. Rock Monday, and the wake in summer, shrovings, the wakeful ketches on Christmas Eve, the hoky, or seed cake, these he yearly keeps, yet holds them no reliques of popery. He is not so inquisitive after news derived from the privy closet, when the finding an eyry of hawks in his own grounds, or the foaling of a colt come of a good strain, are tidings more pleasant, more profitable. He is lord paramount within himself, though he hold by never so mean a tenure ; and dies the more contentedly (though he leave his heir young) in regard he leaves him not liable to a covetous guardian. Lastly, to end him ; he cares not when his end comes, he needs not fear his audit, for his *quietus* is in heaven.

(From the Same.)

ROBERT BURTON

[Few books give a more distinct idea of the personality of their author than that given by the *Anatomy of Melancholy*. But the accounts which we have of that author and his history are somewhat meagre. He was born on 8th February 1577 at Lindley in Leicestershire, his family being of gentle birth and of some landed estate, and was educated at the grammar schools of Nuneaton and Sutton Coldfield. He entered Brasenose College, Oxford, in 1593, and was elected on the foundation at Christ Church six years later. He took orders, and was presented by the Dean and Chapter to St. Thomas's, Oxford, in 1616, and later by Lord Berkeley to the rectory of Segrave in his native county. He constantly resided at Christ Church, but kept his livings till his death in 1640, a death which gossip, without any evidence, chose to consider self-helped, if not self-inflicted, partly because of his ambiguous epitaph, "cui vitam dedit *et mortem* melancholia," partly because he had calculated his nativity so as pretty exactly to forecast the time. It has been pointed out that he actually died at sixty-three—an age more usually fatal than any other. Despite his residence of full forty years in a single college, and of nearly half a century in the same university, almost nothing is known of him, and the few traditions or assertions about his melancholy, its occasional alleviations, his facility of quotation, and so forth, are vague, and in rather suspicious accordance with the notion which, as has been said, any one would form from his book.]

IT is a commonplace that in the most absurd error there may generally be discovered, if not some considerable ground or background of truth, yet some fragment of explanation. There is such an explanation for the absurd craze which has induced its monomaniacs to include Robert Burton's work among those, dating from the last quarter of the sixteenth century and the first of the seventeenth, which they father upon Francis Bacon, or a secret society headed by him. To no one possessing one grain of critical power of separation could the work of Shakespeare, of Bacon, and of Burton seem to come from the same hand. But each stands apart from all his other contemporaries in a certain combination, different in each, of universality of comprehension, with intense individuality of expression. Burton's form of this

combination of gifts lay in the union of almost universal reading
with the application of that reading to the setting forth and illustration of a peculiar temperament of mind—the temperament
which is expressed by writers as ancient as the Preacher, and as
modern as Schopenhauer.   To dwell on the way in which, as far
as matter goes, he deals with the subject of Melancholy would be
here impossible.   It is sufficient to say that he had read almost
everything—classical, mediaeval, and modern, theology, science
(as science then went), law, history, poetry.   He will quote Ovid
one moment and Chaucer the next, a schoolman on this page,
and—rarest of all quotations to be found in his own contemporaries—a contemporary playwright on that.   The whole is cast
into the form of a scientific investigation of the causes, symptoms,
varieties, and cure of what he calls Melancholy.   But as the
manner of his age was (though no one else shows it in quite such
perfection) the investigation passes into, or is continually accompanied by, an endless chain of citation from his innumerable
authors.   Nor is the fashion of this citation less peculiar than its
abundance.   For the most part the borrowed passages are not
given singly to support and illustrate single sentences or paragraphs of the author's own.   They run on into endless series with
each other, or are twisted in alternate strands with Burton's own
writing.   Sometimes his sentences read as if a string of references in a footnote had by some inadvertence cropped up in the
text ; often as if the clauses were written in shorthand—notes for
the author's own use in future extension or selection.   Now he will
give the original of his version, or a paraphrase in a note ; now
he will quote his author in Latin or another tongue, and follow
this up with a sort of half-gloss, half-version in English.   To a
careless reader, or to one quite out of sympathy with Burton's
own mood, the method may seem either a cumbrous conglomera-
tion, due to lack of taste, skill, and energy, or the lost labour of
elaborate eccentricity.   Not so to any one who takes the trouble
to master Burton's own introduction, or who starts in harmony
with the spirit of the book.   If the *Anatomy of Melancholy* be
regarded as mere outpouring of commonplace books, with a
pretext of unity in purpose and subject, it is no great thing.   To
be understood it must be regarded as at once the exhibition of a
temperament, and the discussion of a case.

Burton occupied rather more than twenty years, from the
time of his election to a position of learned ease, in shaping

his book for its first appearance in 1621 : he spent rather less than another twenty in refashioning and perfecting the work. Frequently as it has been reprinted, no attempt has ever yet been made to execute a critical edition, indicating the variations which were thus introduced by him on the four occasions when reissues were called for in his own lifetime. These alterations and additions are very numerous and very considerable, and the author not unfrequently draws attention to them in the text. But he has never, in making them, broken through the singular unity and control of treatment which the book shows. As far as the *minutiæ* of style are concerned, Burton's characteristics are well marked, and not very numerous. His method of quotation obliges him of necessity to immense sentences, or rather clause-heaps. But it is noteworthy that when he intermits citation and narrates or argues in his own person. he is less, not more, given than his contemporaries to the long sentence, and frequently has a distinctly terse and crisp arrangement of the members of his paragraph. Of definite mannerisms he chiefly affects apposition, the omission of conjunctions and connecting words of all kinds, and a very curious and characteristic use of the demonstrative he and its cases, which covers with him a range of senses from "that well-known person " to "anybody."

These details of form, however, though adding to the fantastic personality of the book, are as nothing compared to the idiosyncrasies of its matter and spirit. Apt as Burton is to digress— indeed he has a formal defence of the practice—and enormous as is the range of his digression, he has contrived to make all this huge congeries of material subservient to his purpose of illustrating a new "vanity of vanities," of combining, as it were, in one book the knowledge of Solomon, and his reflections on the futility of the things known and the knowing of them. Rigidly precise in appearance as is the scheme he lays out, its sweep and ramifications are so great and intricate that hardly anything introduced by him can be said to be absolutely irrelevant. He contrives to see all things in Melancholy, and yet to make his treatment of them anything but melancholic. Indeed with all his plunges in the *balneum diaboli*, all his love for quaint out-of-the-way knowledge, there is in Burton a strong vein of plain common-sense which is sometimes almost prosaic, in the transferred and uncomplimentary sense, and which emerges now and then, especially in his long and famous discourse of Love-melancholy.

His own verse translations, too, are such mere doggrel for the most part that one almost suspects a trick and deliberation. But there are few things, indeed, that deserve censure in Burton, the perpetual refuge and delight of scholarly English readers, an unmatched storehouse of learning, and one not easily matched for wisdom, a writer who, by force of genius, has turned into an organic whole the hugest and most apparently heterogeneous stock of materials that ever an architect of letters set himself to build withal.

GEORGE SAINTSBURY.

DEMOCRITUS HIS UTOPIA

UTOPIAN parity is a kind of government, to be wished for, rather than effected, *Respub. Christianopolitana*, Campanella's *City of the Sun*, and that new *Atlantis*, witty fictions, but mere chimeras : and Plato's community in many things is impious, absurd, and ridiculous ; it takes away all splendour and magnificence. I will have several orders, degrees of nobility, and those hereditary, not rejecting younger brothers in the mean time ; for they shall be sufficiently provided for by pensions, or so qualified, brought up in some honest calling, they shall be able to live of themselves. I will have such a proportion of ground belonging to every barony : he that buys the land, shall buy the barony ; he that by riot consume his patrimony, and ancient demesnes, shall forfeit his honours. As some dignities shall be hereditary, so some again by election or gift (besides free offices, pensions, annuities) like our bishoprics, prebends, the Bassa's palaces in Turkey, the procurators' houses, and offices in Venice, which (like the golden apple) shall be given to the worthiest and best deserving both in war and peace, as a reward of their worth and good service, as so many goals for all to aim at (*honos alit artes*), and encouragements to others. For I hate those severe, unnatural, harsh, German, French, and Venetian decrees, which exclude plebeians from honours : be they never so wise, rich, virtuous, valiant, and well qualified, they must not be patricians, but keep their own rank : this is *naturæ bellum inferre*, odious to God and men ; I abhor it. My form of government shall be monarchical ;

> " . . . *nunquam libertas gratior exstat,*
> *Quam sub rege pio,*" etc.

few laws, but those severely kept, plainly put down, and in the mother tongue, that every man may understand. Every city shall have a peculiar trade or privilege, by which it shall be chiefly maintained : and parents shall teach their children (one of three at least), bring up and instruct them in the mysteries of their own trade. In each town these several tradesmen shall be so aptly disposed as they shall free the rest from danger or offence. Fire-trades, as smiths, forge-men, brewers, bakers, metal-men, etc., shall dwell apart by themselves ; dyers, tanners, fel-mongers, and such as use water, in convenient places by themselves : noisome or fulsome for bad smells, as butchers' slaughter-houses, chandlers, curriers, in remote places, and some back lanes. Fraternities and companies I approve of, as merchants' burses, colleges of druggers, physicians, musicians, etc., but all trades to be rated in the sale of wares, as our clerks of the market do bakers and brewers ; corn it self, what scarcity soever shall come, not to exceed such a price. Of such wares as are transported or brought in, if they be necessary, commodious, and such as nearly concern man's life, as corn, wood, coal, etc., and such provision we cannot want, I will have little or no custom paid, no taxes ; but for such things as are for pleasure, delight, or ornament, as wine, spice, tobacco, silk, velvet, cloth of gold, lace, jewels, etc., a greater impost. I will have certain ships sent out for new discoveries every year, and some discreet men appointed to travel into all neighbour kingdoms by land, which shall observe what artificial inventions and good laws are in other countries, customs, alterations, or ought else, concerning war, or peace, which may tend to the common good ;—ecclesiastical discipline, *penes episcopos*, subordinate as the other ; no impropriations, no lay patrons of church livings, or one private man, but common societies, corporations, etc , and those rectors of benefices to be chosen out of the universities, examined and approved as the *literati* in China. No parish to contain above a thousand auditors. If it were possible, I would have such priests as should imitate Christ, charitable lawyers should love their neigh-bours as themselves, temperate and modest physicians, politicians contemn the world, philosophers should know themselves, noble-men live honestly, tradesmen leave lying and cozening, magistrates corruption, etc. But this is impossible ; I must get such as I may. I will therefore have of lawyers, judges, advocates, physicians, chirurgions, etc., a set number ; and every man, if it be possible, to plead his own cause, to tell that tale to the judge, which he doth to his advocate, as at Fez in Africk, Bantam, Aleppo, Raguse, *suam quisque caussam dicere tenetur ;*—those advocates, chirurgions, and physicians, which are allowed to be maintained out of the common treasure ; no fees to be given or taken, upon pain of losing their places ; or, if they do, very small fees, and when the cause is fully ended. He that sues any man shall put in a pledge, which if it be proved he hath wrongfully sued his adversary, rashly or maliciously, he shall forfeit and lose. Or else, before any suit begin, the plaintiff shall have his complaint approved by a set delegacy to that purpose : if it be of moment, he shall be suffered, as before, to proceed ; if otherwise, they shall determine it. All causes shall be pleaded *suppresso nomine*, the parties' names concealed, if some circumstances do not otherwise require. Judges and other officers shall be aptly disposed in each province, villages, cities, as common arbitrators to hear causes, and end all controversies ; and those not single, but three at least on the bench at once, to determine or give sentence ; and those again to sit by turns or lots, and not to continue still in the same office. No controversy to depend above a year, but, without all delays and further appeals, to be speedily dispatched, and finally concluded in that time allotted. These and all other inferior magistrates, to be chosen as the *literati* in China, or by those exact suffrages of the Venetians ; and such again not be eligible, or capable of magistracies, honours, offices, except they be sufficiently qualified for learning, manners, and that by the strict approbation of deputed examinators : first, scholars to take place, then, soldiers ; for I am of Vegetius his opinion, a scholar deserves better than a soldier, because *unius ætatis sunt quæ fortiter fiunt, quæ vero pro utilitate reipub. scribuntur, æterna :* a soldier's work lasts for an age, a scholar's for ever. If they misbehave themselves, they shall be deposed, and accordingly punished ; and, whether their offices be annual or otherwise, once a year they shall be called in question, and give an account : for men are partial and passionate, merciless, covetous, corrupt, subject to love, hate, fear, favour, etc., *omne sub regno graviore regnum.* Like Solon's Areopagites, or those Roman censors, some shall visit others, and be visited *invicem* themselves ; they shall oversee that no prowling officer, under colour of authority, shall insult over his inferiors, as so many wild beasts, oppress, domineer, flay, grind, or trample on, be partial or corrupt, but that there be *æquabile jus*, justice equally done, live as friends and brethren together ; and (which Sesellius would have and so much desires in his kingdom of France) a diapason and sweet harmony of kings, princes, nobles, and plebeians, so mutually tied and involved in love, as well as laws and authority, as that they never disagree, insult, or incroach one upon another. If any man deserve well in his office, he shall be rewarded ;

> " . . . *quis enim virtutem amplectitur ipsam,*
> *Præmia si tollas ?* . . ."

He that invents any thing for public good in any art or science, writes a treatise, or performs any noble exploit at home or abroad, shall be accordingly enriched, honoured, and preferred. I say, with Hannibal in Ennius, *Hostem qui feriet, mihi erit Carthaginiensis :* let him be of what condition he will, in all offices, actions, he that deserves best shall have best.

(From *Democritus Junior to the Reader.*)

LOVE OF SOLITUDE

COZEN german to idleness, and a concomitant cause which goes hand in hand with it, is *nimia solitudo*, too much solitariness— by the testimony of all physicians, cause and symptom both ; but as it is here put for a cause, it is either coact, enforced, or else voluntary. Enforced solitariness is commonly seen in students, monks, friars, anchorites, that, by their order and course of life, must abandon all company, society of other men, and betake themselves to a private cell ; *otio superstitioso seclusi* (as Bale and Hospinian well term it), such as are the Carthusians of our time, that eat no flesh (by their order), keep perpetual silence, never go abroad ; such as live in prison, or some desert place, and cannot have company, as many of our country gentlemen do in solitary houses ; they must either be alone without companions, or live beyond their means, and entertain all comers as so many hosts, or else converse with their servants and hinds, such as are unequal, inferior to them, and of a contrary disposition ; or else, as some do, to avoid solitariness, spend their time with lewd fellows in taverns, and in ale-houses, and thence addict themselves to some unlawful disports, or dissolute courses. Divers again are cast upon this rock of solitariness for want of means, or out of a strong apprehension of some infirmity, disgrace ; or, through bashfulness, rudeness, simplicity, they cannot apply themselves to others' company. *Nullum solum infelici gratius solitudine, ubi nullus sit qui miseriam exprobret.* This enforced solitariness takes place, and produceth his effect soonest, in such as have spent their time jovially, peradventure in all honest recreations, in good company, in some great family or populous city, and are upon a sudden confined to a desert country cottage far off, restrained of their liberty, and barred from their ordinary associates. Solitariness is very irksome to such, most tedious, and a sudden cause of great inconvenience.

Voluntary solitariness is that which is familiar with melancholy, and gently brings on, like a Siren, a shooing-horn, or some Sphinx, to this irrevocable gulf: a primary cause Piso calls it; most pleasant it is at first, to such as are melancholy given, to lie in bed whole days, and keep their chambers, to walk alone in some solitary grove, betwixt wood and water, by a brook side, to meditate upon some delightsome and pleasant subject, which shall affect them most ; *amabilis insania*, and *mentis gratissimus error.* A most incomparable delight it is so to melancholize, and build castles in the air, to go smiling to themselves, acting an infinite variety of parts, which they suppose, and strongly imagine they represent, or that they see acted or done. *Blanda quidem ab initio*, saith Lemnius, to conceive and meditate of such pleasant things sometimes, "present, past, or to come," as Rhasis speaks. So delightsome these toys are at first, they could spend whole days and nights without sleep, even whole years alone in such contemplations, and phantastical meditations, which are like unto dreams ; and they will hardly be drawn from them, or willingly interrupt. So pleasant their vain conceits are, that they hinder their ordinary tasks and necessary business ; they cannot address themselves to them, or almost to any study or employment : these phantastical and bewitching thoughts so covertly, so feelingly, so urgently, so continually, set upon, creep in, insinuate, possess, overcome, distract, and detain them, they cannot, I say, go about their more necessary business, stave off or extricate themselves, but are ever musing, melancholizing, and carried along, as he (they say) that is led round about an heath with a *Puck* in the night. They run earnestly on in this labyrinth of anxious and solicitous melancholy meditations, and cannot well or willingly refrain, or easily leave off, winding and unwinding themselves, as so many clocks, and still pleasing their humours, until at last the scene is turned upon a sudden, by some bad object ; and they, being now habituated to such vain meditations and solitary places, can endure no company, can ruminate of nothing but harsh and distasteful subjects. Fear, sorrow, suspicion, *subrusticus pudor*, discontent, cares, and weariness of life, surprise them in a moment ; and they can think of nothing else : continually suspecting, no sooner are their eyes open, but this infernal plague of melancholy seizeth on them, and terrifies their souls, representing some dismal object to their minds, which now, by no means, no labour, no persuasions, they can avoid ; *hæret lateri letalis arundo ;* they may not be rid of it ; they cannot resist. I may not deny but that there is some profitable meditation, contemplation, and kind of solitariness, to be embraced, which the fathers so highly commended—Hierom, Chrysostom, Cyprian, Austin, in whole tracts, which Petrarch, Erasmus, Stella, and others, so much magnify in their books—a paradise, an heaven on earth, if it be used aright, good for the body, and better for the soul ; as many of those old monks used it, to divine contemplations ; as Simulus a courtier in Adrian's time, Diocletian the emperor, retired themselves, etc., in that sense, *Vatia solus scit vivere ;* Vatia lives alone ; which the Romans were wont to say, when they commended a country life ; or to the bettering of their knowledge, as Democritus, Cleanthes, and those excellent philosophers, have ever done, to sequester themselves from the tumultuous world ; or, as in Pliny's villa Laurentana, Tully's Tusculan, Jovius' study, that they might better *vacare studiis et Deo*, serve God and follow their studies. Methinks, therefore, our too zealous innovators were not so well advised in that general subversion of abbeys and religious houses, promiscuously to fling down all. They might have taken away those gross abuses crept in amongst them, rectified such inconveniencies, and not so far to have raved and raged against those fair buildings, and everlasting monuments of our forefathers' devotion, consecrated to pious uses. Some monasteries and collegiate cells might have been well spared, and their revenues otherwise employed ; here and there one, in good towns or cities at least, for men and women of all sorts and conditions to live in, to sequester themselves from the cares and tumults of the world, that were not desirous or fit to marry, or otherwise willing to be troubled with common affairs, and know not well where to bestow themselves, to live apart in, for more conveniency, good education, better company sake ; to follow their studies (I say) to the perfection of arts and sciences common good, and, as some truly devoted monks of old had done, freely and truly to serve God : for these men are neither solitary, nor idle, as the poet made answer to the husbandman in Æsop, that objected idleness to him, he was never so idle as in his company ; or that Scipio Africanus in Tully, *numquam minus solus, quam quum solus; numquam minus otiosus, quam quum esset otiosus;* never less solitary, than when he was alone, never more busy, than when he seemed to be most idle. It is reported by Plato, in his dialogue *de Amore*, in that prodigious commendation of Socrates, how, a deep meditation coming into Socrates' mind by chance, he stood still musing, *eodem vestigio cogitabundus*, from morning to noon ; and, when as then he had not yet finished his meditation, *perstabat cogitans;* he so continued till the evening ; the soldiers (for he then followed the camp) observed him with admiration, and on set purpose watched all night ; but he persevered immoveable *ad exortum solis*, till the sun rose in the morning, and then, saluting the sun, went his ways. In what humour constant Socrates did thus, I know not, or how he might be affected ; but this would be pernicious to another man ; what intricate business might so really possess him, I cannot easily guess. But this is *otiosum otium;* it is far otherwise with these men, according to Seneca : *omnia nobis mala solitudo persuadet;* this solitude undoeth us ; *pugnat cum vitâ sociali;* 'tis a destructive solitariness. These men are devils, alone, as the saying is ; *homo solus aut deus aut dæmon;* a man, alone, is either a saint or a devil ; *mens ejus aut languescit, aut tumescit;* and *væ soli!* in this sense ; woe be to him that is so alone ! These wretches do frequently degenerate from men, and, of sociable creatures, become beasts, monsters, inhumane, ugly to behold, *misanthropi;* they do even loathe themselves, and hate the company of men, as so many Timons, Nebuchadnezzars, by too much indulging to these pleasing humours, and through their own default. So that which Mercurialis (*Consil. II.*) sometimes expostulated with his melancholy patient, may be justly applied to every solitary and idle person in particular ; *natura de te videtur conqueri posse*, etc., nature may justly complain of thee, that, whereas she gave thee a good wholesome temperature, a sound body, and God hath given thee so divine and excellent a soul, so many good parts and profitable gifts, thou hast not only contemned and rejected, but hast corrupted them, polluted them, overthrown their temperature, and perverted those gifts with riot, idleness, solitariness, and many other ways ; thou art a traitor to God and Nature, an enemy to thy self and to the world. *Perditio tua ex te;* thou hast lost thy self wilfully, cast away thy self; thou thy self art the efficient cause of thine own misery, by not resisting such vain cogitations, but giving way unto them.

(From the *Causes of Melancholy*.)

OF REPULSE

REPULSE and disgrace are two main causes of discontent, but, to an understanding man, not so hardly to be taken. Cæsar himself hath been denied ; and when two stand equal in fortune, birth, and all other qualities alike, one of necessity must lose. Why shouldst thou take it so grievously ? It hath been a familiar thing for thee thy self to deny others. If every man might have what he would, we should all be deified, emperors, kings, princes ; if whatsoever vain hope suggests, unsatiable appetite affects, our preposterous judgment thinks fit were granted, we should have another chaos in an instant, a mere confusion. It is some satisfaction to him that is repelled, that dignities, honours, offices, are not always given by desert or worth, but for love, affinity, friendship, affection, great men's letters, or as commonly they are bought and sold. Honours in court are bestowed, not according to men's virtues and good conditions (as an old courtier observes) ; but, as every man hath means, or more potent friends, so he is preferred. With us in France (for so their own countryman relates) most part the matter is carried by favour and grace ; he that can get a great man to be his mediator, runs away with all the preferment. *Indignissimus plerumque præfertur, Vatinius Catoni, illaudatus laudatissimo :*

> "   .   .   .   *servi dominantur ; aselli*
> *Ornantur phaleris ; dephalerantur equi.*"

An illiterate fool sits in a man's seat, and the common people hold him learned, grave, and wise. One professeth (Cardan well notes) for a thousand crowns ; but he deserves not ten ; when as he that deserves a thousand cannot get ten. *Salarium non dat multis salem.* As good horses draw in carts, as coaches ; and oftentimes, which Machiavel seconds, *principes non sunt, qui ob insignem virtutem principatu digni sunt;* he that is most worthy wants employment ; he that hath skill to be a pilot wants a ship ; and he that could govern a commonwealth, a world itself, a king in conceit, wants means to exercise his worth, hath not a poor office to manage. And yet all this while he is a better man than is fit to reign, *etsi careat regno*, though he want a kingdom, than he that hath one, and knows not how to rule it. A lion serves not always his keeper, but oftentimes the keeper the lion ; and, as Polydore Virgil hath it, *multi reges, ut pupilli, ob inscitiam non regunt, sed reguntur.* Hieron of Syracuse was a brave king, but wanted a kingdom ; Perseus of Macedon had nothing of a king but the bare name and title ; for he could not govern it ; so great places are often ill bestowed, worthy persons unrespected. Many times too the servants have more means than the masters whom they serve ; which Epictetus counts an eyesore and inconvenient. But who can help it ? It is an ordinary thing in these days to see a base impudent ass, illiterate, unworthy, unsufficient, to be preferred before his betters, because he can put himself forward, because he looks big, can bustle in the world, hath a fair outside, can temporise, collogue, insinuate, or hath good store of friends and money ; whereas a more discreet, modest, and better deserving man shall lie hid or have a repulse. 'Twas so of old, and ever will be, and which Tiresias advised Ulysses in the poet—

" Accipe, qua ratione queas ditescere," etc.

is still in use ; lie, flatter, and dissemble ; if not, as he concludes,

" Ergo pauper eris,"

then go like a beggar, as thou art. Erasmus, Melancthon, Lipsius, Budæus, Cardan, lived and died poor. Gesner was a silly old man, *baculo innixus*, amongst all those huffing cardinals, swelling bishops, that flourished in his time, and rode on foot-clothes. It is not honesty, learning, worth, wisdom, that prefers men (the race is not to the swift, nor the battle to the strong), but, as the wise man said, chance, and sometimes a ridiculous chance : *casus plerumque ridiculus multos elevavit.* 'Tis fortune's doings, as they say, which made Brutus now dying exclaim, *O misera virtus ! ergo nihil quam verba eras ! atqui ego te tanquam rem exercebam ; sed tu serviebas fortunæ.* Believe it hereafter, O my friends ! Virtue serves fortune. Yet be not discouraged (O my well deserving spirits) with this which I have said ; it may be otherwise ; though seldom, I confess, yet sometimes it is.

But, to your farther content, I'll tell you a tale. In Moronia pia, or Moronia felix, I know not whether, nor how long since, nor in what cathedral church, a fat prebend fell void. The carcase scarce cold, many suitors were up in an instant. The first had rich friends, a good purse; and he was resolved to outbid any man before he would lose it; every man supposed he should carry it. The second was my Lord Bishop's chaplain (in whose gift it was); and he thought it his due to have it. The third was nobly born; and he meant to get it by his great parents, patrons, and allies. The fourth stood upon his worth; he had newly found out strange mysteries in chemistry, and other rare inventions, which he would detect to the public good. The fifth was a painful preacher; and he was commended by the whole parish where he dwelt; he had all their hands to his certificate. The sixth was the prebendary's son lately deceased; his father died in debt (for it, as they say), left a wife and many poor children. The seventh stood upon fair promises, which to him and his noble friends had been formerly made for the next place in his lordship's gift. The eighth pretended great losses, and what he had suffered for the church, what pains he had taken at home and abroad; and besides he brought noble men's letters. The ninth had married a kinswoman, and he sent his wife to sue for him. The tenth was a foreign doctor, a late convert, and wanted means. The eleventh would exchange for another; he did not like the former's site, could not agree with his neighbours and fellows upon any terms; he would be gone. The twelfth and last was (a suitor in conceit) a right honest, civil, sober man, an excellent scholar, and such a one as lived private in the university; but he had neither means nor money to compass it; besides he hated all such courses; he could not speak for himself, neither had he any friends to solicit his cause, and therefore made no suit, could not expect, neither did he hope for, or look after it. The good bishop, amongst a jury of competitors, thus perplexed, and not yet resolved what to do, or on whom to bestow it, at the last, of his own accord, mere motion, and bountiful nature, gave it freely to the university student, altogether unknown to him but by fame; and, to be brief, the academical scholar had the prebend sent him for a present. The news was no sooner published abroad, but all good students rejoiced, and were much cheered up with it, though some would not believe it; others, as men amazed, said it was a miracle; but one amongst the rest thanked God for it, and said, "*Nunc juvat tandem studiosum esse, et Deo integro corde servire.*" You have heard my tale ; but, alas ! it is but a tale, a mere fiction ; 'twas never so, never like to be ; and so let it rest.

(From the *Cure of Melancholy*.)

CHARITY, THE WANT OF IT

A FAITHFUL friend is better than gold, a medicine of misery, an only possession ; yet this love of friends, nuptial, heroical, profitable, pleasant, honest, all three loves put together, are little worth, if they proceed not from a true Christian illuminated soul, if it be not done *in ordine ad Deum*, for God's sake. "Though I had the gift of prophecy, spake with tongues of men and angels, though I feed the poor with all my goods, give my body to be burned, and have not this love, it profiteth me nothing " (1 Cor. xiii. 1, 3) ; 'tis *splendidum peccatum*, without charity. This is an all-apprehending love, a deifying love, a refined, pure, divine love, the quintessence of all love, the true philosopher's stone : *non potest enim* (as Austin infers) *veraciter amicus esse hominis, nisi fuerit ipsius primitus veritatis :* he is no true friend that loves not God's truth. And therefore this is true love indeed, the cause of all good to mortal men, that reconciles all creatures, and glues them together in perpetual amity, and firm league, and can no more abide bitterness, hate, malice, than fair and foul weather, light and darkness, sterility and plenty, may be together. As the sun in the firmament (I say), so is love in the world ; and for this cause 'tis love without an addition, love κατ' ἐξοχὴν, love of God, and love of men. The love of God begets the love of man ; and by this love of our neighbour, the love of God is nourished and increased. By this happy union of love, all well governed families and cities are combined, the heavens annexed, and divine souls complicated, the world itself composed, and all that is in it conjoined in God, and reduced to one. This love causeth true and absolute virtues, the life, spirit, and root of every virtuous action ; it finisheth prosperity, easeth adversity, corrects all natural incumbrances, inconveniences, sustained by faith and hope, which, with this our love, make an indissoluble twist, a Gordian knot, an æquilateral triangle ; and yet the greatest of them is love (1 Cor. xiii. 13) which inflames our souls with a divine heat, and being so inflamed, purgeth, and, so purged, elevates to God, makes an atonement, and reconciles us unto him. That other love infects the soul of man ; this cleanseth : that depresses ; this erears : that causeth cares and troubles ; this quietness of mind ; this informs, that deforms our life : that leads to repentance, this to heaven.   For, if once we be truly link't and touched with this charity, we shall love God above all, our neighbour as ourself, as we are enjoined (Mark xii. 31 ; Matt. xix. 19), perform those duties and exercises, even all the operations of a good Christian.

This love suffereth long ; it is bountiful, envieth not, boasteth not itself ; is not puffed up : it deceiveth not ; it seeketh not his own things, is not provoked to anger ; it thinketh not evil ; it rejoiceth not in iniquity, but in truth.   It suffereth all things, believeth all things, hopeth all things (1 Cor. xiii. 4, 5, 6, 7) ; it covereth all trespasses (Prov. x. 12), a multitude of sins (1 Peter iv. 8), as our Saviour told the woman in the Gospel, that washed His feet, many sins were forgiven her, for she loved much (Luke vii. 47) : it will defend the fatherless and the widow (Isa. i. 17), will seek no revenge, or be mindful of wrong (Levit. xix. 18), will bring home his brother's ox if he go astray, as it is commanded (Deut. xxii. 1), will resist evil, give to him that asketh, and not turn from him that borroweth, bless them that curse him, love his enemies (Matt. v.), bear his brother's burthen (Gal. vi. 2).   He that so loves, will be hospitable, and distribute to the necessities of the saints : he will, if it be possible, have peace with all men, feed his enemy if he be hungry ; if he be athirst, give him drink ; he will perform those seven works of mercy ; he will make himself equal to them of the lower sort, rejoice with them that rejoice, weep with them that weep (Rom. xii. 15) : he will speak truth to his neighbour, be courteous and tender hearted, forgiving others for Christ's sake, as God forgave him (Eph. iv. 32) ; he will be like minded (Phil. ii. 2), of one judgment ; be humble, meek, long suffering (Colos. iii. 12), forbear, forget, and forgive (13, 22): and what he doth shall be heartily done to God, and not to men : be pitiful and courteous (1 Peter iii. 8, 11), seek peace and follow it.   He will love his brother, not in word and tongue, but in deed and truth (1 John iii. 18) ; and he that loves God, Christ will love him that is begotten of him (1 John v. 1, etc.)   Thus should we willingly do, if we had a true touch of this charity, of this divine love, if we would perform this which we

are enjoined, forget and forgive, and compose ourselves to those
Christian laws of love.

> " O felix hominum genus,
>   Si vestros animos Amor,
>   Quo cœlum regitur, regat ! "

Angelical souls, how blessed, how happy should we be, so loving,
how might we triumph over the devil, and have another heaven
upon earth !

But this we cannot do ; and, which is the cause of all our
woes, miseries, discontent, melancholy, want of this charity. We
do *invicem angariare*, contemn, insult, vex, torture, molest, and
hold one another's noses to the grindstone hard, provoke, rail,
scoff, calumniate, challenge, hate, abuse (hard-hearted, implacable,
malicious, peevish, inexorable as we are), to satisfy our lust or
private spleen, for toys, trifles, and impertinent occasions, spend
our selves, goods, friends, fortunes, to be revenged on our adversary, to ruin him and his. 'Tis all our study, practice, and
business, how to plot mischief, mine, countermine, defend and
offend, ward ourselves, injure others, hurt all ; as if we were born
to do mischief, and that with such eagerness and bitterness, with
such rancour, malice, rage, and fury, we prosecute our intended
designs, that neither affinity or consanguinity, love or fear of God
or men, can contain us : no satisfaction, no composition, will be
accepted, no offices will serve, no submission ; though he shall,
upon his knees, as Sarpedon did to Glaucus in Homer, acknow-
ledging his error, yield himself with tears in his eyes, beg his
pardon, we will not relent, forgive, or forget, till we have confounded him and his, " made dice of his bones," as they say, see
him rot in prison, banish his friends' followers, *et omne invisum
genus*, rooted him out, and all his posterity. Monsters of men
as we are, dogs, wolves, tigers, fiends, incarnate devils, we do
not only contend, oppress, and tyrannise ourselves, but, as so
many firebrands, we set on, and animate others : our whole life
is a perpetual combat, a conflict, a set battle, a snarling fit : *Eris
Dea* is settled in our tents : *Omnia de lite*, opposing wit to wit,
wealth to wealth, strength to strength, fortunes to fortunes, friends
to friends, as at a sea fight, we turn our broadsides, or two mill-
stones with continual attrition, we fire ourselves, or break
another's backs, and both are ruined and consumed in the end.
Miserable wretches ! to fat and enrich ourselves, we care not how
we get it : *Quocunque modo rem :* how many thousands we undo,

whom we oppress, by whose ruin and downfall we arise, whom we injure, fatherless children, widows, common societies, to satisfy our own private lust. Though we have myriads, abundance of wealth and treasure (pitiless, merciless, remorseless, and uncharitable in the highest degree) and our poor brother in need, sickness, in great extremity, and now ready to be starved for want of food, we had rather, as the fox told the ape, his tail should sweep the ground still, than cover his buttocks : rather spend it idly, consume it with dogs, hawks, hounds, unnecessary buildings, in riotous apparel, ingurgitate, or let it be lost, than he should have part of it ; rather take from him that little which he hath, than relieve him.

(From *Love-Melancholy.*)

BISHOP HALL

[Joseph Hall was born at Ashby-de-la-Zouch in 1574, educated at Emanuel College, Cambridge, and, after spending several years at the University, became Rector of Halsted, in Suffolk, in 1601. After travelling with Sir Edmund Bacon in the Low Countries, and having already given to the world his *Satires* (written in imitation of Persius) and his *Meditations*, he attracted the notice of Henry, Prince of Wales. From Halsted he was collated to Waltham, where he remained twenty-two years, during which he was more than once employed abroad, most notably as the representative of King James in the ecclesiastical contentions of the Netherlands. In 1608 he became involved in controversy with the Brownists : and this controversy served as a counterbias to the puritanical inclination, which for a time rendered him an object of some suspicion to the party of Archbishop Laud. In 1627 he became Bishop of Exeter ; and his controversial faculty was still further sharpened by the Smectymnuus dispute as to the divine right of Episcopacy, in which he had Milton for one of his opponents. After the meeting of the Long Parliament, and the more violent steps taken against the Church, his position as defender of Episcopacy made him the object of bitter hatred on the part of the Parliamentary party. He was translated to the See of Norwich in 1641. But his time there was short and troubled. The most severe measures were dealt out to him by the victorious faction, whose theories he had combated. He was imprisoned and stript of all the temporalities of his see, and died in 1656, before the Restoration reversed the fate of the struggle.]

JOSEPH HALL'S father was the agent and representative of the Earl of Huntingdon, and was thus in a position to secure for his son some patronage of the kind to which so many notable men of the time in Church and State were indebted for their University training. But Hall seems to have been most influenced by the character of his mother, whose portrait, which her son has painted in a few striking lines, gives us the impression of greater force than attractiveness. She emulated the famous women of antiquity in her sanctity, which had more than a tincture of puritanic gloom in its composition. Much of each day was spent in private devotion : " whence," says her son,

" she would still come forth, with a countenance of undesembled mortification." Other symptoms which he describes as proof of her indubitable piety, savour strongly of hypochondria ; but gloomy as she must have made her surroundings, she undoubtedly retained a strong hold upon the reverence and affection of her son, and to her he doubtless owed that early puritanic leaning, which subsequent experience curbed, but did not altogether eradicate.

From a home where the chief impression was one of sincere but gloomy and melancholy piety, Hall passed to the University of Cambridge, where he evidently acquired a position such as would nowadays be gained by one who secured the highest honours of the Schools. He was one of the teaching staff of his college ; and his literary reputation, as the author of the *Satires*, must have given him some position and notoriety, although in his own reminiscences we hear nothing of these early efforts. His later years were occupied with other fights, carried on with very different weapons ; and as the *Satires* were cast up as a reproach to him by Milton in the Smectymnuus controversy, Hall found it neither convenient nor congenial to recall these youthful poems. Criticism of the *Satires* does not fall within the scope of the present notice; but they have much interest for any one who would appreciate Hall's later prose work. They are not only remarkable as the productions of a youth who was little past his majority (they were published in 1597), but they also link Hall with the literature of a previous generation. His compeers then were the last of the Elizabethan dramatists ; the chief object of his admiration was Spenser. In language the *Satires* are artificially archaic : and the tone that pervades them has very little in common with the spirit of his later work. But they brought a freedom and a vigour to his prose style which it never lost, and the practice which they gave him in his early years not only added force and liveliness to his later controversial style, but also gave to his religious writings the quick movement, the variety and the lavish illustration, which are their chief characteristics.

Hall thus combined some elements which are rarely found in combination. Educated amongst puritanic influences and under the shadow of a religion that regarded each individual accident as brought about by the special intervention of providence ; passing from this to the classical influences of the University, and finding his models in antiquity ; thrusting himself as a youth into the literary struggles of the day—he brought to his later work as a divine some unique qualities. His earliest religious writings are devout and earnest, but they borrow their illustrations largely from secular sources; they have no strongly marked dogmatic features, and their language has a freedom and a force that are peculiar. Hating the Romanists he was nevertheless most conspicuously the opponent of the sects that accused the Church of England of Romanist inclination. During a great part of his life, Hall strove to maintain a position which had much to commend it, which was inspired by right-minded charity, which had entirely good objects, but which inevitably exposed him to misconstruction, involved him in disputes with his ecclesiastical superiors, and necessarily gave to his writing, in spite of its force and freedom, something of incompleteness in point of logic. He strove to maintain a middle course. He talked much of the evils of uncharitable judgment. He deprecated division, except upon what he deemed to be fundamentals, forgetting that the most complete cleavage between man and man must necessarily arise from differences as to what is, and what is not, fundamental. Undoubtedly this gives to his religious writings something of platitude, which is not saved by the freedom and force of his literary touch. There is a want of conviction, which no earnestness can quite supply. Yet side by side with this, there is the self-satisfaction which comes from the puritanical tenet, that all his life is ordered for him by providence, and that the misfortunes which befall an opponent are the contrivance of divine power. He preaches on the one hand the duty of charity, and on the other the evils of laxity, from a standpoint which is none the less narrow because it is midway between two extremes. "If," he says, "men be allowed a latitude of opinions in some unnecessary verities, it may not be endured that in matter of religion every man should think what he lists, and utter what he thinks, and defend what he utters, and publish what he defends, and gather disciples to what he publisheth. This liberty, or rather licentiousness, would be the bane of any church." He forgets that men cannot he brought to agree as to what are "verities," but yet "unnecessary"; and that no utterance such as this brings us, for practical purposes, one whit nearer to agreement.

No wonder that he was suspected by such a man as Laud; no wonder that he writes as an outsider, and that his devotional writings often reflect the pagan moralist. In the end, fate was too strong for him : and when the flood-gates were opened, he speaks like a man, overwhelmed and confounded by the fierceness of controversies, the logical importance of which he never rightly appreciated. Yet at times, baffled as he is between authority and private judgment, he hits the mark with unerring accuracy, as a student of human nature. " The Romanists," he says "are all for blind obedience : the Romanists therefore go away with peace, without truth ; ours, under pretence of striving for some truths, abandon peace."

Besides his devotional writings we have from Hall some treatises on casuistry. Such treatises have never thriven in England. They do not appeal to a wide audience, and are therefore scarcely literature in the proper sense. Hall's casuistical writings lack the subtlety of the Romanist casuists, and they have none of his own special characteristics. They have none of the free and almost reckless vigour of his controversial writing ; little of the variety of illustration of his devotional treatises ; and only now and then, as when he covertly attacks Milton, in dealing with the question of divorce, do they show any of the vigour which we associate with his pen.

His most striking prose works are those of devotion and of Scriptural exegesis, which are often wordy, but always free and flowing in point of composition. They bear the impress of pulpit oratory, in which, as he tells us himself, he followed the practice of composing the whole sermon beforehand, but delivering it from memory and not from a manuscript. " Never," he says, " durst I climb into the pulpit to preach any sermon, whereof I had not before, in my poor and plain fashion, penned every word in the same order, wherein I *hoped* to deliver it ; although in the expression I listed not to be a slave to syllables."

H. CRAIK.

To THE HIGH AND MIGHTY MONARCH

Our dear and dread Sovereign Lord

JAMES,

By the good Providence of God, King of Great Britain, France,
and Ireland, the most worthy and most able Defender
of the Faith, and most Gracious Patron of the
Church : all peace and happiness.

MOST GRACIOUS SOVEREIGN—I cannot so over-love this issue
of my own brain, as to hold it worthy of your Majesty's judicious
eyes : much less of the highest patronage under heaven : yet
now, my very duty hath bidden me look so high, and tells me
it would be no less than injurious, if I should not lay down my
work, where I owe my service ; and that I should offend, if I
presume not. Besides ; whither should the rivers run, but into
the sea ? It is to your Majesty (under the Highest) that we
owe both these sweet opportunities of good, and all the good
fruits of these happy opportunities : if we should not, therefore,
freely offer to your Majesty some præmetial handfuls of that
crop, whereof you may challenge the whole harvest, how could
we be but shamelessly unthankful ? I cannot praise my present,
otherwise than by the truth of that heart from which it proceedeth :
only this I may say, that seldom any man hath offered to your
royal hands a greater bundle of his own thoughts (some whereof,
as it must needs fall out amongst so many, have been confessed
profitable), nor perhaps more variety of discourse. For here
shall your Majesty find morality, like a good handmaid, waiting
on divinity ; and divinity, like some great lady, every day in
several dresses ; speculation interchanged with experience ;
positive theology with polemical ; textual with discursory ; popular
with scholastical.

I cannot dissemble my joy to have done this little good ; and if it be the comfort and honour of your unworthy servant, that the God of heaven hath vouchsafed to use his hand in the least service of His Church ; how can it be but your crown and rejoicing, that the same God hath set apart your Majesty, as a glorious instrument of such an universal good to the whole Christian world ? It was a mad conceit of that old Heresiarch, which might justly take his name from madness, than an huge giant bears up the earth with his shoulder ; which he changes every thirtieth year for ease ; and, with the removal, causes an earthquake. If by the device he had meant only an emblem of kings (as our ancient mythologists, under their Saint George, and Christopher, have described the Christian soldier and good pastor), he had not done amiss : for surely, the burden of the whole world lies on the shoulders of sovereign authority ; and it is no marvel if the earth quake in the change. As kings are to the world, so are good kings to the Church. None can be so blind, or curious, as not to grant, that the whole Church of God upon earth rests herself principally (next to her stay above) upon your Majesty's royal supportation : you may truly say with David, *Ego sustineo columnas ejus.* What wonder is it, then, if our tongues and pens bless you ; if we be ambitious of all occasions, that may testify our cheerful gratulations of this happiness to your Highness, and ours in you ? Which, our humble prayers unto Him, by whom kings reign, shall labour to continue, till both the earth and heavens be truly changed.— The unworthiest of your Majesty's servants,

JOSEPH HALL.

(Prefatory Letter to *Contemplations.*)

MEDIATION IN CHURCH CONTROVERSIES

IT was not long after, that his Majesty, finding the exigence of the affairs of the Netherlandish churches to require it, both advised them to a synodical decision ; and, by his incomparable wisdom, promoted the work. My unworthiness was named for one of the assistants of that honourable, grave, and reverend meeting, where I failed not of my best service to that woefully distracted Church. By the time I had stayed some two months there, the unquietness of the nights in those garrison towns working upon the tender disposition of my body, brought me to such weakness through want of rest, that it began to disable me from attending the Synod : which yet, as I might, I forced myself unto ; as wishing that my zeal could have discountenanced my infirmity. Where, in the meantime, it is well worthy of my thankful remembrance, that being in an afflicted and languishing condition for a fortnight together with that sleepless distemper, yet it pleased God, the very night before I was to preach the Latin sermon to the Synod, to bestow upon me such a comfortable refreshing of sufficient sleep, as thereby my spirits were revived, and I was enabled with much vigour and vivacity to perform that service : which was no sooner done, than my former complaint renewed upon me, and prevailed against all the remedies that the counsel of physicians could advise me unto ; so as, after long strife, I was compelled to yield unto a retirement, for the time, to the Hague ; to see if change of place and more careful attendance, which I had in the house of our right honourable ambassador, the Lord Carleton, now Viscount Dorchester, might recover me. But when, notwithstanding all means, my weakness increased so far as that there was small likelihood left of so much strength remaining as might bring me back into England, it pleased his gracious majesty, by our noble ambassador's solicitation, to call me off, and to substitute a worthy divine, Mr. Doctor Goade, in my unwillingly forsaken room. Returning by Dort, I sent in my sad farewell to that grave assembly ; who, by common vote, sent to me the president of the synod and the assistants, with a respective and gracious valediction. Neither did the deputies of my lords the States neglect after a very respectful compliment sent from them to me by Daniel Heinsius, to visit me : and, after a noble acknowledgement of more good service from me than I durst own, dismissed me with an honourable retribution : and sent after me a rich medal of gold, the portraiture of the synod, for a precious monument of their respects to my poor endeavours ; who failed not, while I was at the Hague, to impart unto them my poor advice, concerning the proceeding of that synodical meeting. The difficulties of my return, in such weakness, were many and great ; wherein, if ever, God manifested His special providence to me, in overruling the cross accidents of that passage ; and, after many dangers, and despairs, contriving my safe arrival.

After not many years' settling at home, it grieved my soul to see our own Church begin to sicken of the same disease, which we had endeavoured to cure in our neighbours. Mr. Montague's tart and vehement assertions of some positions, near of kin to the Remonstrants of Netherland, gave occasioner of raising no small broil in the Church. Sides were taken ; pulpits everywhere rang of these opinions ; but parliaments took notice of the division, and questioned the occasion. Now, as one that desired to do all good offices to our dear and common mother, I set my thoughts on work, how so dangerous a quarrel might be happily composed : and, finding that mistaking was more guilty of this dissension, than misbelieving (since it plainly appeared to me, that Mr. Montague meant to express, not Arminius, but B. Overall, a more moderate and safe author, however he sped in delivery of him) ; I wrote a little project of pacification, wherein I desired to rectify the judgment of men, concerning this misapprehended controversy ; showing them the true party in this unreasonable plea ; and, because B. Overall went a midway, betwixt the two opinions which he held extreme, and must needs therefore somewhat differ from the commonly-received tenet in these points, I gathered out of B. Overall on the one side, and out of our English divines at Dort on the other, such common propositions concerning these five busy articles, as wherein both of them are fully agreed. All which being put together, seemed unto me to make up so sufficient a body of accorded truth, that all other questions moved hereabouts appeared merely superfluous ; and every moderate Christian might find where to rest himself without hazard of contradiction. These I made bold, by the hands of Dr. Young, the worthy dean of Winchester, to present to his excellent Majesty, together with an humble motion of a peaceable silence to be enjoined to both parts, in those other collateral and needless disquisitions ; which, if they might befit the schools of academical disputants, could not certainly sound well from the pulpits of popular auditories. Those reconciliatory papers fell under the eyes of some grave divines on both parts. Mr. Montague professed that he had seen them, and would subscribe to them very willingly : others, that were contrarily minded, both English, Scottish, and French divines, proffered their hands to a no less ready subscription. So as much peace promised to result out of that weak and poor enterprise, had not the confused noise of the misconstructions of those who never saw the work, crying it down for the very name's sake, meeting with the royal edict of a general inhibition, buried it in a secure silence.

I was scorched a little with this flame, which I desired to quench : yet this could not stay my hand from thrusting itself into a hotter fire.

Some insolent Romanists, Jesuits especially, in their bold disputations (which, in the time of the treaty of the Spanish match and the calm of that relaxation, were very frequent), pressed nothing so much as a catalogue of the professors of our religion, to be deduced from the primitive times ; and, with the peremptory challenge of the impossibility of this pedigree, dazzled the eyes of the simple : while some of our learned men, undertaking to satisfy so needless and unjust a demand, gave, as I conceived, great advantage to the adversary. In a just indignation to see us thus wronged by misstating the question betwixt us, as if we, yielding ourselves to another church, originally and fundamentally different, should make good our own erection upon the ruins, yea, the nullity of theirs ; and, well considering the infinite and great inconveniences that must needs follow upon this defence, I adventured to set my pen on work ; desiring to rectify the opinions of those men, whom an ignorant zeal had transported, to the prejudice of our holy cause ; laying forth the damnable corruptions of the Roman Church, yet making our game of the outward visibility thereof ; and, by this means putting them to the probation of those newly obtruded corruptions, which are truly guilty of the breach betwixt us. The drift whereof being not well conceived by some spirits that were not so wise as fervent, I was suddenly exposed to the rash censures of many well affected and zealous Protestants ; as if I had, in a remission of my wonted zeal to the truth, attributed too much to the Roman Church, and strengthened the adversaries' hands and weakened our own. This envy I was fain to take off by my speedy apologetical advertisement, and, after that, by my Reconciler, seconded with the unanimous letters of such reverend, learned, sound divines, both Bishops and doctors, as whose undoubtable authority was able to bear down calumny itself ; which done, I did, by a seasonable moderation, provide for the peace of the Church, in silencing both my defendants and challengers, in this unkind and ill-raised quarrel.

Immediately before the publishing of this tractate (which did not a little aggravate the envy and suspicion), I was by his majesty raised to the bishopric of Exeter ; having formerly, with much humble deprecation, refused the see of Gloucester earnestly proffered unto me. How, beyond all expectation, it pleased God to place me in that Western charge ; which, if the Duke of Buckingham's letters, he being then in France, had arrived but some hours sooner, I had been defeated of ; and, by what strange means it pleased God to make up the competency of that provision, by the unthought of addition of the rectory of St. Breok within that diocese ; if I should fully relate the circumstances, would force the confession of an extraordinary hand of God in the disposing of those events.

I entered upon that place, not without much prejudice and suspicion on some hands ; for some, that sat at the stern of the Church, had me in great jealousy for too much favour of Puritanism. I soon had intelligence who were set over me for espials. My ways were curiously observed and scanned. However, I took the resolution to follow those courses which might most conduce to the peace and happiness of my new and weighty charge. Finding, therefore, some factious spirits very busy in that diocese, I used all fair and gentle means to win them to good order ; and therein so happily prevailed, that, saving two of that numerous clergy, who continuing in their refractoriness fled away from censure, they were all perfectly reclaimed ; so as I had not one minister professedly opposite to the anciently received orders (for I was never guilty of urging any new impositions) of the church in that large diocese.

Thus we went on comfortably together, till some persons of note in the clergy, being guilty of their own negligence and disorderly courses, began to envy our success ; and, finding me ever ready to encourage those whom I found conscionably forward and painful in their places, and willingly giving way to orthodox and peaceable lectures in several parts of my diocese, opened their mouths against me, both obliquely in the pulpit and directly at the court : complaining of my too much indulgence to persons disaffected, and my too much liberty of frequent lecturings within my charge. The billows went so high, that I was three several times upon my knee to his majesty, to answer these great criminations ; and what contestation I had with some great lords concerning these particulars, it would be too long to report : only this, under how dark a cloud I was hereupon I was so sensible that I plainly told the lord Archbishop of Canterbury, that rather than I would be obnoxious to those slanderous tongues of his misinformers, I would cast up my rochet. I knew I went right ways, and would not endure to live under undeserved suspicions.

(From *Observations on some Specialities of Divine Providence in the Life of Joseph Hall, Bishop of Norwich*.)

BESIEGED IN HIS PALACE

BUT after the covenant was appointed to be taken, and was generally swallowed of both clergy and laity, my power of ordination was, with some strange violence, restrained : for when I was going on in my wonted course, which no law or ordinance had inhibited, certain forward volunteers in the city, banding together, stir up the mayor and aldermen and sheriffs to call me to an account for an open violation of their covenant.

To this purpose, divers of them came to my gates at a very unseasonable time : and, knocking very vehemently, required to speak with the bishop. Messages were sent to them to know their business : nothing would satisfy them but the bishop's presence. At last I came down to them, and demanded what the matter was : they would have the gate opened, and then they would tell me. I answered that I would know them better first : if they had anything to say to me I was ready to hear them. They told me they had a writing to me, from Mr. Mayor, and some other of their magistrates. The paper contained both a challenge of me for breaking covenant, in ordaining ministers ; and, withal, required me to give in the names of those, which were ordained by me both then and formerly since the covenant. My answer was, that Mr. Mayor was much abused by those who had misinformed him, and drawn that paper from him ; that I would the next day give a full answer to the writing. They moved that my answer might be my personal appearance at the Guildhall. I asked them when they ever heard of a bishop of Norwich appearing before a mayor. I knew mine own place ; and would take that way of answer which I thought fit ; and so dismissed them, who had given out that day, that had they known before of mine ordaining, they would have pulled me and those whom I ordained out of the chapel by the ears.

While I received nothing, yet something was required of me. They were not ashamed, after they had taken away and sold all my goods and personal estate, to come to me for assessments and monthly payments for that estate which they had taken ; and took distresses from me upon my most just denial ; and vehemently required me to find the wonted arms of my predecessors, when they had left me nothing.

Many insolencies and affronts were, in all this time, put upon us. One while a whole rabble of volunteers came to my gates late, when they were locked up, and called for the porter to give them entrance : which being not yielded, they threatened to make by force : and had not the said gates been very strong, they had done it. Others of them clambered over the walls and would come into my house ; their errand they said, was to search for delinquents ; what they would have done I know not, had not we by a secret way sent to raise the officers for our rescue. Another while, the Sheriff Toftes and Alderman Linsey, attended with many zealous followers, came into my chapel to look for superstitious pictures and relics of idolatry, and sent for me, to let me know they found those windows full of images, which were very offensive, and must be demolished. I told them they were the pictures of some ancient and worthy bishops, as St. Ambrose, Austin, etc. It was answered me, that they were so many popes ; and one younger man amongst the rest (Townsend as I perceived afterwards) would take upon him to defend that every diocesan bishop was pope. I answered him with some scorn ; and obtained leave that I might, with the least loss and defacing of the windows, give order for taking off that offence ; which I did by causing the heads of those pictures to be taken off, since I knew the bodies could not offend.

There was not that care and moderation used in reforming the cathedral church bordering upon my palace. It is no other than tragical to relate the carriage of that furious sacrilege, whereof our eyes and ears were the sad witnesses, under the authority and presence of Linsey, Toftes the sheriff, and Greenwood. Lord, what work was here ! what clattering of glasses ! what beating down of walls ! what tearing up of monuments ! what pulling down of seats ! what wresting out of irons and brass from the windows and graves ! what defacing of arms ! what demolishing of curious stone-work, that had not any representation in the world, but only of the cost of the founder, and skill of the mason ! what tooting and piping upon the destroyed organ-pipes ! and what a hideous triumph on the market-day before all the country ; when, in a kind of sacrilegious and profane procession, all the organ pipes, vestments, both copes and surplices, together with the leaden cross which had been newly sawn down from over the Green-yard pulpit, and the service-books and singing-books that could be had, were carried to the fire in the public market-place ; a lewd wretch walking before the train, in his cope trailing in the dirt, with a service-book in his hand, imitating in an impious scorn the tune, and usurping the words of the litany used formerly in the church. Near the public cross, all these monuments of idolatry must be sacrificed to the fire : not without much ostentation of a zealous joy, in discharging ordinance, to the cost of some, who professed how much they had longed to see that day. Neither was it any news, upon this guild day, to have the cathedral, now open on all sides, to be filled with musketeers waiting for the major's return ; drinking and tobacconing as freely as if it had turned ale-house.

Still yet I remained in my palace, though with but a poor retinue and means ; but the house was held too good for me. Many messages were sent by Mr. Corbet to remove me thence. The first pretence was, that the committee, who now was at charge for a house to sit in, might make their daily session there ; being a place both more public, roomy, and chargeless. The committee, after many consultations, resolved it convenient to remove thither ; though many overtures and offers were made to the contrary. Mr. Corbet was impatient of my stay there ; and procures and sends peremptory messages for my present dislodging ; we desired to have some time allowed for providing some other mansion, if we must needs be cast out of this ; which my wife was so willing to hold, that she offered, if the charge of the present committee-house were the thing stood upon, she would be content to defray the sum of the rent of that house of her fifth part : but that might not be yielded ; out we must, and that in three weeks' warning by Midsummer Day then approaching : so as we might have lain in the street for aught I know, had not the providence of God so ordered it, that a neighbour in the close, one Mr. Gostlin, a widower, was content to void his house for us.

This hath been my measure; wherefore I know not: Lord, thou knowest, who only canst remedy, and end, and forgive or avenge this horrible oppression.

(From *Bishop Hall's Hard Measure.*)

BALAAM AND THE ASS

THAT no man may marvel to see Balaam have visions from God and utter prophecies from Him, his very ass hath his eyes opened to see the angel, which his master could not, and his mouth opened to speak more reasonably than his master.   There is no beast deserves so much wonder as this of Balaam, whose common sense is advanced above the reason of his rider; so as for the time the prophet is brutish, and the beast prophetical. Who can but stand amazed at the eye, at the tongue of this silly creature?   For so dull a sight, it was much to see a bodily object that were not too apparent, but to see that spirit which his rider discerned not was far beyond nature.   To hear a voice come from that mouth, which was used only to bray, it was strange and uncouth : but to hear a beast, whose nature is noted for incapacity, to out-reason his master, a professed prophet, is in the very height of miracles; yet can no heart stick at these, that considers the dispensation of the Almighty in both.   Our eye could no more see a beast, than a beast can see an angel, if He had not given this power to it.   How easy is it for Him that made the eye of man and beast, to dim or enlighten it at His pleasure; and if His power can make the very stones to speak, how much more a creature of sense.   That evil spirit spake in the serpent to our first parent; why is it more that a spirit should speak in the mouth of a beast?   How ordinarily did the heathen receive their oracles out of stones and trees !   Do not we ourselves teach birds to speak those sentences they understand not ? we may wonder, we cannot distrust, when we compare the act with the Author; which can as easily create a voice without a body as a body without a voice.   Who now can hereafter plead his simplicity and dulness of apprehending spiritual things, when he sees how God exalts the eyes of a beast, to see a spirit?   Who can be proud of seeing visions, since an angel appeared to a beast?   Neither was his skin better after it than others of his kind. Who can complain of his own rudeness and inability to reply in a good cause, when the very beast is enabled by God to convince his master? There is no mouth into which God cannot put words; and how often doth he choose the weak and unwise to confound the learned and mighty!

What had it been better for the ass to see the angel, if he had rushed still upon his sword? Evils were as good not seen, as not avoided; but now he declines the way, and saves his burthen. It were happy for perverse sinners, if they could learn of this beast, to run away from foreseen judgments. The revenging angel stands before us: and though we know we shall as sure die as sin, yet we have not the wit or grace to give back: though it be with the hurt of a foot to save the body; with the pain of the body to save the soul.

I see, what fury and stripes the impatient prophet bestows upon this poor beast, because he will not go on; yet if he had gone on, himself had perished. How often do we wish those things, the not obtaining whereof is mercy! We grudge to be staid in the way to death, and fly upon those which oppose our perdition.

I do not (as who would not expect) see Balaam's hair stand upright, nor himself alighting and appalled at this monster of miracles: but, as if no new thing had happened, he returns words to the beast, full of anger, void of admiration; whether his trade of sorcering had so inured him to receive voices from his familiars, in shape of beasts, that this event seemed not strange to him; or, whether his rage and covetousness had so transported him, that he had no leisure to observe the unnatural unusualness of the event. Some men make nothing of those things, which overcome others with horror and astonishment.

(From *Contemplations.*)

TO MY REVEREND BRETHREN OF THE DIOCESE OF NORWICH

WORTHY BRETHREN—Ye cannot but have taken notice of the silence, that hath lately possessed my tongue, which was wont to be vocal enough. Besides some external reasons, it is my care and zeal of peace, that stops my mouth for the time ; and bids me refrain, even from good works. In the meanwhile, the same dear respect to peace employs my hand ; and bids it supply the place of my tongue, as that which shall speak louder and to more eyes than my tongue could to ears : both of them are heartily devoted to peace, and strive whether shall more express it.

It was ever the desire of my soul, even from my first entrance upon the public service of the Church, according to my known signature, with Noah's Dove, to have brought an olive branch to the tossed Ark : and God knows how sincerely I have endeavoured it : but, if my wings have been too short, and the wind too high for me, to carry it home, I must content myself with the conscience of my faithful devotions. Some little hint whereof, notwithstanding, I have thought fit to give to the world, in this present discourse, lest I should seem to be, like itself, all pretence ; and that I might by this essay of mine, open the way to some more able undertakers.

Now therefore, let me recommend this subject to your seriousest thoughts ; and beseech you all, in the bowels of our common Saviour, to join with me, in the zealous prosecution of what I here treat of, peace.

It is a useful rule of our Romish casuists, that he who will have benefit of their large indulgences, must *porrigere manus adjutrices*. Surely, it holds much better, in the present case. Whoever will hope to reap the comfort of this incomparable blessing of peace, must put forth his helping hand, towards the procuring it. Oh, let not our studies, nor prayers, nor tears, nor counsels, nor solicitations, nor engagements, nor endeavours, be wanting to it : no ; nor, if need were, our blood. What the price of it is, since the fruition of it did not teach us, we have too well learnt in the want.

Alas, my brethren, we cannot help one another sufficiently to condole the miseries under which we, yea this whole Church, yea this whole bleeding monarchy, yea the whole Christian world, at this time groaneth, by reason of that woeful and deadly debate, that rageth everywhere. All the whole earth is on fire : the flame reacheth up to heaven, and calls for more thence. Woe is me ! our very punishment is our sin. What should we do, but pour out floods of tears, towards the quenching of it : and say, with the lamenting prophet, " Oh that my head were waters, and mine eyes a fountain of tears, that I might weep day and night for the slain of the daughter of my people!"—Jer. ix. 1.

But, as Chrysostom said long ago in the like case to Innocentius, it is not wailing will serve the turn, if we do not bestir ourselves, what we may, for redress. When we see our house on fire, do we stand still and cry? do we not ring bells, and call neighbours, and bring ladders, and fetch buckets, and pour on water, and pull down reeds and rafters, and whatever may feed that flame? And why should we not do so, in this common conflagration? Oh, let every man of us put his hand to the work; and labour to withdraw that hellish fuel which nourisheth and increaseth this fearful combustion; and, if each man can but pull away one stick, it shall be his comfort and joy in that great day. But far, far be it from us, that any of us should mis-employ himself as an incendiary.

It is felony, by our municipal laws, for a man to burn but the frame of a building intended for a house: how heinously flagratious shall the God of Heaven account it, to set on fire His complete spiritual house the Church, whereof every believer is a living stone! Doubtless, how slight account soever the world makes of these spiritual distempers, it shall be easier in the day of judgment for thieves and whoremongers and adulterers than for the breakers of public peace. Never was there any so fearful vengeance inflicted upon any malefactors, as upon Korah and his combination. Surely, if we consider the sin in itself, other offences had been far more heinous: but in that it was a presumptuous mutiny, tending to the affront of allowed authority, to the violation of peace, and to the destruction of community, the earth could not stand under it: hell only is fit to receive it.

I speak not this to intimate the least suspicion, much less accusation, of any of you, my dear brethren; but, by way of a tender precaution and loving cohortation, to excite you and myself to the improvement of all the powers of our souls, for the recovery and perpetuation of the Church's peace: a duty, which both our blessed Saviour, and his holy Apostles, hath so vehemently urged, as if there were no life of Christianity without it.

As we honour the God of Love and Peace whom we serve, as we love the Prince of Peace in whom we believe, as we tender the success of the Gospel of Peace which we preach, as we wish and hope for the comfort of the peace of God in our own bosoms, let us seek peace where it is missing, let us follow after it when it flies from us, let us never leave the chase, by importuning God and men, till we overtake it, till we re-enjoy it, and all the blessings that accompany it ; which shall be ever the prayer and endeavour of—Your faithful and loving fellow-labourer,

JOSEPH NORWICH.

(Prefatory Letter to The Peace Maker.)

THE CHRISTIAN'S DISPOSITION

THE Christian is a man and more, an earthly saint, an angel clothed in flesh, the only lawful image of his Maker and Redeemer, the abstract of God's Church on earth, a model of heaven, made up in clay, the living temple of the Holy Ghost.

For his disposition, it hath in it as much of heaven as his earth may make room for.

He were not a man, if he were quite free from corrupt affections ; but these he masters, and keeps in with a strait hand ; and if, at any time, they grow testy and headstrong, he breaks them with a severe discipline, and will rather punish himself than not tame them. He checks his appetite with discreet but strong denials, and forbears to pamper nature lest it grow wanton and impetuous.

He walks on earth, but converses in heaven ; having his eyes fixed on the invisible, and enjoying a sweet communion with his God and Saviour. While all the rest of the world sits in darkness, he lives in a perpetual light : the heaven of heavens is open to none but him ; thither his eye pierceth and beholds those beams of inaccessible glory which shine in no face but his.

The deep mysteries of godliness, which to the great clerks of the world are as a book clasped and sealed up, lie open before him fair and legible ; and, while those bookmen know whom they have heard of, he knows whom he hath believed.

He will not suffer his Saviour to be ever out of his eye ; and if, through some wordly interceptions, he lose the sight of that blessed object for a time, he zealously retrieves him,—not without a hungry check of his own mis-carriage,—and is now so much the more fixed by his former slackening so as he will henceforth sooner part with his soul than his Redeemer.

The terms of entireness wherein he stands with the Lord of Life are such as he can feel, but cannot express though he should borrow the language of angels : it is enough that they are one Spirit.

His reason is willingly captivated to his faith, his will to his reason, and his affections to both.

He fears nothing that he sees, in comparison of that which he sees not ; and displeasure is more dreadful to him than smart.

Good is the adequate object of his love : which he duly proportions, according to the degrees of its eminence ; affecting the chief good, not without a certain ravishment of spirit ; the lesser, with a wise and holy moderation.

Whether he do more hate sin, or the evil spirit that suggests it, is a question.

Earthly contents are too mean grounds whereon to raise his joy ; these, as he balks not when they meet him in his way, so he doth not too eagerly pursue ; he may taste of them, but so as he would rather fast than surfeit.

He is not insensible of those losses which casualty or enmity may inflict, but that which lies most heavily upon his heart is his sin. This makes his sleep short and troublesome, his meals stomachless, his recreations listless, his everything tedious, till he find his soul acquitted by his great surety in heaven ; which done, he feels more peace and pleasure in his calm than he found horror in the tempest.

His heart is the storehouse of most precious graces. That faith whereby his soul is established triumphs over the world, whether it allure or threaten ; and bids defiance to all the powers of darkness, not fearing to be foiled by any opposition. His hope cannot be discouraged with the greatest difficulties ; but bears up against natural impossibilities, and knows how to reconcile contradictions. His charity is both extensive and fervent, barring out no one that bears the face of a man ; but pouring out itself upon the household of faith : that studies good constructions of men and actions, and keeps itself free both from suspicion and censure.

Grace doth more exalt him than his humility depresses him. Were it not for that Christ who dwells in him, he could think himself the meanest of all creatures : now, he knows he may not disparage the Deity of Him by whom he is so gloriously inhabited, in whose only right he can be as great in his own thoughts as he is despicable in the eyes of the world.

He is wise to Godward, however it be with him for the world ; and, well knowing he cannot serve two masters, he cleaves to the better, making choice of that good part which cannot be taken from him, not so much regarding to get that which he cannot keep, as to possess himself of that good which he cannot lose.

He is just in all his dealings with men, hating to thrive by injury and oppression, and will rather leave behind something of his own than filch from another's heap.

He is not closefisted, where is just occasion of his distribution, willingly parting with those metals which he regards only for use, not caring for either their colour or substance ; earth is to him no other than itself, in what hue soever it appeareth.

In every good cause he is bold as a lion, and can neither fear faces nor shrink at dangers, and is rather heartened with opposition ; pressing so much the more, where he finds a large door open, and many adversaries, and, when he must suffer, doth as resolutely stoop, as he did before valiantly resist.

He is holily temperate in the use of all God's blessings, as knowing by whom they are given, and to what end ; neither dares either to mis-lay them, or to mis-spend them lavishly, as duly weighing upon what terms he receives them, and fore-expecting an account.

Such a hand doth he carry upon his pleasures and delights, that they run not away with him ; he knows how to slacken the reins without a debauched kind of dissoluteness, and how to straiten them without a sullen rigour.

(From *The Christian.*)

UNDUTIFUL SONS

In your next section, like ill-bred sons, you spit in the face of your mother—a mother too good for such sons—the Church of England ; and tell us of " Papists, that dazzle the eyes of poor people with the glorious name of the Holy Mother the Church." If they be too fond of their mother, I am sure your mother hath little cause to be fond of you, who can and dare compare her to those

Ethiopian strumpets, which were common to all comers. For your whole undutiful carriage towards her, take heed of the ravens of the valley. As if we were no less strangers than you enemies to the Church of England, you tell the world, that we know not who she is ; and that we wonder when we are asked the question, and run descant upon the two archbishops, bishops, Convocation, even what your luxuriant wit shall please ; and, at last, you make up your mouth with a merry jest, telling your reader that the Remonstrant, out of his simplicity, never heard nor thought of any more Churches of England than one." *Ridiculum caput!* Sit you merry, brethren ; but, truly, after all your sport, still my " simplicity " tells me there is but one Church of England. There are many Churches in England, but many Churches of England were never till now heard of. You had need fetch it as far as the " Heptarchy." And, to show how far you are from the objected simplicity, ye tell us, in the shutting up, that England, Scotland, and Ireland are all one Church of England. *Nullum magnum ingenium sine mixturâ dementiæ.*

(From *A Defence of The Humble Remonstrance.*)

WEARY LOQUACITY

AND now forbear, if you can, readers, to smile in the parting, at the grave counsel of our wise Smectymnuus ; who, after he hath tired his reader with a tedious volume, in answer to my short " Defence," adviseth me very sadly, that my " words " may be " less in number."

Yet, howsoever his weary loquacity may, in this causeless exprobration, deserve to move your mirth ; I shall resolve to make good use of his counsel. *Est olitor sæpe opportuna locutus.* In the sequel, my words, which were never yet taxed for an offensive superfluity, shall be very few ; and such as, to your greater wonder, I shall be beholden for, to my kind adversaries.

The rereward of my late *Defence* was backed by the sound testimony of Dr. Abraham Scultetus, the famous Professor of Heidelberg, and the great oracle in his time of the Palatinate ; who, in both the tenets of Episcopacy by Divine Right, and the unwarrantableness of Lay Presbytery, agrees so fully with me as

I do with myself : the grounds whereof, I dare confidently say, are such, as no wit of man can overthrow or weaken.

Now what say my Smectymnuans to this ? " For brevity sake, we will content ourselves with what that learned Rivet spake, when these two treatises of Scultetus were showed to him, by a great prelate amongst us, and his judgment required : *Hæc omnia jamdudum sunt protrita et profligata;* all these have been long since overworn, and beaten out, and baffled."

In good time, brethren ! And why should not I take leave to return the same answer to you, in this your tedious velitation of Episcopacy ? There is not one new point in this your overswoln and unwieldy bulk. No hay-cock hath been oftener shaken abroad, and tossed up and down in the wind, than every argument of yours hath been agitated by more able pens than mine : *Hæc omnia jamdudum sunt protrita et profligata.* Why should I abuse my good hours ; and spend my last age, devoted to better thoughts, in an unprofitable babbling ?

You may, perhaps, expect to meet with fitter matches, that have more leisure. The cause is not mine alone ; but common to this whole Church, to the whole Hierarchy, to all the Fathers of the Church throughout the world, to all the dutiful sons of those Fathers wheresoever. You may not hope, that so many learned and eminent divines, who find themselves equally interested in this quarrel, can suffer either so just a cause unseconded, or so high insolence unchastised.

For myself, I remember the story that Plutarch tells of the contestation between Crassus and Deiotarus ; men well stricken in age, and yet attempting several exploits, not so proper for their gray hairs. "What," said Crassus to Deiotarus, "dost thou begin to build a city, now in the latter end of the day?" "And truly," said Deiotarus to him again, "I think it somewhat with the latest for you to think of conquering the Parthians." Some witty lookers-on will, perhaps, apply both these to me. It is the city of God, the evangelical Jerusalem, which some factious hands have miserably demolished : is it for shaking and wrinkled hands to build up again, now in the very setting and shutting-in of the day ? They are dangerous and not inexpert Parthians, who shoot out their arrows, even bitter invectives, against the sacred and apostolical government of the Church ; and such, as know how to fight, fleeing : are these fit for the vanquishing of a decrepit leader ?

Shortly, then, since I see that our Smectymnuans have vowed, like as some impetuous scolds are wont to do, to have the last word ; and have set up a resolution, by taking advantage of their multitude, to tire out their better-employed adversary, with mere length of discourse ; and to do that by bulk of body, which by clean strength they cannot ; I have determined to take off my hand from this remaining controversy of Episcopacy (wherein I have said enough already, without the return of answer ; and, indeed, anticipated all those threadbare objections, which are here again regested to the weary reader), and to turn off my combined opposites to matches more meet for their age and quality : with this profession, notwithstanding, that, if I shall find, which I hope I never shall, this just and holy cause, whether out of insensibleness or cautious reservedness, neglected by more able defenders, I shall borrow so much time from my better thoughts, as to bestow some strictures, where I may not afford a large confutation.   I have ever held μέγα βιβλίον μέγα κακὸν : which, as it holds in whatsoever matter of discourse, so especially in this so beaten subject of Episcopacy ; wherein, since I find it impossible for my adversaries to fall upon any but former notions, oft urged, oft answered, "For brevity sake we will content ourselves with what that learned Rivet spake of the two treatises of Scultetus, *Hæc omnia jamdudum sunt protrita et profligata,*" with this yet for a conclusion, that if, in this their wordy and wearisome volume, they shall meet with any one argument, which they dare avow for new, they shall expect their answer by the next post.

(From *An Answer to Smectymnuus's Vindication.*)

JAMES USSHER

[James Ussher was born at Dublin on the 4th of January 1581. He was nephew of Henry Ussher, Archbishop of Armagh, and of Richard Stanihurst, translator of four books of the Æneid. At the age of thirteen he was admitted as the second on the roll of scholars of the newly-founded Trinity College, Dublin. Subsequently he became Fellow of the same Society. At the death of his father in 1598, he abandoned most of the property that came to him, and devoted himself to study. From 1601 to 1619 he read the fathers daily. He became famous as a theologian and antiquary, and was the friend of Camden, Selden, Cotton, and Evelyn. In 1607 he was made Professor of Divinity at Dublin, in 1620 Bishop of Meath, and in 1625 Archbishop of Armagh. In 1640 he crossed the Channel to live in England, where he died on the 21st of March 1656.

Ussher's *magnum opus* is his Latin *Annales Veteris et Novi Testamenti*. His principal English works are treatises on *The Religion of the Ancient Irish and British; Imperial Laws in Great Britain and Ireland; Corbes, Herenachs, and Termon Lands; Immanuel, or the Mystery of the Incarnation; An Answer to the Challenge of a Jesuit; The Power of the Prince*. A complete edition of Ussher's writings, with a Life, was published by Professor Elrington and the Rev. J. Todd, in 17 vols. 1841-64.]

THE fame of Archbishop Ussher has long been but a *nominis umbra*, nor shall anything here be said to recall his ghost from the quiet gardens of oblivion. Seventeen volumes of his treatises gather dust upon the shelves; as one takes them down one remembers the disinterment of some buried hero from his burrow among the hills. The very topics are sufficiently alarming—The Chronology of the Old Testament; The Primitive Celtic Church; Corbes, Termons, and Herenachs. Such themes repel the ordinary man, and for the specialist the treatment is out of date. There are qualities of style, indeed, whereby the most abstruse disquisitions, like flies in amber, survive. One reads Burton without regard to his faded theories on the physical basis of love. But to style as an end in itself Ussher paid little heed. Controversy was his business; his interest, antiquities. He used his prose in the spirit of the scholar rather than the artist; as the instrument of his labours, not their object. And since all mere scholarship must needs be superseded, Ussher's writings have lost their savour; he lingers, if at all, in the popular mind only as the discoverer of two dates—that of 4 B.C. for the birth of Christ; that of 4004 B.C., which figures on the margin of our Bibles for the creation. Nor can there be a better essay in the study of evidence than to consider why the methods which led him to so sound a conclusion in the one case proved so untrustworthy in the other.

Argument means for Ussher the accumulation of authorities; authorities, indeed, weighed with precision, criticised as to their authenticity, but in the last result accepted as authoritative. And with this is connected his renunciation of style; for to style the abundance of quotation must needs be fatal. Fragments pieced together from other men's works, even where translation is freely used, cannot but lack the unity which the impress of a single personality gives. Ussher's writing is always a mosaic of quotations. His learning is immense. At an early age, so his biographers tell us, he sat down and read the fathers straight through. Chroniclers, schoolmen, the writers of Greece and Rome, all are at his fingers' ends. He has wandered in the byeways of Celtic and Scandinavian lore. And in this he was happy, that by his time the sum-total of things knowable had not so swelled as to be beyond the compass of one intellect; so that he does not appear a mere specialist, but a true scholar, with a wide sweep and an adequate survey of knowledge. Moreover, he has at least one gift—an architectonic gift—of style; he marshals his authorities with a due regard to balance and proportion, keeping always in mind the clear design of his argument, and the impression he intends it to produce. Another side of Ussher's disregard of the purely literary element in composition is apparent in his two or three short dogmatic treatises. In these copious citation would have been out of place; but in its stead he adopts the method of question and answer—of catechism, in fact. Where he does write a few pages for himself, his English is at least dignified, if a trifle Ciceronian. It must not be forgotten that more than half his work was composed in Latin, and that the habit of using the dead language naturally affected his mode of expressing himself in the living. Yet now and then he has touches racy with the raciness of a countryman of St. Patrick.

Most of Ussher's treatises, where their interest is not purely antiquarian, bear more or less directly upon the controversy with Rome. He generally escapes the vulgarities of polemic. The Catholic Church, indeed, is " Babylonish" and "a dunghill of errors." But of the personal abuse, which tarnishes the gold of Milton, for instance, there is but little. As in life, so in speech, he is humane, and without asperity. One of his tracts, that *On the Power of the Prince*, belongs to the political side of theology. It is a pronouncement in favour of divine right ; and this, together with his friendship with Laud, effectually disposes of his supposed leanings to Calvinism. A number of sermons are included in the complete edition of his works ; but as these were published in spite of his expressed injunction, they need hardly be taken into account.

EDMUND K. CHAMBERS.

OF PURGATORY, AND PRAYER FOR THE DEAD

THE next point that offereth itself unto our consideration is that of purgatory. Whereof if any man do doubt, Cæsarius, a German monk of the Cistercian order, adviseth him for his resolution to make a journey into Scotland (the greater Scotland he meaneth) and there to enter into St. Patrick's purgatory, and then he giveth him his word, that " he shall no more doubt of the pains of purgatory." If Dr. Terry, who commendeth this unto us as the testimony " of a most famous author," should chance to have a doubtful thought hereafter of the pains of purgatory, I would wish his ghostly father to enjoin him no other penance but the undertaking of a pilgrimage unto St. Patrick's purgatory ; to see whether he would prove any wiser when he came from thence, than when he went thither. In the meantime, until he hath made some further experiment of the matter, he shall give me leave to believe him that hath been there, and hath cause to know the place as well as any (the island wherein it is seated, being held by him as part of the inheritance descended unto him from his ancestors) and yet professeth, that he found nothing therein, which might afford him any argument to think there was a purgatory. I pass by that Nennius and Probus and all the elder writers of the life of St. Patrick that I have met withal, speak not one word of any such place ; and that Henry the monk of Saltrey, in the days of king Stephen, is the first in whom I could find any mention thereof ; this only would I know of the doctor, what the reason might be, that where he bringeth in the words of Giraldus Cambrensis touching this place, as " an authentical authority" ; he passeth over that part of his relation, wherein he affirmeth, that St. Patrick intended by this means to bring the rude people to a persuasion of the certainty " of the infernal pains of the reprobate, and of the true and everlasting life of the elect after death ? "

The Grecians allege this for one of their arguments against purgatory : that whereas "their fathers had delivered unto them many visions and dreams, and other wonders concerning the everlasting punishment," wherewith the wicked should be tormented in hell ; yet none of them had "declared anything concerning a purgatory temporary fire." Belike the doctor was afraid that we would conclude, upon the same ground, that St. Patrick was careful to plant in men's minds the belief of a heaven and hell, but of purgatory taught them never a word. And sure I am, that in the book ascribed unto him, *De Tribus Habitaculis*, which is to be seen in his Majesty's library, there is no mention of any other place after this life, but of these two only. I will lay down here the beginning of that treatise, and leave it to the judgment of any indifferent man, whether it can well stand with that which the Romanists teach concerning purgatory at this day. "There be three habitations under the power of Almighty God : the first, the lowermost, and the middle. The highest whereof is called the kingdom of God, or the kingdom of heaven, the lowermost is termed hell, the middle is named the present world, or the circuit of the earth. The extremes whereof are altogether contrary one to another : for what fellowship can there be betwixt light and darkness, betwixt Christ and Belial ? but the middle hath some similitude with the extremes. For in this world there is a mixture of the bad and of the good together, whereas in the kingdom of God there are none bad, but all good : but in hell there are none good but all bad. And both these places are supplied out of the middle. For of the men of this world some are lifted up to heaven, others are drawn down to hell. Namely, like are joined unto like, that is to say, good to good, and bad to bad : just men to just angels, wicked men to wicked angels ; the servants of God to God, the servants of the devil to the devil. The blessed are called to the kingdom prepared for them from the beginning of the world : the cursed are driven into the everlasting fire that is prepared for the devil and his angels." Thus far there.

Hitherto also may be referred that ancient canon of one of our Irish synods, wherein it is affirmed that the soul being separated from the body is "presented before the judgment seat of Christ, who rendereth its own unto it, according as it hath done" : and that "neither the archangel can lead it into life, until the Lord hath judged it, nor the devil transport it unto pain, unless the Lord do damn it"; as the writings of Sedulius likewise, that after the end of this life "either death or life succeedeth," and that "death is the gate by which we enter into our kingdom": together with that of Claudius; that "Christ did take upon him our punishment without the guilt, that thereby he might loose our guilt, and finish also our punishment." Cardinal Bellarmine, indeed allegeth here against us the vision of Furseus, who "rising from the dead, told many things which he saw concerning the pains of purgatory," as Bede, he saith, doth write. But, by his good leave, we will be better advised, before we build articles of faith upon such visions and dreams as these, many whereof deserved to have a place among "the strange narrations of souls appearing after death," collected by Damasius the heathen idolater, rather than among the histories and discourses of sober Christians.

As for this vision of Furseus: all that Bede relateth of it to this purpose, is concerning great fires above the air, appointed to "examine every one according to the merits of his works," which peradventure may make something for Damasius his purgatory *in circulo lacteo* (for in that circle made he a way for the souls that went to the hades in heaven; and would not have us wonder, that there they should be purged by the way); but nothing for the papist's purgatory, which Bellarmine by the common consent of the schoolmen determineth to be in the bowels of the earth. Neither is there anything else in the whole book of the life of Furseus, whence Bede borrowed these things, that looketh toward purgatory, unless peradventure that speech of the devil may be thought to give some advantage unto it. "This man hath not purged his sins upon earth; neither doth he receive punishment for them here. Where is therefore the justice of God?" as if God's justice were not sufficiently satisfied by the sufferings of Christ: but man also must needs give further satisfaction thereunto by penal works or sufferings, either here, or in the other world, which is the ground upon which our Romanists do lay the rotten frame of their devised purgatory.

The latter visions of Malachias, Tundal, Owen, and others that lived within these last five hundred years, come not within the compass of our present enquiry: nor yet the fables that have been framed in those times, touching the lives and actions of elder saints, whereof no wise man will make any reckoning. Such, for example, is that which we read in the life of St. Brendan: that the question being moved in his hearing "whether the sins of the dead could be redeemed by the prayers or almsdeeds of their friends remaining in this life," for that was still a question in the church, he is said to have told them, that on a certain night, as he sailed on the great ocean, the soul of one Colman, who "had been an angry monk, and a sower of discord betwixt brethren," appeared unto him, who complaining of his grievous torments, entreated that prayers might be made to God for him, and after six days thankfully acknowledged that by means thereof he had gotten into heaven. Whereupon it is concluded, "that the prayer of the living doth profit much the dead." But of St. Brendan's sea pilgrimage, we have the censure of Molanus, a learned Romanist, that there be "many apocryphal fooleries in it ; and whosoever readeth the same with any judgment, cannot choose but pronounce of it, as Photius doth of the strange narrations of Damasius, formerly mentioned ; that it containeth not only apocryphal, but also "impossible, incredible, ill-composed, and monstrous" fooleries. Whereof though the old legend itself were not free as by the heads thereof, touched by Glaber Rodulphus and Giraldus Cambrensis, may appear, yet for the tale that I recited out of the new legend of England, I can say, that in the manuscript books which I have met withal here, in St. Brendan's own country (one whereof was transcribed for the use of the friars minors of Kilkenny, about the year of our Lord one thousand three hundred and fifty), there is not the least footstep thereof to be seen.

(From *Religion of the Ancient Irish.*)

JOHN SELDEN

[John Selden (1584-1654), the only son of a yeoman, was born at Salvington on the Sussex coast, and was educated at Chichester Grammar Schoo and at Hart Hall, Oxford. In 1604 he was admitted to the Inner Temple, where he rapidly gained a name for his antiquarian erudition. In 1621 Selden, though not a member, assisted the Commons in drawing up a protest against the King's refusal to receive the petition of grievances ; for this he suffered a five weeks' imprisonment. In 1624 he entered Parliament, and for twenty years took a prominent part in the struggle between Commons and Crown. In 1627 he supported Hampden in his resistance to Charles' forced loan, and the following year helped to frame the Petition of Right. For his share in the proceedings of the Parliament of 1629, when protests against tonnage and poundage were read while the Speaker was forcibly held in the chair, Selden was again imprisoned—this time for nearly two years. In the Long Parliament Selden's firm moderation opposed the zeal of the more violent reformers as well as the unwarranted pretensions of the royal prerogative. He was one of the committee appointed to draw up a remonstrance on the state of the nation ; but he voted against Strafford's impeachment, and attempted to defeat the Declaration against Episcopacy in 1641. When matters came to a head shortly after with the impeachment of the five members, Selden maintained the illegality alike of the King's Commission of Array, and of the Commons' Ordinance for the Militia. He was a member of the Assembly of Divines, in which, according to Whitelock, " Mr. Selden spake admirably, and confuted divers of them in their own learning." His closing years were spent under the roof of the Dowager-Countess of Kent. His library is preserved in the Bodleian, Oxford. The list of Selden's legal and Rabbinical treatises in Latin is too long for insertion here. His two principal works in English are *Titles of Honour* (1614), and *History of Tithes* (1618), which was suppressed by James I. on the ground that it denied their "divine right." The *Table-Talk* — collected and recorded by Selden's amanuensis, the Rev. Richard Millward—was not printed till 1689. But it seems probable, from Millward's dedication to Selden's executors, that he had prepared it for publication soon after Selden's death.]

IT is by his conversation rather than by his writings that Selden claims a place in this series. Most of his learned treatises were written in Latin, and the few that are in English can hardly be regarded as specimens of English prose. Documents and records in all languages form the body of his works. Selden does little more than arrange and cement them together. This method of writing history has evident advantages, but they are not of a literary character. In the *Titles of Honour* there is not one page of consecutive English. The passage quoted below— where for once he tells a legend in his own words instead of quoting the original — is the longest uninterrupted piece of English in *The History of Tithes*, with the exception of the preface. Selden contents himself with quoting his authorities; for his aim in all his works is an exposition of facts, and he allows them to speak for themselves.

There is no reason to doubt Millward's statement in his dedication of the *Table-Talk* to Selden's friends, that "the sense and notion here is wholly his (Selden's), and most of the words." "You will quickly perceive them to be his," he adds, "by the familiar illustrations wherewith they are set off, and in which way you know he was so happy, that, with a marvellous delight to those that heard him, he would presently convey the highest points of religion, and the most important affairs of state, to an ordinary apprehension." And this appeal is sustained by the evidence of Clarendon—which might serve for a description of the *Table-Talk*—that "in his conversation he was the most clear discourser, and had the best faculty of making hard things easy, and of presenting them to the understanding of any man that hath been known." The ordinary reader, ignorant of the circumstances which from time to time gave occasion to the *Table-Talk*, must miss the full significance of much that is contained in it. Even an apophthegm or anecdote loses half its flavour apart from context and circumstances; and Millward, though he desires his readers to "carry along with them the *When* and the *Why* many of these things were spoken" gives them no help. The detached notes, taken at different times over a period of twenty years, are classified under headings according to subject. It would have been better, since there was no attempt to edit them, had they been left in chronological sequence. "We can no more know," says Selden, in one of these *obiter dicta*, "what a minister said in his sermon by two or three words picked out of it, than we can tell what tune a musician played last upon the lute by two or three single notes." In some degree the same applies to these fragments of conversation. Yet, if put together as a whole the reader may trace in them, as in a broken mirror, some reflection of Selden's personality. A greater part of them forms a commentary on the exciting events and problems of his time — prerogative, divine right, episcopacy, parliament, etc. His statements are naturally less restrained here than in his more public utterances, and serve as a key to his political position during the years in which he acted as the bulwark of the constitution and arbiter of the rights of king and of commons. His favourite text, "All is as the State pleases," gives the central principle of his political philosophy. He considers that the rights and authority of King, Church, and Commons alike take their origin from, and are subject to, "the laws of the kingdom," of which he takes the purely empirical view of a practical lawyer. Selden adds to his marvellous range of learning a wide experience of life and keen analytic powers. His usual method of exposition is to reduce the subject at issue to its simplest form, and to illustrate it by homely analogy. Take, as an example, this on "Consecrated Places." "All things are God's already; we can give him no right, by consecrating any, that he had not before, only we set it apart to his service. Just as a gardener brings his lord and master a basket of apricots and presents them, his lord thanks him, perhaps gives him something for his pains, and yet the apricots were as much his lord's before as now." For refutation he frequently uses the *reductio ad absurdum*, as in the following : " If we once come to leave that outloose, as to pretend conscience against law, who knows what inconvenience may follow ? For thus, suppose an Anabaptist comes and takes my horse. I sue him ; he tells me he did according to his conscience ; his conscience tells him all things are common amongst the saints, what is mine is his ; therefore you do ill to make such a law, 'If any man takes another's horse he shall be hanged.' What can I say to this man ? He does according to his conscience." Selden's judgments, though occasionally betraying his dislikes, are given without acerbity or passion. He speaks with the quiet assurance of a man who knows his facts, and discusses the issues which were so deeply moving his contemporaries with the calmness of a retrospective historian. His advice in practical affairs now and then recalls the worldly wisdom of Bacon's *Essays.* " In a troubled state," he says in one passage, " we must do as in foul weather upon the Thames, not think to cut directly through, so the boat may be quickly full of water, but rise and fall as the waves do, give as much as conveniently we can." And in another place he says : " 'Tis not juggling that is to be blamed, but much juggling ; for the world cannot be governed without it." His humour is characteristic. At times it takes the form of epigram, as in the following : " They talk (but blasphemously enough) that the Holy Ghost is president of their general councils, when the truth is, the odd man is still [always] the Holy Ghost." At others, it suggests a ludicrous parallel. " Doctor Prideaux, in his lectures, several days used arguments to prove predestination ; at last he tells his auditory they are damned that do not believe it ; doing herein just like schoolboys, when one of them has got an apple, or something the rest have a mind to, they use all the arguments they can to get some of it from him. *I gave you some t'other day ; you shall have some with me another time.* When they cannot prevail, they tell him he's a jackanapes, a rogue, and a rascal." Selden has the limitations of one whose feet are always planted firmly on solid earth. He is a guide, a critic ; not a leader, an inspirer. As he is untouched by the fanaticisms, he is incapable of the fine enthusiasms of his day. His remarks on poetry show no powers of literary appreciation. Clarendon justly remarked upon his "undervaluing of style." In his writings his sentences are usually ponderous, and often involved—a striking contrast to the homeliness and lucidity of his conversations, which, however, show also carelessness as to form. Yet in both there is an entire absence of pedantry. Selden estimated knowledge at its true value. " No man," he says, " is the wiser for his learning ; it may administer matter to work in, or objects to work upon ; but wit and wisdom are born with a man." It is matter for regret that one who was pre-eminent in his age for both learning and wisdom should have devoted himself so exclusively to the pursuit of the former as to leave us nothing of the latter except a few fragments collected after his death by his secretary.

W. S. M'CORMICK.

A SCHOLAR'S DEFENCE

NEITHER at all wish I that this of mine should gain any strength of truth from my name alone, but from those authorities which I have designed and brought, both for elder, late and present times, out of such both printed and manuscript *Annals*, *Histories*, *Councils*, *Chartularies*, *Laws*, *Lawyers*, and *Records* only as were to be used in the most accurate way of search that might furnish for the subject. Yet also I have not neglected the able judgments of such of the learned of later time, as give light to former ages. But I so preferred the choicest and most able, that I have wholly abstained from any mention or use here of those many ignorants that (while they write) rather instruct us in their own wants of ability, than direct to anything that may satisfy. If through ignorance I have omitted anything in the *History* or the *Review* that deserved place in them, who ever shall admonish me of it shall have a most willing acknowledgment of his learning and courtesy. But all the bad titles that are ever due to abuse of the holiest obtestation be always my companions, if I have purposely omitted any good authority of ancient or late time, that I saw necessary, or could think might give further or other light to any position or part of it! For I sought only Truth ; and was never so far engaged in this or aught else as to torture my brains or venture my credit to make or create premises for a chosen conclusion, that I rather would than could prove. My premises made what conclusions or conjectures I have, and were not bred by them. And although both of them here not a little sometimes vary from what is vulgarly received, yet that happened not at all from any desire to differ from common opinion, but from another course of disquisition than is commonly used : that is, by examination of the truth of those suppositions which patient idleness too easily takes for clear and granted. For the old sceptics that never would profess that they had found a truth, showed yet the best way to search for any, when they doubted as well of what those of the dogmatical sects too credulously received for infallible principles, as they did of the newest conclusions. They were indeed questionless too nice, and deceived themselves with the nimbleness of their own sophisms, that permitted no kind of established truth. But plainly, he that avoids their disputing levity, yet, being able, takes to himself their liberty of enquiry, is in the only way that in all kinds of studies leads and lies open even to the sanctuary of truth ; while others, that are servile to common opinion and vulgar suppositions, can rarely hope to be admitted nearer than into the base court of her temple, which too speciously often counterfeits her inmost sanctuary. And to this purpose also is that of Quintilian, most worthy of memory, *Optimus est in discendo, patronus incredulus.*

(From the Preface to *The History of Tithes.*)

THE FIRST PAYMENT OF TITHES IN ENGLAND.

FOR the practice of payment among Christians, both Britons and Saxons, might we believe the common tale of that Augustine, the first Archbishop of Canterbury province, his coming to Cometon in Oxfordshire, and doing a most strange miracle there ; touching the establishing of the doctrine of due payment of tithes, we should have as certain and express authority for the ancient practice of such payment, as any other church in Christendom can produce. But as the tale is, you shall have it, and then censure it. About the year (they say) DC. Augustine coming to preach at Cometon, the priest of the place makes complaint to him, that the lord of the manor having been often admonished by him, would yet pay him no tithes. Augustine questioning the lord about that default in devotion, he stoutly answered, that the tenth sheaf doubtless was his that had interest in the nine, and therefore would pay none. Presently Augustine denounces him excommunicate, and turning to the altar to say mass, publicly forbad that any excommunicate person should be present at it, when suddenly a dead corpse, that had been buried at the church door, arose (pardon me for relating it) and departed out of the limits of the churchyard, standing still without, while the mass continued. Which ended, Augustine comes to this living dead, and charges him in the name of the Lord God to declare who he was. He tells him, that in the time of the British State he was *huius villæ Patronus*, and although he had been often urged by the doctrine of the priest to pay his tithes, yet he never could be brought to it ; for which he died, he says, excommunicate, and was carried to Hell. Augustine desired to know where the priest that excommunicated him, was buried. This dead showed him the place ; where he makes an invocation of the dead priest, and bids him arise also, because they wanted his help. The priest rises. Augustine asks him, if he knew that other that was risen. He tells him, yes ; but wishes he had never known him. For (saith he) he was in all things ever adverse to the Church, a detainer of his tithes, and a great sinner to his death, and therefore I excommunicated him. But Augustine publicly declares, that it was fit mercy should be used towards him, and that he had suffered long in Hell for his offence (you must suppose, I think, the author meant Purgatory) ; wherefore he gives him absolution, and sends him to his grave, where he fell again into dust and ashes. He gone, the priest new risen tells, that his corpse had lain there above clxx. years ; and Augustine would gladly have had him continue upon earth again, for instruction of souls, but could not thereto entreat him. So he also returns to his former lodging. The lord of the town standing by all this while, and trembling, was now demanded if he would pay his tithes ; but he presently fell down at Augustine's feet, weeping and confessing his offence ; and receiving pardon, became all his life time a follower of Augustine's. Had this legend truth in it, who could doubt, but that payment of tithes was in practice in the infancy of the British Church ? The priest that rose from the dead, lived (if he ever lived) about cccxxx. after Christ, and would not surely have so taxed the lord of this manor only, if the payment had not been usually among other good Christians here, not taught only, but performed also. Neither need I admonish much of the authority of it : the whole course of it directs you how to smell out the original. Beside the common Legend of our Saints, it is in some volumes put alone, for a most observable monument ; and I found it bound up at the end of the MS. life of Thomas Becket, Archbishop of Canterbury, written by John de Grandisono ; and it remains in the public library of Oxford.

(From *The History of Tithes.*)

MEASURE OF THINGS

WE measure from ourselves ; and as things are for our use and purpose, so we approve them.   Bring a pear to the table that is rotten, we cry it down, 'tis naught ; but bring a medlar that is rotten, and 'tis a fine thing ; and yet I'll warrant you the pear thinks as well of itself as the medlar does.

—We measure the excellency of other men by some excellency we conceive to be in ourselves.   Nash a poet, poor enough (as poets us'd to be), seeing an alderman with his gold chain upon his great horse, by way of scorn, said to one of his companions, "Do you see yon fellow, how goodly, how big he looks ?   Why, that fellow cannot make a blank verse."

—Nay, we measure the goodness of God from ourselves ; we measure his goodness, his justice, his wisdom, by something we call just, good, or wise in ourselves ; and in so doing, we judge proportionably to the country-fellow in the play, who said if he were a King, he would live like a lord, and have peas and bacon every day, and a whip that cried slash.

(From the *Table-Talk*.)

OPINION

OPINION and affection extremely differ.   I may affect a woman best, but it does not follow I must think her the handsomest woman in the world.   I love apples best of any fruit, but it does not follow, I must think apples to be the best fruit.   Opinion is something wherein I go about to give reason why all the world should think as I think.   Affection is a thing wherein I look after the pleasing of myself.

—'Twas a good fancy of an old Platonic : The gods, which are above men, had something whereof man did partake, an intellect, knowledge, and the gods kept on their course quietly. The beasts, which are below man, had something whereof man did partake, sense and growth, and the beasts lived quietly in their way.   But man had something in him, whereof neither gods nor beasts did partake, which gave him all the trouble, and made all the confusion in the world ; and that is opinion.

—'Tis a foolish thing for me to be brought off from an opinion, in a thing neither of us know, but are led only by some cobweb-stuff; as in such a case as this, *Utrum angeli in vicem colloquantur?* If I forsake my side in such a case, I show myself wonderful light, or infinitely complying, or flattering the other party: but if I be in a business of nature, and hold an opinion one way, and some man's experience has found out the contrary, I may with a safe reputation give up my side.

—'Tis a vain thing to talk of a heretic, for a man for his heart can think no otherwise than he does think. In the primitive times there were many opinions, nothing scarce but some or other held. One of these opinions being embraced by some prince, and received into his kingdom, the rest were condemned as heresies; and his religion, which was but one of the several opinions, first is said to be orthodox, and so have continued ever since the Apostles.

(From the Same.)

LOGIC AND RHETORIC

FIRST in your sermons use your logic, and then your rhetoric. Rhetoric without logic is like a tree with leaves and blossoms, but no root; yet I confess more are taken with rhetoric than logic, because they are catched with a free expression, when they understand not reason. Logic must be natural, or it is worth nothing at all; your rhetoric figures may be learned. That rhetoric is best which is most seasonable and most catching. An instance we have in that old blunt commander at Cadiz, who showed himself a good orator; being to say something to his soldiers, which he was not used to do, he made them a speech to this purpose: "What a shame will it be, you Englishmen, that feed upon good beef and brewess, to let those rascally Spaniards beat you, that eat nothing but oranges and lemons"; and so put more courage into his men than he could have done with a more learned oration. Rhetoric is very good, or stark naught: there is no medium in rhetoric. If I am not fully persuaded I laugh at the orator.

(From the Same.)

LORD HERBERT OF CHERBURY

[Edward Herbert (1583-1648), Lord Castle-Island (1624), Lord Herbert of Cherbury in the Peerage of England (1629), published his most important work, the treatise *De Veritate*, in 1624, and continued his philosophical speculations in the *Religio Laici* (1645), and *De Religione Gentilium* (published in 1663). His *History of King Henry VIII*. was printed in 1649. The Autobiography was written about 1643 ("my age is now past three-score"), and first published by Horace Walpole in 1764. A valuable edition, with an introduction and a full historical commentary by Mr. S. L. Lee, appeared in 1886. The *Poems of Lord Herbert of Cherbury, English and Latin*, have been edited by Mr. J. Churton Collins (1881).]

THE philosophical works of Lord Herbert of Cherbury are written in Latin : his English prose works are his *History of King Henry VIII*. and his own *Life*. In neither of these latter is it possible to find much excellence of rhetoric. The *History* was intended to challenge comparison with Bacon's *Henry VII*., but all the labour of its author failed to secure for it anything like the spring and liveliness of Bacon's narrative. The *Autobiography* cannot be called tedious or heavy, but the author's manner is uncertain, and there is a provoking discrepancy between the arrogant valour of the sentiments, and the ill-cut phrases and loose construction of the language. In a mere philosopher this negligence might pass.

The *Autobiography* was edited by Horace Walpole in a spirit of mischief. "I was resolved the world should not think I admired it seriously, though there are really fine passages in it, and good sense too. I drew up an equivocal preface in which you will discover my opinion." This "equivocal preface" states the contrast which first attracted Walpole, and which still brings readers to the book : the contrast between the philosophical solemnity of the author and his inexpugnable self-confidence in respect of gallantry and the point of honour. This is what preserves his name—not the mere stories of his adventures, though they are good, nor any skill in writing ; not his metaphysics nor his religious advice ; but the impression of his singular character.

In that character there was no flaw : it was incapable of any suspicion of itself, and being proof against that danger it was proof against all other weakness. His metaphysical system and his moral and religious arguments are the expansion and the evolution of his individual consciousness of rectitude. From the beginning to the end of his life he is anxious to make all the world of the same mind as himself ; from the beginning to the end he is vexed rather than surprised at the dulness and unreadiness of all the world in face of this opportunity of enlightenment. He explained to the regent of the English College at Rome his tolerance of errors in religion ; on his deathbed he explained to Archbishop Ussher his reasonable, tolerant, and infinitesimal desire for the last rites of the Church, and among his latest thoughts must have been one of forgiveness for Ussher, who refused the request of a gentleman so free from prejudices. More interesting than most passages in his *Life of Henry VIII.* is the speech introduced by him in the report of the parliament of 1529, where a nameless orator is put up to expound the doctrines of the *Religio Laici* and *De Veritate* :—

> Each nation may be permitted the beliefe of any pious miracle that conduceth to God's glory ; without that on this occasion we need to scandalize or offend each other. The common truths in religion formerly mentioned, being firmer bonds of unity, than that anything emergent out of traditions (whether written or unwritten) should dissolve them. Let us therefore establish and fix these catholike or universall notions. They will not hinder us to believe whatsoever else is faithfully taught upon the authority of the Church. So that whether the Eastern, Western, Northern, or Southern teachers, etc., and particularly whether my Lord of Rochester, Luther, Eccius, Zuinglius, Erasmus, Melancthon, etc., be in the right, wee laiques may so build upon these catholike and infallible grounds of religion, as whatsoever superstructures of faith be rais'd, these foundations yet may support them.

The historian does not report King Henry's opinion about this tolerant reasoner : the ghostly orator escapes.

The Life of Lord Herbert is full of adventures and of encounters with great personages. The adventures are well told ; there is seldom anything very striking in the descriptions of people. King Louis XIII. and the fair maid of an inn are described more particularly than the rest : the writer has little to say of Casaubon or

Grotius, of Henry IV. or Queen Margaret. Spinola, though there is not much about him, is represented as a soldier and a gallant gentleman, whom Herbert offered to follow " if ever he did lead an army against the infidels." The fortunes and the ideas of Herbert are generally sufficient for him : he is not much interested in other people. The story comes to an end in 1624 ; the writer did not go on to tell of his difficulty in understanding what the civil war of England was all about, and of the inconvenience which it caused him.

W. P. KER.

LORD HERBERT OF CHERBURY IN PARIS;

1623, 1624

I SHALL not enter into a narration of the passages occurring in the Spanish court, upon his Highness's arrival thither, though they were well known to me for the most part, by the information the French Queen was pleased to give me, who, among other things, told me that her sister did wish well unto the prince. I had from her, also, intelligence of certain messages sent from Spain to the Pope, and the Pope's messages to them; whereof, by her permission, I did afterwards inform his Highness. Many judgments were now made concerning the event which this treaty of marriage was likely to have; the Duke of Savoy said that the prince's journey thither was *Un tiro di quelli cavallieri antichi che andavano cosi per il mondo a diffare li incanti* (that it was a trick of those ancient knights-errant, who went up and down the world after that manner to undo enchantments); for as that Duke did believe that the Spaniard did intend finally to bestow her on the Imperial house, he conceived that he did only entertain the treaty with England, because he might avert the king my master from treating in any other place, and particularly in France, howbeit, by the intelligence I received in Paris, which I am confident was very good, I am assured the Spaniard meant really at that time, though how the match was broken, I care not here to relate, it being a more perplexed and secret business than I am willing to insert into the narration of my life.

New propositions being now made, and other counsels thereupon given, the Prince taking his leave of the Spanish court, came to St. Andrews in Spain, where, shipping himself with his train, arrived safely at Portsmouth, about the beginning of October 1623; the news whereof being shortly brought into France, the Duke of Guise came to me, and said he found the Spaniards were not so able men as he thought, since they had neither married the Prince in their country, nor done anything to break his match elsewhere ; I answered that the Prince was more dexterous than that any secret practice of theirs could be put upon him ; and as for violence, I thought the Spaniards durst not offer it.

The war against those of the religion continuing in France, Père Séguerend, confessor to the king, made a sermon before his majesty on the text—That we should forgive our enemies ; upon which argument, having said many good things, he at last distinguished forgiveness, and said : We were indeed to forgive our enemies, but not the enemies of God ; such as were heretics, and particularly those of the religion ; and that his Majesty, as the most Christian king, ought to extirpate them wheresoever they could be found. This particular being related to me, I thought fit to go to the Queen-mother without further ceremony, for she gave me leave to come to her chamber whensoever I would, without demanding audience, and to tell her that though I did not usually intermeddle with matters handled within their pulpits, yet because Père Séguerend, who had the charge of the King's conscience, had spoken so violently against those of the religion, that his doctrine was not limited only to France, but might extend itself in its consequences beyond the seas, even to the dominions of the King my master ; I could not but think it very unreasonable, and the rather that as her Majesty well knew that a treaty of marriage betwixt our Prince and the Princess her daughter was now begun, for which reason I could do no less than humbly desire that such doctrines as these henceforth might be silenced by some discreet admonition, she might please to give to Père Séguerend, or others that might speak to this purpose. The Queen, though she seemed very willing to hear me, yet handled the business so, that Père Séguerend was together informed who had made this complaint against him, whereupon also he was so distempered, that by one Monsieur Gaellac, a Provençal, his own countryman, he sent me this message ; that he knew well who had accused him to her Majesty, and that he was sensible thereof; that he wished me to be assured, that wheresoever I was in the world, he would hinder my fortune. The answer I returned by Monsieur Gaellac was, that nothing in all France but a friar or a woman durst have sent me such a message.

Shortly after this, coming again to the Queen-mother, I told her that what I had said concerning Père Séguerend was spoken with a good intention, and that my words were now discovered to him in that manner, that he sent me a very affronting message, adding after a merry fashion these words, that I thought Séguerend so malicious, that his malice was beyond the malice of women; the Queen, being a little startled hereat, said : _A moy femme, et parler ainsi ?_ to me a woman and say so ? I replied gently ; _Je parle a votre majesté comme reyne, et non pas comme femme;_ I speak to your Majesty as a Queen, and not as a woman, and so took my leave of her. What Père Séguerend did afterwards, in the way of performing his threat, I know not ; but sure I am, that had I been ambitious of worldly greatness, I might have often remembered his words, though as I ever loved my book and a private life, more than any busy preferments, I did frustrate and render vain his greatest power to hurt me.

My book, _De veritate prout distinguitur a revelatione verisimili, possibili, et a falso,_ having been begun by me in England, and formed there in all its principal parts, was about this time finished ; all the spare hours which I could get from my visits and negociations, being employed to perfect this work, which was no sooner done, but that I communicated it to Hugo Grotius, that great scholar, who, having escaped his prison in the Low Countries, came into France, and was much welcomed by me and Monsieur Tielenus also, one of the greatest scholars of his time, who, after they had perused it, and given it more commendations than is fit for me to repeat, exhorted me earnestly to print and publish it ; howbeit, as the frame of my whole book was so different from anything which had been written heretofore, I found I must either renounce the authority of all that had written formerly concerning the method of finding out truth, and consequently insist upon my own way, or hazard myself to a general censure concerning the whole argument of my book ; I must confess it did not a little animate me, that the two great persons above mentioned did so highly value it, yet as I knew it would meet with much opposition, I did consider whether it was not better for me a while to suppress it. Being thus doubtful in my chamber, one fair day in the summer, my casement being opened towards the south, the sun shining clear, and no wind stirring, I took my book, _De Veritate,_ in my hand, and kneeling on my knees, devoutly said these words :—

"O Thou eternal God, Author of the light which now shines upon me, and Giver of all inward illuminations, I do beseech

Thee, of Thy infinite goodness, to pardon a greater request than a sinner ought to make ; I am not satisfied enough whether I shall publish this book, *De Veritate;* if it be for Thy glory, I beseech Thee give me some sign from heaven ; if not, I shall suppress it."

I had no sooner spoken these words, but a loud though gentle noise came from the heavens, for it was like nothing on earth, which did so comfort and cheer me, that I took my petition as granted, and that I had the sign I demanded, whereupon also I resolved to print my book. This, how strange soever it may seem, I protest before the Eternal God is true, neither am I any way superstitiously deceived herein, since I did not only clearly hear the noise, but in the serenest sky that ever I saw, being all without cloud, did to my thinking see the place from whence it came.

And now I sent my book to be printed in Paris at my own cost and charges, without suffering it to be divulged to others than to such as I thought might be worthy readers of it ; though afterwards reprinting it in England, I not only dispersed it among the prime scholars of Europe, but was sent to not only from the nearest but furthest parts of Christendom, to desire the sight of my book, for which they promised anything I should desire by way of return ; but hereof more amply in its place.

The treaty of a match with France continuing still, it was thought fit for the concluding thereof, that the Earl of Carlisle and the Earl of Holland should be sent Extraordinary Ambassadors to France.

(From the *Life*, last pages.)

JOHN HALES

[John Hales was born at Bath in 1584. From the Grammar School there he passed to Cambridge at the age of thirteen, and took the degree of B.A. Remarkable learning and philosophic acumen secured him a Fellowship at Merton, and, having gained distinction by his private lectures in Greek, he became Public Lecturer in the same language to the University in 1612. The following year, having been for some time in orders, he delivered a funeral oration in Latin on Sir Thomas Bodley, which was his first and only publication. The same year, he was elected a Fellow of Eton. In 1618, Hales attended the Synod of Dort, as reporter of the proceedings to Sir Dudley Carleton, English ambassador to the Hague, whose chaplain he was at the time. The speech of Episcopius, the Arminian leader there, according to Farindon, led Hales to "bid John Calvin good night." He retired to Eton on his Fellowship in 1619, and from that time till his death in 1656, he lived a hermit's life, visiting London but seldom, although his company was much desired in Ben Jonson's "Apollo." He formed a fine collection of books, and enjoyed the reputation of great learning. Laud made him a canon of Windsor in 1629. Two years later, however, he was deprived by the Parliamentary Committee, and, in 1649, he lost his Fellowship. He was able, however, to support himself and other deprived scholars till his death, out of the proceeds of the sale of his library.]

AMONG the English rationalists of the seventeenth century, the "ever memorable" John Hales of Eton is in a manner overshadowed by the greater figure which Falkland makes in history; his memory suffers, in comparison even with Chillingworth's, in consequence of his extreme reticence. Yet in strict temporal sequence, Hales precedes both in the line of spiritual descent from Colet, Cranmer, and Hooker. And he yields to neither—who, though much younger men, predeceased him—in scholarship, or in clearness of mental vision. The materials for an estimate of Hales are, indeed, scanty. He himself published nothing but his funeral oration on Sir Thomas Bodley. His *Works* in three volumes, which Lord Hailes edited in 1765, contain, besides merely occasional tracts, including the famous *On Schism and Schismaticks,* sermons, and his letters from the Synod of Dort. Still, even if not a line of his had survived we should be obliged to accept the testimony offered as to his exceptional scholarship by Clarendon, Bishop Pearson, Andrew Marvell, Dr. Heylin, and Bishop Stillingfleet. Anthony Wood styles him "a walking library." In the brief passage which may be styled his *apologia* he wrote, "The pursuit of truth hath been my only care, ever since I understood the meaning of the word. For this I have forsaken all hopes, all desires, all friends which might bias me, and hinder me from driving right at what I aimed." Clarendon furnished the complement of his character in words which he gives out to be Hales's own :—"His opinions, he was sure, did him no harm, but he was far from being confident that they might not do others harm who entertained them, and might entertain other results from them than he did. There is then no mystery about the lifelong seclusion and reticence of 'one of the clearest heads and best prepared hearts of Christendom.'" It is easy enough to discern the genesis of his quiescent temper, if not of his thirst for truth in his early experience of theological controversy at Dort. Hales began his report of the proceedings with a strong Calvinistic bias, and though he could never quite cast off his prejudices against the (Arminian) Remonstrants his tone was in the later letters distinctly modified. Yet he left the Synod—as he had entered it, a Calvinist. Though he professed to "bid Calvin good night," he did not, as the late Principal Tulloch puts it, "say good morning to Arminius." He came away from Dort disgusted with the violence of the dogmatic disputations he had listened to, and convinced that truth could not be compressed into creed or system. He went straight into residence at Eton, and, for seventeen years he, of his own freewill, gave no writing to the world. Two Latin treatises, dated respectively 1628 and 1633, which have been attributed to him, but without warrant, are worthy of notice because they provide the ground for the untrue charge of Socinianism brought against him, chiefly by Anthony Wood. The tract *On Schism and Schismaticks* appears to have been written about 1636, most probably for the benefit of Chillingworth, whose *Religion of Protestants* appeared in the following year. It was little more than a brief categorical statement of what he had long been in the habit of maintaining in conversation—that it was only pride and passion which kept Christendom from agreeing upon such a liturgy as might bring the world into one communion. "Why may I not go," he asked, "if occasion require, into an Arian church, so there be no Arianism expressed in their liturgy?" Schisms, he held, had crept into the Church by one of three ways, upon matter of fact, upon matter of opinion, or upon a point of ambition. The kernel of the tract was the contention "that in cases of separation among Christians those who would impose burdens on others, and enforce an unnecessary conformity, were really responsible for the schism, and that episcopal ambition had been the great cause of frequent, continuous, and bloody schisms." But Hales's clearness of mental sight and rational thoroughness are really nowhere so manifest as in the posthumously published tract *On the Sacrament of the Lord's Supper*. He assailed Protestants as well as Catholics for holding that the words of consecration were anything but "a mere trope." Turning to the question whether the Church might err in fundamentals, he poured contempt on the doctrine of the Infallibility of Councils. "It was never heard," he said, "in any profession that the conclusion of truth went by plurality of voices, the Christian profession only excepted ; and I have often mused how it comes to pass that the way which in all other sciences is not able to warrant the poorest conclusion, should be thought sufficient to give authority to conclusions in divinity, the supremest empress of sciences." Hales is most distinctively modern, perhaps, in his sermon *Of Enquiry and Private Judgment in Religion*. Infallibility was, he argued, not a favour peculiar to any one man ; all must have it. A man must know not only what he has to believe, but why he has to believe. Hales's literary style is, in the main, the reflection of his lucid manner of thinking. When he argues, he goes straight to the point, and, barring a certain looseness in the construction of his sentences, he is a master of exposition. His illustrations, though copious, never weary the reader, being always the natural overflow of a mind well stocked with learning, and not a mere display of pedantry. There runs through his writings a thin thread of humour characteristic of the man — himself in earnest, but scorning the earnestness about non-essentials which he discovers in others.

W. WALLACE.

ALL DIFFERENCES DO NOT INVOLVE SCHISM

It hath been the common disease of Christians from the beginning, not to content themselves with that measure of faith, which God and the Scriptures have expressly afforded us ; but out of a vain desire to know more than is revealed, they have attempted to discuss things, of which we can have no light, neither from reason nor revelation : neither have they rested here, but upon pretence of church authority, which is none, or tradition, which for the most part is but figment ; they have peremptorily concluded, and confidently imposed upon others, a necessity of entertaining conclusions of that nature ; and to strengthen themselves, have broken out into divisions and factions, opposing man to man, synod to synod, till the peace of the church vanished, without all possibility of recall. Hence arose those ancient and many separations amongst Christians occasioned by Arianism, Eutychianism, Nestorianism, Photinianism, Sabellianism, and many more both ancient and in our time ; all which indeed are but names of schism, howsoever in the common language of the fathers, they were called heresies. For heresy is an act of the will, not of reason ; and is indeed a lie, not a mistake : else how could that known speech of Austin go for true : *Errare possum, hæreticus esse nolo ?* Indeed, Manichæism, Valentinianism, Marcionism, Mahometanism, are truly and properly heresies ; for we know that the authors of them received them not, but minted them themselves, and so knew that which they taught to be a lie. But can any man avouch that Arius and Nestorius, and others that taught erroneously concerning the Trinity, or the person of our Saviour, did maliciously invent what they taught, and not rather fall upon it by error and mistake ? Till that be done, and that upon good evidence, we will think no worse of all parties than needs we must, and take these rents in the church to be at the worst but schisms upon matter of opinion. In which case what we are to do, is not a point of any great depth of understanding to discover, so be distemper and partiality do not intervene. I do not yet see, that *opinionum varietas, et opinantium unitas*, are ἀσύστατα; or that men of different opinions in Christian religion, may not hold communion *in sacris*, and both go to one church. Why may I not go, if occasion require, to an Arian church, so there be no Arianism expressed in their liturgy ? And were liturgies and public forms of service so framed as that they admitted not of particular and private fancies, but contained only such things, as in which all Christians do agree, schisms on opinion were utterly vanished. For consider of all the liturgies that are or ever have been, and remove from them whatsoever is scandalous to any party, and leave nothing but what all agree on ; and the event shall be, that the public service and honour of God shall no ways suffer : whereas to load our public forms with the private fancies upon which we differ, is the most sovereign way to perpetuate schism unto the world's end. Prayer, confession, thanksgiving, reading of Scriptures, exposition of Scripture, administration of sacraments in the plainest and simplest manner, were matter enough to furnish out a sufficient liturgy, though nothing either of private opinion, or of church pomp, of garments, of prescribed gestures, of imagery, of music, of matter concerning the dead, of many superfluities, which creep into the churches under the name of order and decency, did interpose itself. For to charge churches and liturgies with things unnecessary, was the first beginning of all superstition ; and when scruples of conscience began to be made or pretended, then schisms began to break in. If the spiritual guides and fathers of the Church would be a little sparing of incumbering churches with superfluities, and not over rigid, either in reviving obsolete customs, or imposing new, there were far less danger of schism or superstition ; and all the inconvenience were likely to ensue would be but this, they should in so doing yield a little to the imbecilities of inferiors, a thing which St. Paul would never have refused to do. Meanwhile, wheresoever false or suspected opinions are made a piece of the church-liturgy, he that separates is not the schismatic ; for it is alike unlawful to make profession of known or suspected falsehoods, as to put in practice unlawful or suspected actions.

(From *A Tract concerning Schism and Schismatics.*)

FALSE PROOFS

NOW to remove you yet a little further from this fancy of casting yourself into the arms of others, and to concilate you the more to God and your reason, I will open one thing farther unto you, which is this, That you put off the care of your faith and religion from yourselves on other men sundry ways, when you think you do nothing less ; for when we plead for the truth of our profession, and appeal either to our education or breeding, " thus we have been brought up, thus we have been taught " ; or to antiquity, " thus have our ancients delivered unto us " ; or to universality, " this hath been the doctrine generally received " ; or to synods, councils, and consent of churches, " this is the doctrine established by ecclesiastical authority " : all these are nothing else but deceitful forms of shifting the account and reason of our faith and religion from ourselves, and casting it upon the back of others. I will shew it you by the particular examination of every one of these ; which I will the willinger do, because I see these are the common hackney reasons which most men use in flattering themselves in their mistakes ; for all this is nothing else but man's authority thrust upon us under divers shapes. For, first of all, education and breeding is nothing else but the authority of our teachers taken over our childhood. Now there is nothing which ought to be of less force with us, or which we ought more to suspect : for childhood hath one thing natural to it, which is a great enemy to truth, and a great furtherer of deceit ; what is that ? Credulity. Nothing is more credulous than a child : and our daily experience shows how strangely they will believe either their ancients, or one another, in most incredible reports. For, to be able to judge what persons, what reports are credible, is a point of strength, of which that age is not capable ; " The chiefest sinew and strength of wisdom," saith Epicharmus, " is not easily to believe." Have we not then great cause to call to better account, and examine by better reason, whatsoever we learnt in so credulous and easy an age, so apt, like the softest wax, to receive every impression ? Yet notwithstanding this singular weakness, and this large and real exception which we have against education, I verily persuade myself, that if the best and strongest ground of most men's religion were opened, it would appear to be nothing else.

Secondly, Antiquity, what is it else (God only expected) but man's authority born some ages before us? Now for the truth of things, time makes no alteration; things are still the same they are, let the time be past, present, or to come. Those things which we reverence for antiquity, what were they at their first birth? were they false? time cannot make them true; were they true? time cannot make them more true. The circumstance therefore of time, in respect of truth and error, is merely impertinent. Yet thus much must I say for antiquity, that amongst all these balancing and halting proofs, if truth have any advantage against error and deceit, it is here. For there is an antiquity which is proper to truth, and in which error can claim no part; but then it must be an antiquity most ancient. This cannot be but true, for it is God, and God is truth. All other parts of antiquity, deceit and falsehood will lay claim to as well as truth. Most certain it is, truth is more ancient than error; for error is nothing else but deviation and swerving from the truth. Were not truth therefore first, there could be no error, since there could be no swerving from that which is not. When therefore antiquity is pleaded for the proof of any conclusion commended to you for true, be you careful to know whether it be most ancient, yea or no: if it be so, then is it an invincible proof, and pleads for nothing but the truth; if otherwise, though it be as ancient, I say not as Inachus, but as Satan himself, yet it is no proof of truth.

Thirdly, Universality is such a proof of truth, as truth itself is ashamed of; for universality is nothing but a quainter and a trimmer name to signify the multitude. Now human authority at the strongest is but weak, but the multitude is the weakest part of human authority; it is the great patron of error, most easily abused, and most hardly disabused. The beginning of error may be, and mostly is, from private persons, but the maintainer and continuer of error is the multitude. Private persons first beget errors in the multitude, and make them public; and publicness of them begets them again in private persons. It is a thing which our common experience and practice acquaints us with, that when some private persons have gained authority with the multitude, and infused some error into them, and made it public, the publicness of the error gains authority to it, and interchangeably prevails with private persons to entertain it. The most singular and strongest part of human authority is properly in the wisest and most virtuous; and these, I trow, are not the most universal.   If truth and goodness go by universality and multitude, what mean then the prophets and holy men of God everywhere in Scripture so frequently, so bitterly, to complain of the small number of good men, careful of God and truth ?   Neither is the complaint proper to Scripture, it is the common complaint of all that have left any records of antiquity behind them.   Could wishing do any good, I could wish well to this kind of proof; but it will never go so well with mankind that the most shall be the best.   The best that I can say of argument and reason drawn from universality and multitude, is this, such reason may, per- chance, well serve to excuse an error, but it can never serve to warrant a truth.

Fourthly, Councils and synods, and consent of churches, these indeed may seem of some force, they are taken to be the strongest weapons which the church had fought with ; yet this is still human authority after another fashion ; let me add one thing, that the truth hath not been more relieved by these than it hath been distressed.   At the council at Nice met 318 bishops to defend the divinity of the Son of God ; but at Ariminum met well near 600 bishops to deny it.   I ask then, What gained the truth here by a synod ? Certainly in the eye of reason it more endangered it ; for it discovered the advantage that error had among the multitude above the truth ; by which reason truth might have been greatly hazarded.   I have read that the nobility of Rome, upon some fancy or other, thought fit, that all servants should wear a kind of garment proper to them, that so it might be known who were servants, who were freemen : but they were quickly weary of this conceit ; for perceiving in what multitudes servants were in most places, they feared that the singularity of their garment might be an item to them to take notice of their multitude, and to know their own strength, and so at length take advantage of it against their masters.   This device of calling councils was but like that fancy of the Roman gentlemen ; for many times it might well have proved a great means to have endangered the truth, by making the enemies thereof to see their own strength, and work upon that advantage ; for it is a speedy way to make them to see that, which for the most part is very true, that there are more which run against the truth, than with it.   (From *Private Judgment in Religion.*)

WILLIAM DRUMMOND

[William Drummond (1585-1649) was educated at the High School, and at the recently founded University of Edinburgh. After some years of law study on the Continent, he in 1610 succeeded his father as laird of Hawthornden. There he spent a life of quiet seclusion, in study and in composition, at first mainly poetical, His notes, and the catalogue of his library, show that he was a student of Greek, Latin, Italian, and French, and a diligent reader of the English writers of his time. In 1618 he was visited by Ben Jonson, of whose conversations he took careful notes. In 1623, after a serious illness, Drummond published *A Cypress Grove*, a philosophical meditation on Death. The popularity of this work is proved by the publication of a second edition in 1630. It was probably the connection of his family with the Stuarts, by the marriage of Robert III. with Annabella Drummond, that impelled him to take up the *History of Scotland during the Reigns of the Five Jameses*. The troubles which preceded the Civil War drew from him a number of contributions, advocating a mediating policy from the royalist side. The best of these are *Irene, or a Remonstrance for Concord, Amity, and Love* (1638), and Σκιαμαχία (1643) ; but they were not allowed more than a MS. circulation. In spite of his reputation as a malignant, Drummond did not suffer seriously at the hands of the later Presbyterian tyranny. The defeat of his friend Montrose at Philiphaugh (1645) crushed his last hope of a settled government, and his remaining years were clouded by despondency and failing health. He died in December 1649.

A Cypress Grove is Drummond's only prose work that was published in his lifetime. *The History of the Jameses* was printed in 1655, with several "Memorials of State," and a few letters ; his royalist tracts were first included in the collected edition of 1711. Extracts from Drummond's unpublished manuscripts were printed by Laing in the *Archæologia Scotica*, iv. 57-110, 224-270.]

A Cypress Grove is a remarkable, and in some respects unique, example of sonorous poetic prose. Detached passages of similar eloquence are to be found in the prose of Drummond's contemporaries and immediate successors ; none of them has maintained the same height of imaginative contemplation throughout a piece of equal length. *A Cypress Grove* is the first original work in which an English writer has deliberately set himself to make prose do service for poetry. It is a dignified " Meditation upon Death," tinged with melancholy ; and the whole has unity of tone and conception. Opening with a picture of his fears as "in the quiet solitariness of the night " he thinks " on the last of human terrors," the author reflects upon the necessity and universality of death ; upon the vexations, disasters, indignities, and meanness of life—where beauty, greatness, knowledge, are but vanity, " on so small a round as is this earth, and bounded with so short a course of time " ; where to die young is to leave the feast before satiety ; where fame is defeated by oblivion. Then, from these purely mundane views, he breaks into a train of idealistic thoughts which are put into the form of an apostrophe to his soul. Having at last fallen asleep, he sees in a dream the vision of a lost friend who reveals to him the meaning of death and the joys of eternity. *A Cypress Grove* is, therefore, not a series of " dispersed meditations," as Bacon defines his " Essay"; nor is its argument intended as a chain of connected reasoning. The meditation is imaginatively conceived ; it is presented as the expression of an individual mood, rising to a natural climax, and placed in an artistic setting.

This essential character of the work has been neglected by some of its critics. It has been objected that its argument is one-sided ; that the author has not given a more wholesome and bracing view of life as the scene of joyous and passionate endeavour. This is no doubt true ; yet the objection is beside the mark. For it applies an alien standard to what is not an essay, but a reverie. It blames what is practically a poem on resignation to death for not depicting the joys of life. One might as reasonably complain that Milton had not mingled the moods of *L'Allegro* and *Il Penseroso*. The critic is not called upon to refute poetical reflections by formal logic. His true criterion is congruity. And it is part of the success of *A Cypress Grove* that no dissonant note mars its pensive melancholy.

The most characteristic qualities of Drummond's style are wealth of imagery, variety of sentence-structure, and rhythmic flow. His metaphors are apt and pregnant ; he uses similes less frequently than the writers of his age, and seldom draws them out beyond a line. The antithesis of some of the apophthegms which break the continuity of his periods is not over-strained. Two cases of word-play occur, but they are venial. The composition, though carefully elaborated, is seldom laboured or overcharged with ornament ; and his ear is rarely, if ever, betrayed into a preference of sound to sense. The even pitch of subdued eloquence at which the style is maintained would prove monotonous but for the ever-changing and contrasting formation of the sentences. This skilful variation of construction, by diversifying the length and cadence of the clauses, gives to the pages of *A Cypress Grove* the peculiar charm of richly modulated music.

Drummond's idealistic bent is seen in the recurrence of certain ideas—at times of phrases and allusions. The pettiness of earthly life is a constant refrain. The earth is "a mote of dust encircled by a pond"; another time, "an anthill, and men as many pismires and grasshoppers." Again, "This globe of the earth, which seemeth huge to us, in respect of the universe and compared with that wide pavilion of heaven, is less than little, of no sensible quantity, and but as a point." He returns more than once to the image of the Ptolemaic cosmos for his conception of "the All."

On a theme so common among the Elizabethan writers, it is not strange that Drummond's treatment should occasionally echo theirs. In the Platonic apostrophe to his soul one is reminded of Spenser's Hymn to Beauty, and his stanzas on Mutability. Passages here and there seem to be paraphrases or expansions of the monologues of Hamlet and of Prospero. There is even at times a similarity of phrase, as in "The goodly fabric of this world," "This fair and admirable frame," "The rank weeds in this garden of the world," and in the recurring comparisons of the world to a stage, of life to a dream, and of death to sleep. Drummond was, as his library shows, a diligent reader of the English literature of his time; yet these parallels may be accidental. But the exact reproduction of some of Bacon's phrases in his Essay on Death proves that this at least had been closely studied. In the following—"So do little *children fear to go in the dark, and their fear is increased with tales*"; "Death nor painful is, nor evil, except *in contemplation of the cause*"—the parts italicised are transcripts of the words in Bacon's two opening sentences. When Drummond speaks of death as "being of itself as indifferent as birth," and of "the marble colours of obsequies, weeping and funeral pomp," adding "much more ghastliness unto it than otherwise it hath," he paraphrases Bacon more loosely. But Bacon's sentence (in the 1612 edition), "*There is no passion* in the mind of man *so weak*, but *masters* the fear of death," is copied as literally as Drummond's context will allow. It must not be supposed, however, that these coincidences detract from the originality of *A Cypress Grove*. The contrast between Drummond's and Bacon's works has been already emphasised.

Mr. Masson's comparison of *A Cypress Grove* with *Hydrio-taphia* has been repeated by later critics. Beyond the similarity of subject there is little or nothing upon which to base it. No resemblance is traceable between the learning and wit of Sir Thomas Browne's reflections on ancient burial rites, and the poetic melancholy of Drummond. Had Browne read *A Cypress Grove* he might have applied to the author words from his *Urn-Burial :* "Many are too early old"; "Pious spirits who pass their days in raptures of futurity, make little more of this world than the world that was before it." The idealistic creed common to both writers affords some parallels of thought among the concluding pages of the *Religio Medici*. But the healthy zest in life of the busy physician is a contrast to the relaxing introspection of the recluse of Hawthornden ; and their styles, where it is possible to compare them, reflect the difference between their characters.

A Cypress Grove was written under the inspiration of affliction and depression, when, as we learn from a letter to Sir William Alexander, " The loss of friends had estranged him from himself," and after he had

> " Twice been at the doors of death,
> And twice found shut those gates which ever mourn."

It was published with his " Flowers of Zion," its counterpart in verse. We have no previous prose of his except some notes and letters, and his later writings are disappointing. The *History of the Five Jameses*, much the longest of his works, is a dull and commonplace chronicle, of no historical and small literary value. His *Irene* and Σκιαμαχία contain some trenchant pages ; but, with the rest of his tracts, their main interest consists in their revela-tion of Drummond's attitude during the political and ecclesiastical troubles through which he lived. He longed, like the saner spirits of his time, for tolerance and peace ; and, though a royalist, he did not scruple on occasion to criticise the policy of Charles.

Though Drummond's life, except for a few short intervals, was spent in Scotland, his work belongs properly to English literature. The pure Scots dialect had in his time almost fallen out of literary use. Even Knox's prose is anglicised, and the Union of the

Crowns had completed what the Reformation had begun. Drummond's friend, Sir William Alexander, with the other Scottish poets who had followed James to his English court, had taken English models for their verses. But Drummond may be regarded as the earliest prose writer in Scotland who uses English as a mother-tongue; for James, even in his later work, occasionally falls back on a northern word or idiom. As in his sonnets he attaches himself to the school of Spenser, so his prose has its place alongside that of Sidney, Raleigh, and Bacon. He was the one star in the "Σκοτία Scotorum" of his age : a late survival of the Scottish renaissance which had already disappeared before the reforming zeal of presbyteries.

W. S. M'CORMICK.

A REVERIE ON DEATH

HAVING often and diverse times, when I had given myself to rest in the quiet solitariness of the night, found my imagination troubled with a confused fear, or sorrow or horror, which, interrupting sleep, did astonish my senses, and rouse me all appalled, and transported in a sudden agony and amazedness : of such an unaccustomed perturbation not knowing, not being able to dive into any apparent cause, carried away with the stream of my then doubting thoughts, I began to ascribe it to that secret foreknowledge and presaging power of the prophetic mind, and to interpret such an agony to be to the spirit, as a sudden faintness and universal weariness useth to be to the body, a sign of following sickness ; or as winter lightnings, earthquakes, and monsters are to commonwealths and great cities, harbingers of wretched events, and emblems of their sudden destinies.

Hereupon, not thinking it strange, if whatsoever is human should befal me, knowing how providence overcomes grief, and discountenances crosses ; and that, as we should not despair in evils which may happen to us, we should not be too confident, nor lean much to those goods we enjoy ; I began to turn over in my remembrance all that could afflict miserable mortality, and to forecast everything which could beget gloomy and sad apprehensions, and with a mask of horror show itself to human eyes : till in the end, as by unities and points mathematicians are brought to great numbers and huge greatness, after many fantastical glances of the woes of mankind, and those incumbrances which follow upon life, I was brought to think, and with amazement, on the last of human terrors, or (as one termed it) the last of all dreadful and terrible evils, Death.

For to easy censure it would appear, that the soul, if it can foresee that divorcement which it is to have from the body, should not without great reason be thus over-grieved, and plunged in inconsolable and unaccustomed sorrow : considering their near union, long familiarity and love, with the great change, pain, and ugliness, which are apprehended to be the inseparable attendants of Death.

They had their being together, parts they are of one reasonable creature, the harming of the one is the weakening of the working of the other. What sweet contentments doth the soul enjoy by the senses! They are the gates and windows of its knowledge, the organs of its delight. If it be tedious to an excellent player on the lute, to abide but a few months the want of one, how much more the being without such noble tools and engines be painful to the soul? And if two pilgrims which have wandered some few miles together, have a heart's-grief when they are near to part, what must the sorrow be at parting of two so loving friends and never-loathing lovers, as are the body and soul?

Death is the violent estranger of acquaintance, the eternal divorcer of marriage, the ravisher of the children from the parents, the stealer of parents from their children, the interrer of fame, the sole cause of forgetfulness, by which the living talk of those gone away as of so many shadows or age-worn stories. All strength by it is enfeebled, beauty turned into deformity and rottenness, honour into contempt, glory into baseness. It is the reasonless breaker off of all actions, by which we enjoy no more the sweet pleasures of earth, nor contemplate the stately revolutions of the heavens. The sun perpetually setteth, stars never rise unto us: It in one moment robbeth us of what with so great toil and care in many years we have heaped together: By this are succession of lineages cut short, kingdoms left heirless, and greatest states orphaned: It is not overcome by pride, soothed by flattery, tamed by entreaties, bribed by benefits, softened by lamentations, nor diverted by time. Wisdom, save this, can prevent and help everything. By Death we are exiled from this fair city of the world: it is no more a world unto us, nor we any more a people unto it. The ruins of fanes, palaces, and other magnificent frames yield a sad prospect to the soul; and how should it without horror view the wreck of such a wonderful masterpiece as is the body?

That Death naturally is terrible and to be abhorred, it cannot well and altogether be denied, it being a privation of life, and a not being; and every privation being abhorred of nature, and evil in itself, the fear of it too being ingenerated universally in all creatures. Yet I have often thought that even naturally, to a mind by nature only resolved and prepared, it is more terrible in conceit than in verity, and at the first glance than when well pryed into ; and that rather by the weakness of our fantasy than by what is in it ; and that the marble colours of obsequies, weeping, and funeral pomp (which we ourselves paint it with) did add much more ghastliness unto it than otherwise it hath. To aver which conclusion, when I had gathered my wandering thoughts, I began thus with myself.

If on the great theatre of this earth among the numberless number of men, *to die* were only proper to thee and thine, then undoubtedly thou had reason to repine at so severe and partial a law. But since it is a necessity, from which never any age bypast hath been exempted, and unto which they which be, and so many as are to come, are thralled (no consequent of life being more common and familiar), why shouldst thou with unprofitable and nought-availing stubbornness, oppose so inevitable and necessary a condition ? This is the high-way of morality, and our general home : Behold what millions have trod it before thee, what multitudes shall after thee, with them which at that same instant run. In so universal a calamity (if Death be one) private complaints cannot be heard : with so many royal palaces, it is no loss to see thy poor cabin burn. Shall the heavens stay their ever-rolling wheels (for what is the motion of them but the motion of a swift and ever-whirling wheel, which twineth forth and again uprolleth our life), and hold still time to prolong thy miserable days, as if the highest of their working were to do homage unto thee ? Thy death is a pace of the order of this *All*, a part of the life of this world ; for while the world is the world, some creatures must die, and others take life. Eternal things are raised far above this sphere of generation and corruption, where the first matter, like an ever flowing and ebbing sea, with divers waves, but the same water, keepeth a restless and never tiring current ; what is below in the universality of the kind, not in itself doth abide : *Man* a long line of years hath continued, *This man* every hundred is swept away. This globe environed with air is the sole region of Death, the grave where everything that taketh life must rot, the stage of fortune and change, only glorious in the inconstancy and varying alterations of it, which though many, seem yet to abide one, and being a certain entire one, are ever many. The never agreeing bodies of the elemental brethren turn one into another ; the earth changeth her countenance with the seasons, sometimes looking cold and naked, other times hot and flowery : nay, I cannot tell how, but even the lowest of those celestial bodies, that mother of months, and empress of seas and moisture, as if she were a mirror of our constant mutability, appeareth (by her too great nearness unto us) to participate of our changes, never seeing us twice with that same face; now looking black, then pale and wan, sometimes again in the perfection and fulness of her beauty shining over us. Death no less than life doth here act a part, the taking away of what is old being the making way for what is young. This earth is as a table-book, and men are the notes ; the first are washen out, that new may be written in. They who fore-went us did leave a room for us, and should we grieve to do the same to those which should come after us ? Who, being suffered to see the exquisite rarities of an antiquary's cabinet, is grieved that the curtain be drawn, and to give place to new pilgrims ? And when the Lord of this Universe hath shewed us the amazing wonders of his various frame, should we take it to heart, when he thinketh time, to dislodge ? This is his unalterable and inevitable decree : As we had no part of our will in our entrance into this life, we should not presume to any in our leaving it, but soberly learn to will that which he wills, whose very will giveth being to all that it wills ; and reverencing the Orderer, not repine at the order and laws, which al-where and always are so perfectly established, that who would essay to correct and amend any of them, he should either make them worse, or desire things beyond the level of possibility. All that is necessary and convenient for us, He hath bestowed upon us, and freely granted ; and what He hath not bestowed or granted us, neither is it necessary nor convenient that we should have it.

If thou dost complain that there shall be a time in which thou shalt not be, why dost thou not also grieve that there was a time in which thou was not ; and so that thou art not as old as that enlivening planet of time ? For not to have been a thousand years before this moment, is as much to be deplored, as not to live a thousand after it, the effect of them both being one : that will be after us, which, long long before we were, was. Our children's children have that same reason to murmur, that they were not young men in our days, which we have to complain that we shall not be old in theirs. The violets have their time, though they impurple not the winter, and the roses keep their season, though they disclose not their beauty in the spring.

Empires, states, and kingdoms have, by the doom of the supreme Providence, their fatal periods ; great cities lie sadly buried in their dust ; arts and sciences have not only their eclipses, but their wanings and deaths. The ghastly wonders of the world, raised by the ambition of ages, are overthrown and trampled : some lights above, not idly entitled stars, are lost, and never more seen of us : the excellent fabric of this universe itself shall one day suffer ruin, or a change like ruin ; and should poor earthlings thus to be handled complain ?

. . . . . .

But that, perhaps, which anguisheth thee. most, is to have this glorious pageant of the world removed from thee in the spring and most delicious season of thy life ; for though to die be usual, to die young may appear extraordinary. If the present fruition of these things be unprofitable and vain, what can a long continuance of them be ? If God had made life happier, he had also made it longer. Stranger and new halcyon, why would thou longer nestle amidst these unconstant and stormy waves ? Hast thou not already suffered enough of this world, but thou must yet endure more ? To live long, is it not to be long troubled ? But number thy years, which are now —— and thou shalt find that whereas ten have outlived thee, thousands have not attained this age. One year is sufficient to behold all the magnificence of nature, nay, even one day and night ; for more is but the same brought again. This sun, that moon, these stars, the varying dance of the spring, summer, autumn, winter, is that very same which the Golden Age did see. They which have the longest time lent them to live in, have almost no part of it at all, measuring it either by the space of time which is past, when they were not, or by that which is to come. Why shouldst thou then care, whether thy days be many or few, which, when prolonged to the uttermost, prove, paralleled with eternity, as a tear is to the ocean ? To die young, is to do that soon, and in some fewer days, which once thou must do ; it is but the giving over of a game, that after never so many hazards must be lost. When thou hast lived to that age thou desirest, or one of Plato's years, so soon as the last of thy days riseth above thy horizon, thou wilt then, as now, demand longer respite, and expect more to come. The oldest are most unwilling to die. It is hope of long life that maketh life seem short. Who will behold, and with the eye of judgment behold, the many changes attending human affairs, with the after-claps of fortune, shall never lament to die young. Who knows what alterations and sudden disasters in outward estate or inward contentments, in this wilderness of the world, might have befallen him who dieth young, if he had lived to be old? Heaven foreknowing imminent harms, taketh those which it loves to itself before they fall forth. Death in youth is like the leaving a superfluous feast before the drunken cups be presented. Pure, and (if we may so say) virgin souls carry their bodies with no small agonies, and delight not to remain long in the dregs of human corruption, still burning with a desire to turn back to the place of their rest ; for this world is their inn, and not their home. That which may fall forth every hour, cannot fall out of time. Life is a journey on a dusty way, the furthest rest is Death, in this some go more heavily burdened than others : Swift and active pilgrims come to the end of it in the morning or at noon, which tortoise-paced wretches, clogged with the fragmentary rubbish of this world, scarce with great travail crawl unto at midnight. Days are not to be esteemed after the number of them, but after the goodness. More compass maketh not a sphere more complete, but as round is a little as a large ring ; nor is that musician most praiseworthy who hath longest played, but he in measured accents who hath made sweetest melody. To live long hath often been a let to live well. Muse not how many years thou mightest have enjoyed life, but how sooner thou mightest have losed it ; neither grudge so much that it is no better, as comfort thyself that it hath been no worse. Let it suffice that thou hast lived till this day, and (after the course of this world) not for nought thou hast had some smiles of fortune, favours of the worthiest, some friends, and thou hast never been disfavoured of Heaven.

As those images were pourtrayed in my mind (the morning star now almost arising in the East), I found my thoughts in a mild and quiet calm ; and not long after, my senses, one by one, forgetting their uses, began to give themselves over to rest, leaving me in a still and peaceable sleep, if sleep it may be called, when the mind awaking is carried with free wings from our fleshly bondage. For heavy lids had not long covered their lights, when I thought, nay sure, I was, where I might discern all in this great *All*, the large compass of the rolling circles, the brightness and continual motion of those rubies of the night, which by their distance here below cannot be perceived ; the silver-countenance of the wandering Moon, shining by another's light ; the hanging of the Earth, as environed with a girdle of crystal ; the Sun enthronised in the midst of the planets, eye of the heavens, and gem of this precious ring, the World. But whilst with wonder and amazement I gazed on those celestial splendours and the beaming lamps of that glorious temple, like a poor country man brought from his solitary mountains and flocks to behold the magnificence of some great city, there was presented to my sight a Man, as in the spring of years, with that self-same grace, comely features, and majestic look, which the late —— was wont to have ; on whom I had no sooner set mine eyes, when (like one planet-stricken) I became amazed : But he, with a mild demeanour, and voice surpassing all human sweetness, appeared (methought) to say :

"What is it doth thus anguish and trouble thee ? Is it the remembrance of Death, the last period of wretchedness, and entry to these happy places ; the lantern which lighteneth men to see the mystery of the blessedness of Spirits, and that glory which transcendith the curtain of things visible ? Is thy fortune below on that dark globe (which scarce by the smallness of it appeareth here) so great, that thou are heart-broken and dejected to leave it ? What if thou wert to leave behind thee a —— so glorious in the eye of the world (yet but a mote of dust encircled with a pond) as that of mine, so loving——, such great hopes, these had been apparent occasions for lamenting ; and but apparent. Dost thou think thou leav'st life too soon ? Death is best young. Things fair and excellent are not of long endurance upon earth. Who liveth well liveth long. Souls most beloved of their Maker are soonest relieved from their bleeding cares of life, and most swiftly wafted through the surges of human miseries. Opinion, that great enchantress and poiser of things, not as they are but as they seem, hath not in anything more than in the conceit of Death, abused man : who must not measure himself, and esteem his estate, after his earthly being, which is but as a dream ; for, though he be born on the earth, he is not born for the earth, more than the embryo for the mother's womb. It complaineth to be delivered of its bands, and to come to the light of this world ; and man bewaileth to be loosed from the chains with which he is fettered in that valley of vanities."

'From *A Cypress Grove*.)

GEORGE HERBERT

[George Herbert (1593-1633), the fifth of seven sons of Richard Herbert, of the famous Monmouthshire family of that name, was educated at Westminster School, and Trinity College, Cambridge, where he graduated in 1611, and became Fellow in 1615. In 1619 he was elected Public Orator for the University, in the discharge of the duties of which office he attracted the attention of King James, who appointed him to a sinecure office of £120 a year. The death of many friends, and later of the king, having weakened his position at court, and his health becoming increasingly feeble, he took Holy Orders, the profession for which his character and talents from the first pointed him out. In 1629 he married, and in 1630 was inducted to the living of Bemerton, near Salisbury, where he continued until his death three years later. During these three years, he wrote his *Country Parson*, which was not, however, printed until after his death.]

IN his *Life of George Herbert*, Izaak Walton informs us that when Herbert delivered his first sermon at Bemerton, after his induction to that living, the discourse was "after a most florid manner, both with great learning and eloquence"; but that at the close he warned his congregation that it "should not be his constant way of preaching . . . but that for their sakes his language and his expressions should be more plain and practical in his future sermons." As far as I am aware, this opening sermon was never printed and given to the world, so that it is impossible to compare Herbert's style when "eloquent" with that other style which was plain and practical; but this is certain, that the only prose work of Herbert's of any length that we possess, his *Country Parson*, partakes of the latter character. In fact, when we recall the incessant effort after simile and analogy in his poems, this prose treatise is curiously simple and straightforward, and owes its effectiveness to just these qualities. The later euphuism was indeed abundantly conspicuous in Herbert's verse, but it was the euphuism of thought and fancy, rather than of style. His similes are often as far fetched as those of Lovelace or Cowley, but they are rarely, if ever, grotesque.

They are, in fact, chastened and kept in check by a genuine earnestness and religious power which are never absent. Apart from the thoughts expressed, the literary diction of Herbert's verse is as free from ornament as Wordsworth's. He is rarely, if ever, florid or rhetorical. The taste of the age for conceits finds its gratification in other ways—in puns and quibbles, as well as in tricks of construction, such as verses arranged in the shape of wings or altars, or in mechanical ingenuity like the following—

> What open force or hidden CHARM
> Can blast my fruit or bring me HARM
> While the enclosure is Thine ARM?

No trace of such misapplied cleverness is to be found in Herbert's prose ; and we cannot doubt that the same restraining force was at work, and for the same reasons, as dictates the style of his later Bemerton sermons. Not for the first or last time in our literature was it to be shown that the euphuistic tendency is killed when the writer begins to think more of his topic than of himself.

The style of Herbert's simple prose treatise was no doubt further determined by the form he chose for it. Its complete title is *A Priest to the Temple,* or *The Country Parson, his Character and Rule of Holy Life.* The word " Character," printed in large capitals, was perhaps meant to convey that the " Characters " of Theophrastus was in the author's mind. He may have wished to suggest that the acts and habits of the Country Parson were as well worth record and analysis as some of the more frivolous types of the Greek philosopher. Moreover, to write " Characters," had become a fashion. Overbury's had appeared after his death in 1614, and Earle's *Microcosmography* in 1628. For the rest, there are traces here and there of the antithesis, and the balanced sentence of Lyly and the earlier euphuists, which is only saying that the dexterous manipulation of language was still a little too evident, and that style, which means the perfection of such skill, had not yet fully learned the *ars celare artem.*

But throughout, the style is what may be called "well-bred," and the native sweetness and courtesy of George Herbert are reflected even in the choice and arrangement of his words and phrases.

ALFRED AINGER.

THE PARSON PREACHING

THE Country Parson preacheth constantly; the pulpit is his joy and his throne. If he at any time intermit, it is either for want of health, or against some great festival, that he may the better celebrate it, or for the variety of the hearers, that he may be heard at his return more attentively. When he intermits, he is ever very well supplied by some able man, who treads in his steps, and will not throw down what he hath built; whom also he entreats to press some point, that he himself hath often urged with no great success, that so, in the mouth of two or three witnesses, the truth may be more established. When he preacheth he procures attention by all possible art, both by earnestness of speech (it being natural to men to think that where is much earnestness there is somewhat worth hearing), and by a diligent and busy cast of his eye on his auditors, with letting them know that he observes who marks and who not; and with particularising of his speech—now to the younger folk, then to the elder; now to the poor, and now to the rich: "This is for you, and this is for you;" for particulars ever touch and awake more than generals. Herein also he serves himself of the judgments of God, as those of ancient times, so especially of the late ones; and those most which are nearest to his parish; for people are very attentive at such discourses, and think it behoves them to be so, when God is so near them, and even over their heads. Sometimes he tells them stories and sayings of others, according as his text invites him; for them also men heed and remember better than exhortations, which though earnest, yet often die with the sermon, especially with country people, which are thick and heavy, and hard to raise to a point of zeal and fervency, and need a mountain of fire to kindle them; but stories and sayings they will well remember. He often tells them that sermons are dangerous things, that none goes out of Church as he came in, but either better or worse; that none is careless before his Judge,

and that the Word of God shall judge us.   By these and other
means the parson procures attention ; but the character of his
sermon is holiness : he is not witty, or learned, or eloquent, but
holy ; a character that Hermogenes never dreamed of, and therefore he could give no precept thereof.   But it is gained, first, by
choosing texts of devotion, not controversy, moving and ravishing
texts, whereof the Scriptures are full.   Secondly, by dipping and
seasoning all our words and sentences in our hearts before they
come into our mouths, truly affecting and cordially expressing all
that we say, so that the auditors may plainly perceive that every
word is heart-deep.   Thirdly, by turning often, and making many
apostrophes to God, as, " O Lord, bless my people and teach them
this point " ; or, " O my Master, on whose errand I come, let
me hold my peace, and do Thou speak Thyself, for Thou art
love, and when Thou teachest all are scholars."   Some such irra-
diations scatteringly in the sermon, carry great holiness in them.
The prophets are admirable in this.   So Isaiah lxiv. : " Oh that
Thou wouldst rend the heavens, that Thou wouldst come down ! "
etc. ; and Jeremiah x., after he had complained of the desolation
of Israel, turns to God suddenly, " O Lord, I know that the way
of man is not in himself," etc.   Fourthly, by frequent wishes of
the people's good, and joying therein, though he himself were with
St. Paul even sacrificed upon the service of their faith ; for there
is no greater sign of holiness than the procuring and rejoicing in
another's good.   And herein St. Paul excelled in all his Epistles.
How did he put the Romans in all his prayers ! (Rom. i. 9) ; and
ceased not to give thanks for the Ephesians (Eph. i. 16) ; and
for the Corinthians (chap. i. 4) ; and for the Philippians made
request with joy (chap. i. 4) ; and is in contention for them
whether to live or die ; be with them or Christ (verse 23) ; which,
setting aside his care of his flock, were a madness to doubt of.
What an admirable epistle is the second to the Corinthians ! how
full of affections !—he joys and he is sorry, he grieves and he
glories : never was there such care of a flock expressed, save in
the great Shepherd of the fold, who first shed tears over Jerusalem,
and afterwards blood.   Therefore this care may be learned there,
and then woven into sermons, which will make them appear
exceeding reverend and holy.   Lastly, by an often urging of the
presence and majesty of God, by these or suchlike speeches :—
" Oh, let us all take heed what we do !   God sees us, He sees
whether I speak as I ought, or you hear as you ought ; He sees

hearts as we see faces : He is among us ; for if we be here, He must be here, since we are here by Him, and without Him could not be here." Then turn the discourse to His majesty, "And He is a great God and terrible : as great in mercy, so great in judgment. There are but two devouring elements, fire and water : He hath both in Him ; His voice is the sound of many waters (Revelation i.) ; and He himself is a consuming fire (Hebrews xii.)." Such discourses show very holy. The parson's method in handling of a text consists of two parts : first, a plain and evident declaration of the meaning of the text ; and secondly, some choice observations drawn out of the old text as it lies entire and unbroken in the Scripture itself. This he thinks natural and sweet and grave. Whereas the other way of crumbling a text into small parts, as, the person speaking or spoken to, the subject and object and the like, hath neither in it sweetness, nor gravity, nor variety, since the words apart are not Scripture, but a dictionary, and may be considered alike in all the Scripture. The parson exceeds not an hour in preaching, because all ages have thought that a competency, and he that profits not in that time, will less afterwards, the same affection which made him not profit before making him then weary, and so he grows from not relishing to loathing.

(From *A Priest to the Temple*.)

THE PARSON ON SUNDAYS

THE Country Parson, as soon as he awakes on Sunday mornings presently falls to work, and seems to himself so as a market man is when the market day comes, or a shopkeeper when customers use to come in. His thoughts are full of making the best of the day, and contriving it to his best gains. To this end, besides his ordinary prayers, he makes a peculiar one for a blessing on the exercises of the day. That nothing befall him unworthy of that Majesty before which he is to present himself, but that all may be done with reverence to His glory, and with edification to his flock, humbly beseeching his Master that how or whenever He punish him, it be not in his ministry ; then he turns to request for his people that the Lord would be pleased to sanctify them all, that they may come with holy hearts and awful minds into the congregation, and that the good God would pardon all those who come with less prepared hearts than they ought. This done, he sets himself to the consideration of the duties of the day, and if there be any extraordinary addition to the customary exercises, either from the time of the year, or from the state, or from God, by a child born or dead, or any other accident, he contrives how and in what manner to induce it to the best advantage. Afterwards, when the hour calls, with his family attending him, he goes to church, at his first entrance humbly adoring and worshipping the invisible majesty and presence of Almighty God, and blessing the people, either openly or to himself. Then having read Divine service twice fully, and preached in the morning, and catechised in the afternoon, he thinks he hath in some measure, according to poor and frail man, discharged the public duties of the congregation. The rest of the day he spends either in reconciling neighbours that are at variance, or in visiting the sick, or in exhortations to some of his flock by themselves, whom his sermons cannot or do not reach. And every one is more awaked when we come and say, "Thou art the man." This way he finds exceeding useful and winning ; and these exhortations he calls his privy purse, even as princes have theirs, besides their public disbursements. At night, he thinks it a very fit time, both suitable to the joy of the day and without hindrance to public duties, either to entertain some of his neighbours or to be entertained of them, where he takes occasion to discourse of such things as are both profitable and pleasant, and to raise up their minds to apprehend God's good blessing to our Church and state—that order is kept in the one, and peace in the other, without disturbance or interruption of public divine offices. As he opened the day with prayer, so he closeth it, humbly beseeching the Almighty to pardon and accept our poor services, and to improve them, that we may grow therein, and that our feet may be like hinds' feet, ever climbing up higher and higher unto Him.

(From the Same.)

THOMAS HOBBES

[The philosopher of Malmesbury, as it used to be the fashion to call him, was born at that town on the 5th of April, 1588, and was the son of the vicar of Charlton, a village in the immediate neighbourhood, then a seat of the Knyvets, which early in Hobbes' life went by marriage to the Howards, and before his death was connected with Dryden. He went early to Magdalen Hall at Oxford, and took his degree. Somewhat before his majority he was recommended to the Cavendish family, as tutor to the future (second) Earl of Devonshire, and for the greater part of a century he remained a client of the house, and not unfrequently a member of the household. He made the grand tour with his pupil in 1610, and returning to London became acquainted with most of the literary society of James the First's time, being closely associated with Bacon. His own first literary effort was late and not original, being a translation of Thucydides which he published in 1628, his fortieth year. It is, though not rigidly exact, a very good translation—as good as his subsequent attempt on Homer is bad. In the same year his pupil died. He returned to his old business, and conducted the son of Sir Gervase Clifton over the Continent, but he soon resorted again to the Devonshire family, making his third journey abroad as tutor in charge of his first pupil's son. He now, in the middle of the fourth decade of the century, was introduced to the strongly mathematical and philosophical group of Parisian men of letters. He plunged, not with happy results, into mathematics ; he attacked philosophy with results, in part at least, very happy. On his return to England he took the Royalist side, and, being always a very timid person, fled abroad again, lest the Parliament should take notice of his published or MS. works. Of these *De Cive* appeared in 1642 ; *Leviathan* in 1651. The wonderful little *Human Nature* had been written as early as 1640, but was not published till much later. As he had fled from England to France, so he fled from France to England, owing to some slight from Charles II. to whom he had been tutor for a time. But after the Restoration Charles gave him a pension. He enjoyed it for nearly twenty years and died at Hardwick Hall, on 4th December, 1679, in his ninety-second year. His works are chiefly known in the edition (16 vols.) of Molesworth, which, though the print and paper are excellent, is simply not edited at all. A Danish scholar, Dr. Tönnies, has recently given some careful recensions of particular works from MS.]

BUT slight reference need, or indeed can, be made here to the matter of the remarkable works of Hobbes. His philosophy, so-called, was a philosophy rather of the eighteenth than of his own century, almost destitute of a metaphysic, and contenting itself chiefly with certain nominalist or anti-idealist glances in the ontological direction, while it busied itself with law, religion, politics, ethics, psychology, and, to some extent, physics. Man was quite the centre of the universe to Hobbes, though he had no very exalted idea of humanity: and the reproachful use of the term "Hobbist" in his later days and after his death to signify Deist, is to be justified, if justified at all, less by any actively anti-Christian doctrine in his writings than by his uncompromising anthropology. Hobbes might have defined man as an extremely troublesome animal who sometimes has brains enough to see the necessity of keeping his own and others' troublesome instincts in order for his own and others' good. And this is the basis alike of his politics, his ethics, and, so far as he indulges in it, his psychology.

His manner, which is here of more interest to us than his matter, is also extremely remarkable and curious. He wrote, as has been said above, late; he constantly produced (not always in exact counterpart) his works both in English and in Latin; and in some cases, if not in most, it would appear that the Latin was his own work and the English that merely of an amanuensis, though much revised and altered by himself. This, however, though odd and a little disquieting to the critic, is not of much real importance, the personal and individual impression in his English work being so distinct and so uniform that the exact circumstances and process of composition may be neglected.

It would hardly be possible to take Hobbes for anything but a seventeenth-century writer, even if his work were anonymous and undated, but he possesses among the English writers of the seventeenth century very marked characteristics. They have been to some extent traced to the influence of Ben Jonson, of whom Hobbes saw much in early middle life, and whose style in his *Discoveries* is by no means unlike that of Hobbes, though it is less unadorned. But in truth the resemblances of Hobbes to Jonson in form, as well as his resemblances to Bacon, another early associate or patron of his, in some other respects, are not resemblances of imitation. To whatever causes they were due on the side of the elder writers, they came on Hobbes's part from idiosyncrasy, from study, and from the working of his peculiar theories. To a very mature period of life he wrote nothing, it would seem, but Latin (remarkably strong and clear Latin, but bare of all ornament or

Ciceronianism, and indeed rather ugly), or else the severe and un-adorned English of his *Thucydides*. His study—though his contempt of the schoolmen is almost ultra-Baconian—had evidently been much in school divinity and philosophy, as well as in technical writers on law and other " dry " subjects. But the character of his philosophy itself must have had even more influence than these things on the character of his style. Hobbes is a Nominalist of Nominalists. He will have no other universals than names ; he pours scorn on "*nesses* and *tudes* and *ties*." " Define what you mean by your words ; define it strictly and exactly, and then add, subtract, divide, and otherwise treat the quantities so defined as confidently as in actual computation "—this is the summary, almost in his own words, of his method. Philosophically, of course, the result is frequently faulty. In the effort to reject the vague, Hobbes often leaves large parts of his problems unaccounted for ; and in the effort to secure the precise he often attaches non-natural meanings to words of which men feel, but which they cannot sharply express, the natural meanings. Thus, for instance, he makes a point, though perhaps a point more apparent than real, when he scornfully dismisses the supposed " corruptions " of the Three Governments—anarchy for democracy, oligarchy for aristocracy, and tyranny for monarchy—as names given to the things themselves by those who do not like them. But when he says that *pulchrum* is " that which promises good " his reader can only reply, " Philosopher of Malmesbury, when you and I talk of beauty we talk of two different things," and when he says, " *Contempt* or little sense of the calamity of others is that which men call CRUELTY," his reader can only say, " You may be of such men, I am not."

Still every one must see what a character, what an intense force and personality, this exaltation of names and this constant endeavour to identify them as exactly as possible with ideas, must impress upon style if the writer's power of expression be suitable to his design. In Hobbes the power was so suitable. His style is not engaging. It is frequently arid and hard ; the life-blood seems to have been squeezed out of it, and only a dried preparation to remain. At times, indeed, as in some famous passages of the *Human Nature* and the *Leviathan*, the dry bones are agitated by a curious gust of more human feeling ; but this is rare. Hobbes' process of argument is the articulating of a skeleton rather than anything else ; but the articulation is faultless, and the " subject " is superbly treated. He is never unimpressive ; he is never, as writers who aim at extreme precision and the rejection of all superfluity often are, trivial ; he is very seldom, indeed, to any reader who takes the slightest genuine interest in his subject, dull. His language always has a stuff and substance of thought, though it may sometimes, as has been said, be rather twisted and non-natural thought : his thought never fails to clothe itself in clear and accurate language. Difficult he may sometimes be, but he is hardly ever obscure, and he is absolutely free from a common vice both of easy and difficult philosophers, the vice of talking without really saying anything. Crabbed is the favourite, and on the whole the most appropriate, epithet for him ; but it may be questioned whether it does not apply better to the harsh and un-grateful character of his ethical teaching than the peculiarities of style which usually receive that name in writing. It is to be observed that in actual controversy Hobbes does not show at his best. His objections to Descartes verge on the petty and quibbling. It is possible that school divinity may be, as he says, "the kingdom of darkness." But when you condescend to argue with an inhabitant of that or any kingdom, you must adopt his language, or get him to accept yours, or arrange for a common interpreter. To argue with a school divine as Hobbes does with Bramhall by saying, "*actus simplicissimus* signifieth nothing" is but weak.

It is when he is not jangling with others, but speaking in his own pulpit that Hobbes is at his best. The two first parts of the " Tripos," *Human Nature* and *De Corpore Politico* (for the third, " Liberty and Necessity," is a mere controversial appendix) the *Philosophical Elements*, the *Leviathan*, and the critical-narrative *Behemoth* (somewhat better presented in Dr. Tönnies' edition) are the places to see him thus. It is true that like other philosophers he is more convincing in appearance than on examination. The rigid definition of every term, of every idea as it occurs, has a noble appearance of equity ; but as each definition gives room for a fresh assumption it is perhaps not quite so equitable as it looks. This, however, is a purely material objection. As far as the out-ward dress of philosophy goes, and no doubt often a good deal farther, Hobbes, yielding to many in beauty, yields to none in a certain majesty of form. His disdain for ornament carries with it more than an apparent, it carries with it a real freedom from sophistry. His fallacies, such as they are, lie open for any tolerably acute reasoner to detect : they are not masked and wimpled in a cloud of words. Nor for all his love of names does he ever descend to that barren playing with terminology which is so common in philosophical writing. Almost all great philosophers have had, as it were inevitably, the style of their philosophy, but none has had it so much as Hobbes. His style is bare, uninviting, uncompromising, rugged, but strong, ready at any moment for defence or attack, without an ounce of superfluous ornament or flesh—a style like the armour and condition of a veteran legionary.

GEORGE SAINTSBURY.

THE CAUSES OF MUTUAL FEAR

THE cause of mutual fear consists partly in the natural equality of men, partly in their mutual will of hurting: whence it comes to pass, that we can neither expect from others, nor promise to ourselves the least security. For if we look on men full-grown, and consider how brittle the frame of our human body is, which perishing, all its strength, vigour, and wisdom itself perisheth with it; and how easy a matter it is, even for the weakest man to kill the strongest: there is no reason why any man, trusting to his own strength, should conceive himself made by nature above others. They are equals, who can do equal things one against the other; but they who can do the greatest things, viz., kill, can do equal things. All men therefore among themselves are by nature equal; the inequality we now discern, hath its spring from the civil law.

All men in the state of nature have a desire and will to hurt, but not proceeding from the same cause, neither equally to be condemned. For one man, according to that natural equality which is among us, permits as much to others as he assumes to himself; which is an argument of a temperate man, and one that rightly values his power. Another, supposing himself above others, will have a license to do what he lists, and challenges respect and honour, as due to him before others; which is an argument of a fiery spirit. This man's will to hurt ariseth from vain glory, and the false esteem he hath of his own strength; the other's from the necessity of defending himself, his liberty, and his goods, against this man's violence.

Furthermore, since the combat of wits is the fiercest, the greatest discords which are, must necessarily arise from this contention. For in this case it is not only odious to contend against, but also not to consent. For not to approve of what a man saith, is no less than tacitly to accuse him of an error in that thing which he speaketh; as in very many things to dissent, is as much as if you accounted him a fool whom you dissent from. Which may appear hence, that there are no wars so sharply waged as between sects of the same religion, and factions of the same commonweal, where the contestation is either concerning doctrines or politic prudence. And since all the pleasure and jollity of the mind consists in this, even to get some, with whom comparing, it may find somewhat wherein to triumph and vaunt itself; it is impossible but men must declare sometimes some mutual scorn and contempt, either by laughter, or by words, or by gesture, or some sign or other; than which there is no greater vexation of mind, and than from which there cannot possibly arise a greater desire to do hurt.

But the most frequent reason why men desire to hurt each other, ariseth hence, that many men at the same time have an appetite to the same thing; which yet very often they can neither enjoy in common, nor yet divide it; whence it follows that the strongest must have it, and who is strongest must be decided by the sword.

(From the *Philosophical Elements of a True Citizen*.)

THE STATE OF WAR

WHATSOEVER therefore is consequent to a time of war, where every man is enemy to every man; the same is consequent to the time, wherein men live without other security, than what their own strength, and their own invention shall furnish withal. In such condition, there is no place for industry; because the fruit thereof is uncertain : and consequently no culture of the earth ; no navigation, nor use of the commodities that may be imported by sea ; no commodious building ; no instruments of moving and removing such things as require much force ; no knowledge of the face of the earth ; no account of time ; no arts ; no letters ; no society ; and, which is worst of all, continual fear, and danger of violent death ; and the life of man solitary, poor, nasty, brutish, and short.

It may seem strange to some man that has not well weighed these things, that nature should thus dissociate, and render men apt to invade, and destroy one another : and he may therefore, not trusting to this inference, made from the passions, desire perhaps to have the same confirmed by experience. Let him therefore consider with himself, when taking a journey, he arms himself, and seeks to go well accompanied; when going to sleep, he locks his doors; when even in his house he locks his chests; and this when he knows there be laws, and public officers, armed, to revenge all injuries shall be done him; what opinion he has of his fellow-subjects, when he rides armed; of his fellow-citizens, when he locks his doors; and of his children and servants, when he locks his chests. Does he not there as much accuse mankind by his actions, as I do by my words? But neither of us accuse man's nature in it. The desires and other passions of man are in themselves no sin. No more are the actions that proceed from those passions, till they know a law that forbids them; which, till laws be made, they cannot know: nor can any law be made, till they have agreed upon the person that shall make it.

It may peradventure be thought, there was never such a time, nor condition of war as this; and I believe it was never generally so over all the world; but there are many places where they live so now. For the savage people in many places of America, except the government of small families, the concord whereof dependeth on natural lust, have no government at all; and live at this day in that brutish manner, as I said before. Howsoever, it may be perceived what manner of life there would be, where there were no common power to fear, by the manner of life which men that have formerly lived under a peaceful government, used to degenerate into, in a civil war.

But though there had never been any time, wherein particular men were in a condition of war one against another; yet in all times, kings and persons of sovereign authority, because of their independency, are in continual jealousies, and in the state and posture of gladiators: having their weapons pointing, and their eyes fixed on one another; that is, their forts, garrisons, and guns upon the frontiers of their kingdoms; and continual spies upon their neighbours; which is a posture of war. But, because they uphold thereby the industry of their subjects; there does not follow from it, that misery, which accompanies the liberty of particular men.

To this war of every man against every man, this also is consequent, that nothing can be unjust. The notions of right and wrong, justice and injustice, have there no place. Where there is no common power, there is no law: where no law, no injustice. Force and fraud are in war the two cardinal virtues.

Justice, and injustice are none of the faculties neither of the body, nor mind. If they were, they might be in a man that were alone in the world, as well as his senses, and passions. They are qualities, that relate to men in society, not in solitude. It is consequent also to the same condition, that there be no propriety, no dominion, no *mine* and *thine* distinct; but only that to be every man's, that he can get; and for so long, as he can keep it. And thus much for the ill condition, which man by mere nature is actually placed in : though with a possibility to come out of it, consisting partly in the passions, partly in his reason.

(From the *Leviathan*.)

NATURAL RELIGION

CURIOSITY, or love of the knowledge of causes, draws a man from the consideration of the effect to seek the cause; and again, the cause of that cause; till of necessity he must come to this thought at last, that there is some cause, whereof there is no former cause, but is eternal; which is it men call God. So that it is impossible to make any profound inquiry into natural causes, without being inclined thereby to believe there is one God eternal; though they cannot have any idea of Him in their mind, answerable to His nature. For as a man that is born blind, hearing men talk of warming themselves by the fire, and being brought to warm himself by the same, may easily conceive, and assure himself, there is somewhat there, which men call *fire*, and is the cause of the heat he feels : but cannot imagine what it is like, nor have an idea of it in his mind, such as they have that see it : so also by the visible things in this world, and their admirable order, a man may conceive there is a cause of them, which men call God : and yet not have an idea, or image of Him in his mind.

And they that make little or no inquiry into the natural causes of things, yet from the fear that proceeds from the ignorance itself, of what it is that hath the power to do them much good or harm, are inclined to suppose, and feign unto themselves, several kinds of powers invisible; and to stand in awe of their own imaginations; and in time of distress to invoke them; as also in the time of an expected good success, to give them thanks; making the creatures of their own fancy, their gods. By which means it hath come to pass, that from the innumerable variety of fancy, men have created in the world innumerable sorts of gods. And this fear of things invisible, is the natural seed of that which every one in himself calleth religion ; and in them that worship, or fear that power otherwise than they do, superstition.

And this seed of religion, having been observed by many ; some of those that have observed it, have been inclined thereby to nourish, dress, and form it into laws ; and to add to it of their own invention, any opinion of the causes of future events, by which they thought they should be best able to govern others, and make unto themselves the greatest use of their powers.

(From the Same.)

THE RACE

THE comparison of the life of man to a race, though it hold not in every part, yet it holdeth so well for this our purpose, that we may thereby both see and remember almost all the passions before mentioned. But this *race* we must suppose to have no other *goal*, nor other *garland*, but being foremost, and in it :

To endeavour, is *appetite*.
To be remiss, is *sensuality*.
To consider them behind, is *glory*.
To consider them before, is *humility*.
To lose ground with looking back, *vain glory*.
To be holden, *hatred*.
To turn back, *repentance*.
To be in breath, *hope*.
To be weary, *despair*.
To endeavour to overtake the next, *emulation*.
To supplant or overthrow, *envy*.
To resolve to break through a stop foreseen, *courage*.
To break through a sudden stop, *anger*.
To break through with ease, *magnanimity*.
To lose ground by little hindrances, *pusillanimity*.
To fall on the sudden, is disposition to *weep*.
To see another fall, is disposition to *laugh*.

To see one out-gone whom we would not, is *pity*.
To see one out-go whom we would not, is *indignation*.
To hold fast by another, is to *love*.
To carry him on that so holdeth, is *charity*.
To hurt one's-self for haste is *shame*.
Continually to be out-gone, is *misery*.
Continually to out-go the next before, is *felicity*.
And to forsake the course, is to *die*.

(From *Human Nature.*)

LOVE

OF *love*, by which is understood the joy man taketh in the fruition of any present good, hath been already spoken of in the first section, chapter vii. under which is contained the love men bear to one another, or pleasure they take in one another's company; and by which nature, men are said to be sociable. But there is another kind of love, which the Greeks call Ἔρως and is that which we mean, when we say that a man is in love: forasmuch as this passion cannot be without diversity of sex, it cannot be denied but that it participateth of that indefinite love mentioned in the former section. But there is a great difference betwixt the desire of a man indefinite, and the same desire limited *ad hunc;* and this is that love which is the great theme of poets: but notwithstanding their praises, it must be defined by the word need: for it is a conception a man hath of his need of that one person desired. The cause of this passion is not always nor for the most part beauty, or other quality in the beloved, unless there be withal hope in the person that loveth: which may be gathered from this, that in great difference of persons, the greater have often fallen in love with the meaner; but not contrary. And from hence it is, that for the most part they have much better fortune in love, whose hopes are built upon something in their person, than those that trust to their expressions and service; and they that care less, than they that care more: which not perceiving, many men cast away their services, as one arrow after another, till, in the end, together with their hopes, they lose their wits.

(From the Same.)

THE INCONVENIENCES OF GOVERNMENT

THE inconvenience arising from government in general to him that governeth, consisteth partly in the continual care and trouble about the business of other men that are his subjects ; and partly, in the danger of his person. For the head always is that part, not only where the care resideth, but also against which the stroke of an enemy most commonly is directed. To balance this in-commodity, the sovereignty, together with the necessity of this care and danger, comprehendeth so much honour, riches, and means, whereby to delight the mind, as no private man's wealth can attain unto. The inconveniences of government in general to a subject are none at all, if well considered, but in appearance. There be two things that may trouble his mind, or two general grievances ; the one is, loss of liberty ; the other, the uncertainty of *meum* and *tuum*. For the first, it consisteth in this, that a subject may no more govern his own actions according to his own discretion and judgment, or, which is all one, conscience, as the present occasions from time to time shall dictate to him ; but must be tied to do according to that will only, which once for all he had long ago laid up, and involved in the wills of the major part of an assembly, or in the will of some one man. But this is really no inconvenience. For, as it hath been showed before, it is the only means, by which we have any possibility of preserving ourselves. For if every man were allowed this liberty of follow-ing his conscience, in such difference of consciences, they would not live together in peace an hour. But it appeareth a great inconvenience to every man in particular, to be debarred of this liberty, because every one apart considereth it as in himself, and not as in the rest : by which means, liberty appeareth in the like-ness of rule and government over others. For where one man is at liberty, and the rest bound, there that one hath government ; which honour, he that understandeth not so much, demanding by the name simply of liberty, thinketh it a great grievance and in-jury to be denied it. For the second grievance concerning *meum* and *tuum*, it is also none, but in appearance only ; it consisteth in this, that the sovereign power taketh from him that which he used to enjoy, knowing no other propriety, but use and custom. But without such sovereign power, the right of men is not propriety to anything, but a community, no better than to have no right at all, as hath been showed, Part I. chapter i. section 10. Propriety therefore being derived from the sovereign power, is not to be pretended against the same, especially, when by it every subject hath his propriety against every other subject, which when sovereignty ceaseth, he hath not, because in that case they return to war amongst themselves. Those levies therefore which are made upon men's estates, by the sovereign authority, are no more but the price of that peace and defence which the sovereignty maintaineth for them. If this were not so, no money nor forces for the wars, nor any other public occasion, could justly be levied in the world. For neither king, nor democracy, nor aristocracy, nor the estates of any land, could do it, if the sovereignty could not. For in all those cases, it is levied by virtue of the sovereignty. Nay more, by the three estates here, the land of one man may be transferred to another, without crime of him from whom it was taken, and without pretence of public benefit, as hath been done : and this without injury, because done by the sovereign power. For the power whereby it is done, is no less than sovereign, and cannot be greater. Therefore this grievance for *meum* and *tuum* is not real, unless more be exacted than is necessary ; but it seemeth a grievance, because to them that either know not the right of sovereignty, or to whom that right belongeth, it seemeth an injury ; and injury, how little soever the damage, is always grievous, as putting us in mind of our disability to help ourselves, and into envy of the power to do us wrong.

(From *De Corpore Politico*.)

HOW THE PRESBYTERIANS GREW STRONG

IT was not their own art alone that did it, but they had the concurrence of a great many gentlemen, that did no less desire a popular government in the civil state than these ministers did in the Church. And as these did in the pulpit draw the people to their opinions, and to a dislike of the Church government, Canons, and Common-Prayer book, so did the other make them in love with the democracy by their harangues in the Parliament, and by their discourses and communication with people in the country, continually extolling liberty and inveighing against tyranny, leaving the people to collect of themselves that this tyranny was the present government of the state. And as the Presbyterians brought with them into their churches their divinity from the universities, so did many of the gentlemen bring their politics from thence into the Parliament; but neither of them did this very boldly in the time of Queen Elizabeth. And though it be not likely that all of them did it out of malice, but many of them out of error, yet certainly the chief leaders were ambitious ministers, and ambitious gentlemen; the ministers envying the authority of bishops, whom they thought less learned; and the gentlemen envying the privy-council, whom they thought less wise than themselves. For it is a hard matter for men, who do all think highly of their own wits, when they have also acquired the learning of the university, to be persuaded that they want any ability requisite for the government of a commonwealth, especially having read the glorious histories and the sententious politics of the ancient popular governments of the Greeks and Romans, amongst whom kings were hated and branded with the name of tyrants, and popular government (though no tyrant was ever so cruel as a popular assembly) passed by the name of liberty. The Presbyterian ministers, in the beginning of the reign of Queen Elizabeth, did not, because they durst not, publicly preach against the discipline of the Church. But not long after, by the favour perhaps of some great courtier, they went abroad, preaching in most of the market-towns of England, as the preaching friars had formerly done, upon working-days in the morning; in which sermons, these and others of the same tenets, that had charge of souls, both by the manner and matter of their preaching, applied themselves wholly to the winning of the people to a liking of their doctrines and good opinion of their persons.

And first, for the manner of their preaching; they so framed their countenance and gesture at their entrance into the pulpit, and their pronunciation both in their prayer and sermon, and used the Scripture phrase (whether understood by the people or not), as that no tragedian in the world could have acted the part of a right godly man better than these did; insomuch that a man unacquainted with such art, could never suspect any ambitious plot in them to raise sedition against the state, as they then had designed; or doubt that the vehemence of their voice (for the same words with the usual pronunciation had been of little force)

and forcedness of their gesture and looks, could arise from anything else but zeal to the service of God. And by this art they
came into such credit, that numbers of men used to go forth of
their own parishes and towns on working-days, leaving their
calling, and on Sundays leaving their own churches, to hear them
preach in other places, and to despise their own and all other
preachers that acted not so well as they. And as for those
ministers that did not usually preach, but instead of sermons did
read to the people such homilies as the Church had appointed,
they esteemed and called them dumb dogs.

Secondly, for the matter of their sermons, because the anger
of the people in the late Roman usurpation was then fresh, they
saw there could be nothing more gracious with them than to
preach against such other points of the Romish religion as the
bishops had not yet condemned ; that so receding further from
popery than they did, they might with glory to themselves leave
a suspicion on the bishops, as men not yet well purged from
idolatry.

Thirdly, before their sermons, their prayer was or seemed to
be *extempore*, which they pretended to be dictated by the spirit
of God within them, and many of the people believed or seemed
to believe it. For any man might see, that had judgment, that
they did not take care beforehand what they should say in their
prayers. And from hence came a dislike of the Common-Prayer
book, which is a set form, premeditated, that men might see to
what they were to say *Amen*.

Fourthly, they did never in their sermons, or but lightly,
inveigh against the lucrative vices of men of trade or handicraft ;
such as are feigning, lying, cozening, hypocrisy, or other uncharitableness, except want of charity to their pastors and to the
faithful : which was a great ease to the generality of citizens and
the inhabitants of market-towns, and no little profit to themselves.

Fifthly, by preaching up an opinion that men were to be
assured of their salvation by the testimony of their own private
spirit, meaning the Holy Ghost dwelling within them. And
from this opinion the people that found in themselves a sufficient
hatred towards the Papists, and an ability to repeat the sermons
of these men at their coming home, made no doubt but that they
had all that was necessary, how fraudulently and spitefully soever
they behaved themselves to their neighbours that were not
reckoned amongst the saints, and sometimes to those also.

Sixthly, they did, indeed, with great earnestness and severity, inveigh often against two sins, carnal lusts and vain swearing ; which, without question, was very well done. But the common people were thereby inclined to believe, that nothing else was sin, but that which was forbidden in the third and seventh commandments (for few men do understand by the name of lust any other concupiscence, than that which is forbidden in that seventh commandment ; for men are not ordinarily said to lust after another man's cattle, or other goods or possessions) : and therefore never made much scruple of the acts of fraud and malice, but endeavoured to keep themselves from uncleanness only, or at least from the scandal of it. And, whereas they did, both in their sermons and writings, maintain and inculcate, that the very first motions of the mind, that is to say, the delight men and women took in the sight of one another's form, though they checked the proceeding thereof so that it never grew up to be a design, was nevertheless a sin, they brought young men into desperation and to think themselves damned, because they could not (which no man can, and is contrary to the constitution of nature) behold a delightful object without delight. And by this means they became confessors to such as were thus troubled in conscience, and were obeyed by them as their spiritual doctors in all cases of conscience.

(From *Behemoth.*)

THOMAS MAY

[He was the son of Sir Thomas May of Mayfield, Sussex, and was born in 1594. A Fellow-commoner of Sidney Sussex College, Cambridge, a student at Gray's Inn, and a courtier, he occupied his leisure in penning tragedies, comedies, descriptive poems, and translations from Virgil and Lucan. During the Civil Wars he was employed as secretary and historiographer to the Long Parliament. In this capacity he published in 1647 his *History of the Parliament of England, which began 3rd Nov.* 1640. This work however only extends to the battle of Newbury in 1643. In a *Breviary* of the same history, published in 1650, he carries the story some years further. May's *History* was reprinted by Baron Maseres in 1812, and by the Clarendon Press in 1854 ; his *Breviary* is included in Maseres' *Select Tracts relating to the Civil Wars* (1815). His comedies are, *The Heir* and *The Old Couple:* his tragedies, *Cleopatra, Agrippina,* and *Antigone.* To these Mr. Fleay would add the anonymous play of *Nero,* and if this be really May's it is his masterpiece. There exists a rare book entitled *An Epitome of the English History by Thomas May, Esq., a late Member of Parliament, 3rd ed.* 1690; but as this is written in an anti-Cromwellian vein, and as the events narrated go down to 1660, it can hardly be the work of our author, who died in 1650.]

MAY is a man of letters playing the historian. He flaunts you his Latin at every turn, decking his narrative with quotations from Claudian, Petronius, Lucan, and stopping to translate them with superfluous nicety. He conceives of history rather as an art than a science ; his object is to instruct ignorance, not to assist investigation ; he will insert a document here and there, but for the most part you must take his word for his authorities. And, as is the wont of literary men, it is the personal note that attracts him most, not as with the modern school, analysis of hidden cause and obvious effect ; so that the best part of his book is to be found in the touches of characterisation, in the sketches of Pym, of Strafford. As a describer of battles he is hardly vigorous or picturesque enough. Indeed to style in writing he never attains. He has not the gift of the paragraph ; page after page is a string of disconnected notes. And his diction is so far Latinised as to become bald, without catching the felicities which Latinisms sometimes convey. A recent essayist writes "that to possess that half of the language within which Latin heredities lurk and Roman-esque allusions are at play, is to possess the state and security of a dead tongue without the death." And this is true for the geniuses, for Shakespeare with his "extravagant and erring spirit," for Sir Thomas Browne and a few others, but for the rest, for such as May, it is only a pitfall, a short cut to tediousness and the easy commonplace. Against this it must be set that May is not pretentious, that his judgment is sober, and his temper just. Such praises one may bestow on the journeymen of literature.

EDMUND K. CHAMBERS.

THE ARGUMENT OF HIS HISTORY

THE subject of this work is a civil war; a war indeed as much more than civil, and as full of miracle, both in the causes and effects of it, as was ever observed in any age; a war as cruel as unnatural, that has produced as much rage of swords, as much bitterness of pens, both public and private, as was ever known; and has divided the understandings of men, as well as their affections, in so high a degree, that scarce could any virtue gain due applause, any reason give satisfaction, or any relation obtain credit, unless amongst men of the same side. It were therefore a presumptuous madness to think that this poor and weak discourse, which can deserve no applause from either side, should obtain from both so much as pardon; or that those persons should agree in the judgment they will form of it who could never agree in anything else.

I cannot therefore be so stupid as not to be fully sensible of the difficulty of the task imposed on me, or the great envy which attends it; which other men who have written histories, upon far less occasion, have discoursed of at large in their prefaces. And Tacitus himself, complaining of those ill times which were the unhappy subject of his *Annals* (though he wrote not in the time of the same princes under whom those things were acted), yet (because the families of many men who had then been ignominious were yet in being) could not but discourse how much happier those writers had been, who had taken more ancient and prosperous times for their argument; such (as he there expresses it) as those times in which the great and glorious actions of the old Romans, their honourable achievements, and exemplary virtues, are recorded.

And I could have wished more than my life (being myself inconsiderable) that, for the sake of the public, my theme could rather have been the prosperity of these nations, the honour and happiness of the king, and such a blessed condition of both, as might have reached all the ends for which government was first ordained in the world, than the description of shipwrecks, ruin, and desolations. Yet these things, truly recorded and observed, may be of good use, and may benefit posterity in divers kinds. For though the present actions, or rather sufferings, of these (once happy) nations, are of so high a mark and consideration, as might, perchance, throw themselves into the knowledge of posterity by tradition and the weight of their own fame, yet it may much conduce to the benefit that may arise from that knowledge, to have the true causes, original, and growth of them represented by an honest pen.

For the truth of this plain and naked discourse, which is here presented to the public view, containing a brief narration of those distractions which have fallen amongst us during the sitting of this present parliament, as also some passages and visible actions of the former government (whether probably conducing to these present calamities or not, of which let the reader judge), I appeal only to the memory of any Englishman, whose years have been enough to make him know the actions that were done, and whose conversation has been enough public to let him hear the common voice and discourses of people upon those actions ; to his memory, I say, do I appeal, whether such actions were not done and such judgments made upon them as are here related. In which, perchance, some readers may be put in mind of their own thoughts heretofore, which thoughts have since, like Nebuchadnezzar's dream, departed from them. An English gentleman, who went to travel when this parliament was called, and returned when these differences were grown among us, hearing what discourses were daily made, affirmed that the parliament of England (in his opinion) was more misunderstood in England than at Rome ; and that there was a greater need to remind our own countrymen than to inform strangers of what was past ; so much, said he, have they seemed to forget both the things themselves and their own former notions concerning them.

- (From *The History of the Long Parliament.*)

STRAFFORD

BUT now a greater actor is brought upon the stage, Thomas Wentworth, Earl of Strafford, Lieutenant of Ireland, a man too great to be let escape ; no sooner accused but surprised, and secured for a trial.

Which trial of his, if we consider all things—the high nature of the charge against him ; the pompous circumstances and stately manner of the trial itself ; the time that it lasted ; the preciousness of that time so consumed ; and, lastly, of what moment and consequence the success of it must prove—I may safely say, that no subject in England, and probably in Europe, ever had the like.

So great it was, that we can hardly call it the trial of Strafford only ; the king's affections toward his people and parliament, the future success of this parliament, and the hopes of three kingdoms depending on it, were all tried when Strafford was arraigned.

Many subjects in Europe have played louder parts upon the theatre of the world, but none left it with greater noise ; nor was the matter of his accusation confined within one realm ; three whole kingdoms were his accusers, and eagerly sought, in one death, a recompense of all their sufferings ; that we may say of his case, as Claudian says of Ruffinus,

> *Offensis Ruffinum divide terris.*

Within ten days after the parliament began, the Earl of Strafford, newly returned from the north, was sitting in the House of Lords ; when master Pymme, an ancient gentleman, of great experience in parliamentary affairs, and no less known fidelity to his country, came up to the Lords, and, in the name of all the Commons of England, accused Thomas Earl of Strafford, Lord Lieutenant of Ireland, of high treason ; and desired their lordships that he might be sequestered from parliament and forthwith committed to prison ; as also to let them know that the Commons, within very few days, would resort to their lordships with the particular articles and grounds of this accusation.

(From the Same.)

THE QUEEN MOTHER

IT was her misfortune (how far her crime I cannot tell) that, during her abode here, the two kingdoms of England and

Scotland were embroiled in great troubles, which the people were apt to impute in some measure to her counsels, knowing what power the queen her daughter had with the king.

Others taxed her not at all, but looked upon other causes, the same counsels, which, long before her arrival, had distempered England ; but the people made their judgment upon it from her actions or successes in other places.

But, however it were, the queen was fearful of the people here, and had not long before desired to have a guard allowed her, pretending fear of her life, by reason of some attempts which she conceived to have been made against her ; upon which a guard was set about her house.

Her regency in France had not been happy, nor according to the interest of that kingdom ; though that, perchance, may be accounted a fault not so particular to her as commonly incident to the regency of queen mothers in that land : inasmuch as Thuanus commends the saying of Charles the Ninth (a prince whom otherwise he doth not praise) upon his deathbed. That, since he must die at that age (being four and twenty), he thanked God he had no son, lest France should fall under a regency, of which he had found the sad effects. His mother was Katherine de Medicis, of the same family with this queen.

After the time of her regency, her actions had been such, that the king her son would not harbour her in his own kingdom, nor was she welcome into the territories of her son-in-law the king of Spain. But the people there were no less desirous of her departure than afterward in England.

Insomuch as she afterward became a strange example of the instability of human fortunes, that so great a queen, and mother to so many mighty princes, should want a quiet harbour for her age.

Not long after her departure from England she died at Culleine, and might seem a parallel, in some things, to the famous Empress of Rome who founded that city, and there planted a Roman colony, Agrippina, the wife of Claudius Cæsar and the mother of Nero. They both had tasted of power, been active in it, but not pleasing to the people. They were both taught that the greatness of their sons was not so much advantage to their power as they had hoped, and had learned, that all power dependent upon another is of small validity and less stability ; as Tacitus observes, speaking of the same Agrippina,

Nihil rerum mortalium tam instabile et fluxum est, quam fama potentiæ non sua vi nixæ.

(From the Same.)

THE BATTLE OF EDGEHILL

THE cannon on both sides with a loud thunder began the fight, in which the success was not equal, the parliament's cannon doing great execution upon their enemies, but theirs very little. The Earl of Lindsey, general for the king, with a pike in his hand, led on the main body of that army, in which was the king's own regiment, encountered by the Lord-General Essex, who exposed himself to all the danger that a battle could make, first leading on his troop, then his own regiment of foot, and breathing courage into them, till, being dissuaded by divers from engaging himself too far, he returned to the rest of the army to draw them on. The chief regiments having begun the battle, Sir Philip Stapleton, with a brave troop of gentlemen (which were the general's life-guard, and commanded by him), charged the king's regiment on their right flank with their pikes, and came off without any great hurt, though those pikemen stoutly defended themselves, and the musketeers, being good firemen, played fiercely upon them. The battle was hot at that place, and so many of the king's side slain, that the parliament army began to be victorious there ; they took the standard royal, the bearer thereof, Sir Edmund Varney, being slain, and the general, the Earl of Lindsey, sore wounded, was taken prisoner. But the same fortune was not in every part ; for the king's right wing, led by prince Rupert, charged fiercely upon the left wing of the other (consisting most of horse), and prevailed altogether, for the parliament troops ran almost all away in that wing, and many of their fool companions, dismayed with their flight, fled all away before they had stood one charge ; Colonel Essex, being utterly forsaken by that whole brigade which he commanded, went himself into the van, where he performed excellent service, both by direction and execution, till at the last he was shot in the thigh, of which he shortly after died ; (some part of their disheartening was caused by the revolt of their own side ; for Sir Faithful Fortescue, at the beginning of the fight, instead of charging the enemy, discharged his pistol to the ground, and with his troop, wheeling about, ran to the king's army, to whom he had formerly given notice thereof by his cornet). The parliament army had undoubtedly been ruined that day, if prince Rupert and his pursuing troops had been more temperate in blundering so untimely as they did, and had wheeled about to assist their distressed friends in other parts of the army ; for prince Rupert followed the chase to Keynton town, where the carriages of the army were, which they presently pillaged, using great cruelty, as was afterwards related, to the unarmed waggoners and labouring men. A great number of the flying parliament soldiers were slain in that chase, which lasted two miles beyond Keynton, and so far, till the pursuers were forced to retire, having met with Colonel Stampden, who marched with the other brigade of the army, that brought on the artillery and ammunition, before spoken of. Colonel Stampden discharged five pieces of cannon against them ; some were slain, and the rest ceasing the pursuit retired hastily to the field, where they found all their infantry, excepting two regiments, quite defeated ; for in the meantime, Sir William Balfore, lieutenant-general of the horse, with a regiment of horse, charged a regiment of the king's foot, before any foot of his own side could come up to him, and, breaking most bravely into it, had cut most of them off ; and afterward, by the assistance of some foot who were come up to him, he defeated another regiment, and so got up to the greatest part of the king's ordnance, taking some of them, cutting off the gears of the horses that drew them, and killing the gunners, but was enforced to leave them without any guard, by reason that he laboured most to make good the day against several regiments of the king's foot, who still fought with much resolution, especially that which was of the king's guard, where his standard was ; by which Sir William Balfore's regiment rode, when they came back from taking the ordnance, and were by them mistaken for their own side. Their passing without any hostility was the cause, that immediately afterward, Sir William, riding up toward the Lord-General Essex's regiment of horse, they gave fire upon Sir William Balfore's men, supposing them to be enemies, but soon discovering each other, they joined companies, and were led up with half the lord-general's regiment, by his excellency himself, against the king's main strength, where a terrible and bloody encounter happened ; at the same time Colonel Ballard, who led a brigade there of the lord-general's regiment and the

Lord Brook's, forced a stand of the king's pikes, and broke through two of his regiments.

In this great conflict the standard royal (as aforesaid) was taken, and Sir Edmund Varney slain, the Earl of Lindsey with his son, taken prisoners, together with colonel Vavasor, lieutenant colonel of that regiment; colonel Munroe also was there slain.

The standard thus taken, and put into the lord-general's hand, was by him delivered to his secretary, master Chambers; but the secretary, after he had carried it some time in his hand, suffered it to be taken from him by an unknown person, and so privately it was conveyed away. There also was great service performed by the Lord Gray, son to the Earl of Stamford, and Sir Arthur Haslerig, and a considerable help given to the turning of the day, by defeating a regiment of the king's called the blue regiment.

By this time all the king's foot, excepting two regiments, were dispersed, and the parliamentarians had gotten the advantage of the wind, and that ground which their enemies had fought upon. Those two regiments of the king's retiring themselves, and finding their ordnance behind them without any guard, took stand there, and made use of their cannon, discharging many shot against their enemies. But at that time the parliament foot began to want powder, otherwise (as was observed by a commander in that army) they had charged them both with horse and foot; which in all probability would have utterly ruined the king's infantry, consisting in a manner but of two regiments.

Thus the parliament army, partly for want of ammunition, and partly being tired with so long a fight (for the whole brunt of the battle had been sustained by two regiments of their horse and four or five of their foot), made no great haste to charge any more.

The king's horse, who had been long pillaging about Keynton, by this time had leisure to come about on both hands, and join themselves, to their foot; but as they came back on the left hand of their enemies, Sir Philip Stapleton with his horse gave them a terrible charge, which they were not long able to endure, but, finding a gap in an hedge, got from him upon the spur as fast as they could, to the rest of their broken troops, and so at last joined with their foot that stood by the ordnance. And now on both sides the horse were gathered to their own foot, and so stood together both horse and foot, one against another, till it was night.

The parliament army being wholly possessed of the ground which their enemies had chosen to fight upon, stood upon it all night, and in the morning returned to a warmer place near Keynton, where they had quartered the night before ; for they were much pinched with cold, and the whole army in extreme want of victuals.

The king's army had withdrawn to the top of the hill for their more security, where they made great fires all the night long.

(From the Same.)

JAMES HOWELL

[The author of the *Familiar Letters*, which have made one of the most popular books of English literature, was born about 1594. His pedigree loses itself in the usual mists of Welsh royalty or chieftaincy, after the fashion to be expected in a country where surnames were a late and doubtful importation ; but his father was the parson of Abernant, in Carmarthenshire, and his relationship to good Welsh families seems indisputable. His school was Hereford, his college Jesus, Oxford, where he took his degree in 1613. Howell, however, was pre-eminently a man of affairs. He obtained a recommendation to his countryman Sir Robert Mansel, who with others had obtained a patent for the manufacture of glass, and was anxious to procure workmen from abroad. Howell was sent to Venice and elsewhere on this business, as he was later to Spain in hopes of recovering sums due to English merchants, at the favourable moment of the Prince of Wales's intended marriage to the Infanta. During the reign of Charles the First he had many public and semi-public employments, and at last, just at the outbreak of the civil war, was made Clerk to the Council. The employment brought him little but imprisonment at the hands of the Parliament, and he lay in the Fleet till the war was over. At the Restoration (though Howell's royalism, for all his imprisonment, was not of a very thorough-going character) he was made Historiographer-Royal. He survived that date six years and died in 1666. His *Epistolæ Ho-Elianæ* or *Familiar Letters*, in four books, appeared at intervals from 1645 to 1655. He was also the author of a vast number of separate works, some of which will be noticed below. The *Letters* were extremely popular, and after their collection went into ten editions in about three-quarters of a century, while they have had a considerable modern revival of popularity, and have never been neglected by students and literary men. The most complete and careful modern edition is that of Mr. Jacobs in 1890. The older ones are easily accessible, and may have greater charms for some readers. Howell's *Instructions for Foreign Travel* was reprinted by Mr. Arber.]

IT has been observed more than once, and certainly with great truth, of Howell, that he was a journalist born before his time ; and it may be added that he was not only this, but even, by anticipation, that peculiar and late kind of journalist known as the special correspondent. He had a considerable knowledge of literature, and, it would seem, a real, if not a very critical, love of books ; but his bent was neither towards original production nor towards pure study. To be active in affairs and to write about them ; to make popular summaries of history, politics, all manner of matters, especially those of passing interest—these were the tasks for which he was most inclined : and in undertaking and discharging them he was aided by a restless and rather adventurous temperament and a very considerable linguistic faculty. Hardly any kind of writing came amiss to him, prose, verse, or dictionary-making ; but of all his forty or fifty books or pamphlets there is no doubt that the *Familiar Letters* bear the bell. The four "books" of which they are composed are of very unequal value and, so to speak, genuineness. It has been suspected, and with great reason, that even in the earlier instalments Howell frequently patched and wrote up his old letters, and may sometimes have invented them whole. But there can be little doubt that many, if not most of the later epistles, are pure literary exercises, popular tractates or pamphlets in the guise of letters. Even these however are mostly readable ; and the earlier pieces are delightful. Howell has been accused of being a prig, which is harsh, and of being a coxcomb, which is true enough ; and he has other qualities which are not in themselves gifts or graces. But his pedantry, his egotism, his adroit, if seldom quite abject flattery of the great, his spice of ill-nature now and then, his self-seeking and intriguing, present, as they are reflected in his style and matter, a spectacle by no means ugly, and very decidedly lively. And in this distinct and lively style he has abundance of interesting things to tell. His scraps and doles of book-learning are constantly contrasted with, and thrown up by, passages of sheer reporting, but reporting which is almost that of genius. In his travels and affairs he always had his eyes open, and could always describe what he saw. We may not attach strict credence to what he tells us of Raleigh's fate and Ben Jonson's foibles, of his own activity and ability, and of other people's mishaps or peccadilloes. But whether he is talking of these things, or of the manufacture of "barillia," or of the Oxenham white bird, or of the shocking adventure of Lieutenant Jaquette, with a much earlier and more mischievous Lady of Lyons, or of almost anything but the subjects of his later vamped-up essays and sometimes even of these—there is the attraction of the best "light" or "miscellaneous" writing. The thing is not specially edifying, but it is almost always amusing : if there is no great profit or any very exquisite pleasure in the reading, it is always an agreeable pastime. Howell had had more predecessors than is generally thought in the attempt to furnish pastime of this kind ; but no one had yet acquired the perfect knack of furnishing it. He has something of the Boswellian touch in him, of the faculty of making us despise himself a little, but take an almost increased interest in his work, by reason of the way in which we look down on him. And much of his effect is due to pure matters of style and treatment, to his perfect clearness, to his mixture of the vernacular and the pedantic, nay to his very tags of mostly bad verse. A great writer he was not, but an extraordinarily clever and amusing one, with abundant distinction and idiosyncrasy, he was, and after more than two centuries, still is.

GEORGE SAINTSBURY.

THE MURDER OF BUCKINGHAM

(To the Right Honourable the Lady Scroop, Countess of
Sunderland : from Stamford.)

MADAM—I lay yesternight at the post-house at Stilton, and this
morning betimes the post-master came to my bed's head and
told me the Duke of Buckingham was slain : my faith was not
then strong enough to believe it, till an hour ago I met in the
way with my Lord of Rutland (your brother) riding post towards
London ; it pleased him to alight, and show me a letter wherein
there was an exact relation of all the circumstances of this sad
tragedy.

Upon Saturday last, which was but next before yesterday,
being Bartholomew Eve, the Duke did rise up in a well-disposed
humour out of his bed, and cut a caper or two, and being ready,
and having been under the barber's hands (when the murderer
had thought to have done the deed, for he was leaning upon the
window all the while) he went to breakfast attended by a great
company of Commanders, where Monsieur Soubize came unto
him, and whispered him in the ear that Rochelle was relieved,
the Duke seemed to slight the news, which made some think
that Soubize went away discontented : after breakfast the Duke
going out, Colonel Fryer stepped before him, and stopping him
upon some business, and Lieutenant Felton being behind, made a
thrust with a common tenpenny knife over Fryer's arm at the
Duke, which lighted so fatally, that he slit his heart in two,
leaving the knife sticking in the body : the Duke took out the
knife, and threw it away, and laying his hand on his sword, and
drawing it half out said, " The villain hath killed me " (meaning,
as some think, Colonel Fryer), for there had been some difference
betwixt them, so reeling against a chimney he fell down dead :
the Duchess being with child hearing the noise below, came
in her nightgears from her bed-chamber, which was in an upper

room, to a kind of rail, and thence beheld him weltering in his own blood. Felton had lost his hat in the crowd, wherein there was a paper sewed, wherein he declared that the reason which moved him to this act was no grudge of his own, though he had been far behind for his pay, and had been put by his Captain's place twice, but in regard he thought the Duke an enemy to the state, because he was branded in Parliament, therefore what he did was for the public good of his country. Yet he got clearly down, and so might have gone to his horse which was tied to a hedge hard by ; but he was so amazed that he missed his way, and so struck into the *pastry*, where although the cry went that some Frenchman had done it, he thinking the word was Felton, he boldly confessed, 'twas he that had done the deed, and so he was in their hands. Jack Stamford would have run at him, but he was kept off by Mr. Nicholas, so, being carried up to a tower, Captain Mince tore off his spurs, and asking how he durst attempt such an act, making him believe the Duke was not dead, he answered boldly that he knew he was dispatched, for 'twas not he, but the hand of heaven that gave the stroke, and though his whole body had been covered over with armour of proof he could not have avoided it. Captain Charles Price went post presently to the King four miles off, who being at prayers on his knees when it was told him, yet he never stirred, nor was he disturbed a whit till all divine service was done. This was the relation, as far as my memory could bear, in my Lord of Rutland's letter, who willed me to remember him unto your Ladyship, and tell you that he was going to comfort your niece (the Duchess) as fast as he could : and so I have sent the truth of this sad story to your Ladyship, as fast as I could by this Post, because I cannot make that speed myself, in regard of some business I have to dispatch for my Lord in the way ; so I humbly take my leave, and rest

Your Ladyship's most dutiful servant,

J. H.

STAMFORD, *Aug.* 5, 1628.

(From *Familiar Letters*.)

THE WHITE BIRD

To Mr. E. D.

SIR—I thank you a thousand times for the noble entertainment you gave me at Berry, and the pains you took in shewing me the antiquities of that place. In requital, I can tell you of a strange thing I saw lately here, and I believe 'tis true: as I passed by St. Dunstan's in Fleet Street the last Saturday, I stepped into a lapidary, or stone-cutter's shop, to treat with the master for a stone to be put upon my father's tomb : and casting my eyes up and down, I spied a huge marble with a large inscription upon it, which was thus to my best remembrance :

"Here lies John Oxenham, a goodly young man, in whose chamber, as he was struggling with the pangs of death, a bird with a white breast was seen fluttering about his bed, and so vanished.

" Here lies also Mary Oxenham, the sister of the said John, who died the next day, and the same apparition was seen in the room."

Then another sister is spoke of. Then—

" Here lies hard by James Oxenham, the son of the said John, who died a child in his cradle a little after, and such a bird was seen fluttering about his head, a little before he expired, which vanished afterwards."

At the bottom of the stone there is,

" Here lies Elizabeth Oxenham, the mother of the said John, who died sixteen years since, when such a bird with a white breast was seen about her bed before her death."

To all these there be divers witnesses, both Squires and ladies, whose names are engraven upon the stone : this stone is to be sent to a town hard by Exeter, where this happened.

Were you here, I could raise a choice discourse with you hereupon. So hoping to see you the next term, to requite some of your favours, I rest

Your true friend to serve you,

J. H.

WESTMINSTER, 3 *July*, 1632.

(From the Same.)

HOWELL'S SABBATH DEVOTIONS

'TIS true, though there be rules and rubrics in our liturgy sufficient to guide every one in the performance of all holy duties, yet I believe every one hath some mode and model or formulary of his own, especially for his private cubicular devotions.

I will begin with the last day of the week, and with the latter end of that day, I mean Saturday evening, on which I have fasted ever since I was a youth in Venice, for being delivered from a very great danger: this year I use some extraordinary acts of devotion to usher in the ensuing Sunday in hymns, and various prayers of my own penning before I go to bed. On Sunday morning I rise earlier than upon other days, to prepare myself for the sanctifying of it ; nor do I use barber, tailor, shoemaker, or any other mechanic that morning, and whatsoever diversions, or lets may hinder me the week before, I never miss, but in case of sickness, to repair to God's Holy House that day, where I come before prayers begin, to make myself fitter for the work by some previous meditations, and to take the whole service along with me ; nor do I love to mingle speech with any in the interim about news or worldly negotiations in God's Holy House. I prostrate myself in the humblest and decentest way of genuflection I can imagine : nor do I believe there can be any excess of exterior humility in that place : therefore I do not like those squatting unseemly bold postures upon one's tail, or muffling the face in the hat, or thrusting it in some hole, or covering it with one's hand : but with bended knee, and an open confident face, I fix my eyes on the east part of the church, and heaven. I endeavour to apply every tittle of the service to my own conscience and occasions, and I believe the want of this, with the huddling up, and careless reading of some ministers, with the commonness of it, is the greatest cause that many do undervalue, and take a surfeit of our public service.

For the reading and singing psalms, whereas most of them are either petitions or eucharistical ejaculations, I listen to them more attentively, and make them my own ; when I stand at the creed, I think upon the custom they have in Poland, and elsewhere, for gentlemen to draw their swords all the while, intimating thereby, that they will defend it with their lives and blood : And for the Decalogue, whereas others use to rise, and sit, I ever kneel at it in the humblest and trembling'st posture of all, to crave remission for the breaches passed of any of God's holy commandments (especially the week before), and future grace to observe them.

I love a holy devout sermon, that first checks, and then cheers the conscience, that begins with the Law, and ends with the Gospel : but I never prejudicate or censure any preacher, taking him as I find him.

And now that we are not only *adulted*, but ancient christians, I believe the most acceptable sacrifice we can send up to heaven, is Prayer and Praise, and that sermons are not so essential as either of them to the true practice of devotion. The rest of the holy Sabbath, I sequester my body and mind as much as I can from wordly affairs.   (From the Same.)

THE PIED PIPER

TO MR. E. P.

SIR—I saw such prodigious things daily done these few years past, that I had resolved with myself to give over wondering at anything, yet a passage happened this week, that forced me to wonder once more, because it is without parallel. It was that some odd fellows went skulking up and down London streets, and with figs and raisins allured little children, and so purloined them away from their parents, and carried them a ship-board, far beyond sea, where by cutting their hair, and other devices, they so disguised them that their parents could not know them. This made me think upon that miraculous passage in Hamelen, a town in Germany, which I hoped to have passed through when I was in Hamburg, had we returned by Holland, which was thus (nor would I relate it unto you were there not some ground of truth for it). The said town of Hamelen was annoyed with rats and mice : and it chanced that a pied-coated Piper came thither, who covenanted with the chief burghers for such a reward, if he could free them quite from the said vermin, nor would he demand it till a twelvemonth and a day after : the agreement being made, he began to play on his pipes, and all the rats and the mice followed him to a great lough hard by, where they all perished ;

so the town was infected no more. At the end of the year, the Pied Piper returned for his reward, the burghers put him off with slightings, and neglect, offering him some small matter, which he refusing, and staying some days in the town, one Sunday morning at high mass, when most people were at church, he fell to play on his pipes, and all the children up and down followed him out of the town, to a great hill not far off, which rent in two, and opened, and let him and the children in, and so closed up again. This happened a matter of two hundred and fifty years since : and in that town, they date their bills and bonds, and other instruments in law, to this day from the year of the going out of their children : besides, there is a great pillar of stone at the foot of the said hill, whereon this story is engraven.

No more now, for this is enough in conscience for one time : so I am

Your most affectionate servitor,

J. H.

FLEET, 1 *Octob.* 1643.

(From the Same.)

WINES

FRANCE participating of the climes of all the countries about her, affords wines of quality accordingly, as towards the Alps and Italy she hath a luscious rich wine called Frontignac ; in the country of Provence towards the Pyrenees : in Languedoc there are wines concustable with those of Spain : one of the prime sort of white wines is that of Beaume, and of clarets that of Orleans, though it be interdicted to wine the King's cellar with it in respect of the corrosiveness it carries with it. As in France so in all other wine-countries the white is called the female, and the claret or red wine is called the male, because commonly it hath more sulphur, body and heat in't : the wines that our merchants bring over grow upon the river Garonne, near Bordeaux, in Gascony, which is the greatest mart for wines in all France ; the Scot, because he hath always been an useful confederate to France against England, hath (among other privileges) right of preemption or first choice of wines in Bordeaux ; he is also permitted to carry his ordnance to the very walls of the town, whereas the English are forced to leave them at Blaye a good way distant down the river. There is a hard green wine that grows about Rochelle, and the islands thereabouts, which the cunning Hollander sometimes use to fetch, and he hath a trick to put a bag of herbs, or some other infusions into it (as he doth brimstone in Rhenish), to give it a whiter tincture, and more sweetness ; then they re-embark it for England, where it passeth for good Bachrag, and this is called *stooming* of wines. In Normandy there's little or no wine at all grows, therefore the common drink of that country is cider, specially in Low Normandy : there are also many beer-houses in Paris and elsewhere, but though their barley and water be better than ours, or that of Germany, and though they have English and Dutch brewers among them, yet they cannot make beer in that perfection.

The prime wines of Germany grow about the Rhine, specially in the Pfalts or lower Palatinate about Bachrag, which hath its etymology from *Bacchiara*, for in ancient times there was an altar erected there to the honour of Bacchus, in regard of the richness of the wines. Here and all France over, 'tis held a great part of incivility for maidens to drink wine until they are married, as it is in Spain for them to wear high shoes, or to paint till then. The German mothers, to make their sons fall into hatred of wine, do use when they are little to put some owl's eggs into a cup of Rhenish, and sometimes a little living eel, which twingling in the wine while the child is drinking so scares him, that many come to abhor and have an antipathy to wine all their lives after. From Bachrag the first stock of vines which grow now in the Grand Canary Island were brought, which, with the heat of the sun and the soil, is grown now to that height of perfection, that the wine which they afford are accounted the richest, the most firm, the best-bodied, and lastingest wine, and the most defecated from all earthly grossness of any other whatsoever, it hath little or no sulphur at all in't, and leaves less dregs behind, though one drink it to excess : French wines may be said to pickle meat in the stomach, but this is the wine that digests, and doth not only breed good blood, but it nutrifieth also, being a glutinous substantial liquor : of this wine, if of any other, may be verified that merry induction, That good wine makes good blood, good blood causeth good humours, good humours cause good thoughts, good thoughts bring forth good works, good works carry a man to heaven, *ergo* good wine carrieth a man to heaven. If this be true surely more English go to heaven this way than any other, for I think there's more Canary brought into England than to all the world besides. I think also there is a hundred times more drunk under the name of Canary wine than there is brought in, for Sherries and Malagas well mingled pass for Canaries in most taverns, more often than Canary itself, else I do not see how 'twere possible for the vintner to save by it: or to live by his calling, unless he were permitted sometimes to be a brewer. When Sacks and Canaries were brought in first among us, they were used to be drunk in *Aquavitae* measures, and 'twas held fit only for those to drink of them who were used to carry their *legs in their hands, their eyes upon their noses*, and an *Almanack in their bones:* but now they go down every one's throat both young and old like milk.

(From the Same.)

HEYLYN

[Peter Heylyn was born at Burford in Oxfordshire in 1600. From the School at Burford he passed first to Hart Hall (afterwards Magdalen Hall, and now Hertford College) and then to Magdalen College, Oxford, of which he became a Fellow in 1618. He soon acquired a reputation by his energy and learning, and in 1621, published the first edition of his *Geography*. Presently he entered upon the more dangerous ground of ecclesiastical controversy, and became involved in disputes with Dr. Prideaux, whose leanings to Puritanism he disliked. Taken under the protection of Laud and the Court he became the chief literary exponent of the principles upon which Laud's policy was based. In the struggles which followed he was an extreme supporter of the Royalist party, and his chief antagonist was Williams, Bishop of Lincoln. He played a notable part in the prosecution of Prynne, the author of *Histriomastix*, and naturally when the tide turned he was one of the first marked out for vengeance by the Parliament and the Puritans. Misfortunes, poverty, persecution, and eventually blindness, did not quench his spirit. On the Restoration he recovered his position as Sub-dean of Westminster (which he had held along with other church preferments, although he never reached high ecclesiastical rank), but did not live long to enjoy the triumph of his party, dying in 1662.]

HEYLYN was a man of undoubted sincerity, of quick and active, if somewhat superficial, intellect, and of a temper which found satisfaction only in controversy. If, in his triumph, he often pressed the advantage hard against his antagonists, he accepted, with undaunted spirit, the fate of the conquered, and throughout his life he neither gave nor asked for quarter. His memory was enormous, and his learning various, although ill digested : and while he grasped clearly and tenaciously the principles of Laud's policy, and frequently had the best of his antagonists in arguments, he was without judgment, imagination, or any sense of proportion. He did not altogether lack wit, but his sarcasm is rough and boisterous rather than keen : and he rates Fuller for his digressions and his waywardness, being utterly incapable of sympathy with the happier moods of Fuller's humour. Wood gives us a portrait of the man—"of very mean port and presence";

so worn as to be "like a skeleton" : and it answers to his mental equipment—narrow and precise in opinion ; unassailable in self-confidence ; condemning with equally unsparing hand the Romanists and the Puritans : but yet brave and honest according to his lights, and commanding respect for his invincible courage, and undaunted cheerfulness in defeat. Personally, he is said to have been kind and hospitable, although irascible and quick-tempered.

His controversial works were very numerous, and perhaps the most characteristic is the *Examen Historicum*, in which he attacked Fuller's *Church History*, and Sanderson's *History of King Charles*. His more important works were completed at the close of his busy life (when he was obliged, by failing eyesight, constantly to employ an amanuensis—on whose defects he is amusingly frank, as when he declares that he cannot quote a Greek verse, because his transcriber could not copy it correctly), and they were mostly published after his death. They are *Ecclesia Restaurata* or the *History of the Reformation : Cyprianus Anglicus* (the life of Archbishop Laud) : and *Aerius Redivivus* (the history of Presbyterianism), in the title of which we may perhaps trace the same line of satire which made Swift ridicule the dissenters as Æolists. In all of them the character of the man shines through the style. They are written with considerable force and verve, which is most marked perhaps in the last, where he was attacking with all his heart a sect whom he detested. The diction is correct, but rarely rises to anything like eloquence, and owes its variety chiefly to an occasional homely raciness. But like all his contemporaries, Heylyn always avoids a slipshod style : and we are never allowed to forget that he belonged to a school which followed, as closely as it might, the classical models, and aimed at least, if it did not always succeed in its aim, at giving to history a worthy and dignified literary dress.

H. CRAIK.

FULLER AS AN HISTORIAN

PROCEED we in the next place to verses and old ends of poetry, scattered and dispersed in all parts of the history, from one end to the other; for which he hath no precedent in any historian, Greek or Latin, or any of the national histories of these latter times: the histories of Herodotus Xenophon, Thucydides, and Plutarch, amongst the Greeks; of Cæsar, Livy, Sallust, Tacitus, and Suetonius amongst the Latins afford him neither warrant nor example for it: the like may be affirmed of Eusebius, Socrates, Sozomen, Theodoret, Ruffin, and Evagrius, Church historians all; though they had all the best choice and the most excellent poets of the world to befriend them in it: and he that shall consult the histories of succeeding times, through all the ages of the Church to this present day, will find them all as barren of any encouragements in this kind as the ancients were: nay, whereas Bishop Goodwin in his annals gives us an epitaph of two verses only made on Queen Jane Seymour, and afterwards a copy of eighteen verses on the martyrdom of Archbishop Cranmer; he ushers in the last with this short apology, "*Contra morem Historiæ liceat quæso inserere,*" etc. Let me (saith he), I beseech you, insert these following verses, though otherwise against the rule and laws of history. But what, alas! were eighteen or twenty verses compared with those many hundred (six or seven hundred at the least) which we find in our author; whether to show the universality of his reading in all kind of writers, or his faculty in translating (which when he meets with hard copies he knows how to spare) I shall not determine at the present: certain I am, that by his interlarding of his prose with so many verses he makes the book look rather like a Church-romance (our late romancers being much given to such kind of mixtures) than a well-built ecclesiastical history. And if it be a matter so unconvenient to put a new piece of cloth on an old garment; the putting of so many old

patches on a new piece of cloth must be more unfashionable.
Besides that, many of those old ends are so light and ludicrous,
so little pertinent to the business which he has in hand, that they
serve only to make sport for children (*ut pueris placeas et declam-
atio fias*), and for nothing else.

This leads me to the next impertinency, his raking into the
channel of old popish legends, writ in the darker times of superstition, but written with an honest zeal, and a good intention : as
well to raise the reader to the admiration of the person of whom
they write, as to the emulation of his virtues : but being mixed
with some monkish dotages, the most learned and ingenious men
in the Church of Rome have now laid them by ; and it had been
very well if our author had done so too, but that there must be
something of entertainment for the gentle reader, and to inflame
the reckoning which he pays not for.   But above all things recommend me to his merry tales, and scraps of trencher-jests, frequently
interlaced in all parts of the history ; which, if abstracted from the
rest, and put into a book by themselves, might very well be served
up for a second course to the Banquet of Jests, a supplement to
the old book entitled *Wits, Fits, and Fancies;* or an additional
century to the old *Hundred Merry Tales*, so long since extant.
But standing as they do, they neither do become the gravity of a
Church-historian, nor are consistent with the nature of a sober
argument.   But, as it seems, our author came with the same
thoughts to the writing of this present history as poets anciently
addressed themselves to the writing of comedies, of which thus my
Terence :—

> Poeta cum primum animum ad scribendum appulit,
> Id sibi negotii credidit solum dari,
> Populo ut placerent quas fecisset fabulas.

That is to say,

> Thus poets, when their mind they first apply
> In looser verse to frame a comedy,
> Think there is nothing more for them to do.
> Than please the people whom they speak unto.

(From *Examen Historicum.*)

A ROYAL PROGRESS

HAVING secured herself by this peace with France, and being
at no open enmity with the King of Spain, she resolves to give

herself some pleasure, and thereupon prepareth for her summer's progress. In the course whereof she bestowed a visit upon Cambridge on the 5th of August, where she was honourably received by Mr. Secretary Cecil, being then Chancellor of that University, together with all the Heads of Houses and other students, attired in their academical habits, according to their several and distinct degrees. Her lodging was provided in King's College; the days of her abode there spent in scholastical exercises of philosophy, physic, and divinity; the nights in comedies and tragedies, and other pleasing entertainments. On Wednesday the 7th of the same month she rode through the town, and took a view of all the colleges and halls—the goodly monuments of the piety of her predecessors, and of so many men and women famous in their generations. Which done, she took leave of Cambridge in a Latin oration, in which she gave them great encouragement to pursue their studies; not without giving them some hopes, that if God spared her life and opportunity, she would erect some monument among them of her love to learning, which should not be inferior unto any of her royal ancestors. In which diversion she received such high contentment, that nothing could have seemed to be equal to it, but the like at Oxon, where she was entertained about two years after for seven days together, with the same variety of speeches, interludes, disputations, and other academical expressions of a public joy. In one point, that of Oxford seemed to have the pre-eminence, all things being there both given and taken with so even an hand, that there could be no ground for any emulation, strife, or discord to ensue upon it. But in the midst of these contentments which she had at Cambridge were sown the seeds of those divisions and combustions with which the Church hath been continually distracted to this very day. For so it happened, that Mr. Thomas Preston of King's College, and Mr. Thomas Cartwright of Trinity College were appointed for two of the opponents in a disputation; in which the first, by reason of his comely gesture, pleasing pronunciation, and graceful personage, was both liked and rewarded by her, the other receiving neither reward nor commendation; which so incensed the proud man, too much opinionated of himself and his own abilities, that he retired unto Geneva, where, having thoroughly informed himself of all particulars, both of doctrine and discipline, wherein the Churches of that platform differed from the Church of England, he returned home with an intent to repair his credit, or rather to get himself a name (as did Erostratus in the burning of Diana's temple) by raising such a fire, such combustions in her, as were never to be extinguished (like the fire of Taberah) but by the immediate hand of heaven.

(From *Ecclesia Restaurata.*)

STRAFFORD AND THE KING

BUT now we must look back on the Earl of Strafford, the prosecution of whose impeachment had long been delayed upon some probable hope, that the displeasures of his greatest adversaries might be mitigated by some Court preferments. In order where-unto it was agreed upon (if my intelligence or memory fail not) that the Earl of Bedford should be made lord treasurer, and Pym chancellor of the Exchequer, the Earl of Essex governor of the prince, and that Hampden should be made his tutor, the Lord Saye master of the wards, and Hollis principal secretary in place of Windebank ; the deputyship of Ireland was disposed of also, and some command appointed for the Earl of Warwick in the royal navy. Which earls, together with the Earl of Hertford, and the Lord Kimbolton (eldest son to the Earl of Manchester) were taken at this time into his majesty's council, that they might witness to the rest of that party with what sincerity and piety his majesty's affairs were governed at the council table. And in relation to this purpose the Bishop of London delivered to the king the treasurer's staff, the Earl of Newcastle relinquished the governance of the prince, and the Lord Cottington relinquished his offices both in the Exchequer and the Court of Wards ; there being no doubt but that Bishop Duppa in order to so good a work would relinquish the tutorship of the prince when it should be required of him : so gallantly did these great persons deny them-selves to advance the service of their master. But before all these things were fully settled and performed, the king's mind was altered (but by whom altered, hath been more conjectured than affirmed for certain), which so exasperated them who were con-cerned in this designation, that they pursued the Earl of Strafford with the greatest eagerness. And somewhat to this purpose was hinted in the king's declaration of the 18th of August ; in which he signified what overtures had been made by them, and with what importunity for offices and perferments, what great services should have been done for him, and what other undertaking even to have saved the life of the Earl of Strafford. By which discovery as he blemished the reputes of some principal members in the eyes of many of the people ; so he gave no small cause of wonder to many others, when they were told from his own pen at how cheap rate (a rate which would have cost him nothing) he might have saved the life of such an able and deserving minister.

This design being thus unhappily dashed, the earl was called unto his trial on the 22nd day of March last past ; which being continued many days with great expectation, his adversaries (though the ablest men in the House of Commons) perceived that his defences were so strong, and their proof so weak, that they thought it not safe to leave the judgment of the cause to the House of Peers in way of judicature. For finding that their proofs amounted not to a legal evidence ; and that nothing but legal evidence could prevail in a court of judicature, they resolved to steer their course by another wind, and to call the legislative power to their assistance ; according unto which both Lords and Commons might proceed by the light of their own understanding without further testimony. And so it was declared by Saint John, then solicitor-general, in a conference between the committees of both Houses, April 29, 1641. Where it is said, that although single testimony might be sufficient to satisfy private consciences, yet how far it would have been satisfactory in a judicial way, where forms of law are more to be stood upon, was not so clear ; whereas in this way of Bill, private satisfaction to each man's conscience is sufficient, although no evidence had been given in at all. Thus they resolved it in this case ; but knowing of what dangerous consequence it might be to the lives and fortunes of themselves and the rest of subjects, a saving clause was added to the Bill of Attainder, that it should not be drawn into example for the time to come. By which it was provided, that no judge or judges, justice or justices whatever, shall adjudge or interpret any act or thing to be treason, nor hear or determine any treason, nor in any other manner, than he or they should or ought to have done before the making of this Act, and as if this Act had never been made.

His Majesty understanding how things were carried, resolved to use his best endeavours to preserve the man who had deserved so bravely of him. And therefore, in a speech to both Houses of

Parliament on the first May, absolved him from all treasons
charged upon him ; conjuring them by the merit of his former
graces, and the hopes of greater, not to compel him to do anything against his conscience, to which no worldly consideration
whatever should be able to tempt him. This put the Lords to
such a stand, who were before inclinable enough to that unfortunate gentleman, that multitudes of the rabble were brought
down out of London and Southwark, to cry for speedy justice and
execution ; the names of such as had not voted to the bill, being
posted up in the Palace Yard, by the title of Straffordians and
enemies to the Commonwealth. Which course so terrified the
Lords, that most of them withdrawing themselves from the House of
Peers, the attainder passed, and certain bishops were nominated to
attend the king, for satisfying his conscience, and persuading him
to sign that destructive bill. Never was poor prince brought to
so sad an exigent, between his conscience on one side and the
fears of such a public rupture on the other as seemed to threaten
nothing but destruction to himself and his family. But human
frailty, and the continual solicitation of some about him, so prevailed at last, that on Monday morning, the 9th of May, he put a
most unwilling hand to that fatal bill, issuing a commission unto
certain lords to pass the same into an Act, and with the same to
speed another (which he had also signed with the same penful of
ink) for the continuance of the present Parliament during the
pleasure of the Houses. The Act thus passed on Monday
morning, the earl was brought unto the scaffold on the Wednesday following, desiring earnestly, but in vain, to exchange some
words with the archbishop before his death ; which gave occasion
to a report that a little before his death he had charged his
misfortunes, oversights, and misdemeanours upon the Archbishop
of Canterbury, as the prime author of the same, and had bitterly
cursed the day of their first acquaintance ; which being so
scandalous and dishonourable to this great prelate, I shall lay
down the whole truth in this particular, as it came from the archbishop's own mouth, in the presence of Balfour, a Scot, and then
lieutenant of the Tower, who was required to attest to each
period of it.   (From *Cyprianus Anglicus*.)

JOHN KNOX

THE castle being yielded, and the country quieted, the French returned with their booty, of which their prisoners which they brought along with them made the principal part, not made the tamer by their sufferings in the enemy's galleys, insomuch that when the image of the Virgin Mary was offered to them to be kissed on some solemn occasion, one of them snatched it into his hands, flung it into the sea, and said unto them that brought it, in a jeering manner, that her ladyship was light enough, and might learn to swim. Which desperate and unadvised action (as it was no other) is said by Knox to have produced this good effect, that the Scots were never after tempted to the like idolatries. Knox at this time was prisoner in the galleys among the rest, and, with the rest, released upon the peace made between France and England, at the delivering up of Boulogne ; for which he passed over into England, where he was first made preacher at Berwick, next at Newcastle, afterwards to some church of London, and finally in some other places of the South : so that removing like our late itinerants from one church to another, as he could meet with entertainment, he kept himself within that sanctuary till the death of King Edward, and then betook himself to Geneva for his private studies. From hence he published his desperate doctrine of predestination, which he makes not only to be an impulsive to, but the compulsive cause of men's sins and men's wickednesses : from hence he published his traitorous and seditious pamphlet, entitled *The First Blast of the Trumpet*, in which he writes most bitterly, amongst other things, against the Regimen of Women, aiming therein particularly at the two Maries Queens of Scotland, Mary Queen of England, and Mary Queen-Dowager of Hungary, Governess of the Low Countries for Charles the Fifth : and finally, from hence he published another of the like nature, entitled *An Admonition to Christians ;* in which he makes the Emperor Charles to be worse than Nero, and Mary Queen of England to be nothing better than Jezebel. According to which good beginning, he calls her in his history (but not published hence), that idolatrous and mischievous Mary of the Spaniard's blood, a cruel persecutrix of God's people, as the acts of her unhappy reign did sufficiently witness. In which he comes as close to Calvin as could be desired.

By this means he grew great with Calvin, and the most leading men of the Consistorians, who looked upon him as a proper engine to advance their purposes ; but long he had not stayed amongst them, when he received an invitation from some friends of his of the same temper and affections, as it after proved, to take charge of the Church of Frankfort, to which some learned men and others of the English nation had retired themselves in the reign of Queen Mary : which call he first communicated unto Calvin, by whose encouragement and persuasion he accepted of it, and by his coming rather multiplied than appeased the quarrels which he found amongst them ; but siding with the inconformable party, and knowing so much of Calvin's mind touching the liturgy and rites of the Church of England, he would by no means be persuaded to officiate by it ; and for that cause was forced by Dr. Cox, and others of the learned men who remained there, to forsake the place, as hath been shown at large in another place. Outed at Frankfort, he returns again to his friends at Geneva ; and being furnished with instructions for his future carriage in the cause of his ministry, he prepares for his journey into Scotland, passeth to Dieppe, from thence to England, and at last came, a welcome man, to his native country, which he found miserably divided into sides and factions. Mary their infant Queen had been transported into France at six years of age ; the regency, taken from James, Earl of Arran, given to Mary of Lorraine, the Queen's mother, not well obeyed by many of the nobility and great men of the country, but openly opposed and reviled by those who seemed to be inclinable to the Reformation. To these men Knox applied himself with all care and cunning, preaching from place to place, and from house to house, as opportunity was given him. In which he gathered many churches, and set up many congregations, as if he had been the apostle-general of the Kirk of Scotland ; in all points holding a conformity unto Calvin's platform, even to the singing of David's Psalms in the English metre, the only music he allowed of in God's public service. From villages and private houses he ventured into some of the great towns and more eminent cities, and at the last appeared in Edinburgh itself, preaching in all, and ministering the communion in many places, as he saw occasion. This was sufficient to have raised a greater storm against him than he could have been able to endure ; but he must make it worse by a new provocation. For at the per-suasion of the Earl of Glencairn, and some others of his principal followers, he writes a long letter to the Queen Regent, in which he earnestly persuades her to give ear to the Word of God, according as it was then preached by himself and others : which letter being communicated by the queen to the Archbishop of Glasgow, and dispersed in several copies by Knox himself, gave such a hot alarm to the bishops and clergy, that he was cited to appear in Blackfriars' Church in Edinburgh, on the 15th of May : and though upon advertisement that he came accompanied with so great a train, that it could not be safe for them to proceed against him, he was not troubled at that time, yet he perceived that having made the queen his enemy, he could not hope to remain longer in that kingdom, but first or last he must needs fall into their hands.

(From *Aerius Redivivus.*)

WILLIAM CHILLINGWORTH

[William Chillingworth, the son of a citizen of Oxford, was born in 1602 ; Laud, then a Fellow of St. John's, was his godfather.   Entered at Trinity College in 1618, he graduated two years later, and, in 1628, he was elected a Fellow of his College.   He took from the first an active part in the " Romish " controversy, which then agitated the University, frequently meeting in debate one John Fisher, a Jesuit, who ultimately convinced him that the only refuge from distracting religious conflict was in the bosom of the infallible Roman Catholic Church.   Chillingworth went to Douay in 1630, but returned to Oxford in the following year, and, three years later, declared himself to be again a Protestant, though not yet an Anglican.   It was not till after the publication of his great work, *The Religion of Protestants a safe way to Salvation*, that he consented to subscribe the Articles, and accept the Chancellorship of Salisbury.   Chillingworth was a close friend of Lord Falkland, and with him took the side of Charles the First against the Parliament.   He was taken prisoner on the fall of Arundel Castle, where he had lain ill during the siege, and was almost literally talked to death in January 1644 by Francis Cheynell, a Puritan minister, who attended his funeral, and buried his " corrupt rotten book " with him.]

CHILLINGWORTH had not the reputation of great scholarship. He was rather an incomparable debater.   The picture of him walking in Trinity Gardens looking for some one to argue with shows the habit of the man.   Yet he never argued merely to secure a triumph over an adversary.   His temporary conversion to Roman Catholicism proves his earnestness.   Yet it may fairly be said that this single translation of theory into practice sufficed him.   He did not again face the practical issues of his specula- tions.   Though he arrived at a rationalism that was inconsistent with the idea of a Church, he signed the Articles, as a basis of peace and union, with a subscription which satisfied Laud. Rationalism and toleration were Chillingworth's guiding principles. He recognised the voice of God spoken in Scripture as the only authority in religion, and he allowed the free right of individual reason to interpret the Bible.   The final appeal to the Bible separated him from the Anglicans of Laud's school on the one hand ; and on the other his latitudinarianism roused the bitter hatred of Cheynell and his Puritan friends. *The Religion of Protestants* was a contribution to a controversy between Edward Knott, a Jesuit, and Dr. Potter, Provost of Queen's College, Oxford. Knott opened with a book styled *Charity mistaken, with the want whereof Catholics are unjustly charged for affirming, as they do with grief, that Protestancie, unrepented, destroys Salvation.* Potter retorted with a volume styled *Want of Charity justly charged on all such Romanists as dare (without truth and modesty) affirm that Protestancie destroyeth Salvation.* It was to the Jesuit's second assault, a pamphlet headed *Mercy and Truth or Charity maintained by Catholics*, that Chillingworth set himself to reply in his *Religion of Protestants*. This work is a model of elaborate and close reasoning. Indeed, its elaborateness and closeness stagger the modern student, who is not accustomed to find a matter so taken from the root up. Chillingworth aimed at perfect balance and absolute fairness. He fought his adversary preface by preface, and chapter by chapter, and placed every argument he had to meet before the reader in full and in front of his own answer to it. It is necessary, therefore, to penetrate a dense mass of minor ideas and issues, mainly irrelevant, before reaching the heart of the matter. Yet Chillingworth never relaxes hold of his chief argumentation, never loses sight of the real end which he has in view, and which is not so much to put down the arrogance of Rome and defend the dignity of the Church of England, as to assert the right of free inquiry, and the necessity for personal conviction. The desideratum of both disputants was an infallible means of determining religious truth. Knott maintained that the source of certitude was the Roman Catholic Church. Chillingworth on the other hand, held that the Bible, and the Bible only, was the religion of Protestants. That, of course, is the common doctrine of Protestantism. It is valid only so long as there is general agreement as to the interpretation of the Bible. Chillingworth's contribution to theology is this gloss upon it, that the great principles of religion, as contained in Scripture, are too plain to be mistaken—they are embraced in the Apostle's Creed ; Christians may safely differ upon those matters of speculation which divide the sects. For a plain workaday rule he lays it down that " nothing is necessary to be believed but what is plainly revealed." Scripture tested, save in fundamentals, by the free open mind—the " right reason " he called it—was for Chillingworth the sole source of religious certainty. He bowed to no authority, save the universal tradition which was the common warrant for belief in the Bible. Reason must rule—it being, indeed, a plain improbability for any man to submit his reason but to reason. Chillingworth's argumentative clearness was regarded by Locke as a model. His style is, indeed, admirably suited at once to the matter and to the form of his work. He commands a considerable vocabulary, and although his sentences are often loosely constructed, he writes, when he is at his best, with point and carefully chosen phrase. His rhetorical weapons are retort and homely illustration. His manner of building up an argument is, indeed, worthy of Locke's encomium. If he desires to deal a specially heavy blow he reduces his reasoning to a formal syllogism, and crushes his opponent with it. He has a keen scent for a fallacy, and exposes one when he finds it with trenchant humour. He never condescends to quibbling, but all throughout an argument maintains a dignity which, more than anything else, gave him his strength in debate. It was a mind of no common order that could give unity to a work constructed on such a plan as *The Religion of Protestants*. Even in the graces of composition, Chillingworth excels his contemporaries. The flexibility and pointedness of his style are virtues as great as the richness and power of Hooker's and Bacon's, and, for his purpose, of greater value. The heat of debate sometimes hurries him into undue vehemence, but he never loses his temper. His other works are not important. These are nine sermons, a series of tracts entitled *Additional Discourses*, and a fragment called *The Apostolic Institution of Episcopacy demonstrated*, in which he maintains that Episcopacy is not repugnant to the government settled in and for the Church by the Epistles.

W. WALLACE.

SCRIPTURE INTELLIGIBLE

BUT, speaking truly and properly, the Scripture is not a judge, nor cannot be, but only a sufficient rule for those to judge by that believe it to be the Word of God (as the Church of England and the Church of Rome both do), what they are to believe, and what they are not to believe. I say, sufficiently perfect and sufficiently intelligible in things necessary to all that have understanding, whether they be learned or unlearned. And my reason hereof is convincing and demonstrative, because nothing is necessary to be believed but what is plainly revealed. For to say, that when a place of Scripture, by reason of ambiguous terms, lies indifferent between divers senses, whereof one is true and the other is false, that God obliges men, under pain of damnation, not to mistake through error and human frailty, is to make God a tyrant ; and to say that He requires us certainly to attain that end, for the attaining whereof we have no certain means ; which is to say, that, like Pharoah, He gives no straw, and requires brick ; that He reaps where He sows not ; that He gathers where He strews not ; that He will not be pleased with our utmost endeavours to please Him, without full, and exact, and never-failing performance ; that His will is that we should do what He knows we cannot do ; that He will not accept of us according to that which we have, but requireth of us what we have not. Which whether it can consist with His goodness, and His wisdom, and with His Word, I leave to honest men to judge. If I should send a servant to Paris, or Rome, or Jerusalem, and he using his utmost diligence not to mistake his way, yet notwithstanding meeting often with such places where the road is divided into several ways, whereof every one is as likely to be true and as likely to be false as any other, should at length mistake and go out of the way, would not any man say that I were an impotent, foolish, and unjust master, if I should be offended with him for so doing ? And shall we not tremble to impute that to God which we would take in foul scorn if it were imputed to ourselves ?

Certainly, I for my part fear I should not love God if I should think so strangely of Him.

Again, when you say that unlearned and ignorant men cannot understand Scripture, I would desire you to come out of the clouds, and tell us what you mean; whether, that they cannot understand any Scripture, or that they cannot understand so much as is sufficient for their direction to heaven. If the first, I believe the learned are in the same case. If the second, every man's experience will confute you; for who is there that is not capable of a sufficient understanding of the story, the precepts, the promises, and the threats of the Gospel? If the third, that they may understand something but not enough for their salvation; I ask you, first, Why then doth St. Paul say to Timothy, The Scriptures are able to make him wise unto salvation? Why doth St. Austin say, *Ea quæ manifeste posita sunt in sacris scripturis, omnia continent quæ pertinent ad fidem, moresque vivendi?* Why does every one of the four Evangelists entitle their book, The Gospel, if any necessary and essential part of the Gospel were left out of it? Can we imagine that either they omitted something necessary out of ignorance, not knowing it to be necessary? or, knowing it to be so, maliciously concealed it? or, out of negligence, did the work they had undertaken by halves. If none of these things can without blasphemy be imputed to them, considering they were assisted by the Holy Ghost in this work, then certainly it most evidently follows that every one of them writ the whole Gospel of Christ; I mean, all the essential and necessary parts of it. So that if we had no other book of Scripture but one of them alone, we should not want anything necessary to salvation. And what one of them hath more than another, it is only profitable, and not necessary; necessary indeed to be believed, because revealed; but not therefore revealed because it is necessary to be believed.

Neither did they write only for the learned, but for all men. This being one special means of the preaching of the Gospel, which was commanded to be preached, not only to learned men, but to all men. And therefore, unless we will imagine the Holy Ghost and them to have been wilfully wanting to their own desire and purpose, we must conceive that they intended to speak plain, even to the capacity of the simplest; at least, touching all things necessary to be published by them and believed by us.

(From *The Religion of Protestants a Safe Way to Salvation.*)

FAITH AND UNDERSTANDING

THE third condition you require to faith is, that our assent to
Divine truths should not only be unknown and unevident by any
human discourse, but that absolutely also it should be obscure in
itself, and, ordinarily speaking, be void even of supernatural
evidence.   Which words must have a very favourable construction,
or they will not be sense.   For who can make anything of these
words, taken properly, that faith must be an unknown, unevident
assent, or an assent absolutely obscure ?   I had always thought
that known and unknown, obscure and evident, had been affections
not of our assent, but the object of it ; not of our belief, but
the thing believed.   For well may we assent to a thing unknown,
obscure, or unevident ; but that our assent itself should be called
therefore unknown or obscure, seems to me as great an im-
propriety, as if I should say, your sight were green or blue,
because you see something that is so.   In other places, therefore,
I answer your words, but here I must answer your meaning ;
which I conceive to be, that it is necessary to faith that the
objects of it, the points which we believe, should not be so
evidently certain, as to necessitate our understanding to an
assent, that so there might be some merit in faith, as you love to
speak (who will not receive, no, not from God himself, but a
pennyworth for a penny), but as we, some obedience in it, which
can hardly have place where there is no possibility of disobedi-
ence ; as there is not, where the understanding does all, and the
will nothing.   Now, seeing the religion of Protestants, though it
be much more credible than yours, yet is not pretended to have
the absolute evidence of sense or demonstration ; therefore I
might let this doctrine pass without exception, for any prejudice
that can redound to us by it.   But yet I must not forbear to tell
you, that your discourse proves indeed this condition requisite to
the merit, but yet not to the essence of faith ; without it faith were
not an act of obedience, but yet faith may be faith without it ;
and this you must confess, unless you will say either the apostles
believed not the whole Gospel which they preached, or that they
were not eye-witnesses of a great part of it ; unless you will
question St. John for saying, " That which we have seen with our
eyes, and which our hands have handled, etc., declare we unto

you "; nay, our Saviour himself for saying, "Thomas, because thou seest, thou believest; blessed are they which have not seen, and yet have believed." Yet, if you will say, that in respect of the things which they saw, the apostles' assent was not pure and proper and mere faith, but somewhat more, an assent containing faith, but superadding to it, I will not contend with you, for it will be a contention about words. But then again I must crave leave to tell you, that the requiring this condition is, in my judgment a plain revocation of the former. For had you made the matter of faith either naturally or supernaturally evident, it might have been a fitly attempered and duly proportioned object for an absolute certainty natural or supernatural, but requiring as you do, "that faith should be an absolute knowledge of a thing not absolutely known, an infallible certainty of a thing, which though it is in itself, yet is not made to us to appear to be, infallibly certain," to my understanding you speak impossibilities. And truly for one of your religion to do so, is but a good decorum. For the matter and object of your faith being so full of contradictions, a contradictious faith may very well become a contradictious religion. Your faith, therefore, if you please to have it so, let it be a free, necessitated, certain, uncertain, evident, obscure, prudent and foolish, natural and supernatural, unnatural assent. But they which are unwilling to believe nonsense themselves, or persuade others to do so, it is but reason they should make the faith, wherewith they believe, an intelligible, compossible, consistent thing, and not define it by repugnances. Now nothing is more repugnant, than that a man should be required to give most certain credit unto that which cannot be made to appear most certainly credible; and if it appear to him to be so, then it is not obscure that it is so. For if you speak of an acquired rational, discursive faith, certainly these reasons, which make the object seem credible, must be the cause of it; and consequently the strength and firmity of my assent must rise and fall, together with the apparent credibility of the object. If you speak of a supernatural infused faith, then you either suppose it infused by the former means, and then that which was said before must be said again; for whatsoever effect is wrought merely by means, must bear proportion to, and cannot exceed, the virtue of the means by which it is wrought. As nothing by water can be made more cold than water, nor by fire more hot than fire, nor by honey more sweet than honey, nor by gall more bitter than gall : or if you will suppose it infused without means, then that power which infuseth into the understanding assent, which bears analogy to sight in the eye, must also infuse evidence, that is, visibility into the object : and look what degree of assent is infused into the understanding, at least, the same degree of evidence must be infused into the object. And for you to require a strength of credit beyond the appearance of the object's credibility, is all one as if you should require me to go ten mile an hour upon a horse that will go but five ; to discern a man certainly through a mist or cloud, that makes him not certainly discernible ; to hear a sound more clearly than it is audible ; to understand a thing more fully than it is intelligible : and he that doth so, I may well expect that his next injunction will be, that I must see something that is invisible, hear something inaudible, understand something that is wholly unintelligible. For he that demands ten of me, knowing I have but five, does in effect as if he demanded five, knowing that I have none : and by like reason, you requiring that I should see things further than they are visible, require I should see something invisible ; and in requiring that I believe something more firmly than it is made to me evidently credible, you require in effect that I believe something which appears to me incredible, and while it does so. I deny not but that I am bound to believe the truth of many texts of Scripture, the sense whereof is to me obscure, and to human understandings incomprehensible ; but then it is to be observed, that not the sense of such texts, nor the manner of these things, is that which I am bound to believe, but the truth of them. But that I should believe the truth of anything, the truth whereof cannot be made evident with an evidence proportionable to the degree of faith required of me, this I say for any man to be bound to do is unjust and unreasonable, because to do it is impossible.

(From the Same.)

SAMUEL RUTHERFORD

[Rutherford was born near Jedburgh in 1600, and educated at Edinburgh University, where he became Professor of Humanity in 1623. In 1625 he left the University, and from 1627 to 1639 (with a temporary ejection for non-conformity), he was minister of Anwoth in Galloway. In 1639 he was appointed Professor of Divinity at St. Andrews. From 1642 to 1647 he was in London as a member of the Westminster Assembly of Divines. On his return he became Principal of the New College in St. Andrews, and subsequently Rector of the University. He died in 1661. His principal works were *Exercitationes Apologeticæ* (Amsterdam, 1636), *Plea for Paul's Presbytery in Scotland* (1642), *The Due Right of Presbyteries*, and *Lex, Rex* (1644), *The Trial and Triumph of Faith* (sermons, 1645), *Divine Right of Church Government and Excommunication* (1646), *Christ Dying and Drawing Sinners to Himself* (sermons, 1647), *A Survey of the Spiritual Antichrist* (1648), *A Free Disputation against Pretended Liberty of Conscience* (1649), *The Covenant of Life Opened* (1655), *Influences of the Life of Grace* (1659), and *An Examination of Arminianism*, and the *Letters* (dating from 1639 to 1661), both of which were published posthumously. Several editions of the *Letters* have been issued in the present century, and at least one of *Lex, Rex*.]

RUTHERFORD is a writer most of whose works have a memorial only in the graveyard of history. There was a moment when the Church which Knox had founded in the North seemed about to triumph in England also. Rutherford was at that moment the literary champion of Presbytery, and as such he was pilloried by Milton in the famous sonnet : "On the new Forcers of Conscience," ending in the line " New presbyter is but old priest writ large." His principal controversial work, *Lex, Rex : The Law and the Prince, a Dispute for the just Prerogative of King and People*, is a medley of politics and theology. In this book the revolutionary theories of the Scottish school which Buchanan and Knox had inaugurated, were for the first time expounded for the practical guidance of Englishmen. Fifty years before, Sir Robert Cecil expressed the current theory of sovereignty, when he described himself as " A vassal to the Creator's celestial crea-

ture," Queen Elizabeth. Fifty years later, the great preacher
Bourdaloue, who was nothing if not sincere, assured James the
Second's exiled queen, Mary of Modena, in a sermon before the
French Court, that God had chosen her " to display united in her
person all the perfection of Christianity, with all the greatness of
the age." Rutherford sought to bring kings and queens from
heaven to earth. He argued that the right to rule is divine only
in so far as it is based upon a justly observed contract, express
or implied, between ruler and people. " What excellency he hath
as a man is the excellency of one mortal man, and cannot make
him eminent in dignity, and in the absolute consideration of the
excellency of a man, to be above many men and a whole
kingdom." Nor is the ruler above criticism, for "in the
Pastors, Doctors, and Elders of the Church, there is a ministerial
power, as servants under Christ, in His authority and name, to
rebuke and censure kings." On such a theory self-defence
against a sovereign, and even retaliation, are obviously in certain
circumstances quite justifiable. *Lex, Rex* was not a philosophical
treatise, such as the *Leviathan*. Both in form and in substance
it was a long pamphlet, adapted to the needs of the moment ; it
had a great vogue in the five years preceding the execution of
Charles I., and again, in the next generation, among the Cove-
nanters. The Revolution of 1688 justified its principles, but at
the same time extinguished its vitality, for it had not the saving
gift of style, and its scholastic argumentation could not in any
case have long outlived the seventeenth century. Rutherford's
other controversial works are mainly directed against the Arminians and Antinomians, who have ceased to be interesting save
in the pages of *Hudibras*.

We pass from the brawls of the market-place to the cloistered,
star-lit seclusion of those *Letters*, which the evangelical succession, from Baxter to Spurgeon, has united to declare seraphic
and divine. Like Knox, Rutherford was a great father-confessor
or director of souls. Knox, however, was no mystic. Rutherford
had a quasi-oriental faculty of self-absorption in his ideal of
" heavenly love." This quality received partial expression in his
sermons, but it is in his letters, where he was under no restraint,
that its full development appears. The letters are the unstringing
of a bent bow, the channel by which he delivered his soul. They
are full of sympathy, but it is the sympathy rather of an angel
writing from the seventh heaven than of a fellow-man. As an

illustration, it may suffice to compare his efforts at consolation
with those of two other men of a different stamp. Take a letter
from Oliver Cromwell to his brother-in-law, whose son had been
killed at Marston Moor. " Sir, God hath taken away your eldest
son by a cannon-shot. It brake his leg. We were necessitated
to have it cut off, whereof he died. Sir, you know my own trials
this way ; but the Lord supported me with this, that the Lord
took him into the happiness we all pant for, and live for. . . .
You have cause to bless the Lord. He is a glorious saint in
heaven ; wherein you ought exceedingly to rejoice." Here the
sympathy is concrete and visible, but the tone is almost Roman
in its repression. Take again, a letter from Fénélon to the Duc
de Chevreuse. " Monsieur votre fils réussissait au milieu du
monde empesté : c'est ce succès qui afflige, et c'est ce succès qui
a fait trancher le fil de ses jours, par un conseil de miséricorde
pour lui et pour les siens. Il faut adorer Dieu, et se taire."
What an admirable delicacy and tenderness of touch, with just a
shade of artifice ! The cause for rejoicing, which Cromwell
expresses with a soldier's bluntness, Fénélon barely suggests.
Now take one of Rutherford's letters to a mother on the death of
her child. " A going down star is not annihilated, but shall
appear again. If he hath casten his bloom and flower, the bloom
is fallen in heaven in Christ's lap ; and as he was lent a while to
time, so is he given now to eternity, which will take yourself ;
and the difference of your shipping and his to heaven and
Christ's shore, the land of life, is only in some few years, which
weareth every day shorter, and some short and soon-reckoned
summers will give you a meeting with him. But what, with
him ? Nay, with better company—with the Chief and Leader of
the heavenly troops, that are riding on white horses, that are
triumphing in glory. . . . Let all your visitations speak all the
letters of your Lord's summons. They cry, O vain world ! O
bitter sin ! O short and uncertain time ! O fair eternity, that is
above sickness and death ! O kingly and princely bridegroom !
hasten glory's marriage, shorten time's short-spun and soon-
broken thread, and conquer sin ! O happy and blessed death,
that golden bridge laid over by Christ my Lord, betwixt time's
clay-banks and heaven's shore ! " Rutherford, let it be noticed,
first presents a vivid picture of those aspects of death which
are most consolatory, and so far he is at one with Fénélon and
Cromwell ; but having done this, he goes further : he becomes

aggressor instead of suppliant, and commands, rather than entreats, the sufferer to share his own ecstatic vision.   This gift of
communicating a fervid enthusiasm is the secret of his style, as
it appears in the letters ; but it has powerful allies in the aptness
of his comparisons, in an abundant flow of racy Scottish idiom,
in the simplicity and vigour of his metaphors (which with two
principal exceptions are mainly chosen from out-door country
life), and in his ready mintage of golden sayings which can be
withdrawn and enshrined.   The exceptional metaphors that give
an air of alternate extravagance and quaintness to nearly every
page of the *Letters* are borrowed, somewhat incongruously, from
the imagery of the Song of Solomon, and from the devious
practice of old Scots Law.   Those of the former class at times
sound in modern ears painfully grotesque and irreverent, and
blemish the artistic form of a correspondence otherwise, of its
kind, unmatched in our literature.   But similar allusions may be
found in the works of Crashaw and Baxter, to mention only two
of Rutherford's contemporaries, and we must not forget that the
seventeenth-century Puritan revelled in symbolical interpretation,
and demanded an unrestrained expression of personal religious
experience.   The *Letters*, as a Puritan classic, deserve a place
beside *The Saint's Rest* and *The Pilgrim's Progress*.

JAMES MILLER DODDS.

FLIGHT NO LAWFUL MEANS OF ESCAPE FOR AN OPPRESSED PEOPLE

Now a private man may fly, and that is his second necessity, and violent re-offending is the third mean of self-preservation. But with leave, violent re-offending is necessary to a private man, when his second mean, to wit, flight, is not possible, and cannot attain the end, as in the case of David : if flight do not prevail, Goliah's sword and an host of armed men are lawful. So to a church and a community of Protestants, men, women, aged, sucking children, sick, and diseased, who are pressed either to be killed, or forsake religion and Jesus Christ, flight is not the second mean, nor a mean at all, because, (1) not possible, and therefore not a natural mean of preservation : for 1st, the aged, the sick, the sucking infants, and sound religion in the posterity cannot flee, flight here is physically and by nature's necessity unpossible, and therefore no lawful mean. 2nd, if Christ have a promise that the ends of the earth (Ps. ii. 8) and the isles shall be His possession (Isa. xlix. 1), I see not how natural defence can put us to flee, even all Protestants, and their seed, and the weak and sick, whom we are obliged to defend as ourselves, both by the law of nature and grace. I read that seven wicked nations and idolatrous were cast out of their land to give place to the Church of God, to dwell there ; but show me a warrant in nature's law and in God's word that three kingdoms of Protestants, their seed, aged, sick, sucking children, should flee out of England, Scotland, Ireland, and leave religion and the land to a king and to papists, prelates and bloody Irish, and atheists : and therefore to a church and community having God's right and man's law to the land, violent re-offending is their second mean (next to supplications and declarations, etc.), and flight is not required of them, as of a private man. Yea, flight is not necessarily required of a private man, but where it is a possible mean of self-preservation, violent and unjust invasion of a private man, which is unavoidable may be obviated with violent re-offending. Now the unjust invasion made on Scotland in 1640, for refusing the service-book, or rather the idolatry of the Mass, therein intended, was unavoidable, it was unpossible for the Protestants, their old and sick, their women and sucking children to flee over sea, or to have shipping betwixt the king's bringing an army on them at Dunslaw, and the prelates charging of the ministers to receive the mass-book. Althusius saith well, " Though private men may flee ; but the estates if they flee, they do not their duty to commit a country, religion and all to a lion." Let not any object, we may not devise a way to fulfil the prophecy (Ps. ii. 8, 9, Isa. xlix. 1). It is true, if the way be our own sinful way ; nor let any object, a colony went to New-England and fled the persecution. Answer, true, but if fleeing be the only mean after supplication, there was no more reason that one colony should go to New-England, than it is necessary and by a divine law obligatory, that the whole Protestants in the three kingdoms according to Royalists' doctrine, are to leave their native country and religion to one man and to popish idolators and atheists willing to worship idols with them ; and whether then shall the Gospel be, which we are obliged to defend with our lives ?

(From *Lex, Rex.*)

LETTER TO JEAN BROWN

MISTRESS—grace, mercy, and peace be to you. I am glad that ye go on at Christ's back in this dark and cloudy time. It were good to sell other things for Him ; for when all these days are over, we shall find it our advantage that we have taken part with Christ. I confidently believe His enemies shall be His footstool, and that He shall make green flowers, dead, withered hay, when the honour and glory shall fall off them, like the bloom or flower of a green herb shaken with the wind. It were not wisdom for us to think that Christ and the Gospel will come and sit down at our fireside ; nay, but we must go out of our warm houses and seek Christ and His Gospel. It is not the sunny side of Christ that we must look to, and we must not forsake Him for want of that ; but must set our face against what may befall us in following on, till He and we be through the briars and bushes on the dry ground. Our soft nature would be borne through the troubles of this miserable life in Christ's arms. And it is His wisdom, who knoweth our mould, that His bairns go wet-shod and cold-footed to heaven. Oh how sweet a thing were it for us to learn to make our burdens light by framing our hearts to the burden, and making our Lord's will a law! I find Christ and His cross not so ill to please, nor yet such troublesome guests as men call them. Nay, I think patience should make Christ's water good wine, and this dross good metal; and we have cause to wait on, for ere it be long our Master will be at us, and bring this whole world out before the sun and the daylight in their blacks and whites. Happy are they who are found watching. Our sand-glass is not so long as we need to weary: time will eat away, and root out our woes and sorrow: our heaven is in the bud, and growing up to an harvest, why then should we not follow on, seeing our span-length of time will come to an inch? Therefore, I commend Christ to you, as your last living and longest living Husband, and the staff of your old age: let Him have now the rest of your days; and think not much of a storm upon the ship that Christ saileth in; there shall no passenger fall overboard; but the crazed ship and the sea-sick passenger shall come to land safe. I am in as sweet communion with Christ as a poor sinner can be; and am only pained that He hath much beauty and fairness, and I little love; He great power and mercy, and I little faith; He much light, and I bleared eyes. O, that I saw him in the sweetness of His love, and in His marriage clothes, and were over head and ears in love with that Princely One, Christ Jesus my Lord! Alas, my riven dish and running-out vessel can hold little of Christ Jesus! I have joy in this, that I would not refuse death before I put Christ's lawful heritage in men's trysting; and what know I, if they would have pleased both Christ and me? Alas! that this land hath put Christ to open rouping, and to an "Any man more bids?" Blessed are they who would hold the crown on His head, and buy Christ's honour with their own losses. I rejoice to hear your son John is coming to visit Christ and taste of His love. I hope he shall not lose his pains, or rue of that choice. I had always (as I said often to you) a great love to dear Mr. John Brown, because I thought I saw Christ in him more than in his brethren; fain would I write to him, to stand by my sweet

Master, and I wish ye would let him read my letter, and the joy
I have, if he will appear for, and side with my Lord Jesus.
Grace, grace be with you.—Yours, in his sweet Lord Jesus.

S. R.

ABERDEEN, 13*th March* 1637.

. (From the *Letters.*)

VIOLENT AND NATURAL DEATH

VIOLENCE more or less is an accident of death, as it is the same
hand folded in, or the fingers stretched out ; violent death is but
death on horseback, and with wings, or a stroke with the fist, as
the other death is a blow with the palms of the hand.   Natural
death is death going on foot, and creeping with a slower pace ;
violent death unites all its forces at once, and takes the city by
storm, and comes with sourer and blacker visage.   Death natural
divides itself in many several bits of deaths ; old age being a long
spun out death, and nature seems to render the city more
willingly, and death comes with a whiter and a milder visage ;
the one has a salter bite, and teeth of steel and iron ; the other
has softer fingers, and takes asunder the boards of the clay-
tabernacle more leisurely, softly, tenderly, and with less din, as
not willing that death should appear death, but a sleep ; the
violent death is as when apples green and raw are plucked off
the tree, or when flowers in the bud, and young, are plucked up
by the roots ; the other way of dying is, as when apples are
ripened and are filled with well-boiled summer sap, and fall off
the tree of their own accord in the eater's mouth ; or when
flowers wither on the stalk.   Some dying full of days have like
banqueters, a surfeit of time, others are suddenly plucked away
when they are green ; but which of the ways you die, not to die
in the Lord is terrible ; ye may know ye shall die by the fields
ye grow on, while ye live ; a believer on Christ, breathes in
Christ, speaks, walks, prays, believes, eateth, drinketh, sickens,
dies in Christ ; Christ is the soil he is planted in, he groweth on
the banks of the paradise of God ; when he falleth, he cannot fall
wrong ; some are trees growing on the banks of the river of fire
and brimstone ; when God hews down the tree, and death fells them,
the tree can fall no otherwise than in hell ; O how sweet to be

in Christ, and to grow as a tree planted on the banks of the river of life, when such die they fall in Christ's lap and in His bosom ; be the death violent or natural ! it is all one whether a strong gale and a rough storm shore the child of God on the new Jerusalem's dry land, or if a small calm blast, even with rowing of oars, bring the passenger to heaven, if once he be in that goodly land.

(From *Christ Dying*.)

JOHN EARLE

[Born at York about 1601. According to Wood, graduated B.A. and was elected to a fellowship at Merton College, Oxford, in 1619. He was a resident in the University in 1628, the date of the publication, by Edward Blount, of his *Microcosmography, or A Piece of the World discovered in Essays and Characters.* King Charles II., whose tutor he had been, and whose fortunes he had followed in exile, conferred upon him in 1662 the Bishopric of Worcester, whence in 1663 he was promoted to Salisbury. He died at Oxford in 1665.]

EARLE'S epitaph in Merton College Chapel, conformably with the fact that he lived in an age of academical studies from which we are but just emerging, based his literary reputation upon his presumably excellent Latin versions of two standard English books. But although no reference was allowed on his tomb to the one work in the vulgar tongue which has secured to him a place among our men of letters, the inscription suggests precisely enough the antithetical mixture which distinguished him " as an author," while it commended him " as a man." " *Potuit in aulâ vivere, et mundum spernere :* he contrived to live at court, while contemning the world." No sentence could better summarise that which attracts and that which edifies in the character-sketches of this quick-witted observer and high-minded censor of his times.

It would be rather absurd to treat a slender collection of " detached leaves " like the *Microcosmography* (to which in later editions new detachments were from time to time added) as a classic of our prose-literature ; but there is no difficulty in accounting for its prolonged popularity, and good reason for approving the soundness of the judgment with which it found favour. It fell in, as is the case with all but possibly a very few successful books (and I think I might omit the qualification), with a current of public predilection ; yet its author knew how to preserve, or preserved unconsciously, the individual note.

These books of *Characters*—short essays delineating in brief and quasi-aphoristic form particular types of men or women—were an appropriate product of what may (roughly) be called the Jacobean age. On the one hand, the creativeness of dramatic characterisation had exhausted, or was exhausting itself; on the other, the introspection which Puritanism had begun to enforce called for the comparisons without which no examination of self seems to be altogether complete. The literary form suited to this still real, however extenuated, demand was ready to hand. Its inventor Theophrastus had, like Earle, lived in an age marked, to borrow the words of Professor Jebb, by a reaction from creating to analysing ; and the century in which the *Microcosmography* was written gave birth to scores of imitations of so congenial a model. Earle, who unlike some of these had most certainly read Theophrastus, is differentiated from them all—including the Master—by characteristics of his own. Inasmuch as while the Greek original at once inspired and controlled his method, the *Characters* which Earle had immediately before him were undoubtedly those of Overbury, it may suffice to compare these two series. The wider variety of observation on the part of the courtier is more than compensated by the greater depth and refinement in the university scholar ; but while Overbury displays on occasion a graphic skill of which Earle's sketches, as it were, offer hardly more than a promise, he cannot be said to be Earle's superior either in pure wit, or I think in the conception of those grave counterfoils so effectively introduced by both authors. What, in the former way, could be better than the turn in Earle's very first Character, *A Child :* " The older he grows, he is a stair lower from God ; and, like his first father, much worse in his breeches ? " Or the touches in the Character of *A Plain Country Fellow*, who " never praises God but on good ground "; and who thinks " Noah's flood the greatest plague that ever was, not because it drowned the world, but spoiled the grass ? " Or, as a mere matter of quaint novelty of style, the final reference of *A Young Raw Preacher* to " a chamber-maid, with whom we will leave him now in the bonds of wedlock. Next Sunday you shall have him again ? "

The seventy-eight types which in the most enlarged edition of the book make up the *World in Small*, display less diversity than might perhaps have been expected from so numerous a selection. But the writer, it must be remembered, had, unlike Overbury, not yet begun his travels, and was a resident college fellow in a University whose praiseworthy efforts to be a world in itself were limited by circumstance even more narrowly in his time than in ours. Accordingly, though his ideal is the *Contemplative Man*, who "is a scholar in this great university, the world," he excels in the presentation of academical and clerical types, in which, down to the days of *Robert Elsmere*, there has remained individuality enough to furnish forth excellent tragicomedy. Such are the *Young Raw Preacher* and his admirable "opposite," the *Grave Divine;* and that other pair of contrasts, the *Down-right Scholar*, who "cannot speak to a dog in his own dialect," and the *Mere Young Gentleman of the University*, who "of all things, endures not to be mistaken for a scholar." These portraits, together with such *pendants* as *An Old College Butler* and *A University Dun*, are drawn from the life; whereas those taken from town-life, like the *Tobacco-seller* and *Paul's Walk*, are comparatively colourless. But the University or scholar's point of view is apparent throughout in the illustrations which spring up ready to the author's use; in him it is not far-fetched to define the *Self-conceited Man* as one who "prefers Ramus before Aristotle, and Paracelsus before Galen, and whosoever with most paradox is commended, and Lipsius his hopping style, before either Tully or Quintilian"; or to paraphrase a *Shopkeeper* as "the title-page or index of that well-stuffed book, his shop." But Earle is preserved from pedantry by the liveliness of his wit, while his wit itself has in it a salt nobler than the Attic—the savour of pure and unaffected piety. The vicissitudes of his career united with the characteristics of his intellect to make him an opponent of Puritanism, but not a mocking opponent; and it is noticeable how, in his forcible character of *A Profane Man*, he describes him as one who "will take upon him with oaths to pelt some tenderer man out of his company, and makes good sport at his conquest over the Puritan fool." He makes no secret of his aversion from extravagances which even as a mere matter of style he must have naturally been inclined to dislike, above all when he sees them exaggerated, as all such things are exaggerated when taken up by women, in a *She Precise Hypocrite*, one of his most vigorous likenesses. But his sympathies, as the later Characters make it specially evident, are with earnestness of faith, as well as with the clearness of judgment which he misses in *A Sceptic in Religion*. Again, it is interesting to note how this type of academic half-heartedness rather than double-facedness should have survived to days when Socinus and Vorstius, as well as "the zeal of Amsterdam," have been superseded by other heresiarchs, and by other short roads to salvation. Like most satirists (though no doubt there are notable instances on the other side) Earle was a conservative to the core ; but not one of the rank and file who, like his *Vulgar-Spirited Man*, " have no lifting thoughts."

A. W. WARD.

A PRETENDER TO LEARNING

IS one that would make others more fools than himself; for though he know nothing, he would not have the world know so much. He conceits nothing in learning but the opinion, which he seeks to purchase without it, though he might with less labour cure his ignorance, than hide it. He is indeed a kind of scholar-mountebank, and his art, our delusion. He is trickt out in all the accoutrements of learning, and at the first encounter none passes better. He is oftener in his study, than at his book, and you cannot pleasure him better, than to deprehend him. Yet he hears you not till the third knock, and then comes out very angry, as interrupted. You find him in his slippers, and a pen in his ear, in which formality he was asleep. His table is spread wide with some classic folio, which is as constant to it as the carpet, and hath laid open in the same page this half year. His candle is always a longer sitter up than himself, and the boast of his window at midnight. He walks much alone in the posture of meditation, and has a book still before his face in the fields. His pocket is seldom without a Greek Testament, or Hebrew Bible, which he opens only in the church, and that when some stander by looks over. He has his sentences for company, some scatterings of Seneca and Tacitus, which are good upon all occasions. If he read any thing in the morning, it comes up all at dinner: and as long as that lasts, the discourse is his. He is a great plagiary of tavern-wit: and comes to sermons only that he may talk of Austin. His parcels are the mere scrapings from company, yet he complains at parting what time he has lost. He is wondrously capricious to seem a judgment, and listens with a sour attention to what he understands not. He talks much of Scaliger and Causabon and the Jesuits, and prefers some un-heard-of Dutch name before them all. He has verses to bring in upon these and these hints, and it shall go hard but he will wind in his opportunity. He is critical in a language he cannot construe, and speaks seldom under Arminius in divinity. His business and retirement and caller away is his study, and he protests no delight to it comparable. He is a great nomenclator of authors, which he has read in general in the catalogue, and in particular in the title, and goes seldom so far as the dedication. He never talks of any thing but learning, and learns all from talking. Three encounters with the same men pump him, and then he only puts in, or gravely says nothing. He has taken pains to be an ass, though not to be a scholar, and is at length discovered and laught at.

(From *Microcosmographie*.)

A SCEPTIC IN RELIGION

Is one that hangs in the balance with all sorts of opinions, whereof not one but stirs him and none sways him. A man guiltier of credulity than he is taken to be ; for it is out of his belief of every thing that he fully believes nothing. Each religion scares him from its contrary : none persuades him to itself. He would be wholly a Christian, but that he is something of an atheist, and wholly an atheist, but that he is partly a Christian ; and a perfect heretic, but that there are so many to distract him. He finds reason in all opinions, truth in none : indeed the least reason perplexes him, and the best will not satisfy him. He is at most a confused and wild Christian, not specialised, by any form, but capable of all. He uses the land's religion, because it is next him, yet he sees not why he may not take the other, but he chooses this, not as better, but because there is not a pin to choose. He finds doubts and scruples better than resolves them, and is always too hard for himself. His learning is too much for his brain, and his judgment too little for his learning, and his over-opinion of both spoils all. Pity it was his mischance of being a scholar : for it does only distract and irregulate him and the world by him. He hammers much in general upon our opinions' uncertainty, and the possibility of erring makes him not venture on what is true. He is troubled at this naturalness of religion to countries, that Protestantism should be born so in England and Popery abroad, and that fortune and the stars should so much share in it. He likes not this connexion of the Common-weal and divinity, and fears it may be an arch-practice of state. In our differences with Rome he is strangely unfixt, and a new man every day, as his last discourse-book's meditations transport him. He could like the grey hairs of Popery, did not some dotages there stagger him; he would come to us sooner, but our new name affrights him. He is taken with their miracles but doubts an imposture; he conceives of our doctrine better, but it seems too empty and naked. He cannot drive into his fancy the circumscription of truth to our corner, and is as hardly persuaded to think their old legends true. He approves well of our faith, and more of their works, and is sometimes much affected at the zeal of Amsterdam. His conscience interposes itself betwixt duellers, and whilst it would part both, is by both wounded. He will sometimes propend much to us upon the reading a good writer and at Bellarmine recoils as far back again; and the fathers jostle him from one side to another. Now Socinus and Vorstius afresh torture him, and he agrees with none worse than himself. He puts his foot into heresies tenderly, as a cat in the water, and pulls it out again, and still something unanswered delays him, yet he bears away some parcel of each, and you may sooner pick all religions out of him than one. He cannot think so many wise men should be in error, nor so many honest men out of the way, and his wonder is doubled, when he sees these oppose one another. He hates authority as the tyrant of reason, and you cannot anger him worse than with a Father's *dixit*, and yet that many are not persuaded with reason, shall authorise his doubt. In sum, his whole life is a question, and his salvation a greater, which death only concludes, and then he is resolved.

(From the Same.)

A VULGAR-SPIRITED MAN

IS one of the herd of the world. One that follows merely the common cry, and makes it louder by one. A man that loves none but who are publicly affected, and he will not be wiser than the rest of the town. That never owns a friend after an ill name, or some general imputation though he knows it most unworthy. That opposes to reason, Thus men say, and Thus most do, and

Thus the world goes ; and thinks this enough to poise the other. That worships men in place, and those only, and thinks all a great man speaks oracles. Much taken with my lord's jest, and repeats you it all to a syllable. One that justifies nothing out of fashion, nor any opinion out of the applauded way. That thinks certainly all Spaniards and Jesuits very villains, and is still cursing the Pope and Spinola. One that thinks the gravest cassock the best scholar : and the best clothes the finest man. That is taken only with broad and obscene wit, and hisses any thing too deep for him. That cries Chaucer for his money above all our English poets, because the voice has gone so, and he has read none. That is much ravisht with such a noble man's courtesy, and would venture his life for him, because he put off his hat. One that is foremost still to kiss the King's hand, and cries " God bless his Majesty " loudest. That rails on all men condemned and out of favour, and the first that says, Away with the traitors : yet struck with much ruth at executions, and for pity to see a man die, could kill the hangman. That comes to London to see it, and the pretty things in it, and the chief cause of his journey the bears : that measures the happiness of the kingdom by the cheapness of corn ; and conceives no harm of state, but ill trading. Within this compass, too, come those that are too much wedged into the world, and have no lifting thoughts above those things that call to thrive, to do well, and preferment only the grace of God. That aim all studies at this mark, and show you poor scholars as an example to take heed by. That think the prison and want, a judgment for some sin, and never like well hereafter of a jail-bird. That know no other content but wealth, bravery, and the town-pleasures ; that think all else but idle speculation, and the philosophers mad-men : in short, men that are carried away with all outwardnesses, shows, appearances, the stream, the people ; for there is no man of worth but has a piece of singularity, and scorns something.

(From the Same.)

OWEN FELLTHAM

[Owen Felltham was born early in the seventeenth century. Very little is known of his history, even the dates of his birth and death are uncertain. He was the son of one Thomas Felltham of Suffolk, gent., and it is inferred was attached to the household of the Earl of Thomond. He appears to have been happily married. He seems to have had a liberal education, and to have been possessed of means. He is supposed to have died about 1677.]

THE most celebrated of the writings of Owen Felltham is his little volume of *Resolves, divine, moral, and political.* In addition to this he wrote a *Brief character of the Low Countries under the States,* some lay sermons or *Practical Reflections* on certain Scripture texts ; poems, and letters.

Part of the *Resolves* was written in his nineteenth year. It is uncertain when the little book first made its appearance ; the earliest edition we possess is the second, published in 1628, and it is supposed that the first had appeared some two years previously.

Felltham writes pleasantly and well. Each essay or resolve is well turned, and in itself a work of art. Like most of his learned contemporaries he adorns his pages with classical allusions and quotations, but not oppressively so. He was censured for not giving his references. He defended himself against this charge somewhat curiously, saying that he did not profess to be a scholar, and for a gentleman he held such accuracy "a little pedantical."

His metaphors and analogies are for the most part felicitous. He does not labour after effect, but writes with the easy grace of a refined, but not profound, student of literature.

The *Resolves* may be best described as satires. They are temperate, judicial, wise. There is no ardent enthusiasm, but considerable earnestness and good sense in Felltham's writings.

His style is easy without being colloquial ; dignified without being stilted. It is that of an amiable, pious, sensible man of the

world, who aimed at as much virtue as was conveniently practicable ; and who, without affecting to be a saint, patiently endeavoured not to be too much of a sinner.

His sentences are never lengthy nor involved, and always perfectly intelligible. There is no loftiness of diction, neither is there
any attractive homeliness. Sustained, harmonious, dignified, he
inspires our respect, if he does not win our love.

A shrewd and graceful humour, seldom wandering into coarse-
ness, distinguishes his writings, notably his *Brief Character of the
Low Countries*.

Ignorant as we are of his whole life, ignorant even of the dates
of his entering and leaving the world, we yet feel as we close this
book of his *Resolves*, written primarily for his own guidance, and
modestly offered to the world, on the chance of possibly helping
others, that we know and like the man with his quiet, sensible
spirit, and earnest gentlemanlike utterance.

A. I. FITZROY.

A FRIEND AND ENEMY, WHEN MOST DANGEROUS

I WILL take heed both of a speedy friend and a slow enemy.
Love is never lasting which flames before it burns; and hate,
like wetted coals, throws a fiercer heat when fire gets the
mastery. As quick wits have seldom sound judgments which
should make them continue: so friendship kindled suddenly is
rarely found to consist with the durability of affection. Enduring
love is ever built on virtue, which no man can see in another at
once. He that fixes upon her shall find a beauty which will
every day take him with some new grace or other. I like that
love which, by a soft ascension, by degrees possesses itself of the
soul. As for an enemy who is long a making, he is much the
worse for being ill no sooner. He hates not without cause who
is unwilling to hate at all.

(From *Resolves, Divine, Moral, and Political.*)

OF PREACHING

THE defect of preaching has made the pulpit slighted; I mean
the much bad oratory we find come from it. It is a wonder to
me how men can preach so little, and so long: so long a time,
and so little matter; as if they thought to please by the inculca-
tion of their vain tautologies. I see no reason why so high a
princess as divinity is should be presented to the people in the
sordid rags of the tongue; nor that he who speaks from the
Father of Languages should deliver his embassage in an ill one.
A man can never speak too well while he speaks not obscurely.
Long and diffusive sentences are both tedious to the ear and
difficult to retain. A sentence well couched takes both the senses
and the understanding. I love not those cart-rope speeches.

which are longer than the memory of man can fathom. I see not but that divinity, put into apt *significants*, might ravish as well as poetry. They are sermons but of baser metal, which lead the eyes to slumber. He answered well that, after often asking, said still, that action was the chief part of an orator. Surely that oration is most powerful where the tongue is eloquent, and speaks in a native decency, even in every limb. A good orator should pierce the ear, allure the eye, and invade the mind of his hearer. And this is Seneca's opinion : fit words are better than fine ones : I like not those which are injudiciously employed ; but such as are expressively pertinent, which lead the mind to something beside the naked term. And he that speaks thus must not look to speak thus every day. A *kembed* oration will cost both labour and the rubbing of the brain. And *kembed* I wish it, not *frizzled* nor *curled*. Divinity should not be wanton. Harmless jests I like well ; but they are fitter for the tavern than the majesty of the temple. Christ taught the people with authority. Gravity becomes the pulpit. I admire the valour of some men who, before their studies, dare ascend the pulpit ; and do there take more pains than they have done in their library. But having done this, I wonder not that they there spend sometimes three hours, only to weary the people into sleep. And this makes some such fugitive divines that, like cowards, they run away from their text. Words are not all, nor is matter all, nor gesture ; yet, together they are. It is very moving in an orator when the soul seems to speak as well as the tongue. St. Augustin says, Tully was admired more for his tongue than his mind ; Aristotle more for his mind than his tongue : but Plato for both. And surely nothing is more necessary in an oration, than a judgment able well to conceive and utter. I know God hath chosen by weak things to confound the wise : yet I see not but, in all times, attention has been paid to language. And even the Scriptures (though not the Hebrew) I believe are penned in a tongue of deep expression, wherein almost every word has a metaphorical sense, which illustrates by some allusion. How political is Moses in his Pentateuch ! How philosophical Job ! How massy and sententious is Solomon in his proverbs ! how grave and solemn in his Ecclesiastes ; that in the world, there is not such another dissection of the world as it ! How were the Jews astonished at Christ's doctrine ! How eloquent a pleader is Paul at the bar ; in disputation how subtle ! And he who reads the Fathers shall find them as if written with a fine pen. . . . I wish no man to be too dark and full of shadow. There is a way to be pleasingly plain; and some have found it. Mercury himself may move his tongue in vain if he has none to hear him but a non-intelligent. They that speak to children assume a pretty lisping. Birds are caught by the counterfeit of their own shrill notes. There is a magic in the tongue which can charm even the rude and untaught. Eloquence is a bridle, wherewith a wise man rides the monster of the world, the people. The affections of the hearer depend upon the tongue of the speaker.

> Flet, si flere jubes; gaudet, gaudere coactus:
> Et te dante, capit Judex quum non habet iram. —LUCAN.

> Thou may'st give smiles, or tears which joys do blot;
> Or wrath to Judges, which themselves have not.

I grieve that any thing so excellent as divinity should fall into a sluttish handling. Surely, though other obstructions do eclipse her, yet this is a principal one. I never yet knew a good tongue that wanted ears to hear it. I will honour her in her plain trim; but I would desire her in her graceful jewels; not that they give addition to her goodness, but that she is thereby rendered more persuasive in working on the soul she meets with. When I meet with worth which I cannot overlove, I can well endure that art which is a means to heighten liking.

(From the Same.)

DESCRIPTION OF A DUTCH HOUSE

WHEN you are entered the house the first thing you encounter is a looking-glass. No question but a true emblem of politic hospitality; for though it reflects yourself in your own figure, 'tis yet no longer than while you are there before it. When you are gone once, it flatters the next comer, without the least remembrance that you ere were there.

The next are the vessels of the house marshalled about the room like watchmen. All as neat as if you were in a citizens' wives' cabinet: for unless it be themselves, they let none of God's creatures lose anything of their native beauty.

Their houses, especially in their cities, are the best eye beauties of their country. For cost and sight they far exceed our English, but they want their magnificence. Their lining is yet more rich than their outside ; not in hangings, but in pictures, which even the poorest are there furnisht with. Not a cobbler but has his toys for ornament. Were the knacks of all their houses set together, there would not be such another Bartholomew Fair in Europe.

Whatsoever their estates be, their house must be fair. Therefore from Amsterdam they have banished sea-coal, lest it soil their buildings, of which the statelier sort are sometimes sententious, and in the front carry some conceit of the owner. As to give you a taste in these :

> Christus Adjutor Meus ;
> Hoc abdicato Perenne Quæro ;
> Hic Medio tutius Itur.

Every door seems studded with diamonds. The nails and hinges hold a constant brightness, as if rust there were not a quality incident to iron. Their houses they keep cleaner than their bodies ; their bodies than their souls. Go to one you shall find the andirons shut up in net-work. At a second, the warming-pan muffled in Italian cut-work. At a third the sconce clad in cambric.

(From *A Brief Character of the Two Countries.*)

SIR KENELM DIGBY

[Kenelm Digby was the son of Sir Everard Digby, executed for his participation in the Gunpowder Plot. He was born in 1603, at Gayhurst, Bucks,
an estate which was preserved to him by the care of his mother. For a time
he seems to have been educated as a Protestant under the charge of Laud,
then Dean of Gloucester; but although there are doubts as to the date of his
adherence to the Roman Catholic Church, he certainly became an avowed
Roman Catholic before 1636. He studied first at Gloucester Hall (afterwards
Worcester College) in the University of Oxford, and next in the University of
Paris, and spent a large part of his early manhood abroad. In 1623, he
received the honour of knighthood, and in 1624 was privately married to
Venetia Stanley, descended from the Earls of Derby and the house of Percy—
a lady of great beauty and talents, with whose reputation, however, scandal
had been busy. In 1627, he started, under royal licence, as head of a
privateering expedition, in which he defeated a Venetian and French fleet.
On the outbreak of the disputes between the Crown and the Parliament, he
fell under the suspicion of the Parliamentary party and was banished; and it
was while in France, under the protection of Henrietta Maria and her mother,
that he published his chief work, *On the Nature of Bodies, and the Nature of
Man's Soul*. The sincerity of his political principles is rendered doubtful by
his subsequent friendly relations with Cromwell; but strangely enough, he
seems never to have broken off his connection with the Royalist party, and
was well received at Court after the Restoration. He took an interest in the
establishment of the Royal Society in 1663, and died in London in 1665.]

AMONGST the many strange personalities of the 17th century,
there are few whose character it is more difficult to gauge than
that of Kenelm Digby. He played his part as courtier, man of
fashion, romancer, critic, soldier, virtuoso, and philosopher; and
although he was distinguished in each, there was no sphere in
which some suspicion of charlatanism did not attach to him. It
is indeed difficult to avoid the conclusion that an element of
madness entered into his composition, or at least that his versatility was united to an abnormal eccentricity, which, if it partly
relieves him of the worst charges, yet explains how small his
influence was in any single sphere of activity. His vanity was

prodigious, and is naturally most conspicuous where his writings (as is frequently the case) relate to his own actions.

His *Private Memoirs*, first printed from his MS. in 1827, give us an account of his life down to 1628 ; and the larger part is occupied with a singular history of his early love and marriage with Venetia Stanley. The story is told as a romance under assumed names, and it is impossible to tell what part of it is true and what part pure romancing. In style it is inflated and turgid, and exhibits all the absurd magniloquence of diction characteristic of the romances of the day, with a strange perversity in its moralisings which is peculiar to Digby himself. Besides this we have some shorter narratives ; one entitled *Sir Kenelm Digby's Honour Maintained*, in which his prowess in resenting an insult to his king by single combat is set forth ; and another, the journal of his privateering expedition, which is simple and direct narrative. In 1643, he printed his *Observations on Religio Medici*, written in feverish haste, and with something of captious criticism of Browne's work ; in 1644, his *Observations* on an obscure passage in Spenser's Fairie Queene ; and in the same year his chief philosophical work, *On the Nature of Bodies, and the Nature of Man's Soul*.

Some of his most marked peculiarities are best exhibited by the contrast between Browne and himself, which appears in his *Observations on Religio Medici*. In Browne's mysticism the imagination is always stronger than the ingenuity, and the breadth of a generous and liberal sympathy is more conspicuous than any definiteness of formal belief. But Digby is always straining after a system ; and he evidently wrote the criticism under the influence of the philosophical theory which he sets forth more elaborately in the longer treatise on the *Nature of Bodies and the Nature of Man's Soul*. What attracts us most in Browne is his keen perception of the bearing of religious belief upon the faculties of man ; he never obtrudes any dogmatism, but he steers his way through the labyrinth of creeds, with a calm and steady equipoise which never loses its courteous dignity. Digby, with far less of philosophic calm, is much more of the schoolman ; without attacking any religious dogma, he yet pursues, with greater pertinacity, a sort of rationalistic system. He will not subscribe to Browne's gentle contempt for the impotence of human reason, but would fain base religion upon the foundations of reason. The germ of freethinking was there ; and it is difficult to avoid the belief that Swift, whose writings are full of reminiscences both of Browne and of Digby, found in Digby's sprightly philosophising a type of the mental complacency against which he directed his satire.

His more elaborate philosophical work begins by tracing the operations of physical nature, and through them, explains the action of instinct in animals. He distinguishes sharply between these instincts (the result, as he maintains, solely of physical causes), and the operations of the human intellect, even when these approach most nearly to the semblance of the instincts in animals. From this distinction he argues that there must be some basis for these operations which is not physical; that this basis is the sole foundation for a belief in the existence of the soul; and enunciates in a somewhat different form, the thesis *Cogito ergo sum.* And because this basis is not physical and is not therefore subject to physical laws, it must be immortal. The theory is open to assault at many points; but it is worked out with much care and ingenuity; and by the very care and accuracy of his argument, Digby's style becomes clear, exact, and forcible. He has not the boldness or the mastery of language which invents new expressions or clothes new thoughts in words. But he writes with the polished ease and grace which in his carriage and his manner so vividly impressed all his contemporaries, even when they were compelled to admit his total want of veracity. He has the confidence, and, at the same time, the breadth of view, acquired by converse with every phase of life. His prose has not the quaint turns, and the sympathetic subtlety of Browne's; but as the extracts given below will show, he can rise occasionally to very lofty heights of dignity and eloquence. With all this, however, there is a pervading impression of artificiality, as of one whose character was above all things theatrical; and of superficial confidence, as of one to whom philosophical lucubrations were only a phase of eccentric and ill-balanced restlessness. The best description of Digby is that given by a master of word-por-traiture—Clarendon.

" Sir Kenelm Digby was a person very eminent and notorious throughout the whole course of his life, from his cradle to his grave; of an ancient family and noble extraction, and inherited a fair and plentiful fortune notwithstanding the attainder of his father. He was a man of a very extraordinary person and presence, which drew the eyes of all men upon him, which were more fixed by a wonderful graceful behaviour, a flowing courtesy and civility, and such a volubility of language, as surprised and delighted ; and though in another man it might have appeared to have somewhat of affectation, it was marvellous graceful in him, and seemed natural to his size and mould of person, to the gravity of his motion, and the tune of his voice and delivery. He had a fair reputation in arms, of which he gave an early testimony in his youth in some encounters in Spain and Italy, and afterwards in an action in the Mediterranean Sea, where he had the command of a squadron of ships of war, set out at his own charge under the king's commission. . . . In a word, he had all the advantages that nature and art, and an excellent education could give him ; which, with a great confidence and presentness of mind, buoyed him up against all those prejudices and disadvantages (as the attainder and execution of his father for a crime of the highest nature ; his own marriage with a lady, though of an extraordinary beauty, of as extraordinary a fame ; his changing and re-changing his religion ; and some personal vices and licences in his life) which would have suppressed and sunk any other man, but never clouded or eclipsed him from appearing in the best places, in the best company, and with the best estimation and satisfaction."

To this portrait we may add the following sentence of Anthony Wood :—

" Had (Sir Kenelm Digby) been dropt out of the clouds in any part of the world he would have made himself respected ; but the Jesuits who cared not for him, spoke spitefully, and said, ''Twas true, but he must not have stayed above six weeks.' "

H. CRAIK.

AN EXTRACT FROM A SHIP'S LOG

I GAVE order for the speedy dispatch of the polacra, and with half of my ships went to Delphos, which is a very good port, and there I spent my time taking in some marble stones and statues till the Vice-Admiral and polacra and sattia came to me, which was the 3rd of September. Then the wind being contrary I unladed the sattia, and took the rest of her goods (which the Vice-Admiral and Hopewell had left) into my ship.

The reasons that moved me to come to Micono were these. Mr. Taverner said the polacra was so leaky and in evil plight that he would not venture to sail in her to Patras, and to stay at Milo to careen and fit her I saw was very inconvenient, for it was a place that administered means of such debauchedness that I found by experience I could have no command of my men there, and the wind came fair to carry us to Micono in a day, and it was too soon by three weeks to come into our port to make provisions, for it was so hot that all men said in a month yet meat could not take salt, and wine is extremely cheap at Micono, so that I intended to make all my provisions there of that, but was frustrated, for they had filled up all their old cask and store with new wines which were naught for beverage, and in the little channel between Tino and Micono did pass all those vessels that went for Constantinople, Scio, or Smyrna, where I heard there were six Frenchmen ready to come out, and more daily expected to come thither. But being at Micono I found that my men likewise haunted that shore, which yet was not comparably so bad as Milo, and were uneasy to be kept aboard; so that I went with most of my ships to Delphos, a desert island, where staying till the rest were ready, because idleness should not fix their minds upon any untoward fancies (as is usual among seamen), and together to avail myself of the convenience of carrying away some antiquities there, I busied them in rolling of stones to the seaside, which they did with such eagerness as though it had been the earnestest business that they came out for, and they mastered prodigious massy weights ; but one stone, the greatest and fairest of all, containing four statues, they gave over after they had been, three hundred men, a whole day about it, while the dispatching some business with some Venetians come from Tino detained me aboard. But the next day I contrived a way with masts of ships and another ship to ride over against it, that brought it down with much ease and speed. In the little Delphos there are brave marble stones heaped up in the great ruins of Apollo's temple, and within the circuit of it is a huge statue, but broken in two pieces about the waist, which the Greeks told me was Apollo's. It weigheth at least thirty tons, and time hath worn out much of the softnesses and gentlenesses of the work, yet all the proportions remain perfect and in gross : the yieldings of the flesh and the musculous parts are visible, so that it is still a brave noble piece, and hath by divers been attempted to be carried away, but they have all failed in it.

(From *Journal of a Voyage into the Mediterranean.*)

THE MAXIMS OF SELF-CONTENTMENT

THERE is no man certainly that seeth so far as I do into these contentments and blessings, but will desire them as vehemently as I do ; but there may be this difference between us, that they may want courage and resolution to possess and defend them ; and I deem it a greater weakness to disguise one's passions than to entertain them. Other men's opinions shall never drive me from maintaining the rules that I have prescribed to myself ; then since this so mainly importeth my happiness I will not fail to justify myself to the world for giving way to my affections ; and then, although I may not gain the opinion of wisdom suitable to those times, yet I hope I shall have the ancients my friends, in that I seek to get a habitude that breedeth full pleasure and interior delight, and banish far from my consideration those things that are without me, to the end that not being afraid of the censures of the world, I may not drown my life in perpetual disquiet. But if what I have said to that effect, do not relish to other men's

fantasies ; and that it be like too solid meat for weak stomachs
and tender teeth, as the vulgar's are, I will proceed with them in
a more gentle, or rather submissive way ; if they will not absolve
me, let them pardon me ; let my friends be so indulgent to me as
to pass by this one action, and I will not fail their hopes or their
desires in any thing else.   Although I cannot persuade myself
that I am in an error in this, yet since others believe it, it will
make me strive to behave myself so in all things else, that I may
rectify myself in their good opinion, and, to that effect, strain myself in virtuous actions beyond what otherwise I should have done.
If it be a fault in me, yet it would be a greater injustice in them to
condemn all that may be good besides, for so small a mixture of
the contrary ; what discreet man ever threw away a fair and rich
garment for having a small spot in some one corner of it !   It
importeth no man but himself ; then it is reason that no man but
myself should trouble himself about it ; yet if they will still search
into me, let them remember, that in the choice of friends those are
to be esteemed good that are the least ill, since none are positively
good ; and if all men have something of evil, let them examine
the nature and weight of what evil is inherent to every one, and
make their choice accordingly.   And if herein I strive not to
better myself, let them conceive the cause proceedeth as much out
of my design as out of my weakness, for I have learned, and from
an author of unquestionable authority, that even the mending of a
state is not worth the disordering and troubling it.   And if I yield
more to the tempest that carryeth me away, than some may like
of, let them consider that a ship tossed in a violent storm maketh
fairest weather before the wind ; wherefore I judge it folly for any
man to force and strain his nature, to raise a civil war within
himself.   Besides, I care not for mending myself by halves :
with me if anything be awry, let all that hangeth upon that string
be so too.   If my affection be a fault, I must confess I cannot
help it, for herein we are under the conduct of the stars, and then
I will never go about to prescribe its limits ; and sure it is better
to have some evil increased, than all one's good troubled.   But
withal I will say this in my own behalf, that I think who hath
given testimony of wisdom in other things, shall never be accounted
a fool for his affections when he can give himself a good account
of them ; and they that live in the memory of after ages, shall not
be judged by their loves, but by their other actions.   Let them in
me look upon those, and cover this, as they did in ancient times

that sold a good horse ; they covered those parts of him that were not essential to be observed in judging of his goodness, lest they might carry away the buyer's eye from marking the principal limbs, by the which they might make a judgment of the rest. Howsoever, since this may be liable to dispute, whether I have done well or ill, let men suspend their sentences till the event give the verdict one way ; let them follow that wise man's advice that would have none judge of another's happiness till after his death ; and in this, censure me by the tenor of my future life, wherein I dare boldly promise to myself that, whensoever I shall avow her for such, she will prove an exact pattern of a virtuous wife, and I of a happy man ; and this not through any prophetic revelation or credulous fantasy, but upon infallible grounds and the certain knowledge of her nature, which is such that it will be my fault if she prove not as I would have her ; and I am confident that her life will belie any rumour that may have been spread abroad to her disadvantage by malicious persons, and believed by others that take up their opinions upon trust.

To end then this long, and I fear tedious discourse of mine, let me put you in mind, how some ancient and much esteemed philosophers were of opinion that a man of vigorous spirits and of a clear understanding might not only love, but without blame use the liberty of his own election and inclinations, and ought to oppose the original rules of nature against vulgar laws and customs ; and that limited and artificial ordinances are only for weak minds, who are not able to judge of things truly as they are by the dim light of their own feeble nature. And while it remaineth in controversy what is best for a man to do, let him in the mean time at least do what pleaseth him most : and for my part, I can never deem those humours very vain that are very pleasing, since content is the true seasoning of all other blessings, and that without it they are all nothing ; nor guide my actions by other men's censures, which hurt not at all when they are neglected or patiently endured, nor be afflicted when they condemn me ; and thus I shall be free from the servitude that most men live in, who are more troubled by the opinions of evils than by their real essence ; and then the world shall see that my happiness and content is not proportioned to the estimation that they make of it, which will soon be forgotten and vanish away ; but to what I truly enjoy and feel in myself, which will remain in me for ever. And to express fully the exact character of my mind in this particular, give me leave to make use of the sententious poet's words, though applied to my purpose somewhat differing from his sense, where he saith :

> Prætulerim delirus inersque videri
> Dum mea delectent mala me, vel denique fallant,
> Quam sapere et ringi.— HORAT.

And then I will entreat them to think of me as I do of others ; which is, that no man of a competent understanding and judgment is to be lamented or pitied for finding any means, whatsoever it be, to please and satisfy himself.

(From *Private Memoirs.*)

THE SOUL'S EXCELLENCE

AND now I hope I may confidently say I have been as good as my word : and I doubt not but my reader will find it so, if he spend but half as much time in perusing these two treatises as the composing of them hath cost me. They are too nice (and indeed unreasonable) who expect to attain without pains unto that which hath cost others years of toil. Let them remember the words of holy Job, that wisdom is not found in the land of those who live at their ease. Let them cast their eyes on every side round about them, and then tell me, if they meet with any employment that may be compared to the attaining unto these, and such like principles ; whereby a man is enabled to govern himself understandingly and knowingly, towards the happiness both of the next life and of this ; and to comprehend the wise man's theme ; what is good for a man in the days of his vanity, whiles he playeth the stranger under the sun. Let us fear God's judgments. Let us carefully pursue the hidden bounties He hath treasured up for us. Let us thank Him for the knowledge He hath given us : and admire the excellency of Christian religion ; which so plainly teaches us that unto which it is so extreme hård to arrive by natural means. Let us bless Him that we are born unto it. And let us sing to Him ; That it is He, who preached His doctrine to Jacob, and giveth His laws to Israel. He hath not done the like to all nations ; nor hath He manifested His secret truths unto them.

But before I cut off this thread, which hath cost me so much pains to spin out to this length, I must crave my reader's leave to make some use of it for my own behoof. Hitherto my discourse hath been directed to him, now I shall entreat his patience that I may reflect it in a word or two upon myself. And as I am sure I have profited myself not a little by talking all this while to him, that obliging me to polish my conceptions with more care, and to range them into better order, than while they were but rude meditations within my own breast, so I hope that a little conversation with myself upon this important subject (which is to be studied for use and practice, not for speculative science) may prove advantageous unto him, if his warmed thoughts have tuned his soul to such a key, as I am sure these considerations have wound up mine unto.

To thee then, my soul, I now address my speech. For since by long debate, and toilsome rowing against the impetuous tides of ignorance and false apprehensions which overflow thy banks and hurry thee headlong down the stream, whilst thou are imprisoned in thy clayey mansion, we have with much ado arrived at some little atom of thy vast greatness ; and with the hard and tough blows of strict and wary reasoning we have stricken out some few sparkles of that glorious light which environeth and swelleth thee, or, rather, which is thee : it is high time I should retire myself out of the turbulent and slippery field of eager strife and litigious disputation, to make my accounts with thee, where no outward noise may distract us, nor any way intermeddle between us, excepting only that eternal verity, which by thee shineth upon my faint and gloomy eyes, and in which I see whatever doth or can content thee in me. I have discovered that thou (my soul) wilt survive me : and so survive me as thou will also survive the mortality and changes which belong to me, and which are but accidentary to thee, merely because thou art in me. Then shall the vicissitude of time, and the inequality of dispositions in thee be turned into the constancy of immortality : and into the evenness of one being, never to end, and never to receive a change, or succession to better or worse.

When my eye of contemplation hath been fixed upon this bright sun as long as it is able to endure the radiant beams of it ; whose redundant light veileth the looker on with a dark mist ; let me turn it for a little space upon the straight passage and narrow gullet through which thou strivest (my soul) with faint and weary steps during thy hazardous voyage upon the earth to make thyself away; and let me examine what comparison there is between thy two conditions, the present one wherein thou now findest thyself immersed in flesh and blood, and the future state that will betide thee, when thou shalt be melted out of this gross ore, and refined from this mean alloy. Let my term of life be of a thousand long years, longer than ever happened to our aged forefathers, who stored the earth with their numerous progeny, by outliving their skill to number the diffused multitudes that swarmed from their loins; let me, during this long space, be sole emperor and absolute lord of all the huge globe of land and water encompassed with Adam's offspring; let all my subjects be prostrate at my feet, with obedience and awe, distilling their activest thoughts in studying night and day to invent new pleasures and delights for me; let nature conspire with them to give me a constant and vigorous health, a perpetual spring of youth, that may to the full relish whatsoever good all they can fancy; let gravest prelates, and greatest princes, serve instead of flatterers to heighten my joys, and yet those joys be raised above their power of flattery; let the wise men of this vast family (whose sentiments are maxims and oracles, to govern the world's beliefs and actions) esteem, reverence, and adore me in the secretest and the most recluse withdrawings of their hearts; let all the wealth which to this very day hath ever been torn out of the bowels of the earth, and all the treasures which the sea hideth from the view of greedy men, well round about me, whilst all the world besides lyeth gaping to receive the crumbs that fall neglected by me from my full loaden table; let my imagination be as vast as the unfathomed universe, and let my felicity be as accomplished as my imagination can reach unto, so that wallowing in pleasure I be not able to think how to increase it, or what to wish for more than that which I possess and enjoy.

Thus when my thoughts are at a stand, and can raise my present happiness no higher; let me call to mind how this long lease of pleasant days will in time come to an end: this bottom of a thousand joyful years will at length be unwound, and nothing remain of it; and then (my soul) thy infinitely longer lived immortality will succeed; thy never-ending date will begin a new account, impossible to be summed up, and beyond all proportion infinitely exceeding the happiness we have rudely aimed to express, so that no comparison can be admitted between them. For suppose first that such it were, as the least and shortest of those manifold joys, which swell it to that height we have fancied, were equal to all the contentment thou shalt receive in a whole million of years, yet millions of years may be so often multiplied, as at length the slender and limited contentments supposed in them may equalise and outgo the whole heap of overflowing bliss, raised so high in the large extent of these thousand happy years, which when they are cast into a total sum ; and that I compare it with the immeasurable eternity which only measureth thee ; then I see that all this huge product of algebraical multiplication appeareth as nothing, in respect of the remaining, and never-ending survivance, and is less than the least point in regard of the immense universe. But then, if it be true (as it is most true) that thy least spark and moment of real happiness in that blessed eternity thou hopest for is infinitely greater and nobler than the whole mass of fancied joys of my thousand years' life here on earth, how infinitely will the value of thy duration exceed all proportion, in regard of the felicity I had imagined myself ? And seeing there is no proportion between them, let me sadly reflect upon my own present condition, let me examine what it is, I so busily and anxiously employ my thoughts and precious time upon ; let me consider my own courses, and whither they lead me ; let me take a survey of the lives and actions of the greatest part of the world, which make so loud a noise about my ears, and then may I justly sigh out from the bottom of my anguished heart, to what purpose have I hitherto lived ? to what purpose are all these millions of toilsome ants, that live and labour about me ? To what purpose were Cæsars and Alexanders ? To what Aristotles and Archimedeses ? How miserably foolish are those conquering tyrants, that divide the world with their lawless swords ? What senseless idiots those acute philosophers, who tear men's wits in pieces by their different ways, and subtle logic ! striving to show men beatitudes in this world, and seeking for that, which if they had found, were but nothing of a nothing in respect of true beatitude ! He only is truly wise, who, neglecting all that flesh and blood desireth, endeavoureth to purchase at any rate this felicity which thy survivance promiseth ; the least degree of which so far surmounteth all the heaps which the giants of the earth are able to raise by throwing hills upon hills, and striving in vain to scale and reach those eternities which reside above the skies. Alas, how fondly doth mankind suffer itself to be deluded ! How true it is that the only thing necessary proveth the only thing that is neglected ! Look up, my soul, and fix thine eye upon that truth, which eternal light maketh so clear unto thee, shining upon thy face with so great evidence, as defyeth the noontide sun in its greatest brightness. And this it is, that every action of thine, be it never so slight, is mainly mischievous ; or be it never so bedecked with those specious considerations which the wise men of the world judge important, is foolish, absurd, and unworthy of a man, and unworthy of one that understandeth, and acknowledgeth thy dignity, if in it there be any speck, or if through it there appear any spark of those mean and false motives which with a false bias draw any way aside from attaining that happiness we expect in thee. That happiness ought to be the end and mark we level at ; that the rule and model of all our actions ; that the measure of every circumstance, of every atom, of whatsoever we bestow so precious a thing upon, as the employment of thee is.

(From *Two Treatises of the Nature of Bodies and the Nature of Man's Soul.*)

SIR THOMAS URQUHART

[Sir Thomas Urquhart (or as he spelt it himself "Urchard") is supposed to have been born about the year 1605. His family, the Urquharts of Cromarty, was an exceedingly ancient one, and he himself traced a complete genealogy to Adam ; but, as one of his editors observes with admirable moderation, "some of the entries are undoubtedly fictitious." His mother was Christiana, daughter of Lord Elphinstone, and she figures last in the list which Eve heads ; nor is it improbable that Urquhart had her name partly in mind when he signed as he sometimes did "C. P." (Christianus Presbyteromastix). Little is known of his youth except that he had ample means and travelled a good deal. When the troubles approached he, a strong cavalier, took part in the demonstration called the "Trot of Turriff" (1639), and was knighted by the King in 1641. Thenceforward he had difficulties with creditors and cove-nanters, was proclaimed a traitor at the Cross of Edinburgh, fought at Wor-cester and elsewhere, survived till the Restoration, and is said to have died of excessive laughter and joy at hearing thereof. He is best known to the present generation by his partial translation of Rabelais, published in 1653, where the extraordinary style which he had fostered and practised earlier in his own work harmonises so well with the subject as almost to create a second original. His own compositions are of the wildest eccentricity, but possess considerable interest. They begin with a mathematical work called *Trissotetras*, a title which is but a mild specimen of the singular Greek compounds which Urquhart borrowed or, much more often, invented for the titles, sub-titles, and details of all his books. Others are *Pantochronocanon* or the *Promptuary of Time ; Ekscubalauron*, a treatise nominally on a jewel picked out of the dirt at Worcester ; *Logopandecteision*, a scheme of an universal language. All are a strange medley of learning, whimsicality, family pride, and egotistical prattle, couched in a style which is something like Euphuism crossed and dashed with the most liberal borrowings from classical and modern tongues alike, especially French. They are unluckily accessible with great difficulty, the only modern and complete edition being the handsome one privately printed for the Maitland Club in 1834.]

SIR THOMAS URQUHART is one of those personages—pro-portionally rather numerous during the seventeenth century, and certainly more numerous then than at any other time—who seem to be characters of fiction strayed into the world of fact. That Sir Walter Scott, who must have known all about him, did not put him into one of his books is chiefly to be taken as a proof of Scott's shrewd judgment, for Urquhart was complete already as presented by himself. Indeed Sir Walter may be said to have decomposed him : and flashes of Urquhart appear in Dugald Dalgetty, in the Baron of Bradwardine, in King James, and elsewhere. That is to say, Sir Thomas was an exaggeratedly typical example of a certain class of Scottish gentleman of his time—learned to pedantry, original to the verge of madness, proud as a peacock, brave and faithful as steel. The extracts which follow will show him better than any description in short space can do, though not so well, perhaps, as a very large number of scraps sifted and arranged from his extraordinary works. His most famous, and perhaps his best single passage is his long account of the Admirable Crichton, who seems to represent his own ideal—an account on which most subsequent writers who have depicted that half-mythical personage have drawn. But it is much too long for insertion here as a whole, and would be injured by curtailment. The shorter sketch of Dr. Seaton here given, and the introduction to one of the books of *Logopandecteision* will probably suffice to exhibit, as well as can be done, the strange jumble of his matter, the lawless freedom of his vocabulary, and the way in which any subject, even the most remote, is brought somehow or other round to the interests and fortunes of the Urquhart family in general, and to those of " C. P." in particular. It may be suspected that Urquhart, like some others whose naturally fantastic brains were superheated by those troublous times, was not entirely sane. But his learning, or at least his reading, was thoroughly genuine : the *Trissotetras* is not unworthy of a countryman and contemporary of Napier, and the *Logopandecteision* in the midst of its exuberant oddities displays acuteness enough. In language Urquhart is merely an extreme example of the deliberately extravagant quaintness which characterised his time, but it must be admitted that he is one of the most extreme, and that it would be nearly impossible to go beyond him. How far the study of Rabelais, and perhaps of other French writers of the same school encouraged his natural tendencies, and how far these tendencies inclined him to the study of Rabelais, are questions which in the absence of data it is not very profitable to discuss. But he is certainly one of our greatest translators, despite the liberties which he sometimes takes with his text.

GEORGE SAINTSBURY.

DOCTOR SEATON

THERE was another called Doctor Seaton, not a Doctor of Divinity, but one that had his degrees at Padua, and was Doctor *utriusque juris;* for whose pregnancy of wit, and vast skill in all the mysteries of the civil and canon laws, being accounted one of the ablest men that ever breathed, he was most heartily desired by Pope Urbane the eighth to stay at Rome ; and the better to encourage him thereto, made him chief Professor of the Sapience, a college in Rome so called ; where, although he lived a pretty while with great honour and reputation, yet at last, as he was a proud man, falling at some odds with *il Collegio Romano,* the supremest seat of the Jesuits, and that wherein the general of that numerous society hath his constant residence, he had the courage to adventure coping with them where they were strongest, and in matter of any kind of learning to give defiance to their greatest scholars ; which he did do with such a height of spirit, and in such a lofty and *bravashing* humour, that, although there was never yet that ecclesiastical incorporation wherein there was so great universality of literature, or multiplicity of learned men, he nevertheless, misregarding what estimation they were in with others, and totally reposing on the stock or basis of his own knowledge, openly gave it out, that if those Teatinos, his choler not suffering him to give them their own name of Jesuits, would offer any longer to continue in vexing him with their frivolous chat and captious argumentations, to the impugning of his opinions, and yet in matters of religion they were both of one and the same faith, he would, like a Hercules amongst so many myrmidons, fall in within the very midst of them, so besquatter them on all sides, and, with the *granads* of his invincible arguments, put the brains of all and each of them in such a fire, that they should never be able, pump as they would, to find in all the

cellules thereof one drop of either reason or learning wherewit
to quench it.

This unequal undertaking of one against so many, wheree
some were greater courtiers with his Papal Holiness than he
shortened his abode at Rome, and thereafter did him so muc
prejudice in his travels through Italy and France, that when at
any time he became scarce of money, to which exigent his
prodigality often brought him, he could not as before, expect an
ayuda de costa, as they call it, or *viaticum*, from any Prince of
the territories through which he was to pass, because the channels
of their liberality were stopped, by the rancour and hatred of his
conventual adversaries.

When, nevertheless, he was at the lowest ebb of his fortune,
his learning, and incomparable facility in expressing any thing
with all the choicest ornaments of, and incident variety to the
perfection of the Latin elocution, raised him to the dignity of
being possessed with the chair of Lipsius, and professing humanity,
in Italy called *buone letere*, in the famous university of Louvain ;
yet, like Mercury, unapt to fix long in any one place, deserting
Louvain, he repaired to Paris, where he was held in exceeding
great reputation for his good parts, and so universally beloved,
that both laics and churchmen, courtiers and scholars, gentlemen
and merchants, and almost all manner of people, willing to learn
some new thing or other, for, as says Aristotle, every one is
desirous of knowledge, were ambitious of the enjoyment of his
company, and ravished with his conversation. For besides that
the matter of his discourse was strong, sententious, and witty, he
spoke Latin as if he had been another Livy or Salustius : nor,
had he been a native of all the three countries of France, Italy,
and Germany, could he have expressed himself, as still he did when
he had occasion, with more selected variety of words, nimbler
volubility of utterance, or greater dexterity for tone, phrase, and
accent, in all the languages thereto belonging.

I have seen him circled about at the Louvre with a ring of
French lords and gentlemen, who hearkened to his discourse with
so great attention, that none of them, so long as he was pleased
to speak, would offer to interrupt him, to the end that the pearls
falling from his mouth might be the more orderly congested in
the several treasures of their judgments ; the ablest advocates,
barristers, or counsellors-at-law of all the Parliament of Paris,
even amongst those that did usually plead *en la chambre (*

lid many times visit him at his house, to get his advice in hard
lebatable points. He came also to that sublime pitch of good
diction even in the French tongue, that there having past, by
virtue of a frequent intercourse, several missives in that idiom,
betwixt him and the Sieur de Balzak, who, by the quaintest
Romancealists of France, and daintiest complimenters of all its
luscious youth, was almost uncontrollably esteemed in eloquence
to have surpassed Cicero ; the strain of Seaton's letters was so
high, the fancy so pure, the words so well connexed, and the
cadence so just, that Balzak, infinitely taken with its fluent yet
concise oratory, to do him the honour that was truly due unto
him, most lovingly presented him with a golden pen, in acknowledgement of Seaton's excelling him both in rhetoric and the art
of persuasion ; which gift proceeding from so great an orator,
and for a supereminency in that faculty wherein himself, without
contradiction, was held the chiefest of this and all former ages
that ever were born in the French nation, could not choose but
be accounted honourable. Many learned books were written by
this Seaton in the Latin tongue, whose titles, to speak ingenuously,
I cannot hit upon.

> From Ἐκσκυβάλαυρον: or *The discovery of a most exquisite
> jewel, more precious than diamonds . . . found in
> the kennel of Worcester streets, the day after the fight
> and six before the autumnal equinox, anno 1651, to
> frontal a Vindication of the Honour of Scotland
> . . . wherein the Presbyterian party . . . hath in-
> volved it.*

THE DESIGN OF THE THIRD BOOK, ENTITULED CLERONOMAPORIA

As in the book immediately foregoing, the Author very plainly
hath pointed at the main block which lieth in the way as a
hindrance to the progress of his brain-itineraries ; so in this, the
third of his Introduction, doth he, with great perspicacity, educe
most peremptory reasons out of the clearest springs of both
modern and ancient, divine and human law, why it should be
the, ved. In the meanwhile, the better to prepare the reader

towards a matter of so prime concernment, he begins the purpose
with a peculiar and domestic narrative of the manner how these
impediments were cast in, to the end that the more unjustly he
was dealt with by the persons who did inject them, the greater
justice may appear in his relief from their oppressions. To have
mentioned such particulars, and unfolded them to the view of the
public, did very much damp the genius of the author, who, could
he have otherways done, would undoubtedly have manifested a
most cordial dislike of any motion tending to approve the offering
unto Pan the sacrifice of the household gods, or disclosing to all
the mysteries of penatal rites ; but the thread of the discourse
hanging thereupon, without a gap in its contexture, it could not
be avoided. Especially that generous and worthy knight, the
author's father, having been unparalleledly wronged by false,
wicked, and covetous men, himself being of all men living the
justest, equallest, and most honest in his dealings, his humour
was, rather than to break his word, to lose all he had, and stand
to his most undeliberate promises, what ever they might cost ;
which too strict adherence to the austerest principles of veracity,
proved oftentimes damageable to him in his negotiations with
many cunning sharks, who knew with what profitable odds they
could screw themselves in upon the windings of so good a nature.
He, in all the (near upon) sixty years that he lived, never injured
any man voluntarily, though by protecting and seconding of some
unthankful men he did much prejudge himself ; he never refused
to be surety for any, so cordial he was towards his acquaintance,
yet, contrary to all expectations, his kindness therein was attended
by so much good luck, that he never paid above two hundred
pounds English for all his vadimonial favours. By the unfaithfulness, on the one side, of some of his menial servants, in filching
from him much of his personal estate, and falsehood of several
chamberlains and bailiffs to whom he had intrusted the managing
of his rents, in the unconscionable discharge of their receipts, by
giving up one account thrice, and of such accounts many ; and,
on the other part, by the frequency of disadvantageous bargains,
which the slyness of the subtle merchant did involve him in,
his loss came unawares upon him, and irresistibly, like an armed
man ; too great trust to the one, and facility in behalf of the
other, occasioning so grievous a misfortune, which nevertheless
did not proceed from want of knowledge or ability in natural
parts, for in the business of other men he would have given a

very sound advice, and was surpassing dexterous in arbitrements upon any reference submitted to him, but that he thought it did derogate from the nobility of his house and reputation of his person, to look to petty things in matter of his own affairs. Whereupon, after forty years' custom, being habituated thereunto, he found himself at last, to his great regret, insensibly plunged into inextricable difficulties ; in the large field whereof, the insatiable creditor, to make his harvest by the ruin of that family, struck in with his sickle, and by masking himself with a vizard composed of the rags of the Scottish law, in its severest sense, claims the same right to the whole inheritance that Robin Hood did to Frankindal's money, for being master of the purse wherein it was. Those wretched and unequitable courses, indefatigably prosecuted by merciless men to the utter undoing of the author and exterminion of his name, have induced him, out of his respect to antiquity, his piety to succession, and that *intim* regard of himself which by divine injunction ought to be the rule and measure of his love towards his neighbour, to set down in this parcel of his Introduction, the cruel usage wherewith he hath been served these many years past by that inexorable race, the lamentable preparatives which, by granting their desires, would ensue to the extirpation of worthy pedigrees, and the unexemplifiable injustice thereby redounding to him who never was in any thing obliged to them. The premisses he enlargeth with divers quaint and pertinent similes, and after a neat apparelling of usury in its holiday garments, he deduceth, from the laws and customs of all nations, the tender care that ought to be had in the preservation of ancient families ; the particulars whereof, in matter of ordonance he evidenceth by the acts of Solon, the decrees of the decemvirs, and statutes of the Twelve Tables ; and for its executional part, in the persons of Q. Fabius, Tiberius the Emperor, and the Israelitish observers of the sacred institution of Jubilees. By which enarration nothing is more clearly inferred, than that, seeing both Jews and Gentiles, Painims and Christians, in their both monarchical and polyarchical governments, have been so zealous in their obsequiousness to so pious a mandate, that the present age being no less concerned in the happy fruits thereof than the good days of old, the splendid authority of this Isle should be pleased not to eclipse their commendation by innovating any thing in the author's case. Who, deciphering the implacability of flagitators, by showing how they throw in obstacles retarding their own payment, thereby tacitly to hasten his destruction, and hinting at the unnatural breach of some of his fiduciaries, he particularizeth the candour of his own endeavours, and *nixuriencie* to give all men contentment ; the discourse whereof, in all its periods, very well deserveth the serious animadversion of the ingenious reader.

SIR THOMAS BROWNE

[Thomas Browne, who was knighted by Charles the Second in the year 1671, was born at London in or near Cheapside, on the 19th October 1605, his father being a mercer, but of a good Cheshire family ; his mother, Ann Garraway of Sussex. The father died early, and the mother married again, her second husband, Sir Thomas Dutton, being probably identical with a soldier of a quick temper who killed his colonel, Sir Hatton Cheeke, in a duel. He seems, however, to have been a friendly stepfather, and can have had nothing to do with the inroad said to have been made on the child's fortune by a dishonest guardian. Nor are there any signs of straitened means in any part of Browne's career. He became a scholar of Winchester in 1616, and matriculated at Broadgate Hall, Oxford (which during his residence became Pembroke College) seven years later. The date of his B.A. degree was 1626, of his M.A. 1629, and about four years later he took the further degree of Doctor of Medicine at Leyden. He is said to have practised earlier in Oxfordshire, to have spent some time in Ireland, and then to have travelled a good deal on the Continent. After returning, and perhaps after some professional stay both in London and in Yorkshire, he settled in 1636 at Norwich, which was his home for the remainder of his life. In 1641 he married a Norfolk lady, Dorothy Mileham, who brought him into relations with some of the best families of the county. He was incorporated as M.D. of his own University in 1637 ; became Fellow of the College of Physicians in 1665 ; was knighted, as above mentioned, and died of a colic on his birthday in the year 1682. His domestic relations, of which we have some memorials in letters, etc., appear to have been uniformly happy, and his entire life was spent quietly in the practice of his profession, and the study of the sciences appertaining to it. His first literary appearance was made with the *Religio Medici*, written, as it would appear, about his thirtieth year, but not published till seven years later (1642) and then, by his own account, surreptitiously. A controversy, for which there is no room here, followed. The *Pseudodoxia Epidemica*, or Vulgar Errors, his longest and most popular work appeared in 1646 ; and he published the *Hydriotaphia* or *Urn Burial*, and the *Garden of Cyrus* in 1658. Nothing more was printed in his lifetime, but additions were subsequently made, the most important of which was the *Christian Morals*, not published till 1716. The standard edition of Browne, a most excellent one, is that of Simon Wilkin, first published in four volumes in 1835, and since included in three volumes of Bohn's Library. Two editions of separate works are sufficiently important to be mentioned, that of *Christian Morals* (1756), with a Life certainly and notes probably (certainly to me) by Dr. Johnson, and that of the same book with the *Religio Medici*, and a *Letter to a Friend*, by Dr. Greenhill, 1881, notable for the extraordinary minuteness of the pains taken with the text and vocabulary.]

GUY PATIN when, very shortly after the appearance of *Religio Medici*, a Latin translation by John Merryweather had brought the book to the notice of continental men of letters, described Browne as " *un mélancholique agréable en ses pensées.*" There may have been a little in this of the traditional estimate of English sadness. But Patin was a man of very shrewd and unprejudiced mind, and there was not as yet in his time the severance between insular and continental thought and letters which the disuse of Latin and the overbearing rise of French power and credit, political and literary, were soon to bring about. And the judgment, though inadequate, is neither inaccurate nor superficial. In temperament, as well as in those perhaps inseparable accidents of temperament, which are called manner and style, Browne strongly resembles, though with remarkable differences, his earlier contemporary, Burton. There was indeed nothing " horrid " about Browne's melancholy, as there is traditionally asserted to have been about Burton's, and the abundant sights which we have of him—writing to his children, mixing in the society of Norwich, noting its antiquities, and the natural history of its neighbourhood —are almost as cheerful as they can be. But it must be remembered that about Burton's private character and ways we really know nothing at all. Comparing the works of the two men we find in Browne a somewhat slighter tendency to regard all things in relation to spiritual valetudinarianism, a more poetical temper, a more rhetorical style, more mysticism, and a more decided piety. But there is in him also the principal mark of the Burtonian melancholy, the ceaseless contemplation of things from the point of view of an unsatisfied and unflinching curiosity, which seems to regard the attempt to satisfy itself as the only panacea, or at least palliative, for the evils of life. Both are humorous, from which it will follow as the night the day that both are melancholy. And though Browne does not necessarily see, and probably was not at all disposed to see all things in melancholy as does his neighbour on the other side of St. Aldate's, there is at least an equally strong undercurrent of this quality in him. Not merely in the famous and almost hackneyed, but here of necessity once more quoted peroration of the *Urn Burial*, where the subject may be said to have demanded it, but always when he is in his most impressive key, the note of sadness, not passionate or querulous, but contemplative and questioning, is heard.

That Browne must have been an exceedingly careful writer is

not only obvious from the most cursory perusal of his work, but may be said to be established beyond a doubt by documentary evidence. In the first place there is the very significant fact that almost all his ornate and most striking passages are to be found in the works which he himself prepared for the press and sent through it ; while the posthumous works, though considerable in bulk, much more rarely exhibit them. In the second place, by a piece of good luck too rare with English authors of the first class, we possess large stores of Browne's MSS. which were bought by Sir Hans Sloane, and thus passed to the British Museum. And these contain numerous variants, first drafts, supplements, and the like, to and of the more elaborate passages. The fact, however, could not be doubted if we had no such evidence. It is perfectly clear that Browne was, in the older and good sense, one of the most artificial writers of English that ever existed. Very few English authors—Shakespeare and Pope are the chief exceptions —have had the benefit of special lexicons such as those which, under the care of M. Adolphe Regnier and his coadjutors and successors, have been gradually compiled for almost all the greater authors of France. But if no one has yet attempted this for the whole of Browne, Dr. Greenhill has done it for three capital *opuscula* which he edited, as a part and a main part of an " index " which fills seventy pages to barely thrice that number of text. There is thus brought together, in an easy conspectus, what all careful readers of Browne must have always had before them dispersedly—his unmatched audacity and fecundity of vocabulary. Disengaged from its accompanying matter, and enriched with a similar glossary to the *Pseudodoxia* and the other works, it would probably constitute the most remarkable repertory of the kind in English.

It is generally and sufficiently known that most of this vocabulary is borrowed from the classical languages, and especially from Latin. It has indeed become a commonplace that Johnson's comparatively early work on Browne determined his own indulgence in this direction ; though Johnson never Latinised with half the temerity of his master. But it would be at once an insufficiency and an injustice to put Browne down as a mere " Limousin student," a mere clumsy corruptor of his native tongue with Latinisms and Græcisms. He was the less likely to be this, inasmuch as he was a diligent reader, and a keen relisher of Rabelais himself, and has left among his letters a Pantagruelist epistle which puzzled the excellent Wilkin, but which is masterly in sense and form, and very easily intelligible to all followers of Master Francis. Still less did he, like a contemporary whose Pantagruelism was equally undoubted, Sir Thomas Urquhart, run wild in classical or pseudo-classical compounds. But Browne never hesitated to use a Latin word in its most idiomatic Latin sense whenever he felt disposed ; and what is more he did not scruple to attach remote connotations of meaning to the words that he borrowed. So, too, he would be indebted to the special sciences for terms of art,—heraldic, medical, philosophic,—and would use them unexplained and at the peril of his auditor whenever their sound or sense pleased him. He would be vernacular whenever he chose ; and contrary to the wont of those who specially affect the ancient tongues of literature, he had no scruple in employing a modern foreign word—French, Italian, or Spanish—when it seemed to him to be desirable. That his license in these respects was, in one of his own most idiomatic words, "controllable" —that is to say exposed to revision and disapproval—it would be extremely rash to deny. That it was in the other sense controlled for the most part by scholarship, by sound sense, and by literary taste, I, for my part, fully believe.

But this coloured, chequered, and almost fantastic vocabulary was only the raw material of Browne's literary art. It was to him something like the marquetry materials, the coloured woods, the ivory, the tortoise-shell, the brass which the great French artists in furniture of his own latest days used in such a surprising manner. It is usual, and not improper, to conjoin Browne, Milton, and Taylor, as the three chief examples of ornate classicising magnificence in seventeenth-century English prose. But Browne deserves distinction from the two great men whose lives and whose styles so nearly coincided with his, for a much greater attention to composition proper. It is true that his syntax, indeed that his whole arrangement is, like his vocabulary, excessively classical. But it has more rarely led him than the others into positive faults of English. Writing as he did, not for pulpit delivery, not under the strain and stress of the necessities of the political pamphlet, but quietly in his study for publication at long intervals of years, he was almost bound to avoid, he certainly did as a rule though not always, avoid, the *anacolutha*, the confusions of English and Latin constructions, the clumsy sentences to which both Milton and Taylor were too prone. And he was more constantly able than they were (though there is no doubt little to choose between the three at their very best) to communicate to his sentences that sound as of the silver trumpet, that wonderful melody of rhythmed though not metrical prose which is the peculiar glory of his age.

Even the most strictly formal criticism must, however, notice elements in the fascination exercised by Browne, which are independent of his strange and gorgeous vocabulary, independent of his unfamiliar but cunning composition, independent even of the attitude of melancholy yet affable irony which was referred to at the beginning of these remarks. His wide, it may almost be said his immense, reading was characteristic of his time, and though an additional, it is not a distinguishing charm. But there is in him something else which is almost wholly his own, which is not in Milton, or in Fuller, or in Glanvill, which is certainly not in Hobbes or Burton, and which makes one disposed to borrow Donne's hyperbole and say of his style that "it's body *thought*." It is observable first of course, and perhaps also most, in *Religio Medici*, to which I should like to affix the sub-titles "Religio Anglicani, Religio generosi, Religio Philosophi." But it is observable also in all works up to what seems to have been the last, though it is not the least, the *Christian Morals*. Some give less room for it than others; but always, wherever there is an opening —in the multifarious miscellany of the *Vulgar Errors*, in the quaint mysticism of the *Garden of Cyrus*, in the affectionate reasoning of the *Letter to a Friend*, in the learned disquisition and glowing rhetoric of the *Urn Burial*—it is there. It is a combination of the profoundest scepticism with the most fervent belief; a perfect ability to exercise the pickaxe and shovel of logic joined to a consciousness that anywhere may be met the wall of adamant against which pickaxe and shovel are powerless; a union of mathematical and mystical proficiency for which we may look elsewhere in vain. And perhaps hardly anything save this combination could have informed his style with its exquisite and unsurpassed quality.

GEORGE SAINTSBURY.

PART OF ADDRESS TO READER

OUR first intentions, considering the common interest of truth, resolved to propose it unto the Latin republick and equal judges of Europe, but, owing in the first place this service unto our country, and therein especially unto its ingenuous gentry, we have declared ourselves in a language best conceived. Although I confess the quality of the subject will sometimes carry us into expressions beyond mere English apprehensions. And, indeed, if elegancy still proceedeth, and English pens maintain that stream we have of late observed to flow from many, we shall, within few years, be fain to learn Latin to understand English, and a work will prove of equal facility in either. Nor have we addressed our pen or style unto the people (whom books do not redress, and who are this way incapable of reduction), but unto the knowing and leading part of learning. As well understanding (at least probably hoping) except they be watered from higher regions, and fructifying meteors of knowledge, these weeds must lose their alimental sap, and wither of themselves. Whose conserving influence could our endeavours prevent, we should trust the rest unto the scythe of time, and hopeful dominion of truth.

We hope it will not be unconsidered, that we find no open tract, or constant manuduction in this labyrinth, but are oft-times fain to wander in the America and untravelled parts of truth. For though, not many years past, Dr. Primrose hath made a learned discourse of Vulgar Errors in Physick, yet have we discussed but two or three thereof. Scipio Mercurii hath also left an excellent tract in Italian, concerning Popular Errors; but, confining himself only unto those in physick, he hath little conduced unto the generality of our doctrine. Laurentius Joubertus, by the same title, led our expectation into thoughts of great relief; whereby, notwithstanding, we reaped no advantage, it answering scarce at all the promise of the inscription. Nor, perhaps (if it were yet extant), should we find any further assistance from that ancient piece of Andreas, pretending the same title. And, therefore, we are often constrained to stand alone against the strength of opinion, and to meet the Goliah and giant of authority, with contemptible pebbles and feeble arguments, drawn from the scrip and slender stock of ourselves. Nor have we, indeed, scarce named any author whose name we do not honour ; and if detraction could invite us, discretion surely would contain us from any derogatory intention, where highest pens and friendliest eloquence must fail in commendation.

And therefore also we cannot but hope the equitable considerations, and candour of reasonable minds. We cannot expect the frown of theology herein ; nor can they which behold the present state of things, and controversy of points so long received in divinity, condemn our sober enquiries in the doubtful appertinences of arts, and receptaries of philosophy. Surely philologers and critical discoursers, who look beyond the shell and obvious exteriours of things, will not be angry with our narrower explorations. And we cannot doubt, our brothers in physick (whose knowledge in naturals will lead them into a nearer apprehension of many things delivered) will friendly accept, if not countenance, our endeavours. Nor can we conceive it may be unwelcome unto those honoured worthies who endeavour the advancement of learning ; as being likely to find a clearer progression, when so many rubs are levelled, and many untruths taken off, which passing as principles with common beliefs, disturb the tranquillity of axioms which otherwise might be raised. And wise men cannot but know that arts and learning want this expurgation ; and if the course of truth be permitted unto itself, like that of time and uncorrected computations, it cannot escape many errors, which duration still enlargeth.

Lastly, we are not magisterial in opinions, nor have we dictator-like obtruded our conceptions ; but, in the humility of enquiries or disquisitions, have only proposed them unto more ocular discerners. And therefore opinions are free ; and open it is for any to think or declare the contrary. And we shall so far encourage contradiction, as to promise no disturbance, or re-oppose any pen, that shall fallaciously or captiously refute us ; that shall only lay hold of our lapses, single out digressions, corollaries, or ornamental conceptions, to evidence his own in as indifferent truths. And shall only take notice of such, whose experimental and judicious knowledge shall solemnly look upon it ; not only to destroy of ours, but to establish of his own ; not to traduce or extenuate, but to explain and dilucidate, to add and ampliate, according to the laudable custom of the ancients in their sober promotions of learning. Unto whom notwithstanding, we shall not contentiously rejoin, or only to justify our own, but to applaud or confirm his maturer assertions ; and shall confer what is in us unto his name and honour ; ready to be swallowed in any worthy enlarger ;—as having acquired our end, if any way, or under any name, we may obtain a work, so much desired, and yet desiderated, of truth.

(From *Pseudodoxia Epidemica*.)

OF GRIFFINS

THAT there are griffins in nature, that is, a mixed and dubious animal, in the forepart resembling an eagle, and behind the shape of a lion, with erected ears, four feet, and a long tail, many affirm, and most, I perceive, deny not. The same is averred by Ælian, Solinus, Mela, and Herodotus—countenanced by the name sometimes found in Scripture, and was an hieroglyphic of the Egyptians.

Notwithstanding we find most diligent enquirers to be of a contrary assertion. For beside that Albertus and Pliny have disallowed it, the learned Aldrovandus hath, in a large discourse rejected it ; Matthias Michovius, who writ of those northern parts wherein men place these griffins, hath positively concluded against it ; and, if examined by the doctrine of animals, the invention is monstrous, nor much inferior unto the figment of sphynx, chimæra, and harpies ; for though there be some flying animals of mixed and participating natures, that is, between bird and quadruped, yet are their wings and legs so set together, that they seem to make each other, there being a commixtion of both, rather than an adaptation or cement of prominent parts unto each other ; as is observable in the bat, whose wings and forelegs are contrived in each other. For though some species there be of middle and participating natures, that is, of bird and beast, as bats and some few others ; yet are their parts so conformed and set together, that we cannot define the beginning or end of either ; there being a commixtion of both in the whole, rather than an adaptation or cement of the one unto the other.

Now for the word γρὺψ or *gryps*, sometimes mentioned in Scripture, and frequently in human authors, properly understood it signifies some kind of eagle or vulture, from whence the epithet *grypus*, for an hooked or aquiline nose. Thus when the Septuagint makes use of this word, Tremellius, and our translation, hath rendered it the ossifrage, which is one kind of eagle. And although the vulgar translation, and that annexed unto the Septuagint, retain the word *gryps*, which in ordinary and school construction is commonly rendered a griffin, yet cannot the Latin assume any other sense than the Greek, from whence it is borrowed. And though the Latin *gryphes* be altered somewhat by the addition of an *h*, or aspiration of the letter π, yet is not this unusual; so what the Greeks call τρόπαιον, the Latin will call *trophæum;* and that person which in the Gospel is named Κλέοπας, the Latins will render Cleophas. And therefore the quarrel of Origen was unjust, and his conception erroneous, when he conceived the food of griffins forbidden by the law of Moses; that is, poetical animals, and things of no existence. And therefore, when in the hecatombs and mighty oblations of the Gentiles, it is delivered they sacrificed *gryphes* or griffins, hereby we may understand some stronger sort of eagles. And therefore also, when it is said in Virgil, of an improper match, or Mopsus marrying Nysa, *Jungentur jam gryphes equis*, we need not hunt after other sense, than that strange unions shall be made, and different natures be conjoined together.

As for the testimonies of ancient writers, they are but derivative, and terminate all in one Aristeus, a poet of Proconesus, who affirmed that near the Arimaspi, or one-eyed nation, griffins defended the mines of gold. But this, as Herodotus delivereth, he wrote by hear-say; and Michovius, who had expressly written of those parts, plainly affirmeth, there is neither gold nor griffins in that country, nor any such animal extant; for so doth he conclude, *Ego vero contra veteres authores, gryphes nec in illa septentrionis, nec in aliis orbis partibus inveniri affirmarim.*

Lastly, concerning the hieroglyphical authority, although it nearest approach the truth, it doth not infer its existency. The conceit of the griffin, properly taken, being but a symbolical fancy, in so intolerable a shape including allowable morality. So doth it well make out the properties of a guardian, or any person entrusted; the ears implying attention; the wings, celerity of execution; the lion-like shape, courage and audacity; the hooked bill, reservance and tenacity. It is also an emblem of valour and magnanimity, as being compounded of the eagle and lion, the noblest animals in their kinds ; and so it is appliable unto princes, presidents, generals, and all heroic commanders ; and so is it also borne in the coat-arms of many noble families of Europe.

But the original invention seems to be hieroglyphical, derived from the Egyptians, and of an higher signification ; by the mystical conjunction of hawk and lion, implying either the genial or the syderous sun, the great celerity thereof, and the strength and vigour in its operations : and therefore, under such hieroglyphics Osyris was described ; and in ancient coins we meet with griffins conjointly with Apollo's *tripodes* and chariot wheels ; and the marble griffins at St. Peter's in Rome, as learned men conjecture, were first translated from the temple of Apollo. Whether hereby were not also mystically implied the activity of the sun in Leo, the power of God in the sun, or the influence of the celestial Osyris, by Moptha, the genius of Nilus, might also be considered. And than the learned Kircherus, no man were likely to be a better Œdipus. (From the Same.)

FAITH IN MYSTERIES

As for those wingy mysteries in divinity, and airy subtleties in religion, which have unhinged the brains of better heads, they never stretched the *pia mater* of mine. Methinks there be not impossibilities enough in religion for an active faith : the deepest mysteries ours contains have not only been illustrated, but maintained, by syllogism and the rule of reason. I love to lose myself in a mystery ; to pursue my reason to an *O altitudo !* 'Tis my solitary recreation to pose my apprehension with those involved enigmas and riddles of the Trinity, incarnation and resurrection. I can answer all the objections of Satan and my rebellious reason with that odd resolution I learned of Tertullian, *Certum est quia impossibile est.* I desire to exercise my faith in the difficultest point ; for, to credit ordinary and visible objects, is not faith but persuasion. Some believe the better for seeing Christ's sepulchre ; and, when they have seen the Red Sea, doubt not of the miracle. Now, contrarily, I bless myself, and am thankful, that I lived not

in the days of miracles ; that I never saw Christ nor His disciples.
I would not have been one of those Israelites that passed the
Red Sea ; nor one of Christ's patients, on whom He wrought His
wonders : then had my faith been thrust upon me ; nor should I
enjoy that greater blessing pronounced to all that believe and
saw not. 'Tis an easy and necessary belief, to credit what our
eye and sense hath examined. I believe He was dead, and
buried, and rose again ; and desire to see Him in His glory,
rather than to contemplate Him in His cenotaph or sepulchre.
Nor is this much to believe : as we have reason, we owe this
faith unto history : they only had the advantage of a bold and
noble faith, who lived before His coming, who, upon obscure
prophecies and mystical types, could raise a belief, and expect
apparent impossibilities. (From *Religio Medici.*)

A PROVIDENCE IN FORTUNE

THIS is the ordinary and open way of His providence, which art
and industry have in a good part discovered ; whose effects we
may foretell without an oracle. To foreshew these is not prophecy
but prognostication. There is another way, full of meanders and
labyrinths, whereof the devil and spirits have no exact ephemerides ;
and that is a more particular and obscure method of His providence ; directing the operations of individual and single essences :
this we call fortune ; that serpentine and crooked line, whereby
He draws those actions His wisdom intends in a more unknown
and secret way : this cryptic and involved method of His providence have I ever admired ; nor can I relate the history of my
life, the occurrences of my days, the escapes, or dangers, and
hits of chance, with a *bezo las manos* to Fortune, or a bare
gramercy to my good stars. Abraham might have thought the
ram in the thicket came thither by accident : human reason
would have said, that mere chance conveyed Moses in the ark
to the sight of Pharaoh's daughter. What a labyrinth is there in
the story of Joseph ! able to convert a stoick. Surely there
are in every man's life certain rubs, doublings, and wrenches,
which pass a while under the effects of chance ; but at
the last, well examined, prove the mere hand of God. 'Twas
not dumb chance that, to discover the fougade, or powder-plot,

contrived a miscarriage in the letter. I like the victory of '88 the better for that one occurrence which our enemies imputed to our dishonour, and the partiality of fortune ; to wit the tempests and contrariety of winds. King Philip did not detract from the nation, when he said, he sent his armada to fight with men, and not to combat with the winds. Where there is a manifest disproportion between the powers and forces of two several agents, upon a maxim of reason we may promise the victory to the superior : but when unexpected accidents slip in, and unthought-of occurrences intervene, these must proceed from a power that owes no obedience to those axioms ; where, as in the writing upon the wall, we may behold the hand, but see not the spring that moves it. The success of that petty province of Holland (of which the grand Seignior proudly said, if they should trouble him, as they did the Spaniard, he would send his men with shovels and pickaxes, and throw it into the sea) I cannot altogether ascribe to the ingenuity and industry of the people, but the mercy of God, that hath disposed them to such a thriving genius ; and to the will of His providence, that dispenseth His favour to each country in their preordinate season. All cannot be happy at once ; for, because the glory of one state depends upon the ruin of another, there is a revolution and vicissitude of their greatness, and must obey the swing of that wheel, not moved by intelligences, but by the hand of God, whereby all estates arise to their zenith and vertical points, according to their predestinated periods. For the lives, not only of men, but of commonwealths and the whole world, run not upon a helix that still enlargeth ; but on a circle, where, arriving to their meridian, they decline in obscurity, and fall under the horizon again.

(From the Same.)

OF THE NATURE OF ANGELS

THEREFORE, for spirits, I am so far from denying their existence, that I could easily believe, that not only whole countries, but particular persons, have their tutelary and guardian angels. It is not a new opinion of the church of Rome, but an old one of Pythagoras and Plato : there is no heresy in it : and if not manifestly defined in Scripture, yet it is an opinion of a good and wholesome use in the course and actions of a man's life ; and would serve as an hypothesis to salve many doubts, whereof common philosophy affordeth no solution. Now, if you demand my opinion and metaphysicks of their natures, I confess them very shallow; most of them in a negative way, like that of God; or in a comparative, between ourselves and fellow-creatures: for there is in this universe a stair, or manifest scale, of creatures, rising not disorderly, or in confusion, but with a comely method and proportion. Between creatures of mere existence and things of life there is a large disproportion of nature: between plants and animals, or creatures of sense, a wider difference: between them and man, a far greater: and if the proportion hold on, between man and angels there should be yet a greater. We do not comprehend their natures, who retain the first definition of Porphyry; and distinguish them from ourselves by immortality: for, before his fall, man also was immortal: yet must we needs affirm that he had a different essence from the angels. Having, therefore, no certain knowledge of their nature, 'tis no bad method of the schools, whatsoever perfection we find obscurely in ourselves, in a more complete and absolute way to ascribe unto them. I believe they have an extemporary knowledge, and, upon the first motion of their reason, do what we cannot without study or deliberation: that they know things by their forms, and define, by specifical difference, what we describe by accidents and properties: and therefore probabilities to us may be demonstrations unto them; that they have knowledge not only of the specifical, but numerical, forms of individuals, and understand by what reserved difference each single hypostasis (besides the relation to its species) becomes its numerical self; that, as the soul hath a power to move the body it informs, so there's a faculty to move any, though inform none: ours upon restraint of time, place, and distance: but that invisible hand that conveyed Habakkuk to the lion's den, or Philip to Azotus, infringeth this rule, and hath a secret conveyance, wherewith mortality is not acquainted. If they have that intuitive knowledge, whereby, as in reflection, they behold the thoughts of one another, I cannot peremptorily deny but they know a great part of ours. They that, to refute the invocation of saints, have denied that they have any knowledge of our affairs below, have proceeded too far, and must pardon my opinion, till I can thoroughly answer that piece of Scripture, "At the conversion of a sinner, the angels in heaven rejoice." I cannot, with those in that great father, securely in-

terpret the work of the first day, *fiat lux*, to the creation of angels ;
though I confess there is not any creature that hath so near a
glimpse of their nature as light in the sun and elements : we style
it a bare accident ; but, where it subsists alone, 'tis a spiritual
substance, and may be an angel ; in brief, conceive light invisible,
and that is a spirit.   From the Same.)

THE SOUL ILLIMITABLE

NOW for my life, it is a miracle of thirty years, which to relate,
were not a history, but a piece of poetry, and would sound to
common ears like a fable.   For the world, I count it not an inn,
but a hospital ; and a place not to live, but to die in.   The world
that I regard is myself ; it is the microcosm of my own frame
that I cast mine eye on : for the other, I use it but like my globe,
and turn it round sometimes for my recreation.   Men that look
upon my outside, perusing only my condition and fortunes, do err
in my altitude ; for I am above Atlas's shoulders.   The earth is
a point not only in respect of the heavens above us, but of that
heavenly and celestial part within us.   That mass of flesh that
circumscribes me limits not my mind.   That surface that tells
the heavens it hath an end cannot persuade me I have any.   I
take my circle to be about three hundred and sixty.   Though
the number of the ark do measure my body, it comprehendeth
not my mind.   Whilst I study to find how I am a microcosm,
or little world, I find myself something more than the great.
There is surely a piece of divinity in us ; something that was
before the elements, and owes no homage unto the sun.   Nature
tells me, I am the image of God as well as Scripture.   He that
understands not thus much hath not his introduction or first lesson,
and is yet to begin the alphabet of man.   Let me not injure the
felicity of others, if I say I am as happy as any.   *Ruat cœlum,
fiat voluntas tua*, salveth all ; so that, whatsoever happens, it is
but what our daily prayers desire.   In brief, I am content ; and
what should providence add more ?   Surely this is it we call
happiness, and this do I enjoy ; with this I am happy in a dream,
and as content to enjoy a happiness in a fancy, as others in a
more apparent truth and reality.   There is surely a nearer apprehension of anything that delights us in our dreams, than in our
waked senses.   Without this I were unhappy ; for my awaked

judgment discontents me, ever whispering unto me that I am from my friend, but my friendly dreams in the night requite me, and make me think I am within his arms. I thank God for my happy dreams, as I do for my good rest ; for there is a satisfaction in them unto reasonable desires, and such as can be content with a fit of happiness. And surely it is not a melancholy conceit to think we are all asleep in this world, and that the conceits of this life are as mere dreams, to those of the next, as the phantasms of the night, to the conceit of the day. There is an equal delusion in both ; and the one doth but seem to be the emblem or picture of the other. We are somewhat more than ourselves in our sleeps ; and the slumber of the body seems to be but the waking of the soul. It is the ligation of sense, but the liberty of reason ; and our waking conceptions do not match the fancies of our sleeps. At my nativity, my ascendant was the earthly sign of *Scorpio*. I was born in the planetary hour of *Saturn*, and I think I have a piece of that leaden planet in me. I am no way facetious, nor disposed for the mirth and galliardise of company ; yet in one dream I can compose a whole comedy, behold the action, apprehend the jests, and laugh myself awake at the conceits thereof. Were my memory as faithful as my reason is then fruitful, I would never study but in my dreams, and this time also would I choose for my devotions : but our grosser memories have then so little hold of our abstracted understandings, that they forget the story, and can only relate to our awaked souls a confused and broken tale of that which hath passed. Aristotle, who hath written a singular tract of sleep, hath not methinks thoroughly defined it ; nor yet Galen, though he seems to have corrected it ; for those *noctambulos* and night-walkers, though in their sleep, do yet enjoy the action of their senses. We must therefore say that there is something in us that is not in the jurisdiction of Morpheus ; and that those abstracted and ecstatick souls do walk about in their own corpses, as spirits with the bodies they assume, wherein they seem to hear, see, and feel though indeed the organs are destitute of sense, and their natures of those faculties that should inform them. Thus it is observed, that men sometimes, upon the hour of their departure, do speak and reason above themselves. For then the soul begins to be freed from the ligaments of the body, begins to reason like herself, and to discourse in a strain above mortality.   (From the Same.)

SLEEP

But the quincunx of heaven runs low, and 'tis time to close the five ports of knowledge. We are unwilling to spin out our awaking thoughts into the phantasms of sleep, which often continueth precogitations ; making cables of cobwebs, and wildernesses of handsome groves. Beside Hippocrates hath spoke so little, and the oneirocritical masters have left such frigid interpretations from plants, that there is little encouragement to dream of paradise itself. Nor will the sweetest delight of gardens afford much comfort in sleep ; wherein the dulness of that sense shakes hands with delectable odours ; and though in the bed of Cleopatra, can hardly with any delight raise up the ghost of a rose.

Night, which Pagan theology could make the daughter of Chaos, affords no advantage to the description of order ; although no lower than that mass can we derive its genealogy. All things began in order, so shall they end, and so shall they begin again ; according to the ordainer of order and mystical mathematicks of the city of heaven.

Though Somnus in Homer be sent to rouse up Agamemnon, I find no such effects in these drowsy approaches of sleep. To keep our eyes open longer were but to act our antipodes. The huntsmen are up in America, and they are already past their first sleep in Persia. But who can be drowsy at that hour which freed us from everlasting sleep ? or have slumbering thoughts at that time, when sleep itself must end, and as some conjecture all shall awake again. (From the *Garden of Cyrus.*)

THE VANITY OF AMBITION

Now since these dead bones have already out-lasted the living ones of Methuselah, and, in a yard under ground and thin walls of clay, out-worn all the strong and specious buildings above it ; and quietly rested under the drums and tramplings of three conquests : what prince can promise such diuturnity unto his relicks, or might not gladly say,

Sic ego componi versus in ossa velim ?

Time, which antiquates antiquities, and hath an art to make dust of all things, hath yet spared these minor monuments. In vain we hope to be known by open and visible conservatories, when to be unknown was the means of their continuation, and obscurity their protection. If they died by violent hands, and were thrust into their urns, these bones become considerable, and some old philosophers would honour them, whose souls they conceived most pure, which were thus snatched from their bodies, and to retain a stronger propension unto them; whereas they weariedly left a languishing corpse, and with faint desires of reunion. If they fell by long and aged decay, yet wrapt up in the bundle of time, they fall into indistinction, and make but one blot with infants. If we begin to die when we live, and long life be but a prolongation of death, our life is a sad composition; we live with death, and die not in a moment. How many pulses made up the life of Methuselah, were work for Archimedes: common counters sum up the life of Moses his man. Our days become considerable, like petty sums, by minute accumulations; where numerous fractions make up but small round numbers; and our days of a span long, make not one little finger.

If the nearness of our last necessity brought a nearer conformity into it, there were a happiness in hoary hairs, and no calamity in half senses. But the long habit of living indisposeth us for dying; when avarice makes us the sport of death, when even David grew politickly cruel, and Solomon could hardly be said to be the wisest of men. But many are too early old, and before the date of age. Adversity stretcheth our days, misery makes Alcmena's nights, and time hath no wings unto it. But the most tedious being is that which can unwish itself, content to be nothing, or never to have been, which was beyond the mal-content of Job, who cursed not the day of his life, but his nativity; content to have so far been, as to have a title to future being, although he had lived here but in an hidden state of life, and as it were an abortion.

What song the Syrens sang, or what name Achilles assumed when he hid himself among women, though puzzling questions, are not beyond all conjecture. What time the persons of these ossuaries entered the famous nations of the dead, and slept with princes and counsellors, might admit a wide solution. But who were the proprietaries of these bones, or what bodies these ashes made up, were a question above antiquarism; not to be resolved by man, nor easily perhaps by spirits, except we consult the provincial guardians, or tutelary observators. Had they made as good provision for their names, as they have done for their relicks, they had not so grossly erred in the art of perpetuation. But to subsist in bones, and be but pyramidally extant, is a fallacy in duration. Vain ashes which in the oblivion of names, persons, times, and sexes, have found unto themselves a fruitless continuation, and only arise unto late posterity, as emblems of mortal vanities, antidotes against pride, vain-glory, and madding vices. Pagan vain-glories which thought the world might last for ever, had encouragement for ambition ; and, finding no *atropos* unto the immortality of their names, were never damped with the necessity of oblivion. Even old ambitions had the advantage of ours, in the attempts of their vain-glories, who acting early, and before the probable meridian of time, have by this time found great accomplishment of their designs, whereby the ancient heroes have already out-lasted their monuments and mechanical preservations. But in this latter scene of time, we cannot expect such mummies unto our memories, when ambition may fear the prophecy of Elias, and Charles the Fifth can never hope to live within two Methuselahs of Hector.

And therefore, restless inquietude for the diuturnity of our memories unto present considerations seems a vanity almost out of date, and superannuated piece of folly. We cannot hope to live so long in our names, as some have done in their persons. One face of Janus holds no proportion unto the other. 'Tis too late to be ambitious. The great mutations of the world are acted, or time may be too short for our designs. To extend our memories by monuments, whose death we daily pray for, and whose duration we cannot hope, without injury to our expectations in the advent of the last day, were a contradiction to our beliefs. We, whose generations are ordained in this setting part of time, are providentially taken off from such imaginations ; and, being necessitated to eye the remaining particle of futurity, are naturally constituted unto thoughts of the next world, and cannot excusably decline the consideration of that duration, which maketh pyramids pillars of snow, and all that's past a moment.

(From *Urn Burial*.)

IMAGINATION SWEETENS LIFE

JULIUS SCALIGER, who in a sleepless fit of the gout could make two hundred verses in a night, would have but five plain words upon his tomb. And this serious person, though no minor wit, left the poetry of his epitaph unto others; either unwilling to commend himself or to be judged by a distich, and perhaps considering how unhappy great poets have been in versifying their own epitaphs: wherein Petrarca, Dante, and Ariosto, have so unhappily failed, that if their tombs should out-last their works, posterity would find so little of Apollo on them, as to mistake them for Ciceronian poets.

In this deliberate and creeping progress unto the grave, he was somewhat too young and of too noble a mind, to fall upon that stupid symptom observable in divers persons near their journey's end, and which may be reckoned among the mortal symptoms of their last disease; that is, to become more narrow minded, miserable, and tenacious, unready to part with any thing, when they are ready to part with all, and afraid to want when they have no time to spend; meanwhile physicians, who know that many are mad but in a single depraved imagination, and one prevalent decipiency; and that beside and out of such single deliriums a man may meet with sober actions and good sense in Bedlam; cannot but smile to see the heirs and concerned relations gratulating themselves on the sober departure of their friends; and though they behold such mad, covetous passages, content to think they die in good understanding, and in their sober senses.

Avarice, which is not only infidelity but idolatry, either from covetous progeny or questuary education, had no root in his breast, who made good works the expression of his faith, and was big with desires unto public and lasting charities; and surely where good wishes and charitable intentions exceed abilities, theorical beneficency may be more than a dream. They build not castles in the air who would build churches on earth; and though they leave no such structures here, may lay good foundations in heaven. In brief, his life and death were such, that I could not blame them who wished the like, and almost to have been himself; almost I say; for though we may wish the prosperous appurtenances of others, or to be another in his happy accidents, yet so intrinsical is every man unto himself, that some doubt may be made, whether any would exchange his being, or substantially become another man.

He had wisely seen the world at home and abroad, and thereby observed under what variety men are deluded in the pursuit of that which is not here to be found. And although he had no opinion of reputed felicities below, and apprehended men widely out in the estimate of such happiness ; yet his sober contempt of the world wrought no Democritism or Cynicism, no laughing or snarling at it, as well understanding there are not felicities in this world to satisfy a serious mind ; and therefore, to soften the stream of our lives, we are fain to take in the reputed contentions of this world, to unite with the crowd in their beatitudes, and to make ourselves happy by consortion, opinion, or co-existimation : for strictly to separate from received and customary felicities, and to confine unto the rigour of realities, were to contract the consolation of our beings unto too uncomfortable circumscriptions.

(From the *Letter to a Friend.*)

SOMETHING TO BE LOVED IN ALL

WHEN thou lookest upon the imperfections of others, allow one eye for what is laudable in them, and the balance they have from some excellency, which may render them considerable. While we look with fear or hatred upon the teeth of the viper, we may behold his eye with love. In venomous natures something may be amiable : poisons afford antipoisons : nothing is totally, or altogether uselessly bad. Notable virtues are sometimes dashed with notorious vices, and in some vicious tempers have been found illustrious acts of virtue ; which makes such observable worth in some actions of king Demetrius, Antonius, and Ahab, as are not to be found in the same kind in Aristides, Numa, or David. Constancy, generosity, clemency, and liberality have been highly conspicuous in some persons not marked out in other concerns for example or imitation. But since goodness is exemplary in all, if others have not our virtues, let us not be wanting in theirs ; nor scorning them for their vices whereof we are free, be condemned by their virtues wherein we are deficient. There is dross, alloy, and embasement in all human tempers ; and he flieth without wings who thinks to find ophir or pure metal in any. For perfection is not, like light, centered in any one body ; but, like the dispersed seminalities of vegetables at the creation, scattered through the whole mass of the earth, no place producing all and almost all some. So that 'tis well, if a perfect man can be made out of many men, and, to the perfect eye of God, even out of mankind. Time, which perfects some things, imperfects also others. Could we intimately apprehend the ideated man, and as he stood in the intellect of God upon the first exertion by creation, we might more narrowly comprehend our present degeneration, and how widely we are fallen from the pure exemplar and idea of our nature : for after this corruptive elongation from a primitive and pure creation, we are almost lost in degeneration ; and Adam hath not only fallen from his Creator, but we ourselves from Adam our tycho and primary generator.

(From *Christian Morals.*)

WALK NOT WITH LEADEN SANDALS

SINCE thou hast an alarum in thy breast, which tells thee thou hast a living spirit in thee above two thousand times in an hour ; dull not away thy days in slothful supinity and the tediousness of doing nothing. To strenuous minds there is an inquietude in over quietness, and no laboriousness in labour ; and to tread a mill after the slow pace of the snail, or the heavy measures of the lazy of Brazilia, were a most tiring penance, and worse than a race of some furlongs at the Olympics. The rapid courses of the heavenly bodies are rather imitable by our thoughts, than our corporeat motions ; yet the solemn motions of our lives amount unto a greater measure than is commonly apprehended. Some few men have surrounded the globe of the earth ; yet many in the set locomotions and movements of their days have measured the circuit of it, and twenty thousand miles have been exceeded by them. Move circumspectly, not meticulously, and rather carefully solicitous, than anxiously solicitudinous. Think not there is a lion in the way, nor walk with leaden sandals in the paths of goodness ; but in all virtuous motions let prudence determine thy measures. Strive not to run like Hercules, a furlong in a breath : festination may prove precipitation ; deliberating delay may be wise cunctation, and slowness no slothfulness.

(From the Same.)

TEMPERANCE IN PLEASURE

PUNISH not thyself with pleasure ; glut not thy sense with palative delights ; nor revenge the contempt of temperance by the penalty of satiety. Were there an age of delight or any pleasure durable, who would not honour Volupia ? but the race of delight is short, and pleasures have mutable faces. The pleasures of one age are not pleasures in another, and their lives fall short of our own. Even in our sensual days, the strength of delight is in its seldomness or rarity, and sting in its satiety : mediocrity is its life, and immoderacy its confusion. The luxurious emperors of old inconsiderately satiated themselves with the dainties of sea and land, till, wearied through all varieties, their refections became a study unto them, and they were fain to feed by invention : novices in true epicurism ! which, by mediocrity, paucity, quick and healthful appetite, makes delights smartly acceptable ; whereby Epicurus himself found Jupiter's brain in a piece of Cytheridian cheese, and the tongues of nightingales in a dish of onions. Hereby healthful and temperate poverty hath the start of nauseating luxury ; unto whose clear and naked appetite every meal is a feast, and in one single dish the first course of Metellus ; who are cheaply hungry and never lose their hunger, or advantage of a craving appetite, because obvious food contents it ; while Nero, half famished, could not feed upon a piece of bread, and, lingering after his snowed water, hardly got down an ordinary cup of Calda. By such circumscriptions of pleasure the contemned philosophers reserved unto themselves the secret of delight, which the helluos of those days lost in their exorbitances. In vain we study delight ; it is at the command of every sober mind, and in every sense born with us ; but nature who teacheth us the rule of pleasure, instructeth also in the bounds thereof, and where its line expireth. And, therefore, temperate minds, not pressing their pleasures until the sting appeareth, enjoy their contentations contentedly, and without regret, and so escape the folly of excess, to be pleased unto displacency. (From the Same.)

THE LIMITS OF FELICITY

COURT not felicity too far, and weary not the favourable hand of fortune. Glorious actions have their times, extent, and *non ultras*.

To put no end unto attempts were to make prescription of successes, and to bespeak unhappiness at the last : for the line of our lives is drawn with white and black vicissitudes, wherein the extremes hold seldom one complexion. That Pompey should obtain the surname of great at twenty-five years, that men in their young and active days should be fortunate and perform notable things, is no observation of deep wonder ; they having the strength of their fates before them, nor yet acted their parts in the world for which they were brought into it ; whereas men of years, matured for counsels and designs, seem to be beyond the vigour of their active fortunes, and high exploits of life, providentially ordained unto ages best agreeable unto them. And, therefore, many brave men finding their fortune grow faint, and feeling its declination, have timely withdrawn themselves from great attempts, and so escaped the ends of mighty men, disproportionable to their beginnings. But magnanimous thoughts have so dimmed the eyes of many, that forgetting the very essence of fortune, and the vicissitude of good and evil, they apprehend no bottom in felicity ; and so have been still tempted on unto mighty actions, reserved for their destructions. For fortune lays the plot of our adversities in the foundation of our felicities, blessing us in the first quadrate, to blast us more sharply in the last. And since in the highest felicities there lieth a capacity of the lowest miseries, she hath this advantage from our happiness to make us truly miserable : for to become acutely miserable we are to be first happy. Affliction smarts most in the most happy state, as having somewhat in it of Belisarius at beggar's bush, or Bajazet in the grate. And this the fallen angels severely understand ; who have acted their first part in heaven, are made sharply miserable by transition, and more afflictively feel the contrary state of hell.

(From the Same.)

UN-MAN NOT THYSELF

LIVE unto the dignity of thy nature, and leave it not disputable at last, whether thou hast been a man ; or, since thou art a composition of man and beast, how thou hast predominantly passed thy days, to state the denomination. Un-man not, therefore thyself by a bestial transformation, nor realise old fables. Expose not thyself by four-footed manners unto monstrous draughts, and caricature representations. Think not after the old Pythagorean conceit, what beast thou may'st be after death. Be not under any brutal metempsychosis, while thou livest and walkest about erectly under the scheme of man. In thine own circumference, as in that of the earth, let the rational horizon be larger than the sensible, and the circle of reason than of sense : let the divine part be upward, and the region of beast below ; otherwise, 'tis but to live invertedly, and with thy head unto the heels of thy antipodes. Desert not thy title to a divine particle and union with invisibles. Let true knowledge and virtue tell the lower world thou art a part of the higher. Let thy thoughts be of things which have not entered into the hearts of beasts : think of things long past, and long to come : acquaint thyself with the choragium of the stars, and consider the vast expansion beyond them. Let intellectual tubes give thee a glance of things which visive organs reach not. Have a glimpse of incomprehensibles ; and thoughts of things, which thoughts but tenderly touch. Lodge immaterials in thy head ; ascend unto invisibles ; fill thy spirit with spirituals, with the mysteries of faith, the magnalities of religion, and thy life with the honour of God ; without which, though giants in wealth and dignity, we are but dwarfs and pygmies in humanity, and may hold a pitiful rank in that triple division of mankind into heroes, men, and beasts. For though human souls are said to be equal, yet is there no small inequality in their operations ; some maintain the allowable station of men ; many are far below it ; and some have been so divine, as to approach the apogeum of their natures, and to be in the confinium of spirits.

Behold thyself by inward opticks and the crystalline of thy soul. Strange it is that in the most perfect sense there should be so many fallacies, that we are fain to make a doctrine, and often to see by art. But the greatest imperfection is in our inward sight, that is, to be ghosts unto our own eyes ; and while we are so sharp-sighted as to look through others, to be invisible unto ourselves ; for the inward eyes are more fallacious than the outward. The vices we scoff at in others, laugh at us within ourselves. Avarice, pride, falsehood lie undiscerned and blindly in us, even to the age of blindness ; and, therefore, to see ourselves interiorly, we are fain to borrow other men's eyes ; wherein true friends are good informers, and censurers no bad friends. Conscience only, that can see without light, sits in the areopagy and dark tribunal of our hearts, surveying our thoughts and condemning their obliquities. Happy is that state of vision that can see without light, though all should look as before the creation, when there was not an eye to see, or light to actuate a vision : wherein, notwithstanding, obscurity is only imaginable respectively unto eyes ; for unto God there was none : eternal light was ever ; created light was for the creation, not Himself ; and, as He saw before the sun, may still also see without it. In the city of the new Jerusalem there is neither sun nor moon ; where glorified eyes must see by the archetypal sun, or the light of God, able to illuminate intellectual eyes, and make unknown visions. Intuitive perceptions in spiritual beings may, perhaps, hold some analogy unto vision : but yet how they see us, or one another, what eye, what light, or what perception is required unto their intuition, is yet dark unto our apprehension ; and even how they see God, or how unto our glorified eyes the beatifical vision will be celebrated, another world must tell us, when perceptions will be new, and we may hope to behold invisibles. (From the Same.)

IZAAK WALTON

[Izaak Walton was born at Stafford in August 1593. He came early up to London, and took a shop in Cornhill. In 1617-18 he was made one of the Ironmongers' Company. In 1624 we find him a linen-draper in Fleet Street, near Chancery Lane, and in 1630 he bought a house in the latter thoroughfare. He possessed many noble and clerical friends, whose acquaintance he sedulously cultivated. To the *LXXX. Sermons* of Dr. Donne he prefixed in 1640 his *Life* of that worthy. His *Life of Sir Henry Wotton* appeared in the same year. During the Civil War he retired to Stafford. His *Complete Angler* made its first appearance in 1653. He published the *Life of Hooker* in 1662 ; the *Life of George Herbert* in 1670 in a first complete edition of the four *Lives;* the *Life of Sanderson* followed in 1678 ; and, possibly, a work called *Love and Truth* in 1680. He spent the close of his career in the house of his son-in-law, Prebendary Hawkins, in Winchester, where he died in his ninety-first year on the 15th day of December 1683, and was buried in Winchester Cathedral.]

IZAAK WALTON closes his most celebrated work with the words, " Study to be quiet." This is the fit colophon to his literary achievement. His work as an author and as a man is summed up in the phrase. Born to stirring times, it was his fortune to live into times that were more than stirring—times that were turbulent, resonant, vociferous. He loved peaceful chatting with gracious elderly persons about pastoral and meditative themes. He liked to walk by still waters, through quiet, dreamy meadows. But it was his fate to find the civic stillness which he delighted in broken up by arms and onsets, and to see the sword of Civil War vambrashed from one end of England to the other. These conditions did not change the current of his style ; they only forced it to dig a deeper channel, and so helped to develop that delicate and pensive product which is the prose of Izaak Walton.

It would have greatly surprised and scandalised the author of the *Complete Angler* to have been told that in two centuries' time everybody would still be reading him, when only scholars continued to turn the pages of his magnificent friend, Dr. Donne.

How clear and strong, in spite of its modesty, was the individuality of Walton is shown by the fact that his unbounded admiration of Donne as a preacher and a theological essayist has in no way affected his own manner of writing. After the brutality of so much of Elizabethan prose, especially of the lighter sort, the note of most sweet amenity comes to us refreshingly in Walton. But it does not appear that it was audible to his own contemporaries. He was hardly considered until the eighteenth century as a writer at all, but only as the purveyor of certain interesting and accurate professional observations. In his youth Greene and Nash had been read, and there still remained a tradition that a certain violence was requisite to garnish prose of the entertaining variety. Perhaps the very qualities which we delight in in Walton —the extraordinary simplicity and lucidity—seemed undignified to the stately taste of the seventeenth century.

The prose of Walton is very original in character. In his use of the dialogue form he may have owed something to the graceful pastoral pamphlets of Nicholas Breton. Perhaps he had admired the essays of the unfortunate Sir Thomas Overbury. In all essential respects, however, his pleasant amalgam of science and poetry, of learning and experience, appears to be an invention of his own. His discourse "seems to be music, and charms us to an attention." The curious disease of Euphuism is seen to be quite cured by the time we reach Walton ; not a trace of it is left in him, though it was to be met with long afterwards in writers of far greater pretension. His vocabulary is very modern. Sometimes the easy nature of the style betrays it into incorrectness, but even this is modern. When Walton is roused by some exciting topic, whether it be "the lost credit of the poor despised chubb," or the desirability of drinking "a civil cup to all otter-hunters," he is often startlingly felicitous. We feel inclined to say to him, as Venator did to Piscator, "Ay, marry, sir ! now you talk like an artist."

The famous milkmaid passage, which we quote among our selections, is perhaps the most admirable which Walton has left us. It is introduced abruptly, yet not without art ; it is evident that the gentle author perceived the patch to be a purple one. All the little side-pictures which are introduced in this portion of the *Complete Angler* are wonderfully graphic. The otter-hunt is as picturesque as any of our modern naturalists could make it. Yet perhaps the best example of sustained felicity in Walton is the long Lucianic dispute between Piscator, Venator, and Auceps, each extolling his trade. There is something Greek in the simplicity and extreme naturalness of this triologue, in which air, earth, and water seem contending in the gallant persons of the Falconer, the Fox-Hunter, and the Fisherman. It seems a pity that Walton wrote so little in this broad and philosophic manner, celebrating the arts of active life and the ideals of the sportsman with blossoming hawthorn for a background, and the lark and throstle for an orchestra.

A certain happy strain in English prose may be said to start with Izaak Walton. Of the same stock have followed Sterne and Lamb and Mr. Robert Louis Stevenson. These are the delicate moralists that make a flute of our language, and pipe to us in a mode that is "free and pleasant and civilly merry" so artlessly that we are in danger of forgetting that it is the very consummation of art. The humour of Walton is charming. We can imagine Charles Lamb gravely inquiring, "How could Cleopatra have feasted Mark Antony with eight wild boars roasted whole at one supper if the earth had not been a bountiful mother?" No one before him had just this turn of phrase, this playful archness, and we conceive his fun to have trotted about quite unnoticed between the legs of the elephantine Jacobean facetiousness. It is to be noted too, as a point which links him more with the later humourists of our country, that his sentences are often admirably terse, and that he was disengaged from those coils of verbiage in which his contemporaries writhed like Laocoons.

As a biographer, again, Walton was an innovator. The five short lives which he published, though pale by the side of such work in biography as the end of the eighteenth century introduced, are yet notable as among the earliest which aim at giving us a vivid portrait of the man, instead of a discreet and conventional testimonial. It is to Walton, too, that we owe the idea of illustrating and developing biography by means of correspondence. Without doubt his incorrigible optimism entered into his study of the character of his friends, and it is no part of his inexperience as a portrait-painter that he mixes his colours with so much rose-water. He saw his distinguished acquaintances in that light; he saw them pure, radiant, and stately beyond a mortal guise, and he could not be true to himself unless he gave them the superhuman graces at which we may now smile a little. We sometimes feel that the stiffness of the biographical portrait is irksome to him. But here, as elsewhere, the artist is true to himself. Between the production of his *Life of Donne* and his *Life of Sanderson* nearly forty years elapsed, and prose style had in the meantime undergone extraordinary changes. But Walton is unchanged, the same graceful loquacity, the same limpid and serious sweetness, the same distinguished presentation of experience, mark the first biography and the latest. He is not seen quite so often at his best in the *Lives* as in the *Complete Angler*, where he may weave into his composition as many verses and as much music, as many flowers and as much fancy, as his heart desires,

EDMUND GOSSE.

WHAT WE OWE TO THE BIRDS

NAY, more, the very birds of the air, those that be not hawks, are both so many and so useful and pleasant to mankind, that I must not let them pass without some observations ; they both feed and refresh him——feed him with their choice bodies, and refresh him with their heavenly voices.   I will not undertake to mention the several kinds of fowl by which this is done, and his curious palate pleased by day, and which with their very excrements afford him a soft lodging at night.   These I will pass by, but not those little nimble musicians of the air, that warble forth their curious ditties with which Nature has furnished them to the shame of art.

At first the lark, when she means to rejoice, to cheer herself and those that hear her, she then quits the earth and sings as she ascends higher into the air ; and, having ended her heavenly employment, grows then mute and sad to think she must descend to the dull earth, which she would not touch but for necessity.

How do the blackbird and thrassel with their melodious voices bid welcome to the cheerful spring, and in their fixed months warble forth such ditties as no art or instrument can reach to !

Nay, the smaller birds also do the like in their particular seasons, as namely the laverock, the titlark, the little linnet, and the honest robin, that loves mankind both alive and dead.

But the nightingale, another of my airy creatures, breathes such sweet loud music out of her little instrumental throat, that it might make mankind to think miracles are not ceased.   He that at midnight, when the very labourer sleeps securely, should hear, as I have very often, the clear airs, the sweet descants, the natural rising and falling, the doubling and redoubling of her voice, might well be lifted above earth, and say, "Lord, what music hast Thou provided for the saints in heaven, when Thou affordest bad men such music on earth ?"

(From *The Complete Angler.*)

ANGLING AN ART

Piscator. Well, now, Mr. Venator, you shall neither want time nor my attention to hear you enlarge your discourse concerning hunting.

Venator. Not I, sir. I remember you said that angling itself was of great antiquity, and a perfect art, and an art not easily attained to; and you have so won upon me in your former discourse, that I am very desirous to hear what you can say further concerning those particulars.

Pisc. Sir, I did say so, and I doubt not but if you and I did converse together but a few hours, to leave you possessed with the same high and happy thoughts that now possess me of it; not only of the antiquity of angling, but that it deserves commendations, and that it is an art, and an art worthy the knowledge and practice of a wise man.

Ven. Pray, sir, speak of them what you think fit, for we have yet five miles to the Thatched House, during which walk I dare promise you my patience, and diligent attention shall not be wanting. And if you shall make that to appear which you have undertaken; first, that it is an art, and an art worth the learning, I shall beg that I may attend you a day or two a-fishing, and that I may become your scholar, and be instructed in the art itself which you so much magnify.

Pisc. O sir, doubt not but that angling is an art. Is it not an art to deceive a trout with an artificial fly? a trout that is more sharp-sighted than any hawk you have named, and more watchful and timorous than your high-mettled merlin is bold! and yet I doubt not to catch a brace or two to-morrow for a friend's breakfast. Doubt not, therefore, sir, but that angling is an art, and an art worth your learning; the question is rather, whether you be capable of learning it? for angling is somewhat like poetry, men are to be born so—I mean with inclinations to it, though both may be heightened by discourse and practice; but he that hopes to be a good angler must not only bring an inquiring, searching, observing wit, but he must bring a large measure of hope and patience, and a love and propensity to the art itself; but having once got and practised it, then doubt not but angling will prove to be so pleasant that it will prove to be like virtue, a reward to itself.   (From the Same.)

THE OTTER HUNT

Venator. My friend Piscator, you have kept time with my thoughts ; for the sun is just rising, and I myself just now come to this place, and the dogs have just now put down an Otter. Look down at the bottom of the hill there in what meadow, checkered with water-lilies and lady-smocks ; there you may see what work they make. Look ! Look ! you may see all busy, men and dogs, dogs and men, all busy.

Piscator. Sir, I am right glad to meet you, and glad to have so fair an entrance into this day's sport, and glad to see so many dogs and more men all in pursuit of the Otter. Let's compliment no longer, but join unto them. Come, honest Venator, let's be gone, let us make haste ; I long to be doing : no reasonable hedge or ditch shall hold me.

Ven. Gentleman, Huntsman, where found you this Otter ?

Huntsman. Marry, Sir, we found her a mile from this place, a-fishing ; she has this morning eaten the greatest part of this trout ; she has only left thus much of it, as you see, and was fishing for more. When we came, we found her just at it : but we were here very early, we were here an hour before sunrise, and have given her no rest since we came ; sure she will hardly escape all these dogs and men. I am to have the skin if we kill her.

Ven. Why, Sir, what's the skin worth ?

Hunt. 'Tis worth ten shillings to make gloves ; the gloves of an Otter are the best fortification for your hands that can be thought on against wet weather.

Pisc. I pray, honest Huntsman, let me ask you a pleasant question : Do you hunt a beast or a fish ?

Hunt. Sir, it is not in my power to resolve you. I leave it to be resolved by the College of Carthusians, who have made vows never to eat flesh. But I have heard the question hath been debated among many great clerks, and they seem to differ about it ; yet most agree that her tail is fish : and if her body be fish too, then I may say that a fish will walk upon land, for an Otter does so sometimes five, or six, or ten miles in a night, to catch for her young ones, or to glut herself with fish, and I can tell you that pigeons will fly forty miles for a breakfast ; but, Sir, I am sure the Otter devours much fish, and kills and spoils much more than he eats : and I can tell you that this Dog-fisher, for so the Latins call him, can smell a fish in the water an hundred yards from him : Gesner says much farther ; and that there is an herb, Benione, which being hung in a linen-cloth near a fish-pond, or any haunt that he uses, makes him to avoid the place ; which proves he smells both by water and land. And I can tell you there is brave hunting this water-dog in Cornwall ; where there have been so many, that our learned Camden says there is a river called Ottersey, which was so named by reason of the abundance of Otters that bred and fed in it. (From the Same.)

THE MILKMAID'S SONG

Piscator. Nay, stay a little, good Scholar ; I caught my last Trout with a worm ; now I will put on a minnow and try a quarter of an hour about yonder trees for another, and so walk towards our lodging. Look you, Scholar, thereabout we shall have a bite presently, or not at all. Have with you, Sir ! o' my word, I have hold of him. Oh ! it is a great logger-headed Chub ; come, hang him upon that willow-twig, and let's be going. But turn out of the way a little, good Scholar, towards yonder high honeysuckle hedge ; there we'll sit and sing whilst this shower falls so gently upon the teeming earth, and gives yet a sweeter smell to the lovely flowers that adorn these verdant meadows.

Look, under that broad beech-tree I sat down, when I was last this way a-fishing, and the birds in the adjoining grove seemed to have a friendly contention with an echo, whose dead voice seemed to live in a hollow tree, near to the brow of that primrose hill ; there I sat viewing the silver streams glide silently towards their centre, the tempestuous sea ; yet sometimes opposed by rugged roots, and pebble-stones, which broke their waves, and turned them into foam : and sometimes I beguiled time by viewing the harmless lambs, some leaping securely in the cool shade, whilst others sported themselves in the cheerful sun ; and saw others craving comfort from the swollen udders of their bleating dams. As I thus sat, these and other sights had so fully possessed my soul with content, that I thought, as the poet has happily expressed it,

> " I was for that time lifted above earth,
> And possessed joys not promised in my birth."

As I left this place, and entered into the next field, a second pleasure entertained me ; 'twas a handsome Milkmaid that had not yet attained so much age and wisdom as to load her mind with any fears of many things that will never be, as too many men too often do ; but she cast away all care, and sung like a nightingale. Her voice was good, and the ditty fitted for it ; 'twas that smooth song, which was made by Kit Marlowe, now at least fifty years ago : and the Milkmaid's mother sung an answer to it, which was made by Sir Walter Raleigh in his younger days.

They were old-fashioned poetry, but choicely good, I think much better than the strong lines that are now in fashion in this critical age. Look yonder ! on my word, yonder they both be a-milking again. I will give her the Chub, and persuade them to sing those two songs to us.

God speed you, good woman ! I have been a-fishing, and am going to Bleak Hall to my bed ; and having caught more fish than will sup myself and my friend, I will bestow this upon you and your daughter, for I use to sell none.

Milk-Woman. Marry, God requite you ! Sir, and we'll eat it cheerfully ; and if you come this way a-fishing two months hence, a-grace of God I'll give you a syllabub of new verjuice in a new-made hay-cock for it, and my Maudlin shall sing you one of her best ballads ; for she and I both love all Anglers, they be such honest, civil, quiet men. In the mean time will you drink a draught of red cow's milk ? you shall have it freely.

Pisc. No, I thank you ; but I pray do us a courtesy that shall stand you and your daughter in nothing, and yet we will think ourselves still something in your debt : it is but to sing us a song that was sung by your daughter when I last passed over this meadow, about eight or nine days since.

Milk-W. What song was it, I pray ? Was it " Come, Shepherds, deck your herds ? " or, " As at noon Dulcina rested ? " or " Philida flouts me ? " or Chevy Chace ? or Johnny Armstrong ? or Troy Town ?

Pisc. No, it is none of those : it is a song that your daughter sung the first part, and you sung the answer to it.

Milk-W. Oh, I know it now ; I learned the first part in my golden age, when I was about the age of my poor daughter ; and the latter part, which indeed fits me best now, but two or three years ago, when the cares of the world began to take hold of me ; but you shall, God willing, hear them both, and sung as well as we can, for we both love Anglers.   Come, Maudlin, sing the first part to the gentlemen with a merry heart, and I'll sing the second, when you have done.   (From the Same.)

THE BLESSING OF CONTENT

Venator. Well sung, master !   This day's fortune and pleasure, and this night's company and song, do all make me more and more in love with angling.   Gentlemen, my master left me alone for an hour this day, and I verily believe he retired himself from talking with me, that he might be so perfect in this song ; was it not, master ?

Piscator. Yes, indeed, for it is many years since I learned it, and having forgotten a part of it, I was forced to patch it up by the help of mine own invention, who am not excellent at poetry, as my part of the song may testify ; but of that I will say no more, lest you should think I mean by discommending it to beg your commendations of it.   And therefore, without replications, let's hear your catch, scholar, which I hope will be a good one, for you are both musical and have a good fancy to boot.

Ven. Marry, and that you shall, and as freely as I would have my honest master tell me some more secrets of fish and fishing as we walk and fish towards London to-morrow.   But, master, first let me tell you that, that very hour which you were absent from me, I sat down under a willow-tree by the water-side, and considered what you had told me of the owner of that pleasant meadow in which you then left me ; that he had a plentiful estate, and not a heart to think so ; that he had at this time many lawsuits depending, and that they both damped his mirth, and took up so much of his time and thoughts, that he himself had not leisure to take the sweet content that I, who pretended no title to them, took in his fields ; for I could there sit quietly, and, looking on the water, see some fishes sport themselves in the silver streams, others leaping at flies of several shapes and colours ; looking on the hills I could behold them spotted with woods and groves ; looking down the meadows, could see here a boy gathering lilies and lady-smocks, and there a girl cropping culverkeyes and cowslips, all to make garlands suitable to this present month of May. These, and many other field-flowers, so perfumed the air, that I thought that very meadow like that field in Sicily, of which Diodorus speaks, where the perfumes arising from the place make all dogs that hunt in it to fall off, and to lose their hottest scent. I say, as I thus sat, joying in my own happy condition, and pitying this poor rich man that owned this and many other pleasant groves and meadows about me, I did thankfully remember what my Saviour said, that the meek possess the earth—or rather, they enjoy what the other possess and enjoy not; for anglers, and meek, quiet-spirited men, are free from those high, those restless thoughts which corrode the sweets of life; and they, and they only, can say, as the poet has happily expressed it—

> " Hail! blest estate of lowliness!
> Happy enjoyments of such minds,
> As, rich in self-contentedness,
> Can, like the reeds in roughest winds,
>   By yielding make that blow but small
>   At which proud oaks and cedars fall."

(From the Same.)

A VISION

AT this time of Mr. Donne's and his wife's living in Sir Robert's house, the Lord Hay was, by King James, sent upon a glorious embassy to the then French king, Henry the Fourth, and Sir Robert put on a sudden resolution to accompany him to the French Court, and to be present at his audience there. And Sir Robert put on a sudden resolution to solicit Mr. Donne to be his companion in that journey. And this desire was suddenly made known to his wife, who was then with child, and otherwise under so dangerous a habit of body as to her health, that she professed an unwillingness to allow him any absence from her, saying, " Her divining soul boded her some ill in his absence," and therefore desired him not to leave her. This made Mr. Donne lay aside all thoughts of the journey, and really to resolve against it. But Sir Robert became restless in his persuasions for it, and Mr. Donne was so generous as to think he had sold his liberty, when he received so many charitable kindnesses from him, and told his wife so ; who did therefore, with an unwilling-willingness, give a faint consent to the journey, which was proposed to be but for two months ; for about that time they determined their return. Within a few days after this resolve, the ambassador, Sir Robert, and Mr. Donne, left London, and were the twelfth day got all safe to Paris. Two days after their arrival there, Mr. Donne was left alone in that room in which Sir Robert and he and some other friends had dined together. To this place Sir Robert returned within half an hour ; and as he left, so he found, Mr. Donne alone, but in such an ecstasy, and so altered as to his looks, as amazed Sir Robert to behold him, insomuch that he earnestly desired Mr Donne to declare what had befallen him in the short time of his absence. To which Mr. Donne was not able to make a present answer ; but, after a long and per-plexed pause, did at last say, " I have seen a dreadful vision since I saw you. I have seen my dear wife pass twice by me through this room, with her hair hanging about her shoulders, and a dead child in her arms ; this I have seen since I saw you." To which Sir Robert replied, " Sure, sir, you have slept since I saw you ; and this is the result of some melancholy dream, which I desire you to forget, for you are now awake." To which Mr. Donne's reply was, " I cannot be surer that I now live than that I have not slept since I saw you ; and am as sure, that at her second appearing, she stopped, and looked me in the face, and vanished." Rest and sleep had not altered Mr. Donne's opinion the next day, for he then affirmed this vision with a more deliberate, and so confirmed a confidence that he inclined Sir Robert to a faint belief that the vision was true. It is truly said that desire and doubt have no rest, and it proved so with Sir Robert, for he immediately sent a servant to Drewry House, with a charge to hasten back, and bring him word whether Mrs. Donne were alive, and, if alive, in what condition she was as to her health. The twelfth day the messenger returned with this account—That he found and left Mrs. Donne very sad and sick in her bed, and that, after a long and dangerous labour, she had been delivered of a dead child. And, upon examination, the abortion proved to be the same day, and about the very hour, that Mr. Donne affirmed he saw her pass by him in his chamber.

(From the *Lives*.)

GEORGE HERBERT AT BEMERTON

IT was not many days before he returned back to Bemerton to view the church, and repair the chancel, and indeed to rebuild almost three parts of his house which was fallen down or decayed by reason of his predecessor's living at a better parsonage house, namely, at Minal, sixteen or twenty miles from this place. At which time of Mr. Herbert's coming alone to Bemerton, there came to him a poor old woman, with an intent to acquaint him with her necessitous condition, as also with some troubles of her mind; but after she had spoken some few words to him, she was surprised with a fear, and that begot a shortness of breath, so that her spirits and speech failed her; which he perceiving, did so compassionate her, and was so humble, that he took her by the hand, and said, "Speak, good mother, be not afraid to speak to me, for I am a man that will hear you with patience, and will relieve your necessities too, if I be able, and this I will do willingly; and therefore, mother, be not afraid to acquaint me with what you desire." After which comfortable speech, he again took her by the hand, made her sit down by him, and understanding she was of his parish he told her "He would be acquainted with her and take her into his care." And having with patience heard and understood her wants—and it is some relief for a poor body to be heard with patience—he, like a Christian clergyman, comforted her by his meek behaviour and counsel; but because that cost him nothing, he relieved her with money too, and so sent her home with a cheerful heart, praising God and praying for him. Thus worthy, and, like David's blessed man, thus lowly, was Mr. George Herbert in his own eyes, and thus lovely in the eyes of others.

At his return that night to his wife at Bainton, he gave her an account of the passages betwixt him and the poor woman; with which she was so affected, that she went next day to Salisbury, and there bought a pair of blankets, and sent them as a token of her love to the poor woman; and with them a message, "That she would see and be acquainted with her when her house was built at Bemerton." (From the Same.)

DR. SANDERSON AT BOOTHBY PANNEL

AND this excellent man did not think his duty discharged by only reading the Church prayers, catechising, preaching, and administering the sacraments seasonably ; but thought—if the law or the canons may seem to enjoin no more, yet—that God would require more than the defective laws of man's making can or do enjoin ; the performance of that inward law, which Almighty God hath imprinted in the conscience of all good Christians, and inclines those whom He loves to perform. He, considering this, did therefore become a law to himself, practising what his conscience told him was his duty, in reconciling differences, and preventing lawsuits, both in his parish and in the neighbourhood. To which may be added his often visiting sick and disconsolate families, persuading them to patience, and raising them from dejection by his advice and cheerful discourse, and by adding his own alms, if there were any so poor as to need it : considering how acceptable it is to Almighty God, when we do as we are advised by St. Paul, Gal. vi. 2, " Help to bear one another's burden," either of sorrow or want ; and what a comfort it will be, when the Searcher of all hearts shall call us to a strict account for that evil we have done, and the good we have omitted, to remember we have comforted and been helpful to a dejected or distressed family.

And that his practice was to do good, one example may be, that he met with a poor dejected neighbour, that complained he had taken a meadow, the rent of which was £9 a year ; and when the hay was made ready to be carried into his barn, several day's constant rain had so raised the water, that a sudden flood carried all away, and his rich landlord would bate him no rent ; and that unless he had half abated, he and seven children were utterly undone. It may be noted, that in this age there are a sort of people so unlike the God of Mercy, so void of the bowels of pity, that they love only themselves and children : love them so, as not to be concerned, whether the rest of mankind waste their days in sorrow or shame : people that are cursed with riches, and a mistake that nothing but riches can make them and theirs happy. But it was not so with Dr. Sanderson : for he was concerned, and spoke comfortably to the poor dejected man : bade him go home and pray, and not load himself with sorrow, for he would go to his landlord next morning : and if his landlord would not abate what he desired, he and a friend would pay it for him.

To the landlord he went the next day, and, in a conference, the Doctor presented to him the sad conditions of his poor dejected tenant ; telling him how much God is pleased when men compassionate the poor : and told him, that though God loves sacrifice, yet he loves mercy so much better, that He is best pleased when called the God of Mercy. And told him the riches he was possessed of were given him by that God of Mercy, who would not be pleased, if he, that had so much given, yea, and forgiven him too, should prove like the rich steward in the gospel, "that took his fellow servant by the throat to make him pay the utmost farthing." This he told him : and told him, that the law of this nation—by which law he claims his rent—does not undertake to make men honest or merciful ; but does what it can to restrain men from being dishonest or unmerciful, and yet was defective in both ; and that taking any rent from his poor tenant, for what God suffered him not to enjoy, though the law allowed him to do so, yet if he did so, he was too like that rich steward which he had mentioned to him ; and told him that riches so gotten, and added to his great estate, would, as Job says, "prove like gravel in his teeth" : would in time so corrode his conscience, or become so nauseous when he lay upon his death-bed, that he would then labour to vomit it up, and not be able ; and therefore advised him, being very rich, to make friends of his unrighteous Mammon, before that evil day come upon him : but however, neither for his own sake, nor for God's sake, to take any rent of his poor, dejected, sad tenant ; for that were to gain a temporal, and lose his eternal happiness. These, and other such reasons were urged with so grave and compassionate an earnestness, that the landlord forgave his tenant the whole rent.

The reader will easily believe that Dr. Sanderson, who was so meek and merciful, did suddenly and gladly carry this comfortable news to the dejected tenant : and will believe that at the telling of it there was a mutual rejoicing. It was one of Job's boasts that "he had seen none perish for want of clothing : and that he had often made the heart of the widow to rejoice," Job xxxi. 19. And doubtless Dr. Sanderson might have made the same religious boast of this and very many like occasions. But, since he did not, I rejoice that I have this just occasion to do it for him ; and that I can tell the reader, I might tire myself and him, in telling how like the whole course of Dr. Sanderson's life, was to this which I have now related.

(From the Same.)

MRS. HUTCHINSON

[Lucy, daughter of Sir Allen Apsley, lieutenant of the Tower, married (July 1638) Mr. John Hutchinson of Owthorpe in the county of Nottingham. Her *Life of Colonel Hutchinson* was published first in 1806 ; there are several later editions. In Mr. C. H. Firth's edition there are a number of additional documents. Two theological essays by Mrs. Hutchinson were published in 1817 : (1) "On the Principles of the Christian Religion" (addressed to her daughter) ; (2) "Of Theologie" (incomplete : the first part is a clear and orderly discussion of natural theology ; the second part, beginning with the "pure antediluvian theology," comes down no further than the birth of the giants). Mrs. Hutchinson's MS. translation of Lucretius, in couplets, is in the British Museum.]

In all Mrs. Hutchinson's writings there is a struggle between two opposite tendencies—one having its source in her natural and ingenuous strength of mind ; the other in her education and adopted principles. It would be easy, by making unfair selections from her works, to compose a picture of unamiable virtue and female pedantry. This would be unjust ; at the same time, it cannot be denied that she gives the materials for such a description of her character, as well as the complementary evidence, which proves that she was something more than a bookish woman with strict principles. The fragment of her autobiography contains what deserves to be the *locus classicus* on the topic of early piety :—

"Play among other children I despised, and when I was forced to entertain such as came to visit me, I tired them with more grave instructions than their mothers, and plucked all their babies to pieces, and kept the children in such awe, that they were glad when I entertained myself with older company ; to whom I was very acceptable, and being in the house with many persons that had a great deal of wit, and very profitable serious discourses being frequent at my father's table and in my mother's drawing-room, I was very attentive to all, and gathered up things that I would utter again, to great admiration of many that took my memory and imitation for wit. . . . I used to exhort my mother's maids much, and to turn their idle discourses to good subjects ; but I thought when I had done this on the Lord's day, and every day performed my due tasks of reading and praying, that then I was free to anything that was not sin ; for I was not at that time convinced of the vanity of conversation which was not scandalously wicked. I thought it no sin to learn or hear witty songs and amorous sonnets or poems, and twenty things of that kind, wherein I was so apt that I became the confidante in all the loves that were managed among my mother's young women ; and there was none of them but had many lovers, and some particular friends beloved above the rest."

If this passage is to be treasured as a description of a good child, the last sentence must be abandoned. For an estimate of the character of Mrs. Hutchinson, this last sentence is valuable. It is in this way that she makes it impossible for the reader to regard her as an abstract virtue, or one of the Puritan graces. Her quickness of understanding and her energy preserve her from these extremes of perfection.

Mrs. Hutchinson was not a mere learned woman, though it might be possible to collect out of her two theological essays and her apology for her translation of Lucretius evidence enough to justify such an opinion of her. Her account of her study of Lucretius is a companion piece to the account of her childhood. She has become, she says, convinced of the sin of amusing herself with such vain philosophy, "which even at the first I did not employ any serious study in, for I turned it into English in a room where my children practised the several qualities they were taught with their tutors, and I numbered the syllables of my translation by the threads of the canvas I wrought in, and set them down with a pen and ink that stood by me." She goes on to treat her poet with much severity for "his and his master's ridiculous, impious, execrable doctrines," "*the foppish, casual dance of atoms.*" Her discourse on natural theology is full of references to the heathen poets and philosophers, without much respect for any of them. It is open to any one to describe her as a woman disagreeably and vainly learned, without any appreciation of her classical authors except in so far as they can be used to humiliate the ignorant, and make them uncomfortable. This view, again, would be an unfair one. It is possible to admire the picture of Mrs. Hutchinson taking Lucretius along with her tambour in the children's schoolroom, and at the same time to recognise that her learning is often better employed than in this translation, and that her liking for pens and ink is justified by the freshness and liveliness of her style.

Mrs. Hutchinson's style is not remarkable for anything except this natural vigour, and this is to be found in her theological essays as well as in the life of her husband. She wrote because she had something to say. The life of her husband is more interesting than her theology, but her theological discourses are in their way equally spontaneous.

The *Life of Colonel Hutchinson* is not one of the biographies that excel in the art of making small things interesting. But the narrative does not leave hold of particulars. Situations and adventures are often represented in a summary way, but though Mrs. Hutchinson may renounce the picturesque details, she gives the essential parts of the drama. Instances of this may easily be found. The best is the passage that relates how Lambert's troopers, trying to bully Colonel Hutchinson in his own house at Owthorpe, were quieted by suddenly coming upon fifty or sixty men, who happened to be there that day as representatives of three parishes which had quarrelled over a pauper (ii. p. 230). This is not treated as a great narrative author would have given it ; but the important things are there, the incident is boldly and clearly recounted.

That part of the *Life* which refers to Cromwell is less satisfactory. That "the colonel saw through him" is Mrs. Hutchinson's opinion ; but the conversations between Cromwell and Hutchinson, in which Hutchinson rebuked ambition and was answered by "serious, lying professions," are not fully reported. This part of the story lay beyond Mrs. Hutchinson's own view, and Cromwell is not seen distinctly in the indirect report of his ambition and "dissimulations."

W. P. KER.

THE colonel having set things in order in the country, had an intent to have carried his family that winter with him to London ; when just that week he was going, news was brought that Lambert had once more turned out the parliament, and the colonel rejoiced in his good fortune that he was not present.

Lambert was exceedingly puffed up with his cheap victory, and cajoled his soldiers ; and, before he returned to London, set on foot among them their old insolent way of prescribing to the parliament by way of petition.

The parliament, after the submission of the army, had voted that there should no more be a general over them, but, to keep that power in their own hands, that all the officers should take their commissions immediately from the Speaker. The conspiracy of the army, to get a leader in their rebellion, was laid, that they should petition for generals and such like things as might facilitate their intents. Among others that were taken in arms against the parliament, Lord Castleton was one of the chief heads of the insurrection. Him Lambert brought along with him in his coach, not now as a prisoner, but ·unguarded, as one that was to be honoured. The parliament hearing of this, sent and fetched him out of his company and committed him to prison, and then the army's saucy petition was delivered, and, upon the insolent carriage of nine colonels they were by vote disbanded. Lambert being one of them, came in a hostile manner and plucked the members out of the house ; Fleetwood, whom they trusted to guard them, having confederated with Lambert and betrayed them. After that, setting up their army court at Wallingford-house, they began their arbitrary reign, to the joy of all the vanquished enemies of the parliament, and to the amazement and terror of all men that had any honest interest : and now were they all devising governments, and some honourable members, I know not through what fatality of the times, fell in with them. When Colonel Hutchinson came into the country some time before Lambert's revolt, Mr. Robert Pierrepont, the son of the late Colonel Francis Pierrepont, sent friends to entreat the Colonel to receive him into his protection. Upon the entreaty of his uncle he took him into his own house, and entertained him civilly there, whilst he writ to the Speaker, urging his youth, his surrender of himself, and all he could do in favour of him, desiring to know how they would please to dispose of him. Before the letters were answered Lambert had broken the parliament, and the colonel told him he was free again to do what he pleased; but the young gentleman begged of the colonel that he might continue under his sanctuary, till these things came to some issue. This the colonel very freely admitted, and entertained him till the second return of the parliament, not without much trouble to his house, of him and his servants, so contrary to the sobriety and holiness the colonel delighted in, yet for his father's and his uncle's sakes he endured it about six months.

Some of Lambert's officers, while he marched near Nottinghamshire, having formerly served under the colonel's command, came to his house at Owthorpe and told him of the petition that was set on foot in Lambert's brigade, and consulted whether they should sign it or no. The colonel advised them by no means to do it, yet notwithstanding, they did, which made the colonel exceedingly angry with them, thinking they rather came to see how he stood affected, than really to ask his counsel. When Lambert had broken the House, the colonel made a short journey to London to inform himself how things were, and found some of the members exceedingly sensible of the sad estate the kingdom was reduced unto by the rash ambition of these men, and resolving that there was no way but for every man that abhorred it to improve their interest in their countries, and to suppress these usurpers and rebels. Hereupon the colonel took measures to have some arms bought and sent him, and had prepared a thousand honest men, whenever he should call for their assistance; intending to improve his *posse comitatus* when occasion should be offered. To provoke him more particularly to this, several accidents fell out. Among the rest, six of Lambert's troopers came to gather money, laid upon the country by an assessment of parliament, whom the colonel telling that in regard it was levied by that authority, he had paid it, but otherwise would not; two of them only who were in the room with the colonel, the rest being on horseback in the court, gave him such insolent terms, with such insufferable reproaches of the parliament, that the colonel drew a sword which was in the room to have chastised them. While a minister that was by held the colonel's arm, his wife, not willing to have them killed in her presence, opened the door and let them out, who presently ran and fetched in their companions in the yard with cocked pistols. Upon the bustle, while the colonel having disengaged himself from those that held him, was run after them with the sword drawn, his brother came out of another room, upon whom, the soldiers pressing against a door that went into the great hall, the door flew open, and about fifty or sixty men appeared in the hall, who were there upon another business. For Owthorpe, Kinolton, and Hickling, had a contest about a cripple that was sent from one to the other, but at last, out of some respect they had for the colonel, the chief men of the several towns were come to him, to make some accommodation, till the law should be again in force. When the colonel heard the soldiers were come, he left them shut up in his great hall, who by accident thus appearing, put the soldiers into a dreadful fright. When the colonel saw how pale they looked, he encouraged them to take heart, and calmly admonished them for their insolence, and they being changed and very humble through their fear, he called for wine for them, and sent them away. To the most insolent of them he said, " These carriages would bring back the Stewarts." The man, laying his hand upon his sword, said, " Never while he wore that." Among other things they said to the colonel, when he demanded by what authority they came, they showed their swords, and said, "That was their authority." After they were dismissed, the colonel, not willing to appear because he was sheriff of the county, and had many of their papers sent him to publish, concealed himself in his house, and caused his wife to write a letter to Fleetwood, to complain of the affronts had been offered him, and to tell him that he was thereupon retired, till he could dwell safely at home. To this Fleetwood returned a civil answer, and withal sent a protection, to forbid all soldiers from coming to his house, and a command to Swallow who was the colonel of these men, to examine and punish them. Mrs. Hutchinson had sent before to Swallow, who then quartered at Leicester, the next day after it was done, to inform him, who sent a letter utterly disowning their actions, and promising to punish them. This Mrs. Hutchinson sent to show the soldiers who then lay abusing the country at Colson ; but when they saw their officer's letter they laughed at him, and tore it in pieces. Some days after he, in a civil manner, sent a captain with them and other soldiers to Owthorpe, to inquire into their misdemeanours before their faces ; which being confirmed to him, and he beginning to rebuke them, they set him at light, even before Mrs. Hutchinson's face, and made the poor man retire *sneaped* to his colonel ; while these six rogues, in one week's space, besides the assessments assigned them to gather up, within the compass of five miles, took away violently from the country, for their own expense, above five-and-twenty pounds.

(From *Memoirs of Colonel Hutchinson.*)

BULSTRODE WHITELOCKE

[The author of *Memorials of the English Affaires* was the son of a judge, and was born in London in 1605. He was educated at Oxford under the eye of Laud, studied law, and was called to the bar before the accession of Charles I., at which point in history his *Memorials* begin. After a youth noted, it would seem, by frivolity, he was elected to the Long Parliament, and soon made his mark in it. Of all his impeachers, Strafford said " Palmer and Whitelocke used him like gentlemen." Originally a moderate Royalist, he offered a determined resistance to the attempt to make Presbytery *jure Divino*. Although he was a member of the Westminster Assembly, he lost no opportunity of fostering a reconciliation between King and Parliament, and was indeed fiercely assailed in the House of Commons for alleged treachery in the course of a private interview which Hollis and he had with Charles at Oxford. Later on, impelled by various motives, he veered round to the side of the more uncompromising opponents of the King. He even became the confidant of Cromwell, and had the courage, when sounded on the subject, to dissuade his chief from assuming the title of King. He was sent by Cromwell as ambassador to Sweden, and on his return resumed his place in Parliament and a practice at the bar, which, though often broken in upon by the exigencies of public affairs was, at some periods of his life, positively enormous. He was included in the Act of Oblivion, and died in 1675 in his house in Wiltshire. Whitelocke, who was married three times, was distinguished by his religious though not ultra-puritanical sentiments, and by a love of his family which justified, in his own eyes at least, the scrupulous care for his own interests that characterised his action at many critical moments in his life.]

WHITELOCKE wrote complete Annals of his life, of which the *Memorials* are mere extracts. Judged by the latter, which have alone survived, he has no claim to the title of historian. The *Memorials* are a diary, the mere raw material of history, For philosophical deductions and general views the reader must have recourse to the diarist's Parliamentary speeches, which are scattered liberally throughout the text. Apart from these, and the accounts of conversations, the work is the bald record of events almost no care being bestowed either on arrangement of facts or on style. Neither the excitement of debate nor the heat of battle seems to quicken his pulse or disturb the even flow of his pen.

Yet his language is naturally apt, and he has a keen appreciation of the value of the personal in narrative. Thus he hastily summarises an important but tedious portion of the proceedings against Strafford after this fashion : " A Bill was brought into the House of Commons to attaint the earl of high treason ; upon debate whereof they noted him guilty of high treason." Yet he can spare time and space for a genuinely picturesque passage like this :—" The Earl was brought to the bar by the lieutenant of the Tower ; his habit black, wearing his George in a gold chain ; his countenance nearly black, his person proper, but a little stooping with his distemper or habit of body ; his behaviour exceedingly graceful, and his speech full of weight, reason, and pleasingness." Only Whitelocke's speeches and records of conversations smell of the closet lamp. Yet, granted that he was able in the subsequent writing of his orations to heighten their polish, it is evident that he was an effective speaker. Though the best service he rendered to the public was the passing of a measure " for putting all the books of law and proceedings in the Courts of Justice into the English tongue," he did not disdain the rhetorical device of quotation, and his speeches are much more thickly studded with Latin phrases than with appeals to passion. The conversations which he commits to paper are stilted and formal. To sum up, the motto on the title-page of the *Memorials* is an index to the value of the book. It is important because it deals with events of which Whitelocke could say, *Quæque ipse miserrima vidi, et quorum pars magna fui.* He set down his impressions while they were fresh, and there is nothing in his character, so far as it is known, to lead us to suspect his *bona fides.* In his later years, living in enforced retirement, he wrote many religious books which were never published, but there is extant a posthumous volume of *Essays, Ecclesiastical and Civil.*

W. WALLACE.

SHIP MONEY

MR. JOHN HAMPDEN, my countryman and kinsman, a gentleman of an ancient family in Buckinghamshire, and of a great estate and parts, denied the payment of ship money, as an illegal tax. He often advised in this great business with Holborn, St. John, myself, and others of his friends and council. Several other gentlemen refused the payment of this tax of ship money: whereupon the king was advised by the Lord Chief Justice Finch, and others, to require the opinion of his judges, which he did, stating the case in a letter to them.

After much solicitation by the chief Justice Finch, promising preferment to some, and highly threatening others whom he found doubting, as themselves reported to me, he got from them in answer to the king's letter and case, their opinions in these words:

We are of opinion, that when the good and safety of the kingdom in general is concerned, and the whole kingdom in danger, your majesty may by writ under the great seal of England, command all your subjects of this your kingdom, at their charge, to provide and furnish such number of ships, with men, victuals, and ammunition, and for such time as your majesty shall think fit, for the defence and safeguard of the kingdom, from such peril and danger. And that by law your majesty may compel the doing thereof in case of refusal, or refractoriness. And we are also of opinion, that in such case your majesty is the sole judge, both of the dangers, and when, and how the same is to be prevented and avoided.

This opinion was signed by Bramston, Finch, Davenport, Denham, Hutton, Jones, Croke, Trever, Vernon, Berkley, Crawley, Weston.

This opinion and subscription of the judges, was inrolled in all the courts of Westminster, and much distasted many gentlemen of the country, and of their own profession, as a thing extrajudicial, unusual, and of very ill consequence in this great business, or in any other.

The king, upon this opinion of his judges, gave order for proceeding against Hampden in the exchequer, where he pleaded, and the king's council demurring, the point in law came to be argued for the king by his council, and for Hampden by his council, and afterwards the judges particularly argued this great point at the bench, and all of them (except Hutton and Croke) argued, and gave their judgments for the king.

The arguments both at the bar and bench, were full of rare and excellent learning, especially in matter of record and history; but they are too voluminous to be here inserted.

Judge Croke (of whom I speak knowingly) was resolved to deliver his opinion for the king, and to that end had prepared his argument. Yet a few days before he was to argue, upon discourse with some of his nearest relations, and most serious thoughts of this business, and being heartened by his lady, who was a very good and pious woman, and told her husband upon this occasion, that she hoped he would do nothing against his conscience, for fear of any danger or prejudice to him, or his family; and that she would be contented to suffer want or any misery with him, rather than be an occasion for him to do, or say any thing against his judgment and conscience.

Upon these and many the like encouragements, but chiefly upon his better thoughts, he suddenly altered his purpose and arguments; and when it came to his turn, contrary to expectation, he argued and declared his opinion against the king.

But Hampden, and many others of quality and interest in their countries, were unsatisfied with this judgment, and continued to the utmost of their power in opposition to it; yet could not at that time give any farther stop or hindrance to the prosecution of the business of ship money, but it remained *alta mente repostum*. (From *Memorials.*)

A CONFERENCE WITH THE KING

HOLLIS and I thought ourselves obliged in civility and courtship to return a visit to the Earl of Lindsey. But (all the commissioners having agreed that none of us should singly give any visit to any of the king's officers or great lords, nor in company without acquainting our fellow - commissioners therewith) we thought fit to tell them our intentions (with their leave) to return a visit to the Earl of Lindsey, who had so courteously first sent to visit us, and all our fellow-commissioners approved thereof, and wished us to do as we intended.

The same evening about eight or nine of the clock, Hollis and I went to the court to the Earl of Lindsey's lodgings, whom we found ill, and in his bed, and divers lords with him ; among the rest the Lord Savile, then newly made Earl of Sussex.

The Earl of Lindsey expressed much contentment, and that he took it extreme kindly that we would come to visit him, and treated us with extraordinary respect and courtesy ; and no man with him was so forward to compliment us as was the Lord Savile.

When we had been there about a quarter of an hour, the king and Prince Rupert, and divers great lords came into the chamber, where we were. Whether sent to, after we came, or by accident, we knew not. The king saluted us very civilly, and began to discourse with us, part whereof was to this effect.

King. I am sorry, gentlemen, that you could bring to me no better propositions for peace, nor more reasonable than these are.

Hollis. They are such, sir, as the parliament thought fit to agree upon, and I hope a good issue may be had out of them.

Whitelocke. We are but their servants to present them to your majesty, and very willing to be messengers of peace.

King. I know you could bring no other than what they would send. But I confess I do not a little wonder at some of them, and particularly at the qualifications.

Hol. Your majesty will be pleased to consider of them as a foundation for peace.

King. Surely you yourselves cannot think them to be reasonable or honourable for me to grant.

Hol. Truly, sir, I could have wished that some of them had been otherwise than they are, but your majesty knows that those things are all carried by the major vote.

King. I know they are, and am confident that you who are here and your friends (I must not say your party) in the House endeavoured to have had them otherwise, for I know you are well-willers to peace.

Whit. I have had the honour to attend your majesty often heretofore upon this errand, and am sorry it was not to better effect.

King. I wish, Mr. Whitelocke, that others had been of your judgment, and of Mr. Hollis's judgment, and then I believe we had had an happy end of our differences before now.

Hol. We are bound to your majesty for your gracious and true opinion of us, and wish we had been, or may be capable to do your majesty better service.

King. Your service, Mr. Hollis and the rest of those gentlemen, whose desire hath been for peace, hath been very acceptable to me, who do earnestly desire it my self, and in order to it, and out of the confidence I have of you two that are here with me, I ask your opinion and advice what answer will be best for me to give at this time to your propositions, which may probably further such a peace as all good men desire.

Hol. Your majesty will pardon us if we are not capable in our present condition to advise your majesty.

Whit. We now by accident have the honour to be in your majesty's presence, but our present employment disables us from advising your majesty if we were otherwise worthy to do it in this particular.

King. For your abilities I am able to judge, and I now look not on you in your employments from the parliament, but as friends and my private subjects I require your advice.

Hol. Sir, to speak in a private capacity, your majesty sees that we have been very free, and touching your answer, I shall say further, that I think the best answer would be your own coming amongst us.

Whit. Truly, Sir, I do believe that your majesty's personal presence at your parliament, would sooner put an end to our unhappy distractions than any treaty.

King. How can I come thither with safety?

Hol. I am confident there would be no danger to your person to come away directly to your parliament.

King. That may be a question, but I suppose your principals who sent you hither will expect a present answer to your message.

Whit. The best present, and most satisfactory answer, I humbly believe, would be your majesty's presence with your parliament, and which I hope might be without any danger

Hol. We should be far from advising anything which might be of the least danger to your Majesty's person : and I believe your coming to your parliament would be none ; but we most humbly submit that to your majesty's own pleasure and great wisdom.

King. Let us pass by that, and let me desire you two, Mr. Hollis and Mr. Whitelocke to go into the next room, and a little to confer together, and to set down somewhat in writing, which you apprehend may be fit for me to return in answer to your message ; and that in your judgments may facilitate and promote this good work of peace.

Hol. We shall obey your majesty's command and withdraw.

We went together into another room, where we were private, and upon discourse together we apprehended that it would be no breach of trust in us to observe the king's desire herein ; but that it might be a means to facilitate the work about which we came, the most desirable business of peace.

Therefore by Mr. Hollis's intreaty, and as we both agreed I wrote down what was our sense in this matter, and what might be fit for the substance of the king's answer to our message ; but I wrote it not in my usual hand, nor with any name to it, nor was any person present but we two when it was written, nor did the king admit of any others to hear the discourse which passed betwixt him and us.

The paper which was thus written we left upon the table in the withdrawing room ; and the king went in, and took it, and then with much favour and civility, bid us farewell, and went away himself, after which, and a few compliments passed between the Earl of Lindsey and us, we took leave of him and the rest of the company, and returned to our own lodgings.

(From the Same.)

THE TRIAL OF THE KING

THE High Court of Justice sat in Westminster Hall, the President in his scarlet robe, and many of the commissioners in their best habit.

After the calling the court, the king came in, in his wonted posture with his hat on ; as he passed by in the Hall a cry was made, Justice, Justice, Execution, Execution. This was by some soldiers and others of the rabble.

The king desired to be heard, the president answered, that he must hear the court ; and sets forth the intentions of the court to proceed against the prisoner, and withal offered that the king might speak, so it were not matter of debate.

The king desired, that in regard he had something to say, for the peace of the kingdom and liberty of the subject, before sentence were given, he might be heard before the Lords and Commons in the Painted Chamber.

Upon this the court withdrew into the court of wards, and the king to Sir Robert Cotton's House ; and after about an hour's debate, they returned again into Westminster Hall.

The court resolved, that what the king had tendered, tended to delay ; yet if he would speak anything for himself in court, before sentence, he might be heard.

Many of the commissioners in the debate of it in the court of wards, were against this resolution, and pressed to satisfy the king's desire, and themselves, to hear what the king would say to them in the Painted Chamber, before sentence ; but it was voted by the major part in the negative. Upon which Colonel Harvey, and some others of the commissioners went away in discontent, and never sat with them afterwards ; this proposal of the king's being denied by the commissioners, the king thereupon declared himself, that he had nothing more to say.

Then the president made a large speech of the king's misgovernment, and that by law, kings were accountable to their people, and to the law, which was their superior, and he instanced in several kings, who had been deposed, and imprisoned, by their subjects, especially in the king's native country, where, of one hundred and nine kings, most were deposed, imprisoned, or proceeded against for mis-government, and his own grandmother removed, and his father an infant crowned.

After this the clerk was commanded to read the sentence, which recited the charge, and the several crimes of which he had been found guilty.

For all which treasons and crimes, the court did adjudge that he, the said Charles Stuart, as a tyrant, traitor, murderer, and public enemy, shall be put to death by the severing of his head from his body.

The king then desired to be heard, but it would not be

permitted, being after sentence, and as he returned through the hall, there was another cry for Justice and Execution.

Here we may take notice of the abject baseness of some vulgar spirits, who seeing their king in that condition, endeavoured in their small capacity, further to promote his misery, that they might a little curry favour with the present powers and pick thanks of their then superiors.

Some of the very same persons were afterwards as clamorous for justice against those that were the king's judges.

A prince is not exempt from the venom of these mad dogs.

(From the Same.)

THOMAS FULLER

[Thomas Fuller was born in the rectory of Aldwinkle St. Peter's, North-amptonshire (the same village but not the same parish, and consequently not in the same house which saw the birth of Dryden some twenty years later), in 1608. His father was a prebendary of Salisbury, as well as rector of Aldwinkle ; and, as his mother's brother, Dr. Davenant, who was president of Queens' College, Cambridge, afterwards became Bishop of the same diocese, he had more than one connection therewith. He was entered at his uncle's college, and graduated there, but migrated to Sidney Sussex. He held a curacy in Cambridge, but as soon as he had taken priest's orders, was presented by his uncle to a prebend in Salisbury, receiving a little later, 1634, the rectory of Broad Windsor, in Dorsetshire. He began to write early, attempting verse without any success ; but when he published the first of his well-known books, *The Holy War*, he was thirty-one. Three years later, in 1642, he produced the still more characteristic *Holy and Profane State*, a book in which the whole Fuller appears in microcosm. He had before this removed to London, where he was preacher at the Savoy. When the Rebellion broke out he served as army chaplain at Basing, at Oxford, at Exeter, and peripatetically with Hopton's army. During this time he wrote another of his best books, *Good Thoughts in Bad Times* (1645), which had sequels later. Considering the active part he had taken on the king's side (though indeed it is said that extreme royalists thought him lukewarm), he was fortunate during the Commonwealth, for though he lost his country benefices, and could not remain at the Savoy, or in Eastcheap, where he preached for some time, he was appointed to and remained undisturbed in the curacy of Waltham Abbey. *A Pisgah Sight of Palestine* (1650), and his great *Church History of Britain* (1655), which brought him into contro-versy with Heylin, were the chief results of this time. The Restoration, when it came, restored him to his benefices, made him a royal chaplain extraordinary, and put him in a good way for a bishopric ; but he died of fever on August 16, 1661, being only fifty-three. He had been married twice — once in quite early life, and again in 1651 to a daughter of Lord Baltinglass. His largest, if not his most important work, the *Worthies of England*, was pub-lished in an unfinished state a year after his death, by his son. His sermons were never collected till 1891, when an edition of them, which had been begun by Mr. J. E. Bailey, a lifelong student of Fuller and collector of books, relating to him, was completed and published by Mr. Axon of Manchester. There is no complete edition of his work ; but a selection from the whole of it appeared under the editorship of Dr. Jessopp at the Clarendon Press, 1892.]

THE *locus classicus* of English criticism respecting Fuller has long been, and no doubt will long be, Coleridge's marginal note, beginning " Wit was the stuff and substance of Fuller's intellect." It is not easy to speak or think too highly of the genius of Coleridge ; but it is much easier to overvalue separate *obiter dicta* of his, especially *dicta* of the critical character. For he was as little given to co-ordinate and check his thoughts as to take any other sort of intellectual trouble, and the very genius which made him so often clothe those thoughts in memorable form, makes it necessary to be doubly careful in mistaking the form for the " stuff and substance." His *dictum* on Fuller, however, has so far received general acceptance from competent persons that probably few critics would refuse to bracket Fuller with Sydney Smith as the wittiest of Englishmen. Some differences of the pair will be found further noticed in these volumes, on the later of them. Here, and as regards Fuller, it may be sufficient to note others. One of his latest editors, Dr. Jessopp, who has also made the comparison with Sydney Smith, has taken occasion, with all due apologies, to tone down, albeit carefully and without any direct antagonism or depreciation, the lofty eulogies which Coleridge and Lamb had bestowed on the author of the *Worthies of England*. It must have been an ungrateful, but was to some extent a necessary task. For excessive laudation has this drawback, that it constantly creates revulsion in readers who, not quite adjusted to the point of view, endeavour to take it at the bidding of their betters and fail. Such a result would be specially lamentable in Fuller's case, because he is, taken rightly and enjoyed rightly, one of the most delectable of English authors. But it is very likely to happen when such a reader as has just been glanced at goes from extracts and specimens, still more from critical laudations, to his complete works. His two great contemporaries and analogues, Burton and Browne, have nothing to fear from any such process ; Fuller perhaps has, and it may possibly be due to a sort of feeling of this that, though he has never wanted for fervent admirers, they seem always rather to have shrunk from paying him the greatest and the most necessary, if the most trying, honour that can be paid to an author by issuing a complete edition of his works. There are many curious contradictions in Fuller's character, both personal and literary, and it is not impossible that the presence of them communicates to his personality and his literature the almost unmatched piquancy which both possess, and which have never failed to attract fit persons. A Puritan Cavalier (Dr. Jessopp calls him a Puritan, and though I should hardly go so far myself, there is no doubt that Fuller leaned far more to the extreme Protestant side than most of his comrades in loyalty), a man of the sincerest and most unaffected piety, who never could resist a joke, an early member of the exact or antiquarian school of historians, who was certainly not a very profound or wide scholar, and who constantly laid himself open to the animadversions of others by his defects in scholarship—Fuller is a most appetising bundle of contradictions. But his contradictions undoubtedly sometimes disgust ; and perhaps even some almost insatiable lovers of "the humour of it" may occasionally think that he carries the humour of it too far.

It is however his positive rather than his negative side with which we have chiefly to do. From this side Fuller may be described as having had an extraordinary loyalty to and affection for his native country, which led him to acquire the mass of information laid up in his *Church History* and *Worthies* ; a sincere, though not a very erudite theology ; and the above-mentioned wit, which, being the ruling characteristic of his nature, showed itself at all times and in all places. Its direct and immediate effects, if not always exactly suitable to time and place, are always delightful. The memorable anthology in quintessence of Fullerisms which Charles Lamb has collected might be very largely increased, and indeed the work of Dr. Jessopp, to which reference has been made, does so increase it. But though, as has been hinted, the reading of the great mass of Fuller's work may induce a certain occasional revulsion, it may be doubted whether the full virtue of the Fullerian wit is perceptible till such reading has been undertaken. Only then can the mild wisdom, which hardly ever fails of mildness unless the Roman Catholic Church is concerned, be fully appreciated, and the vivid wit which accompanies it be fully comprehended. The singular fertility in conjoining strange societies of thought, which has generally been considered the essence of wit, is present everywhere, and always delightful. The imagination—or fancy, rather—which supplies Fuller with these conjunctions is not poetical, as it was in his nearer contemporary, Browne ; it is not erudite and all-compelling, as in the case of his somewhat older contemporary, Burton. It is a little desultory, a very little "Philistine," sometimes a little childish but it is always and everywhere delightful, and sometimes strangely stimulative and informing.

The indirect literary effects of this peculiarity of Fuller's on his style are noteworthy. For it can hardly be doubted that Fuller's essential quality of thought, the quaint and perpetual bubbling up within him of odd jests, comparisons, and what not, had a good deal to do with his comparative freedom from the besetting sin of his time—the sin of long, complicated, over-weighted sentences. Although a parenthesis or an additional clause will sometimes suffice for such spirts and fireworks of jest as those in which Fuller, be the subject sacred or profane, be the form of his utterance sermon, essay, history, or what not, must needs indulge, it will not always suffice for them ; and there are many reasons for putting the jest in a sentence by itself, and so leaving the most serious part of the narrative or argument ostensibly uninterrupted. However this may be, it is certain that Fuller, his quaintness excepted, is one of the least antique or obsolete of mid-seventeenth-century writers. That he is one of the most agreeable and also one of the most instructive is the unanimous verdict of competent critics ; and if some of those critics dwell most on their sense of pleasure, and others most on the limitations which they perceive in the giver of it, that is not a very serious difference. But it is impossible not to express regret at the absence of a really complete edition of his works. Comparatively few people may have noticed how great is the effect of diversity in mechanical presentment of books on the mind of the reader, but his must be an unusually critical mind who brings exactly the same faculties of appreciation to a seventeenth-century folio, to one of the stately quartos of the close of the eighteenth and the beginning of this, to a bookseller's octavo of the early Victorian period, and to batches of reprints of all shapes and sizes since. There ought to be a complete Fuller ; and in any country but England there would long since have been one.

GEORGE SAINTSBURY.

THE NATURAL COMMODITIES OF HAMPSHIRE

RED DEER

GREAT store of these were lately in the New Forest, so called because newly made by King William the Conqueror. Otherwise, ten years hence, it will be six hundred years old. Indeed, as Augustus Cæsar is said to have said of Herod King of Judæa, that it was better to be his hog than his child; so was it most true of that King William, that it was better to have been his stag than his subject; the one being by him spared and preserved, the other ruined and destroyed: such was the devastation he made of towns in this country, to make room for his game. And it is worth our observing the opposition betwixt the characters of

KING EDGAR
" Templa Deo, templis monachos, monachis dedit agros."

KING WILLIAM
" Templa adimit Divis, fora civibus, arva colonis."

And now was the south-west of this country made a forest indeed, if, as an antiquary hath observed, a forest be so called, *quia foris est*, because it is set open and abroad. The stags therein were stately creatures, jealous, revengeful; insomuch that I have been credibly informed, that a stag, unable for the present to master another who had taken his hind from him, waited his opportunity, till his enemy had weakened himself with his wantonness, and then killed him. Their flesh may well be good, whose very horns are accounted cordial. Besides, there is a concave in the neck of a green-headed stag, when above his first crossing, wherein are many worms, some two inches in length, very useful in physic, and therefore carefully put up by Sir Theodore Mayerne and other skilful physicians. But, I believe, there be few stags now in New Forest, fewer harts, and not any harts-royal (as escaping the chase of a king) ; though in time there may be some again.

HONEY

Although this country affordeth not such lakes of honey as some authors relate found in hollow trees in Muscovy; nor yieldeth combs equal to that which Pliny reporteth seen in Germany, eight feet long ; yet produceth it plenty of this necessary and profitable commodity.

Indeed Hampshire hath the worst and best honey in England ; worst, on the heath, hardly worth five pounds the barrel ; best, in the champaign, where the same quantity will well nigh be sold for twice as much. And it is generally observed, the finer the wheat and wool, both which are very good in this county, the purer the honey of that place.

Honey is useful for many purposes, especially that honey which is the lowest in any vessel. For it is an old and true rule "the best oil is in the top ; the best wine in the middle ; and the best honey in the bottom." It openeth obstructions, cleareth the breast from those humours which fall from the head ; with many other sovereign qualities, too many to be reckoned up in a winter's day.

However, we may observe three degrees, or kinds rather, of honey :—(1) *Virgin honey*, which is the purest, of a late swarm which never bred bees. (2) *Chaste honey*, for so I may term all the rest which is not sophisticated with any addition. (3) *Harlot honey*, as which is adulterated with meal and other trash mingled therewith.

Of the first and second sort I understand the counsel of Solomon, " My son, eat honey, for it is good : " good absolutely in the substance, though there may be excess in the quantity thereof.

WAX

This is the cask, where honey is the liquor ; and, being yellow by nature, is by art made white, red, and green, which I take to be the dearest colours, especially when appendant on parchment. Wax is good by day and by night, when it affordeth light, for sight the clearest ; for smell the sweetest ; for touch the cleanliest. Useful in law to seal instruments ; and in physic, to mollify sinews, ripen and dissolve ulcers, etc. Yea, the ground and foundation of all cere-cloth (so called from *cera*) is made of wax.

HOGS

Hampshire hogs are allowed by all for the best bacon, being our English Westphalian, and which, well ordered, hath deceived the most judicious palates. Here the swine feed in the forest on plenty of acorns (men's meat in the golden, hogs' food in this iron age); which, going out lean, return home fat, without either care or cost of their owners. Nothing but fulness stinteth their feeding on the mast falling from the trees, where also they lodge at liberty (not pent up, as in other places, to stacks of peas), which some assign the reason of the fineness of their flesh; which, though not all *glorre* (where no banks of lean can be seen for the deluge of fat), is no less delicious to the taste, and more wholesome for the stomach.

Swine's flesh, by the way, is observed most nutritive of men's bodies, because of its assimilation thereunto. Yet was the eating thereof forbidden to the Jews, whereof this reason may be rendered (besides the absolute will of the law-giver), because in hot countries men's bodies are subject to the measles and leprosies, who have their greatest repast on swine's flesh. For the climate of Canaan was all the year long as hot as England betwixt May and Michaelmas; and it is penal for any butchers with us in that term to kill any pork in the public shambles.

As for the manufacture of clothing in this county (diffused throughout the same) such as deny the goodness of Hampshire cloth, and have occasion to wear it, will be convinced of its true worth by the price which they must pay for it.

(From the *History of the Worthies of England.*)

JOHN OF TREVISA AND GEOFFREY CHAUCER

THIS year a godly, learned, and aged servant of God ended his days; namely, John de Trevisa, a gentleman of an ancient family (bearing Gules, a Garbe, Or,), born at Crocadon in Cornwall, a secular priest, and Vicar of Berkeley; a painful and faithful translator of many and great books into English, as *Polychronicon*, written by Ranulphus of Chester, Bartholomæus *De Rerum Proprietatibus*, etc. But his masterpiece was the translating of the

Old and New Testament; justifying his act herein by the example of Bede, who turned the Gospel of St. John in English.

I know not which more to admire, his ability, that he could—his courage, that he durst—or his industry, that he did—perform so difficult and dangerous a task; having no other commission than the command of his patron, Thomas Lord Berkeley: which lord, as the said Trevisa observeth, had the Apocalypse in Latin and French, then generally understood by the better sort as well as English, written on the roof and walls of his chapel at Berkeley; and which not long since (namely, *anno* 1622), so remained, as not much defaced. Whereby we may observe, that, midnight being past, some early risers even then began to strike fire, and enlighten themselves from the Scriptures.

It may seem a miracle, that the bishops being thus busy in persecuting God's servants, and Trevisa so obnoxious to their fury for this translation, that he lived and died without any molestation. Yet was he a known enemy to monkery; witness that (among many other) of his speeches, that he "had read how Christ had sent apostles and priests into the world, but never any monks or begging friars." But, whether it was out of reverence to his own aged gravity, or respect to his patron's greatness, he died full of honour, quiet, and age, little less than ninety years old. For, (1) He ended his translation of *Polychronicon*, (as appeareth by the conclusion thereof,) the 29th of Edward III. when he cannot be presumed less than thirty years of age. (2) He added to the end thereof, fifty (some say more) years of his own historical observations. Thus as he gave a Garbe or Wheatsheaf for his arms, so, to use the prophet's expression, "the Lord gathered him as a sheaf into the floor," Micah iv. 12, even full ripe and ready for the same.

We may couple with him his contempo ary, Geoffrey Chaucer, born (some say) in Berkshire, others in Oxfordshire, most and truest in London. If the Grecian Homer had seven, let our English have three places contest for his nativity. Our Homer, I say; only herein he differed: *Mæonides nullas ipse reliquit opes:* "Homer himself did leave no pelf:" whereas our Chaucer left behind him a rich and worshipful estate.

His father was a vintner in London; and I have heard his arms quarrelled at, being Argent and Gules strangely contrived, and hard to be blazoned. Some more wits have made it the dashing of white and red wine, (the parents of our ordinary claret), as nicking his father's profession. But were Chaucer alive, he would justify his own arms in the face of all his opposers, being not so devoted to the Muses, but he was also a son of Mars. He was the prince of English poets ; married the daughter of Pain Roëc, king of arms in France, and sister to the wife of John of Gaunt, king of Castile.

He was a great refiner and illuminer of our English tongue ; and, if he left it so bad, how much worse did he find it ! Witness Leland thus praising him :—

> *Prædicat Algerum merito Florentia Dantem,*
> *Italia et numeros tota, Petrarche, tuos.*
> *Anglia Chaucerum veneratur nostra Poëtam,*
> *Cui Veneres debet patria lingua suas,*

> " Of Alger Dants Florence doth justly boast,
> Of Petrarch brags all the Italian coast.
> England doth poet Chaucer reverence,
> To whom our language owes its eloquence."

Indeed, Verstegan, a learned antiquary, condemns him, for spoiling the purity of the English tongue by the mixture of so many French and Latin words. But he who mingles wine with water, though he destroys the nature of water, improves the quality thereof.

I find this Chaucer fined in the Temple two shillings for striking a Franciscan friar in Fleet Street ; and it seems his hands ever after itched to be revenged, and have his pennyworths out of them, so tickling religious Orders with his tales, and yet so pinching them with his truths, that friars, in reading his books, know not how to dispose their faces betwixt crying and laughing. He lies buried in the south aisle of St. Peter's, Westminster ; and since hath got the company of Spenser and Drayton, a pair royal of poets, enough almost to make passengers' feet to move metrically, who go over the place where so much poetical dust is interred.

(From the *Church History of Britain*.)

THE GOOD YEOMAN

THE good yeoman is a gentleman in ore, whom the next age may see refined ; and is the wax capable of a genteel impression, when the prince shall stamp it. Wise Solon (who accounted

Tellus the Athenian the most happy man, for living privately on his own lands) would surely have pronounced the English yeomanry "a fortunate condition," living in the temperate zone betwixt greatness and want; an estate of people almost peculiar to England. France and Italy are like a die, which hath no points between cinque and ace—nobility and peasantry. Their walls, though high, must needs be hollow, wanting filling-stones. Indeed, Germany hath her boors, like our yeoman; but, by a tyrannical appropriation of nobility to some few ancient families, their yeomen are excluded from ever rising higher, to clarify their bloods. In England, the temple of honour is bolted against none who have passed through the temple of virtue; nor is a capacity to be genteel denied to our yeoman, who thus behaves himself:—

MAXIM I

He wears russet clothes, but makes golden payment.—Having tin in his buttons, and silver in his pocket. If he chance to appear in clothes above his rank, it is to grace some great man with his service; and then he blusheth at his own bravery. Otherwise, he is the surest landmark whence foreigners may take aim of the ancient English customs; the gentry more floating after foreign fashions.

MAXIM II

In his house he is bountiful both to strangers and to poor people. —Some hold, when hospitality died in England, she gave her last groan amongst the yeomen of Kent. And still, at our yeoman's table, you shall have as many joints as dishes; no meat disguised with strange sauces; no straggling joint of a sheep in the midst of a pasture of grass, beset with salads on every side; but solid, substantial food. No servitors (more nimble with their hands, than the guests with their teeth) take away meat, before stomachs are taken away. Here you have that which in itself is good, made better by the store of it, and best by the welcome to it.

MAXIM III

He hath a great stroke in making the knight of the shire.— Good reason, for he makes a whole line in the subsidy book; where, whatsoever he is rated, he pays without any regret, not caring how much his purse is let blood, so it be done by the advice of the physicians of the State.

Maxim IV

He seldom goes far abroad, and his credit stretcheth further than his travel.—He goes not to London, but *se defendendo* to save himself of a fine, being returned of a jury; where seeing the king once, he prays for him ever afterwards.

Maxim V

In his own country he is a main man in juries.—Where, if the judge please to open his eyes in matter of law, he needs not to be led by the nose in matters of fact. He is very observant of the judge's *item*, when it follows the truth's *imprimis;* otherwise (though not mutinous in a jury,) he cares not whom he displeaseth, so he pleaseth his own conscience.

Maxim VI

He improveth his land to a double value by his good husbandry.—Some grounds that wept with water, or frowned with thorns, by draining the one, and clearing the other, he makes both to laugh and sing with corn. By marl and limestones burnt, he bettereth his ground; and his industry worketh miracles, by turning stones into bread. Conquest and good husbandry both enlarge the king's dominions; the one, by the sword, making the acres more in number; the other, by the plough, making the same acres more in value. Solomon saith, "The king himself is maintained by husbandry." Pythis, a king, having discovered rich mines in his kingdom, employed all his people in digging of them; whence tilling was wholly neglected, insomuch as a great famine ensued. His queen, sensible of the calamities of the country, invited the king her husband to dinner, as he came home hungry from overseeing his workmen in the mines. She so contrived it, that the bread and meat were most artificially made of gold; and the king was much delighted with the conceit thereof, till at last he called for real meat to satisfy his hunger. "Nay," said the queen, "if you employ all your subjects in your mines, you must expect to feed upon gold; for nothing else can your kingdom afford."

Maxim VII

In time of famine, he is the Joseph of the country, and keeps the poor from starving.—Then he *tameth* his stacks of corn, which not his covetousness but providence hath reserved for time of need ; and to his poor neighbours abateth somewhat of the high price of the market. The neighbour gentry court him for his acquaintance ; which either he modestly waveth, or thankfully accepteth, but no way greedily desireth. He insults not on the ruins of a decayed gentleman, but pities and relieves him ; and, as he is called "Goodman," he desires to answer to the name, and to be so indeed.

Maxim VIII

In war, though he serveth on foot, he is ever mounted on a high spirit.—As being a slave to none, and a subject only to his own prince. Innocence and independence make a brave spirit , whereas, otherwise, one must ask his leave to be valiant on whom one depends. Therefore, if a State run up all to noblemen and gentlemen, so that the husbandmen be only mere labourers or cottagers, (which one calls "but housed beggars,") it may have good cavalry, but never good bands of foot ; so that their armies will be like those birds called *apodes*, "without feet," always only flying on their wings of horse. Wherefore, to make good infantry, it requireth men bred, not in a servile or indigent fashion, but in some free and plentiful manner. Wisely, therefore, did that knowing prince, King Henry VII., provide laws for the increase of his yeomanry, that his kingdom should not be like to coppice woods ; where, the *staddles* being left too thick, all runs to bushes and briars, and there is little clean underwood. For, enacting that houses used to husbandry should be kept up with a competent proportion of land, he did secretly sow Hydra's teeth ; whereupon, according to the poet's fiction, should rise up armed men for the service of this kingdom.

(From *The Holy State*.)

EJACULATIONS : THEIR PRIVILEGE

EJACULATIONS take not up any room in the soul. They give liberty of callings, so that at the same instant one may follow his proper vocation. The husbandman may dart forth an ejaculation and not make a *balk* the more. The seaman nevertheless steer his ship right, in the darkest night. Yea, the soldier at the same time may shoot out his prayer to God, and aim his pistol at his enemy, the one better hitting the mark for the other.

The field wherein bees feed is no whit the barer for their biting ; when they have taken their full repast on flowers or grass, the ox may feed, the sheep fat, on their reversions. The reason is because those little chemists distil only the refined part of the flower, leaving the gross or substance thereof. So ejaculations bind not men to any bodily observance, only busy the spiritual half, which maketh them consistent with the prosecution of any other employment.

(From *Good Thoughts in Bad Times.*)

AN ILL MATCH

DIVINE Providence is remarkable in ordering, that a fog and a tempest never did, nor can, meet together in nature. For as soon as a fog is fixed the tempest is allayed ; and as soon as a tempest doth arise the fog is dispersed. This is a great mercy ; for otherwise such small vessels as boats and barges, which want the conduct of the card and compass, would irrecoverably be lost.

How sad, then, is the condition of many sectaries in our age ; which in the same instant have a fog of ignorance in their judgments, and a tempest of violence in their affections, being too blind to go right, and yet too active to stand still.

(From the Same.)

THE IMPRISONMENT AND RANSOM OF KING RICHARD

KING RICHARD setting sail from Syria, the sea and wind favoured him till he came into the Adriatic (Oct. 8) ; and on the coasts of Istria he suffered shipwreck ; wherefore he intended to pierce through Germany by land, the nearest way home. But the nearness of the way is to be measured not by the shortness but the safeness of it.

He disguised himself to be one Hugo, a merchant, whose only commodity was himself, whereof he made but a bad bargain. For he was discovered in an inn in Austria, because he disguised his person, not his expenses ; so that the very policy of an hostess, finding his purse so far above his clothes, did detect him (Dec. 20) ; yea, saith mine author, *Facies orbi terrarum nota, ignorari non potuit.* The rude people, flocking together, used him with insolencies unworthy him, worthy themselves ; and they who would shake at the tail of this loose lion, durst laugh at his face now they saw him in a grate ; yet all the weight of their cruelty did not bow him beneath a princely carriage.

Leopold Duke of Austria hearing hereof, as being lord of the soil, seized on this royal stray (Dec. 20) ; meaning now to get his pennyworths out of him, for the affront done unto him in Palestine.

Not long after the duke sold him to Henry the emperor, for his harsh nature surnamed *Asper*, and it might have been *Sævus*, being but one degree from a tyrant. He kept King Richard in bands, charging him with a thousand faults committed by him in Sicily, Cyprus, and Palestine. The proofs were as slender as the crimes gross, and Richard having an eloquent tongue, innocent heart, and bold spirit, acquitted himself in the judgment of all the hearers. At last he was ransomed for a hundred and forty thousand marks, *collen* weight. A sum so vast in that age, before the Indies had overflowed all Europe with their gold and silver, that to raise it in England they were forced to sell their church plate, to their very chalices. Whereupon out of most deep divinity it was concluded, that they should not celebrate the sacrament in glass, for the brittleness of it ; nor in wood, for the sponginess of it, which would suck up the blood ; nor in alchymy, because it was subject to rusting; nor in copper, because that would provoke vomiting ; but in chalices of latten, which belike was a metal without exception. And such were used in England for some hundred years after, until at last John Stafford, Archbishop of Canterbury, when the land was more replenished with silver, inknotteth that priest in the greater excommunication that should consecrate *poculum stanneum.*

(From the *History of the Holy War.*)

FULLER'S FAREWELL TO EXETER ON THE EVE OF ITS SURRENDER

AND now I am to take my final farewell of this famous city of Exeter. I have suffered from some for saying several times, that I thought this or this would be my last sermon, when afterwards I have preached again. Yet I hope the guests are not hurt, if I bring them in a course more than I promised or they expect. Such would have forborne their censures had they consulted with the Epistle to the Romans. In the fifteenth chapter, verse 33, the apostle seems to close and conclude his discourse, ' Now the God of Peace be with you all, Amen.' And yet presently he beginneth afresh and continueth his epistle a whole chapter longer. Yea, in the sixteenth chapter, verse 20, St. Paul takes a second solemn *vale*, ' The grace of our Lord Jesus Christ be with you all, Amen ; ' and, notwithstanding, still he spins out his matter three verses farther, till that full and final period, verse 27, ' To God only wise be glory through Jesus Christ for ever, Amen.' Thus loath to depart is the tune of all loving friends : the same I may plead for myself, so often taking my farewell, wherein if any were deceived, none I am sure were injured.

Now this is all : the Rabbins have a conceit that manna relished so to the palates of the Jews just as the eater thereof did fancy or desire. Consult with yourselves, and wish your own spiritual and temporal conveniences, wish what you will, for body, soul, both ; you, yours, your private, the public ; confine not your happiness with too narrow measure of your own making. And my constant prayer to God shall be, that he would be pleased to be to you all in general, each one in particular, that very thing which you for your own good do most desire, Amen.

(From *Fear of losing the Old Light*, a Sermon preached in Exeter.)

LORD CLARENDON

[Edward Hyde was descended from a family of old standing in Cheshire, and was born in Wilts in 1608. He was sent to Oxford to be bred for the Church; but after taking his degree began the study of the law at the Middle Temple, his uncle being a lawyer of great influence in the profession, afterwards Lord Chief Justice. By an early marriage in 1629, he became connected with the Duke of Buckingham. His first wife died in six months; and three years later, he married the daughter of Sir Thomas Aylesbury, and settled himself seriously to the work of his profession, in which he attained much success. At first he joined the popular party, not from a desire of violent change, nor from any wish to encroach upon the prerogative, but from his jealousy of that tampering with the law of which the unconstitutional courts, that had lately sprung up, were guilty. This attitude he maintained until the open attacks upon the Church, of which he was the ardent defender, broke his connection with the popular party; and he soon became the trusted adviser of the king. In 1643 he became Chancellor of the Exchequer, at a time when his duties consisted chiefly in contriving means of raising contributions amongst the king's adherents; and being sent to Jersey, as minister attending upon the Prince of Wales, he accompanied him afterwards to France, remained with him as titular minister, and played a leading part in the negotiations that ended in the Restoration. For seven years he maintained himself, amidst many ignoble factions, as the leading authority in the State, holding the office of Lord Chancellor, and being created Earl of Clarendon. In 1667 the intrigues against him succeeded; he was exiled, and died in France in 1674. His works, beyond those which are rather of the nature of State papers, are the *History of the Rebellion*, not published till 1702, and the *Life and Continuation of the History*, not published till 1759.]

In the case of a man like Clarendon, the chief part of whose life was the making of history, and only a very secondary part the writing of it, we must look much more to his experiences than to any literary principles or model, in order to find out what determined his methods and his style. For his University he always maintained an ungrudging devotion, but his literary tastes were formed in another school; and he tells us himself that he "left it, rather with the opinion of a young man of parts and pregnancy of wit, than that he had improved it much by industry." He counted it a piece of good fortune that he left it early ; and his first mental training was in the discipline of the law. To that he joined close association with a singularly choice band of friends ; and he " dedicated himself to the profession of the law, without declining the politer learning to which his humour and his conversation always kept him very indulgent." The study of the law was, indeed, scarcely congenial to him ; he had " to lay some obligation on himself" to continue it ; and, although in thought and action he was dominated by its influence, he never became a great lawyer. In youth his health was weak ; and when he lost by death his first wife, " a young lady very fair and beautiful, . . . nearly allied to many noble families in England," he tells us that " nothing but his entire duty and reverence to his father kept him from giving over all thoughts of books, and transporting himself beyond the seas to enjoy his own melancholy." Of a temper keen, ardent, and impulsive, it was only by severe self-discipline that he forced himself again into the routine of his profession ; but this was made more easy by his marriage with his second wife, " with whom he lived very comfortably in the most uncomfortable times, and very joyfully in those times when matter of joy was administered, for the space of five or six and thirty years." To his father, who was, as he tells us, *omnifariam doctus*, he owed much ; and his training in life was an admirable one. While pursuing actively the career of a practising lawyer, he sweetened his life and enlarged his range by mixing, as one of themselves, amidst a society of choice spirits —chief amongst them, Ben Jonson, John Selden, Sir Kenelm Digby, and Thomas Carew. " If he had anything good in him," he was wont to say, " in his humour, or in his manners, he owed it to the example and the information he had received in and from that company, with most of whom he had an entire friendship." Their characters he has sketched for us with that skill which stood him in such good stead when he came to portray the actors on a wider and a more momentous stage.

His first introduction to public life was through Archbishop Laud ; and, while in the early struggles between the Court and the Parliament, his ardent constitutionalism led him to oppose some encroachments of the prerogative, it would be a mistake to conceive him as an active supporter of the popular party. As the designs of that party became more evident, and especially as their opposition to the Church became more marked, Hyde was distinctly estranged from them; and before the war broke out, he was the trusted, but candid, adviser of the king. In spite of bitter vexation, caused by designs which were opposed to his own, and of which he clearly saw the inexpediency, he never swerved from his loyalty to that cause. The Restoration brought to him the outward semblance of reward, but with it a responsibility that weighed heavily upon him, as he saw the fatal danger which the corruption of the time, and the laxity of Charles II., were storing up for the future. For seven years he was able to maintain himself against a strange coalition, which banded against him what was most corrupt in the Court, and most progressive in the nation; and when he fell, it was after he had given his labour, his strength, and his peace to establish in his country his own ideal of orderly and constitutional government, which he saw to be threatened chiefly by the acts of those to whom his loyalty was ungrudgingly pledged. It is an easy criticism to urge against Clarendon that he was incapable of appreciating the new forces that were at work in English history. But the same criticism may always be urged against one who has formed a definite ideal, and will not swerve from it; and it remains none the less true that there is scarcely any prime minister of England who left upon her so firm an impress of his own personality—an impress which remained fresh to a period within living memory, and traces of which are not wanting even now.

To such an experience as Clarendon's, the making of history was far more than the writing of it; and the habits bred of action in a great scene and in a great crisis, the varied tasks which had been thrust upon him, the tragic significance of the long struggle that constituted his life, have, in combination with those literary interests that from first to last sweetened his toil, given to his style its special and inimitable characteristics. It is often cumbrous and prolix; its construction is frequently irregular; the arrangement is sometimes confusing, and the sense of proportion seems to be lost. But its chief note is one of almost tragic dignity. His *History of the Rebellion*—be it noted, the first history which our literature possesses from the hand of a great actor in the struggle it portrays—has something of the burden of an epic. But it is enlivened by those inimitable characters which his careful study of human nature, his intense desire to know those who were worthy to be known, enabled him to draw ; portraits in which every feature is given in its due proportion, and in which no trait, however homely, is omitted which can add to their dramatic force.   But these frequently recurring sketches, to which all readers of the *Life* and of the *Rebellion* will turn with chief pleasure, do not exhaust the great qualities of Clarendon in literature.   In every page we see marks of that acquaintance with great administrative affairs that dispels the mists of pedantry which are apt to gather round the mere student of history.   Even when he is cumbrous in his sentences, we seem to hear the voice of one accustomed to speak to great assemblies, and who, as Pepys tells us, gave such an impression of easy mastery in his parliamentary orations.   The habit of the orator to supply the place of logical sequence and orderly arrangement, by variations of tone, of manner, of action, is evident throughout every page of Clarendon, but is chiefly evident when his feelings are most moved.   It is then that he indulges in phrases almost conversational in their familiarity, but none the less forcible.   " To warm the people into rebellion ; " " the incurable disease of want of money ; " " artillery, commonly a sponge that can never be filled ; " " the gamesters who were to play this game looked into their hands ; " such phrases as these are constantly recurring where his narrative is most quick and dramatic.   He groups together the light and dark shades in his portraits, the favourable and adverse criticisms of special actions, just as the dramatist or the orator might group them, so as to lead his audience gradually into his own mental attitude, and to produce an impression which even those most opposed to him find it hard to throw off.   He gives to his narrative the deepest force of reality, because the habits of a lifetime had made him familiar with great affairs.   He gives to it the sternness of tragedy, because he had maintained for years a losing struggle, and had exchanged ease and comfort for the burden and hardships of exile.   His unique experience, in uniting the literary friendships of his early manhood with the heavy task of his later years, helps him to give to it grace and variety.   But above all—and it is in this that our chief literary inheritance from Clarendon consists—he wears his habit as a writer easily and lightly, as one who wore it not merely as the student, or the scholar, or the historian, but as the dress in which he is to tell the momentous history where he himself played so large and so dignified a part.   Such literary work as that of Clarendon does more than anything else to disencumber literature of pedantry, and to make it instinct with the life and movement of human affairs.

H. CRAIK.

THE DEATH OF STRAFFORD

DURING these perplexities, the Earl of Strafford, taking notice of the straits the king was in, the rage of the people still increasing (from whence he might expect a certain outrage and ruin), how constant soever the king continued to him; and, it may be, knowing of an undertaking (for such an undertaking there was) by a great person, who had then a command in the Tower, "that if the king refused to pass the bill, to free the kingdom from the hazard it seemed to be in, he would cause his head to be stricken off in the Tower,") writ a most pathetical letter to the king, full of acknowledgment of his favours; but lively presenting "the dangers, which threatened himself and his posterity, by his obstinacy in those favours;" and therefore by many arguments conjuring him "no longer to defer his assent to the bill, that so his death might free the kingdom from the many troubles it apprehended."

The delivery of this letter being quickly known, new arguments were applied: "that this free consent of his own clearly absolved the king from any scruple that could remain with him;" and so in the end they extorted from him, to sign a commission to some lords to pass the bill: which was as valid as if he had signed it himself; though they comforted him even with that circumstance, "that his own hand was not in it."

It may easily be said, that the freedom of the parliament, and his own negative voice, being thus barbarously invaded, if his majesty had, instead of passing that act, come to the house and dissolved the parliament; or if he had withdrawn himself from that seditious city, and put himself in the head of his own army; much of the mischief, which hath since happened, would have been prevented. But whoever truly considers the state of affairs at that time; the prevalency of that faction in both houses; the rage and fury of the people; the use that was made by the schismatical preachers (by whom all the orthodox were silenced) of the late protestation in their pulpits ; the fears and jealousies they had infused into the minds of many sober men, upon the discourse of the late plot; the constitution of the council-table, that there was not an honest man durst speak his conscience to the king, for fear of his ruin ; and that those, whom he thought most true to him, betrayed him every hour, insomuch as his whispers in his bedchamber were instantly conveyed to those against whom those whispers were ; so that he had very few men to whom he could breathe his conscience and complaint, that were not suborned against him, or averse to his opinions : that on the other side, if some expedient were not speedily found out, to allay that frantic rage and combination in the people, there was reason enough to believe, their impious hands would be lifted up against his own person, and (which he much more apprehended) against the person of his royal consort ; and lastly, that (besides the difficulty of getting thither except he would have gone alone) he had no ground to be very confident of his own army : I say, whoever sadly contemplates this, will find cause to confess, the part which the king had to act was not only harder than any prince, but than any private gentleman, had been incumbent to ; and that it is much easier, upon the accidents and occurrences which have since happened, to determine what was not to have been done, than at that time to have foreseen, by what means to have freed himself from the labyrinth in which he was involved.

All things being thus transacted, to conclude the fate of this great person, he was on the twelfth day of May brought from the Tower of London (where he had been a prisoner near six months) to the scaffold on Tower-hill ; where, with a composed, undaunted courage, he told the people, "he was come thither to satisfy them with his head ; but that he much feared, the reformation which was begun in blood would not prove so fortunate to the kingdom, as they expected, and he wished :" and after great expressions "of his devotion to the church of England, and the protestant religion established by law, and professed in that church ; of his loyalty to the king, and affection to the peace and welfare of the kingdom ;" with marvellous tranquillity of mind, he delivered his head to the block, where it was severed from his body at a blow ; many of the standers by, who had not been over charitable to him in his life, being much affected with the courage and Christianity of his death.

Thus fell the greatest subject in power, and little inferior to any in fortune, that was at that time in any of the three kingdoms ; who could well remember the time when he led those people, who then pursued him to his grave. He was a man of great parts, and extraordinary endowments of nature ; not unadorned with some addition of art and learning, though that again was more improved and illustrated by the other ; for he had a readiness of conception, and sharpness of expression, which made his learning thought more than in truth it was. His first inclinations and addresses to the court were only to establish his greatness in the country ; where he apprehended some acts of power from the old lord Savile, who had been his rival always there, and of late had strengthened himself by being made a privy counsellor, and officer at court ; but his first attempts were so prosperous that he contented not himself with being secure from his power in the country, but rested not, till he had bereaved him of all power and place in court ; and so sent. him down, a most abject, disconsolate, old man, to his country, where he was to have the superintendency over him too, by getting himself at that time made lord president of the north. These successes, applied to a nature too elate and arrogant of itself, and a quicker progress into the greatest employments and trust, made him more transported with disdain of other men, and more contemning the forms of business, than happily he would have been, if he had met with some interruptions in the beginning, and had passed in a more leisurely gradation to the office of a statesman.

He was, no doubt, of great observation, and a piercing judgment, both into things and persons ; but his too good skill in persons made him judge the worse of things ; for it was his misfortune to be of a time wherein very few wise men were equally employed with him ; and scarce any (but the Lord Coventry, whose trust was more confined) whose faculties and abilities were equal to his ; so that upon the matter he wholly relied upon himself : and discerning many defects in most men, he too much neglected what they said or did. Of all his passions, his pride was most predominant ; which a moderate exercise of ill fortune might have corrected and reformed ; and which was by the hand of Heaven strangely punished, by bringing his destruction upon him by two things that he most despised, the people and Sir Harry Vane. In a word, the epitaph, which Plutarch records that Sylla wrote for himself, may not be unfitly applied to him : "that no man did ever pass him, either in doing good to his friends, or in doing mischief to his enemies ;" for his acts of both kinds were most exemplary and notorious.

(From the *History of the Rebellion.*)

THE CITY OF LONDON

THE city of London, as the metropolis of England, by the situation the most capable of trade, and by the most usual residence of the court, and the fixed station of the courts of justice for the public administration of justice throughout the kingdom, the chief seat of trade, was, by the successive countenance and favour of princes, strengthened with great charters and immunities, and was a corporation governed within itself ; the mayor, recorder, aldermen, sheriffs, chosen by themselves ; several companies incorporated within the great corporation ; which, besides notable privileges, enjoyed lands and perquisites to a very great revenue. By the incredible increase of trade, which the distractions of other countries, and the peace of this, brought, and by the great license of resort thither, it was, since the access of the crown to the king, in riches, in people, in buildings, marvellously increased, insomuch as the suburbs were almost equal to the city ; a reformation of which had been often in contemplation, never pursued, wise men foreseeing that such a fulness could not be there, without an emptiness in other places ; and whilst so many persons of honour and estates were so delighted with the city, the government of the country must be neglected, besides the excess, and ill husbandry, that would be introduced thereby. But such foresight was interpreted a morosity, and too great an oppression upon the common liberty ; and so, little was applied to prevent so growing a disease.

As it had these and many other advantages and helps to be rich, so it was looked upon too much of late time as a common stock not easy to be exhausted, and as a body not to be grieved by ordinary acts of injustice ; and therefore, it was not only a resort, in all cases of necessity, for the sudden borrowing great sums of money, in which they were commonly too good merchants for the crown, but it was thought reasonable, upon any specious pretences, to void the security, that was at any time given for money so borrowed.

So after many questionings of their charter, which were ever removed by considerable sums of money, a grant made by the king in the beginning of his reign (in consideration of great sums of money) of good quantities of land in Ireland, and the city of Londonderry there, was avoided by a suit in the star-chamber; all the lands, after a vast expense in building and planting, resumed into the king's hands, and a fine of fifty thousand pounds imposed upon the city. Which sentence being pronounced after a long and public hearing, which time they were often invited to a composition, both in respect of the substance, and the circumstances of proceeding, made a general impression in the minds of the citizens of all conditions, much to the disadvantage of the court; and though the king afterwards remitted to them the benefit of that sentence, they imputed that to the power of the parliament, and rather remembered how it had been taken from them, than by whom it was restored; so that, at the beginning of the parliament, the city was as ill affected to the court as the country was; and therefore chose such burgesses to sit there, as had either eminently opposed it, or accidentally been oppressed by it.

The chief government and superintendency of the city is in the mayor and aldermen; which, in that little kingdom, resembles the house of peers; and as subordinate the common council is the representative body thereof, like the house of commons, to order and agree to all taxes, rates, and such particulars belonging to the civil policy. The common council are chosen every year, so many for every parish, of the wisest and most substantial citizens, by the vestry and common convention of the people of that parish; and as the wealthiest and best reputed men were always chosen, so, though the election was once a year, it was scarce ever known that any man once chosen was afterwards rejected or left out, except upon discovery of an enormous crime, or decaying in fortune to a bankrupt; otherwise, till he was called to be alderman, or died, he continued, and was every year returned of the common council.

After the beginning of this parliament, when they found by their experience in the case of the Earl of Strafford, of what consequence the city might be to them, and afterwards found, by the courage of the present lord mayor, Sir Richard Gurney, who cannot be too often nor too honourably mentioned, that it might be kept from being disposed by them; and that the men of wealth and ability, who at first had concurred with them, began now to discern that they meant to lead them further than they had a mind to go ; they directed their confidants, that at the election of the common councilmen by the concurrence and number of the meaner people, all such who were moderate men, and lovers of the present government, should be rejected ; and in their places men of the most active and pragmatical heads, of how mean fortunes soever, should be elected ; and by this means all that body consisted of upstart, factious, indigent companions, who were ready to receive all advertisements and directions from those who steered at Westminster, and as forward to encroach upon their superiors, the mayor and aldermen, as the other was upon the house of peers. And so this firebrand of privilege inflamed the city at that time.

(From the Same.)

CHARACTER OF HAMPDEN

MR. HAMPDEN was a gentleman of a good family in Buckinghamshire, and born to a fair fortune, and of a most civil and affable deportment. In his entrance into the world, he indulged to himself all the license in sports and exercises, and company, which was used by men of the most jolly conversation. Afterwards, he retired to a more reserved and melancholy society, yet preserving his own natural cheerfulness and vivacity, and above all, a flowing courtesy to all men, though they who conversed nearly with him, found him growing into a dislike of the ecclesiastical government of the church, yet most believed it rather a dislike of some churchmen, and of some introducements of theirs, which he apprehended might disquiet the public peace. He was rather of reputation in his own country, than of public discourse, or fame in the kingdom, before the business of ship-money : but then he grew the argument of all tongues, every man inquiring who and what he was, that durst, at his own charge, support the liberty and property of the kingdom, and rescue his country, as he thought, from being made a prey to the court. His carriage, throughout this agitation, was with that rare temper and modesty, that they who watched him narrowly to find some advantage against his person, to make him less resolute in his cause, were compelled to give him a just testimony. And the judgment that was given against him infinitely more advanced him, than the service for which it was given. When this parliament began (being returned knight of the shire for the county where he lived), the eyes of all men were fixed on him, as their *patriæ pater*, and the pilot that must steer the vessel through the tempests and rocks which threatened it. And I am persuaded, his power and interest, at that time, was greater to do good or hurt, than any man's in the kingdom, or than any man of his rank hath had at any time : for his reputation of honesty was universal, and his affections seemed so publicly guided, that no corrupt or private ends could bias them.

He was of that rare affability and temper in debate, and of that seeming humility and submission in judgment, as if he brought no opinion with him, but a desire of information and instruction ; yet he had so subtle a way of interrogating, and, under the notion of doubts, insinuating his objections, that he left his opinions with those from whom he pretended to learn and receive them. And even with them who were able to preserve themselves from his infusions, and discerned those opinions to be fixed in him, to which they could not comply, he always left the character of an ingenious and conscientious person. He was indeed a very wise man, and of great parts, and possessed with the most absolute spirit of popularity, that is the most absolute faculties to govern the people, of any man I ever knew. For the first year of the parliament, he seemed rather to moderate and soften the violent and distempered humours, than to inflame them. But wise and dispassioned men plainly discerned that that moderation proceeded from prudence, and observation that the season was not ripe, rather than that he approved of the moderation ; and that he begat many opinions and motions, the education whereof he committed to other men ; so far disguising his own designs, that he seemed seldom to wish more than was concluded ; and in many gross conclusions, which would hereafter contribute to designs not yet set on foot, when he found them sufficiently backed up by majority of voices, he would withdraw himself before the question, that he might seem not to consent to so much visible unreasonableness ; which produced as great a doubt in some, as it did approbation in others, of his integrity. What combination soever had been originally with the Scots for the invasion of England, and what farther was entered into afterwards in favour of them, and to advance any alteration [of the government] in parliament, no man doubts was at least with the privity of this gentleman.

After he was among those members accused by the king of high treason, he was much altered; his nature and carriage seeming much fiercer than it did before. And without question, when he first drew his sword, he threw away the scabbard; for he passionately opposed the overture made by the king for a treaty from Nottingham, and as eminently, any expedients that might have produced any accommodations in this that was at Oxford; and was principally relied on, to prevent any infusions which might be made into the Earl of Essex towards peace, or to render them ineffectual, if they were made; and was indeed much more relied on by that party, than the general himself. In the first entrance into the troubles, he undertook the command of a regiment of foot, and performed the duty of a colonel, on all occasions, most punctually. He was very temperate in diet, and a supreme governor over all his passions and affections, and had thereby a great power over other men's. He was of an industry and vigilance not to be tired out, or wearied by the most laborious; and of parts not to be imposed upon by the most subtle or sharp; and of a personal courage equal to his best parts; so that he was an enemy not to be wished wherever he might have been made a friend; and as much to be apprehended where he was so, as any man could deserve to be. And therefore his death was no less congratulated on the one party, than it was condoled in the other. In a word, what was said of Cinna might well be applied to him: "he had a head to contrive, and a tongue to persuade, and a hand to execute, any mischief." His death therefore seemed to be a great deliverance to the nation.

(From the Same.)

THE CHARACTER OF LORD FALKLAND

BUT I must here take leave a little longer to discontinue this narration; and if the celebrating the memory of eminent and extraordinary persons, and transmitting their great virtues, for the imitation of posterity, be one of the principal ends and duties of history, it will not be thought impertinent, in this place, to remember a loss which no time will suffer to be forgotten, and no success or good fortune could repair. In this unhappy battle was slain the Lord Viscount Falkland ; a person of such prodigious parts of learning and knowledge, of that inimitable sweetness and delight in conversation, of so flowing and obliging a humanity and goodness to mankind, and of that primitive simplicity and integrity of life, that if there were no other brand upon this odious and accursed civil war, than that single loss, it must be most infamous and execrable to all posterity.

Turpe mori, post te, solo non posse dolore.

Before this parliament, his condition of life was so happy that it was hardly capable of improvement.   Before he came to twenty years of age, he was master of a noble fortune, which descended to him by the gift of a grandfather, without passing through his father or mother, who were then both alive and not well enough contented to find themselves passed by in the descent.   His education for some years had been in Ireland, where his father was lord deputy ; so that, when he returned into England, to the possession of his fortune, he was unentangled with any acquaintance or friends, which usually grow up by the custom of conversation ; and therefore was to make a pure election of his company ; which he chose by other rules than were prescribed to the young nobility of that time.   And it cannot be denied, though he admitted some few to his friendship for the agreeableness of their natures, and their undoubted affection to him, that his familiarity and friendship, for the most part, was with men of the most eminent and sublime parts, and of untouched reputation in point of integrity, and such men had a title to his bosom.

He was a great cherisher of wit, and fancy, and good parts in any man ; and, if he found them clouded with poverty or want, a most liberal and bountiful patron towards them, even above his fortune ; of which, in those administrations, he was such a dispenser, as, if he had been trusted with it to such uses, and if there had been the least of vice in his expense, he might have been thought too prodigal.   He was constant and pertinacious in whatsoever he resolved to do, and not to be wearied by any pains that were necessary to that end.   And therefore having once resolved not to see London, which he loved above all places, till he had perfectly learned the Greek tongue, he went to his own house in the country, and pursued it with that indefatigable industry, that it will not be believed in how short a time he was master of it, and accurately read all the Greek historians.

In this time, his house being within ten miles of Oxford, he contracted familiarity and friendship with the most polite and accurate men of that university; who found such an immenseness of wit, and such a solidity of judgment in him, so infinite a fancy bound in by a most logical ratiocination, such a vast knowledge, that he was not ignorant in any thing, yet such an excessive humility, as if he had known nothing, that they frequently resorted, and dwelt with him, as in a college situated in a purer air; so that his house was a university in a less volume; whither they came not so much for repose as study; and to examine and refine those grosser propositions which laziness and consent made current in vulgar conversation.

Many attempts were made upon him by the instigation of his mother (who was a lady of another persuasion in religion, and of a most masculine understanding, alloyed with the passion and infirmities of her own sex) to pervert him in his piety to the church of England and to reconcile him to that of Rome, which they prosecuted with the more confidence, because he declined no opportunity or occasion of conference with those of that religion, whether priests or laics; having diligently studied the controversies, and exactly read all, or the choicest of the Greek and Latin fathers, and having a memory so stupendous, that he remembered, on all occasions, whatsoever he read. And he was so great an enemy to that passion and uncharitableness, which he saw produced, by difference of opinion, in matters of religion, that in all those disputations with priests, and others of the Roman church, he affected to manifest all possible civility to their persons, and estimation of their parts; which made them retain still some hope of his reduction, even when they had given over offering farther reasons to him to that purpose. But this charity towards them was much lessened, and any correspondence with them quite declined, when, by sinister arts, they had corrupted his two younger brothers, being both children, and stolen them from his house, and transported them beyond seas, and perverted his sisters; upon which occasion he writ two large discourses against the principal positions of that religion, with that sharpness of style, and full weight of reason, that the church is deprived of great jewels in the concealment of them, and that they are not published to the world.

He was superior to all those passions and affections which attend vulgar minds, and was guilty of no other ambition than of knowledge, and to be reputed a lover of all good men ; and that made him too much a contemner of those arts, which must be indulged in the transactions of human affairs. In the last short parliament, he was a burgess in the house of commons ; and, from the debates which were then managed with all imaginable gravity and sobriety, he contracted such a reverence to parliaments, that he thought it really impossible they could ever produce mischief or inconvenience to the kingdom ; or that the kingdom could be tolerably happy in the intermission of them. And from the unhappy and unseasonable dissolution of that convention, he harboured, it may be, some jealousy and prejudice to the court, towards which he was not before immoderately inclined ; his father having wasted a full fortune there, in those offices and employments by which other men used to obtain a greater. He was chosen again this parliament to serve in the same place, and, in the beginning of it, declared himself very sharply and severely against those exorbitancies, which had been most grievous to the state, for he was so rigid an observer of established laws and rules, that he could not endure the least breach or deviation from them ; and thought no mischief so intolerable as the presumption of ministers of state to break positive rules, for reasons of state ; or judges to transgress known laws, upon the title of conveniency, or necessity ; which made him so severe against the earl of Strafford, and the Lord Finch, contrary to his natural gentleness and temper ; insomuch as they who did not know his composition to be as free from revenge as it was from pride, thought that the sharpness to the former might proceed from the memory of some unkindnesses, not without a mixture of injustice, from him towards his father. But without doubt he was free from those temptations, and was only misled by the authority of those, who, he believed, understood the laws perfectly ; of which himself was utterly ignorant ; and if the assumption, which was scarce controverted, had been true, " that an endeavour to overthrow the fundamental laws of the kingdom had been treason," a strict understanding might make reasonable conclusions to satisfy his own judgment, from the exorbitant parts of their several charges.

The great opinion he had of the uprightness and integrity of those persons who appeared most active, especially of Mr. Hampden, kept him longer from suspecting any design against the peace of the kingdom ; and though he differed from them commonly in conclusions, he believed long their purposes were honest. When he grew better informed what was law, and discerned in them a desire to control that law by a vote of one or both houses, no man more opposed those attempts, and gave the adverse party more trouble by reason and argumentation, insomuch as he was, by degrees, looked upon as an advocate for the court, to which he contributed so little, that he declined those addresses, and even those invitations which he was obliged almost by civility to entertain. And he was so jealous of the least imagination that he should incline to preferment, that he affected even a morosity to the court, and to the courtiers; and left nothing undone which might prevent and divert the king's or queen's favour towards him, but the deserving it. For when the king sent for him once or twice to speak with him, and to give him thanks for his excellent comportment in those councils, which his majesty graciously termed "doing him service," his answers were more negligent, and less satisfactory, than might be expected; as if he cared only that his actions should be just, not that they should be acceptable, and that his majesty should think that they proceeded only from the impulsion of conscience, without any sympathy in his affections; which, from a stoical and sullen nature, might not have been misinterpreted; yet, from a person of so perfect a habit of generous and obsequious compliance with all good men, might very well have been interpreted by the king as more than an ordinary averseness to his service; so that he took more pains, and more forced his nature to actions unagreeable, and unpleasant to it, that he might not be thought to incline to the court, than most men have done to procure an office there. And if any thing but not doing his duty could have kept him from receiving a testimony of the king's grace and trust at that time, he had not been called to his council; not that he was in truth averse to the court or from receiving public employment; for he had a great devotion to the king's person, and had before used some small endeavour to be recommended to him for a foreign negociation, and had once a desire to be sent ambassador into France; but he abhorred an imagination or doubt should sink into the thoughts of any man, that, in the discharge of his trust and duty in parliament, he had any bias to the court, or that the king himself should apprehend that he looked for a reward for being honest.

For this reason, when he heard it first whispered, " that the king had a purpose to make him a counsellor," for which there was, in the beginning, no other ground, but because he was known sufficient (*haud semper errat fama, aliquando et eligit*), he resolved to decline it ; and at last suffered himself only to be overruled, by the advice and persuasions of his friends, to submit to it. Afterwards, when he found that the king intended to make him secretary of state, he was positive to refuse it ; declaring to his friends, "that he was most unfit for it, and that he must either do that which would be great disquiet to his own nature, or leave that undone which was most necessary to be done by one that was honoured with that place ; for that the most just and honest men did, every day, that which he could not give himself leave to do." And indeed he was so exact and strict an observer of justice and truth, *ad amussim*, that he believed those necessary condescensions and applications to the weakness of other men, and those arts and insinuations which are necessary for discoveries, and prevention of ill, would be in him a declension from his own rules of life ; which he acknowledged fit, and absolutely necessary to be practised in those employments ; and was, in truth, so precise in the practice of the principles he prescribed to himself (to all others he was as indulgent), as if he had lived *in republica Platonis, non in fæce Romuli.*

Two reasons prevailed with him to receive the seals, and but for those he had resolutely avoided them. The first, the consideration that it (his refusal) might bring some blemish upon the king's affairs, and that men would have believed that he had refused so great an honour and trust, because he must have been with it obliged to do somewhat else not justifiable. And this he made matter of conscience, since he knew the king made choice of him, before other men, especially because he thought him more honest than other men. The other was, lest he might be thought to avoid it out of fear to do an ungracious thing to the House of Commons, who were sorely troubled at the displacing Sir Harry Vane, whom they looked upon as removed for having done them those offices they stood in need of ; and the disdain of so popular an incumbrance wrought upon him next to the other. For as he had a full appetite of fame by just and generous actions, so he had an equal contempt of it by any servile expedients ; and he so much the more consented to and approved the justice upon Sir Harry Vane, in his own private judgment, by how much he surpassed most men in the religious observation of a trust, the violation whereof he would not admit of any excuse for.

For these reasons he submitted to the king's command, and became his secretary, with as humble and devout an acknowledgment of the greatness of the obligation, as could be expressed, and as true a sense of it in his heart. Yet two things he could never bring himself to, whilst he continued in that office, that was to his death ; for which he was contented to be reproached, as for omissions in a most necessary part of his place. The one, employing of spies, or giving any countenance or entertainment to them. I do not mean such emissaries, as with danger would venture to view the enemy's camp, and bring intelligence of their number, or quartering, or such generals as such an observation can comprehend ; but those, who by communication of guile, or dissimulation of manners, wound themselves into such trusts and secrets, as enabled them to make discoveries for the benefit of the state. The other, the liberty of opening letters, upon a suspicion that they might contain matter of dangerous consequence. For the first, he would say, " such instruments must be void of all ingenuity, and common honesty, before they could be of use ; and afterwards they could never be fit to be credited : and that no single preservation could be worth so general a wound, and corruption of human society, as the cherishing such persons would carry with it." The last, he thought " such a violation of the law of nature, that no qualification by office could justify a single person in the trespass " ; and though he was convinced by the necessity and iniquity of the time, that those advantages of information were not to be declined, and were necessarily to be practised, he found means to shift it from himself ; when he confessed he needed excuse and pardon for the omission ; so unwilling he was to resign any thing in his nature to an obligation in his office.

In all other particulars he filled his place plentifully, being sufficiently versed in languages to understand any that are used in business, and to make himself again understood. To speak of his integrity and his high disdain of any bait that might seem to look towards corruption, *in tanto viro, injuria virtutum fuerit.* Some sharp expressions he used against the archbishop of Canterbury, and his concurring in the first bill to take away the votes of bishops in the House of Peers, gave occasion to some to believe, and opportunity to others to conclude and publish, " that he was no friend to the church, and the established government of it," and troubled his very friends much, who were more confident of the contrary, than prepared to answer the allegations.

The truth is, he had unhappily contracted some prejudice to the archbishop ; and having only known him enough to observe his passion, when, it may be, multiplicity of business, or other indisposition, had possessed him, did wish him less entangled and engaged in the business of the court, or state ; though, I speak it knowingly, he had a singular estimation and reverence of his great learning, and confessed integrity ; and really thought his letting himself to those expressions, which implied a disesteem of him, or at least an acknowledgment of his infirmities, would enable him to shelter him from part of the storm he saw raised for his destruction ; which he abominated with his soul.

The giving his consent to the first bill for the displacing the bishops, did proceed from two grounds ; the first, his not understanding the original of their right and suffrage there ; the other, an opinion that the combination against the whole government of the church by bishops, was so violent and furious, that a less composition than the dispensing with their intermeddling in secular affairs, would not preserve the order. And he was persuaded to this by the profession of many persons of honour, who declared, "they did desire the one, and would not then press the other" ; which, in that particular, misled many men. But when his observation and experience made him discern more of their intentions, than he before suspected, with great frankness he opposed the second bill that was preferred for that purpose ; and had, without scruple, the order itself in perfect reverence ; and thought too great encouragement could not possibly be given to learning, nor too great rewards to learned men ; and was never in the least degree swayed or moved by the objections which were made against that government (holding them most ridiculous), or affected to the other, which those men fancied to themselves.

He had a courage of the most clear and keen temper, and so far from fear, that he was not without appetite of danger ; and therefore, upon any occasion of action, he always engaged his person in those troops, which he thought, by the forwardness of the commanders, to be most like to be farthest engaged ; and in all such encounters he had about him a strange cheerfulness and companiableness, without at all affecting the execution that was then principally to be attended, in which he took no delight, but took pains to prevent it, where it was not, by resistance, necessary ; insomuch that at Edgehill, when the enemy was routed, he was like to have incurred great peril, by interposing to save those who had thrown away their arms, and against whom, it may be, others were more fierce for their having thrown them away ; insomuch as a man might think, he came into the field only out of curiosity to see the face of danger, and charity to prevent the shedding of blood. Yet in his natural inclination he acknowledged he was addicted to the profession of a soldier ; and shortly after he came to his fortune, and before he came to age, he went into the Low Countries, with a resolution of procuring command : and to give himself up to it, from which he was converted by the complete inactivity of that summer ; and so he returned into England, and shortly after entered upon that vehement course of study we mentioned before, till the first alarum from the north ; and then again he made ready for the field, and though he received some repulse in the command of a troop of horse, of which he had a promise, he went a volunteer with the Earl of Essex.

From the entrance into this unnatural war, his natural cheerfulness and vivacity grew clouded, and a kind of sadness and dejection of spirit stole upon him, which he had never been used to ; yet being one of those who believed that one battle would end all differences, and that there would be so great a victory on one side, that the other would be compelled to submit to any conditions from the victor (which supposition and conclusion generally sunk into the minds of most men, and prevented the looking after many advantages, that might then have been laid hold of), he resisted those indispositions, *et in luctu, bellum inter remedia erat.* But after the king's return from Brentford, and the furious resolution of the two houses not to admit any treaty for peace, those indispositions, which had before touched him, grew into a perfect habit of uncheerfulness ; and he, who had been so exactly unreserved and affable to all men, that his face and countenance was always present, and vacant to his company, and held any cloudiness, and less pleasantness of the visage, a kind of rudeness or incivility, became, on a sudden, less communicable ; and thence, very sad, pale, and exceedingly affected with the spleen. In his clothes and habit, which he had intended before always with more neatness, and industry, and expense than is usual to so great a mind, he was not now only incurious, but too negligent ; and in his reception of suitors, and the necessary or casual addresses to his place, so quick and sharp and severe, that there wanted not some men (who were strangers to his nature and disposition), who believed him proud and imperious, from which no mortal man was ever more free.

The truth is, that as he was of a most incomparable gentleness, application, and even demissiveness and submission to good, and worthy, and entire men, so he was naturally (which could not but be more evident in his place, which objected him to another conversation and intermixture, than his own election had done), *adversus malos injucundus :* and was so ill a dissembler of his dislike and disinclination to ill men, that it was not possible for such not to discern it. There was once, in the House of Commons, such a declared acceptation of the good service an eminent member had done to them, and, as they said, to the whole kingdom, that it was moved, he being present, "that the speaker might, in the name of the whole house, give him thanks ; and then, that every member might, as a testimony of his particular acknowledgment, stir or move his hat towards him " ; the which (though not ordered) when very many did, the Lord Falkland (who believed the service itself not to be of that moment, and that an honourable and generous person could not have stooped to it for any recompense), instead of moving his hat, stretched both his arms out, and clasped his hands together upon the crown of his hat, and held it close down to his head ; that all men might see how odious that flattery was to him, and the very approbation of the person, though at that time most popular.

When there was any overture or hope of peace, he would be more erect and vigorous, and exceedingly solicitous to press any thing which he thought might promote it ; and sitting among his friends, often, after a deep silence and frequent sighs, would, with a shrill and sad accent, ingeminate the word *Peace, Peace ;* and would passionately profess, "that the very agony of the war, and the view of the calamities and desolation the kingdom did and must endure, took his sleep from him, and would shortly break his heart." This made some think, or pretend to think, "that he was so much enamoured on peace, that he would have been glad the king should have bought it at any price " ; which was a most unreasonable calumny. As if a man, that was himself the most punctual and precise in every circumstance that might reflect upon conscience or honour, could have wished the king to have committed a trespass against either. And yet this senseless scandal made some impression upon him, or at least he used it for an excuse of the daringness of his spirit ; for at the leaguer before Gloucester, when his friends passionately reprehended him for exposing his person unnecessarily to danger (as he delighted to visit the trenches, and nearest approaches, and to discover what the enemy did), as being so much beside the duty of his place, that it might be understood against it, he would say merrily, " that his office could not take away the privileges of his age ; and that a secretary in war might be present at the greatest secret of danger " ; but withal alleged seriously, " that it concerned him to be more active in enterprises of hazard, than other men ; that all might see that his impatiency for peace proceeded not from pusillanimity, or fear to adventure his own person."

In the morning, before the battle, as always upon action, he was very cheerful, and put himself into the first rank of the Lord Byron's regiment, who was then advancing upon the enemy, who had lined the hedges on both sides with musketeers ; from whence he was shot with a musket in the lower part of the belly, and in the instant falling from his horse, his body was not found till the next morning ; till when, there was some hope he might have been a prisoner ; though his nearest friends, who knew his temper, received small comfort from that imagination. Thus fell that incomparable young man, in the four and thirtieth year of his age, having so much despatched the business of life, that the oldest rarely attain to that immense knowledge, and the youngest enter not into the world with more innocence ; whosoever leads such a life, needs not care upon how short warning it be taken from him.

(From the Same.)

THE CHARACTER OF CHARLES I.

To speak first of his private qualifications as a man, before the mention of his princely and royal virtues ; he was, if ever any, the most worthy of the title of an honest man ; so great a lover of justice, that no temptation could dispose him to a wrongful action, except it was so disguised to him that he believed it to be just. He had a tenderness and compassion of nature, which restrained him from ever doing a hardhearted thing ; and there-

fore he was so apt to grant pardon to malefactors, that the judges
of the land represented to him the damage and insecurity to the
public, that flowed from such his indulgence. And then he
restrained himself from pardoning either murders or highway
robberies, and quickly discerned the fruits of his severity by a
wonderful reformation of those enormities. He was very punctual
and regular in his devotions ; he was never known to enter upon
his recreations or sports, though never so early in the morning,
before he had been at public prayers ; so that on hunting days
his chaplains were bound to a very early attendance. He was
likewise very strict in observing the hours of his private cabinet
devotions ; and was so severe an exactor of gravity and reverence
in all mention of religion, that he could never endure any light or
profane word, with what sharpness of wit soever it was covered ;
and though he was well pleased and delighted with reading verses
made upon any occasion, no man durst bring before him any
thing that was profane or unclean. That kind of wit had never
any countenance then. He was so great an example of conjugal
affection, that they who did not imitate him in that particular did
not brag of their liberty ; and he did not only permit, but direct
his bishops to prosecute those scandalous vices, in the ecclesiastical
courts, against persons of eminence, and near relation to his
service.

His kingly virtues had some mixture and alloy, that hindered
them from shining in full lustre, and from producing those fruits
they should have been attended with. He was not in his nature
very bountiful, though he gave very much. This appeared more
after the Duke of Buckingham's death, after which those showers
fell very rarely ; and he paused too long in giving, which made
those, to whom he gave, less sensible of the benefit. He kept
state to the full, which made his court very orderly ; no man
presuming to be seen in a place where he had no pretence to be.
He saw and observed men long, before he received them about
his person ; and did not love strangers ; nor very confident men.
He was a patient hearer of causes ; which he frequently accustomed
himself to at the council board, and judged very well, and was
dexterous in the mediating part ; so that he often put an end to
causes by persuasion, which the stubbornness of men's humours
made dilatory in courts of justice.

He was very fearless in his person ; but not very enterprising.
He had an excellent understanding, but was not confident enough

of it ; which made him oftentimes change his own opinion for a worse, and follow the advice of men that did not judge so well as himself. This made him more irresolute than the conjuncture of his affairs would admit ; if he had been of a rougher and more imperious nature he would have found more respect and duty. And his not applying some severe cures to approaching evils proceeded from the lenity of his nature, and the tenderness of his conscience, which, in all cases of blood, made him choose the softer way, and not hearken to severe counsels, how reasonably soever urged. This only restrained him from pursuing his advantage in the first Scottish expedition, when, humanly speaking, he might have reduced that nation to the most slavish obedience that could have been wished. But no man can say he had then many who advised him to it, but the contrary, by a wonderful indisposition all his council had to fighting, or any other fatigue. He was always an immoderate lover of the Scottish nation, having not only been born there, but educated by that people, and besieged by them always, having few English about him till he was king ; and the major number of his servants being still of that nation, who he thought could never fail him. And among these, no man had such an ascendant over him, by the humblest insinuations, as Duke Hamilton had.

As he excelled in all other virtues, so in temperance he was so strict, that he abhorred all debauchery to that degree, that, at a great festival solemnity, where he once was, when very many of the nobility of the English and Scots were entertained, being told by one who withdrew from thence, what vast draughts of wine they drank, and "that there was one earl, who had drank most of the rest down, and was not himself moved or altered," the king said "that he deserved to be hanged "; and that earl coming shortly after into the room where his majesty was, in some gaiety, to show how unhurt he was from that battle, the king sent one to bid him withdraw from his majesty's presence ; nor did he in some days after appear before him.

So many miraculous circumstances contributed to his ruin, that men might well think that heaven and earth and the stars designed it. Though he was, from the first declension of his power, so much betrayed by his own servants, that there were very few who remained faithful to him ; yet that treachery proceeded not from any treasonable purpose to do him any harm, but from particular and personal animosities against other men.

And, afterwards, the terror all men were under of the parliament, and the guilt they were conscious of themselves, made them watch all opportunities to make themselves gracious to those who could do them good ; and so they became spies upon their master, and from one piece of knavery were hardened and confirmed to undertake another ; till at last they had no other hope of preservation but by the destruction of their master.　And after all this, when a man might reasonably believe that less than a universal defection of three nations could not have reduced a great king to so ugly a fate, it is most certain that, in that very hour when he was thus wickedly murdered in the sight of the sun, he had as great a share in the hearts and affections of his subjects in general, was as much beloved, esteemed, and longed for by the people in general of the three nations, as any of his predecessors had ever been.　To conclude, he was the worthiest gentleman, the best master, the best friend, the best husband, the best father, and the best Christian that the age in which he lived produced. And if he were not the best king, if he were without some parts and qualities which have made some kings great and happy, no other prince was ever unhappy who was possessed of half his virtues and endowments, and so much without any kind of vice.

(From the Same.)

CHARACTER OF CROMWELL

HE was one of those men, *quos vituperare ne inimici quidem possunt, nisi ut simul laudent;* (whom his very enemies could not condemn without commending him at the same time :) for he could never have done half that mischief without great parts of courage, industry, and judgment.　He must have had a wonderful understanding in the natures and humours of men, and as great a dexterity in applying them ; who, from a private and obscure birth, (though of a good family) without interest or estate, alliance or friendship, could raise himself to such a height, and compound and knead such opposite and contradictory tempers, humours, and interests into a consistence, that contributed to his designs, and to their own destruction ; whilst himself grew insensibly powerful enough to cut off those by whom he had climbed, in the instant that they projected to demolish their own building.　What

Velleius Paterculus said of Cinna may very justly be said of him, *ausum eum, quæ nemo auderet bonus; perfecisse, quæ a nullo, nisi fortissimo, perfici possent:* (he attempted those things which no good man durst have ventured on : and achieved those in which none but a valiant and great man could have succeeded). Without doubt, no man with more wickedness ever attempted any thing, or brought to pass what he desired more wickedly, more in the face and contempt of religion, and moral honesty ; yet wickedness as great as his could never have accomplished those trophies without the assistance of a great spirit, an admirable circumspection and sagacity, and a most magnanimous resolution.

When he appeared first in the parliament, he seemed to have a person in no degree gracious, no ornament of discourse, none of those talents which use to reconcile the affections of the stander by ; yet as he grew into place and authority, his parts seemed to be raised, as if he had concealed faculties, till he had occasion to use them ; and when he was to act the part of a great man, he did it without any indecency, notwithstanding the want of custom.

After he was confirmed and invested protector by the humble petition and advice, he consulted with very few upon any action of importance, nor communicated any enterprise he resolved upon, with more than those who were to have principal parts in the execution of it ; nor with them sooner than was absolutely necessary. What he once resolved, in which he was not rash, he would not be dissuaded from, nor endure any contradiction of his power and authority ; but extorted obedience from them who were not willing to yield it.

When he had laid some very extraordinary tax upon the city, one Cony, an eminent fanatic, and one who had heretofore served him very notably, positively refused to pay his part, and loudly dissuaded others from submitting to it, "as an imposition notoriously against the law, and the property of the subject, which all honest men were bound to defend." Cromwell sent for him, and cajoled him with the memory of "the old kindness and friendship, that had been between them ; and that of all men he did not expect this opposition from him in a matter that was so necessary for the good of the commonwealth." But it was always his fortune to meet with the most rude and obstinate behaviour from those who had formerly been absolutely governed by him, and they commonly put him in mind of some expressions and sayings of his own, in cases of the like nature ; so this man remembered

him how great an enemy he had expressed himself to such grievances, and had declared "that all who submitted to them, and paid
illegal taxes, were more to blame, and greater enemies to their
country than they who had imposed them ; and that the tyranny
of princes could never be grievous, but by the tameness and
stupidity of the people. When Cromwell saw that he could not
convert him, he told him "that he had a will as stubborn as his,
and he would try which of them two should be master." Thereupon, with some terms of reproach and contempt, he committed
the man to prison, whose courage was nothing abated by it, but
as soon as the term came he brought his *habeas corpus* in the
King's Bench, which they then called the Upper Bench. Maynard,
who was of council with the prisoner, demanded his liberty with
great confidence, both upon the illegality of the commitment, and
the illegality of the imposition, as being laid without any lawful
authority. The judges could not maintain or defend either, and
enough declared what their sentence would be, and therefore the
protector's attorney required a farther day to answer what had been
urged. Before that day, Maynard was committed to the Tower
for presuming to question or make doubt of his authority, and
the judges were sent for and severely reprehended for suffering
that license ; when they, with all humility, mentioned the law and
magna charta, Cromwell told them "their *magna charta* should
not control his actions, which he knew were for the safety of the
commonwealth." He asked them, "who made them judges !
Whether they had any authority to sit there but what he gave
them ? and if his authority were at an end, they knew well enough
what would become of themselves ; and therefore advised them to
be more tender of that which could only preserve them," and so
dismissed them with the caution, "that they should not suffer the
lawyers to prate what it would not become them to hear."

Thus he subdued a spirit that had been often troublesome to
the most sovereign power, and made Westminster-hall as obedient,
and subservient to his commands, as any of the rest of his quarters.
In all other matters which did not concern the life of his jurisdiction, he seemed to have great reverence for the law, rarely interposing between party and party. As he proceeded with this kind
of indignation and haughtiness with those who were refractory and
dared to contend with his greatness, so towards all who complied
with his good pleasure and courted his protection, he used a
wonderful civility, generosity, and bounty

To reduce three nations, which perfectly hated him, to an entire obedience to all his dictates ; to awe and govern those nations by an army that was indevoted to him and wished his ruin, was an instance of a very prodigious address. But his greatness at home was but a shadow of the glory he had abroad. It was hard to discover which feared him most, France, Spain, or the Low Countries, where his friendship was current at the value he put upon it. As they did all sacrifice their honour and their interest to his pleasure, so there is nothing he could have demanded that either of them would have denied him. To manifest which there needs only two instances. The first is when those of the valley of Lucerne had unwarily rebelled against the Duke of Savoy, which gave occasion to the Pope and the neighbour princes of Italy to call and solicit for their extirpation, and their prince positively resolved upon it, Cromwell sent his agent to the Duke of Savoy, a prince with whom he had no correspondence or commerce, and so engaged the cardinal, and even terrified the Pope himself, without so much as doing any grace to the English Roman Catholics, (nothing being more usual than his saying, "that his ships in the Mediterranean should visit Civita Vecchia ; and that the sound of his cannon should be heard in Rome,") that the Duke of Savoy thought it necessary to restore all that he had taken from them, and did renew all those privileges they had formerly enjoyed, and newly forfeited.

The other instance of his authority was yet greater, and more incredible. In the city of Nismes, which is one of the fairest in the province of Languedoc, and where those of the religion do most abound, there was a great faction at that season when the consuls (who are the chief magistrates) were to be chosen. Those of the reformed religion had the confidence to set up one of themselves for that magistracy ; which they of the Roman religion resolved to oppose with all their power. The dissension between them made so much noise, that the intendant of the province, who is the supreme minister in all civil affairs throughout the whole province, went thither to prevent any disorder that might happen. When the day of election came, those of the religion possessed themselves with many armed men of the town-house, where the election was to be made. The magistrates sent to know what their meaning was ; to which they answered, "they were there to give their voices for the choice of the new consuls, and to be sure that the election should be fairly made." The bishop of the city, the intendant of the province, with all the officers of the church and the present magistrates of the town, went together in their robes to be present at the election, without any suspicion that there would be any force used. When they came near the gate of the town-house, which was shut, and they supposed would be opened when they came, they within poured out a volley of musket-shot upon them, by which the dean of the church and two or three of the magistrates of the town were killed upon the place and very many others wounded ; whereof some died shortly after. In this confusion the magistrates put themselves into as good a posture to defend themselves as they could, without any purpose of offending the other till they should be better provided ; in order to which they sent an express to the court with a plain relation of the whole matter of fact, "and that there appeared to be no manner of combination with those of the religion in other places of the province ; but that it was an insolence in those of the place, upon the presumption of their great numbers, which were little inferior to those of the catholics." The court was glad of the occasion, and resolved that this provocation, in which other places were not involved, and which nobody could excuse, should warrant all kind of severity in that city, even to the pulling down their temples and expelling many of them for ever out of the city ; which, with the execution and forfeiture of many of the principal persons, would be a general mortification to all of the religion in France ; with whom they were heartily offended ; and a part of the army was forthwith ordered to march towards Nismes, to see this executed with the utmost rigour.

Those of the religion in the town were quickly sensible into what condition they had brought themselves ; and sent, with all possible submission, to the magistrates to excuse themselves, and to impute what had been done to the rashness of particular men, who had no order for what they did. The magistrates answered, "that they were glad they were sensible of their miscarriage ; but they could say nothing upon the subject till the king's pleasure should be known ; to whom they had sent a full relation of all that had passed." The others very well knew what the king's pleasure would be, and forthwith sent an express, one Moulins, a Scotch-man, who had lived many years in that place and in Montpelier, to Cromwell, to desire his protection and interposition. The express made so much haste, and found so good a reception the first hour he came, that Cromwell, after he had received the whole account, bade him "refresh himself after so long a journey, and he would take such care of his business, that by the time he came to Paris he should find it despatched"; and that night sent away another messenger to his ambassador, Lockhart; who, by the time Moulins came thither, had so far prevailed with the cardinal, that orders were sent to stop the troops, which were upon their march towards Nismes; and within few days after, Moulins returned with a full pardon and amnesty from the king, under the great seal of France, so fully confirmed with all circumstances, that there was never farther mention made of it, but all things passed as if there had never been any such thing. So that nobody can wonder that his memory remains still in those parts, and with those people, in great veneration.

He would never suffer himself to be denied anything he ever asked of the cardinal, alleging, "that the people would not be otherwise satisfied"; which the cardinal bore very heavily, and complained of to those with whom he would be free. One day he visited Madam Turenne, and when he took his leave of her, she, according to her custom, besought him to continue gracious to the churches. Whereupon the cardinal told her, "that he knew not how to behave himself; if he advised the king to punish and suppress their insolence, Cromwell threatened him to join with the Spaniard; and if he shewed any favour to them, at Rome they accounted him an heretic."

He was not a man of blood, and totally declined Machiavel's method, which prescribes, upon any alteration of government, as a thing absolutely necessary, to cut off all the heads of those, and extirpate their families, who are friends to the old one. It was confidently reported that, in the council of officers, it was more than once proposed, "that there might be a general massacre of all the royal party, as "the only expedient to secure the government": but that Cromwell would never consent to it; it may be, out of too much contempt of his enemies. In a word, as he had all the wickednesses against which damnation is denounced, and for which hell-fire is prepared, so he had some virtues which have caused the memory of some men in all ages to be celebrated; and he will be looked upon by posterity as a brave bad man.

(From the Same.)

CLARENDON'S EARLY FRIENDS

MR. SELDEN was a person whom no character can flatter, or transmit in any expressions equal to his merit and virtue. He was of so stupendous learning in all kinds and in all languages, (as may appear in his excellent and transcendent writings), that a man would have thought he had been entirely conversant amongst books, and had never spent an hour but in reading and writing; yet his humanity, courtesy, and affability was such, that he would have been thought to have been bred in the best courts, but that his good nature, charity, and delight in doing good, and in communicating all he knew, exceeded that breeding. His style in all his writings seems harsh and sometimes obscure; which is not wholly to be imputed to the abstruse subjects of which he commonly treated, out of the paths trod by other men; but to a little undervaluing the beauty of a style, and too much propensity to the language of antiquity; but in his conversation he was the most clear discourser, and had the best faculty of making hard things easy, and presenting them to the understanding of any man that hath been known. Mr. Hyde was wont to say, that he valued himself upon nothing more than upon having had Mr. Selden's acquaintance from the time he was very young; and held it with great delight as long as they were suffered to continue together in London; and he was very much troubled always when he heard him blamed, censured, and reproached, for staying in London, and in the parliament, after they were in rebellion, and in the worst times, which his age obliged him to do; and how wicked soever the actions were which were every day done, he was confident he had not given his consent to them; but would have hindered them if he could with his own safety, to which he was always enough indulgent. If he had some infirmities with other men, they were weighed down with wonderful and prodigious abilities and excellencies in the other scale.

Charles Cotton was a gentleman born to a competent fortune, and so qualified in his person and education, that for many years he continued the greatest ornament of the town, in the esteem of those who had been best bred. His natural parts were very great, his wit flowing in all the parts of conversation: the superstructure of learning not raised to a considerable height; but having passed some years in Cambridge, and then in France, and conversing always with learned men, his expressions were ever proper and significant, and gave great lustre to his discourse upon any argument ; so that he was thought by those who were not intimate with him, to have been much better acquainted with books than he was. He had all those qualities which in youth raise men to the reputation of being fine gentlemen ; such a pleasantness and gaiety of humour, such a sweetness and gentleness of nature, and such a civility and delightfulness in conversation, that no man in the court or out of it, appeared a more accomplished person ; all these extraordinary qualifications being supported by as extraordinary a clearness of courage and fearlessness of spirit, of which he gave too often manifestation. Some unhappy suits in law, and waste of his fortune in those suits, made some impression upon his mind ; which being improved by domestic afflictions, and those indulgences to himself which naturally attend those afflictions, rendered his age less reverenced than his youth had been ; and gave his best friends cause to have wished that he had not lived so long.

John Vaughan was then a student of the law in the Inner Temple, but at that time indulged more to the politer learning ; and was in truth a man of great parts of nature, and very well adorned by arts and books, and so much cherished by Mr. Selden, that he grew to be of entire trust and friendship with him, and to that owed the best part of his reputation ; for he was of so magisterial and supercilious a humour, so proud and insolent a behaviour, that all Mr. Selden's instructions, and authority, and example, could not file off that roughness of his nature, so as to make him very grateful. He looked most into those parts of the law which disposed him to least reverence to the crown, and most to popular authority ; yet without inclination to any change in government ; and therefore, before the beginning of the civil war, and when he clearly discerned the approaches to it in parliament (of which he was a member), he withdrew himself into the fastnesses of his own country, North Wales, where he enjoyed a secure, and as near an innocent life, as the iniquity of that time would permit ; and upon the return of King Charles the Second, he appeared under the character of a man who had preserved his loyalty entire, and was esteemed accordingly by all that party.

His friend Mr. Hyde, who was then become Lord High Chancellor of England, renewed his old kindness and friendship towards him, and was desirous to gratify him all the ways he could, and earnestly pressed him to put on his gown again, and take upon him the office of a judge ; but he excused himself upon his long discontinuance (having not worn his gown, and wholly discontinued the profession from the year 1640, full twenty years), and upon his age, and expressly refused to receive any promotion ; but continued all the professions of respect and gratitude imaginable to the chancellor, till it was in his power to manifest the contrary, to his prejudice, which he did with circumstances very uncommendable. (From the *Life*.)

CLARENDON'S EARLY MANHOOD

UNDER this universal acquaintance and general acceptation, Mr. Hyde led for many years as cheerful and pleasant a life as any man did enjoy, as long as the kingdom took any pleasure in itself. His practice grew every day as much as he wished, and would have been much more if he had wished it, by which he not only supported his expense, greater much than men of his rank and pretences used to make, but increased his estate by some convenient purchases of land adjoining to his other ; and he grew so much in love with business and practice that he gave up his whole heart to it ; resolving by a course of severe study, to recover the time he had lost upon less profitable learning, and to intend nothing else but to reap all those benefits to which that profession could carry him, and to the pursuing whereof he had so many and so unusual encouragements ; and towards which it was not the least that God had blessed him with an excellent wife, who perfectly resigned herself to him, and who then had brought him, before any troubles in the kingdom, three sons and a daughter, which he then and ever looked upon as his greatest blessing and consolation.

Because we shall have little cause hereafter to mention any other particulars in the calm part of his life, whilst he followed the study and practice of the law, it will not in this place appear a very impertinent digression to say that he was, in that very time when fortune seemed to smile and to intend well towards him, and often afterwards, throughout the whole course of his life, wont to say that, " when he reflected upon himself and his past actions, even from the time of his first coming to the Middle Temple, he had much more cause to be terrified upon the reflection than the man who had viewed Rochester bridge in the morning that it was broken, and which he had galloped over in the night ; that he had passed over more precipices than the other had done, for many nights and days and some years together ; from which nothing but the immediate hand of God could have preserved him." For though it is very true the persons before mentioned were the only men in whose company, in those seasons of his life, he took delight, yet he frequently found himself in the conversation of worse, and, indeed, of all manner of men ; and it being in the time when the war was entered into against the two crowns, and the expeditions made to, and unprosperous returns from, Cadiz and the Isle of Rhè, the town was full of soldiers, and of young gentlemen who intended to be soldiers, or as like them as they could ; great license used of all kinds, in clothes, in diet, in gaming, and all kinds of expenses equally carried on by men who had fortunes of their own to support it, and by others who, having nothing of their own, cared not what they spent whilst they could find credit : so that there was never an age in which, in so short a time, so many young gentlemen, who had not experience in the world, or some good tutelar angel to protect them, were insensibly and suddenly overwhelmed in that sea of wine, and women, and quarrels, and gaming, which almost overspread the whole kingdom and the nobility and gentry thereof. And when he had, by God's immediate blessing, disentangled himself from these labyrinths, (his nature and inclination disposing him rather to pass through those dissolute quarters than to make any stay in them), and was enough composed against any extravagant excursions ; he was still conversant with a rank of men (how worthy soever) above his quality, and engaged in an expense above his fortune, if the extraordinary accidents of his life had not supplied him for those excesses ; so that it brought no prejudice upon him, except in the censure of severe men, who thought him a person of more license than in truth he was, and who, in a short time, were very fully reconciled to him.

He had without doubt great infirmities, which, by a providential mercy, were reasonably restrained from growing into vices, at least into any that were habitual. He had ambition enough to keep him from being satisfied with his own condition, and to raise his spirit to great designs of raising himself ; but not to transport him to endeavour it, by any crooked and indirect means. He was never suspected to flatter the greatest men, or in the least degree to dissemble his own opinions or thoughts, how ingrateful soever it often proved ; and even an affected defect in, and contempt of those two useful qualities cost him dear afterwards.   He indulged his palate very much, and took even some delight in eating and drinking well, but without any approach to luxury ; and, in truth, rather discoursed like an epicure, than was one ; having spent much time in the eating hours with the earl of Dorset, the Lord Conway, and the Lord Lumley ; men who excelled in gratifying their appetites. He had a fancy, sharp and luxuriant, but so carefully cultivated and strictly guarded, that he never was heard to speak a loose or profane word, which he imputed to the chastity of the persons where his conversation usually was, where that rank sort of wit was religiously detested ; and a little discountenance would quickly root those unsavoury weeds out all discourses where persons of honour are present.

He was in his nature inclined to pride and passion, and to a humour between wrangling and disputing very troublesome, which good company in a short time so much reformed and mastered, that no man was more affable and courteous to all kind of persons, and they who knew the great infirmity of his whole family, which abounded in passion, used to say, he had much extinguished the unruliness of that fire.   That which supported and rendered him generally acceptable was his generosity (for he had too much a contempt of money), and the opinion men had of the goodness and justice of his nature, which was transcendent in him, in a wonderful tenderness, and delight in obliging.   His integrity was ever without blemish, and believed to be above temptation.   He was firm and unshaken in his friendships, and, though he had great candour towards others in the differences of religion, he was zealously and deliberately fixed in the principles, both of the doctrine and discipline of the church : yet he used to say to his nearest friends, in that time, when he expected another kind of calm for the remainder of his life, " though he had some glimmering light of, and inclination to virtue in his nature, that the whole progress of his life had been full of desperate hazards : and that only the merciful hand of God Almighty had prevented his being both an unfortunate and a vicious man " ; and he still said that " God had vouchsafed that signal goodness to him, for the piety and exemplar virtue of his father and mother " ; whose memory he had always in veneration : and he was pleased with what his nearest ally and bosom friend, Sergeant Hyde (who was afterwards chief justice of the King's Bench), used at that time to say of him, that his cousin had passed his time very luckily and with notable success, and was like to be very happy in the world; but he would never advise any of his friends to walk in the same paths, or to tread in his steps.

It was about the year 1639, when he was little more than thirty years of age, and when England enjoyed the greatest measure of felicity that it had ever known: the two crowns of France and Spain worrying each other by their mutual incursions and invasions; whilst they had both a civil war in their own bowels; the former, by frequent rebellions from their own factions and animosities, the latter, by the defection of Portugal, and both laboured more to ransack and burn each other's dominions than to extinguish their own fire. All Germany weltering in its own blood, and contributing to each other's destruction, that the poor crown of Sweden might grow great out of their ruins, and at their charge; Denmark and Poland being adventurers in the same destructive enterprises. Holland and the United Provinces, wearied and tired with their long and chargeable war, how prosperous soever they were in it; and beginning to be more afraid of France, their ally, than of Spain, their enemy. Italy every year infested by the arms of Spain and France, which divided the princes thereof into the several factions.

Of all the princes of Europe, the king of England alone seemed to be seated upon that pleasant promontory that might safely view the tragic sufferings of all his neighbours about him, without any other concernment than what arose from his own princely heart and Christian compassion, to see such desolation wrought by the pride, and passion, and ambition of private persons, supported by princes who knew not what themselves would have. His three kingdoms flourishing in entire peace and universal plenty, in danger of nothing but their own surfeits, and his dominions every day enlarged, by sending out colonies upon large and fruitful plantations; his strong fleets commanding all seas; and the numerous shipping of the nation bringing the trade of the world into his ports; nor could it with unquestionable security be carried any whither else; and all these blessings enjoyed under a prince of the greatest clemency and justice, and of the greatest piety and devotion, and the most indulgent to his subjects and most solicitous for their happiness and prosperity.

O fortunati nimium, bona si sua norint.

In this blessed conjuncture, when no other prince thought he wanted anything to compass what he most desired to be possessed of, but the affection and friendship of the king of England, a small, scarce discernible cloud arose in the north, which was shortly after attended with such a storm that never gave over raging till it had shaken, and even rooted up the greatest and tallest cedars of the three nations ; blasted all its beauty and fruitfulness, brought its strength to decay, and its glory to reproach, and almost to desolation, by such a career and deluge of wickedness and rebellion, as by not being enough foreseen, or in truth suspected, could not be prevented.

(From the Same.)

CHARACTER OF HIMSELF

MR. HYDE was, in his nature and disposition, different from both the other ; which never begot the least disagreement between the Lord Falkland and him. He was of a very cheerful and open nature, without any dissimulation ; and delivered his opinion of things or persons, where it was convenient, without reserve or disguise ; and was at least tenacious enough of his opinion, and never departed from it out of compliance with any man. He had a very particular devotion and passion for the person of the king ; and did believe him the most, and the best Christian in the world. He had a most zealous esteem and reverence for the constitution of the government ; and believed it so equally poised, that if the least branch of the prerogative was torn off, or parted with, the subject suffered by it, and that his right was impaired ; and he was as much troubled when the crown exceeded its just limits, and thought its prerogative hurt by it ; and therefore not only never consented to any diminution of the king's authority, but always wished that the king would not consent to it, with what importunity or impetuosity soever it was desired and pressed.

He had taken more pains than such men use to do, in the examination of religion ; having always conversed with those of different opinions with all freedom and affection, and had very much kindness and esteem for many, who were in no degree of his own judgment ; and upon all this, he did really believe the church

of England the most exactly formed and framed for the encouragement and advancement of learning and piety, and for the preservation of peace, of any church in the world : that the taking away
any of its revenue, and applying it to secular uses, was robbery,
and notorious sacrilege; and that the diminishing the lustre it
had, and had always had in the government, by removing the
bishops out of the house of peers, was a violation of justice; the
removing a landmark, and the shaking the very foundation of
government; and therefore he always opposed, upon the impulsion of conscience, all mutations in the church; and did
always believe, let the season or the circumstance be what it
would, that any compliance was pernicious ; and that a peremptory
and obstinate refusal, that might put men in despair of what they
laboured for, and take away all hope of obtaining what they
desired, would reconcile more persons to the government than
the gratifying them in part ; which only whetted their appetite to
desire more, and their confidence in demanding it.

Though he was of a complexion and humour very far from
despair, yet he did believe the king would be oppressed by that
party which then governed, and that they who followed and
served him would be destroyed ; so that it was not ambition of
power, or wealth, that engaged him to embark in so very
hazardous an employment, but abstractly the consideration of
his duty ; and he often used to apply those words of Cicero to
himself, *Mea ætas incidit in id bellum, cujus altera pars sceleris
nimium habuit, altera felicitatis parum.* It is very probable,
that if his access at that time had been as frequent to the king
as Sir John Colepepper's was, or the Lord Falkland's might have
been, some things might have been left undone the doing whereof
brought much prejudice to the king ; for all his principles were
much more agreeable to his majesty's own judgment, than those
of either of the other ; and what he said was of equal authority
with him ; and when any advice was given by either of the other,
the king usually asked, "whether Ned Hyde were of that opinion";
and they always very ingenuously confessed, that he was not :
but his having no relation of service, and so no pretence to be
seen often at court, and the great jealousy that was entertained
towards him, made it necessary to him to repair only in the
dark to the king upon emergent occasions, and leave the rest to
be imparted by the other two ; and the differences in their natures
and opinions never produced any disunion between them in those

councils which concerned the conduct of the king's service ; but they proceeded with great unanimity, and very manifestly much advanced the king's business from the very low state it was in when they were first trusted ; the other two having always much deference to the Lord Falkland, who allayed their passions ; to which they were both enough inclined.

(From the Same.)

FEALTY AGAINST CONSCIENCE

MR. HYDE was wont often to relate a passage in that melancholic time, when the standard was set up at Nottingham, with which he was much affected. Sir Edmund Varney, knight-marshal, who was mentioned before as standard-bearer, with whom he had great familarity, who was a man of great courage, and generally beloved, came one day to him, and told him, " he was very glad to see him in so universal a damp, under which the spirits of most men were oppressed, retain still his natural vivacity and cheerfulness ; that he knew that the condition of the king, and the power of the parliament, was not better known to any man than to him ; and therefore he hoped that he was able to administer some comfort to his friends, that might raise their spirits, as well as it supported his own." He answered, that he was, in truth, beholden to his constitution, which did not incline him to despair ; otherwise, that he had no pleasant prospect before him, but thought as ill of affairs as most men did ; that the other was as far from being melancholic as he, and was known to be a man of great courage (as indeed he was of a very cheerful and a generous nature, and confessedly valiant), and that they could not do the king better service, than by making it their business to raise the dejected minds of men, and root out those apprehensions which disturbed them, of fear and despair, which could do no good, and did really much mischief."

He replied smiling, " I will willingly join with you the best I can, but I shall act it very scurvily. My condition," he said, "is much worse than yours, and different, I believe, from any other man's ; and will very well justify the melancholy that, I confess to you, possesses me. You have satisfaction in your conscience that you are in the right ; that the king ought not to grant what is required of him ; and so you do your duty and your business together : but for my part, I do not like the quarrel, and do heartily wish that the king would yield and consent to what they desire ; so that my conscience is only concerned in honour and in gratitude to follow my master. I have eaten his bread, and served him near thirty years, and will not do so base a thing as to forsake him ; and choose rather to lose my life (which I am sure I shall do) to preserve and defend those things which are against my conscience to preserve and defend : for I will deal freely with you, I have no reverence for the bishops, for whom this quarrel subsists." It was not a time to dispute ; and his affection to the church had never been suspected. He was as good as his word ; and was killed, in the battle of Edge-hill, within two months after this discourse. And if those who had the same and greater obligations, had observed the same rules of gratitude and generosity, whatever their other affections had been, that battle had never been fought, nor any of that mischief been brought to pass that succeeded it.   (From the Same.)

HOPES OF PEACE FRUSTRATED

It was about the beginning of March (which by that account was about the end of the year 1642, and about the beginning of the year 1643) that the commissioners of the parliament came to Oxford, to treat with his Majesty ; and were received graciously by him ; and by his order lodged conveniently, and well accommodated in all respects.

The parliament had bound up their commissioners to the strictest letter of their propositions ; nor did their instructions at this time (which they presented to the king) admit the least latitude to them, to interpret a word or expression, that admitted a doubtful interpretation. Insomuch as the king told them, " that he was sorry that they had no more trust reposed in them ; and that the parliament might as well have sent their demands to him by the common carrier, as by commissioners so restrained." They had only twenty days allowed them to finish the whole treaty : whereof they might employ six days in adjusting a cessation, if they found it probable to effect it in that time ; otherwise they were to decline the cessation, and enter upon the conditions of the peace ; which, if not concluded before the end of the twenty days, they were to give it over, and to return to the parliament.

These propositions and restrictions much abated the hopes of a good issue of the treaty. Yet every body believed, and the commissioners themselves did not doubt, that if such a progress should be made in the treaty, that a peace was like to ensue, there would be no difficulty in the enlargement of the time ; and therefore the articles for a cessation were the sooner declined, that they might proceed in the main business. For though what was proposed by them in order to it was agreeable enough to the nature of such an affair ; yet the time allowed for it was so short, that it was impossible to make it practicable ; nor could notice be timely given to all the quarters on either side to observe it.

Besides that, there were many particulars in it, which the officers on the king's side (who had no mind to a cessation) formalised much upon ; and (I know not from what unhappy root, but) there was sprung up a wonderful aversion in the town against a cessation. Insomuch as many persons of quality of several counties, whereof the town was full, applied themselves in a body to the king, not to consent to a cessation till a peace might be concluded ; alleging, that they had several agitations in their countries, for his majesty's and their own conveniences, which would be interrupted by the cessation ; and if a peace should not afterwards ensue, would be very mischievous. Which suggestion, if it had been well weighed, would not have been found to be of importance. But the truth is, the king himself had no mind to the cessation, for a reason which shall be mentioned anon, though it was never owned ; and so they waived all further mention of the cessation, and betook themselves to the treaty ; it being reasonable enough to believe, that if both sides were heartily disposed to it, a peace might as soon have been agreed upon as a cessation could be. All the transactions of that treaty having been long since published, and being fit only to be digested into the history of that time, are to be omitted here. Only what passed in secret, and was never communicated, nor can otherwise be known, since at this time no man else is living who was privy to that negociation but the chancellor of the exchequer, will have a proper place in this discourse.

The propositions brought by the commissioners in the treaty were so unreasonable, that they well knew that the king would never consent to them ; but some persons amongst them, who were known to wish well to the king, endeavoured underhand to bring it to pass. And they did therefore, whilst they publicly pursued their instructions, and delivered and received papers upon their propositions, privately use all the means they could, especially in conferences with the Lord Falkland and the chancellor of the exchequer, that the king might be prevailed with in some degree to comply with their unreasonable demands.

In all matters which related to the church, they did not only despair of the king's concurrence, but did not in their own judgments wish it; and believed, that the strength of the party which desired the continuance of the war, was made up of those who were very indifferent in that point; and that, if they might return with satisfaction in other particulars, they should have power enough in the two houses, to oblige the more violent people to accept or submit to the conditions. They wished therefore that the king would make some condescensions in the point of the militia; which they looked upon as the only substantial security they could have, not to be called in question for what they had done amiss. And when they saw nothing could be digested of that kind, which would not reflect both upon the king's authority and his honour, they gave over insisting upon the general; and then Mr. Pierrepoint (who was of the best parts, and most intimate with the earl of Northumberland) rather desired than proposed, that the king would offer to grant his commission to the earl of Northumberland, to be lord high admiral of England. By which condescension he would be restored to his office, which he had lost for their sakes; and so their honour would be likewise repaired, without any signal prejudice to the king; since he should hold it only by his majesty's commission, and not by any ordinance of parliament; and he said, if the king would be induced to gratify them in this particular, he could not be confident that they should be able to prevail with both houses to be satisfied therewith, so that a peace might suddenly be concluded; but, as he did not despair even of that, he did believe, that so many would be satisfied with it, that they would from thence take the occasion to separate themselves from them, as men who would rather destroy their country than restore it to peace.

And the earl of Northumberland himself took so much notice of this discourse to secretary Nicholas (with whom he had as much freedom as his reserved nature was capable of) as to protest to him, that he desired only to receive that honour and trust from the king, that he might be able to do him service ; and thereby to recover the credit he had unhappily lost with him.   In which he used very decent expressions towards his majesty ; not without such reflections upon his own behaviour, as implied that he was not proud of it ; and concluded, that if his majesty would do him that honour, as to make that offer to the houses, upon the proposition of the militia, he would do all he could that it might be effectual towards a peace ; and if it had not success, he would pass his word and honour to the king, that as soon, or whensoever his majesty would please to require it, he would deliver up his commission again into his hands ; he having no other ambition or desire, than by this means to redeliver up the royal navy to his majesty's as absolute disposal, as it was when his majesty first put it into his hands ; and which he doubted would hardly be done by any other expedient, at least not so soon.

When this proposition (which, from the interest and persons who proposed it, seemed to carry with it some probability of success, if it should be accepted) was communicated with those who were like with most secrecy to consult it ; secretary Nicholas having already made some approach towards the king upon the subject, and found his majesty without inclination to hear more of it ; it was agreed and resolved by them, that the chancellor of the exchequer should presume to make the proposition plainly to the king, and to persuade his majesty to hear it debated in his presence ; at least, if that might not be, to enlarge upon it himself as much as the argument required : and he was not unwilling to embark himself in the affair.

When he found a fit opportunity for the representation, and his majesty at good leisure, in his morning's walk, when he was always most willing to be entertained ; the chancellor related ingenuously to him the whole discourse, which had been made by Mr. Pierrepoint, and to whom ; and what the earl himself had said to secretary Nicholas ; and what conference they, to whom his majesty gave leave to consult together upon his affairs, had between themselves upon the argument, and what occurred to them upon it ; in which he mentioned the earl's demerit towards his majesty with severity enough, and what reason he had not to be willing to restore a man to his favour, who had forfeited it so unworthily.   Yet he desired him to consider his own ill condition ; and how unlike it was that it should be improved by the continuance of the war ; and whether he could ever imagine a possibility of getting out of it upon more easy conditions than what was now proposed ; the offer of which to the parliament could do him no signal prejudice, and could not but bring him very notable advantages ; for if the peace did not ensue upon it, such a rupture infallibly would, as might in a little time facilitate the other. And then he said as much to lessen the malignity of the earl as he could, by remembering, how dutifully he had resigned his commission of admiral upon his majesty's demand, and his refusal to accept the commission the parliament would have given him ; and observed some vices in his nature, which would stand in the place of virtues, towards the support of his fidelity to his majesty, and his animosity against the parliament, if he were once reingratiated to his majesty's trust.

The king heard him very quietly without the least interruption, which he used not to do upon subjects which were not grateful to him ; for he knew well that he was not swayed by any affection to the man, to whom he was more a stranger than he was to most of that condition ; and he, upon occasions, had often made sharp reflections upon his ingratitude to the king. His majesty seemed at the first to insist upon the improbability that any such concession by him would be attended with any success ; that not only the earl had not interest in the houses to lead them into a resolution that was only for his particular benefit, but that the parliament itself was not able to make a peace, without such conditions as the army would require ; and then he should suffer exceedingly in his honour, for having shewn an inclination to a person who had requited his former graces so unworthily : and this led him into more warmth than he used to be affected with. He said, "indeed he had been very unfortunate in conferring his favours upon many very ungrateful persons ; but no man was so inexcusable as the earl of Northumberland." He said "he knew that the earl of Holland was generally looked upon as the man of the greatest ingratitude ; but," he said, "he could better excuse him than the other : that it was true, he owed all he had to his father's and his bounties, and that himself had "conferred great favours upon him ; but that it was as true, he had frequently given him many mortifications, which, though he had deserved, he knew had troubled him very much ; that he had oftener denied him, than any other man of his condition ; and that he had but lately refused to gratify him in a suit he had made to him, of which he had been very confident ; and so might have some excuse (how ill soever) for being out of humour, which led him from one ill to another : but that he had lived always without intermission with the earl of Northumberland as his friend, and courted him as his mistress ; "that he had never denied any thing he had ever asked, and therefore his carriage to him was never to be forgotten."

And this discourse he continued with more commotion, and in a more pathetical style than ever he used upon any other argument. And though at that time it was not fit to press the matter further, it was afterwards resumed by the same person more than once ; but without any other effect, than that his majesty was contented that the earl should not despair of being restored to that office, when the peace should be made ; or upon any eminent service performed by him, when the peace should be despaired of. The king was very willing and desirous that the treaty should be drawn out in length ; to which purpose a proposition was made to the commissioners for an addition of ten days, which they sent to the parliament, without the least apprehension that it would be denied. But they were deceived ; and for answer, received an order upon the last day but one of the time before limited, by which they were expressly required to leave Oxford the next day. From that time all intercourse and commerce between Oxford and London, which had been permitted before, was absolutely interdicted under the highest penalties by the parliament.

If this secret underhand proposition had succeeded, and received that encouragement from the king that was desired, and more application of the same remedies had been then made to other persons (for alone it could never have proved effectual), it is probable, that those violent and abominable counsels, which were but then in projection between very few men of any interest, and which were afterwards miserably put in practice, had been prevented. And it was exceedingly wondered at, by those who were then privy to this overture, and by all who afterwards came to hear of it, that the king should in that conjuncture decline so advantageous a proposition ; since he did already discern many ill humours and factions, growing and nourished, both in his court and army, which would every day be uneasy to him ; and did with all his soul desire an end of the war. And there was nothing more suitable and agreeable to his magnanimous nature, than to forgive those, who had in the highest degree offended him : which temper was notorious throughout his whole life. It will not be therefore amiss, in this discourse, to enlarge upon this fatal rejection, and the true cause and ground thereof.

The king's affection to the queen was of a very extraordinary alloy; a composition of conscience, and love, and generosity, and gratitude, and all those noble affections which raise the passion to the greatest height; insomuch as he saw with her eyes, and determined by her judgment; and did not only pay her this adoration, but desired that all men should know that he was swayed by her: which was not good for either of them. The queen was a lady of great beauty, excellent wit and humour, and made him a just return of noblest affections; so that they were the true idea of conjugal affection, in the age in which they lived. When she was admitted to the knowledge and participation of the most secret affairs (from which she had been carefully restrained by the duke of Buckingham whilst he lived), she took delight in the examining and discussing them, and from thence in making judgment of them; in which her passions were always strong.

She had felt so much pain in knowing nothing, and meddling with nothing, during the time of that great favourite, that now she took pleasure in nothing but knowing all things, and disposing all things; and thought it but just, that she should dispose of all favours and preferments as he had done; at least, that nothing of that kind might be done without her privity: not considering that the universal prejudice that great man had undergone, was not with reference to his person, but his power; and that the same power would be equally obnoxious to murmur and complaint, if it resided in any other person than the king himself. And she so far concurred with the king's inclination, that she did not more desire to be possessed of this unlimited power, than that all the world should take notice that she was the entire mistress of it; which in truth (what other unhappy circumstances soever concurred in the mischief) was the foundation upon which the first and the utmost prejudices to the king and his government were raised and prosecuted. And it was her majesty's and the kingdom's misfortune, that she had not any person about her, who had either ability or affection, to inform and advise her of the temper of the kingdom, or humour of the people; or who thought either worth the caring for.

When the disturbances grew so rude as to interrupt this harmony, and the queen's fears, and indisposition, which proceeded from those fears, disposed her to leave the kingdom, which the king, to comply with her, consented to (and if that fear had not been predominant in her, her jealousy and apprehension, that the king would at some time be prevailed with to yield to some unreasonable conditions, would have dissuaded her from that voyage); to make all things therefore as sure as might be, that her absence should not be attended with any such inconvenience, his majesty made a solemn promise to her at parting, that he would receive no person into any favour or trust, who had disserved him, without her privity and consent; and that, as she had undergone so many reproaches and calumnies at the entrance into the war, so he would never make any peace, but by her interposition and mediation, that the kingdom might receive that blessing only from her.

This promise (of which his majesty was too religious an observer) was the cause of his majesty's rejection, or not entertaining this last overture; and this was the reason that he had that aversion to the cessation, which he thought would inevitably oblige him to consent to the peace, as it should be proposed; and therefore he had countenanced an address, that had been made to him against it, by the gentlemen of several counties attending the court: and in truth they were put upon that address by the king's own private direction. Upon which the chancellor of the exchequer told him, when the business was over, that he had raised a spirit he would not be able to conjure down; and that those petitioners had now appeared in a business that pleased him, but would be as ready to appear, at another time, to cross what he desired; which proved true. For he was afterwards more troubled with application and importunity of that kind, and the murmurs that arose from that liberty, when all men would be counsellors, and censure all that the council did, than with the power of the enemy.

About the time that the treaty began, the queen landed in the north; and she resolved, with a good quantity of ammunition and arms, to make what haste she could to the king; having at her first landing expressed, by a letter to his majesty, her apprehension of an ill peace by that treaty; and declared, that she would never live in England, if she might not have a guard for the security of her person: which letter came accidentally afterwards into the hands of the parliament; of which they made use to the queen's disadvantage. And the expectation of her majesty's arrival at Oxford, was the reason that the king so much desired the prolongation of the treaty. And if it had pleased God that she had come thither time enough, as she did shortly after, she would have probably condescended to many propositions for the gratifying particular persons, as appeared afterwards, if thereby a reasonable peace might have been obtained.

(From the Same.)

CAUSES OF THE CORRUPTION WHICH FOLLOWED THE RESTORATION

THIS unhappy temper and constitution of the royal party with whom he had always intended to have made a firm conjunction against all accidents and occurrences which might happen at home or from abroad, did wonderfully displease and trouble the king ; and, with the other perplexities, which are mentioned before, did so break his mind, and had that operation upon his spirits, that finding he could not propose any such method to himself, by which he might extricate himself out of those many difficulties and labyrinths in which he was involved, nor expedite those important matters which depended upon the good-will and despatch of the parliament, which would proceed by its own rules, and with its accustomed formalities, he grew more disposed to leave all things to their natural course, and God's providence ; and by degrees unbent his mind from the knotty and ungrateful part of his business, grew more remiss in his application to it, and indulged to his youth and appetite that license and satisfaction that it desired, and for which he had opportunity enough, and could not be without ministers abundant for any such negotiations ; the time itself, and the young people thereof of either sex having been educated in all the liberty of vice, without reprehension or restraint. All relations were confounded by the several sects in religion which discountenanced all forms of reverence and respect, as relics and marks of superstition. Children asked not blessing of their parents ; nor did they concern themselves in the education of their children ; but were well content that they should take any course to maintain themselves, that they might be free from that expense. The young women conversed without any circumspection or modesty, and frequently met at taverns and common eatinghouses; and they who were stricter and more severe in their comportment, became the wives of the seditious preachers, or of officers of the army. The daughters of noble and illustrious families bestowed themselves upon the divines of the time, or other low and unequal matches. Parents had no manner of authority over their children, nor children any obedience or submission to their parents; but "every one did that which was good in his own eyes." This unnatural antipathy had its first rise from the beginning of the rebellion, when the fathers and sons engaged themselves in the contrary parties, the one choosing to serve the king, and the other the parliament; which division and contradiction of affections was afterwards improved to mutual animosities and direct malice, by the help of the preachers and the several factions in religion, or by the absence of all religion: so that there were never such examples of impiety between such relations in any age of the world, Christian or heathen, as that wicked time, from the beginning of the rebellion to the king's return; of which the families of Hotham and Vane are sufficient instances; though other more illustrious houses may be named, where the same accursed fruit was too plentifully gathered, and too notorious to the world. The relation between masters and servants had been long since dissolved by the parliament, that their army might be increased by the prentices against their masters' consent, and that they might have intelligence of the secret meetings and transactions in those houses and families which were not devoted to them; from whence issued the foulest treacheries and perfidiousness that were ever practised: and the blood of the master was frequently the price of the servant's villany.

Cromwell had been most strict and severe in the forming the manners of his army, and in chastising all irregularities; insomuch that sure there was never any such body of men so without rapine, swearing, drinking, or any other debauchery, but the wickedness of their hearts: and all persons cherished by him, were of the same leaven, and to common appearance without the practice of any of those vices which were most infamous to the people, and which drew the public hatred upon those who were notoriously guilty of them. But then he was well pleased with the most scandalous lives of those who pretended to be for the king, and wished that all his were such, and took all the pains he could that they might be generally thought to be such; whereas in truth the greatest part of those who were guilty of those disorders were young men, who had never seen the king, and had been born and bred in those corrupt times, " when there was no king of Israel." He was equally delighted with the luxury and voluptuousness of the presbyterians, who, in contempt of the thrift, sordidness, and affected ill-breeding of the independents, thought it became them to live more generously, and were not strict in restraining or mortifying the unruly and inordinate appetite of flesh and blood, but indulged it with too much and too open scandal, from which he reaped no small advantage ; and wished all those, who were not his friends, should not only be infected, but given over to the practice of the most odious vices and wickedness.

In a word, the nation was corrupted from that integrity, good nature, and generosity, that had been peculiar to it, and for which it had been signal and celebrated throughout the world ; in the room whereof the vilest craft and dissembling had succeeded. The tenderness of the bowels, which is the quintessence of justice and compassion, the very mention of good nature was laughed at and looked upon as the mark and character of a fool ; and a roughness of manners, or hardheartedness and cruelty was affected. In the place of generosity, a vile and sordid love of money was entertained as the truest wisdom, and any thing lawful that would contribute towards being rich. There was a total decay, or rather a final expiration of all friendship ; and to dissuade a man from any thing he affected, or to reprove him for any thing he had done amiss, or to advise him to do any thing he had no mind to do, was thought an impertinence unworthy a wise man, and received with reproach and contempt. These dilapidations and ruins of the ancient candour and discipline were not taken enough to heart, and repaired with that early care and severity that they might have been ; for they were not then incorrigible ; but by the remissness of applying remedies to some, and the unwariness in giving a kind of countenance to others, too much of that poison insinuated itself into minds not well fortified against such infection : so that much of the malignity was transplanted, instead of being extinguished, to the corruption of many wholesome bodies, which, being corrupted, spread the diseases more powerfully and more mischievously.

(From the Same.)

THE STUART FAMILY

THE truth is, it was the unhappy fate and constitution of that family, that they trusted naturally the judgments of those who were as much inferior to them in understanding as they were in quality, before their own, which was very good; and suffered even their natures, which disposed them to virtue and justice, to be prevailed upon and altered and corrupted by those who knew how to make use of some one infirmity that they discovered in them; and by complying with that, and cherishing and serving it, they by degrees wrought upon the mass, and sacrificed all the other good inclinations to that single vice. They were too much inclined to like men at first sight, and did not love the conversation of men of many more years than themselves, and thought age not only troublesome but impertinent. They did not love to deny, and less to strangers than to their friends; not out of bounty or generosity, which was a flower that did never grow naturally in the heart of either of the families, that of Stuart or the other of Bourbon, but out of an unskilfulness and defect in the countenance; and when they prevailed with themselves to make some pause rather than to deny, importunity removed all resolution, which they knew neither how to shut out nor to defend themselves against, even when it was evident enough that they had much rather not consent; which often made that which would have looked like bounty lose all its grace and lustre.

(From the Same.)

CLARENDON'S LETTER TO THE KING

MAY it please your Majesty,

I am so broken under the daily insupportable instances of your Majesty's terrible displeasure, that I know not what to do, hardly what to wish. The crimes which are objected against me, how passionately soever pursued, and with circumstances very unusual, do not in the least degree fright me. God knows I am innocent in every particular as I ought to be; and I hope your Majesty knows enough of me to believe that I had never a violent appetite for money, that could corrupt me. But, alas! your Majesty's declared anger and indignation deprives me of the comfort and support even of my own innocence, and exposes me to the rage and fury of those who have some excuse for being my enemies ; whom I have sometimes displeased, when (and only then) your Majesty believed them not to be your friends. I hope they may be changed ; I am sure I am not, but have the same duty, passion, and affection for you that I had when you thought it most unquestionable, and which was and is as great as ever man had for any mortal creature. I should die in peace (and truly I do heartily wish that God Almighty would free you from further trouble by taking me to Himself) if I could know or guess at the ground of your displeasure, which I am sure must proceed from your believing, that I have said or done somewhat I have neither said nor done. If it be for any thing my Lord Berkeley hath reported, which I know he hath said to many, though being charged with it by me he did as positively disclaim it ; I am as innocent in that whole affair, and gave no more advice or counsel or countenance in it, than the child that is not born ; which your Majesty seemed once to believe, when I took notice to you of the report, and when you considered how totally I was a stranger to the persons mentioned, to either of whom I never spake word, or received message from either in my life. And this I protest to your Majesty is true, as I have hope in heaven ; and that I have never wilfully offended your Majesty in my life, and do upon my knees beg your pardon for any over-bold or saucy expressions I have ever used to you ; which, being a natural disease in old servants who have received too much countenance, I am sure hath always proceeded from the zeal and warmth of the most sincere affection and duty.

I hope your Majesty believes, that the sharp chastisement I have received from the best-natured and most bountiful master in the world, and whose kindness alone made my condition these many years supportable, hath enough mortified me as to this world ; and that I have not the presumption or the madness to imagine or desire ever to be admitted to any employment or trust again. But I do most humbly beseech your Majesty, by the memory of your father, who recommended me to you with some testimony, and by your own gracious reflection upon some one service I may have performed in my life, that hath been acceptable to you ; that you will by your royal power and interposition put a stop to this severe prosecution against me, and that my concernment may give no longer interruption to the great affairs of the kingdom ; but that I may spend the small remainder of my life, which cannot hold long, in some parts beyond the seas, never to return ; where I will pray for your Majesty, and never suffer the least diminution in the duty and obedience of,

> May it please your Majesty,
> > Your Majesty's
> > > Most humble and most
> > > > Obedient subject and servant,
> > > > > CLARENDON.

*From my house
this 16th of November.*

(From the Same.)

JOHN MILTON

[John Milton, born in Bread Street, London, 9th December 1608 ; entered at Christ's College, Cambridge, 12th February 1624 ; left the University as M.A., and retired to Horton, Bucks, 1632 ; set out for Italy 1637, returning in 1639 ; took up his abode in London, first in St. Bride's Churchyard, then in Aldersgate Street ; in 1643 married Mary Powell, by whom he had three daughters ; after her death in 1653 he married Catherine Woodcock, who died about a year after her marriage, in 1657, having borne him a daughter. In March 1649 Milton had been appointed Secretary for Foreign Tongues to the Council of State, an office which he held till the downfall of the Commonwealth. The Restoration involved him in personal peril ; but after the passing of the Act of Oblivion he came forth from his concealment, and settled in a house in Holborn near Red Lion Square, whence, in 1662, he removed to Artillery Walk near Bunhill Fields. In 1665 he married his third wife, Elizabeth Marshall. He died 8th November 1674, and was buried in the church of St. Giles, Cripplegate.]

MILTON, it seems, succeeded imperfectly in defending the English people against the imputation that he allowed himself on its behalf to be diverted from the service of the Muses. The charge, frequently made, once more found expression in the late Mark Pattison's admirable biographical essay.

Although with divers reservations dictated by his own candour, this distinguished scholar virtually repeated the accusation of Johnson, that Milton " lent his breath "—they omit to say by whom that breath was inspired—" to blow the flames of contention." The censure, whether uttered in so many words, or insinuated, or implied, is based on the obsolete fallacy of drawing a distinction between a great writer, or for that matter a great intellectual worker of any kind, and the same personage viewed as " a man." I have no room for discussing it here ; nor am I in the secret of Milton's " mission " to his nation or to mankind. Indeed, the question might be asked on a lower plane, whether posterity can judge so accurately of the relation of the mind of Milton even to his own age and to its problems, as to decide *ex cathedrâ* upon the capacity in which he would have best fulfilled the purpose of his life. We may regret, no doubt, for the sake not only of our highest pleasures, but also because of the absolute value of the gift bestowed upon mankind in poetry like Milton's, that he should have allowed an "episode" of twenty years to interrupt his poetical productivity. We may further regret that the prose writing to which he mainly devoted himself during this period of his literary life, should have been of a kind which, following the fashion of his times in particular, and the tendency of controversial writing in general, largely led him into excesses or obliquities, into invective, vituperation, and the inveracities of passion or spleen, such as it is painful to have to associate with his lofty name. Yet, if he conceived it his duty (and who can suppose that he conceived otherwise?) to devote himself during these years to the service of a cause and a rule which for him embodied freedom sanctified by the fear of God, he would have been false to himself had he hesitated instead of making his choice. The critics who disapprove of Milton's having "prostituted his genius to political party" are, after all, as blind as those who quarrel with Goethe for not having played a prominent part as a "Liberation" patriot, instead of contenting himself with doing his duty to his prince, his people and mankind, as that duty presented itself to him. If a man, be he or be he not a great poet, can at any time do a nobler thing than his duty, Milton and Goethe were alike at fault. Since his *Defensio Secunda* was written by him in Latin, I may here, instead of below, quote from it a passage showing that he deliberately chose what he thought the course dictated to him by his duty to his country, to the Church of God, and to many of his fellow-Christians : "When the liberty of speech was no longer subject to control, all mouths began to be opened against the Bishops, some complaining of the vices of the individuals, others of those of the Order. They said it was unjust that they alone (*i.e.* they of the Established Church) should differ from the model of other reformed churches ; that the government of the Church should be according to the pattern of other churches, and particularly the Word of God. *This awakened all my attention and my zeal. I saw that a way was opening for the establishment of real liberty ;* that the foundation was laying for the deliverance of man from the yoke of slavery and superstition ; that the principles of religion, which were the first objects of our care, would exert a salutary influence on the manners and institutions of the republic ; and, as I had from my youth up studied the distinction between religious and civil rights, I perceived that if I ever wished to be of use, I ought at least not to be wanting to my country, to the Church, and to many of my fellow-Christians, in a cause of so much danger ; *I therefore determined to relinquish the other pursuits in which I was engaged, and to transfer the whole force of my talents and my industry to this one important object.*" Still more striking are certain passages in the Preface to the Second Book on *The Reason of Church Government*, which will be found in one of the extracts given in the text.

Milton's earlier verse is in the memory of all ; and it is therefore unnecessary to recall how the great conflict which occupies the great body of his prose writings, casts its premonitory shadow over the most exquisite of all his contributions to our literature. What the *Hymn on Christ's Nativity* had with a directness at once naïve and impassioned exhibited as a struggle in which "the damned crew" of heathen divinities was compelled to yield to "the dreaded Infant's hand," in the *Allegro* and *Penseroso* becomes a psychological contrast, tending to an unmistakable choice. In *Comus* the conflict has deepened into a spiritual trial issuing in the acceptance of that view of life which shows the light of a great poet's imagination, reflecting itself in historic Puritanism, as the sunlight reflects itself in the raindrops. The transition to the lower level of satirical invective is made in *Lycidas*, which with a more than Spenserian boldness mixes up the controversial with the plaintive element, and thus serves as a link between the prose of Milton and the earlier music of his lute.

It would be easy to show how little (to compare him again with Goethe) there was that Milton in his Italian journey desired to cast off and leave behind him on this side of the Alps. His unbending Protestantism, notwithstanding Sir Henry Wotton's seasonable warning, never sought to conceal itself, either at Rome or elsewhere, and entailed upon him a certain measure of surveillance in the Papal city. The few extant records of a sojourn, which exercised so lasting an effect upon his poetic and in a secondary degree upon his prose style, show him both maintaining among changing scenes a mind unchanged, and trusting in a Higher Power to "stoop" to the aid of his weakness. How freely he breathed in the atmosphere of Geneva on his way home ; and how sympathetically he had in Italy—then suffering from a decay only too plainly visible to an observer trained in historical studies—entered into the complaints of scholars less fortunate (as they deemed) than himself! " I could recount," he afterwards wrote in the *Areopagitica*, "what I have seen and heard in other countries, where this kind of inquisition" (the censorship of the press) "tyrannises, when I have sat among their learned men (for that honour I had) *and have been counted happy to be born in such a place of philosophic freedom as they supposed England was*, while themselves did nothing but bemoan the servile condition into which learning amongst them was brought, that this was it which had damped the glory of Italian wits, that nothing had been there written now these many years but flattery and fustian."

In the winter 1639-40 Milton settled in the city as a private tutor, an occupation provocative of needless "merriment" in Johnson, because of the inadequacy of its immediate results. Yet no mode of life could have been better adapted for the process of digesting his accumulations of learning and experience, which in Milton went hand in hand with that of pondering over old and new themes and schemes. He was thus engaged when his own times, so to speak, knocked at his study door and imperiously claimed his attention. 1641 was the year in which he first became a writer of controversial prose.

Of the great questions of the age in England the church question was the most fundamentally important, and came most directly home to Milton, who, as has been seen, had carried it in his mind since his college days, and whose views concerning it had already in some measure directed the course of his life. He was, moreover, at this period in frequent intercourse with Puritan ministers of his acquaintance, one of whom had formerly been his tutor. Thus, when in 1641, by the introduction of the Root and Branch Bill, due to the rejection by the House of Lords of the proposal to exclude bishops from a seat in it, this church question had been narrowed into the choice between the continuance of the Episcopal system and its complete overthrow, Milton felt that his hour had arrived. Already before the Bill had begun to be debated in the Commons, a storm of pamphlets on the subject had darkened the atmosphere; and one of these, the *Humble Remonstrance* of Bishop Hall of Norwich, who had previously come forward as the champion of *Episcopacy by Divine Right*, produced the celebrated *Answer* by "*Smectymnuus.*" Soon (probably about two months later, *i.e.* in May or June 1641) after the appearance of this joint manifesto of five more or less prominent Puritan divines, Milton put forth anonymously his first prose treatise, *Of Reformation in England, and the causes that hitherto have hindered it: Two Books, written to a Friend.*

In this essay, which displays the freshness of the combatant newly entering the arena, unhampered by a wish to reserve any of his strength, most of the essential characteristics of Milton as a prose-writer are already perceptible. It smells of the lamp, of course, but by no means oppressively ; for among the best sons of the Church of Rome cited as deploring the choking of her life by her endowments, are not only Dante and Petrarch and Ariosto, but also "our Chaucer," whom it is not surprising to find wrongly identified with the author of *The Ploughman's Tale ;* nor does the writer yield to the temptation of falling into a " paroxysm of citations," as he calls it, from the Fathers, although clearly capable of holding his own in this direction with Prynne himself. But his learning is not index-learning, his historical illustrations of the charge of worldliness as inseparable from the connexion between Church and State are close-fitting as well as telling, and vary from indignant invective to polite irony. Edward VI.'s bishops " suffered themselves to be the common stales, to countenance with their prostituted gravities every politic fetch that was then on foot, as oft as the potent statists pleased to employ them." Elizabeth's "found a good tabernacle ; they sat under a spreading vine, their lot was fallen in a fair inheritance." And, finally, we recognise in the first of Milton's tracts, more especially at its close, the eloquence of a spirit moved to its depths by the actual theme of discourse ; though here as yet there still clings to his style something of the pulpit-peroration manner, which he was before long to shake off.

Milton's second prose pamphlet, which appeared in the same year as the first, *Of Prelatical Episcopacy*, is short and of little significance, except as showing the combative readiness of the author, who saw what some heroic fighters in similar struggles fail to notice, that, in a conflict turning on establishments, their moderate defenders, familiar with the history of the subject, deserve to be answered. The third of this earliest group of his controversial writings, the *Animadversions upon the Remonstrant's Defence against Smectymnuus*, is a retort upon a reply by Bishop Hall which "*Smectymnuus*" had already met by a *Vindication* from head-quarters. Milton's contribution was not, however, superfluous, for he afterwards spoke of himself as held to have on this occasion "brought a timely succour to the ministers who were hardly a match for the eloquence of their opponents." Doubtless, at the same time, this tract, so far as he is himself concerned, exhibits the dangers of the path on which he had entered, and the declivities to which it is prone. These *Animadversions* are in dialogue form, and occasionally approach with hazardous closeness to colloquialism :

"*Remonst.* No one clergy in the whole Christian world yields so many eminent scholars, learned preachers, grave, holy, and accomplished divines as this Church of England doth at this day.

"*Answ.* Ha, ha, ha !"

Elsewhere, however, the writer emancipates himself from the very form which he has chosen, and soars on the wings of a true enthusiasm into aspects of his theme beyond the range of mere passing controversies. Where he describes the blessings of an unfettered ministry of religion, his eloquence has a force and a fire inseparable from the influence of personal sentiment, which had a peculiar interest to these early outpourings, and we remember how brief had been the interval since he had deemed himself (in his own phrase) as one "shoved away from the shearer's feast."

Events now thickened ; and, as is invariably the case in critical times, the personal responsibility of those who had chosen their side became more definite. When, early in 1642, Milton published his *Reason of Church Government urged against Prelaty*, he appended his name to the treatise. As its title implied, he here, although according to the fashion of his age, directing his arguments against a particular essay (or collection of essays) on the opposite side, passed to the philosophical line of reasoning, in other words, to first principles. Although his views on the question of Church Government had not yet reached their extreme point, the necessity of the separation of Church from State had now already become to him an axiom, with regard both to religious life and to civil society. In a passage in the exordium of the Second Book, partially extracted below, he offers his own apology for resolving to devote his powers to the paramount problem of his times. He foresees the possibility of a reaction which might involve him in the reproach of having shrunk from taking his part in the actual struggle, and he vindicates his present resolution to avert, at the cost of literary fame as a great English writer, such an imputation upon his sense of his highest responsibilities. But the biographical interest of this Second Book should not be allowed to overshadow its argumentative dignity, or to hide the beauty of such passages as that which seeks to oppose to the " No King, no Bishop " cry, the conception, half ironical, of a true leader of the people who, like unto that " mighty Nazarite Samson," " grows up to a noble strength and perfection with those his illustrious and sunny locks, the laws, waving and curling about his godlike shoulders."

The fifth and last in this, the first series of Milton's prose treatises, was *An Apology against a Pamphlet called a Modest Confutation of the Animadversions of the Remonstrant against Smectymnuus* (1642), directed against the tardy reply put forth by Bishop Hall, with the assistance as has been supposed of his son, to Milton's previous attack. This *Apology* abounds in a kind of recrimination one might well wish away (for what answer is it to the false assertion that Milton had been " vomited out " by his University, to indulge in scornful reflexions upon the condition of that university under prelatical government, and in particular upon the academical plays whereby budding bishops and deans were taught manners and morals ?) But it also contains yet another autobiographical passage, which Professor Masson considers to be " without exception, the profoundest thing that Milton has told us about himself," and which I therefore cannot refrain from extracting below. This declaration is not one to be bandied about with cavils or reservations in biographical or other controversy ; if Milton here strayed from the truth, then his whole life was a lie ; in the opposite event, how instinct with living force becomes the ethical teaching of *Comus*, the product of this pure and unsullied period of the poet's youth !

The first group of Milton's prose writings, as he tells us himself, established him as the literary representative of the Puritan side ; and this was in itself no small achievement, when the cause of Prelacy had found a champion in a veteran of Hall's learning and experience as a controversialist, gifted with satirical power, and blessed with moderation of temper. With such an adversary the apologist of *Smectymnuus* might in some points have seemed ill-matched, more especially as he was deficient in all the gentler forms of humour, and scorned most of the varieties of tact. But such deficiencies count for little in the blaze of passion which in these early pieces manifestly requires no fanning, and which again and again bursts forth with an impetus that must have taken some at least of his readers by storm. The sincerity of the impulse which had led to their production in rapid succession upon one another is apparent in the treatises themselves ; nor have many writers, whose genius was so wonderfully fertile as Milton's, restricted themselves with the same consistency to themes by which their minds are not only attracted but occupied.

It was to serve his country by upholding the religious ideal which to him seemed to have been so perilously obscured in both Church and State that he had first become a publicist. In the ensuing years he turned aside, partly from motives or under influences which it could have been no satisfaction to him to make very clear to himself, into a different, though in some measure cognate, field of controversy. The series of publications in question began with *The Doctrine and Discipline of Divorce* (1643), republished in an enlarged form with an introductory letter *To the Parliament of England, with the* [Westminster] *Assembly* (1644). It is noticeable how in this Preface, instead of, as in his earlier treatises, leaving it to learned or lay to take what they choose from the case laid before them, he declares with uneasy pride : " I seek not to seduce the simple and illiterate ; my errand is to find out the choicest and learnedest, who have this high gift of wisdom—to answer solidly, or to be convinced." But the dignity of this attitude was in the present instance assumed only. He was in a hurry, as literary men of sensitive minds and powerful imaginations too often are, to make public deductions from his private experiences. Even had his contention been unanswerable that divorce should be allowed on grounds such as seem to have caused his own separation from his wife— that is to say, " for no visible reason "—Parliament, Assembly, and public could have waited a little longer for the urging of it. There was no necessity for him publicly to advocate this particular reform before the first year of his married life—or, according to one not improbable view, his " honeymoon "—had come to an end. In the second tract of the series he appealed to the authority of *Martin Bucer* (1644) an eminent Reformation divine, to whom peculiar respect has for special reasons deservedly been paid by English Protestantism, but to whose authority in this particular kind of questions there exist equally special reasons for demurring ; in the third and fourth, published on the same day (in 1645), Milton reviewed the many passages in Scripture bearing on the subject, and "pilloried" those opponents who still remained unexposed. Prynne, while censured for misrepresenting Milton's argument as equivalent to the advocacy of "divorce at pleasure," is almost tenderly blamed for giving Truth cause to leave him defenceless "after having suffered much and long in her defence." But upon the anonymous author of a reply to *The Doctrine and Discipline*, the vials of Milton's wrath are emptied, and at the close he allows "fate to extort from him a talent of sport, which he had thought to hide in a napkin." He was, in fact, very sore about the reception accorded to his "new subject," as well as to his Greek titles ; very possibly the age of Henry VIII., to which he made appeal in a sonnet against his detractors, would have been more tolerant in both directions. The most important effect of the entire episode was to add intensity to the forces which at the time were driving Milton away from the halting-place of orthodox Presbyterianism towards the unfenced, but not on that account less tenable, position of the right of private judgment. The spirit of freedom was abroad both in things political and in things religious ; the agitation of the Sects typified the desire for spiritual independence, and the New Modelling of the army showed how it was proposed to secure the victory. To the period immediately preceding the accomplishment of the measures which ultimately brought about the collapse of the Presbyterian *régime* belongs the publication of Milton's one enduringly popular prose work, the *Areopagitica* (1644).

How unconfined are the operations of a spirit like that to which I have referred, both in a genius of the prophetic type and in a great age, had, however, been shown by the appearance earlier in the same year of another prose tractate by Milton— *On Education*. It was addressed to a remarkable man of his acquaintance, Samuel Hartlib, a naturalised Prussian merchant, settled in London, who in his turn had introduced to English readers the educational theories of his friend, the Moravian, John Amos Comenius. Milton's essay, written under these influences, is as radical a plea for reform as any that about this time proceeded from his pen. But though in its critical portion this brief deliverance on an all-important theme deals effectively enough with the failure of the existing methods, the system of education which, as a really progressive and scientific one, he wished to substitute for them, is elaborated by him under conditions that, no doubt, give to the essay an essentially speculative — or, why not say,

fanciful ?—tinge.   Nor can it, I think, be supposed that the ous
was any pretence on Milton's part, who knew more than enov'ion
of the practical difficulties and complications of the problem; ring
have exhausted them.   His tract, after all, had little d ours
significance for his own times ; and was little more than a ritics
of fly-leaf which might possibly prove suggestive, should   The
taken out of its pigeon-hole by some later generation of refor e con-

The *Areopagitica : A Speech for the Liberty of Unli* le the
Printing, in direct contrast with the above, addressed *tures*
directly to an actual Order of the Long Parliament, subje frag-
the printing-press to the necessity of official licences analogo r (of
those imposed seven years before, by the (since abolished) (with
of Star-Chamber.   It is needless (were it possible) to enquir more
to what extent either personal grievances in connexion wii the
authority thus assumed, or a growing personal conviction bles
the way in which it was certain to continue to be used by th ct
dominant Presbyterian majority in Parliament, contributed y
stimulate the energy of Milton's onslaught.   The form in whic ."
he clothed it is for the present purpose of more importan be
The *Areopagiticus* of Isocrates is a rhetorical pamphlet un n
the guise of a speech, but designed directly to influence e
political life of Athens.   Its purpose was to commend and s
enforce the extended authority which the Areopagus had assun e
or resumed, and to urge an appeal to a better past as against t
uncertainties of a distracted present.   A certain concession
therefore implied in Milton's choice of title ; but the parallel i
inexact, and is used by him chiefly in order to contrive a courteou
opening for an attack that would not be put into the form of
indictment.   The treatise maintains throughout the form of
speech, and has accordingly a greater variety of light and shad
than is to be found in any other of Milton's prose works.   Indeed
one passage at least, extracted below, in which the author deal
with the impossibility of " licensing " all the pleasures of life, ha t
a playful charm generally foreign to his prose style.   In h e
argument he shows, in the first instance historically, the vicio of
origin of the power which the Parliament has assumed, tracin nd
from the Inquisition to " inquisiturient " prelates and presby age,
He next proves the radical falsity of the system, as deduced y so
the fundamental conditions of the conflict between truth
falsehood, ignorance and better knowledge ; and illustra earned
proved practical absurdity of attempting to purify literature er less

a progressive or by a retrospective *index*. Lastly, he shows
positive harm which must result from the imposition of such
·ncubus upon authorship, as the soil where thought should
᠁ ᠁ree ; and appeals to that trust in liberty, without which its
᠁tions are valueless. In place of accountability to a licensing
᠁ or boards, he vindicates to authorship the responsibility
᠁ upon the writer speaking the truth as it is in him, and
᠁ he talents entrusted to man by his Maker.

᠁ significance of this work, which exhibits more than any
᠁on's prose writings the power of generalisation, or, if the
᠁sion be preferred, the art of broadening particular issues,
᠁teristic of the highest kind of eloquence, is not of course to
᠁᠁sured by any conclusions as to its direct effect, and still
᠁ to Milton's subsequent relations with the political agency
᠁ operations he had impugned. Concerning these relations,
᠁vill only say that while I remain somewhat sceptical as to the
᠁tigating influence of Milton upon the treatment of press offences
᠁en himself officially associated with the censorship, I agree
᠁ this question does not really affect that of his consistency.
᠁᠁t is rightly observed by Professor Masson that "the *Areopa-*
᠁*ta* had not committed its author to the doctrine of the Liberty
᠁he Press in the sense that everything or anything might be
᠁᠁ished with impunity " ; indeed, towards the end of the
᠁᠁ech," he explicitly advises the Parliament to act upon its
᠁᠁er of 1641, requiring the registering in all cases of the names
᠁f printers and authors, as an effective provision for the regulation
᠁f the press. And where would have been the use of registering
᠁᠁es without holding their owners responsible ? Milton was
᠁t personally accountable for the policy adopted towards the
᠁ess after the dissolution of the first Parliament of the Protector-
᠁e, but he undoubtedly identified himself with it by continuing to
᠁᠁ld office under the Protector's government, and thereby, as is often
᠁e᠁ot of officials, contradicted declarations made before he was
᠁ office. For the rest, Milton's own duties in connexion with the
᠁·ss were in substance those of official editor rather than censor ;
᠁nay in addition have occasionally written himself in the columns
᠁e *Mercurius Politicus ;* and it is a pleasing thought of Mr.
᠁᠁n's that, in "the triumphant leading article on the Battle
᠁rcester" (1651), the Secretary's own hand may be traced.
᠁n the time of the publication of the *Areopagitica* to that
᠁xecution of the King, from 1644 to 1649, Milton seems

to have refrained from further interference in political or religi
controversy.   It was the period of his most assiduous self-devo
to the actual work of education, of which his literary labours du
these years formed an organic part.   The results of these lab
are of course lightly put aside as "mere compilations" by c
who favour the art of building without stone or bricks.
Latin treatise on Logic was not published till 1673, and the
templated *Latin Dictionary* never saw the light at all, whi
*Treatise on Christian Doctrine compiled from the Holy Scrip
alone*, likewise in Latin, was issued posthumously as a massive
ment, in two Books since translated by the late Bishop Summe
Winchester).   Of more special interest, as connecting itself
Milton's meditations on poetic themes, is another but
extensive posthumous fragment, the *History of Britain*, i
first book of which he narrates without reserve all the old fa
of Geoffrey of Monmouth, candidly averring as a principal obje
his desire to serve "our English poets and rhetoricians, who
their art will know how to use these reputed tales judiciously
When on historic ground, he knows that it behoves him to
more critical, so that the extinction of the Roman Empire in Brita
draws from him the characteristic comment ; "Henceforth, we a
to steer by another sort of authors ; near enough to the thin
they write, as in their own country, if that would serve ; in tin
not belated, some of equal age ; in expression barbarous, and
say how judicious, I suspend awhile ; this we must expect : in
civil matters to find them dubious relaters, and still to the best
advantage of what they term the Holy Church, meaning indeed
themselves : in most other matters of religion, blind, astonished,
and struck with superstition as with a planet : in one word,
Monks."   That the history of this island during the period ending
with the Battle of Hastings could not be written with sympathetic
warmth by one who thus regarded its principal sources, may b
taken for granted ; even the character of Alfred is drawn withou
enthusiasm, and the account of Edgar, "with whom died all th
Saxon glory," degenerates into scandal.   But in truth the style
this *History* is dry and uninteresting, and conveys to my mi
the impression that, though "revised" by the author in his old
its effectiveness would have been enhanced, had opportuni
served, by further touches from his younger hand.

But from such studies, and excursions, into which his l
curiosity led him from time to time, to "Muscovia and oth

known countries lying eastward of Russia as far as Cathay" (so was the title of the only other historical fragment remaining from Milton's hand) he was once more called away by the demands made upon his conscience by the great issues of his own times. How promptly he, whose personal courage has I believe been impugned because in the days of the outbreak of the Civil War his service in arms was limited to the London Artillery Ground, responded to the call, appears from the fact that he was the first Englishman of any note to publish his approval of the sentence upon the King, while giving in unasked his adhesion to the republican form of government. The full title of his treatise, put forth with the author's well-known initials in Feburary 1649, on *The Tenure of Kings and Magistrates*, invites attention to the extreme consequences of the doctrine of resistance which it develops ; and by devoting part of it to an attempt to rail into approbation the Presbyterians by involving them in the responsibility of the deed, the author conclusively breaks off any possible bridge behind him. The main argument of this manifesto, which Milton was soon to resume in prose writings destined to command a wider celebrity, is indisputably cognate with the teachings of the Jesuit Mariana, and with those that had in an earlier generation proceeded from Calvin, and is strongly influenced by the conception, so long prevalent among political thinkers, that the relations between a people and its magistrates are based upon a compact between them.

An almost inevitable sequel to Milton's wholly voluntary advocacy of the Commonwealth Government, and self-committal to its cause, was his appointment to a post of confidence in its service (March 1679). His activity as Secretary for the Foreign Tongues (*vulgo*, Latin Secretary), under a *régime* by which he held out to the very last, when he is found protesting against its imminent overthrow by public pamphlets and by a private letter to General Monk, may seem to have little or no concern with his contributions to the literature of English prose. But it is worthy of notice that even while he served the State he served it under conditions which both in his official and in what may be called his semi-official writings left to his pen full opportunities for that grave and ample process of composition which had become to it a kind of second nature. In other words, he was not a hack even when in harness ; and if we are unable to conceive of Milton absolving his daily publicistic task with the fevered gaiety of Gentz, neither need we think of him as groaning in spirit like Leibniz over the time lost for more congenial work. But Latin Prose, and English largely modelled upon its example, are apt to create the effect of a more complete leisureliness than may actually have attended what Milton would have termed its "composure," and he was not allowed to let the grass grow under his feet. Passing by, however, the earliest commissions with which he was charged, we come at once to the part taken by him in a controversy of, happily, almost unparalleled notoriety in the features of its course as well as in the circumstances of its origin. If in writing down the *Eikon Basilike* (and this cannot well be said to be a misstatement of the purpose of *Eikonoklastes*), Milton was in truth combating the shadow of a shade, the impression created in England and in Europe at large was to a very different effect. Should it be deemed a hazardous assertion that the worship paid for many generations to the personality of King Charles I. was primarily due to his image as presented in this work, at all events it intensified in an extraordinary degree the horror created by his judicial murder. The question of the genuineness of "the King's book" cannot be discussed here. Cromwell is said to have brutally observed that Charles certainly wrote it, for that he was the greatest hypocrite who ever lived. On the contrary : the style and manner of the book are alike too commonplace and too literary, too redolent of the purely professional to suit themselves very readily to the supposition of the regal authorship. Milton, who strikes no very certain note on the subject, probably comes near the truth in one sense, while missing it in another, when he addresses his censures to "the King or his household rhetorician." In point of fact he treats the King as the author or not the author, according as it suits the turns of his argument ; but he keeps up very effectively from first to last the impression that imposture is the character of this pinchbeck *Imitatio*, however much or however little the Royal Martyr had to do with it. And the king's share in the compound was probably more considerable than critics used to think.

In judging Milton's conduct of the first stage of this controversy, it should be remembered that the fashion of his times still favoured a sort of parallel pursuit, or worrying of an adversary along the whole line of his argument. He most assuredly in this book forewent no opportunity of the kind that presented itself, nor are his powers of sarcastic invective, though too fierce to fall well outside the range of humour, anywhere seen to greater advantage than in passages of the *Eikonoklastes*,

On the other hand an undeniable want of taste allows him to lapse into occasional grossness and (I should not use the expression were I not thinking of a strange trait in Cromwell's behaviour) into occasional horseplay. But, in jest and in earnest, the risks run by Milton in this book are excessive. It was impossible consciously to ignore the very principle of reverence for death to which the irresistible effect of the *Eikon* itself was largely due, without forfeiting the wider sympathy which even invective can ill spare. Vast audiences prefer broad appeals, and even so palpable a hit as the exposure, in the second edition of the *Eikonoklastes* (1650), of the plagiarism of *Pamela's Prayer* was unlikely to affect the general issue of the contest, besides being manifestly made too much of.

That contest had in the meantime widened its circles. For, upon the *Eikon Aklastos*, attributed to Bishop Bramhall, there had followed, also, though in a different sense, "inspired" from the Hague, the *Defensio Regia pro Carolo I.*, composed by the foremost pen (though not, we may confidently add, the foremost intellect) of the age. There was a cold-blooded audacity in the mere notion, reasonable as it may nowadays seem to us, of overtrumping the king of trumps. Indeed, in view of the courageousness of the enterprise as a whole, mere details of daring sink out of sight, such as the famous sally to which Macaulay's schoolboy probably owes his origin ; " what schoolboy, what insignificant little brother in any monastery, but would have pleaded the King's cause more eloquently (*aye, and in better Latin*) than this royal Orator ? " But the *Defensio pro populo Anglicano* (1651), though well Englished in the version attributed by Toland to a Templar of the name of Washington, lies outside our purview, as does the *Defensio Secunda* (1654), translated by Robert Fellowes, produced under a combination of private calamities and discouragements, together with literary and logical disadvantages which must have blunted any weapon forged in a smithy lit by common fires. Undoubtedly, at the same time, some oil of impure mixture had helped to feed the flames. Marvell's eloquence, without its witty application, may therefore be permitted to vary the figure. "When I consider how equally it turns and rises with so many figures, it seems to me a Trajan's column, in whose winding ascent we see embossed the several monuments of your learned victories." It must be allowed that a personal literary quarrel furnished some of the most grotesque supernumeraries to the triumphal procession ; but we are happily dispensed from deviating into side issues which, as Milton himself confessed in his *Pro se Defensio* (1655), dwarfed a memorable contention into a poor personal quarrel.

Throughout the Second Protectorate (1657-8) of Oliver Cromwell, Milton remained the faithful servant of the Government ; but his duties were less onerous, while his personal troubles were more pressing, and the consummation of his blindness announced by him to the readers of the *Defensio Secunda* had actually set in. Thus, his thoughts were more than ever directed to the accomplishment of a task beyond the conditions, wide as they are, of pedestrian speech. Before, however, this task was achieved, events directly related to his individual life intervened such as in their momentousness and swiftness of succession can surely neither before nor since have affected the career of a great writer. Both under the Protectorate of Richard Cromwell and in the period when the supreme authority rested actually or nominally with the restored Rump, the religious policy of Oliver was still, though with more or less hesitation, continued ; and in deprecation of it, Milton once more lifted up his voice as a public writer. In his *Treatise of Civil Power in Ecclesiastical Causes* (1659), he once more undertook to demonstrate on Scriptural grounds the unlawfulness, which even in the mighty hand now cold, had seemed to him to imply the futility, of temporal compulsion in matters of religion. This essay is, more largely perhaps than any other of Milton's writings, with the exception of his long posthumous treatise on *The Christian Doctrine*, interspersed with Scriptural texts as with stepping-stones laid for every stage of the argument ; but the passage I extract may serve as an illustration of the practical limits which in the very heat of theoretical reasoning impose themselves upon him who aspires to mould a policy. The times were out of joint for any such endeavour ; nor, although after the Restoration of the Rump the agitation against the continuance of tithes seemed to promise more decided action, were his *Considerations touching the likeliest means to remove Hirelings out of the Church* (1659)—a title recalling the aspirations of the days of *Lycidas*—more audible amidst the rush of the waters. This tract, which in its antiquities leans upon Selden, and in its appeal to the Waldenses, "whom deservedly I cite so often," possibly rests upon less solid authorities, presents a very vigorous plea for disestablishment and disendowment, in which, though it has less of unction than is to be found in some of Milton's earlier prose, there is more of the "common-sense" tone which possesses hardly less controversial value. I have extracted a passage of this kind; a protest in which, every allowance being made, there remains a rather bitter *residuum*, which may be said to contain the most forcible part of the argument.

Under the Committee of Safety which superseded the pretence of renewed Parliamentary Government, Milton's office had become to all purposes a sinecure; and his *Letter to a Friend concerning The Ruptures of the Commonwealth* (October 1659), was in point of fact only one among many contending attempts to solve a problem to which one hand alone held the master-key. Monk restored the Long Parliament in order that this "Parliament" might appoint him dictator. Early in March 1660 Milton published his *Ready and Easy Way to establish a Free Commonwealth, and the Excellence thereof compared with the Inconveniences and Dangers of readmitting Kingship in this Nation.* The plan which he now proposed was practically that of a permanent and therefore irresponsible Parliament together with a decentralisation of the administrative system. But of greater interest even than those features (the last of importance put forth by him) which drew down upon this treatise an arrowy sheet of criticisms such as hardly any of his previous political speculations had been asked to weather, including the burlesque "censure of the Rota," which reminds us that we are already approaching the age of *Hudibras*, is the firmness with which Milton here once more proclaims his fundamental political principles, among them liberty of conscience, at a time when he will know them to be in extreme, if not in hopeless, peril. I extract, as a concluding passage from Milton's political prose, one which has, in more senses than one, the prophetic note proper to a writer who—he too—looked forward with no faltering eye to a Restoration.

Milton had taken comfort in the thought, that while his argument might commend itself to many "sensible and ingenuous men," he had perchance at the same time spoken to some "whom God might raise of these stones to become children of liberty." Soon he stood among the ruins of the Commonwealth which he had served so amply and yet so freely; and, the period of danger which ensued overpast, his labours in the years remaining to him were "turned to peaceful end."

I pass by what he wrote or published in prose in these later years of his life ; including the brief prefatory note *On that sort of Dramatic Poem which is called Tragedy*, prefixed to his *Samson Agonistes* (1671), and the tract, provoked by the first Declaration of Indulgence, on *True Religion, Heresy, Schism, Toleration* (1673), which, notwithstanding its precision of form, exhibits the historical instincts rather than the logical powers of the writer in its rejection, at any cost, of the toleration of " idolatry." One passage in this tract has, it must be allowed, a faint echo of the well-known ring, " At least, then, let them have leave to write in Latin."

I have thought it permissible, with the aid of Professor Masson's monumental work, to treat the prose writings of Milton in their historical connexion, so far as was possible within the slight framework of an introductory note. It is difficult to imagine that, although by profession, as well as by the character of his genius, a man of letters rather than a statesman, he could have approved of his treatises being primarily dealt with as a whole, in any other fashion. In him throbbed the pulse of the historic movement of his age, and what he wrote as a publicist he wrote for the sake of the matter which he essayed to mould. It could not have occurred to him to take thought of the form of his prose compositions in the first instance, or to speculate on the truism that the effect of things depends on the manner of saying them. The very " pitch " of his style he cannot, after the fashion of more than one eminent historian, have taken thought of accommodating to his themes, although it would contrariwise have been inconceivable to him—or, indeed, to any of the great prose writers of his age—to write down to a particular section of his public. Of his style, as of his matter, his own words hold good, that " though it be an irksome labour to write with industry and judicious pains that which neither weighed nor well-read, shall be judged, without industry or the pains of well-judging, by faction and the easy literature of custom and opinion : it shall be ventured yet."

That, however, a genius such as Milton's should clothe its products in a style of its own, whether the work (in his own phrase) of his " right hand " or of his " left," was at the same time in the nature of things. Upon Milton's prose style an excellent critic, quite recently taken away from us, rightly says that " the most diverse opinions have been pronounced," and necessarily so, " inasmuch as everything depends upon the point of view." Milton's own point of view was to give himself in his prose, so far as the form admitted, wholly and unreservedly. Thus, as will be readily allowed, there are in Milton's prose works, English as well as Latin, passages of a rapt enthusiasm which, though rarer in occurrence, approach in effect the sublimities of his verse. On the other hand, his wrath and indignation—sometimes hardly to be distinguished from spite—set no bounds to the violence of their invective, and he allows his temper to have its own way in flouts and gibes. Too much has, I think, been made of the vituperative qualities of Milton's prose, as if they were of its essence ; they are such in no other sense than that outside the restraint of verse he gave his nature free play, and in this, thanks perhaps to his city breeding, there was an element which finds expression in the copious diction of self-consciousness and (to use plain terms) of arrogant impatience. Again, coming forth as he did from his library, where at the time when he began to publish in prose he was intent upon a series of learned works chiefly in the Latin tongue, he brought his library and his Latin out with him into the open air. Many considerations help to explain the fact (which I suppose will hardly be disputed) that the Latinism of Milton's style was more marked than that of any other great writer's of this period. Among them was his constant habit of writing as well as reading Latin side by side with English, first in the pursuit of his regular literary and educational labours, then in the performance of his official duties as Foreign Secretary. Bacon's case had not been altogether dissimilar ; but he had from his youth up been in close contact with public life, both Parliamentary and forensic. Milton's Ciceronianisms of construction, the prerogative position allowed by him to pronouns both relative and personal, and, above all, his favourite inversion of the usual English order of construction, where the governing verb precedes rather than follows a clause, or series of clauses, dependent upon it, argue a singularly retentive ear, perhaps also a preference for oratorical to historical models. He was not, I think, even in his later verse, altogether unconscious in some of his classicising mannerisms ; but his peculiarities of construction are not, to my mind, so exceptional as they have frequently been asserted to be, nor are his English prose works so full of them as to warrant the censure that they spoil his style. His vocabulary, on the other hand, is abnormally prone to eccentric and occasionally unpleasing forms, not all of which can be set down to the adventurous curiosity which still affected the choice of words in this, the last period, as it might almost be called, of the English Renascence. In both construction and vocabulary, it must be remembered, the age of experiment only passed away when the self-restraint of good taste imposed itself as a law, no longer violable with impunity, in the post-Restoration days. (It will be remembered how Milton himself, in a treatise in which he flings about him such forms as "affatuated" and "imbastardized" and "proditory" and "robustious," takes exception to the new-fangled word "demagogue.") Altogether, while it was indisputably not given to him, as it was to Pascal, to write a prose style with which no modern critic can find fault, his offences against perfection have been partly exaggerated and partly left insufficiently explained.

I am not sure but that both in syntax and diction the ease of Milton's style suffered from the absence of the controlling eye. Most of his prose was written when his sight was either threatening to leave him or had abandoned him altogether. His instincts were rhetorical; the predilections of his reading had probably followed the same bent; and he must, if he paused at all to consider the effect of what he had dictated, have asked for an echo of his own voice and its intentions. Nobody who has written much (in however humble a fashion) for his own oral delivery, but will concede it to be no easy task to write for delivery by others. I feel sure that the complaint frequently urged against the want of harmony in Milton's cadences is at least partially due to the difficulty experienced by casual readers in accommodating themselves, as they read, to a complex manner of eloquence more individual than that of Burke——not to mention Burke's imitators.

I do not deny, in conclusion, that there are traces of pedantry in Milton's prose style, as there are even in the most magnificent exemplars of his verse, and, I am willing to add, in his character and his career. They are most apparent when he descends; nor is it paradoxical that there should be a kind of greatness which best stands erect. Milton's colloquial sallies are at times such as might be expected from an excessive familiarity with epistolary Latin, at other times they are the efforts of a forced sportiveness too grim to be altogether agreeable. But even in these, and how infinitely more in the wealth of illustrations, images, and ideas lavished upon any subject which he is fain to treat, do we recognise the wealth of an imagination which seems at times, within the limits of a single sentence, to master diction and syntax and all the conditions of written speech! To decry such a style as composite is to revive the short-sighted captiousness of an obsolete method of criticism, which was capable of analysing materials, but not of apprehending the power which transfuses what it has appropriated. Milton's prose, all exceptions taken, and all cavils allowed their force, remains the most extraordinary literary prose, and the most wonderful poet's prose, embodied in English literature.

A. W. WARD.

THE DELIVERANCE OF ENGLAND

I DO now feel myself inwrapped on the sudden into those mazes and labyrinths of dreadful and hideous thoughts, that which way to get out, or which way to end, I know not, unless I turn mine eyes, and with your help lift up my hands to that eternal and propitious throne, where nothing is readier than grace and refuge to the distresses of mortal suppliants : and it were a shame to leave these serious thoughts less piously than the heathen were wont to conclude their graver discourses.

Thou, therefore, that sittest in light and glory unapproachable, parent of angels and men ! next, thee I implore, omnipotent King, Redeemer of that lost remnant whose nature thou didst assume, ineffable and everlasting Love ! and thou, the third subsistence of divine infinitude, illumining Spirit, the joy and solace of created things ! one Tripersonal godhead ! look upon this thy poor and almost spent and expiring church, leave her not thus a prey to these importunate wolves, that wait and think long till they devour thy tender flock ; these wild boars that have broke into thy vine-yard, and left the print of their polluting hoofs on the souls of thy servants.   O let them not bring about their damned designs, that stand now at the entrance of the bottomless pit, expecting the watchword to open and let out those dreadful locusts and scorpions, to reinvolve us in that pitchy cloud of infernal darkness, where we shall never more see the sun of thy truth again, never hope for the cheerful dawn, never more hear the bird of morning sing.   Be moved with pity at the afflicted state of this our shaken monarchy, that now lies labouring under her throes, and struggling against the grudges of more dreaded calamities.

O thou, that after the impetuous rage of five bloody inunda-tions, and the succeeding sword of intestine war, soaking the land in her own gore, didst pity the sad and ceaseless revolution of our swift and thick-coming sorrows ; when we were quite breathless, of thy free grace didst motion peace, and terms of covenant with us ; and having first well nigh freed us from antichristian thraldom, didst build up this Britannic empire to a glorious and enviable height, with all her daughter-islands about her ; stay us in this felicity, let not the obstinacy of our half-obedience and will-worship bring forth that viper of sedition, that for these fourscore years hath been breeding to eat through the entrails of our peace ; but let her cast her abortive spawn without the danger of this travailing and throbbing kingdom : that we may still remember in our solemn thanksgivings, how for us, the northern ocean even to the frozen Thule was scattered with the proud shipwrecks of the Spanish armada, and the very maw of hell ransacked, and made to give up her concealed destruction, ere she could vent it in that horrible and damned blast.

O how much more glorious will those former deliverances appear, when we shall know them not only to have saved us from greatest miseries past, but to have reserved us for greatest happiness to come ! Hitherto thou hast but freed us, and that not fully, from the unjust and tyrannous claim of thy foes ; now unite us entirely, and appropriate us to thyself, tie us everlastingly in willing homage to the prerogative of thy eternal throne.

And now we know, O thou our most certain hope and defence, that thine enemies have been consulting all the sorceries of the great whore, and have joined their plots with that sad intelligencing tyrant that mischiefs the world with his mines of Ophir, and lies thirsting to revenge his naval ruins that have larded our seas : but let them all take counsel together, and let it come to nought ; let them decree, and do thou cancel it ; let them gather themselves, and be scattered ; let them embattle themselves, and be broken ; let them embattle, and be broken, for thou art with us.

Then, amidst the hymns and hallelujahs of saints, some one may perhaps be heard offering at high strains in new and lofty measure to sing and celebrate thy divine mercies and marvellous judgments in this land throughout all ages ; whereby this great and warlike nation, instructed and inured to the fervent and continual practice of truth and righteousness, and casting far from her the rags of her whole vices, may press on hard to that high and happy emulation to be found the soberest, wisest, and most Christian people at that day, when thou, the eternal and shortly expected King, shalt open the clouds to judge the several kingdoms of the world, and distributing national honours and rewards to religious and just commonwealths, shalt put an end to all earthly tyrannies, proclaiming thy universal and mild monarchy through heaven and earth ; where they undoubtedly, that by their labours, counsels, and prayers, have been earnest for the common good of religion and their country, shall receive above the inferior orders of the blessed, the regal addition of principalities, legions, and thrones into their glorious titles, and in supereminence of beatific vision, progressing the dateless and irrevoluble circle of eternity, shall clasp inseparable hands with joy and bliss, in over-measure for ever.

But they contrary, that by the impairing and diminution of the true faith, the distresses and servitude of their country, aspire to high dignity, rule, and promotion here, after a shameful end in this life (which God grant them), shall be thrown down eternally into the darkest and deepest gulf of hell, where, under the despiteful control, the trample and spurn of all the other damned, that in the anguish of their torture, shall have no other ease than to exercise a raving and bestial tyranny over them as their slaves and negroes, they shall remain in that plight for ever, the basest, the lowermost, the most dejected, most underfoot, and downtrodden vassals of perdition. (From *Of Reformation in England.*)

NOT THE PRAISE, BUT THE CAUSE

TIMOROUS and ungrateful, the church of God is now again at the foot of her insulting enemies, and thou bewailest. What matters it for thee, or thy bewailing ? When time was, thou couldst not find a syllable of all that thou hast read, or studied, to utter in her behalf. Yet ease and leisure was given thee for thy retired thoughts, out of the sweat of other men. Thou hast the diligence, the parts, the language of a man, if a vain subject were to be adorned or beautified ; but when the cause of God and his church was to be pleaded, for which purpose that tongue was given thee which thou hast, God listened if he could hear thy voice among his zealous servants, but thou wert dumb as a beast ; from henceforward be that which thine own brutish silence hath made thee. Or else I should have heard on the other ear : Slothful, and ever to be set light by, the church hath now overcome her late distresses after the unwearied labours of many her true servants that stood up in her defence; thou also wouldst take upon thee to share amongst them of their joy: but wherefore thou? Where canst thou show any word or deed of thine which might have hastened her peace? Whatever thou dost now talk, or write, or look, is the alms of other men's active prudence and zeal. Dare not now to say or do anything better than thy former sloth and infancy; or if thou darest, thou dost impudently to make a thrifty purchase of boldness to thyself, out of the painful merits of other men; what before was thy sin is now thy duty, to be abject and worthless. These, and such-like lessons as these, I know would have been my matins daily, and my even-song. But now by this little diligence, mark what a privilege I have gained with good men and saints, to claim my right of lamenting the tribulations of the church, if she should suffer, when others, that have ventured nothing for her sake, have not the honour to be admitted mourners. But if she lift up her drooping head and prosper, among those that have something more than wished her welfare, I have my charter and freehold of rejoicing to me and my heirs. Concerning therefore this wayward subject against prelaty, the touching whereof is so distasteful and disquietous to a number of men, as by what hath been said I may deserve of charitable readers to be credited, that neither envy nor gall hath entered me upon this controversy, but the enforcement of conscience only, and a preventive fear lest the omitting of this duty should be against me, when I would store up to myself the good provision of peaceful hours: so, lest it should be still imputed to me, as I have found it hath been, that some self-pleasing humour of vain-glory hath incited me to contest with men of high estimation, now while green years are upon my head; from this needless surmisal I shall hope to dissuade the intelligent and equal auditor, if I can but say successfully that which in this exigent behoves me; although I would be heard only, if it might be, by the elegant and learned reader, to whom principally for a while I shall beg leave I may address myself. To him it will be no new thing, though I tell him that if I hunted after praise, by the ostentation of wit and learning, I should not write thus out of mine own season when I have neither yet completed to my mind the full circle of my private studies, although I complain not of any insufficiency to the matter in hand; or were I ready to my wishes, it were a folly to commit anything elaborately composed to the careless and interrupted listening of these tumultuous times. Next, if I were wise only to my own ends, I would certainly take such a subject as of itself might catch applause, whereas this hath all the disadvantages on the contrary, and such a subject as the publishing whereof might be delayed at pleasure, and time enough to pencil it over with all the curious touches of art, even to the perfection of a faultless picture ; whenas in this argument the not deferring is of great moment to the good speeding, that if solidity have leisure to do her office, art cannot have much. Lastly, I should not choose this manner of writing, wherein knowing myself inferior to myself, led by the genial power of nature to another task, I have the use, as I may account, but of my left hand. And though I shall be foolish in saying more to this purpose, yet, since it will be such a folly, as wisest men go about to commit, having only confessed and so committed, I may trust with more reason, because with more folly, to have courteous pardon. For although a poet, soaring in the high reason of his fancies, with his garland and singing robes about him, might, without apology, speak more of himself than I mean to do ; yet for me, sitting here below in the cool element of prose, a mortal thing among many readers of no empyreal conceit, to venture and divulge unusual things of myself, I shall petition to the gentler sort, it may not be envy to me. I must say, therefore, that after I had for my first years, by the ceaseless diligence and care of my father (whom God recompense !), been exercised to the tongues, and some sciences, as my age would suffer, by sundry masters and teachers, both at home and at the schools, it was found that whether aught was imposed me by them that had the overlooking, or betaken to of mine own choice in English, or other tongue, prosing or versing, but chiefly by this latter, the style, by certain vital signs it had, was likely to live. But much latelier in the private academies of Italy, whither I was favoured to resort, perceiving that some trifles which I had in memory, composed at under twenty or thereabout (for the manner is, that every one must give some proof of his wit and reading there), met with acceptance above what was looked for ; and other things, which I had shifted in scarcity of books and conveniences to patch up amongst them, were received with written encomiums, which the Italian is not forward to bestow on men of this side the Alps ; I began thus far to assent both to them and divers of my friends here at home, and not less to an inward prompting which now grew daily upon me, that by labour and intense study (which I take to be my portion in this life), joined with the strong propensity of nature, I might perhaps leave something so written to aftertimes, as they should not willingly let it die. These thoughts at once possessed me, and these other; that if I were certain to write as men buy leases, for three lives and downward, there ought no regard be sooner had than to God's glory, by the honour and instruction of my country. For which cause, and not only for that I knew it would be hard to arrive at the second rank among the Latins, I applied myself to that resolution, which Ariosto followed against the persuasions of Bembo, to fix all the industry and art I could unite to the adorning of my native tongue; not to make verbal curiosities the end (that were a toilsome vanity), but to be an interpreter and relater of the best and sagest things among mine own citizens throughout this island in the mother dialect. That what the greatest and choicest wits of Athens, Rome, or modern Italy, and those Hebrews of old did for their country, I, in my proportion, with this over and above, of being a Christian, might do for mine; not caring to be once named abroad, though perhaps I could attain to that, but content with these British islands as my world; whose fortune hath hitherto been, that if the Athenians, as some say, made their small deeds great and renowned by their eloquent writers, England hath had her noble achievements made small by the unskilful handling of monks and mechanics.

(From *The Reason of Church Government urged against Prelaty.*)

HIMSELF A TRUE POEM

NOR blame it, readers, in those years to propose to themselves such a reward, as the noblest dispositions above other things in this life have sometimes preferred: whereof not to be sensible when good and fair in one person meet, argues both a gross and shallow judgment, and withal an ungentle and swainish breast. For by the firm settling of these persuasions, I became, to my best memory, so much a proficient, that if I found those authors anywhere speaking unworthy things of themselves, or unchaste of those names which before they had extolled; this effect it wrought with me, from that time forward their art I still applauded, but the men I deplored; and above them all, preferred the two famous renowners of Beatrice and Laura, who never write but honour of them to whom they devote their verse, displaying sublime and pure thoughts, without transgression. And long it was not after, when I was confirmed in this opinion, that he who would not be frustrate of his hope to write well hereafter in laudable things, ought himself to be a true poem; that is, a composition and pattern of the best and honourablest things; not presuming to sing high praises of heroic men, or famous cities, unless he have in himself the experience and the practice of all that which is praiseworthy. These reasonings, together with a certain niceness of nature, an honest haughtiness, and self-esteem either of what I was, or what I might be (which let envy call pride), and lastly that modesty, whereof, though not in the title-page, yet here I may be excused to make some beseeming profession; all these uniting the supply of their natural aid together, kept me still above those low descents of mind, beneath which he must deject and plunge himself, that can agree to saleable and unlawful prostitutions.

Next (for hear me out now, readers), that I may tell ye whither my younger feet wandered; I betook me among those lofty fables and romances, which recount in solemn cantos the deeds of knighthood founded by our victorious kings, and from hence had in renown over all Christendom. There I read it in the oath of every knight, that he should defend to the expense of his best blood, or of his life, if it so befell him, the honour and chastity of virgin or matron; from whence even then I learned what a noble virtue chastity sure must be, to the defence of which so many worthies, by such a dear adventure of themselves, had sworn. And if I found in the story afterward, any of them, by word or deed, breaking that oath, I judged it the same fault of the poet, as that which is attributed to Homer, to have written indecent things of the gods. Only this my mind gave me, that every free and gentle spirit, without that oath, ought to be born a knight, nor needed to expect the gilt spur, or the laying of a sword upon his shoulder to stir him up both by his counsel and his arms, to secure and protect the weakness of any attempted chastity. So that even these books, which to many others have been the fuel of wantonness and loose living, I cannot think how, unless by divine indulgence, proved to me so many incitements, as you have heard, to the love and steadfast observation of that virtue which abhors the society of bordelloes.

Thus, from the laureat fraternity of poets, riper years and the ceaseless round of study and reading led me to the shady spaces of philosophy; but chiefly to the divine volumes of Plato, and his equal Xenophon: where, if I should tell ye what I learnt of chastity and love, I mean that which is truly so, whose charming cup is only virtue, which she bears in her hand to those who are worthy (the rest are cheated with a thick intoxicating potion, which a certain sorceress, the abuser of love's name, carries about); and how the first and chiefest office of love begins and ends in the soul, producing those happy twins of her divine generation, knowledge and virtue.

(From the *Apology for Smectymnuus*.)

THE NEW INQUISITION

FOR if they fell upon one kind of strictness, unless their care were equal to regulate all other things of like aptness to corrupt the mind, that single endeavour they knew would be but a fond labour; to shut and fortify one gate against corruption, and be necessitated to leave others round about wide open. If we think to regulate printing, thereby to rectify manners, we must regulate all recreations and pastimes, all that is delightful to man. No music must be heard, no song be set or sung, but what is grave and doric. There must be licensing dancers, that no gesture, motion, or deportment be taught our youth, but what by their allowance shall be thought honest; for such Plato was provided of. It will ask more than the work of twenty licensers to examine all the lutes, the violins, and the guitars in every house; they must not be suffered to prattle as they do, but must be licensed what they may say. And who shall silence all the airs and madrigals that whisper softness in chambers? The windows also, and the balconies, must be thought on; these are shrewd books, with dangerous frontispieces, set to sale: who shall prohibit them, shall twenty licensers? The villages also must have their visitors to inquire what lectures the bagpipe and the rebec reads, even to the ballatry and the gamut of every municipal fiddler; for these are the countryman's Arcadias, and his Monte Mayors.

And as it is a particular disesteem of every knowing person alive, and most injurious to the written labours and monuments of the dead, so to me it seems an undervaluing and vilifying of the whole nation. I cannot set so light by all the invention, the art, the wit, the grave and solid judgment which is in England, as that it can be comprehended in any twenty capacities, how good soever; much less that it should not pass except their superintendence be over it, except it be sifted and strained with their strainers, that it should be uncurrent without their manual stamp. Truth and understanding are not such wares as to be monopolised and traded in by tickets, and statutes, and standards. We must not think to make a staple commodity of all the knowledge in the land, to mark and license it like our broad-cloth and our woolpacks. What is it but a servitude like that imposed by the Philistines, not to be allowed the sharpening of our own axes and coulters, but we must repair from all quarters to twenty licensing forges?

Had any one written and divulged erroneous things and scandalous to honest life, misusing and forfeiting the esteem had of his reason among men, if after conviction this only censure were adjudged him, that he should never henceforth write, but what were first examined by an appointed officer, whose hand should be annexed to pass his credit for him, that now he might be safely read; it could not be apprehended less than a disgraceful punishment. Whence to include the whole nation, and those that never yet thus offended, under such a diffident and suspectful prohibition, may plainly be understood what a disparagement it is. So much the more whenas debtors and delinquents may walk abroad without a keeper, but unoffensive books must not stir forth without a visible jailor in their title. Nor is it to the common people less than a reproach; for if we be so jealous over them, as that we dare not trust them with an English pamphlet, what do we but censure them for a giddy, vicious, and ungrounded people; in such a sick and weak state of faith and discretion, as to be able to take nothing down but through the pipe of a licenser? That this is care or love of them, we cannot pretend, whenas in those popish places, where the laity are most hated and despised, the same strictness is used over them. Wisdom we cannot call it, because it stops but one breach of licence, nor that neither: whenas those corruptions, which it seeks to prevent, break in faster at other doors, which cannot be shut.

And in conclusion it reflects to the disrepute of our ministers also, of whose labours we should hope better, and of their proficiency which their flock reaps by them, than that after all this light of the gospel which is, and is to be, and all this continual preaching, they should be still frequented with such an unprincipled, unedified, and laic rabble, as that the whiff of every new pamphet should stagger them out of their catechism and Christian walking.   This may have much reason to discourage the ministers, when such a low conceit is had of all their exhortations, and the benefiting of their hearers, as that they are not thought fit to be turned loose to three sheets of paper without a licenser ; that all the sermons, all the lectures preached, printed, vended in such numbers, and such volumes, as have now well-nigh made all other books unsaleable, should not be armour enough against one single Enchiridion, without the castle of St. Angelo of an imprimatur.

And lest some should persuade ye, lords and commons, that these arguments of learned men's discourgement at this your order are mere flourishes, and not real, I could recount what I have seen and heard in other countries, where this kind of inquisition tyrannises ; when I have set among their learned men (for that honour I had), and been counted happy to be born in such a place of philosophic freedom, as they supposed England was, while themselves did nothing but bemoan the servile condition into which learning amongst them was brought ; that this was it which had damped the glory of Italian wits ; that nothing had been there written now these many years but flattery and fustian.   There it was that I found and visited the famous Galileo, grown old, a prisoner to the inquisition, for thinking in astronomy otherwise than the Franciscan and Dominican licensers thought.   And though I knew that England then was groaning loudest under the prelatical yoke, nevertheless I took it as a pledge of future happiness, that other nations were so persuaded of her liberty.

Yet was it beyond my hope, that those worthies were then breathing in her air, who should be her leaders to such a deliverance, as shall never be forgotten by any revolution of time that this world hath to finish.   When that was once begun, it was as little in my fear, that what words of complaint I heard among learned men of other parts uttered against the inquisition, the same I should hear, by as learned men at home, uttered in time of parliament against an order of licensing ; and that so generally, that when I had disclosed myself a companion of their discontent, I might say, if without envy, that he whom an honest quæstorship had endeared to the Sicilians, was not more by them importuned against Verres, than the favourable opinion which I had among many who honour ye, and are known and respected by ye, loaded me with entreaties and persuasions, that I would not despair to lay together that which just reason should bring into my mind, towards the removal of an undeserved thraldom upon learning.

That this is not therefore the disburdening of a particular fancy, but the common grievance of all those who had prepared their minds and studies above the vulgar pitch, to advance truth in others, and from others to entertain it, thus much may satisfy.

(From the *Areopagitica*.)

THE SEARCH AFTER TRUTH

TRUTH indeed came once into the world with her divine master, and was a perfect shape most glorious to look on : but when he ascended, and his apostles after him were laid asleep, then straight arose a wicked race of deceivers, who, as that story goes of the Egyptian Typhon with his conspirators, how they dealt with the good Osiris, took the virgin Truth, hewed her lovely form into a thousand pieces, and scattered them to the four winds. From that time ever since, the sad friends of Truth, such as durst appear, imitating the careful search that Isis made for the mangled body of Osiris, went up and down gathering up limb by limb still as they could find them. We have not yet found them all, lords and commons, nor ever shall do, till her Master's second coming ; he shall bring together every joint and member, and shall mould them into an immortal feature of loveliness and perfection. Suffer not these licensing prohibitions to stand at every place of opportunity forbidding and disturbing them that continue seeking, that continue to do our obsequies to the torn body of our martyred saint.

We boast our light ; but if we look not wisely on the sun itself, it smites us into darkness. Who can discern those planets that are oft combust, and those stars of brightest magnitude that rise and set with the sun, until the opposite motion of their orbs bring them to such a place in the firmament, where they may be seen evening or morning? The light which we have gained was given us, not to be ever staring on, but by it to discover onward things more remote from our knowledge. It is not the unfrocking of a priest, the unmitring of a bishop, and the removing him from off the presbyterian shoulders, that will make us a happy nation : no ; if other things as great in the church, and in the rule of life both economical and political, be not looked into and reformed, we have looked so long upon the blaze that Zuinglius and Calvin have beaconed up to us, that we are stark blind.

There be who perpetually complain of schisms and sects, and make it such a calamity that any man dissents from their maxims. It is their own pride and ignorance which causes the disturbing, who neither will hear with meekness, nor can convince, yet all must be suppressed which is not found in their Syntagma. They are the troublers, they are the dividers of unity, who neglect and permit not others to unite those dissevered pieces, which are yet wanting to the body of truth. To be still searching what we know not, by what we know, still closing up truth to truth as we find it (for all her body is homogeneal, and proportional), this is the golden rule in theology as well as in arithmetic, and makes up the best harmony in a church ; not the forced and outward union of cold, and neutral, and inwardly divided minds.

(From the *Areopagitica*.)

THE PUNISHMENT OF TYRANTS

FOR as to this question in hand, what the people by their just right may do in change of government, or of governor, we see it cleared sufficiently besides other ample authority, even from the mouths of princes themselves. And surely they that shall boast, as we do, to be a free nation, and not have in themselves the power to remove or to abolish any governor supreme, or subordinate, with the government itself upon urgent causes, may please their fancy with a ridiculous and painted freedom, fit to cozen babies ; but we are indeed under tyranny and servitude, as wanting that power, which is the root and source of all liberty, to dispose and economise in the land which God hath given them, as masters of family in their own house and free inheritance.

Without which natural and essential power of a free nation, though bearing high their heads, they can in due esteem be thought no better than slaves and vassals born, in the tenure and occupation of another inheriting lord ; whose government, though not illegal, or intolerable, hangs over them as a lordly scourge, not as a free government ; and therefore to be abrogated.

How much more justly then may they fling off tyranny, or tyrants ; who being once deposed can be no more than private men, as subject to the reach of justice and arraignment as any other transgressors ? And certainly if men, not to speak of heathen, both wise and religious, have done justice upon tyrants what way they could soonest, how much more mild and humane then is it, to give them fair and open trial ; to teach lawless kings, and all who so much adore them, that not mortal man, or his imperious will, but justice, is the only true sovereign and supreme majesty upon earth ? Let men cease therefore, out of faction and hyprocrisy, to make outcries and horrid things of things so just and honourable. Though perhaps till now, no protestant state or kingdom can be alleged to have openly put to death their king, which lately some have written, and imputed to their great glory ; much mistaking the matter. It is not, neither ought to be, the glory of a protestant state, never to have put their king to death ; it is the glory of a protestant king never to have deserved death. And if the parliament and military council do what they do without precedent, if it appear their duty, it argues the more wisdom, virtue, and magnanimity, that they know themselves able to be a precedent to others ; who perhaps in future ages, if they prove not too degenerate, will look up with honour, and aspire towards these exemplary and matchless deeds of their ancestors, as to the highest top of their civil glory and emulation ; which heretofore, in the pursuance of fame and foreign dominion, spent itself vaingloriously abroad ; but henceforth may learn a better fortitude, to dare execute highest justice on them that shall by force of arms endeavour the oppressing and bereaving of religion and their liberty at home. That no unbridled potentate or tyrant, but to his sorrow, for the future may presume such high and irresponsible licence over mankind, to havoc and turn upside down whole kingdoms of men, as though they were no more in respect of his perverse will than a nation of pismires. (From the *Tenure of Kings*.)

THE KING'S MISGOVERNMENT

It were an endless work to walk side by side with the verbosity of this chapter; only to what already hath not been spoken, convenient answer shall be given. He begins again with tumults: all demonstration of the people's love and loyalty to the parliament was tumult; their petitioning tumult; their defensive armies were but listed tumults; and will take no notice that those about him, those in a time of peace listed into his own house, were the beginners of all these tumults; abusing and assaulting not only such as came peaceably to the parliament at London, but those that came petitioning to the king himself at York. Neither did they abstain from doing violence and outrage to the messengers sent from parliament; he himself either countenancing or conniving at them.

He supposes that "his recess gave us confidence, that he might be conquered." Other men suppose both that and all things else, who knew him neither by nature warlike, nor experienced, nor fortunate; so far was any man, that discerned aught, from esteeming him unconquerable; yet such are readiest to embroil others. "But he had a soul invincible." What praise is that? The stomach of a child is ofttimes invincible to all correction. The unteachable man hath a soul to all reason and good advice invincible; and he who is intractable, he whom nothing can persuade, may boast himself invincible; whenas in some things to be overcome, is more honest and laudable than to conquer.

He labours to have it thought, "that his fearing God more than man" was the ground of his sufferings; but he should have known that a good principle not rightly understood may prove as hurtful as a bad; and his fear of God may be as faulty as a blind zeal. He pretended to fear God more than the parliament, who never urged him to do otherwise; he should also have feared God more than he did his courtiers, and the bishops, who drew him as they pleased to things inconsistent with the fear of God. Thus boasted Saul to have "performed the commandment of God," and stood in it against Samuel; but it was found at length, that he had feared the people more than God, in saving those fat oxen for the worship of God, which were appointed for destruction. Not much unlike, if not much worse, was that fact of his, who, for fear to displease his court and mongrel clergy, with the dissolutest of the people, upheld in the church of God, while his power lasted, those beasts of Amalec, the prelates, against the advice of his parliament and the example of all reformation ; in this more inexcusable than Saul, that Saul was at length convinced, he to the hour of death fixed in his false persuasion ; and soothes himself in the flattering peace of an erroneous and obdurate conscience ; singing to his soul vain psalms and exultation, as if the parliament had assailed his reason with the force of arms, and not he on the contrary their reason with his arms ; which hath been proved already, and shall be more hereafter.

He twits them with " his acts of grace " ; proud, and unself-knowing words in the mouth of any king, who affects not to be a god, and such as ought to be as odious in the ears of a free nation. For if they were unjust acts, why did he grant them as of grace ? If just, it was not of his grace, but of his duty and his oath to grant them. "A glorious king he would be, though by his sufferings ; " but that can never be to him whose sufferings are his own doings. He feigns " a hard choice " put upon him, "either to kill his subjects, or be killed." Yet never was king less in danger of any violence from his subjects, till he unsheathed his sword against them ; nay, long after that time, when he had spilt the blood of thousands, they had still his person in a foolish veneration.

He complains " that civil war must be the fruits of his seventeen years reigning with such a measure of justice, peace, plenty, and religion, as all nations either admired or envied." For the justice we had, let the council-table, star-chamber, high-commission speak the praise of it ; not forgetting the unprincely usage, and as far as might be, the abolishing of parliaments, the displacing of honest judges, the sale of offices, bribery, and exaction, not found out to be punished, but to be shared in with impunity for the time to come. Who can number the extortions, the oppressions, the public robberies and rapines committed on the subject both by sea and land, under various pretences ? their possessions also taken from them, one while as forest-land, another while as crown-land ; nor were their goods exempted, no, not the bullion in the mint ; piracy was become a project owned and authorised against the subject.

For the peace we had, what peace was that which drew out

the English to a needless and dishonourable voyage against the Spaniard at Cales ? Or that which lent our shipping to a treacherous and antichristian war against the poor protestants of Rochelle our suppliants ? What peace was that which fell to rob the French by sea, to the embarring of all our merchants in that kingdom ? which brought forth that unblest expedition to the Isle of Rhé, doubtful whether more calamitous in the success, or in the design, betraying all the flower of our military youth and best commanders to a shameful surprisal and execution. This was the peace we had, and the peace we gave, whether to friends or to foes abroad. And if at home any peace were intended us, what meant those Irish billetted soldiers in all parts of the kingdom, and the design of German horse to subdue us in our peaceful houses ?

For our religion, where was there a more ignorant, profane, and vicious clergy, learned in nothing but the antiquity of their pride, their covetousness, and superstition ? whose unsincere and leavenous doctrine, corrupting the people, first taught them looseness, then bondage ; loosening them from all sound know-ledge and strictness of life, the more to fit them for the bondage of tyranny and superstition. So that what was left us for other nations not to pity, rather than admire or envy, all those seventeen years, no wise man could see. For wealth and plenty in a land where justice reigns not is no argument of a flourishing state, but of a nearness rather to ruin or commotion.

These were not "some miscarriages" only of government, "which might escape," but a universal distemper, and reduce-ment of law to arbitrary power ; not through the evil counsels of "some men," but through the constant course and practice of all that were in highest favour : whose worst actions frequently avowing he took upon himself ; and what faults did not yet seem in public to be originally his, such care he took by professing and proclaiming openly, as made them all at length his own adopted sins. The persons also, when he could no longer protect, he esteemed and favoured to the end ; but never otherwise than by constraint yielded any of them to due punishment ; thereby manifesting that what they did was by his own authority and approbation.

(From *Eikonoklastes*.)

JUSTICE ABOVE THE KING

IT might be well thought by him who reads no further than the title of this last essay, that it required no answer. For all other human things are disputed, and will be variously thought of to the world's end. But this business of death is a plain case, and admits no controversy : in that centre all opinions meet. Nevertheless, since out of those few mortifying hours that should have been entirest to themselves, and most at peace from all passion and disquiet, he can afford spare time to inveigh bitterly against that justice which was done upon him ; it will be needful to say something in defence of those proceedings, though briefly, in regard so much on this subject hath been written lately.

It happened once, as we find in Esdras and Josephus, authors not less believed than any under sacred, to be a great and solemn debate in the court of Darius, what thing was to be counted strongest of all other. He that could resolve this, in reward of his excellent wisdom, should be clad in purple, drink in gold, sleep on a bed of gold, and sit next Darius. None but they, doubtless, who were reputed wise had the question propounded to them ; who after some respite given them by the king to consider, in full assembly of all his lords and gravest counsellors, returned severally what they thought. The first held that wine was strongest ; another, that the king was strongest ; but Zorobabel, prince of the captive Jews, and heir to the crown of Judah, being one of them, proved women to be stronger than the king, for that he himself had seen a concubine take his crown from off his head to set it upon her own ; and others beside him have likewise seen the like feat done, and not in jest. Yet he proved on, and it was so yielded by the king himself, and all his sages, that neither wine, nor women, nor the king, but truth of all other things was the strongest.

For me, though neither asked, nor in a nation that gives such rewards to wisdom, I shall pronounce my sentence somewhat different from Zorobabel ; and shall defend that either truth and justice are all one (for truth is but justice in our knowledge, and justice is but truth in our practice), and he indeed so explains himself, in saying that with truth is no accepting of persons, which is the property of justice, or else if there be any odds, that justice, though not stronger than truth, yet by her office, is to put forth and exhibit more strength in the affairs of mankind. For truth is properly no more than contemplation; and her utmost efficiency is but teaching: but justice in her very essence is all strength and activity; and hath a sword put into her hand, to use against all violence and oppression on the earth. She it is most truly, who accepts no person, and exempts none from the severity of her stroke. She never suffers injury to prevail, but when falsehood first prevails over truth; and that also is a kind of justice done on them who are so deluded. Though wicked kings and tyrants counterfeit her sword, as some did that buckler fabled to fall from heaven into the capitol, yet she communicates her power to none but such as, like herself, are just, or at least will do justice. For it were extreme partiality and injustice, the flat denial and overthrow of herself, to put her own authentic sword into the hand of an unjust and wicked man, or so far to accept and exalt one mortal person above his equals, that he alone shall have the punishing of all other men transgressing, and not receive like punishment from men, when he himself shall be found the highest transgressor.

We may conclude, therefore, that justice, above all other things, is and ought to be the strongest; she is the strength, the kingdom, the power, and majesty of all ages. Truth herself would subscribe to this, though Darius and all the monarchs of the world should deny. And if by sentence thus written it were my happiness to set free the minds of Englishmen from longing to return poorly under that captivity of kings from which the strength and supreme sword of justice hath delivered them, I shall have done a work not much inferior to that of Zorobabel; who, by well-praising and extolling the force of truth, in that contemplative strength conquered Darius, and freed his country and the people of God from the captivity of Babylon. Which I shall yet not despair to do, if they in this land, whose minds are yet captive, be but as ingenuous to acknowledge the strength and supremacy of justice, as that heathen king was to confess the strength of truth: or let them but, as he did, grant that, and they will soon perceive that truth resigns all her outward strength to justice: justice therefore must needs be strongest, both in her own, and in the strength of truth. But if a king may do among men whatsoever is his will and pleasure, and notwithstanding be unaccountable to men, then, contrary to his magnified wisdom of Zorobabel, neither truth nor justice, but the king, is strongest of all other things, which that Persian monarch himself, in the midst of all his pride and glory, durst not assume.

Let us see, therefore, what this king hath to affirm, why the sentence of justice, and the weight of that sword, which she delivers into the hands of men, should be more partial to him offending, than to all others of human race. First, he pleads, that "no law of God or man gives to subjects any power of judicature without or against him." Which assertion shall be proved in every part to be most untrue. The first express law of God given to mankind was that to Noah, as a law, in general, to all the sons of men. And by that most ancient and universal law, "Whosoever sheddeth man's blood, by man shall his blood be shed," we find here no exception. If a king therefore do this, to a king, and that by men also, the same shall be done. This in the law of Moses, which came next, several times is repeated, and in one place remarkably, Numbers xxxv. "Ye shall take no satisfaction for the life of a murderer, but he shall surely be put to death : the land cannot be cleansed of the blood that is shed therein, but by the blood of him that shed it." This is so spoken as that which concerned all Israel, not one man alone, to see performed ; and if no satisfaction were to be taken, then certainly no exception. Nay, the king, when they should set up any, was to observe the whole law, and not only to see it done, but to "do it ; that his heart might not be lifted up above his brethren" ; to dream of vain and useless prerogatives or exemptions, whereby the law itself must needs be founded in unrighteousness.

And were that true, which is most false, that all kings are the Lord's anointed, it were yet absurd to think that the anointment of God should be, as it were, a charm against law, and give them privilege, who punish others, to sin themselves unpunishably. The high-priest was the Lord's anointed as well as any king, and with the same consecrated oil ; yet Solomon had put to death Abiathar, had it not been for other respects than that anointment. If God himself say to kings, "Touch not mine anointed," meaning his chosen people, as is evident in that Psalm, yet no man will argue thence, that he protects them from civil laws if they offend ; then certainly, though David, as a private man, and in his own cause, feared to lift his hand against the Lord's anointed, much less can this forbid the law, or disarm justice from having legal power against any king. No other supreme magistrate, in what kind of government soever, lays claim to any such enormous privilege; wherefore then should any king, who is but one kind of magistrate, and set over the people for no other end than they?

(From *Eikonoclastes*.)

PERSECUTION, PAPIST AND PROTESTANT

HOW many persecutions, then imprisonments, banishments, penalties, and stripes; how much bloodshed have the forcers of conscience to answer for, and protestants rather than papists! For the papist, judging by his principles, punishes them who believe not as the church believes, though against the scripture; but the protestant, teaching every one to believe the scripture, though against the church, counts heretical, and persecutes against his own principles, them who in any particular so believe as he in general teaches them; them who most honour and believe divine scripture, but not against any human interpretation though universal; them who interpret scripture only to themselves, which by his own position, none but they to themselves can interpret: them who use the scripture no otherwise by his own doctrine to their edification, than he himself uses it to their punishing; and so whom his docrine acknowledges a true believer, his discipline persecutes as a heretic. The papist exacts our belief as to the church due above scripture; and by the church, which is the whole people of God, understands the pope, the general councils, prelatical only, and the surnamed fathers: but the forcing protestant, though he deny such belief to any church whatsoever, yet takes it to himself and his teachers, of far less authority than to be called the church, and above scripture believed: which renders his practice both contrary to his belief, and far worse than that belief which he condemns in the papist. By all which, well considered, the more he professes to be a true protestant, the more he hath to answer for his persecuting than a papist. No protestant therefore, of what sect soever, following scripture only, which is the common sect wherein they all agree, and the granted rule of every man's conscience to himself, ought by the common doctrine of protestants to be forced or molested for religion. But as for popery and idolatry, why they also may not hence plead to be tolerated, I have much less to say. Their religion the more considered, the less can be acknowledged a religion ; but a Roman principality rather, endeavouring to keep up her old universal dominion under a new name, and mere shadow of a catholic religion ; being indeed more rightly named a catholic heresy against the scripture, supported mainly by a civil, and, except in Rome, by a foreign, power : justly therefore to be suspected, not tolerated, by the magistrate of another country. Besides, of an implicit faith which they profess, the conscience also becomes implicit, and so by voluntary servitude to man's law, forfeits her Christian liberty. Who then can plead for such a conscience, as being implicitly enthralled to man instead of God, almost becomes no conscience, as the will not free, becomes no will ? Nevertheless, if they ought not to be tolerated, it is for just reason of state, more than of religion ; which they who force, though professing to be protestants, deserve as little to be tolerated themselves, being no less guilty of popery in the most popish point. Lastly, for idolatry, who knows it not to be evidently against all scripture, both of the Old and New Testament, and therefore a true heresy, or rather an impiety, wherein a right conscience can have nought to do ; and the works thereof so manifest, that a magistrate can hardly err in prohibiting and quite removing at least the public and scandalous use thereof.

(From *A Treatise of Civil Power in Ecclesiastical Causes.*)

A PERPETUAL GRAND COUNCIL OF THE NATION

MILITARY men hold it dangerous to change the form of battle in view of an enemy : neither did the people of Rome bandy with their senate, while any of the Tarquins lived, the enemies of their liberty ; nor sought, by creating tribunes, to defend themselves against the fear of their patricians, till, sixteen years after the expulsion of their kings, and in full security of their state, they had or thought they had just cause given them by the senate. Another way will be, to well qualify and refine elections : not committing all to the noise and shouting of a rude multitude, but permitting only those of them who are rightly qualified, to nominate as many as they will; and out of that number others of a better breeding, to choose a less number more judiciously, till after a third or fourth sifting and refining of exactest choice, they only be left chosen who are the due number, and seem by most voices the worthiest.

To make the people fittest to choose, and the chosen fittest to govern, will be to mend our corrupt and faulty education, to teach the people faith, not without virtue, temperance, modesty, sobriety, parsimony, justice; not to admire wealth or honour; to hate turbulence and ambition; to place every one his private welfare and happiness in the public peace, liberty, and safety. They shall not then need to be much mistrustful of their chosen patriots in the grand council; who will be then rightly called the true keepers of our liberty, though the most of their business will be in foreign affairs. But to prevent all mistrust, the people then will have their several ordinary assemblies (which will henceforth quite annihilate the odious power and name of committees) in the chief towns of every county, without the trouble, charge, or time lost of summoning and assembling from far in so great a number, and so long residing from their own houses, or removing of their families, to do as much at home in their several shires, entire or subdivided, toward the securing of their liberty, as a numerous assembly of them all formed and convened on purpose with the wariest rotation. Whereof I shall speak more ere the end of this discourse; for it may be referred to time, so we be still going on by degrees to perfection. The people well weighing and performing these things, I suppose would have no cause to fear, though the parliament abolishing that name, as originally signifying but the parley of our lords and commons with the Norman king when he pleased to call them, should, with certain limitations of their power, sit perpetual, if their ends be faithful and for a free commonwealth, under the name of a grand or general council.

Till this be done, I am in doubt whether our state will be ever certainly and throughly settled; never likely till then to see an end of our troubles and continual changes, or at least never the true settlement and assurance of our liberty. The grand council being thus firmly constituted to perpetuity, and still, upon the death or default of any member, supplied and kept in full number, there can be no cause alleged, why peace, justice, plentiful trade, and all prosperity should not thereupon ensue throughout the whole land ; with as much assurance as can be of human things, that they shall so continue (if God favour us, and our wilful sins provoke him not) even to the coming of our true and rightful, and only to be expected King, only worthy as he is our only Saviour, the Messiah, the Christ, the only heir of his eternal Father, the only by him annointed and ordained, since the work of our redemption finished, universal Lord of all mankind.

The way propounded is plain, easy, and open before us ; without intricacies, without the introducement of new or absolute forms or terms, or exotic models ; ideas that would effect nothing ; but with a number of new injunctions to manacle the native liberty of mankind ; turning all virtue into prescription, servitude, and necessity, to the great impairing and frustrating of Christian liberty. I say again, this way lies free and smooth before us ; is not tangled with inconveniencies ; invents no new incumbrances ; requires no perilous, no injurious alteration or circumscription of men's lands and properties ; secure, that in this commonwealth, temporal and spiritual lords removed, no man or number of men can attain to such wealth or vast possession, as will need the hedge of an agrarian law (never successful, but the cause rather of sedition, save only where it began seasonably with first possession) to confine them from endangering our public liberty. To conclude, it can have no considerable objection made against it, that it is not practicable ; lest it be said hereafter, that we gave up our liberty for want of a ready way or distinct form proposed of a free commonwealth. And this facility we shall have above our next neighbouring commonwealth (if we can keep us from the fond conceit of something like a duke of Venice, put lately into many men's hands, by some one or other subtly driving on under that notion his own ambitious ends to lurch a crown), that our liberty shall not be hampered or hovered over by any engagement to such a potent family as the house of Nassau, of whom to stand in perpetual doubt and suspicion, but we shall live the clearest and absolutest free nation in the world.

On the contrary, if there be a king, which the inconsiderate multitude are now so mad upon, mark how far short we are like to come of all those happinesses which in a free state we shall immediately be possessed of. First, the grand council, which, as I showed before, should sit perpetually (unless their leisure give them now and then some intermissions or vacations, easily manageable by the council of state left sitting), shall be called, by the king's good will and utmost endeavour, as seldom as may be. For it is only the king's right, he will say, to call a parliament; and this he will do most commonly about his own affairs rather than the kingdom's, as will appear plainly so soon as they are called. For what will their business then be, and the chief expenses of their time, but an endless tugging between petition of right and royal prerogative, especially about the negative voice, militia, or subsidies, demanded and ofttimes extorted without reasonable cause appearing to the commons, who are the only true representatives of the people and their liberty, but will be then mingled with a court-faction; besides which, within their own walls, the sincere part of them who stand faithful to the people will again have to deal with two troublesome counter-working adversaries from without, mere creatures of the king, spiritual, and the greater part, as is likeliest of temporal lords, nothing concerned with the people's liberty.

If these prevail not in what they please, though never so much against the people's interest, the parliament shall be soon dissolved, or sit and do nothing; not suffered to remedy the least grievance, or enact aught advantageous to the people. Next, the council of state shall not be chosen by the parliament, but by the king, still his own creatures, courtiers, and favourers; who will be sure in all their counsels to set their master's grandeur and absolute power, in what they are able, far above the people's liberty. I deny not but that there may be such a king, who may regard the common good before his own, may have no vicious favourite, may hearken only to the wisest and incorruptest of his parliament: but this rarely happens in a monarchy not elective; and it behoves not a wise nation to commit the sum of their well-being, the whole state of their safety to fortune. What need they? and how absurd would it be, whenas they themselves, to whom his chief virtue will be but to hearken, may with much better management and dispatch, with much more commendation of their own worth and magnanimity, govern without a master? Can the folly be paralleled, to adore and be slaves of a single person, for doing that which it is ten thousand to one whether he can or will do, and we without him might do more easily, more effectually, more laudably ourselves? Shall we never grow old enough to be wise, to make seasonable use of gravest authorities,

experiences, examples? Is it such an unspeakable joy to serve,
such felicity to wear a yoke? to clink our shackles, locked on by
pretended law of subjection, more intolerable and hopeless to be
ever shaken off, than those which are knocked on by illegal
injury and violence?

(From *The Ready Way to Establish a Free Commonwealth.*)

ROBERT LEIGHTON

[Robert Leighton was born in 1611. He was the son of Alexander Leighton, author of *Zion's Plea against the Prelacy*, whose tortures for his faith are famous in the annals of Scotch Presbyterianism. He was educated at Edinburgh, where he graduated in 1631. He travelled in France, visited Douay, and was much influenced by the Jansenists. In 1641 he returned to Scotland, took orders, and became a minister at Newbattle. Here most of his sermons and expositions were written. In 1653 he was chosen Principal and Divinity Professor at Edinburgh. He accepted Episcopacy, at its establishment in 1661, and became successively Bishop of Dunblane in that year, and Archbishop of Glasgow in 1669. Here all his efforts were directed to the promotion of peace between the factions in the Church. Finding this impossible, he resigned his episcopate in 1674 and retired, first to college rooms at Edinburgh, then to Horsted Keynes in Sussex. He died in 1684.

Leighton's chief English works are Commentaries on *The First Epistle of St. Peter*, the first nine chapters of *The Gospel according to St. Matthew*, and other parts of the Bible, a tract entitled *Rules and Instructions for a Holy Life*, and a number of *Sermons*. He also wrote in Latin a series of addresses to university students. These writings were mostly published by Dr. Fall between 1692-1708. Among later editions are those of Doddridge (1748); Jerment (1805-8); Pearson (1825); Aikman (1831). All these editors commit the unpardonable crime of tampering with the original text. More satisfactory in this respect is the recent edition by Dr. West (1869-75, still unfinished). A volume of *Selections from Leighton* was published by Dr. Blair in 1884.]

ROBERT LEIGHTON is as a March swallow among Protestant theologians. Able controversialists, finished scholars, eloquent pulpiters, these the churches of England and Scotland can boast in plenty ; seldom do you find among their borders, more seldom still in their high places, a Pascal or a Thomas à Kempis. Not that such do not exist, but rather that they are inarticulate, bearing their witness by life instead of speech to the truth that is in them. Leighton is a remarkable exception ; above all things a spiritual divine, he has yet the gift of tongues to put his wisdom before the world in decent and profitable shape. It is but a lax prose, not ordered into periods and paragraphs, but ebbing and flowing comment-wise, as the exigencies of a text require it. The phrase is strong and sweet, a little careless perhaps, as of one disregarding the conventions of deliberate art. But at its best it rises into passages of extraordinary height, glowing with the rich fire of jewels, ringing with the harmonies of restrained music. Nor do such passages affect one as conscious rhetoric; they are not merely purple patches; every elevation of style corresponds directly to some moment of intensity or ecstasy in the course of the preacher's thought. Only Leighton lived in an age when sermons might still be literature; before the eighteenth century had ruled that colour and imagination were out of place in the pulpit. In him, as in Jeremy Taylor or in Donne, dignity of speech is not the first consideration; they are not so far removed, Latinised though they be, from the nervous homespun of Latimer.

Yet if Leighton is an artist, he is so, like Plato, in spite of himself; for of all his teaching, the first and last word is renunciation. The resemblance to Plato is no surface one; Plato is the father of all mystics, of all who, in their detachment from the world, confound its good and its ill in one condemnation, while they follow unceasingly the beatific vision. Such an one was Leighton, always aspiring, always ascetic, extravagant sometimes in his rejection of all mundane things, until with Guinevere, one often feels it impossible to

> " Breathe in that fine air,
> That pure severity of perfect light."

And with the character thus impressed upon his writing, the testimony of his contemporaries agrees. Burnet tells us, " I never knew him say an idle word, or one that had not a direct tendency to edification, and I never once saw him in any other temper but that which I wished to be in in the last minute of my life. The same spirit explains his indifference to the ecclesiastical disputes of his day. To be a peacemaker was his only part in them. He was asked once, so the story goes, " Whether he preached to the times." " Surely," he said, "you might permit a poor brother to preach Jesus Christ and eternity." It is the note of Leighton, both in his life and his writing, to have all the graces; but one misses some of the humanities. Burnet never saw him laugh, and very seldom even smile. So that his gospel is a little ineffective for want of sympathy with the heart of things—the laugh of things, " Broad as ten thousand beeves at pasture." Yet he has always been a consolation to the spiritually-minded. Bishop Jebb called him "a human seraph," and Coleridge, who based upon him the whole of his *Aids to Reflection*, " Plato fortified by St. Paul."

EDMUND K. CHAMBERS.

THE FLOWER OF THE GRASS

THIS is elegantly added. There is indeed a great deal of seeming difference betwixt the outward conditions of life amongst men. Shall the rich and honourable and beautiful and healthful go in together, under the same name, with the baser and unhappier part, the poor, wretched sort of the world, who seem to be born for nothing but sufferings and miseries? At least, hath the wise no advantage beyond the fools? Is all grass? Make you no distinction? No; all is grass, or if you will have some other name, be it so, once this is true, that all flesh is grass; and if that glory which shines so much in your eyes must have a difference, then this is all it can have,—it is but the flower of that same grass; somewhat above the common grass in gayness, a little comelier, and better apparelled than it, but partaker of its frail and fading nature; it hath no privilege nor immunity that way, yea, of the two, it is the less durable, and usually shorter lived; at the best it decays with it: "The grass withereth and the flower thereof falleth away."

How easily and quickly hath the highest splendour of a man's prosperity been blasted, either by men's power or by the immediate hand of God! "The Spirit of the Lord blows upon it" (as Isaiah says, chap. xl. 7), and by that, not only the grass withers, but the flower fades, though never so fair. "When thou correctest man for iniquity," says David, "thou makest his beauty to consume away like a moth," Psalm xxxix. 11. How many have the casualties of fire, or war, or shipwreck, in one day, or in one night, or in a small part of either, turned out of great riches into extreme poverty! And the instances are not few, of those who have on a sudden fallen from the top of honour into the foulest disgraces, not by degrees coming down the stair they went up, but tumbled down headlong. And the most vigorous beauty and strength of body, how doth a few days' sickness, or if it escape that, a few years' time, blast that flower ! Yea, those higher advantages which have somewhat both of truer and more lasting beauty in them, the endowments of wit and learning and eloquence, yea, and of moral goodness and virtue, yet they cannot rise above this word, they are still, in all their glory, but the flower of grass ; their root is in the earth. Natural ornaments are of some use in this present life, but they reach no further. When men have wasted their strength, and endured the toil of study night and day, it is but a small parcel of knowledge they can attain to, and they are forced to lie down in the dust in the midst of their pursuit of it : that head that lodges most sciences, shall within a while be disfurnished of them all ; and the tongue that speaks most languages be silenced.

The great projects of kings and princes, and they also themselves, come under this same notion ; all the vast designs that are framing in their heads fall to the ground in a moment ; " They return to their dust and in that day all their thoughts perish," Psalm cxlvi. 4. Archimedes was killed in the midst of his demonstration.

If they themselves did consider this in the heat of their affairs, it would much allay the swelling and loftiness of their minds ; and if they who live upon their favour would consider it, they would not value it at so high a rate, and buy it so dear as often they do. " Men of low degree are vanity," says the Psalmist (Psalm lxii. 9), but he adds, " men of high degree are a lie." From base, mean persons we expect nothing ; but the estate of great persons promises fair, and often keeps not its promise ; therefore they are a lie, although they can least endure that word. They are, in respect of mean persons, as the flower to the grass ; a somewhat fairer lustre they have, but no more endurance, nor exemption from decaying.

(From *Commentary on 1st Epistle of St. Peter.*)

THE VANITY OF LIFE

WHAT is this life we cleave so fast to and hear so unpleasantly of parting with, what is it but a continued train and succession of sorrows, a weary tossing and tottering upon the waves of vanity and misery ? If there be any that find it otherwise, they would do well to speak it out, for surely they would speak that that was never heard of from any other before. No estate or course of life is exempted from the sad causes of that complaint. Consider yourselves and look about you a little, it may be useful for you, ye that so unnecessarily and vainly look so much at and consider one another : take notice of all.

Those of the poorer and meaner sort, they are troubled with necessities and wants and pursuit of those things they have not, to supply their necessities ; and the greater and richer sort, they are troubled with the cares of managing what they have, and sometimes with the loss of it ; and the middle sort between the two, they partake in common of the vexations of both, for their life is spent in turmoil and cares of keeping what they have and getting more ; besides a world of miseries and evils that are common generally, and equally incident to all sorts of men. And this is one of them that is apparent here to have been David's case, sickness and pain of body ; and it is one of the closest and sharpest of evils, one that sits hard upon a man, and that he is least able, by any strength of mind or by any art or rule, to bear off the sense of it. And you will find this guest as often in palaces as in the meanest cottages ; as many groans of sick and diseased persons within silken curtains as in the meanest lodging. And David, that is here our instance, he was a king, and, as is most likely by the circumstances we find, was now well advanced in years and come to the kingdom, and in possession of it ; and yet here he was, sick, smitten and sore vexed, and roared for grief of heart, as almost sinking, and forced to cry out, I am consumed by the blow of Thine hand. And for other things incident to the greatest persons, the ruin of their estates and places and of their greatness, we need not go far off to seek foreign and national examples. We know a very great and fresh instance of that kind, that we have before our eyes ; so that, after fullest survey and inquiry, this conclusion still remains, and is again to be repeated, no instance can be found to infringe it at all ; " Surely every man is altogether vanity."   (From *Expository Lecture on Psalm* xxxix.)

LIFE AND DEATH

NOT only public affairs, or the private concerns of others, but even our own matters should not concern us. It was a maxim of the Stoics that the necessities of life, such as food and raiment, are to be looked after, but that all the rest are great impertinencies. Such things as rich coaches, gorgeous apparel, stately buildings, sumptuous feasts, they are but for the pleasure and show of the world. A man that hath twenty lodgings can be but in one at once ; and though he have twenty different suits of attire, yet hath he but one body to cover, and can wear but one suit at a time ; and he that hath twenty dishes of meat on his table has but one belly to fill ; and for the rest *ad supervacua sudamus*, they are vain superfluities which we strain and strive after. All a rich man's furniture cannot cure a headache ; he may perhaps have more physicians and drugs than others, but for that he may have the less health. As for riches, we have had amongst us lately many lectures of their uncertainty ; they take wings and flee away, leaving those minds that idolised them sinking down to hell and desperation. It is an excellent posture of soul to be so fixed that although the frame of the creation should crack, it would be unmoved. The time is coming when they shall confess this, even when they are stretched upon their death-beds ; believe them then, for then they shall speak truth : like that courtier who, being on his death-bed, and being asked what he would have the king do for him, answered, " Nothing, except he can call back time again that I may repent."

O Death ! why do we not converse more with thee ? Death shall shortly hurry all away before it ; yea, it shall strip the nobles and judges of their robes, and shall pull away the amorous gallant from the embraces of his beautiful mistress, and the bewitched lovers of this world from all which they either have in their possession or grasp after in their hopes. Death shall shake the lap of all men as they go out of this world suffering them to take nothing forth but what they brought into the world with them, save the guilt of their sins, and of their luxury in abusing what God bestowed upon them. That and other sins shall say to a man, *Nos tua sumus, et te sequemur*, we are thine, and we will follow thee. These black troops clapping an arrest upon the soul, quit her not until they have delivered her to the jailor of the bottomless pit.

(From *A Sermon upon Present Duty*.)

DAVID AND SOLOMON: THEIR EXPERIENCE OF LIFE

THIS same verdict we have from his son Solomon, after much experience in all things; who, having the advantage of peace and riches, did particularly set himself to this work, to a most exact enquiry after all things of this earth. He set nature on the rack, to confess its utmost strength for the delighting and satisfying of man; with much pains and art he extracted the very spirit of all, and, after all, he gives the same judgment we have here; his book writ on the subject being a paraphrase on this sentence, dilating the sense and confirming the truth of it. It carries its own sum in those two words which begin and end it; the one, "Vanity of vanities, all is vanity," and the other, "Fear God and keep His commandments, for that is the whole duty of man." And these here are just the equivalent of those two; the former of that beginning word, "I have seen an end of all perfection," and the latter of that concluding one, "But Thy commandment is exceeding broad."

When mean men speak of the vanity of this world's greatness, and poor men cry down riches, it passes but for a querulous, peevish humour to discredit things they cannot reach, or else an ignorant misprision of things they do not understand; or, taking it a little further, but a self-pleasing shift, a willingly under-prizing of these things of purpose to allay the displeasure of the want of them; or, at the best, if something of truth and goodness be in the opinion yet, that the assent of such persons is (like the temperance of sickly bodies) rather a virtue made of necessity than embraced of free choice. But to hear a wise man, in the height of these advantages, proclaim their vanity, yea, kings from the very thrones whereon they sit in their royal robes, give forth this sentence upon all the glories and delights about them, is certainly above all exception. Here are two, the father and the son: the one raised from a mean condition to a crown; instead of a shepherd's staff, to wield a sceptre, and that after many afflictions and dangers in the way to it, which, to some palates, gives a higher relish and sweetness to honour than if it had slid on them ere they could feel it, in the cheap, easy way of an undebated succession. Or, if any think David's best days a little cloudy, by the remains of insurrections and oppositions, in that case usual, as the jumblings of the sea not fully quieted for a while after the storm is over; then, take the son, succeeding to as fair a day as heart can wish, both a complete calm of peace and a bright sunshine of riches and royal pomp, and be able to improve these to the highest. And yet both these are perfectly of the same mind on this great point. The son having peace and time for it, though a king, would make his throne a pulpit, and be a preacher of this one doctrine, to which the father's sentence is the fittest text I have seen.

(From *A Sermon upon Imperfection and Perfection*.)

RENUNCIATION

1. THOU shalt have much to do in mortifying of thy senses or five wits, which must be shut up in the crucified humanity of Christ, and be as they were plainly dead.

2. Thou must learn to have a continual eye inwardly to thy soul and spiritual life, as thou hast used heretofore to have all thy mind and regard to outward pleasure and worldly things.

3. Thou must submit and give thyself up to the discipline of Jesus, and become His scholar, resigning and compelling thyself altogether to obey Him in all things; so that thy willing and nilling thou do utterly cast away from thee, and do nothing without His license: at every word thou wilt speak, at every morsel thou wilt eat, at every stirring or moving of every article or member of thy body, thou must ask leave of Him in thy heart, and ask thyself whether, being so done, they be according to His will and holy example, and with sincere intention of His glory. And even the most necessary actions of thy life, though lawful, yet must be thus offered up with a true intention unto God, in the union of the most holy works and blessed merits of Christ.

4. Pray: "Lord Jesus, bind up in the merits of Thy blessed senses all my feeling and sensation, and all my wits and senses, that I hereafter never use them to any sensuality!"

5. Thus labour to come into this union and knitting up of thy senses in GOD and the Lord Jesus, and remain so fast unto the cross that thou never part from it, and st ll behave thy body and all thy senses as in the presence of the Lord thy God, and commit all things unto the most trusty providence of thy loving

Lord, who will then order all things delectably and sweetly for thee. Reckon all things beside Him for right nought ; and thus mayest thou come to wonderful illuminations and ghostly influences from the Lord thy God, if, for His love, thou canst crucify, renounce, and forsake perfectly thyself and all things.

6. Thou must so crucify thyself to all things, and love and desire God only with thy whole heart, that in this most strong and stedfast knot and union unto the will of God, if He would create hell in thee, or put thee therein, thou mightest be ready to offer thyself, by His grace, for His eternal honour and glory to suffer it, purely for His will and pleasure.

7. Thou must keep thy memory clean and pure, as it were a wedlock chamber, from all strange thoughts, fancies, and imaginations ; and it must be trimmed and adorned with holy imaginations and virtues of Christ's holy crucified life and passion, that God may continually and for ever rest therein. Pray to Him and say,

8. " Lord, instead of knowing Thee, I have sought to know wickedness and sin ; and whereas my will and desire were created to love Thee, I have lost that love, and declined to the creatures. While my memory ought to be filled with Thee ; I have painted it with the memory of innumerable fancies, not only of creatures but of sinful wickedness. Lord, blot out these by Thy blood and imprint Thy own blessed image on my soul, blessed Jesus, by that blood which issued from Thy most loving heart when Thou hangedst on the cross. So knit my soul to Thy most holy will that I may have no other will but Thine, and may be most heartily and fully content with whatsoever Thou wilt do with me in this world and for ever ; yea if Thou wilt put me in hell, to suffer all the pains there, so that I hate not nor sin against Thee, but retain Thy love, I may be content.

(From *Rules and Instructions for a Holy Life.*)

THE COMFORT OF BELIEF

EVERY one trusts to somewhat. As for honour and esteem and popularity, they are airy, vain things ; but riches seem a more solid work and fence, yet they are but a tower in conceit, not really. The rich man's wealth is his strong city and as a high wall is his own conceit ; but the name of the Lord is a strong tower indeed (Prov. xviii. 10, 11). This is the thing that all seek, some fence and fixing ; and here it is. We call you not to vexation and turmoil, but from it, and as St. Paul said, " Whom ye ignorantly worship, Him declare I unto you." Ye blindly and fruitlessly seek after the show and shadow instead of the substance. The true aiming at this fixedness of mind will secure that, though they that aim fall short, yet, by the way they will light on very pretty things that have some virtue in them, as they that seek the philosopher's stone. But the believer hath the thing, the secret itself of tranquillity and joy, and this turns all into gold, even iron chains into a crown of gold : while we look not at the things which are seen, but at the things which are not seen (2 Cor. iv. 17, 18).

This is the blessed and safe estate of believers. Who then can think they have a sad, heavy life ? Oh ! it is the only light-some, sweet, cheerful condition in the world. The rest of men are poor, rolling, unstayed things, every report shaking them, as the leaves of trees are shaken with the wind ; yea, lighter than these, they are as the chaff that the wind drives to and fro at its pleasure (Isa. vii. 2 ; Psa. 1-4). Would men but reflect and look in upon their own hearts, it is a wonder what vain childish things the most would find there, glad and sorry at things as light as the toys of children, at which they laugh and cry in a breath. How easily is the heart puffed up with a thing or a word that pleaseth us, bladder-like, swelled with a little air, and it shrinks in again in discouragement and fear, upon the touch of a needle point, which gives that air some vent.

What is the life of the greatest part but a continual tossing betwixt vain hopes and fears ? All their days are spent in these. Oh ! how vain a thing is man even in his best estate while he is nothing but himself—his heart not united to and fixed on God, disquieted in vain ! And how small a thing will do it. He needs no other than his own heart ; it may prove disquietment enough to himself : his thoughts are his tormentors.

I know some men are, by a stronger understanding and by moral principles, somewhat raised above the vulgar, and speak big of a certain constancy of mind ; but these are but flourishes, an acted bravery. Somewhat there may be that will hold out in some trials, but it will fall far short of this fixedness of faith. Troubles may so multiply as to drive them at length from their posture, and may come on so thick, with such violent blows, as will smite them out of their artificial guard, disorder all their Seneca and Epictetus, and all their own calm thoughts and high resolves. The approach of death, though they make a good mien and set the best face on it, or if not death, yet some other kind of terror, may seize on their spirits, which they are not able to shift off. But the soul trusting in God is prepared for all, not only for the calamities of war, pestilence, famine, poverty, or death, but in the saddest apprehensions of soul, beyond hope, believes in hope ; even in the darkest night casts anchor on God, reposes on Him when it sees no light.

(From *A Sermon on the Believer's Blessedness.*)

THE INHERITANCE

No spot of sin or sorrow there ; all pollution wiped away, and all tears with it ; no envy nor strife ; not as here among men, one supplanting another, one pleading and fighting against another, dividing this point of earth with fire and sword :—no, this inheritance is not the less by division, by being parted among so many brethren ; everyone hath it all, each his crown, and all agreeing on casting them down before His throne from whom they have received them, and in the harmony of His praises.

This inheritance is often called a kingdom, and a crown of glory. This last word may allude to those garlands of the ancients and this is its property, that the flowers in it are all amaranths (as a certain plant is named) and so it is called (1 Pet. v. 4) a crown of glory that fadeth not away.

No change at all there, no winter and summer : not like the poor comforts here, but a bliss always flourishing. The grief of the saints here is not so much for the changes of outward things as of their inward comforts. *Suavis hora, sed brevis mora.* Sweet presences of God they sometimes have, but they are short, and often interrupted ; but there no cloud shall come betwixt them and their sun ; they shall behold Him in His full brightness for ever. As there shall be no change in their beholding, so no weariness nor abatement of their delight in beholding. They sing a new song, always the same, and yet always new. The sweetest of our music, if it were to be heard but for one whole day, would weary them who are most delighted with it. What we have here cloys, but satisfies not; the joys above never cloy and yet always satisfy.

(From *The Commentary on the First Epistle of St. Peter.*)

SPIRITUAL SUNSHINE

WHEN the sun takes its course towards us in the spring season of the year, it drives away the sharp frosts and the heavy fogs of winter; it clears the heavens, decks the earth with variety of plants and flowers, and awakes the birds to the pleasant strains of their natural music. When Christ, after a kind of winter absence, returns to visit a declining church, admirable is the change that he produces : all begin to flourish by His sweet influence ; His house, His worship, His people, are all clothed with a new beauty ; but it is spiritual, and therefore none but spiritual eyes can discern it. When He will thus return, all the power and policy of man can no more hinder Him than it could stay the course of the sun in its circle. In like manner, a deserted, forsaken soul, that can do nothing but languish and droop while Christ withdraws Himself, what inexpressible vigour and alacrity finds it at His returning ! Then those graces which, while they lurked, seemed to have been lost and quite extinguished, bud forth anew with pleasant colour and fragrant smell. It is the light of His countenance that banisheth their false tears, that strengthens their faith, and cures their spiritual infirmities. This sun is indeed the sovereign physician : "Unto you that fear my name, shall the sun of righteousness arise with healing in his wings."

(From *Sermon on Christ the Light and Lustre of the Church.*)

JAMES HARRINGTON

[James Harrington, author of one of the strangest books ever written, even by a man in whom considerable wits were allied to less than doubtful sanity, was the eldest son of Sir Sapcotes Harrington, of Exton, in the county of Rutland. His mother's name was Jane Samuel, and the Harringtons themselves were connected with some of the best English families. James was born in January 1611, and when he was eighteen he entered Trinity College, Oxford, where Chillingworth was his tutor. He succeeded to the family estates while he was still a minor, made the grand tour, served a little, and though he did not marry till very late in life, was a liberal and domestic housekeeper. Although no Royalist he was something of a favourite with Charles I., was gentleman of the chamber to him, accompanied him in the ill-starred " Bishop's War," and after the Rebellion and the surrender at Newcastle was appointed by Parliament one of the King's attendants. He was dismissed as too well affected to his master at the time when Charles was sent to Hurst Castle, and was subsequently imprisoned, but was permitted to attend the King to the very scaffold. It was after this that he took to writing *Oceana*. It was printed during the Protectorate and seized, and though Harrington procured its release it is not improbable that the incident impelled or obliged him to insert the rather fulsome eulogies on Cromwell which may have helped to bring misfortune on him after the Restoration. Until that event, however, he was busy with controversy over his book, which was published in 1656, and with playing at ballot and such like things in the famous Rota Club. In December 1661, he was arrested, partly for his " meddling with politics," partly on suspicion real or feigned of participation in an actual plot. He was imprisoned in the Tower and then at Plymouth, where his health, both of body and mind, suffered severely, and he was at one time actually insane. He was at length released : he married, suffered from gout and paralysis as well as from impaired sanity, and finally died at Westminster on 11th September 1677, having, despite his later troubles, not come very far short of the three-score years and ten. The completest edition of his works is that of Birch, 1737. *Oceana*, which alone of them has much interest, was cheaply reprinted by Mr. Henry Morley a few years ago.]

IT is permissible to a reader of *Oceana*, after adjusting his mind to the exactest political impartiality, to suspect that Harrington was not perfectly sane a good many years before age or unkindness developed his mental malady. The second and third quarters of the seventeenth century no doubt produced abundance of work by men of undoubted sanity, which is in some respects as quaint as this sketch of a "Venetian Constitution" (very different from the meaning later attached to that phrase) for "Oceana" (England), "Marpesia" (Scotland), and "Panopea" (Ireland). But the quaintness of Burton and Browne, of Fuller and Digby, of Glanvill and Wilkins, never induces us to doubt the sanity of the writers for a moment. It is their pleasure to be far-fetched, allusive, abrupt, full of conceits and "metaphysical" oddities, to parade learning in and out of season; but it can hardly be said that their wildest conceits ever run away with them. It is impossible to read even a few pages of *Oceana* without suspecting that in this case the running away is an accomplished fact. Harrington is full of ability, he has studied theoretical politics with immense care, he has observed certain sides of actual politics not without acuteness: he has just censures of *Leviathan* to which his own work is in a manner a counterblast: he is extraordinarily ingenious in the arrangement of the Tribes and the Troops, of the ballot machinery and the "Provincial Orb." But in all this and in the relish with which he draws up accounts for the ballot boxes and the balls of metal and the pavilions, devises elaborate and rather poetical titles for his tribes and their officers, intersperses comic speeches by the "Lord Epimonus" (a genial fanatic of reaction), and adjusts rejoinders to them by the Lord Archon (Cromwell), which are in some respects almost startlingly like Cromwell's own speeches: in all this I say it is almost impossible not to detect what is familiarly called the bee in the bonnet. The abstract principles of Harrington's polity, which may be said to be a fixed maximum of property to be held by individuals, a strict rotation of office-tenure by ballot, and a complicated regulation of all public and even some private details of life, after the model, now of Venice, now of Lacedaemon, might not *in vacuo* be absurd. But it is evident that Harrington had neither the least desire to adjust nor the least faculty of adjusting these abstract ideas to the concrete facts of English character, life, and history. He was seriously taken by his own time, and long afterwards references are found to the *Oceana* in Swift's first serious political work the *Dissensions in Athens and Rome*. But *Oceana* is really moonshine,—a Midsummer Night's Dream of politics, compared with which Utopia and Atlantis are practical projects.

Such things, however, can in literature be very agreeable:

and Harrington's book has many charms. What has been called in other matter " the rich marrowy quality " of it is especially remarkable. Even such a small thing as the constant omission of " law " in the long discussion on the Agrarian provisions of his scheme (" there is in this Agrarian a homage to pure and spotless love," " the Agrarian gives us the sweat of our brows without diminution ") gives a singular zest to the treatise. My Lord Epimonus's speeches have throughout an almost Shakespearean, a more than Jonsonian savour of farce, and though the Archon is frequently unintelligible, as indeed was his great original, he is the equal of that original in pregnancy and his superior in brilliance. The boldness of the metaphors (" this order was thus *fleshed* by the Lord Archon " : " this if they be planted popularly comes to a commonwealth ") is unsurpassed even in the seventeenth century, and certainly not equalled elsewhere in English literary history. This novel and sustaining quality of style carries us through what has been and would otherwise have been justly called the " prolixity dulness, and pedantry " of the book, supports us in its argumentative atmosphere, as of an exhausted receiver, and enables us to do justice, and sometimes perhaps more than justice, to the solid and acute observations which occur from time to time. Harrington was almost certainly mad : and his madness may be a little exasperating when we think of the state of the times and of the necessity which existed for every good citizen to come out of his study and do practical work. But it was a fine madness in its way, and would have been an eminently harmless one in other times.

GEORGE SAINTSBURY.

THE POLITICAL WISDOM OF GIRLS

MANKIND then must either be less just than the creature, or acknowledge also his common interest to be common right. And if reason be nothing else but interest, and the interest of mankind be the right interest, then the reason of mankind must be right reason. Now compute well; for if the interest of popular government come the nearest to the interest of mankind, then the reason of popular government must come the nearest to right reason.

But it may be said that the difficulty remains yet; for be the interest of popular government right reason, a man does not look upon reason as it is right or wrong in itself, but as it makes for him or against him. Wherefore, unless you can show such orders of a government as, like those of God in Nature, shall be able to constrain this or that creature to shake off that inclination which is more peculiar to it, and take up that which regards the common good or interest, all this is to no more end than to persuade every man in a popular government not to carve himself of that which he desires most, but to be mannerly at the public table, and give the best from himself to decency and the common interest. But that such orders may be established as may, nay must, give the upper hand in all cases to common right or interest, notwithstanding the nearness of that which sticks to every man in private, and this in a way of equal certainty and facility, is known even to girls, being no other than those that are of common practice with them in divers cases. For example, two of them have a cake yet undivided, which was given between them: that each of them therefore might have that which is due, "divide," says one to the other, "and I will choose; or let me divide, and you shall choose." If this be but once agreed upon, it is enough; for the divident, dividing unequally, loses, in regard that the other takes the better half; wherefore she divides equally, and so both

have right. " O the depth of the wisdom of God !" and yet "by
the mouths of babes and sucklings has He set forth His strength ; "
that which great philosophers are disputing upon in vain, is
brought to light by two harmless girls, even the whole mystery of
a commonwealth, which lies only in dividing and choosing. Nor
has God (if His works in Nature be understood) left so much to
mankind to dispute upon as who shall divide and who choose, but
distributed them for ever into two orders, whereof the one has the
natural right of dividing, and the other of choosing. For example :

A commonwealth is but a civil society of men : let us take any
number of men (as twenty) and immediately make a commonwealth. Twenty men (if they be not all idiots, perhaps if they
be) can never come so together but there will be such a difference
in them, that about a third will be wiser, or at least less foolish
than all the rest ; these upon acquaintance, though it be but
small, will be discovered, and, as stags that have the largest
heads lead the herd ; for while the six, discoursing and arguing
one with another, show the eminence of their parts, the fourteen
discover things that they never thought on ; or are cleared in
divers truths which had formerly perplexed them. Wherefore,
in matter of common concernment, difficulty, or danger, they
hang upon their lips, as children upon their fathers ; and the
influence thus acquired by the six, the eminence of whose parts
are found to be a stay and comfort to the fourteen, is the authority
of the fathers. Wherefore this can be no other than a natural
aristocracy diffused by God throughout the whole body of mankind
to this end and purpose ; and therefore such as the people have
not only a natural but a positive obligation to make use of as
their guides ; as where the people of Israel are commanded to
"take wise men, and understanding, and known among their
tribes, to be made rulers over them." The six then approved of,
as in the present case, are the senate, not by hereditary right, or
in regard of the greatness of their estates only, which would tend
to such power as might force or draw the people, but by election
for their excellent parts, which tends to the advancement of the
influence of their virtue or authority that leads the people.
Wherefore the office of the senate is not to be commanders, but
counsellors of the people ; and that which is proper to counsellors
is first to debate, and afterward to give advice in the business
whereupon they have debated, whence the decrees of the senate
are never laws, nor so called ; and these being maturely framed,

it is their duty to propose in the case to the people. Wherefore the senate is no more than the debate of the commonwealth. But to debate, is to discern or put a difference between things that, being alike, are not the same ; or it is separating and weighing this reason against that, and that reason against this, which is dividing.

The senate then having divided, who shall choose ? Ask the girls : for if she that divided must have chosen also, it had been little worse for the other in case she had not divided at all, but kept the whole cake to herself, in regard that being to choose too she divided accordingly. Wherefore if the senate have any farther power than to divide, the commonwealth can never be equal. But in a commonwealth consisting of a single council, there is no other to choose than that which divided ; whence it is, that such a council fails not to scramble—that is, to be factious, there being no other dividing of the cake in that case but among themselves.

Nor is there any remedy but to have another council to choose. The wisdom of the few may be the light of mankind ; but the interest of the few is not the profit of mankind, nor of a commonwealth. Wherefore, seeing we have granted interest to be reason, they must not choose lest it put out their light. But as the council dividing consists of the wisdom of the commonwealth, so the assembly or council choosing should consist of the interest of the commonwealth : as the wisdom of the commonwealth is in the aristocracy, so the interest of the commonwealth is in the whole body of the people. And whereas this, in case the commonwealth consist of a whole nation, is too unwieldy a body to be assembled, this council is to consist of such a representative as may be equal, and so constituted, as can never contract any other interest than that of the whole people ; the manner whereof, being such as is best shown by exemplification, I remit to the model. But in the present case, the six dividing, and the fourteen choosing, must of necessity take in the whole interest of the twenty.

(From *Oceana.*)

THE CASE FOR THE AGRARIAN

" My Lords, the Legislators of Oceana.

" My Lord Philautus has made a thing which is easy to seem hard ; if the thanks were due to his eloquence, it would be worthy of less praise than that he owes it to his merit, and the love he has most deservedly purchased of all men : nor is it rationally to be feared that he who is so much beforehand in his private, should be in arrear in his public, capacity. Wherefore, my lord's tenderness throughout his speech arising from no other principle than his solicitude lest the Agrarian should be hurtful to his country, it is no less than my duty to give the best satisfaction I am able to so good a patriot, taking every one of his doubts in the order proposed. And,

" First, Whereas my lord, upon observation of the modern commonwealths, is of opinion that an Agrarian is not necessary : it must be confessed that at the first sight of them there is some appearance favouring his assertion, but upon accidents of no precedent to us. For the commonwealths of Switzerland and Holland, I mean of those leagues, being situated in countries not alluring the inhabitants to wantonness, but obliging them to universal industry, have an implicit Agrarian in the nature of them ; and being not obnoxious to a growing nobility (which, as long as their former monarchies had spread the wing over them, could either not at all be hatched, or was soon broken) are of no example to us, whose experience in this point has been to the contrary. But what if even in these governments there be indeed an explicit Agrarian ? For when the law commands an equal or near equal distribution of a man's estate in land among his children, as it is done in those countries, a nobility cannot grow ; and so there needs no Agrarian, or rather there is one. And for the growth of the nobility in Venice (if so it be, for Machiavel observes in that republic, as a cause of it, a great mediocrity of estates) it is not a point that she is to fear, but might study, seeing she consists of nothing else but nobility ; by which, whatever their estates suck from the people, especially if it comes equally, is digested into the better blood of that commonwealth, which is all, or the greatest, benefit they can have by accumulation. For how unequal soever you will have them to be in their incomes, they have officers of the pomp, to bring them equal in expenses, or at least in the ostentation or show of them. And so unless the advantage of an estate consists more in the measure than in the use of it, the authority of Venice does but enforce our Agrarian ; nor shall a man evade or elude the prudence of it, by the authority of any other commonwealth. For if a commonwealth has been introduced at once, as those of Israel and Lacedemon, you are certain to find her underlaid with this as the main foundation ; nor, if she is obliged more to fortune than prudence, has she raised her head without musing upon this matter, as appears by that of Athens, which through her defect in this point, says Aristotle, introduced her ostracism, as most of the democracies of Greece. But, not to restrain a fundamental of such latitude to any one kind of government, do we not yet see that if there be a sole landlord of a vast territory, he is the Turk ? that if a few landlords overbalance a populous country, they have store of servants ? that if a people be in an equal balance, they can have no lords ? that no government can otherwise be erected, than upon some one of these foundations ? that no one of these foundations (each being else apt to change into some other) can give any security to the government, unless it be fixed ? that through the want of this fixation, potent monarchy and commonwealths have fallen upon the heads of the people, and accompanied their own sad ruins with vast effusions of innocent blood ? Let the fame, as was the merit of the ancient nobility of this nation, be equal to or above what has been already said, or can be spoken, yet have we seen not only their glory, but that of a throne, the most indulgent to and least invasive for so many ages upon the liberty of a people that the world has known, through the mere want of fixing her foot by a proportionable Agrarian upon her proper foundation, to have fallen with such horror as has been a spectacle of astonishment to the whole earth. And were it well argued from one calamity, that we ought not to prevent another ? Nor is Aristotle so good a commonwealthsman for deriding the invention of Phaleas as in recollecting himself, where he says that democracies, when a less part of their citizens overtop the rest in wealth, degenerate into oligarchies and principalities ; and, which comes nearer to the present purpose, that the greater part of the nobility of Tarentum coming accidentally to be ruined, the government of the few came by consequence to be changed into that of the many. (From the Same

THE SPEECH OF THE LORD EPIMONUS DE GARRULA

" MAY it please your Highness, my Lord Archon,—

"Under correction of Mr. Peregrin Spy, our very learned agent and intelligencer, I have seen the world a little, Venice, and (as gentlemen are permitted to do) the great council balloting. And truly I must needs say, that it is for a dumb show the goodliest that I ever beheld with my eyes. You should have some would take it ill, as if the noble Venetians thought themselves too good to speak to strangers, but they observed them not so narrowly. The truth is, they have nothing to say to their acquaintance ; or men that are in council sure would have tongues : for a council, and not a word spoken in it, is a contradiction. But there is such a pudder with their marching and countermarching, as, though never a one of them draw a sword, you would think they were training ; which till I found that they did it only to entertain strangers, I came from among them as wise as I went thither. But in the parliament of Oceana you had no balls nor dancing, but sober conversation ; a man might know and be known, show his parts, and improve them. And now if you take the advice of this same fellow, you will spoil all with his whimsies. Mr. Speaker —cry you mercy, my Lord Archon, I mean—set the wisest man of your house in the great council of Venice, and you will not know him from a fool. Whereas nothing is more certain than that flat and dull fellows in the judgment of all such as used to keep company with them before, upon election into our house, have immediately chitted, like barley in the vat where it acquires a new spirit, and flowed forth into language, that I am as confident as I am here, if there were not such as delight to abuse us, is far better than Tully's ; or, let anybody but translate one of his orations, and speak it in the house, and see if everybody do not laugh at him. This is a great matter, Mr. Speaker ; they do not cant it with your book-learning, your orbs, your centres, your prime magnitudes, and your nebulones, things I profess that would make a sober man run stark mad to hear them ; while we, who should be considering the honour of our country, and that it goes now or never upon our hand, whether it shall be ridiculous to all the world, are going to *nine-holes* or *trow madam* for our business,

like your dumb Venetian, whom this same Sir Politic your resident,
that never saw him do any thing but make faces, would insinuate
into you, at this distance, to have the only knack of state.
Whereas if you should take the pains, as I have done, to look a
little nearer, you would find these same wonderful things to be
nothing else but mere natural fopperies, or *capriccios*, as they call
them in Italian, even of the meanest, of that nation.   For, put
the case you be travelling in Italy, ask your *contadino*, that is, the
next country-fellow you meet, some question, and presently he
ballots you an answer with a nod, which is affirmative ; or a shake
with his head, which is the negative box ; or a shrug with his
shoulder, which is the *bossolo di non sinceri*.   Good !   You will
admire Sandys for telling you, that *grotto di cane* is a miracle :
and I shall be laughed at, for assuring you, that it is nothing else
but such a damp (continued by the neighbourhood of certain
sulphur mines) as through accidental heat does sometimes happen
in our coalpits.   But ingratitude must not discourage an honest
man from doing good.   There is not, I say, such a tongue-tied
generation under heaven as your Italian, that you should not
wonder if he make signs.   But our people must have something
in their diurnals ; we must ever and anon be telling them our
minds ; or if we be at it when we raise taxes, like those gentlemen with the finger and the thumb, they will swear that we are
cutpurses.   Come, I know what I have heard them say, when
some men had money that wrought hard enough for it ; and do
you conceive they will be better pleased when they shall be told
that upon like occasions you are at mumchance or stool-ball ?   I
do not speak for myself ; for though I shall always acknowledge
that I got more by one year's sitting in the house than by my
three years' travels, it was not of that kind.   But I hate that this
same Spy, for pretending to have played at billiards with the most
serene commonwealth of Venice, should make such fools of us
here, when I know that he must have had his intelligence from
some corncutter upon the Rialto ; for a noble Venetian would be
hanged if he should keep such a fellow company.   And yet if I
do not think he has made you all dote, never trust me, my Lord
Archon is sometimes in such strange raptures.   Why, good my
lord, let me be heard as well as your apple squire.   Venice has
fresh blood in her cheeks, I must confess, yet she is but an old
lady.   Nor has he picked her cabinet ; these he sends you are
none of her receipts, I can assure you ; he bought them for a Julio

at St. Mark's of a mountebank. She has no other wash, upon my knowledge, for that same envied complexion of hers but her marshes. My lords, I know what I say, but you will never have done with it, that neither the great Turk, nor any of those little Turks her neighbours, have been able to spoil her! Why you may as well wonder that weasels do not suck eggs in swans' nests. Do you think that it has lain in the devotion of her beads? which you that have puked so much at Popery, are now at length resolved shall consecrate Mr. Parson, and he dropped by every one of his congregation, while those same whimsical intelligences your surveyors (you will break my heart) give the turn to your *primum mobile!* And so I think they will; for you will find that money is the *primum mobile*, and they will turn you thus out of some three or four hundred thousand pounds: a pretty sum for urns and balls, for boxes and pills, which these same quacksalvers are to administer to the parishes; and for what disease I marvel! Or how does it work? Out comes a constable, an overseer, and a churchwarden! Mr. Speaker, I am amazed!"

(From the Same.)

INEQUALITY IN COMMONWEALTHS

UPON these three last orders the Archon seemed to be haranguing at the head of his army in this manner:

"My dear Lords and excellent Patriots,—

"A government of this make is a commonwealth for increase. Of those for preservation, the inconveniences and frailties have been shown; their roots are narrow, such as do not run, have no fibres, their tops weak and dangerously exposed to the weather, except you chance to find one, as Venice, planted in a flower-pot, and if she grows, she grows top-heavy, and falls too. But you cannot plant an oak in a flower-pot; she must have earth for her root, and heaven for her branches.

Imperium Oceano, famam quæ terminet astris.

"Rome was said to be broken by her own weight, but poetically; for that weight by which she was pretended to be ruined, was supported in her emperors by a far slighter foundation. And in the common experience of good architecture, there is nothing more known than that buildings stand the firmer and the longer for their own weight, nor ever swerve through any other internal cause than that their materials are corruptible ; but the people never die, nor, as a political body, are subject to any other corruption than that which derives from their government.   Unless a man will deny the chain of causes, in which he denies God, he must also acknowledge the chain of effects ; wherefore there can be no effect in Nature that is not from the first cause, and those successive links of the chain without which it could not have been. Now except a man can show the contrary in a commonwealth, if there be no cause of corruption in the first make of it, there can never be any such effect.   Let no man's superstition impose profaneness upon this assertion ; for as man is sinful, but yet the universe is perfect, so may the citizen be sinful, and yet the commonwealth be perfect.   And as man, seeing the world is perfect, can never commit any such sin as shall render it imperfect, or bring it to a natural dissolution, so the citizen, where the commonwealth is perfect, can never commit any such crime as will render it imperfect, or bring it to a natural dissolution.   To come to experience : Venice, notwithstanding we have found some flaws in it, is the only commonwealth in the make whereof no man can find a cause of dissolution ; for which reason we behold her (though she consists of men that are not without sin) at this day with one thousand years upon her back, yet for any internal cause, as young, as fresh, and free from decay, or any appearance of it, as she was born ; but whatever in Nature is not sensible of decay by the course of a thousand years, is capable of the whole age of Nature ; by which calculation, for any check that I am able to give myself, a commonwealth, rightly ordered, may for any internal causes be as immortal or long-lived as the world.   But if this be true, those commonwealths that are naturally fallen, must have derived their ruin from the rise of them.   Israel and Athens died not natural but violent deaths, in which manner the world itself is to die.   We are speaking of those causes of dissolution which are natural to government ; and they are but two, either contradiction or inequality.   If a commonwealth be a contradiction, she must needs destroy herself ; and if she be unequal, it tends to strife, and strife to ruin.   By the former of these fell Lacedemon, by the latter Rome.   Lacedemon being made altogether for war, and yet not for increase, her natural progress became her natural dissolution, and the building of her own victorious hand too heavy for her foundation, so that she fell indeed by her own weight. But Rome perished through her native inequality, which how it inveterated the bosoms of the senate and the people each against other, and even to death, has been shown at large.

(From the Same.)

SAMUEL BUTLER

[Samuel Butler was born in 1612 and died in 1680. *The Genuine Remains in Verse and Prose of Mr. Samuel Butler, Author of Hudibras,* were published in 1759 by R. Thyer, Keeper of the Public Library at Manchester. Less than half of the two volumes is in verse; the remainder, in prose, consists of a few tracts, principally of political satire and controversy, a series of *Characters* belonging to the same class of writing as Sir Thomas Overbury's and Earle's *Microcosmography,* and a few selections from Butler's commonplace-books. The editor had manuscript authority for most, not all, of the contents of his book, and the British Museum possesses some of the manuscript sources in Butler's own hand, and some of Mr. Thyer's transcripts. Of these MSS. a considerable portion remains unedited : sixty-six characters transcribed but not sent to the press,—one of them being the character of a publisher,—and a great quantity of miscellaneous notes, for which Butler himself has provided headings, "Learning and Knowledge," "Religion," "Reason," "Opinion," "Nature," "History" (with a notice of the Kingdom of Yvetot), "Princes and Governments," "Contradictions." The last, with "Inconsistent Opinions," is a favourite theme. Of the series of *Characters* there are four in the author's hand, written out fair, numbered and paged, with English headings in Greek letters ; "Bankrupt," numbered *202,* paged *237,* dated 6th October '67 ; "War," *206,* 13th October '67 ; "Horse-courser," *204,* 8th October '67 ; "Churchwarden," *203,* 8th October '67. At least twenty of these essays seem to have been lost. The character of "an Hector" is here printed from the MS. (Add. *32,626*) ; the other three are from the *Remains.*]

HUDIBRAS contains the essence of Butler's studies; the ingredients of his satire are to be found in his prose collections ;[1] his prose essays refer, sometimes explicitly, to the work by which he had made his name. But though *Hudibras* is Butler's master-

---

[1] "I am informed by Mr. Thyer of Manchester, the excellent editor of this author's reliques, that he could show something like *Hudibras* in prose. He has in his possession the commonplace-book, in which Butler reposited, not such events or precepts as are gathered by reading, but such remarks, similitudes, allusions, assemblages, or influences, as occasion prompted, or meditation produced ; those thoughts that were generated in his own mind, and might be usefully applied to some future purpose. Such is the labour of those who write for immortality."—JOHNSON : *Life of Butler.*

piece, it does not reveal the whole of his mind. In *Hudibras*
things are finished and pointed ; but much of the author's life
was spent in what he is fond of calling " owl-light," and in a
mood too sore to be contented with epigram. The resemblance
between Butler and Swift, which is not marked in *Hudibras*,
comes out strongly in Butler's prose. It is not only that both
Butler and Swift are disposed to take the claims of modern
science rather lightly, or to parody Boyle's *Meditations*. The
resemblance is deeper than that ; it lies in their common devotion
to an ideal of a reasonable life, free from exaggeration ; in their
want of mercy for confusion of thought, and disproportion in
studies, for the pretentions of philosophers and theologians, for
the enthusiasms of the dunce, and the infallibility of the churl.
Butler is not hopeful : he loses his good spirits when he takes off
the mask of Harlequin. " In religion and the civil life the wisest
and ablest are fain to comply and submit to the weakest and
most ignorant for their own quiet and convenience." And "all
the business of the world is but diversion, and all the happiness
in it than mankind is capable of, anything that will keep it from
reflecting upon the misery, vanity, and nonsense of it ; and whoever can by any trick keep himself from thinking of it, is as wise
and happy as the best man in it."

In so far as this temper is to be found in the prose fragments,
they are the complement of *Hudibras*, and a better document for
the interpretation of Butler's mind. *Hudibras* is too glaring, and
cannot express the simpler ideas of Butler. His ruling and
characteristic ideas are generally quite simple and unaffected, and
the chief of them is an admiration of simplicity and of good sense.
Together with that, there is the conviction of the rarity of good
sense, and the impression that the ways of the world are generally extravagant. " This age will serve to make a very pretty
farce for the next, if it have any wit to make use of it." The
satire and the fancy of Butler are to be found in *Hudibras*, but
his irony and the sublimer form of contempt are in his prose.

The *Characters* are very various, some of them commonplace,
and not in any striking way distinguishable from the common
form in this kind of writing. Some of them, however, are drawn
from the life, and touched off with all the skill of the master of
surprises and strange analogies. One is an undisguised portrait of
" A Duke of Bucks " : this is the prose counterpart of the character of Zimri. " He endures pleasures with less patience than

other men do their pains." The character of "a small poet" has some general traits in it :—" he calls a slovenly nasty description *great Nature*, and dull flatness *strange easiness*." It is meant, however, as the author is at no trouble to hide, for Edward Benlowes. The Rosicrucian philosophers are portrayed with equal care, and with much less ill-will : " they are now carrying on a *thorough Reformation* in the celestial world—they have repaired the old spheres, that were worn as thin as a cob-web, and fastened the stars in them with a screw, by which means they may be taken off and put on again at pleasure." Among the more general descriptions there are not wanting strokes as cutting as the jerk of the rhymes of *Hudibras*. As in the account of the Ranter :—" he is a monster produced by the madness of this latter age, but if it had been his fate to have been whelp'd in old Rome, he had past for a prodigy, and had been received among raining of stones and the speaking of bulls, and would have put a stop to all public affairs until he had been expiated." In the more conventional characters it is not infrequent to come upon pieces of wit like this variation on the old theme of the moralists —pride in clothes—" his soul dwells in the outside of him, *like that of a hollow tree*"—a figure that is poetically right, and imaginative.

The style of the *Characters* was fixed by tradition when Butler wrote, and he does not reject the established form, except occasionally in the greater length of some of his essays, and in the personal references. Of his other writings many are burlesque or mock-heroic—the *Speech made at the Rota, John Audland's Letter to William Prynne*, and *William Prynne's to John Audland*, and the *Occasional Reflection on Dr. Charlton's Feeling a Dog's Pulse at Gresham College, by R. B., Esq.* The *Two Speeches made in the Rump Parliament, when it was restored by the Officers of the Army in the year* 1659, are more serious arguments, in which the Presbyterians and the Independents are made dramatically to annihilate one another. In *The Royal Martyr vindicated against John Cook, and several others, Pains-takers in the Mysteries of Rebellion*, Butler uses the common weapons of serious controversy.

W. P. KER.

A RABBLE

A RABBLE is a congregation or assembly of the states-general
sent from their respective shops, stalls, and garrets. They are
full of controversy, and every one of a several judgment concerning the business under present consideration, whether it be
mountebank, show, hanging, or ballad-singer. They meet, like
Democritus's atoms *in vacuo*, and by a fortuitous justling together
produce the greatest and most savage beast in the whole world :
for, though the members of it may have something of human nature
while they are asunder, when they are put together, they have
none at all ; as a multitude of several sounds make one great
noise unlike all the rest, in which no one particular is distinguished.
They are a great dunghill, where all sorts of dirty and nasty
humours meet, stink, and ferment ; for all the parts are in a
perpetual tumult. 'Tis no wonder they make strange churches,
for they take naturally to any imposture, and have a great
antipathy to truth and order, as being contrary to their original
confusion. They are a herd of swine possessed with a dry
devil, that run after hanging, instead of drowning. Once a
month they go on pilgrimage to the gallows, to visit the
sepulchres of their ancestors, as the Turks do once a week.
When they come there they sing psalms, quarrel, and return full
of satisfaction and narrative. When they break loose they are
like a public ruin, in which the highest parts be undermost, and
make the noblest fabrics heaps of rubbish. They are like the
sea, that is stirred into a tumult with every blast of wind that
blows upon it, till it becomes a watery Appennine, and heaps
mountain billows upon one another, as once the giants did in the
war with heaven. A crowd is their proper element, in which
they make their way with their shoulders, as pigs creep through
hedges. Nothing in the world delights them so much as the
ruin of great persons, or any calamity in which they have no
share, though they get nothing by it. They love nothing but
themselves in the likeness of one another, and, like sheep, run all

that way the first goes, especially if it be against their governors, whom they have a natural disaffection to.

(From the *Remains*.)

AN OPINIONATER

An opinionater is his own confidant, that maintains more opinions than he is able to support. They are all bastards commonly and unlawfully begotten, but being his own, he had rather, out of natural affection, take any pains, or beg, than they should want a subsistence. The eagerness and violence he uses to defend them argues they are weak, for if they were true, they would not need it. How false soever they are to him he is true to them; and as all extraordinary affections of love or friendship are usually upon the meanest accounts, he is resolved never to forsake them, how ridiculous soever they render themselves and him to the world. He is a kind of a knight errant, that is bound by his order to defend the weak and distressed, and deliver enchanted paradoxes, that are bewitched, and held by magicians and conjurors in invisible castles. He affects to have his opinions as unlike other men's as he can, no matter whether better or worse, like those that wear fantastic clothes of their own devising. No force of argument can prevail upon him; for, like a madman, the strength of two men in their wits is not able to hold him down. His obstinacy grows out of his ignorance; for probability has so many ways, that whosoever understands them will not be confident of any one. He holds his opinions as men do their lands, and, though his tenure be litigious, he will spend all he has to maintain it. He does not so much as know what opinion means, which always supposing uncertainty, is not capable of confidence. The more implicit his obstinacy is, the more stubborn it renders him; for implicit faith is always more pertinacious than that which can give an account of itself; and as cowards, that are well backed, will appear boldest, he that believes as the Church believes is more violent, though he knows not what it is, than he that can give a reason for his faith, and as men in the dark endeavour to tread firmer than when they are in the light, the darkness of his understanding makes him careful to stand fast wheresover he happens, though it be out of his way.

(From the Same.)

A REBEL

A REBEL is a voluntary bandit, a civil renegade, that renounces his obedience to his prince, to raise himself upon the public ruin. He is of great antiquity, perhaps before the creation, at least a preadamite; for Lucifer was the first of his family, and from him he derives himself in an indirect line. He finds fault with the government, that he may get it the easier into his own hands, as men use to undervalue what they have a desire to purchase. He is a botcher of politics, and a state-tinker, that makes flaws in the government, only to mend them again. He goes for a public-spirited man, and his pretences are for the public good, that is, for the good of his own public spirit. He pretends to be a great lover of his country, as if it had given him love powder, but it is merely out of natural affection to himself. He has a great itch to be handling of authority, though he cut his fingers with it; and is resolved to raise himself, though it be but upon the gallows. He is all for peace and truth, but not without lying and fighting. He plays a game with the hangman for the clothes on his back, and when he throws out, he strips him to the skin. He dies in hempen sheets, and his body is hanged, like his ancestor Mahomet's, in the air. He might have lived longer, if the destinies had not spun his thread of life too strong. He is sure never to come to an untimely end; for by the course of law his glass was out long before. He calls rebellion and treason laying out of himself for the public; but being found to be false unlawful coin, he was seized upon, and cut to pieces, and hanged for falsifying himself. His espousing of quarrels proves as fatal to his country as the Parisian wedding did to France. He is like a bell, that is made on purpose to be hanged. He is a diseased part of the body politic, to which all the bad humours gather. He picks straws out of the government like a madman, and startles at them when he has done. He endeavours to raise himself, like a boy's kite, by being pulled against the wind. After all his endeavours and designs he is at length promoted to the gallows, which is performed with a cavalcade suitable to his dignity; and after much ceremony he is installed by the hangman, with the general applause of all men, and dies singing like a swan.

(From the Same.)

AN HECTOR

IS master of the noble science of offence and defence, a mungrel knight-errant, that is always upon adventures. His calling is to call those to accompt, that he thinks have more money, and less to show for their valour than himself. These are his tributaries, and when he is out of repair, he demands reparation of them. His skill consists in the prudent conduct of his quarrels, that he may not be drawn to fight the enemy but upon advantages. He is all for light skirmishes and pickeering, but cares not to engage his whole body, but where he is sure to come off. He is an exact judge of honour, and can hit the very mathematic line between valour and cowardice. He gets more by treaties than fights, as the French are said to have done by the English. When he finds himself overpow'r'd, he draws up his forces as wide in the front as he can, though but three deep, and so faces the enemy, while he draws off in safety, tho' sometimes with the loss of his baggage, that is, his honour. He is as often employ'd as a herald, to proclaim war, defy the enemy, and offer battle, in which desperate service he behaves himself with punctual formality, and is secur'd in his person by the law of nations. He is Py-powder of all quarrels, affronts, and misprisions of affronts, rencounters, rants, assaults, and batteries, and invasions by kick, cudgel, or the lye, that fall out among the sons of Priam, the brethren of the hilt and scabbard, that have taken the croysade upon them, to fight against the Infidel, that will not trust ; and he determines whether they are actionable, and will bear a duel, or not. He never surrenders without flying colours, and bullet in mouth. He professes valour but to put it off, and keeps none for his own use, as doctors never take physic, nor lawyers go to law. When he is engag'd in a quarrel, he talks and looks as big as he can, as dogs when they fall out, set up the bristles of their backs, to seem taller than they are. It is safer for a man to venture his life than his conversation upon him.

(From MSS. in British Museum.)

JEREMY TAYLOR

[Jeremy Taylor (1613-1667), Bishop of Down and Connor, and afterwards also of Dromore, was born at Cambridge, where his father was a barber. This fact may perhaps convey too low an idea of his parentage ; for in the seventeenth century the distinction between trade and profession was not so marked as it is now, and, moreover, the old combination of barber and surgeon was not then altogether extinct. Jeremy Taylor was a descendant of Rowland Taylor of Hadleigh, who suffered martyrdom in the Marian persecution. He was educated at Perse's school, Cambridge, and in 1626 entered as a sizar at Caius College, where, having taken his B.A. degree in 1630-31, he was elected Fellow. He soon attracted attention as a preacher, and became a protégé of Archbishop Laud, through whose intervention he removed from Cambridge to Oxford, and became Fellow of All Souls. In March 1637-38 he was appointed through the influence of the Bishop of London (Dr. Juxon), instigated, no doubt, by Archbishop Laud, Rector of Uppingham. In 1639 he married Phœbe, daughter of Dr. Langsdale, a medical man at Gainsborough, by whom he had three sons, all of whom came to an untimely end. In the Civil War he threw himself heart and soul into the Royalist cause, wrote strongly in defence of Episcopacy, and was made chaplain to Charles I. In the time of the Commonwealth he suffered severely ; his living was sequestrated, and he was several times imprisoned. He tried to make a precarious living by keeping a school in Wales, but the school was broken up through his frequent imprisonments. He then found a refuge at the beautiful seat of Lord Carbery at Golden Grove in Montgomeryshire, where he officiated at the private chapel, and preached some of his grandest sermons. His first wife was now dead, and he married Joanna Bridges, who was possibly, but not certainly, a natural daughter of King Charles I. He made the acquaintance of John Evelyn, who proved a most faithful and liberal friend to him. From Evelyn's *Diary* we find that he was sometimes in London, and that he was allowed to officiate at one of the city churches, or rather connived at in so doing. He next obtained a poor lectureship at Lisburn in Ireland, where he won the friendship of Lord Conway. On the Restoration he was appointed to the bishopric of Down and Connor (1660), to which was added in 1663 the small see of Dromore. Bishop Taylor was not in his element amid a population which consisted mainly of bigoted Presbyterians, and was probably happier in his obscurity than in his advancement. He died in 1667, and was buried in his cathedral at Dromore.]

As a preacher and devotional writer, Bishop Jeremy Taylor stands in the very first rank among the great divines of the golden period of English theology. His sermons are, of their kind, unrivalled. They differ widely from those of his great contemporaries, Barrow, Sanderson, and South ; but they are, in their way, quite equal to any of them. In wealth of illustration, exuberance of fancy grandeur of diction and style, it would be difficult to find their equals in the English language. When Taylor wrote, that language had outgrown the roughness —one might almost say, the grotesqueness—which sometimes marks the earlier prose, and had not degenerated into the commonplace tameness which marks the age of Tillotson. And besides having so noble a vehicle to convey his thoughts, Taylor had other elements of a great preacher. He had a very definite message to deliver, without which the most eloquent preacher will be futile ; and there was a spirit of piety about him which gives his sermons an unction, a sweetness, and a tenderness which commend them to the heart as well as to the head. The unlearned reader may find a difficulty by being, as it were, pulled up constantly by some quotation from a Greek or Latin author ; but Taylor almost always translates it at once, and when he does not, it may generally be ignored without losing the thread of the discourse. The burden of Taylor's teaching, both in his sermons nad in his devotional works, is that, in his own words, "Theology is rather a Divine life than a Divine knowledge." He disliked controversy, and is not seen at his best in his controversial writings. He was not an accurate thinker, and it is sometimes hard to reconcile different passages in his writings. It was perhaps this looseness of thought rather than intentional heresy that led him in some of his works, notably the *Unum Necessarium*, to approach perilously near towards Pelagianism. Hence it is hazardous to appeal to his authority as a theologian, for he might frequently be contradicted by himself. His forte lay not so much in argument as in appeals to the moral and spiritual nature of his readers or hearers, expressed in pure and stately language, and illustrated by magnificent descriptions and apposite quotations from all kinds of authors, sacred and profane. He had a tendency to turn everything he touched to a practical and devotional purpose. Hence his *Life of Christ*, or, to give it its full title, *The History of our Blessed Redeemer, Jesus Christ, or the Great Exemplar*, is quite as much a devotional work as his *Holy Living* or *Holy Dying*. But he is more self-restrained and less ornamental in his devotional works than in his sermons, rarely diverging in them from his mother-tongue. One of his great merits as a devotional writer is the very rare faculty he possessed of composing prayers. His prayers are some of the very few which can bear a moment's comparison with those in the Book of Common Prayer. His light esteem of mere opinions when separated from practice led him to write one of the most remarkable of all his works, " A Discourse of the Liberty of Prophesying, with its just Limits and Temper: showing the unreasonableness of prescribing to other Men's Faith, and the iniquity of persecuting differing Opinions." The title tells its own tale. The theory which Taylor advances, and the arguments by which he supports it, are now so generally admitted that they sound like commonplaces ; but at the time when Taylor wrote on the subject he was far in advance of his age.

We cannot complain that Bishop Taylor was sparing in the use of his powers in that direction in which he was most qualified to shine, for his printed sermons and devotional writings are very voluminous. But with that curious infelicity which great men sometimes show in estimating their own capacities, the work over which he took by far the greatest pains was one in which both his merits and his defects were alike hindrances to his success. In the seventeenth century the word " casuistry " had not yet acquired its evil meaning as almost equivalent to " sophistry." Some of our best casuists, such as Bishops Hall, Sanderson, and Barlow, belong to this period. Bishop Taylor was led, as usual, by purely practical motives to devote himself to this uncongenial work. He thought that " of books of casuistical theology we were almost wholly unprovided ; and, like the children of Israel in the days of Saul and Jonathan, we were forced to go down to the forges of the Philistines, to sharpen every man his share and his coulter, his axe and his mattock. We had swords and spears of our own, enough for defence, and more than enough for disputation ; but in this more necessary part of the conduct of consciences we did receive our answers from abroad, till we found that our old needs were very ill supplied, and new necessities did every day arise." To supply this want he took infinite trouble, devoting some of the best years of his life to elaborating his long work, entitled *Ductor Dubitantium, or Cases of Conscience,* which appeared in 1660. He was himself so far satisfied with the result that he prophesied that his reputation among posterity would rest upon this book—a prophesy which has been signally falsified by the event. For one person who is acquainted with the *Ductor*

Dubitantium, there are probably a hundred who know something, at any rate, about the *Holy Living* and *Holy Dying*, the *Golden Grove*, the *Marriage Ring*, and the *Via Intelligentiæ*. One reason, no doubt, why Taylor's casuistical work had fallen into comparative oblivion is that the subject itself is an obsolete study—not, perhaps, to the advantage of morals. But apart from this, Bishop Tayor was out of his element. A casuist should be terse, logical, severely simple—in short, almost everything that Taylor was not. His illustrations and quotations from the learned languages are even more profuse in the *Ductor* than in the sermons. Bishop Taylor's habit of mind, no less than his style, was essentially of the florid order ; one would have said also, the poetic, had it not been that he tried poetry, and was not very successful. But as a prose writer he was, in his proper department and in his own day, quite unrivalled ; and there are few who have surpassed him since.

J. H. OVERTON.

HOLINESS THE WAY TO KNOWLEDGE

LASTLY : there is a sort of God's dear servants who walk in perfectness, who "perfect holiness in the fear of God"; and they have a degree of clarity and divine knowledge more than we can discourse of, and more certain than the demonstrations of geometry, brighter than the sun, and indeficient as the light of heaven. This is called by the apostle the ἀπαύγασμα τοῦ Θεοῦ. Christ is this "brightness of God," manifested in the hearts of His dearest servants.

> ᾽Αλλ᾽ ἐγὼ ἐς καθαρῶν μερόπων φρένα πυρσὸν ἀνάπτω
> Εὐμαθίης.

But I shall say no more of this at this time, for this is to be felt, and not to be talked of; and they that never touched it with their finger, may secretly, perhaps, laugh at it in their heart, and be never the wiser. All that I shall now say of it is, that a good man is united unto God, κέντρον κέντρῳ συνάψας, as a flame touches a flame, and combines into splendour and to glory; so is the spirit of a man united unto Christ by the Spirit of God. These are the friends of God, and they best know God's mind, and they only that are so, know how much such men do know. They have a special unction from above : so that now you are come to the top of all; this is the highest round of the ladder, and the angels stand upon it : they dwell in love and contemplation, they worship and obey, but dispute not : and our quarrels and impertinent wranglings about religion are nothing else but the want of the measures of this state. Our light is like a candle; every wind of vain doctrine blows it out, or spends the wax, and makes the light tremulous; but the lights of heaven are fixed and bright, and shine for ever.

But that we may speak not only things mysterious, but things intelligible; how does it come to pass, by what means and what

economy is it effected, that a holy life is the best determination
of all questions, and the surest way of knowledge? Is it to be
supposed, that a godly man is better enabled to determine the
questions of purgatory or transubstantiation? is the gift of
chastity the best way to reconcile Thomas and Scotus? and is a
temperate man always a better scholar than a drunkard? To
this I answer, that in all things in which true wisdom consists,
holiness, which is the best wisdom, is the surest way of understanding them. And this, is effected by holiness as a proper and
natural instrument; for naturally every thing is best discerned by
its proper light and congenial instrument.

Γαίη μὲν γὰρ γαῖαν ὀπώπαμεν, ὕδατι δ' ὕδωρ.

For as the eye sees visible objects, and the understanding perceives
the intellectual; so does the Spirit the things of the Spirit. "The
natural man," saith St. Paul, "knows not the things of God, for
they are spiritually discerned:" that is, they are discovered by a
proper light, and concerning these things an unsanctified man
discourses pitifully, with an imperfect idea, as a blind man does
of light and colours which he never saw.

A good man, though unlearned in secular notices, is like the
windows of the temple, narrow without and broad within: he
sees not so much of what profits not abroad, but whatsoever is
within, and concerns religion and the glorifications of God, that
he sees with a broad inspection: but all human learning, without
God, is but blindness and ignorant folly.

But when it is δικαιοσύνη βεβαμμένη εἰς βάθος τῆς ἀληθείας,
—"righteousness dipped in the wells of truth"; it is like an eye
of gold in a rich garment, or like the light of heaven, it shews
itself by its own splendour. What learning is it to discourse of
the philosophy of the sacrament, if you do not feel the virtue of
it? and the man that can with eloquence and subtilty discourse
of the instrumental efficacy of baptismal waters, talks ignorantly
in respect of him who hath "the answer of a good conscience"
within, and is cleansed by the purifications of the Spirit. If the
question concern any thing that can perfect a man and make
him happy, all that is the proper knowledge and notice of the
good man. How can a wicked man understand the purities of
the heart? and how can an evil and unworthy communicant tell
what it is to have received Christ by faith, to dwell with Him, to
be united to Him, to receive Him in his heart? The good man

only understands that : the one sees the colour, and the other feels the substance ; the one discourses of the sacrament, and the other receives Christ ; the one discourses for or against transubstantiation, but the good man feels himself to be changed, and so joined in Christ that he only understands the true sense of transubstantiation, while he becomes to Christ bone of His bone, flesh of His flesh, and of the same spirit with his Lord.

We talk much of reformation, and (blessed be God) once we have felt the good of it ; but of late we have smarted under the name and pretension : the woman that lost her groat, " *everrit domum*," not " *evertit* " ; " she swept the house, she did not turn the house out of doors." That was but an ill reformation that untiled the roof and broke the walls, and was digging down the foundation.

> (From *Via Intelligentiæ, a Sermon preached to the University of Dublin.*)

THE RESPONSIBILITIES OF A BISHOP

THE bishop is like a man that is surety for his friend ; he is bound for many, and for great sums ; what is to be done in this case ; Solomon's answer is the way : " Do this now, my son, deliver thyself, make sure thy friend, give not sleep to thine eyes, nor slumber to thine eyelids " ; that is, be sedulous to discharge thy trust, to perform thy charge ; be zealous for souls, and careless of money : and remember this, that even in Christ's family there was one sad example of an apostate apostle ; and he fell into that fearful estate merely by the desire and greediness of money. Be warm in zeal, and indifferent in thy temporalities : for he that is zealous in temporals, and cold in the spiritual ; he that doth the accessories of his calling by himself, and the principal by his deputies ; he that is present at the feast of sheep-shearing, and puts others to feed the flock ; hath no sign at all upon him of a good shepherd. " It is not fit for us to leave the word of God, and to serve tables," said the apostles. And if it be a less worthy office to serve the tables even of the poor, to the diminution of our care in the dispensation of God's word,—it must needs be an unworthy employment to leave the word of God, and to attend the rich and superfluous furniture of our own tables. Remember the quality of your charges : " *Civitas est, vigilate ad custodiam et concordiam; sponsa est, studete amari; oves sunt, intendite pastui.*" "The Church is a spouse;" the universal Church is Christ's spouse, but your own diocese is yours; "behave yourselves, so that ye be beloved. Your people are as sheep," and they must be fed, and guided, and preserved, and healed, and brought home. "The Church is a city," and you are the watchmen; "take care that the city be kept at unity in itself;" be sure to make peace amongst your people; suffer no hatreds, no quarrels, no suits at law amongst the citizens, which you can avoid; make peace in your dioceses by all the ways of prudence, piety, and authority, that you can; and let not your own corrections of criminals be to any purpose but for their amendment, for the cure of offenders as long as there is hope, and for the security of those who are sound and whole. Preach often, and pray continually; let your discipline be with charity, and your censures slow; let not excommunications pass for trifles, and drive not away the fly from your brother's forehead with a hatchet; give counsel frequently, and dispensations seldom, but never without necessity or great charity; let every place in your diocese say, "*Invenerunt me vigiles,*—The watchmen have found me out," "*hassoverim*"; they that walk the city round have sought me out, and found me. "Let every one of us," as St. Paul's expression is, "show himself a workman that shall not be ashamed"; "*operarium inconfusibilem,*" mark that: "such a labourer shall not be put to shame" for his illness or his unskilfulness, his falseness and unfaithfulness, in that day when the great Bishop of souls shall make his last and dreadful visitation; for, be sure, there is not a carcass nor a skin, not a lock of wool nor a drop of milk of the whole flock, but God shall for it call the idle shepherd to a severe account. And how, think you, will his anger burn, when he shall see so many goats standing at his left hand, and so few sheep at his right? and, upon inquiry, shall find that his ministering shepherds were wolves in sheep's clothing? and that, by their ill example or pernicious doctrines, their care of money and carelessness of their flocks, so many souls perish, who, if they had been carefully and tenderly, wisely and conscientiously handled, might have shined as bright as angels? And it is a sad consideration to remember, how many souls are pitifully handled in this world, and carelessly dismissed out of this world; they are left to live at their own rate, and when they are sick, they are bidden to be of good comfort, and then all is well; who, when they are dead, find themselves cheated of their precious and invaluable eternity. Oh, how will those souls, in their eternal prisons, for ever curse those evil and false guides! And how will those evil guides themselves abide in judgment, when the angels of wrath snatch their abused people into everlasting torments? For will God bless them, or pardon them, by whom so many souls perish? Shall they reign with Christ, who evacuate the death of Christ, and make it useless to dear souls? Shall they partake of Christ's glories, by whom it comes to pass that there is less joy in heaven itself, even because sinners are not converted, and God is not glorified, and the people is not instructed, and the kingdom of God is not filled? Oh, no; the curses of a false prophet will fall upon them, and the reward of the evil steward will be their portion; and they who destroyed the sheep, or neglected them, shall have their portion with goats for ever and ever, in everlasting burnings, in which it is impossible for a man to dwell.

(From a *Consecration Sermon preached at Dublin.*)

OF CONTENTEDNESS IN ALL ESTATES AND ACCIDENTS

VIRTUES and discourses are like friends, necessary in all fortunes; but those are the best, which are friends in our sadnesses, and support us in our sorrows and sad accidents: and, in this sense, no man that is virtuous can be friendless; nor hath any man reason to complain of the Divine Providence, or accuse the public disorder of things, or his own infelicity, since God hath appointed one remedy for all the evils in the world, and that is a contented spirit: for this alone makes a man pass through fire, and not be scorched; through seas, and not be drowned; through hunger and nakedness, and want nothing. For since all the evil in the world consists in the disagreeing between the object and the appetite, as when a man hath what he desires not, or desires what he hath not, or desires amiss; he that composes his spirit to the present accident, hath variety of instances for his virtue, but none to trouble him; because his desires enlarge not beyond his present fortune: and a wise man is placed in the variety of chances, like the nave or centre of a wheel in the midst of all the circumvolutions and changes of posture, without violence or change, save that it turns gently in compliance with its changed parts, and is indifferent which part is up and which is down ; for there is some virtue or other to be exercised, whatever happens ; either patience or thanksgiving, love or fear, moderation or humility, charity or contentedness ; and they are every one of them equally in order to his great end and immortal felicity : and beauty is not made by white or red, by black eyes and a round face, by a straight body and a smooth skin ; but by a proportion to the fancy. No rules can make amiability, our minds and apprehensions make that : and so is our felicity : and we may be reconciled to poverty and a low fortune, if we suffer contentedness and the grace of God to make the proportions. For no man is poor, that does not think himself so : but if, in a full fortune, with impatience he desires more, he proclaims his wants and his beggarly condition. But, because this grace of Contentedness was the sum of all the old moral philosophy, and a great duty in Christianity, and of most universal use in the whole course of our lives, and the only instrument to ease the burdens of the world and the enmities of sad chances ; it will not be amiss to press it by the proper arguments by which God hath bound it upon our spirits : it being fastened by reason and religion, by duty and interest, by necessity and conveniency, by example, and by the proposition of excellent rewards, no less than peace and felicity.

Contentedness in all estates is a duty of religion ; it is the great reasonableness of complying with the Divine Providence which governs all the world, and hath so ordered us in the administration of His great family. He were a strange fool, that should be angry because dogs and sheep need no shoes, and yet himself is full of care to get some. God hath supplied those needs to them by natural provisions, and to thee by an artificial : for He hath given thee reason to learn a trade, or some means to make or buy them ; so that it only differs in the manner of our provision : and which had you rather want, shoes or reason ? And my patron that hath given me a farm is freer to me than if he gives a loaf ready baked. But, however, all these gifts come from Him, and therefore it is fit He should dispense them as He pleases ; and if we murmur here, we may at the next melancholy be troubled that God did not make us to be angels or stars. For, if that which we are or have do not content us, we may be troubled for every thing in the world which is besides our being or our possessions.

God is the master of the scenes ; we must not choose which part we shall act ; it concerns us only to be careful that we do it well, always saying, *if this please God, let it be as it is :* and we, who pray that God's will may be done in earth as it is in heaven, must remember that the angels do whatsoever is commanded them, and go wherever they are sent, and refuse no circumstances : and if their employment be crossed by a higher decree, they sit down in peace and rejoice in the event ; and, when the Angel of Judæa could not prevail in behalf of the people committed to his charge, because the Angel of Persia opposed it ; he only told the story at the command of God, and was as content, and worshipped with as great an extasy in his proportion as the prevailing Spirit. Do thou so likewise : keep the station where God hath placed you, and you shall never long for things without, but sit at home feasting upon the Divine Providence and thy own reason, by which we are taught that it is necessary and reasonable to submit to God.

For, is not all the world God's family ? Are not we His creatures ? Are we not as clay in the hand of the potter ? Do not we live upon His meat, and move by His strength, and do our work by His light ? Are we any thing but what we are from Him ? And shall there be a mutiny among the flocks and herds, because their Lord or their Shepherd chooses their pastures, and suffers them not to wander into deserts and unknown ways ? If we choose, we do it so foolishly that we cannot like it long, and most commonly not at all : but God, who can do what He please, is wise to choose safely for us, affectionate to comply with our needs, and powerful to execute all His wise decrees. Here therefore is the wisdom of the contented man, to let God choose for him : for when we have given up our wills to Him, and stand in that station of the battle where our great General hath placed us, our spirits must needs rest while our conditions have for their security the power, the wisdom, and the charity of God.

Contentedness in all accidents brings great peace of spirit, and is the great and only instrument of temporal felicity. It removes the sting from the accident, and makes a man not to depend upon chance and the uncertain dispositions of men for his well-being, but only on God and his own spirit. We ourselves make our own fortunes good or bad ; and when God lets loose a tyrant

upon us, or a sickness, or scorn, or a lessened fortune, if we fear
to die, or know not to be patient, or are proud, or covetous, then
the calamity sits heavy on us. But if we know how to manage a
noble principle, and fear not death so much as a dishonest action,
and think impatience a worse evil than a fever, and pride to be
the biggest disgrace, and poverty to be infinitely desirable before
the torments of covetousness; then we who now think vice to be
so easy, and make it so familiar, and think the cure so impossible,
shall quickly be of another mind, and reckon these accidents
amongst things eligible.

But no man can be happy that hath great hopes and great
fears of things without, and events depending upon other men, or
upon the chances of fortune. The rewards of virtue are certain,
and our provisions for our natural support are certain; or, if we
want meat till we die, then we die of that disease, and there are
many worse than to die with an atrophy or consumption, or unapt
and coarser nourishment. But he that suffers a transporting
passion concerning things within the power of others, is free from
sorrow and amazement no longer than his enemy shall give him
leave; and it is ten to one but he shall be smitten then and there
where it shall most trouble him: for so the adder teaches us
where to strike, by her curious and fearful defending of her head.
The old Stoics when you told them of a sad story, would still
answer: "*τί πρὸς μέ; What is that to me?*" "Yes, for the
tyrant hath sentenced you also to prison." "Well, what is that?
He will put a chain upon my leg, but he cannot bind my soul."
"No: but he will kill you." "Then I'll die. If presently, let
me go, that I may presently be freer than himself: but if not till
anon or to-morrow, I will dine first, or sleep, or do what reason
and nature calls for, as at other times." This in Gentile philosophy
is the same with the discourse of S. Paul, *I have learned in whatsoever state I am therewith to be content. I know both how to be
abased, and I know how to abound: everywhere and in all things
I am instructed, both how to be full and how to be hungry, both to
abound and suffer need.*

We are in the world like men playing at tables; the chance is
not in our power, but to play it is; and when it is fallen we must
manage it as we can; and let nothing trouble us, but when we
do a base action, or speak like a fool, or think wickedly: these
things God hath put into our powers; but concerning those things
which are wholly in the choice of another, they cannot fall under

our deliberation, and therefore neither are they fit for our passions. My fear may make me miserable, but it cannot prevent what another hath in his power and purpose : and prosperities can only be enjoyed by them who fear not at all to lose them ; since the amazement and passion concerning the future takes off all the pleasure of the present possession. Therefore if thou hast lost thy land, do not also lose thy constancy : and if thou must die a little sooner, yet do not die impatiently. For no chance is evil to him that is content, and to a man nothing miserable, unless it be unreasonable. No man can make another man to be his slave, unless he hath first enslaved himself to life and death, to pleasure or pain, to hope or fear : command these passions, and you are freer than the Parthian kings. (From *Holy Living.*)

OF THE PRACTICE OF PATIENCE

NOW we suppose the man entering upon his scene of sorrows and *passive graces.* It may be he went yesterday to a wedding, merry and brisk, and there he felt his sentence, that he must return home and die (for men very commonly enter into the snare *sing-ing*, and consider not whither their fate leads them); nor feared that then the angel was to strike his stroke, till his knees kissed the earth, and his head trembled with the weight of the rod which God put into the hand of an exterminating angel. But, whatsoever the ingress was, when the man feels his blood boil or his bones weary, or his flesh diseased with a load of a dispersed and dis-ordered humour, or his head to ache, or his faculties discomposed ; then he must consider that all those discourses he hath heard concerning patience and resignation, and conformity to Christ's sufferings, and the melancholic lectures of the Cross, must all of them now be reduced to practice, and pass from an ineffective contemplation to such an exercise as will really try whether we were true disciples of the Cross, or only believed the doctrines of religion when we were at ease, and that they never passed through the ear to the heart, and dwelt not in our spirits. But every man should consider God does nothing in vain ; that He would not to no purpose send us preachers, and give us rules, and furnish us with discourse, and lend us books, and provide sermons, and make examples, and promise His Spirit, and describe the blessedness of holy sufferings, and prepare us with daily alarms, if He did not really purpose to order our affairs so that we should need all this, and use it all. There were no such thing as the grace of Patience, if we were not to feel a sickness, or enter into a state of sufferings."

(From *Holy Dying.*)

ON SET FORMS OF LITURGY

AND here I consider that the true state of the question is only this, Whether it is better to pray to God with consideration, or without ? Whether is the wiser man of the two, he who thinks and deliberates what to say, or he that utters his mind as fast as it comes ? Whether is the better man, he who, out of reverence to God, is most careful and curious that he offend not in his tongue, and, therefore, he himself deliberates, and takes the best guides he can ; or he who, out of the confidence of his own abilities or other exterior assistances, ὅμοιος ἂν εἶναι δόξαιμι τοῖς εἰκῆ, καὶ φορτικῶς, καὶ χύδην,—ὅ,τι ἂν ἐπέλθῃ, λέγουσιν, speaks whatever comes uppermost.

And here I waive the advice and counsel of a very wise man, no less than Solomon, " Be not rash with thy mouth, and let not thy heart be hasty to utter anything before God ; for God is in heaven and thou upon earth ; therefore, let thy words be few." The consideration of the vast distance between God and us, heaven and earth, should create such apprehensions in us, that the very best and choicest of our offertories are not acceptable but by God's gracious vouchsafing and condescension ; and, therefore, since we are so much indebted to God for accepting our best, it is not safe ventured to present Him with a dough-baked sacrifice, and put Him off with that which, in nature and human considera-tion, is absolutely the worst ; for such is all the crude and im-perfect utterance of our more imperfect conceptions : " *Hoc non probo in philosopho, cujus oratio, sicut vita, debet esse composita,*" said Seneca ; " A wise man's speech should be like his life and actions, composed, studied, and considered." And if ever inconsideration be the cause of sin and vanity, it is in our words, and, therefore, is, with greatest care, to be avoided in our prayers, we being, most of all, concerned that God may have no quarrel against them, for folly or impiety.

But, abstracting from the reason, let us consider who keeps the precept best, he that deliberates, or he that considers not when he speaks ? What man in the world is hasty to offer anything unto God ; if he be not, who prays extempore ? And then add to it but the weight of Solomon's reason, and let any man answer me, if he thinks it can well stand with that reverence we owe to the immense, the infinite, and to the eternal God, the God of wisdom, to offer Him a sacrifice which we durst not present to a prince or a prudent governor, "*in re seriâ*," such as our prayers ought to be.

And that this may not be dashed with a pretence it is carnal reasoning, I desire it may be remembered that it is the argument God Himself uses against lame, maimed, and imperfect sacrifices, "Go, and offer this to thy prince," see if he will accept it ; implying that the best person is to have the best present, and what the prince will slight as truly unworthy of him, much more is it unfit for God. For God accepts not of anything we give or do, as if He were bettered by it ; for, therefore, its estimate is not taken by its relation or natural complacency to Him, for, in itself, it is to Him as nothing ; but God accepts it by its proportion and commensuration to us. That which we call our best, and is truly so in human estimate, that pleases God ; for it declares that if we had better we would give it Him. But to reserve the best says too plainly that we think anything is good enough for Him. And, therefore, God, in the law, would not be served by that which was imperfect "*in genere naturæ*' so neither now nor ever will that please Him which is imperfect, "*in genere morum*," or "*materiâ intellectuali*," when we can give a better.

And, therefore, the wisest nations and the most sober persons prepared their verses and prayers in set forms, with as much religion as they dressed their sacrifices, and observed the rites of festivals and burials. Amongst the Romans, it belonged to the care of the priests to worship in prescribed and determined words. "*In omni precatione qui vota effundit sacerdos, Vestam et Janum aliosque deos præscriptis verbis et composito carmine advocare solet.*" The Greeks did so too, receiving their prayers by dictate, word for word. "*Itaque sua carmina suæque precationes singulis diis institutæ sunt ; quas plerumque, ne quid præposterè dicatur, aliquis ex præscripto præire et ad verbum referre solebat.*" Their hymns and prayers were ordained peculiar to every god, which, lest anything should be said preposterously, were usually pronounced, word for word, after the priest, and out of written copies;" and the magi among the Persians were as considerate in their devotions : " *Magos et Persas primo semper diluculo canere diis hymnos et laudes, meditato et solenni precationis carmine;* "The Persians sang hymns to their gods by the morning twilight, in a premeditate, solemn, and metrical form of prayer," said the same author. For, since in all the actions and discourses of men, that which is the least considered is likely to be the worst, and is certainly of the greatest disreputation, it were a strange cheapness of opinion towards God and religion, to be the most incurious of what we say to Him ; and in our religious offices it is strange that everything should be considered but our prayers. It is spoken by Eunapius, to the honour of Proæresius's scholars, that when the proconsul asked their judgments in a question of philosophy, they were προσενεγκόντες τὰ Ἀριστείδου μετὰ πολλῆς σκέψεως καὶ πόνου, ὣς οὐκ εἰσὶ τῶν ἐμούντων, ἀλλὰ τῶν ἀκριβούντων—" they, with much consideration and care, gave in answer those words of Aristides, " That they were not of the number of those that used to vomit out answers, but of those that considered every word they were to speak." " *Nihil enim ordinatum est quod præcipitatur et properat,*" said Seneca ; " Nothing can be regular and orderly that is hasty and precipitate ; " and, therefore, unless religion be the most imprudent, trifling, and inconsiderable thing, and that the work of the Lord is done well enough when it is done negligently, or that the sanctuary hath the greatest beauty when it hath the least order, it will concern us highly to think our prayers and religious offices are actions fit for wise men, and, therefore, to be done as the actions of wise men use to be, that is, deliberately, prudently, and with greatest consideration.

(From *An Apology for authorized and set Forms of Liturgy.*)

ON DIFFERENCE OF OPINION

But men are, nowadays, and indeed always have been, since the expiration of the first blessed ages of Christianity, so in love with their own fancies and opinions, as to think faith and all Christendom is concerned in their support and maintenance ; and whoever is not so fond, and does not dandle them like themselves, it grows up to a quarrel, which, because it is in "*materia theologiæ*," is made a quarrel in religion, and God is entitled to it ; and then if you are once thought an enemy to God, it is our duty to persecute you even to death—we do God good service in it ; when, if we should examine the question rightly, the question is either in "*materia non revelata*," or "*minus evidenti*," or "*non necessaria*," either it is not revealed, or not so clearly, but that wise and honest men may be of different minds ; or else it is not of the foundation of faith, but a remote superstructure ; or else of mere speculation ; or perhaps, when all comes to all, it is a false opinion, or a matter of human interest that we have so zealously contended for ; for to one of these heads most of the disputes of Christendom may be reduced ; so that I believe the present factions, or the most, are from the same cause which St. Paul observed in the Corinthian schism ; "When there are divisions among you, are ye not carnal?" It is not the differing opinions that is the cause of the present ruptures, but want of charity ; it is not the variety of understandings, but the disunion of wills and affections ; it is not the several principles, but the several ends, that cause our miseries ; our opinions commence and are upheld according as our turns are served, and our interests are preserved, and there is no cure for us but piety and charity. A holy life will make our belief holy, if we consult not humanity and its imperfections in the choice of our religion, but search for truth without designs, save only of acquiring heaven, and then be as careful to preserve charity as we were to get a point of faith ; I am as much persuaded we shall find out more truths by this means : or, however, which is the main of all, we shall be secured though we miss them, and then we are well enough.

For if it be evinced that one heaven shall hold men of several opinions, if the unity of faith be not destroyed by that which men call differing religions, and if a unity of charity be the duty of us all, even towards persons that are not persuaded of every proposition we believe, then I would fain know to what purposes are all those stirs and great noises in Christendom, those names of faction, the several names of churches not distinguished by the division of kingdoms, "*ut ecclesia sequatur imperium*," which was the primitive rule and canon, but distinguished by names of sects and men ; these are all become instruments of hatred ; thence come schisms and parting of communions, and then persecutions, and then wars and rebellion, and then the dissolutions of all friendships and societies.   All these mischiefs proceed not from this, that all men are not of one mind, for that is neither necessary nor possible—but that every opinion is made an article of faith, every article is a ground of a quarrel, every quarrel makes a faction, every faction is zealous, and all zeal pretends for God, and whatsoever is for God cannot be too much ; we, by this time, are come to that pass, we think we love not God except we hate our brother, and we have not the virtue of religion unless we persecute all religions but our own, for lukewarmness is so odious to God and man, that we, proceeding furiously upon these mistakes, by supposing we preserve the body, we destroy the soul of religion,—or, by being zealous for faith, or, which is all one, for that which we mistake for faith, we are cold in charity, and so lose the reward of both.

(From *The Liberty of Prophesying*.)

BISHOP WILKINS

[John Wilkins was born at Oxford in 1614, and educated in his early years under the care of a well-known dissenter, Mr. John Dod, who was his grandfather on the mother's side. He afterwards entered at Magdalen Hall, Oxford, and after taking his degree went abroad and became Chaplain to the Count Palatine. Joining the Parliamentary side when the Rebellion broke out, he was made Warden of Wadham in 1648, and Master of Trinity, Cambridge, in 1659, having in 1656 married Robina, sister of Oliver Cromwell, and widow of Peter French, Canon of Christ Church. On the Restoration, he was ejected from Trinity, but became Rector of St. Lawrence Jewry ; and subsequently, through the help of a somewhat compromising patron, the Duke of Buckingham, he was promoted first to the Deanery of Ripon, and then to the Bishopric of Chester, in 1668. He died in 1672.

His works were numerous. In 1638, there appeared *The Discovery of a New World : a Discourse to prove that there may be another habitable world in the Moon.* A second part of this treats of *The Possibility of a Passage to the Moon.* In 1640, appeared *A Discourse Concerning a new Planet : tending to prove that the Earth may be a Planet.* Others of his works were *Mercury, or the Secret Messenger* (1641) ; *Mathematical Magic* (1648) ; *The Principles of Natural Religion* (printed after his death) ; and an *Essay towards a Real Character and Philosophical Language.* This last is a scheme for a universal language, and was written for, and published under the auspices of, the Royal Society, of which Wilkins was a devoted member.]

WILKINS'S curious variations of political adherence, and the fact that his patrons were so strangely assorted as to comprise Cromwell, Charles II., and the Duke of Buckingham, do not lead us to infer that his political faith was very ardent, or that he was troubled with any special delicacy of feeling. But it would be absurd to describe him as a political schemer. His interests were chiefly in other pursuits : such creed as he had was summed up chiefly in the determination to adhere very closely to no creed ; and he was sufficiently astute to make his religious, as well as his political, latitudinarianism, serve his own interests. His friends admit that he was ambitious : and on the other hand, his enemies do not charge against him any dishonourable act. His books have a certain interest of their own, and deserve a place in any collection which is to represent the literary fashion of the day. Wilkins was without enthusiasm, without reverence, and without humour : on the other hand he has unquestionably a certain quaintness and sprightliness of invention, and a certain boldness in argument, in the course of which he puts forward, quite gravely, propositions which, as stated, are extremely droll. Of literary art he has no conception, and the precision with which his argument advances from step to step, while it gives a certain clearness to his prose style, necessarily imparts to it more than the usual amount of formality, and makes any elasticity or ease impossible. Yet it is curious to see how even in a writer so argumentative, and so redolent of the schools, as Wilkins, a reminiscence of that direct colloquial force and freedom so distinctive of our earlier English prose still lingers ; and that even his most scholastic reasoning is enlivened occasionally by a familiar phrase or exclamation.

The characteristic of Wilkins's thought is not profound speculation, and his prose accordingly never becomes intricate or obscure. His chief qualities are, a sort of alert curiosity, a boldness in hazarding conjectures, a determination to be fettered by no authority : and, joined with these, an absence of all hesitation, an air of absolute unconcern as to whether this or that position be true or false, so long as it is conceivably tenable, and a readiness to advance theories which is all the greater because all earnestness of feeling is so entirely wanting. Wilkins was only by accident a theologian. He was for the most part an experimental philosopher, ready and independent, but neither profound nor judicious. He represented one type of the Royal Society. He was not merely the fashionable and dilettante virtuoso : just as little was he one who could materially advance physical science, or extend her sway. He still retains the habit of introducing into his physical speculations, the miscellaneous, ill-digested, uncritical learning which his generation, or a certain section of it, loved, and which seemed an inheritance from the old days of the alchemists. It is easy to see how strong the effect of the Latin construction is upon him. He recurs, sentence after sentence, to what answers to the ablative absolute in Latin. The participle appears in almost every clause : and he seeks to impart a certain logical formality to his argument, by repeatedly following the Latin construction by which the object frequently precedes, and the subject follows, the verb. All this in Wilkins, and in others of his kind, was no doubt helping to form the later fashion of an argumentative style; but it was leading English prose further and further away from the more natural, and perhaps in a literary sense, more healthy, tendency to fix the position of a word rather by the dictates of sound and harmony, than by the exigencies of grammar or logical precision.

H. CRAIK.

A JOURNEY TO THE MOON POSSIBLE

ALL that hath been said concerning the people of the new world is but conjectural, and full of uncertainties ; nor can we ever look for any evident or more probable discoveries in this kind, unless there be some hopes of inventing means for our conveyance thither. The possibility of which shall be the subject of our enquiry in this last proposition.

And if we do but consider by what steps and leisure all arts do usually rise to their growth, we shall have no cause to doubt why this also may not hereafter be found out among other secrets. It hath constantly yet been the method of providence, not presently to show us all, but to lead us on by degrees from the knowledge of one thing to another.

It was a great while ere the planets were distinguished from the fixed stars ; and some time after that, ere the morning and evening star were found to be the same : and in greater space (I doubt not) but this also, and other as excellent mysteries will be discovered. Time, who hath always been the father of new truths, and hath revealed unto us many things which our ancestors were ignorant of, will also manifest to our posterity that which we now desire, but cannot know. *Veniet tempus* (saith Seneca) *quo ista quæ nunc latent, in lucem dies extrahet, et longioris ævi diligentia.* Time will come when the endeavours of after ages shall bring such things to light as now lie hid in obscurity. Arts are not yet come to their solstice ; but the industry of future times, assisted with the labours of their forefathers, may reach that height which we could not attain to. *Veniet tempus quo posteri nostri nos tam aperta nescisse mirentur.* As we now wonder at the blindness of our ancestors, who were not able to discern such things as seem plain and obvious unto us, so will our posterity admire our ignorance in as perspicuous matters.

In the first ages of the world, the islanders thought themselves either to be the only dwellers upon earth, or else if there were any other, they could not possibly conceive how they might have any commerce with them, being severed by the deep and broad sea. But aftertimes found out the invention of ships : in which notwithstanding, none but some bold daring men durst venture, according to that of the tragedian :

> " Audax nimium qui freta primus
> Rate tam fragili perfida rupit. "
>
> Too bold was he, who in a ship so frail
> First ventured on the treacherous waves to sail.

And yet now, how easy a thing is this even to a timorous and cowardly nature ? And, questionless, the invention of some other means for our conveyance to the moon cannot seem more incredible to us than this did at first to them ; and therefore we have no just reason to be discouraged in our hopes of the like success.

Yea, but (you will say) there can be no sailing thither, unless that were true which the poet does but feign, that she made her bed in the sea. We have not now any Drake, or Columbus, to undertake this voyage, or any Dædalus to invent a conveyance through the air.

I answer, though we have not, yet why may not succeeding times raise up some spirits as eminent for new attempts and strange inventions as any that were before them ? It is the opinion of Kepler, that as soon as the art of flying is found out, some of their nation will make one of the first colonies that shall transplant into that other world. I suppose his appropriating this pre-eminence to his own countrymen may arise from an over-partial affection to them. But yet, thus far I agree with him, that whenever that art is invented, or any other whereby a man may be conveyed some twenty miles high, or thereabouts, then it is not altogether improbable that some or other may be successful in this attempt.

For the better clearing of which I shall first lay down, and then answer those doubts that may make it seem utterly impossible.

These are chiefly three.

The first, taken from the natural heaviness of a man's body, whereby it is made unfit for the motion of ascent, together with the vast distance of that place from us.

2. From the extreme coldness of the ætherial air.

3. The extreme thinness of it.

Both which must needs make it impassable, though it were but as many single miles thither as it is thousands.

For the first. Though it were supposed that a man could fly, yet we may well think he would be very slow in it, since he hath so heavy a body, and such a one too, as nature did not principally intend for that kind for motion. It is usually observed, that among the variety of birds, those which do most converse upon the earth, and are swiftest in their running, as a pheasant, partridge, etc., together with all domestic fowl, are less able for flight than others which are for the most part upon the wing, as a swallow, swift, etc. And therefore we may well think that man, not being endowed with any such condition as may enable him for this motion ; and being necessarily tied to a more especial residence on the earth, must needs be slower than any fowl, or less able to hold out. Thus it is also in swimming ; which art though it be grown to a good eminence, yet he that is best skilled in it is not able either for continuance or swiftness, to equal a fish : because he is not naturally appointed to it. So that though a man could fly, yet he would be so slow in it, and so quickly weary, that he could never think to reach so great a journey as it is to the moon.

But suppose withal that he could fly as fast and as long as the swiftest bird, yet it cannot possibly be conceived how he should ever be able to pass through so vast a distance as there is betwixt the moon and our earth. For this planet, according to the common grounds, is usually granted to be at the least fifty-two semidiameters of the earth from us ; reckoning for each semidiameter three thousand four hundred and fifty-six English miles, of which the whole space will be about one hundred and seventy-nine thousand, seven hundred and twelve.

So that though a man could constantly keep on in his journey thither by a straight line, though he could fly a thousand miles in a day, yet he would not arrive thither under a hundred and eighty days, or half-a-year.

And how were it possible for any to tarry so long without diet or sleep !

1. For diet. I suppose there could be no trusting to that fancy of Philo the Jew, who thinks that the music of the spheres should supply the strength of food.

Nor can we well conceive how a man should be able to carry

so much luggage with him as might serve for his viaticum in so tedious a journey.

2. But if he could, yet he must have some time to rest and sleep in. And I believe he shall scarce find any lodgings by the way. No inns to entertain passengers, nor any castles in the air (unless they be enchanted ones) to receive poor pilgrims, or errant knights. And so consequently he cannot have any possible hopes of reaching thither.

Notwithstanding all which doubts, I shall lay down this position.

That supposing a man could fly, or by any other means raise himself twenty miles upwards, or thereabouts, it were possible for him to come unto the moon.

(From *The Discovery of a New World*.)

AUTHORITY OF THE ANCIENTS

IN weighing the authority of others, it is not their multitude that should prevail, or their skill in some things that should make them of credit in everything ; but we should examine what particular insight and experience they had in those things for which they are cited. Now it is plain, that common people judge by their senses, and therefore their voices are altogether unfit to decide any philosophical doubt, which cannot well be examined or explained without discourse and reason. And as for the ancient fathers, though they were men very eminent for their holy lives, and extraordinary skill in divinity, yet they were most of them very ignorant in that part of learning which concerns this opinion ; as appears by many of their gross mistakes in this kind ; as that concerning the antipodes, etc.; and therefore it is not their opinion neither, in this business, that to an indifferent seeker of truth will be of any strong authority.

But against this it is objected. That the instance of the antipodes does not argue any special ignorance in these learned men ; or that they had less skill in such human arts than others ; since Aristotle himself, and Pliny, did deny this as well as they.

I answer :

1. If they did, yet this does make more to the present purpose : for if such great scholars, who were so eminent for their knowledge in natural things, might yet notwithstanding be grossly

mistaken in such matters as are now evident and certain, why then we have no reason to depend upon their assertions or authorities, as if they were infallible.

2. Though these great naturalists, for want of some experience, were mistaken in that opinion, while they thought no place was habitable but the temperate zones : yet it cannot be from hence inferred that they denied the possibility of antipodes : since these are such inhabitants as live opposite unto us in the other temperate zone : and it were an absurd thing to imagine that those who lived in different zones can be antipodes to one another ; and argues that a man did not understand, or else had forgotten that common distinction in geography, wherein the relation of the world's inhabitants unto one another are reckoned up under these three heads ; antaci, periæci, and antipodes. But to let this pass; it is certain that some of the fathers did deny the being of any such, upon other more absurd grounds. Now if such as Chrysostom, Lactantius, etc., who were noted for great scholars ; and such too as flourished in these latter times, when all human learning was more generally professed, should notwithstanding be so much mistaken in so obvious a matter : why then may we not think that these primitive saints, who were the penmen of Scripture, and eminent above others in their time for holiness and knowledge, might yet be utterly ignorant of many philosophical truths, which are commonly known in these days ? It is probable that the Holy Ghost did inform them only with the knowledge of those things whereof they were to be the penmen, and that they were not better skilled in points of philosophy than others. There were, indeed, some of them who were supernaturally endowed with human learning ; yet this was, because they might thereby be fitted for some particular ends, which all the rest were not appointed unto ; thus Solomon was strangely gifted with all kind of knowledge in a great measure ; because he was to teach us by his experience the extreme vanity of it, that we might not so settle our desires upon it, as if it were able to yield us contentment. So too the apostles were extraordinarily inspired with the knowledge of languages, because they were to preach unto all nations. But it will not hence follow, that, therefore, the other holy penmen were greater scholars than others. It is likely that Job had as much human learning as most of them, because his book is more especially remarkable for lofty expressions, and discourses of nature ; and yet it is not likely that he

was acquainted with all those mysteries which later ages have discovered; because when God would convince him of his own folly and ignorance, he proposes to him such questions as being altogether unanswerable, which notwithstanding, any ordinary philosopher in these days might have resolved. As you may see at large in the thirty-eighth chapter of that book.

The occasion was this: Job having before desired that he might dispute with the Almighty concerning the uprightness of his own ways, and the unreasonableness of those afflictions which he underwent, does at length obtain his desire in this kind; and God vouchsafes, in this thirty-eighth chapter, to argue the case with him. Where he does show Job how unfit he was to judge of the ways of providence, in disposing of blessings and afflictions; when he was so ignorant in ordinary matters, being not able to discern the reason of natural and common events. As why the sea should be so bounded from overflowing the land? What is the breadth of the earth? What is the reason of the snow or hail? What was the cause of the rain or dew, of ice and frost, and the like? By which questions, it seems, Job was so utterly puzzled, that he is fain afterwards to humble himself in this acknowledgment: I have uttered that I understood not, things too wonderful for me, which I knew not. Wherefore I abhor myself, and repent in dust and ashes.

So that it is likely these holy men had not these human arts by any special inspiration, but by instruction and study, and other ordinary means; and therefore Moses his skill in this kind is called the learning of the Egyptians. Now, because in those times all sciences were taught only in a rude and imperfect manner; therefore it is likely that they also had but a dark and confused apprehension of things, and were liable to the common errors. And for this reason is it, why Tostatus (speaking of Joshua's bidding the moon stand still as well as the sun) says, *Quod forte erat imperitus circa astrorum doctrinam, sentiens ut vulgares sentiunt:* that perhaps he was unskilful in astronomy, having the same gross conceit of the heavens, as the vulgar had. From all which it may be inferred, that the ignorance of such good men and great scholars concerning these philosophical points can be no sufficient reason why, after examination, we should deny them, or doubt their truth.

(From *A Discourse Concerning a New Planet.*)

MOTION OF THE EARTH POSSIBLE

ANOTHER common argument against this motion is taken from the danger that would thence arise unto all high buildings, which by this would be quickly ruinated, and scattered abroad.

I answer: this motion is supposed to be natural; and those things which are according to nature, have contrary effects to other matters, which are by force and violence. Now it belongs unto things of this latter kind to be inconsistent and hurtful; whereas those of the first kind must be regular, and tending to conversation. The motion of the earth is always equal and like itself; not by fits and starts. If a glass of beer may stand firmly enough in a ship, when it moves swiftly upon a smooth stream, much less then will the motion of the earth, which is more natural, and so consequently more equal, cause any danger unto those buildings that are erected upon it. And therefore to suspect any such event would be like the fear of Lactantius, who would not acknowledge the being of any antipodes, lest then he might be forced to grant that they should fall down unto the heavens. We have equal reason to be afraid of high buildings, if the whole world above us were whirled about with such a mad celerity as our adversaries suppose; for then there would be but small hopes that this little point of earth should escape from the rest.

But supposing (saith Rosse) that this motion were natural to the earth, yet it is not natural to towns and buildings, for these are artificial.

To which I answer: ha, he, he.

(From the Same.)

HENRY MORE

[Henry More was born at Grantham in 1614. His parents were gentlefolk, of small estate and Calvinist principles. He went to Eton, and to Christ's College, Cambridge. He took his degree in 1635, and became a Fellow of his College in 1639. He lived a life of study, refusing all preferment, even the Headship of Christ's. His time was divided between Cambridge and Ragley, in Warwickshire, the home of his friend Lady Conway. Here he found a congenial circle of mystics and wonder-workers. He died in 1687. His writings, controversial and speculative, are very numerous. The most important of them will be found in his *Philosophical Works* (1662), *Divine Dialogues* (1668), *Theological Works* (1675). He published a Latin version of his *Opera Omnia* in 1679. He also wrote poems, which were edited by Dr. Grosart in 1878. There is no modern edition of his prose works. R. Ward's *Life of Henry More* (1710), and the chapter on More in Principal Tulloch's *Rational Theology*, vol. ii., are worth consulting.]

HENRY MORE is unread, rather because he is unreprinted and inaccessible, a mystic in folio, than for any failure to interest essential to his work. For in his day he made the booksellers' fortunes and commanded the attention of all thinking men. He was the heart of the Cambridge movement of the 17th century, that academic reaction against the Hobbesian scheme of things entire ; the heart of it, as Cudworth was its brain. The contribution of this movement to the total process of thought was great : it insisted upon the recognition of the spiritual, as a standpoint for philosophic theory no less imperative, no less to be reckoned with, than that of physical science itself. It made its protest, through the mouth of More and his fellows, on behalf of religion and ethics, against a one-sided system which seemed likely to prove dangerous to both. The protest has been needed, and has been repeated, since then. The emphasis of the spiritual, herein lies More's strength. The saintliness of his personal life, to which his contemporaries bear witness, gave his words their weight : and in all his writing and thinking the ethical intent is clearly visible,

Philosophy other than this assertion of a central principle we shall hardly find in him ; but this is so fruitful and so necessary in itself, that it may excuse the absence of any formal or systematic body of thought. What is less easy to excuse is that More fails to recognise the functions of the intellect in the investigation of the spiritual : he treats it as altogether outside the pale of logic : he believes by preference in the supernatural and the unlikely : nothing, from witchcraft to the mesmeric cures of Valentine Greatrakes, is too much for his faculty of assent. Partly, perhaps, this is the effect of his completely academic life, beguiling him with the cobweb theories and fantastic subtleties of Neoplatonism, which have fascinated generations of solitary thinkers, and which a breath of practical life might have blown away.

He writes excellent English, easy, leisurely, scholarly, with an abundance of learning, which is yet not ponderous, and occasional gleams of humour. He is no pedant; good racy, homespun, coarse words diversify pleasantly his philosophic terminology. Yet in the selection of his language he has the nicety of the exact refined man of letters. Pedantry, indeed would have been impossible to him, for, in spite of his airy mysticisms, he is, like Plato himself, well in touch with earth. His love of nature, of outdoor life, is intense, and colours many a passage of his prose. His chief defect as a writer is a tendency to long-windedness in his periods : none the less he rarely fails to be lucid, often succeeds in being vivid, in the expression of his thought.

E. K. CHAMBERS.

THE DREAM OF BATHYNOUS

IT came to pass, therefore, O Philopolis, that one summer morning, having rose much more early than ordinary, and having walked so long in a certain wood (which I had a good while frequented) that I thought fit to rest myself on the ground, having spent my spirits, partly by long motion of my body, but mainly by want of sleep, and over anxious and solicitous thinking of such difficulties as Hylobares either has already, or, as I descried at first, is likely to propose; I straightway reposed my weary limbs amongst the grass and flowers at the foot of a broad-spread flourishing oak, where the gentle fresh morning air playing in the shade on my heated temples, and with inexpressible pleasure refrigerating my blood and spirits, and the industrious bees busily humming round about me upon the dewy honeysuckles; to which nearer noise was most melodiously joined the distanced singings of the cheerful birds, re-echoed from all parts of the wood; these delights of nature thus conspiring together, you may easily fancy, O Philopolis, would quickly charm my wearied body into a profound sleep. But my soul was then as much as ever awake, and, as it seems, did most vividly dream that I was still walking in these solitary woods with my thoughts more eagerly intent upon those usual difficulties of Providence than ever.

But while I was in this great anxiety and earnestness of spirit, accompanied (as frequently when I was awake) with vehement and devout suspirations and ejaculations towards God, of a sudden there appeared at a distance a very grave and venerable person walking slowly towards me. His stature was greater than ordinary. He was clothed with a loose silk garment of a purple colour, much like the Indian gowns that are now in fashion, saving that the sleeves were something longer and wider; and it was tied about him with a Levitical girdle also of purple; and he wore a pair of velvet slippers of the same colour, but upon his head a

Montero of black velvet, as if he were both a traveller and an inhabitant of that place at once.

Cuphophron. I dare warrant you it was the ghost of some of the worthy ancestors of that noble family to whom these woods did belong.

Hylobares. You forget, Cuphophron, that Bathynous is telling of a dream, as also (this third time) that ghosts, that is, spirits, are nowhere, and therefore cannot be met with in a wood.

Philopolis. Enough of that, Hylobares. I pray you proceed, Bathynous, and describe to us his age and his looks, as well as his clothing.

Cuph. I pray you do, Bathynous. I love alife to hear such things as these punctually related.

Bath. Did not the ruddiness of his complexion and the vivacity of his looks seem to gainsay it, the snowy whiteness of his hair, and large beard, and certain senile strokes in his countenance, seemed to intimate him to be about six score years of age.

Sophr. There is no such contradiction in that, Bathynous. For Moses is said to be an hundred and twenty when he died, and yet his eye was not dim, nor his natural force abated. But, I pray you, proceed.

Bath. While he was at any distance from me, I stood fearless and unmoved, only, in reverence to so venerable a personage, I put off my hat, and held it in my hand. But when he came up closer to me, the vivid fulgour of his eyes, that shone so piercingly bright from under the shadow of his black Montero, and the whole air of his face, though joined with a wonderful deal of mildness and sweetness, did so of a sudden astonish me, that I fell into an excessive trembling, and had not been able to stand, if he had not laid his hand upon my head, and spoken comfortably to me. Which he did in a paternal manner, saying : " Blessed be thou of God, my son, be of good courage, and fear not ; for I am a messenger of God to thee for thy good. Thy serious aspires and breathings after the true knowledge of thy Maker and the ways of His providence (which is the most becoming employment of every rational being) have ascended into the sight of God ; and I am appointed to give into thy hands the two keys of Providence, that thou mayest thereby be able to open the treasures of that wisdom thou so anxiously, and yet so piously, seekest after." And therewithal he put his right hand into his left sleeve, and pulled out two bright shining keys, the one of silver, the other of gold, tied together with a sky-coloured ribbon of a pretty breadth, and delivered them into my hands ; which I received of him, making low obeisance, and professing my thankfulness for so great a gift.

And now by this time I had recovered more than ordinary strength and courage, which I perceived in a marvellous way communicated unto me by the laying of his hand upon my head, so that I had acquired a kind of easy confidence and familiarity to converse with him ; and therefore, though with due civility, yet without all fear, methought I said further to him : " These are a goodly pair of keys, O my father, and very lovely to look upon : but where is the treasure they are to open ? " To which, smiling upon me, he straightway replied : " The treasures, my son, be in the keys themselves." " Then each key," said I, " O my father, will need a farther key to open it." " Each key," said he, " my son, is a key to itself " ; and therewithal bade me take notice of the letters embossed on the silver key, and there was the like artifice on the golden one. Which I closely viewing in both, observed that the keys consisted of a company of rings closely committed together, and that the whole keys were all bespattered with letters very confusedly and disorderly.

" Set the letters of the keys in right order," then said he, " and then pull at their handles, and the treasure will come out." And I took the silver key ; but though I could move the rings by thrusting my nails against the letters, yet I could not reduce the letters into any order, so that they would all lie in straight lines, nor was there any sense in any line. Which when that aged person saw, " You must first know the motto," said he, " my son : That is the key of the key." " I beseech you then," said I, " O my father, tell me the motto." " The motto," said he, " my son, is this :—*Claude fenestras, ut luceat domus.*" Having got the motto, I set to work again, and having reduced those letters that made up that motto into a right line, I, holding the lower part of the key in my left hand, pulled at the handle with my right, and there came out a silver tube, in which was a scroll of thin paper, as I thought, but as strong as any vellum, and as white as driven snow.

Having got this scroll, I took the boldness to open it. The figure thereof was perfectly square, with even margins on all sides, drawn with lines of a sky-coloured blue, very perfect and lovely. In the midst was described the figure of the sun in blazing gold : about the sun were six circles drawn with lines of the same coloured blue. Two of these circles were very near the body of the sun ; the other four more remote both from him and from one another, though not in equal distances. In every one of these circles was there the figure of a little speck like a globe, but of two distinct colours ; the one side towards the sun shining like silver, the other being of a duskish discoloured black. About those little globes in the third and fifth circle there were also drawn lesser circles of blue, one about the third, and four about the fifth, and in each of these circles was there also a small globous speck, of a lesser size than those in the middle. Something there was also about the globe of the sixth circle, but I cannot remember it so distinctly. Beyond these circles there was an innumerable company of star-like figures of gold, of the same hue with that of the sun, but exceeding much less, which, carelessly scattered, some were found a pretty distance from the margin, others towards the margin ; some others were cut in two by the blue line of the margin, as if it were intimated that we should understand that there were still more of those golden stars to an indefinite extent. This scheme entertained my gazing eyes a good time ; for I never had seen such before, and was resolved to impress the lines thereof perfectly in my memory, that I might afterwards discourse more readily thereof with this venerable personage. For I knew the purpose thereof by the inscription on the upper margin, which was, The true System of the World. Having thus satisfied myself, I rolled up the scroll again, and repositing it in the silver tube, easily thrust in the tube into the other part of the key, and disordering the line of letters that contained the motto, all was locked up again safe as before.

Having pleased myself so well with opening this first treasure, I had the more eager desire to assay the other ; and knowing all attempt to be vain without the knowledge of the motto or key of the key, I besought that divine sage to impart it to me. "That I shall do right willingly," said he, "my son : and I pray you take special notice of it. It is, *Amor Dei Lux Animæ*." "An excellent motto indeed," said I, "the key is a treasure in itself." However I set me to work as before, and reducing to such an order that a line of them did plainly contain this motto, I pulled at both ends of the golden key, as I did in the silver one, and in a golden tube continued to the handle of the key there was a scroll of such paper, if I may so call it, as in the other, exceeding white and pure, and, though very thin, yet not at all transparent. The writing was also terminated with even margins on all sides as before ; only it was much more glorious, being adorned richly with flower-work of gold, vermilion, and blue. And I observed that twelve sentences filled the whole area, written with letters of gold. The first was, The measure of providence is the divine goodness, which has no bounds but itself, which is infinite. 2. The thread of time and the expansion of the universe, the same hand drew out the one and spread out the other. 3. Darkness and the abyss were before the light, and the suns or stars before any opaqueness or shadow. 4. All intellectual spirits that ever were, are, or ever shall be, sprung up with the light, and rejoiced together before God in the morning of the creation. 5. In infinite myriads of free agents which were the framers of their own fortunes, it had been a wonder if they had all of them taken the same path ; and therefore sin at the long run shook hands with opacity. 6. As much as the light exceeds the shadows, so much do the regions of happiness those of sin and misery.

These six, Philopolis, I distinctly remember, but had cursorily and glancingly cast mine eye on all twelve. But afterwards fixing my mind orderly upon them, to commit them all perfectly to my memory (for I did not expect that I might carry the keys away with me home), by that time I had got through the sixth aphorism, there had come up two asses behind me out of the wood, one on the one side of the tree, and the other on the other, that set a braying so rudely and so loudly, that they did not only awake, but almost affright me into a discovery that I had all this while been but in a dream. For that aged grave person, the silver and golden keys, and glorious parchment were all suddenly vanished, and I found myself sitting alone at the bottom of the same oak where I fell asleep, betwixt two rudely braying asses.

(From the *Divine Dialogues.*)

THE OBSCURITY OF THE CHRISTIAN RELIGION

That there is a considerable obscurity and abstruseness in Christian religion is easily made evident as well from the cause as the effects of this obscurity. For besides that from the common nature of a mystery Christianity ought to be competently obscure and abstruse, that it may thereby become more venerable and more safely removed out of all danger of contempt ; we cannot but see what a special congruity there is in the matter itself, to have so holy and so highly-concerning a mystery as our religion is, abstruse and obscure. For that divine wisdom that orders all things justly ought not to communicate those precious truths in so plain a manner that the unworthy may as easily apprehend them as the worthy ; but does most righteously neglect the sensual and careless, permitting every man to carry home wares proportionable to the price he would pay in the open market for them : and when they can bestow so great industry upon things of little moment, will not spare to punish their undervaluing this inestimable pearl by the perpetual loss of it. For what a palpable piece of hypocrisy is it for a man to excuse himself from the study of piety, complaining of the intricacies and difficulties of the mystery thereof ; whereas he never yet laid out upon it the tenth part of that pains and affection that he does upon the ordinary trivial things of this world ?

Thus are the careless, voluptuous epicure and over-careful worldling justly met with. But not they alone. For the obscurity of this mystery we speak of is such, that all the knowledge of nature and geometry can never reach the depth of it, or relish the excellency of it ; nor all the skill of tongues rightly interpret it, unless that true interpreter and great mystagogus, the Spirit of God himself, vouchsafe the opening of it unto us, and set it so home in our understandings, that it begets faith in our hearts, so that our hearts misgive us not in the profession of what we would acknowledge as true. For as for the outward letter itself of the Holy Scriptures, God has not so plainly delivered himself therein, that he has given the staff out of his own hands, but does still direct the humble and single-hearted, while he suffers the proud searcher to lose himself in this obscure field of truth. Wherefore disobedient both learning and industry are turned off from obtaining any certain and satisfactory knowledge of this divine mystery, as well as worldliness and voluptuousness. According as our Blessed Saviour has pronounced in that devout doxology :—I thank Thee, O Father, Lord of heaven and earth, because Thou hast hid these things from the wise and prudent, and hast revealed them unto babes. Even so, Father, for so it seemed good in Thy sight.

Nor are the wicked only disappointed, but the goodly very much gratified by the intricacy of this sacred mystery. For the spirit of man being so naturally given to search after knowledge, and his understanding being one of the chiefest and choicest faculties in him, it cannot but be a very high delight to him to employ his noblest endowments upon the divinest objects, and very congruous and decorous they should be so employed. Besides, the present doubtfulness of truth makes the holy soul more devout and dependent on God, the only true and safe guide thereunto. From whence we should be so far from murmuring against Divine Providence for the obscurity and ambiguity of the Holy Scriptures, that we should rather magnify His wisdom therein ; we having discovered so many and so weighty reasons why those divine oracles should be obscure : the wicked thereby being excluded ; the due reverence of the mystery maintained ; and the worthy partakers thereof much advantaged and highly gratified.

For what can indeed more highly gratify a man—whose very nature is reason, and special prerogative speech—than by his skill in arts and languages, by the sagacity of his understanding, and industrious comparing of one piece of those sacred pages with another, to work out, or at least to clear up, some divine truth out of the Scripture to the unexpected satisfaction of himself and general service of the Church ; the dearest faculty of his soul and greatest glory of his nature acting then with the fullest commission, and to so good an end that it need know no bounds, but joy and triumph may be unlimited, the heart exulting in that in which we cannot exceed, viz. the honour of God and the good of His people ? All which gratulations of the soul in her successful pursuits of divine truth would be utterly lost or prevented, if the Holy Scriptures set down all things so fully, plainly, and methodically, that our reading and understanding would everywhere keep equal pace together. Wherefore, that the mind of man may be worthily employed and taken up with a kind of spiritual husbandry, God has not made the Scriptures like an artificial, wherein the walks are plain and regular, the plants sorted and set in order, the fruits ripe, and the flowers blown, and all things fully exposed to our view ; but rather like an uncultivated field, where indeed we have the ground and hidden seeds of all precious things, but nothing can be brought to any great beauty, order, fulness, or maturity without our own industry ; nor indeed with it, unless the dew of His grace descend upon it, without whose blessing this spiritual culture will thrive as little as the labour of the husbandman without showers of rain.

(From the *Mystery of Godliness*.)

DESIGN IN THE ANIMAL WORLD

WE are now come to take a view of the nature of animals. In the contemplation whereof we shall use much what the same method we did in that of plants, for we shall consider in them also their beauty, their birth, their make and fabric of body, and usefulness to mankind. And to dispatch this last first, it is wonderful easy and natural to conceive, that as almost all are made in some sort or other for human uses, so some so notoriously and evidently, that without main violence done to our faculties, we can in no wise deny it. As to instance in those things that are most obvious and familiar ; when we see in the solitary fields a shepherd, his flock, and his dog, how well they are fitted together ; when we knock at a farmer's door, and the first that answers shall be his vigilant mastiff, whom from his use and office he ordinarily names Keeper (and, I remember, Theophrastus, in his character Περὶ ἀγροικίας, tells us that his master, when he has let the stranger in, ἐπιλαβόμενος τοῦ ῥύγχεος, taking his dog by the snout, will relate long stories of his usefulness and the services he does to the house and them in it : Οὗτος φυλάσσει τὸ χωρίον καὶ τὴν οἰκίαν καὶ τοὺς ἔνδον ; "This is he that keeps the yard, the house, and them within ") ; lastly, when we view in the open champaign a brace of swift greyhounds coursing a good stout and well-breathed hare, or a pack of well-tuned hounds and huntsmen on their horsebacks with pleasure and alacrity pursuing their game, or hear them winding their horns near a wood side, so that the whole wood rings with the echo of that music and cheerful yelping of the eager dogs — to say nothing of duck-hunting, of fox-hunting, of otter-hunting, and a hundred more such-like sports and pastimes, that are all performed by this one kind of animal : I say, when we consider this so multifarious congruity and fitness of things in reference to ourselves, how can we withhold from inferring that that which made both dogs and ducks and hares and sheep, made them with a reference to us, and knew what it did when it made them ? And though it be possible to be otherwise, yet it is highly improbable that the flesh of sheep should not be designed for food for men ; and that dogs, that are such a familiar and domestic creature to man, amongst other pretty feats that they do for him, should not be intended to supply the place of a servitor too, and to take away the bones and scraps, that nothing might be lost. And unless we should expect that Nature make jerkins and stockings grow out of the ground, what could she do better than afford us so fit materials for clothing as the wool of the sheep, there being in man wit and art to make use of it ? To say nothing of the silk-worm, that seems to come into the world for no other purpose than to furnish man with more costly clothing, and to spin away her very entrails to make him fine without.

Again, when we view those large bodies of oxen, what can we better conceit them to be, than so many living and walking powdering-tubs, and that they have *animam pro sale*, as Philo speaks of fishes, that their life is but for salt, to keep them sweet till we shall have need to eat them ? Besides, their hides afford us leather for shoes and boots, as the skins of other beasts also serve for other uses. And indeed man seems to be brought into the world on purpose that the rest of the creation might be improved to the utmost usefulness and advantage : for were it not better that the hides of beasts and their flesh should be made so considerable use of to feed and clothe men, than that they should rot and stink upon the ground, and fall short of so noble an improvement as to be matter for the exercise of the wit of man, and to afford him the necessary conveniences of life ? For if man did not make use of them, they would either die of age, or be torn apieces by more cruel masters. Wherefore we plainly see that it is an act of reason and counsel to have made man that he might be a lord over the rest of the creation, and keep good quarter among them.

And being furnished with fit materials to make himself weapons, as well as with natural wit and valour, he did bid battle to the very fiercest of them, and either chased them away into solitudes and deserts, or else brought them under his subjection, and gave laws unto them ; under which they live more peaceably and are better provided for (or at least might be, if men were good) than they could be when they were left to the mercy of the lion, bear, or tiger. And what if he do occasionally and orderly kill some of them for food ? their despatch is quick, and so less dolorous than the paw of the bear, or the teeth of the lion, or tedious melancholy and sadness of old age, which would first torture them, and then kill them, and let them rot upon the ground stinking and useless.

Besides, all the wit and philosophy in the world can never demonstrate that the killing and slaughtering of a beast is any more than the striking of a bush where a bird's nest is, where you fray away the bird, and then seize upon the empty nest. So that if we could pierce to the utmost catastrophe of things, all might prove but a tragic-comedy.

But as for those rebels that have fled into the mountains and deserts, they are to us a very pleasant subject of natural history ; besides, we serve ourselves of them as is to our purpose ; and they are not only for ornament of the universe, but a continual exercise of man's wit and valour when he pleases to encounter. But to expect and wish that there were nothing but such dull tame things in the world that will neither bite nor scratch is as groundless and childish as to wish there were no choler in the body, nor fire in the universal compass of nature.

I cannot insist upon the whole result of this war, nor must forget how that generous animal the horse had at last the wit to yield himself up, to his own great advantage and ours. And verily he is so fitly made for us, that we might justly claim a peculiar right in him above all other creatures. When we observe his patient service he does us at the plough, cart, or under the pack-saddle, his speed upon the highway in matters of importance, his docibleness and desire of glory and praise, and consequently his notable achievements in war, where he will snap the spears apieces with his teeth, and pull his rider's enemy out of the saddle ; and then, that he might be able to perform all this labour with more ease, that his hoofs are made so fit for the art of the smith, and that round armature of iron he puts upon them ; it is a very hard thing not to acknowledge that this so congruous contrivance of things was really from a principle of wisdom and counsel.

There is also another consideration of animals and their usefulness, in removing those evils we are pestered with by reason of the abundance of some other hurtful animals, such as are mice and rats, and the like ; to this end the cat is very serviceable. And there is in the West Indies a beast in the form of a bear, which Cardan calls *Ursus Formicarius*, whose very business it is to eat up all the ants, which some parts of that quarter of the world are sometimes excessively plagued withal.

We might add also sundry examples of living creatures that

not only bear a singular good affection to mankind, but are also fierce enemies to those that are very hurtful and cruel to man : and such are the lizard, an enemy to the serpent ; the dolphin, to the crocodile ; the horse, to the bear ; the elephant, to the dragon, etc.   But I list not to insist upon these things.

(From *An Antidote against Atheism.*)

RICHARD BAXTER

[Richard Baxter (1615-1691), was born at Rowton, in Shropshire, in November 1615. The Baxters were a family of ancient descent, but had somewhat degenerated. He received a desultory education from various tutors, until at the age of fifteen he was sent to the Endowed School at Worcester, where he remained for three years ; but he frequently complains that he never received any competent training. In 1633 he was sent to Court with an introduction to Sir Henry Herbert, Master of the Revels, but a month at Whitehall gave him a distaste for a courtier's life. He returned to his original desire of receiving holy orders, and devoted himself to theological studies. In 1638 he accepted the offer of the head-mastership of a school at Dudley, and in the same year was ordained at Worcester by Bishop Thornborough, from whom also he received a license to teach the school. In 1640 we find him settled at Bridgnorth as "assistant minister" to the Rev. W. Madstard. In the same year was imposed the "*Et cetera*" oath, to which Baxter resolved he would never subscribe. In the following March he was appointed lecturer at Kidderminster, where by his piety and zeal he wrought a moral revolution. On the breaking out of the civil war, he was in a strait ; for he desired to be loyal to the king, and yet his opinions on most points agreed with those of the parliamentary party. He had to leave Kidderminster, and retired to Coventry with thirty other ministers. But he was completely out of sympathy with the sectaries with whom he was brought into contact ; and, with characteristic boldness, he constantly withstood them. After the battle of Naseby he became chaplain to Colonel Whalley's regiment, but he was never really a partisan of either side, and in 1647 he went into retirement for a short time. He then returned to Kidderminster, where he continued his ministry, and also took a leading part in politics, contending for the rights of the people, but opposing the Solemn League and Covenant, the Engagement, the Extirpation of Episcopacy, and the setting aside of Charles II., and holding in horror the execution of Charles I. On the Restoration, which he took part in effecting, he became chaplain to Charles II., and the Bishopric of Hereford was offered to him. But this he could not conscientiously accept ; for he thought the Episcopate of the Church of England was not in accordance with primitive Episcopacy. He took a leading part in the Savoy Conference, being earnestly desirous to remain within the Church, but equally anxious to procure many alterations in its constitution and its liturgy. He could not carry his points, and reluctantly submitted to be evicted by the Act of Uniformity in 1662. He suffered persecution and imprisonment in the reign of Charles II., and still more severely in that of James II., when he was grossly insulted by the notorious Judge Jeffreys. He lost his wife in 1681, and was deeply affected by the bereavement. But he survived her for ten years, exercising his ministry when he had the opportunity, joining with the clergy in resisting the encroachments of James II. in 1688, and joyfully welcoming the Toleration Act of William and Mary. He died on 8th December 1691, and was buried beside his wife in Christ's Church, London, William Bates, who held in the main the same views, as a "moderate Nonconformist" and "unwilling separatist," preaching his funeral sermon.]

RICHARD BAXTER was one of the most voluminous and popular writers of English prose in the 17th century. His *Practical Works* alone fill no less than twenty-two 8vo. volumes; and besides these he wrote a vast amount on a variety of other subjects. Considering the defects of his education, and the incessant whirl in which his life was passed, his literary fecundity is perfectly marvellous. He is said to have taken no pains with his style, and to have written straight from the heart; " he never recast a sentence or bestowed a thought on its rhythm, and the balance of its several parts"; but in spite—or shall we say, in consequence?—of this, his style is in its way remarkably good; there is a freedom and naturalness about it which perhaps would have been lost if he had elaborated his compositions more carefully. Earnestness and robust eloquence breathe through every page. He is seen at his best in his purely practical works; notably in the *Saints' Everlasting Rest*, and *A Call to the Unconverted.* Speaking of the former work, Archbishop Trench has called attention to a remarkable but undoubted fact: " In regard of the choice of words, the book might have been written yesterday. There is hardly one which has become obsolete, hardly one which has drifted away from the meaning which it has in his writings " (*Companions for the Devout Life*, p. 89). In this respect Baxter differs widely from the great writers of his time, such as Jeremy Taylor and Isaac Barrow, who require to be translated, more or less, into popular language. Baxter is essentially a popular writer; he who runs may read almost everything that he has written. A good summary of most of his controversial writings will be found in the Rev. John Hunt's *Religious Thought in England;* but to his practical and devotional works no summary can do justice. Baxter's popularity as a writer in his own day is all the more remarkable, because his views were calculated to please no party entirely. He leaned too much to the Church to please the Nonconformists, and too much to the Nonconformists to please Churchmen; he was too

Calvanistic to suit the Arminians, and too moderate in his Calvinism to suit the hot Calvinists. That, in spite of his independent position, his works were admired, is partly due to the obvious earnestness and sincerity of the man, but partly to the excellence of his matter and style. He was to a great extent a self-taught man, and his writings bear traces of this ; he was not a trained theologian, and can hardly be ranked with the giants of that golden age of theology ; but his works are read where theirs are not.

J. H. OVERTON.

THE KNOWLEDGE OF GOD

THE infinite goodness of God should increase repentance, and win the soul to a more resolute, cheerful service of the Lord. O what a heart is that which can offend, and wilfully offend, so good a God! This is the odiousness of sin, that it is an abuse of an Infinite Good. This is the most heinous, damning aggravation of it, that Infinite Goodness could not prevail with wretched souls against the empty, flattering world, but that they suffered a dream and shadow to weigh down Infinite Goodness in their esteem. And is it possible for worse than this to be found in man? He that had rather the sun were out of the firmament than a hair were taken off his head, were unworthy to see the light of the sun. And surely he that will turn away from God himself, to enjoy the pleasures of his flesh, is unworthy to enjoy the Lord.

It is bad enough that Augustine in one of his epistles saith of sottish worldly men, that " they had rather there were two stars fewer in the firmament than one cow fewer in their pastures, or one tree fewer in their woods or grounds " ; but it is ten thousand times a greater evil that every wicked man is guilty of, that will rather forsake the living God, and lose his part in Infinite Goodness, than he will let go his filthy and unprofitable sins. O sinners, as you love your souls, " despise not the riches of the goodness, and forbearance, and longsuffering of the Lord ; but know that his goodness should lead you to repentance " (Rom. ii. 4). Would you spit at the sun ? Would you revile the stars? Would you curse the holy angels ? If not, O do not ten thousandfold worse, by your wilful sinning against the Infinite Goodness itself.

But for you Christians, that have seen the amiableness of the Lord, and tasted of his perfect goodness, let this be enough to melt your hearts, that ever you have wilfully sinned against him : O what a good did you contemn in the days of your unregeneracy, and in the hour of your sin! Be not so ungrateful and disingenuous as to do so again. Remember, whenever a temptation comes, that it would entice you from the Infinite Good. Ask the tempter, man or devil, whether he hath more than an Infinite Good to offer you : and whether he can outbid the Lord for your affection ?

And now for the time that is before you, how cheerfully should you address yourselves unto his service ! and how delightfully should you follow it on from day to day ! What manner of persons should the servants of this God be, that are called to nothing but what is good ! How good a Master ! how good a work ! and how good company, encouragements and helps ! and how good an end ! All is good, because it is the infinite good, that we serve and seek. And shall we be loitering, unprofitable

(From *The Divine Life.*)

THE HEART IN HEAVEN

CONSIDER, a heart in heaven is the highest excellency of your spirits here, and the noblest part of your Christian disposition : as there is not only a difference between men and beasts, but also among men, between the noble and the base ; so there is not only a common excellency, whereby a Christian differs from the world, but also a peculiar nobleness of spirit, whereby the more excellent differ from the rest : and this lies especially in a higher and more heavenly frame of spirit. Only man, of all inferior creatures, is made with a face directed heavenward ; but other creatures have their faces to the earth. As the noblest of creatures, so the noblest of Christians are they that are set most direct for heaven. As Saul is called a choice and goodly man, higher by the head than all the company ; so is he the most choice and goodly Christian, whose head and heart is thus the highest (1 Sam. iv. 2, and x. 23, 24). Men of noble birth and spirits do mind high and great affairs, and not the smaller things of low poverty. Their discourse is of councils and matters of state, of the government of the commonwealth, and public things : and not of the countryman's petty employments. Oh ! to hear such a heavenly saint, who hath fetched a journey into heaven by faith, and hath been raised up to God in his contemplations, and is newly come down from the views of Christ, what discoveries will he make of those superior regions ! What ravishing expressions drop from his lips ! How high and sacred is his discourse, Enough to make the ignorant world astonished, and perhaps say ! " Much study hath made them mad " (Acts xxvi. 24) ; and enough to convince an understanding hearer that they have seen the Lord : and to make one say, " No man could speak such words as these, except he had been with God." This, this is the noble Christian ; as Bucholcer's hearers concluded, when he had preached his last sermon, being carried between two into the church, because of his weakness, and there most admirably discoursed of the blessedness of souls departed this life, " *Cæteros concionatores a Bucholcero semper omnes, illo autem die etiam ipsum a sese superatum,*" that Bucholcer did ever excel other preachers, but that day he excelled himself ; so may I conclude of the heavenly Christian, he ever excelleth the rest of men, but when he is nearest heaven he excelleth himself. As those are the most famous mountains that are highest ; and those the fairest trees that are tallest ; and those the most glorious pyramids and buildings whose tops do reach nearest to heaven ; so is he the choicest Christian, whose heart is most frequently and delightfully there. If a man have lived near the king, or have travelled to see the sultan of Persia, or the great Turk, he will make this a matter of boasting, and thinks himself one step higher than his private neighbours, that live at home. What shall we then judge of him that daily travels as far as heaven, and there hath seen the King of Kings ? That hath frequent admittance into the Divine presence, and feasteth his soul upon the tree of life ? For my part, I value this man before the ablest, the richest, and the most learned in the world.

(From *The Saints' Everlasting Rest.*)

ABRAHAM COWLEY

[Born in London in 1618 ; educated at Westminster School and at Trinity College, Cambridge ; ejected from his University in 1643-4, when he took up his residence at Oxford. He followed Queen Henrietta Maria to France in 1646, and served the royal family in various ways. On his return to England in 1656 he was arrested by mistake, but released on bail, under which he remained till the Restoration. Disappointed of the Mastership of the Savoy, he was at last enabled, by a favourable lease of royal lands, to retire into country life, and settled, first at Barn Elms, and in 1665 at Porch House, Chertsey, where he died on July 28, 1667.]

COWLEY'S last request to his literary executor was to excise from his works any word or phrase that might give the least offence to religion or good manners. This sincere expression of the piety which was in him—for, notwithstanding the florid exuberance of his pen, Cowley was as a writer, whether of poetry or of prose, quite free from affectation—should be cited at the head of any tribute, however slight, to his literary genius. Fortune plunged him in a long series of dubious activities from the day when he was driven from the gates of Trinity to that when he found refuge at last in his

> " . . . gentle, cool retreat
> From all th' immoderate heat,
> In which this frantic world doth burn and sweat,"

and he drank almost to the dregs the cup of tarnished gold, which is filled with the *miseriæ curialium*. Yet he thought nobly of life and its purposes, and, above all, of that pursuit of letters to which, as a boy, he had been attracted by the copy of Spenser that lay in his mother's parlour, and to which he remained true through all the vicissitudes of his career. Thus, while the decline of his poetic reputation is one which no revival awaits— for it is only out of the decay of another Elizabethan age that another fantastic epoch of literary taste could be generated,—the nearer we can come to him in his prose the more his individuality commends itself to our sympathies ; and in this sense Pope's well-worn "Still I love the language of his heart," may fearlessly be cited once more.

Cowley's prose is but little in quantity, and some of it hardly comes into the category of pure literature. His *Proposition for the Advancement of Experimental Philosophy* is one of the London University—and more especially the London Professorial University—projects of his day, and a very ardent plea for the endowment of research, on conditions (including that of celibacy) which appeared to Cowley indispensable for its prosecution. He was, it should be remembered, not only a fellow, but, so to speak, the poet laureate of the Royal Society. In his discourse by way of *Vision concerning the Government of Oliver Cromwell* he held a brief of a different kind, and this time before a tribunal in little need of being convinced on his side of the question. This piece, though its opening possesses a certain charm, is so rhetorically commonplace in thought that its plan at once sinks from grandeur into grotesqueness, and the Tutelar Angel, to speak profanely, only appears at the wicket in order to be bowled over. Cowley's disposition, it is clear, was magnanimous ; but the turbid political atmosphere of his times, of which not even a Milton could wholly escape the contagion, made it quite impossible for a henchman of the Stuarts to weigh the historic Cromwell. The attempt is a mere ambitious failure. Far happier, and deserving not to be altogether overlooked among its author's prose writings, is the preface to the comedy of *Cutter of Coleman Street* (the revised *Guardian* of Cowley's Cambridge days). He is here on firm ground, moving among the experiences and, it must be allowed, the convictions of his own career, with a temperate dignity commanding respect even for a comic dramatist of the Restoration.

There remain the *Discourses*—they are but eleven in number, and so far as the prose in them is concerned, not one of them is too long—*by way of Essays, in Verse and Prose*. They are rightly considered to form a sort of half-way house between Bacon and Addison, and are thus never likely to fall out of notice. But their chief attraction lies in the personal savour which pervades them all, and makes them, collectively and individually, their author's own. I cannot subscribe altogether to Johnson's *dictum,* that "no author ever kept his verse and prose at a greater distance from each other"; for though Cowley's prose is without the occasional turgidity of his verse, and without the occasional suggestion of a broken pinion in the midst of a Pindaric flight, it equally abounds in witty turns, while happily quotations, as a rule, do duty for mere conceits. Very manifestly (though I do not know that this has been pointed out) his immediate model as a prose essayist was Montaigne, to whom he refers more than once in passing, and with whose ways of thinking and writing, inseparable as these necessarily are in essays of the personal type, he may be supposed to have familiarised himself in the long days of his French exile. Such pieces as those *Of Greatness* and *Of Myself* could hardly have been written except by a diligent student of this exemplar. For the rest, I hardly know why Cowley should be grudged full credit for "the vehement love of retirement," to use Johnson's phrase, announced by the very titles of these essays—*Of Liberty, Of Solitude, Of Obscurity, The Garden, The Dangers of an Honest Man in much Company.* Professor Minto tells us that Cowley, in his constant enunciation of his philosophy of life, was "moved entirely by constitutional sentiment." To be sure there is a difference between weariness and moral indignation; but Cowley's desire for independence was not the less genuine because through most of his life he had been a bondsman, and he loved his fetters none the better because he had worn them till their rust had entered into his very soul.

Nothing further need, I think, be said by way of introduction to extracts which, in this instance, it is easy enough to make, but which can hardly do justice to the pleasant continuity which is one of the principal attractions of essays in Cowley's manner. He may himself have placed more value on the gems of wit glittering on the surface of everything he produced; did he not, forsooth, enter it as a count in his indictment against Oliver Cromwell that the Protector "left no wise or witty apophthegm behind him?" And he may have specially delighted in the echoes for which, in every one of these *Essays*, he found or made opportunity of those "chimes of verse" which "never left ringing in his head" since his boyhood; though, to our taste, this intermixture of prose and metre only serves to give to both something of the sprightly insincerity of the *vaudeville.* The familiar ease, never descending into what would misbecome either the man of breeding or the

man of letters, is the true cause of the pleasure which cultivated readers have never ceased to derive from these *Essays;*
and to enjoy this pleasure to the full, we should pace with
their author the whole length of his modest garden walks; for
his estate was not on the scale of his friend John Evelyn's.

A. W. WARD.

THE USE OF LEISURE

THE first minister of state has not so much business in public, as a wise man has in private : if the one have little leisure to be alone, the other has less leisure to be in company ; the one has but part of the affairs of one nation, the other, all the works of God and nature under his consideration. There is no saying shocks me so much as that which I hear very often : that a man does not know how to pass his time. 'Twould have been but ill spoken by Methusalem, in the nine hundred sixty-ninth year of his life ; so far it is from us, who have not time enough to attain to the utmost perfection of any part of any science, to have cause to complain, that we are forced to be idle for want of work. But this, you'll say, is work only for the learned, others are not capable either of the employments, or divertisements, that arrive from letters. I know they are not : and therefore cannot much recommend solitude to a man totally illiterate. But if any man be so unlearned as to want entertainment of the little intervals of accidental solitude, which frequently occur in almost all conditions (except the very meanest of the people, who have business enough in the necessary provisions for life), it is truly a great shame, both to his parents and himself ; for a very small portion of any ingenious art will stop up all those gaps of our time, either music, or painting, or designing, or chemistry, or history, or gardening ; or twenty other things will do it usefully and pleasantly ; and if he happen to set his affections upon poetry (which I do not advise him to immoderately), that will overdo it : no wood will be thick enough to hide him from the importunities of company or business, which would abstract him from his beloved.   (From the Essay *Of Solitude.*)

A SMALL THING, BUT MINE OWN

I NEVER had any other desire so strong, and so like to covetousness, as that one which I have had always, that I might be master at last of a small house and large garden, with very moderate conveniences joined to them, and there dedicate the remainder of my life only to the culture of them, and study of nature.

And there (with no design beyond my wall), whole and entire to lie,
In no inactive ease, and no unglorious poverty.

Or, as Virgil has said, shorter and better for me, that I might there *studiis florere ignobilis otî* (though I could wish, that he had rather said, *nobilis otî*, when he spoke of his own). But several accidents of my ill fortune have disappointed me hitherto, and do still, of that felicity ; for though I have made the first and hardest step to it, by abandoning all ambitions and hopes in this world, and by retiring from the noise of all business and almost company, yet I stick still in the inn of a hired house and garden, among weeds and rubbish ; and without that pleasantest work of human industry, the improvement of something which we call (not very properly, but yet we call) our own. I am gone out from Sodom, but I am not yet arrived at my little Zoar. " O let me escape thither (is it not a little one ?) and my soul shall live." I do not look back yet ; but I have been forced to stop, and make too many halts. You may wonder, sir (for this seems a little too extravagant and Pindarical for prose), what I mean by all this preface ; it is to let you know, that though I have missed, like a chemist, my great end, yet I account my affections and endeavours well rewarded by something that I have met with by the by : which is, that they have procured to me some part in your kindness and esteem.

(From the Essay *The Garden.*)

A MAXIM CRITICISED

LUCRETIUS, by his favour, though a good poet, was but an ill-natured man, when he said, " it was delightful to see other men in a great storm." And no less ill-natured should I think Democritus, who laughs at all the world, but that he retired himself so much out of it, that we may perceive he took no great pleasure in that kind of mirth. I have been drawn twice or thrice by company to go to Bedlam, and have seen others very much delighted with the fantastical extravagancy of so many various madnesses, which upon me wrought so contrary an effect, that I always returned, not only melancholy, but even sick with the sight. My compassion there was perhaps too tender, for I meet a thousand madmen abroad, without any perturbation ; though to weigh the matter justly, the total loss of reason is less deplorable than the total depravation of it. An exact judge of human blessings, of riches, honours, beauty, even of wit itself, should pity the abuse of them more than the want.

(From the Essay, *The Dangers of an Honest Man in much Company.*)

POETRY AS A MISTRESS

I WAS even then acquainted with the poets (for the conclusion is taken out of Horace); and perhaps it was the immature and immoderate love of them which stamped first, or rather engraved, the characters in me ; they were like letters cut in the bark of a young tree, which with the tree still grow proportionably. But, how this love came to be produced in me so early, is a hard question : I believe I can tell the particular little chance which filled my head first with such chimes of verse, as have never since left ringing there : for I remember when I began to read, and take some pleasure in it, there was wont to lie in my mother's parlour (I know not by what accident, for she herself never in her life read any book but of devotion) ; but there was wont to lie Spenser's works ; this I happened to fall upon, and was infinitely delighted with the stories of the knights, and giants, and monsters, and brave houses, which I found everywhere there (though my understanding had little to do with all this), and by degrees, with the tinkling of the rhyme, and dance of the numbers ; so that I think I had read him all over before I was twelve years old, and was thus made a poet as immediately as a child is made an eunuch. With these affections of mind, and my heart wholly set upon letters, I went to the university ; but was soon torn from thence by that public violent storm which would suffer nothing to stand where it did, but rooted up every plant, even from the princely cedars, to me, the hyssop. Yet I had as good fortune as could have befallen me in such a tempest ; for I was cast by it into the family of one of the best persons, and into the court of one of the best princesses in the world. Now though I was here engaged in ways most contrary to the original design of my life, that is, into much company, and no small business, and into a daily fight of greatness, both militant and triumphant (for that was the state then of the English and the French courts), yet all this was so far from altering my opinion, that it only added the confirmation of reason to that which was before but natural inclination. I saw plainly all the paint of that kind of life, the nearer I came to it; and that beauty which I did not fall in love with, when for aught I knew it was real, was not like to bewitch or entice me, when I saw it was adulterate. I met with several great persons, whom I liked very well, but could not perceive that any part of their greatness was to be liked or desired, no more than I would be glad, or content to be in a storm, though I saw many ships which rid safely and bravely in it. A storm would not agree with my stomach if it did with my courage ; though I was in a crowd of as good company as could be found anywhere, though I was in business of great and honourable trust, though I ate at the best table, and enjoyed the best conveniencies for present subsistence that ought to be desired by a man of my condition in banishment and public distresses ; yet I could not abstain from renewing my old school-boy's wish in a copy of verses to the same effect.

> " Well then ; I now do plainly see,
> This busy world and I shall ne'er agree," &c.

And I never then proposed to myself any other advantage from his Majesty's happy restoration, but the getting into some moderately convenient retreat in the country, which I thought in that case I might easily have compassed, as well as some others, who with no greater probabilities or pretences have arrived to extraordinary fortunes . . . But God laughs at a man who says to his soul, *Take thy ease :* I met presently not only with many little encumbrances and impediments, but with so much sickness, (a new misfortune to me), as would have spoiled the happiness of an Emperor as well as mine : yet I do neither repent nor alter my course. *Non ego perfidum dixi sacramentum :* nothing shall separate me from a mistress which I have loved so long, and have now at last married : though she neither has brought me a rich portion, nor lived yet so quietly with me as I hoped from her. (From the Essay *Of Myself.*)

RALPH CUDWORTH

[Ralph Cudworth was born at Aller in Somersetshire in 1617. His father, also a learned man, died in 1624, and his mother then married Dr. Stoughton, who took the greatest pains with his step-son's education. In 1630 he went to Emmanuel College, Cambridge. In 1640, after a brilliant university career, he was presented to the Rectory of North Cadbury, Somersetshire. He was not long a parish priest, for in 1644 he was appointed Master of Clare and stopped at Cambridge, almost without break, for the remaining forty-four years of his life. He was, in 1645, appointed Regius Professor of Hebrew ; in 1654, Master of Christ's ; and in 1678 Prebendary of Gloucester Cathedral. He died in 1688.

Cudworth is best known by his *True Intellectual System of the Universe* (1678), and his *Treatise on Eternal and Immutable Morality* (not published till 1731). He also wrote a *Discourse concerning the true Notion of the Lord's Supper*, a *Treatise of Free Will*, a couple of sermons, and a work on Daniel's prophecy of the LXX weeks.]

CUDWORTH belonged to the group of scholars and theologians known as the Cambridge Platonists. Henry More, John Smith, Benjamin Whichcote, besides other more or less well known men being of this group. Their chief aim was to defend the freedom of the will against Hobbes and Descartes.

Our author's *True Intellectual System of the Universe*, "wherein all the reason and philosophy of atheism is confuted, and its impossibility demonstrated," is a careful presentment of the various ancient hypotheses as to the nature of the universe, read in the light of the materialistic philosophies of his day. Ueberweg speaks of it as being " at once the most learned and for the time the most critical work, on the history of ancient philosophy which had ever been produced by any English writer." The style is strong and nervous, generally clear and forceful, sometimes even eloquent and graphic. There is every evidence of clearness of head and coolness of judgment about the work. The writer is perhaps open to the charge of making too great a display of learning, but this is a better fault than ignoring all quotation and despising all accuracy of reference.

In the *Treatise concerning Eternal and Immutable Morality* Cudworth purported to defend the freedom of the will against Atheists, Deists, and Christian Theists ; he only completed the first part, however, namely, that against Atheists. The subject is carefully and exhaustively argued, temperately but unflinchingly. The language is occasionally antiquated, and the general style heavier than that of the *Intellectual System*.

The *Treatise of Free Will* is perhaps the most highly finished and generally attractive of Cudworth's philosophical writings. It was suggested by Hobbes' letter to the Marquis of Newcastle. His criticisms are clear and pertinent, the flow of his remarks is not interrupted, as in the *Intellectual System*, by over much quotation from other writers. He is severe in controversy, but never discourteous nor irrelevant.

All Cudworth's writings may be called theological, seeing that the being and nature of God, and the moral responsibility of man, form the chief themes of his philosophical works. Of more specially theological writing we have from him two sermons, and a work on the Lord's Supper.

His sermons are characterised by great breadth of view, which won for him the epithet Latitudinarian in his day, and which would now-a-days cause him to be described as a Broad Church man. Their style is fine ; their diction pure and for the most part simple ; their principal fault, and that a serious one, is their great length.

His discourse on the *Notion of the Lord's Supper* is extremely erudite, garnished with countless quotations from Latin and Greek authors, and with disquisitions upon the Hebrew text of Scripture.

Cudworth's works deserve to be studied by the modern student of English literature, not only for the excellence of their style but for the value of their contents. Many of his strictures upon the materialistic philosophies of his own and of a bygone day still bear on latter-day controversies, while his exhortations to live the Christ-like life rather than wrangle over doctrinal niceties would not come amiss in these times of party shibboleths.

A. I. FITZROY.

ON THE INCORPOREALITY OF THE DEITY

THE Democritics and Epicureans, though consenting with all the other atheists, in this, that whatsoever was unextended, and devoid of magnitude, and therefore nothing (so that there could neither be any substance, nor accident, or mode of any substance, unextended), did notwithstanding distinguish concerning a double nature. First, that which is so extended as to be impenetrable and tangible, or resist the touch; which is body. And secondly, that which is extended also, but penetrably and intangibly; which is space or vacuum: a nature, according to them, really distinct from body, and the only incorporeal thing that is. Now since this space, which is the only incorporeal, can neither do nor suffer anything, but only give place or room to bodies to subsist in, or pass through; therefore can there not be any active, understanding, incorporeal Deity. This is the argumentation of the Democritic atheists.

To which we reply, that if space be indeed a nature distinct from body, and a thing really incorporeal, as they pretend, then will it undeniably follow from this very principle of theirs, that there must be an incorporeal substance; and (this space being supposed by them also to be infinite) an infinite, incorporeal Deity. Because, if space be not the extension of body, nor an affection thereof, then must it of necessity be, either an accident existing alone by itself without a substance, which is impossible; or else the extension, or affection, of some other incorporeal substance, that is infinite. But here will Gassendus step in, to help out his good friends the Democritics and Epicureans at a dead lift, and undertake to maintain, that though space be indeed an incorporeal thing, yet it would neither follow of necessity from thence, that it is an incorporeal substance or affection thereof; nor yet that it is an accident existing alone by itself, without a substance; because this space is really neither accident, nor substance, but a certain middle nature or essence betwixt both.   To which subterfuge of his, that we may not quarrel about words, we shall make this reply ; that unquestionably, whatsoever is, or hath any kind of entity, doth either subsist by itself, or else in an attribute, affection, or mode of something, that doth subsist by itself.   For it is certain, that there can be no mode, accident, or affection of nothing ; and consequently, that nothing cannot be extended, nor mensurable.   But if space be neither the extension of body, nor yet of substance incorporeal, then must it of necessity be the extension of nothing, and the affection of nothing ; and nothing must be mensurable by yards and poles.   We conclude, therefore, that from this very hypothesis of the Democritic and Epicurean atheists, that space is a nature distinct from body, and positively infinite, it follows undeniably, that there must be some incorporeal substance, whose affection its extension is : and because there can be nothing infinite, but only the Deity, that it is the infinite extension of an incorporeal Deity ; just as some learned theists and incorporealists have asserted.   And thus is the argument of these Democritic and Epicurean atheists, against an incorporeal Deity, abundantly confuted ; we having made it manifest, that from that very principle of their own, by which they would disprove the same, it is against themselves demonstrable.

(From the *Intellectual System of the Universe.*)

AGAINST ARBITRARY DECREES

Now the necessary consequence of that which we have hitherto said is this, that it is so far from being true, that all moral good and evil, just and unjust, are mere arbitrary and factitious things, that are created wholly by will ; that (if we would speak properly) we must needs say that nothing is morally good or evil, just or unjust by mere will without nature, because everything is what it is by nature, and not by will.   For though it will be objected here, that when God, or civil powers command a thing to be done, that was not before *debitum* or *illicitum*, " obligatory or unlawful," the thing willed or commanded doth forthwith become Δέον or *debitum*, " obligatory," that which ought to be done by creatures and subjects respectively ; in which the nature of moral good or evil is commonly conceived to consist.   And therefore if all good and evil, just and unjust be not the creatures of mere will (as many assert) yet at least positive things must needs owe all their morality, their good and evil to mere will without nature ; yet notwithstanding, if we well consider it, we shall find that even in positive commands themselves, mere will doth not make the thing commanded just or *debitum*, "obligatory," or beget and create any obligation to obedience; but that it is natural justice or equity, which gives to one the right or authority of commanding, and begets in another duty and obligation to obedience. Therefore it is observable, that laws and commands do not run thus, to will that this or that thing shall become *justum* or *injustum, debitum* or *illicitum*, "just or unjust, obligatory or unlawful," or that men shall be obliged or bound to obey ; but only to require that something be done or not done, or otherwise to menace punishment to the transgressors thereof. For it was never heard of, that anyone founded all his authority of commanding others, and others' obligation or duty to obey his commands, in a law of his own making, that men should be required, obliged, or bound to obey him. Wherefore since the thing willed in all laws is not that men should be bound or obliged to obey ; this thing cannot be the product of the mere will of the commander, but it must proceed from something else ; namely, the right or authority of the commander, which is founded in natural justice and equity, and an antecedent obligation to obedience in the subjects ; which things are not made by laws, but presupposed before all laws to make them valid. And if it should be imagined that any one should make a positive law to require that others should be obliged, or bound to obey him, every one would think such a law ridiculous and absurd ; for if they were obliged before, then this law would be in vain, and to no purpose ; and if they were not before obliged, then they could not be obliged by any positive law, because they were not previously bound to obey such a person's commands ; so that obligation to obey all positive laws is older than all laws, and previous or antecedent to them. Neither is it a thing that is arbitrarily made by will, or can be the object of command, but that which either is or is not by nature. And if this were not morally good and just in its own nature before any positive command of God, that God should be obeyed by His creatures, the bare will of God Himself could not beget an obligation upon any to do what He willed and commanded, because the nature of things do not depend upon will, being not γιγνόμενα but ὄντα, " things that are arbitrarily made," but "things that are." To conclude therefore, even in positive laws and commands it is not mere will that obligeth, but the natures of good and evil, just and unjust, really existing in the world. (From the Same.)

ON THE EXERCISE OF THE WILL

IT cannot be denied but that there are, and may be, many cases in which several objects propounded to our choice at the same time, are so equal, or exactly alike, as that there cannot possibly be any reason or motive in the understanding necessarily to determine the choice to one of them rather than to another of them. As for example, suppose one man should offer to another, out of twenty guinea pieces of gold, or golden balls, or silver globulites, so exactly alike in bigness, figure, colour, and weight, as that he could discern no manner of difference between them, to make his choice of one and no more ; add, also, that these guineas or golden balls may be so placed circularly as to be equidistant from the chooser's hand. Now it cannot be doubted but that, in this case, any man would certainly choose one, and not stand in suspense or demur because he could not tell which to prefer or choose before another. But if being necessitated by no motive or reason antecedent to choose this rather than that, he must determine himself contingently, or fortuitously, or causelessly, it being all one to him which he took, nor could there be any knowledge *ex causis* beforehand which of these twenty would certainly be taken. But if you will say, there was some hidden cause, necessarily determinating in this case, then if the trial should be made an hundred times over and over again, or by a hundred several persons, there is no reason why we must not allow that all of them must needs take the same guinea every time, that is either the first, second, or third, etc. of them, as they lie in order from the right or left hand." (From *Treatise of Free Will.*)

ON CHRIST'S CHRISTIANITY

IT came into the world, not to fill our heads with mere speculations ; to kindle a fire of wrangling and conscientious dispute, among us ; and to warm our spirits against one another, with angry and peevish debates : whilst in the meantime, our hearts remain all ice within towards God, and have not the least spark of true heavenly fire, to melt and thaw them. Christ came not to possess our brains with some cold opinions, that need draw a freezing and benumbing influence upon our hearts. Christ was a Master of Life, not of the schools : and he is the best Christian whose heart beats with the purest pulse towards heaven ; not he whose head spins out the finest cobwebs.

(From *Sermon on They Know Christ, who keep His Commandments*.)

SIR ROGER L'ESTRANGE

[Roger L'Estrange was born in 1616. In the great Rebellion he narrowly escaped the gallows for his loyalty to the King, and upon the Restoration was rewarded by the office of Licenser of the press. Thenceforward he took an active part in political controversy, writing innumerable pamphlets, and conducting more than one journal, notably the *Observator*. After the Revolution he applied himself no less heartily to more serious literature, and translated the history of Josephus, Æsop's *Fables*, Cicero's *Offices*, Seneca's *Morals*, and other works. He died in 1704.]

To the business of the pamphleteer L'Estrange brought excellent natural parts, uncommon zeal, and indefatigable industry. But his tracts were necessarily written with no thought of the morrow, and being calculated to serve a purely temporary purpose, they are, at the best, only good journalism, and so have shared the oblivion which overtakes all that is merely journalism and nothing more. L'Estrange's importance as a writer depends, therefore, not upon the fact that he was the first English professional journalist with any pretension to letters, but, upon the qualities which distinguish his translations, and particularly his version of Æsop, where he allowed himself a very free hand. There is, indeed, to be found in all an easy flow of essentially modern prose, free from elaboration and conceit ; but in the *Æsop* there is something more than simplicity and directness. There are a humour, a vivacity, an irresistible spirit and gusto, which combined with an inimitable vocabulary and the happiest gift of expression, make it a singularly entertaining and delightful book.

L'Estrange has been accused of corrupting the language, and certainly he was not in the habit of inquiring too closely into the parentage or the associations of any term that seemed to him either striking or appropriate. But in literature we are to judge by results, and here the result is plainly a style so idiomatic, so pungent, and so telling as completely to justify his audacity. The flat-nosed, hunch-backed, blubber-lipped, big-bellied, baker-legged

Æsop; the wife of Xanthus, horribly bold, meddling and expensive, easily put off the hooks and hard to be pleased again; the kite who comes powdering down on the frogs and mice; the lark who goes out progging for food for her little ones; the snake lazing at his length in the gleam of the sun; the weasel who tried what she could do with her wits when she could live no longer upon the square;—these and a thousand other vivid and surprising turns of phrase must delight all but the purist as surely as they demonstrate the possibility of a literary employment of "slang" which, if attempted by any but an artist, would result in nothing save imbecility, vulgarity, and nonsense.

J. H. MILLAR.

THE FOX AND THE RAVEN

A CERTAIN fox spied out a raven upon a tree with a morsel in his mouth, that set his chops a watering ; but how to come at it was the question. Oh thou blessed bird ! (says he) the delight of gods, and of men ! and so lays himself forth upon the gracefulness of the raven's person, and the beauty of his plumes ; his admirable gift of augury, etc. And now, says the fox, if thou hadst but a voice answerable to the rest of thy excellent qualities, the sun in the firmament could not show the world such another creature. This nauseous flattery sets the raven immediately a gaping as wide as ever he could stretch, to give the fox a taste of his pipe, but upon the opening of his mouth he drops his breakfast, which the fox presently chopt up, and then bade him remember, that whatever he had said of his beauty, he had spoken nothing yet of his brains.

THE MORAL

There's hardly any man living that may not be wrought upon more or less by flattery : for we do all of us naturally overween in our own favour : but when it comes to be applied once to a vain fool, it makes him forty times an arranter sot than he was before.

(From *Æsop's Fables translated.*)

THE DAW AND BORROWED PLUMES

A DAW that had a mind to be sparkish, tricked himself up with all the gay feathers he could muster together : and upon the credit of these stolen, or borrowed ornaments, he valued himself above all the birds in the air beside. The pride of this vanity got him the envy of all his companions, who upon a discovery of the

truth of the case, fell to pluming of him by consent ; and when
every bird had taken his own feather, the silly daw had nothing
left him to cover his nakedness.

THE MORAL

We steal from one another all manner of ways, and to all
manner of purposes ; wit, as well as feathers ; but where pride
and beggary meet, people are sure to be made ridiculous in the
conclusion.   (From the Same.)

THE FOX AND THE SICK LION

A CERTAIN lion that had got a politic fit of sickness, made it his
observation, that of all the beasts in the forest, the fox never
came at him : And so he wrote him word how ill he was, and
how mighty glad he should be of his company, upon the score of
ancient friendship and acquaintance. The fox returned the
compliment with a thousand prayers for his recovery ; but as for
waiting upon him, he desired to be excused ; for (says he) I find
the traces of abundance of feet going in to your majesty's palace,
and not one that comes back again.

THE MORAL

The kindness of ill-natured and designing people should be
thoroughly considered, and examined, before we give credit to
them.   (From the Same.)

THE APE AND THE DOLPHIN

PEOPLE were used in the days of old to carry gamesome puppies
and apes with them to sea, to pass away the time withal.   Now
there was one of these apes, it seems, aboard a vessel that was
cast away in a very great storm.   As the men were paddling for
their lives, and the ape for company, a certain dolphin, that took
him for a man, got him upon his back, and was making towards

land with him. He had him in a safe road called the Piræus, and took occasion to ask the ape, whether he was an Athenian or not? He told him, yes, and of a very ancient family there. Why then (says the dolphin) you know Piræus: Oh! exceedingly well, says t'other (taking it for the name of a man) why Piræus is my particular good friend. The dolphin, upon this, had such an indignation for the impudence of this Buffon-ape, that he gave him the slip from between his legs, and there was an end of my very good friend, the Athenian.

THE MORAL

Bragging, lying, and pretending, has cost many a man his life and estate. (From the Same.)

NOTES

14. *Proyning*=pruning
18. *A knap.* A hillock or mound, connected with *knob*
19. *Momus.* "In one of Æsop's fables Minerva makes a house, and Momus says it should have been on wheels to get away from bad neighbours" (Ellis)

    l. 4. *mixture.* Understand "want of" (mixture)

    l. 7. *having the commodity.* So it is printed uniformly in the earlier editions ; but probably for "the," we should read "no"

23. *copie*, i.e. *copia*, or abundant flow
28. *spials.* The same word as *espials* (used by Bishop Hall on p. 142 of this vol.), and equivalent to spies
33. *jargons.* Used of any code of terms arranged for a special purpose
37. *kenning*=a distance from which objects could be recognised
    bastons=staves
38. *pistolets* (dimin. from *pistole*) A small Spanish coin
47. *Multitudo ubi religione*, etc. "When the multitude is possessed by superstition it obeys its prophets better than its rulers"

    ut quam minimo, etc. "In order that the change may be

brought about in the republic with as little noise as possible.
61. *fairded*=painted
    Rien contrefait fin = nothing that is counterfeit is fine
    leide=language
    mignard=delicate, dainty
    morgue=mien
    jowking=bowing
62. *fra it be given*=after the time that it has been given
    engine=genius (*ingenium*).
    Nonumque premantur in annum = "and let them be suppressed until the ninth year"
    quia nescit vox missa reverti= "because a word once uttered cannot be recalled"
63. *balladines*=ballad-singers
    danton=tame (*dompter*)
    Μακεδονία οὔ σε χωρεῖ=Macedonia cannot contain thee
72. *delated of heresy*=charged with heresy
80. *fastidious* = wearisome (with nothing of the modern sense "apt to feel weariness or disgust")
98. *Habent venenum*, etc. "They hold poison as their sustenance —nay, even as a delicacy"
100. *digladiations*=combats with the sword, quarrels
114. *ketches*=snatches of song
119. *honos alit artes*=honour fosters arts,

PAGE

153. *Nullum magnum igenium*, etc. = No great genius is free from a mixture of madness
     Est olitor, etc. = Even a market gardener may often speak in season

155. μέγα βιβλίον μέγα κακὸν = a great book is a great evil

160. *the greater Scotland = Scotia major*, or Ireland

170. *Optimus est in discendo*, etc. = the best at learning is the patron who takes not everything on trust

173. *Utrum angeli in vicem*, etc. = whether the angels engage in conversation
     brewess, or *brewis* = broth

187. *that opinionum varietas, et opinantium unitas*, are ἀσύστατα = that difference of opinions, and concord amongst those who hold the opinions, are incompatible

206. *Hermogenes*, a Greek writer on rhetoric, in the age of Marcus Aurelius

229. *Offensis Ruffinum divide terris* = Divide Ruffinus amongst all the lands he has offended

231. *Nihil rerum mortalium*, etc. = amongst all human things none is so unstable and fluctuating, as the reputation of influence that does not rest upon its own power

239. *the pastry* = the room in which pastry was made

243. *wines concustable*, so in the old editions. But it is doubtless an error for *congustable* = wines fit to be tasted with

252. *the fire of Taberah*. See Numbers xi. 3

263. *Ea quæ manifeste posita sunt*, etc. = those things which are plainly set forth in Holy Scriptures, contain all things that pertain to faith and the conduct of life

PAGE

273. *men's trysting*. Here seems equivalent to "trust" or "safe - keeping," although usually it means a pledged meeting

290. *Christus Adjutor Meus*, etc. "Christ my aid;" "Leaving this, I seek an eternal abode;" "Here we journey more safely in a middle course"

295. *polacra* (or *polacca*) and *sattia*, names for vessels used in the Mediterranean

299. *Prætulerim delirus*, etc. = I would rather seem mad and helpless (so long as my ills afford me pleasure, or at least are unknown to me) than be wise and at the same time the aim of envy

307. *bravashing* = swaggering, domineering
     Teatinos, the Theatines, a monkish order founded a few years earlier than the Jesuits
     granads = shot

311. *exterminion*, for extermination; from *exterminium*, like dominion from *dominium*
     intim = close, heartfelt

312. *nixuriencie* = earnestness

321. *Ego vero contra*, etc. I, on the contrary, against the opinion of the older authors, would maintain that griffins are to be found neither in that northern region nor in any other quarter of the globe

322. *a better Œdipus* = a better solver of riddles

323. *bezo las manos* = I kiss my hands

324. *helix* = a spiral coil

325. *hypostasis* = essential substance

328. *oneirocritical* = skilled in the phenomena of dreams
     Sic ego, etc. = so would I choose, when turned to bones, to be laid to rest

329. *Alcmena's nights*, which were

PAGE

made tedious by her protracted travail

330. *atropos* = destroying fate

333. *tycho.* From the Greek τύχων, a god ; either (from τύχη) the god of chance, or (from τεύχω) as a maker or generator (Liddell and Scott)

meticulously = with attention to minute trifles

335. *Belisarius at beggar's bush.* According to the common tradition, Belisarius, after being blinded, begged his daily bread at the gates of the convent of Laurus

Bajazet in the grate. The Sultan Bajazet, in the fourteenth century, was said to have been carried about by his conqueror, Timur, in an iron cage

336. *apogeum.* The point at which heavenly bodies are most distant from the earth

349. *culverkeyes.* The flowers called columbines

361. *sneaped* = snubbed. Cf. "sneaping winds" in *Winter's Tale*

366. *alta mente repostum* = buried in the depths of their mind

377. *Templa Deo*, etc. = He gave churches to God, monks to the churches, lands to the monks

Templa adimit, etc. = He robs the gods of their churches, the citizens of their markets, the husbandmen of their fields

379. *glorre* = grease or fat

384. *tameth.* This is perhaps equivalent to "*teameth*" = carries home by teams ; or perhaps to *teemeth* in the old meaning of "pouring forth"

staddles = trees reserved at the felling of woods, for the growth of timber

385. *balk* = a ridge of land left unploughed

386. *Facies orbi terrarum*, etc. = a face familiar to all the world could not be unknown

386. *collen weight* = Cologne weight

poculum stanneum = a cup of tin

402. *Turpe mori*, etc. = "A poor thing it were not to be able to die after thee, for very grief"

406. *in republica Platonis, non in fœce Romuli* = in Plato's ideal republic, and not in the dregs of actual life

407. *in tanto viro*, etc. = In such a man, would be but to insult his virtues

409. *et in luctu*, etc. = And in his grief, he counted war as one possible remedy

425. *O fortunati nimium*, etc. = O generation, exceeding happy, if only they knew their own mercies

427. *Mea ætas incidit*, etc. My life fell upon a war, one part of which brought an excess of wickedness, the other part a dearth of happiness

471. *rebec.* A sort of guitar

ballatry. A jig or song

Monte Mayors. Referring to G. de Montemayor's Arcadian romance of *Diana Enamorada* (Valencia, 1542)

473. *Enchiridion* = a handbook

474. *he whom an honest quæstorship* = Cicero

475. *Syntagma* = scheme of doctrine

476. *pismires* = ants

511. *chitted* = sprouted

nebulones means "worthless fellows." But it would seem as if Harrington had in his mind *nebulæ* (clouds), with its derivative *nebulosus*

nine-holes or *trow-madam.* Games of different kinds

512. *bossolo di non sinceri* = the box of insincere men

grotto di cane. The grotto near Pozzuolo, the effect of the

END OF VOL. II